THIRD EDITION

The Psychology of Aging

THIRD EDITION

The Psychology of Aging

Theory, Research, and Interventions

Janet K. Belsky

MIDDLE TENNESSEE STATE UNIVERSITY

Brooks/Cole Publishing Company

I⊤P® An International Thomson Publishing Company

Pacific Grove • Albany • Belmont • Bonn • Boston • Cincinnati • Detroit • Johannesburg • London
Madrid • Melbourne • Mexico City • New York • Paris • Singapore • Tokyo • Toronto • Washington

Sponsoring Editor: *Jim Brace-Thompson*
Marketing Team: *Lauren Harp, Donna Shore, Aaron Eden*
Editorial Associate: *Bryon Granmo*
Production Editors: *Nancy L. Shammas; Cecile Joyner*
Manuscript Editors: *Margaret C. Tropp; Lura S. Harrison*
Permissions Editor: *Connie Dowsett*
Interior Design: *Terri Wright Design*
Interior Illustration: *Kathy Joneson*

Cover Design: *Terri Wright Design*
Cover and Chapter Opening Sculptures: *Muriel Kaplan*
Art Editor: *Lisa Torri*
Indexer: *Do Mi Stauber*
Typesetting: *Thompson Type*
Printing and Binding: *R. R. Donnelley & Sons, Crawfordsville*

COPYRIGHT © 1999 by Brooks/Cole Publishing Company
A division of International Thomson Publishing Inc.

I(T)P The ITP logo is a registered trademark used herein under license.

For more information, contact:

BROOKS/COLE PUBLISHING COMPANY
511 Forest Lodge Road
Pacific Grove, CA 93950
USA

International Thomson Publishing Europe
Berkshire House 168-173
High Holborn
London WC1V 7AA
England

Thomas Nelson Australia
102 Dodds Street
South Melbourne 3205
Victoria, Australia

Nelson Canada
1120 Birchmount Road
Scarborough, Ontario
Canada M1K 5G4

International Thomson Editores
Seneca, 53
Colonia Polanco
11560 México, D.F., México

International Thomson Publishing GmbH
Königswinterer Strasse 418
53227 Bonn
Germany

International Thomson Publishing Asia
60 Albert Street
#15-01 Albert Complex
Singapore 189969

International Thomson Publishing Japan
Hirakawacho Kyowa Building, 3F
2-2-1 Hirakawacho
Chiyoda-ku, Tokyo 102
Japan

Printed in the United States of America

10   9   8   7   6

Library of Congress Cataloging-in-Publication Data

Belsky, Janet, [date]
    The psychology of aging : theory, research, and interventions /
Janet K. Belsky. — 3rd ed.
        p.   cm.
    Includes bibliographical references and index.
    ISBN 0-534-35912-4
    1. Aging–Psychological aspects.   2. Aged—Psychology.   3. Aged—
Mental health services.   I. Title.
BF724.55.A35B44   1999
155.67—dc21
                                                    98-17981
                                                      CIP

For my father, Murray Kaplan (1908–1990)
Elegance, Intelligence, and Courage

Contents

🙣 7 *Memory and Dementia* 194

🙣 8 *Personality* 226

🙣 9 *Psychopathology* 260

PART V: The Social Dimension

10 *The Older Family* 292

11 *Life Transitions: Retirement and Widowhood* 328

PART VI: Conclusions

12 *Death and Dying* 366

Preface

When I began revising this book, I thought that the writing would be a cinch. I had just finished a textbook in adult development. This edition of *The Psychology of Aging* would simply involve expanding on the older-adult sections of my previous book. I was wrong.

It is hard to describe my sense of excitement once I focused directly on later life—the thrill of discovering innovative new theories of successful aging and seeing the research leaps in our field within the past few years. Writing this book has been a compelling journey that has rehooked me into being a gerontologist again. I want this text to convey to students the same passion that I feel.

As with my previous books, this edition of *The Psychology of Aging* is not aimed at a single type of student. It is written to appeal to the aspiring PhD as well as to the community-college student taking one course in our field. I think that this balancing act is possible because complex concepts can be explained in terms that everyone can relate to and understand. Textbooks can be both scholarly and easy to read, provided an author cares about the subject, about writing well, and keeps the idea that our research is really all about people firmly in mind.

In this book, my goal is to entice students to enter our field, to teach them to critically evaluate studies and concepts, and to tell the "story" of the psychology of aging in the most interesting way. I want to bring home the evolving quality of our knowledge and of the aging experience itself—that

who we are as older adults is a function both of our ongoing life history and of our living in a particular historical time. Because I believe that having this wider framework is critical to understanding late-life behavior, this book focuses both on traditional areas of psychology and on exploring the societal options, services, and opportunities for older people. It pays special attention to the critical social issues we face as our population ages. It embodies my commitment to the scientist-practitioner model, demonstrating how what we learn in an academic setting translates into interventions to improve the quality of later life. It describes the scientific facts and at the same time strives to bring home the critical, contextual message that making broad factual statements or generalizations about aging is wrong. Diversity and individual differences are the essence of human life. It attempts to offer an *organized* portrait of our field by highlighting how the different studies and concepts in the psychology of aging fit together and relate. In other words, based on my bird's-eye view of the forest, my objective in this book is to integrate (as much as possible) what we psychologists who study aging know.

Here are some techniques that I have used to further these agendas and goals—the features that I believe make this text special:

1. **It is written in a narrative, novelistic style.** This book is written to unfold like a story. The first two chapters set the stage, high-

lighting phenomena and theories that I repeatedly refer to throughout the text. The separate chapters are planned to progress like a story and, as much as possible, to interrelate. This strategy not only makes for more interesting reading, it gives students the sense of reading about an evolving, organic field.

2. **It emphasizes the link between research and practice.** After a full exploration of the research facts, each topic ends with a section describing concrete interventions. These varied interventions—ranging from cognitive remediation studies, to clinical trials designed to show that at-risk behavior can be changed, to environmental modifications for disability, to widowed persons groups—all bring home graphically how basic research translates into actions taken to optimize later life.

3. **It emphasizes the personal dimension of the psychology of aging through first-person accounts.** Because I also want to describe vividly the actual aging experience and give students insights about what it is like to work in gerontology-oriented careers, this book features personal vignettes, primarily interviews I have conducted with older adults and professionals in our field. Features called "Aging in Action" scattered throughout each chapter and introductory chapter vignettes give students a first-hand glimpse into what it is like to be a researcher in the psychology of aging, a psychotherapist in a nursing home, an older widowed person, or an elderly student who has returned to school. I even interviewed a man with Alzheimer's disease!

4. **It emphasizes the historical, societal, and developmental context within which behavior occurs.** In discussing topics such as sexuality or psychopathology, or life-transitions such as retirement or widowhood, I set the stage by describing the historical and earlier life-framework. An in-depth exploration of critical social concerns, such as options in disability, the quality of nursing-home care, poverty in the elderly, and the adequacy of late-life mental health services, is a special focus of this text.

5. **It teaches students to evaluate the studies and concepts in our field.** In order to get students to think critically about our field, I carefully explore the limitations and biases of specific studies, link facts to theoretical frameworks, focus on the ways concepts are defined and measured, and highlight the gaps in what we know.

ACKNOWLEDGMENTS

A project of this magnitude depends on a dedicated publishing team. First and foremost there is the acquisitions editor, the person who is ultimately responsible for getting a book written and into print. Acquisitions editors have a difficult job. They continually travel the country, soliciting potential authors, enlisting reviewers, talking to professors, and attending multiple conventions. They must get authors and reviewers to stick to schedules, decide which critiques are important to improving manuscripts, and prevail on often-recalcitrant writers to make the needed changes. As if that were not enough, they are responsible for producing a good book within the constraints of cost, moderating problems once the manuscript goes "into production," and ensuring that the final product arrives at the right time. Until just this past month, Jim Brace-Thompson had been performing this exhausting feat with grace for more than a decade at Brooks/Cole. He and Vicki Knight, Brooks/Cole's outstanding Executive Editor, deserve a vote of thanks, not just from me and my fellow authors, but from the hundreds of thousands of psychology professors and students who have benefited from this premier publisher's wonderful books over the years.

Then there is the Brooks/Cole production team: the copy editor who goes over the manuscript word by word, improving grammar and punctuation, meticulously checking references, and rewriting sections that don't make sense; the designers and artists whose creative vision makes our contemporary psychology texts genuine works of art. Overseeing this process is the production editor, responsible for coordinating this feat. For this book, Peggy Tropp and Lura Harrison were the copy editors who made my sentences readable. Terri Wright and Kelly Shoemaker were the designers and Lisa Torri was the art editor who produced this beautiful book. Nancy Shammas and Cecile Joyner were the overseers who helped get this edition of *The Psychology of Aging* into print.

I also want to thank the many people not associated with Brooks Cole. I am grateful to the reviewers, whose insights helped lock in my vision for this book: William Bailey, Eastern Illinois University; Kathleen V. Fox, Salisbury State University; Douglas Hardwick, Illinois State University; Janina Jolley, Clarion University of Pennsylvania; Barbara Vance, Brigham Young University; and Michael Vitiello, University of Washington. I am grateful for my friends in the psychology department at Middle Tennessee State University for listening patiently to my trials and tribulations; for the Faculty Research Grant that made this writing possible; to Pam Ahrens for performing the arduous job of checking references and, in the process, saving my mental state; and to the people who consented to tell me the life-stories that make this book come alive. Finally, although I have many other reasons to be grateful to her, I want to thank my mother, Muriel Kaplan, specifically for this book. In addition to her talents at raising four children, my mother has been working for years to produce the beautiful sculptures that grace the cover and each chapter's opening page.

Apart from being lucky to have such a talented mother, I was lucky to come into contact with many talented people over the years: Henry Gleitman and Jacob Nachmias, teachers capable of making Introductory Psychology so captivating that they had 600 college freshman sitting on the edge of our seats; Mary Rootes and Doris Gruenewald, the gifted psychologists who taught me how to do clinical work; and some courageous editors who went out on a limb for me during my writing career. I owe a lifelong debt to Marquita Flemming and my buddy, C. Deborah Laughton, for taking a chance on a total novice twenty years ago when we were young and at Brooks/Cole. (Deb's mission continues to be nurturing promising authors.) I am thankful to Wendy Harris and Joan Gill, who took the heroic step of publishing my previous books after they had been rejected by other companies.

Then there are those exceptional gerontologists, Bob Kahn and Powell Lawton, who shaped my interest in aging. Bob, who I think ranks as the earliest true clinical gerontologist, taught me during my first years of graduate school. Powell was gracious enough to give me my first job after getting my PhD. Although you will be introduced to Powell and his accomplishments in this book, in this section I feel free to plainly spell out my thoughts: I believe that older people and the psychology of aging owe Powell *everything,* as this remarkable man has genuinely built our field. Powell thinks of himself as mainly a researcher, but to me his real genius lies in innovation—his uncanny ability to sense just where gerontology needs to be heading and vigorously taking steps to get us there.

This book is due to my good fortune at finding an ideal husband. David, my role-model for intelligence, wisdom, ethics, and humor, for some strange reason, has decided to make my career and happiness his first priority. (Your dinners are really good, too.) It is the lucky outcome of my being born into a middle-class family who cared about education at this best historical time. This brings up another role-model, the person to whom I have chosen to dedicate this book. This edition of *The Psychology of Aging* was made possible by my father, Murray Kaplan, who spent his life working at a job that did not suit his tremendous intellectual potential in order to allow me and every one of us Kaplan children to fulfill our own intellectual gifts.

Janet K. Belsky

P.S. Please feel free to e-mail me at *jbelsky @frank.mtsu.edu* with any comments or thoughts. In this edition, I want to take full advantage of advanced technology to finally find out what you readers really think!

THIRD EDITION

The Psychology of Aging

Chapter Outline

1

The People and the Field

In 1998, I interviewed three older people, all residents of Murfreesboro, Tennessee. James, age 71, is a retired African American business executive who lives with his wife on a 30-acre farm outside of town. Bertha, age 88, is a resident in a local nursing home. Jan, age 60, is a psychology major at Middle Tennessee State University.

James says he is honored to be interviewed, thrilled to be able to tell the younger generation about his life. What a wise decision it was to buy the farm after retiring! What a fulfilling way to spend the final decades of an interesting life! As an African American growing up during the Depression in the South, James's childhood was hard. He remembers the harsh winters, the outdoor plumbing, the days there was barely enough to eat. Of the boys in the family, all did graduate from high school. But James was the only one to get a college degree. As a young adult, James was active in the civil rights movement. He participated in sit-ins and marched to Montgomery with Martin Luther King. James feels privileged to have been on the scene to witness these events, to have the opportunities provided by living through that remarkable historical time. He is proud of his personal achievements, too. As one of the first minority managers at Nissan, James rose to become vice president, the only person in his family to construct an upper-middle-class life. He is happy about the person he has become in recent years: a more gentle man, more family-oriented, more able to relax. He has anxieties. For now the overall slowing is not so important, the need to be careful about bending, to allow extra time to climb steps. James has no disabilities. He even feels better physically since retiring to a more active life. His main concern is the future, not for himself, but for his wife of 50 years. Rose has arthritis. If James did become disabled, she would not be able to live in this isolated area without help. He does not want to leave his wife with the farm to take care of alone or have her worry over the decision if he does need a nursing home. Will James spend his final years as a burden? What will happen to Rose in 10 or 15 years?

Bertha is in her wheelchair watching TV, an activity that has become standard behavior in recent months. Bertha has trouble following my questions. She seems depleted and apathetic. It is difficult to get her to talk. Since entering the Health Care Center two years ago, Bertha's capacities have steadily declined. She has forgotten the month. She needs help dressing. She can no longer get to the bathroom by herself. Still, Bertha feels she made the right decision in coming here. After breaking her hip, she could not handle life alone. Bertha never married. She worked at a shirt factory to support herself for 45 years. Now it is her time to

rest and have others take care of her needs. For the first time in her life, Bertha has no financial worries. Medicaid takes care of her expenses in the home. Her concerns center around basic activities. Will she be able to get into the wheelchair? Will dinner arrive warm and on time? Will the nurse respond to her call, so she can get to the toilet without having an accident today?

Jan is also finding it difficult to focus on my questions, but not because she isn't interested; she is tired. After taking classes at Middle Tennessee State University and chasing two grandchildren around, it is hard to have the energy for any conversation, even one about her own life. Jan has her own concerns. Her main worry is her daughter. Sara has been so depressed after the divorce. Luckily, she was able to convince her only child to move in and put the children in day care part time. Jan loves being in school. She cannot give up her dream of a career as a social worker to be a full-time parent for a second time. Besides, she may need the income more than ever now that Frank is gone and Sara has to cope with working and raising the children alone. But can she still perform well intellectually? Does she have the same capacity to remember, or learn, or get a job at her age?

roles
The major life activities people engage in

The psychology of aging is about these concerns. It deals with the basic questions we have about our future. How will we function physically, cognitively, and emotionally as we grow old? It explores the **roles,** or major life activities, we associate with our older years: retirement, widowhood, grandparenthood, living in a nursing home. It concerns less expected events, such as going back to school and starting a later life career. How will James change physically in the future? Will Jan be able to do well at school, graduate, and find work at her age? What will make life easier for Bertha as a resident in long-term care?

gerontology
Study of older people and the aging process

Psychologists interested in older people and the aging process, or **gerontology,** search for universal patterns. They want to understand the ways we all develop and change. They also examine the diversity in aging pathways and among older adults. As we saw in these vignettes, James, Jan, and Bertha differ along basic dimensions such as age, ethnicity, gender, and socioeconomic status that are certain to affect their behavior, attitudes, and lifestyles as older adults (see Table 1-1). These people vary in another crucial way. Only one of them fits the negative stereotype of old age.

STEREOTYPES AND THE NEW SENIOR CITIZEN

Table 1-2 lists some demoralizing stereotypes we have about later life. Older people are supposed to be physically feeble and cognitively impaired, emotionally disturbed, financially deprived, and isolated from the world (Butler, 1980; Palmore, 1990). These ideas are deeply ingrained and widespread. They are as common at 70 as at 20 (Hummert, Garstka, & Shaner, 1997) and reveal themselves during our first decade of life (Coyer, Parisi, & Slotterback, 1997). From a very young age, children describe old people as dependent, unattractive, and weak. In such far-flung locations as the Aleutian Islands of Alaska, Paraguay, and Australia, they view the elderly with distaste (Jantz, Seefeldt, Galper, & Serock, 1976; Miller, Blalock, & Ginsberg, 1984–1985).

However, as the table shows, these images are inaccurate. Most people over 65 are vital and active. Only 5% of older Americans live in nursing homes. Even over age 80,

Socioeconomic Status (SES)

Definition   Where a person is on the social stratum as defined by a combination of income, education, and occupation. Although the classic sociological studies of class in America list more differentiated categories, typically Americans are labeled as *working-class* or *blue-collar* when they work in manual jobs and/or do not have a college education and as *middle-class, upper-middle-class,* or *white-collar* when they are college graduates or have higher degrees and work in a professional or managerial job.

Deficiencies   Social class is an ill-defined marker. For instance, one might be middle-class in income, but work in a blue-collar job, or have a Ph.D. and be on welfare. Moreover, the terms *working-class* and *middle-class* were always supposed to involve an implicit set of values, such as middle-class parents are interested in upward mobility and education. These generalizations may not be appropriate today.

Ethnicity

Definition   The group a person fits into based on religion or, more often, country of origin and race.

Deficiencies   Americans are often a mixture of ethnicities, making it impossible to categorize people definitively. Categorizing people into broad groups such as "Hispanic American" can be misleading, as individuals lumped into this category are not alike in customs, values, or country of origin.

Concluding comments   These markers are extremely useful in gerontology, revealing a good deal about inequities in society and offering important information about everything from health status to family life in the older years. However, by using them we also run the risk of stereotyping very diverse people.

most people live independently. Though they often do have disabilities, they do not need institutional care. Although changes in memory and thinking do take place in the latter part of life, the vast majority of older people function well intellectually. Only a small minority suffer from the intense cognitive impairments we link with old age. Moreover, at this point in history, older Americans are emphatically *not* more likely than other age groups to be emotionally disturbed, socially isolated, or extremely financially deprived. In fact, if anything, young people are more likely to suffer from these so-called old-age problems than people over age 65! How have these images fared now that we are confronted with these legions of nonstereotypic older adults?

There is encouraging evidence that our stereotypes are breaking down. In a 1990s' survey conducted by the American Association of Retired Persons, most Americans agreed that the typical older adult was not physically or mentally impaired and that older people could enjoy a variety of activities, including sexual relations and meaningful work. Interestingly, respondents were more negative about the emotional and social, rather than the physical and cognitive, side of life, erroneously believing that psychological distress, interpersonal isolation, and serious financial problems were endemic among older adults (Speas & Obenshain, 1995).

The tendency to stereotype depends on the individual. In this survey, people who were having more trouble with their *own* lives—those who were poorly educated or

TABLE 1-2	Stereotypes and Statistical Facts about Older People

Stereotype 1: *Physical* Most people over 65 are physically impaired. A large percentage live in nursing homes.

Fact: Although most older adults do suffer from at least one chronic disease, the vast majority report *no* impairments in their ability to function. Only 5% of older Americans live in nursing homes. (See Chapters 3, 4, and 5.)

Stereotype 2: *Cognitive* People over 65 are unable to think clearly, remember well, or learn new things. A large percentage are "senile."

Fact Although losses in thinking speed and memory do occur with age, the vast majority of older adults are alert, mentally capable, and definitely able to learn. Only about 5–7% have Alzheimer's disease. (See Chapters 6 and 7.)

Stereotype 3: *Emotional* People over 65 are unhappy, fearful, and depressed. Psychological problems are rampant in old age.

Fact Anxiety, depression, and unhappiness are no more prevalent among the old than the young. In fact, rates of many emotional disorders are at *their lowest ebb* among people over 65. (See Chapters 8 and 9.)

Stereotype 4: *Social* People over 65 are isolated and alone, disconnected from family and friends. Poverty is endemic in the later years.

Fact Older adults are typically in close contact with family and, even over age 85, have at least one close friend. With 12% of older Americans living under the poverty line, compared to *one-fourth* of American children under age 6, dire poverty is twice as common at life's beginning as at its final stage. (See Chapters 10 and 11.)

suffering from emotional problems, impaired health, or money worries—were more likely to attribute these same difficulties to the typical older adult. It depends on the older person, too. Instead of applying to everyone over age 65, negative labels mainly come into play when the person is over age 80 (Hummert, Garstka, & Shaner, 1997) or appears to be ill and infirm (Gekoski & Knox, 1990).

In fact, when Daniel Schmidt and Susan Boland (1986) asked college students to list as many traits as possible linked with being old, they got a hodgepodge of responses. Older people were viewed as frail and incompetent, but also as resilient and tough. They were labeled as quarrelsome and set in their ways, but also as generous, loving, and wise. In other words, while we still think of older people in the traditional ways, these ideas have been supplemented by new perceptions. The strange outcome is a set of firmly held *contradictory* thoughts about what the elderly are like.

So reality is permeating the stereotype. Older people defy generalizations. Many are active, involved, and competent; some are ill and frail. Some are at the height of their powers; others are the embodiment of decline. The words "golden years" sometimes fit this stage of life; at other times, they are a cruel parody. At this time in history, diversity and individual differences are the essence of senior citizen-hood. This diversity is a theme we will be stressing throughout this book.

ageism
Any form of prejudice based on age

The legions of vigorous older people are combating **ageism,** or prejudice on the basis of age. They have made inroads. We have laws prohibiting age discrimination in the workforce and, with some exceptions, mandatory retirement on the basis of age.

We have organizations of elderly marathon runners and counseling services devoted to beginning a postretirement career. While we still may have a way to go before reaching an **age-irrelevant society** (Neugarten, 1977), where everything is equally possible at any age, we have much less rigid rules about what is acceptable at age 70 or 85 than before (O'Rand, 1996; Riley & Riley, 1994). In fact, contrary to our rosy ideas about how older people used to be treated, today we may be living in one of the most age-friendly ages of all. (See Aging in Action 1-1.)

age-irrelevant society
Ideal society in which people can engage in any activity at any time in life

A DEMOGRAPHIC PERSPECTIVE ON AGING PEOPLE

How did we arrive at this age-friendly age? Answers come from getting a bird's-eye view of the territory. **Demography,** the study of populations, offers a statistical picture of today's older adults, tells how later life has changed, and offers hints about older people in the decades to come. Unless otherwise noted, the following information is from the U.S. Senate Special Committee on Aging, 1991a; Bureau of the Census, 1993, 1994, 1995, 1996; and Administration on Aging, 1997.

demography
Statistical study of large populations

An Age Revolution

The main reason for our new view of old age becomes apparent if we look at the most basic fact about later life: The elderly among us are an army. The number one demographic trend of the 20th century has been the dramatic increase in the proportion of people over age 65.

In 1900, only 4% of Americans were elderly. Today, that figure has more than tripled, to almost 13%. Moreover, in the next few decades the ranks of older adults will grow at a rapid pace. The reason is that the huge cohort born immediately after the Second World War has entered the aging phase of life.

Cohort is a crucial term in the psychology of aging. **Cohort,** a word similar to generation, refers to any group of people born during a certain period of time. After World War II, the birthrate soared, producing the bulging cohort called the postwar baby boom. By the year 2030, when the baby boomers have all turned 65, we will be a top-heavy society. The proportion of elderly Americans will swell from 1 in 8 to 1 in 5.

The **baby boom cohort,** defined as people born between 1946 and 1964, has left an indelible imprint on society as its members journey through life. When these children dominated the population during the 1950s and early 1960s, deviations from the two-parent family were discouraged, gender roles were highly traditional, and full-time mothering was expected to be a woman's job in life. Then, as rebellious adolescents during the 1960s and 1970s, this cohort helped engineer a radical transformation in these attitudes and roles. When the baby boomers settled down to working and having their own families during the 1980s, career concerns and children once again assumed center stage, as we entered a more conservative age in politics. Now that this cohort is middle-aged, the phenomenon demographers refer to as the **graying of America** is in

cohort
Group of people born within a specified short period of time, who travel through life at the same point in history

baby boom cohort
Group of people born during the period following World War II, from 1946 to 1964

graying of America
Phrase referring to the fact that a growing fraction of Americans are in the aging phase of life

Aging in Action

1-1 *Ageism through the Ages*

The forehead scowls, the hair is gray. . . . The brows are gone, the eyes are blear. . . . The nose is hooked and far from fair. . . . The ears are rough and pendulous. . . . The face is sallow, dead and drear. . . . The chin is purs'd . . . the lips hang loose. . . . Aye such is human beauty's lot! The arms are short. . . . The hands clench tight; the shoulders tangle in a knot; . . . The breasts in shame they shrink from sight. . . . the thighs are thin; As withered hams, and have a blight of freckles like a sausage-skin.

Thus we mourn for the good old days. Perch'd on our buttocks, wretched crones, huddled together by the blaze. . . . We who have sat on lovers thrones! With many a man 'tis just the same (excerpted from an Old English poem, "Lament of the Fair Heaulmiere," quoted in Minois, 1989, p. 230)

Many of us assume that people had better values and attitudes toward growing old in "the good old days." Poems such as this one suggest the need to take a closer look at this assumption. The following historical summary is based on Minois, 1989, and Fischer, 1977.

In ancient times, many historians believe, old age was seen as a miracle of nature because it was so rare. Where there was no written language, older people were greatly valued for their knowledge. They were given an exalted place. Elders formed the governing bodies in ancient Rome and Greece. The elderly owned the land and resources and so had absolute control over their daughters and sons. However, this elevated status applied only to the elite, and only to males. For slaves, servants, and women, old age was often a cruel time. Moreover, when we look closely at many ancient societies, a different picture emerges.

In some societies, the same elder who was lionized might be subjected to barbaric treatment once he outlived his usefulness—that is, became decrepit or senile. Tribes such as the Samoans killed their aged members outright in elaborate ceremonies in which the victim was required to participate. Others left their older people to die of neglect. Among other groups, strong norms to "respect one's elders" protected older people from such a fate. However, even in cultures Westerners traditionally look up to as models of enlightenment, aging was deprecated and feared. Michelangelo and Sophocles, who were revered as old men, stand out as supposedly typical of the age-accepting attitudes of the social milieus in which they lived. However, the images portrayed in their works of art celebrated youth and beauty. Even in these important cultures, classical Greece and the Renaissance, old age was looked down on as the worst time of life.

Historian Georges Minois (1989) concludes, in a survey of how Western civilization treated its elders: "It is the tendency of every society to live and go on living: it extols the strength and fecundity that are so closely linked to youth and it dreads the . . . decrepitude of old age. Since the dawn of history, . . . young people have regretted the onset of old age. . . . The fountain of youth has always constituted Western man's most irrational hope" (p. 303).

full swing. Society is bracing for a boom in senior citizens when, in 2010, the first of the baby boomers enter their retirement years.

The baby boom is only partly responsible for the graying of America. It does not explain why the ranks of older people have grown so dramatically during the past century or why the older population is mushrooming in almost every country in the world. The main cause for this growth is enduring: an increase in life expectancy during the 20th century unparalleled in human history.

In every culture, some people always lived to old age. However, the chances of reaching one's 70s or 80s were fairly slim. In the Roman empire, only one-fifth of the population made it to middle age. The statistics were no different in America's colonial times; in the Chesapeake colonies, only about 10% of white male children lived to age 60. Because of the high rates of infant and childhood mortality, these societies had a remarkably low **average life expectancy**—one's chances at birth, *on average,* of living to a certain age. In the well-off New England colonies, average life expectancy was about age 30. In Maryland during that same time, it was under age 20, for both masters and their slaves (Fischer, 1977).

During the 18th and especially 19th centuries, life expectancy in the United States and other developed countries improved steadily. By 1900, U.S. life expectancy was age 47.3. Then, in the next half century, it shot up. A U.S. baby born today can expect to live, on the average, to age 76. During this century, average life expectancy has increased by almost 30 years!

The 20th-century **life expectancy revolution** has two phases. In the earlier decades of this century, dramatic gains in life expectancy occurred at younger ages, allowing most people to live past youth. Now our main strides have been made in extending life expectancy in later life. For instance, Americans who turned 65 in 1996 could expect on average to live 17.7 more years. Today, we can expect to be senior citizens for almost as long as we were children and adolescents.

This extension occurred because of a shift in the pattern of disease control. Earlier in this century, medical advances such as immunization and antibiotics wiped out deaths from many **infectious diseases** such as diphtheria. Because these diseases killed both young and old, their eradication allowed most people to live past midlife. Now we have become better able to limit, but not cure, diseases that strike people in middle and later life. People reaching age 65 now live on for years because of declines in mortality from these illnesses of aging called **chronic diseases** (heart disease, cancer, stroke).

Although these advances are due partly to medical breakthroughs such as improved medicines and better surgical techniques, much of the credit belongs to us. Many experts believe that the **lifestyle movement** of the 1960s and 1970s, with its emphasis on exercise and diet, is responsible for the striking decline in mortality from heart disease and stroke that has occurred over the past few decades (Fries, 1990; Kunkel & Harris, 1997; Lesnoff-Caravaglia & Klys, 1987). As we will see in Chapter 3, exercising, eating the right foods, and being concerned with our health earlier really does help slow the onset and pace of certain important age-related chronic diseases.

The rise in late-life expectancy means that unparalleled numbers of people are living into their 9th, 10th, or even 11th decade of life. People over age 85 are now the fastest-growing segment of the population. We can expect their numbers to rise

average life expectancy
Age to which an individual has a 50-50 probability of living from a specific age, most often birth

life expectancy revolution
Phrase referring to the dramatic increase in life expectancy that has taken place during the 20th century

infectious diseases
Category of illnesses that are transmitted by infectious agents or microorganisms

chronic diseases
Category of illnesses that are long-lasting and not typically caused by infectious agents

lifestyle movement
Change in health consciousness during the 1960s and 1970s, emphasizing following good health practices as the key to disease prevention

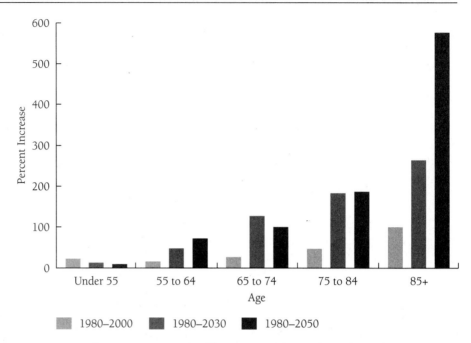

We can expect a dramatic increase in the oldest segment of the population during the next 50 years. How will this transformation change society?
SOURCE: U.S. Senate Special Committee on Aging, 1991a, p. 12.

dramatically in the next few decades. As Figure 1-1 shows, by the middle of the next century, the percentage of the population aged 85 or older is expected to increase almost sixfold.

One consequence is that four-generation families are common (Soldo, 1996). People have the joy of witnessing the birth of a great-grandchild. In their 40s and 50s, they have the pleasure of seeing a parent or a grandparent still alive. There are problems along with this good news. Although we have added time to the end of the life span, we have not necessarily given these family patriarchs—or, more likely, matriarchs—a high-quality life. As we will see in Chapter 5, the increased number of people living into their 80s and 90s means more ill elderly and so an exploding need for medical and nursing care.

By about our ninth decade of life, the chance of being physically disabled by disease increases dramatically. For this reason, gerontologists frequently make a distinction between two groups of older adults: the young-old and the old-old. The **young-old,** defined as people aged 65 to 75, do not often have disabling diseases. They often look and feel middle-aged. They overwhelmingly reject the idea that they are old (Palmore, 1990). The **old-old,** people in their late 70s and beyond, seem in a different

young-old
People in their mid-60s to mid-70s

old-old
People in their late 70s and beyond

While the pride the middle-aged woman in the photo feels in having three adjoining generations is one blessing of living today, along with the pleasure comes liabilities—being burdened with caring for a more fragile younger and older family.

class. Because they are more likely to have physical and mental disabilities, these people are more prone to fit the stereotype of the frail, dependent older adult.

A Revolution in Social Roles

The life expectancy revolution set the stage for our liberated view of old age. With so many vigorous and healthy older people, later life came to be seen as a time of new possibilities as well as decline. However, the real push for this freedom came from a revolution in attitudes and social norms. This change, which occurred when the baby boom cohort "came of age" in the 1960s and early 1970s, encouraged self-expression, not just for the elderly but for all adults.

The "Decade of Protest" began with the civil rights and women's movements and ended with the "counterculture" movement that emphasized liberation in every area of life (Bengtson, 1989). Sexuality before marriage became acceptable. Women entered the workforce in droves. Men were encouraged to share the housework and child care

FIGURE 1-2   *Life Expectancy by Sex, United States, 1970–1992*

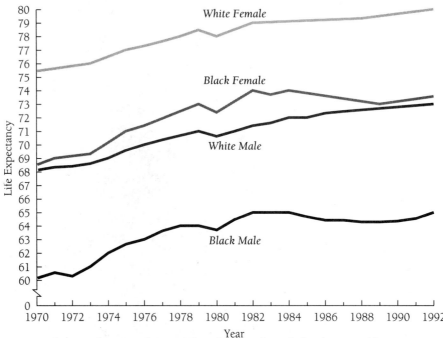

Women outlive men by a significant number of years. The male/female gap in life expectancy is pronounced for both blacks and whites and did not change much over this 22-year period.
SOURCE: *Monthly Vital Statistics Report, 43* (6), March 22, 1995, p. 5.

equally with their wives. Divorce became an acceptable alternative to living in an unhappy marriage. If a woman wanted children, it was no longer absolutely necessary to get married at all. The legacy has been a dramatic change in the family and in the lifestyles of women and men.

Today, a minority of married couples fit the traditional role of breadwinner husband and homemaker wife. Women make up 45% of the labor force. Nearly 60% of women during their prime adult years are working full-time. Even staying at home with young children is no longer typical. As of 1988, more than half of all U.S. women with preschool-age children had paying jobs (Ferber, O'Farrell, & Allen, 1991; Levitan & Conway, 1990).

Today, a minority of people follow the traditional path of marriage for life. With more than half of all marriages ending in divorce, this event has become normal; divorce today is a predictable transition (Furstenberg & Cherlin, 1991; Popenoe, 1988). While divorce rates have stabilized (at a high level), the trend to have children without being married continues to escalate. By the early 1990s, about one-third of all U.S. children were born to unmarried mothers (Council on Families in America, 1995).

This transformation in the younger family has altered the later years. Because single mothers are more likely to be poor, the growth in one-parent families means a needier younger generation—adult children who need more financial help from aging parents than before. As the interview with Jan at the beginning of this chapter reveals, it means more pressure to provide hands-on aid with daily life. The increase in working women and mother-headed families has made the role of grandparent more pivotal, more central than ever to family life.

This transformation will alter how new cohorts of senior citizens negotiate the older years. Today, most women in their 50s have had the experience of working and, increasingly, raising families alone. Men are approaching retirement age having either lived without a spouse or with alternate skills to the breadwinner role. These earlier life experiences may make both sexes more resilient, more able to cope independently with later life losses such as widowhood or leaving one's job.

The same social changes have the potential to create problems as the baby boomers reach later life. As we will see in later chapters, relatives—a spouse and children—do most caring for the infirm elderly. However, with this huge new cohort more likely to be divorced, and having had fewer children on average than their parents' generation did, baby boom older adults will not have as many family members available to care for them in later life (Easterlin, 1996). Divorced men are especially vulnerable. When fathers leave the family when their children are young, the price is often isolation from adult children in old age (Booth & Amato, 1994; Bulcroft & Bulcroft, 1991; Webster & Herzog, 1995). Being less well off financially when young, divorced women and single mothers are not as likely to have adequate savings or pensions to cushion their old age (O'Rand, 1988, 1996). This income problem is especially ominous when we consider how prominent women are in the territory of later life.

Women and Later Life

If the number one demographic fact about the elderly is an increase in numbers, the second concerns who makes up the elderly ranks. The older population is mainly women. The reason is that women live considerably longer than men.

Figure 1-2 illustrates the dramatic gender gap in life expectancy over a 22-year period in the recent past. In 1992, white males had an average life expectancy of 72.3 years. With a life expectancy of close to age 80, white women outlived them by more than 7 years. Moreover, notice that while life expectancy tended to float upward for everyone during these two decades, the gender gap remains wide and transcends race. In 1992, black women outlived black men by almost 9 years (Monthly Vital Statistics Report, 1995).

A complex set of influences accounts for these gender differences in mortality that occur at every phase of life. Although more males are born, boys are more likely to die in infancy, childhood, and adolescence from accidents and diseases. During adulthood, women are much less likely than men to develop heart disease early on.

Since 1970, the gender gap in life expectancy for whites has narrowed slightly. It may decline a bit further if the lifestyle factors contributing to male death rates are reduced. Men are more likely to smoke or drink to excess. They have more hazardous jobs. These environmental differences are thought to partly explain why males have especially high mortality rates from preventable causes of death such as accidents, heart disease and stroke, and lung cancer. But even if we eliminate the external reasons why men die sooner, experts agree, the sex difference in longevity will persist because it has biological causes. Once modern medicine eliminated deaths from childhood illnesses and especially made pregnancy and childbirth safe, women began to outlive men. Today, as Figure 1-3 shows, women outlive men in every developed country, by 4 to 9 years (Nathanson, 1990). Because they must survive childbearing, women are the biologically hardier sex (Verbrugge, 1990).

This means that in every developed country the elderly population is mainly female. The imbalance is especially startling at life's uppermost end. In 1996, at ages 65 to 69, for every 100 U.S. men there were 120 women. In the age group over 85, there were 257!

So, married women can expect to be widowed. They may live as widows for many decades. Because there is also a trend not to live with children, older women often live these final decades alone. They are more at risk of being physically disabled or cognitively impaired, and more likely to spend time in a nursing home. Especially during their old-old years, women are much more likely to be poor (Burkhauser, 1994). Having more time to use up their retirement savings and pensions, plus entering their retired years with fewer assets, means far less money to draw on in advanced old age (Gonyea, 1997).

On the other hand, women bring emotional and social advantages to these problems that are the product of living so long. Because of their lifelong role as relationship experts (and because many of their friends will travel with them to the final stops), women are less likely to be socially isolated and are more connected to family and friends in later life (Moen, 1996). Their attitudes toward illness and disability may offer resilience, too. As we will see in Chapter 5, women tend to be more accepting of sickness, to visit doctors more, and to report more health problems throughout their adult years than men (Verbrugge, 1989, 1990). This gender difference in illness orientation may make it easier for women to cope with the infirmities of advanced old age.

Minorities and Later Life

The demographic statistics relating to minorities are equally revealing about the ranks of older adults. Mainly because African Americans have a much lower life expectancy (see Figure 1-2), the over-65 population is disproportionately white. However, as Figure 1-4 shows, the numbers of minority elderly are growing at a rapid pace. One reason is that as life expectancy in general has risen, more minorities are surviving to old age. Another has to do with a change in the ethnic composition of the industrialized West. Because of a flood of immigrants from Asia, Africa, and Latin America, during the past 40 years Europe, the United States, and Canada have become much more ethnically diverse. Who are the U.S. minority adults?

Although, as we saw in Table 1-1 at the beginning of this chapter, the practice of broadly categorizing people lumps together widely divergent cultural groups, the more than one-fourth of Americans labeled as racial/ethnic minorities in the 1990 census are classified into four groups: African Americans (12.4%); Hispanic Americans (9.4%); Asians and Pacific Islanders (3.1%); and Eskimos and American Indians (.8%). Asian

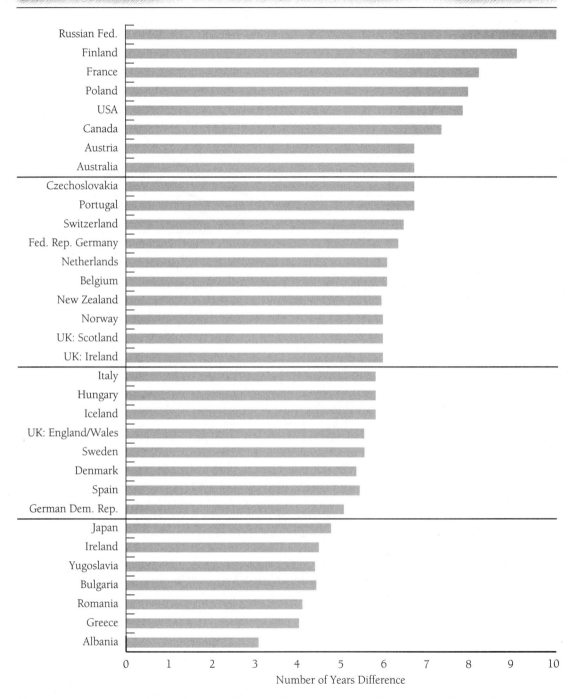

Women outlive men in every developed country. The gap in life expectancy varies dramatically, for largely unknown reasons, from country to country.
SOURCE: Nathanson, 1990.

FIGURE 1-4   *Growth of the Minority Elderly Population, 1960–2050*

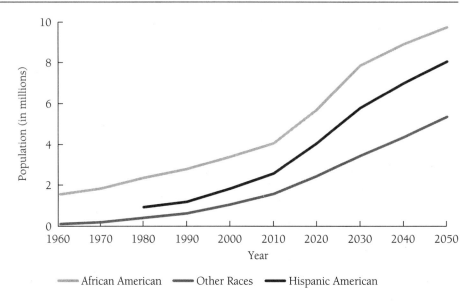

In the future the number of ethnic minority older people will grow rapidly.
SOURCE: Angel & Hogan, 1991.

Americans fare best; African Americans and, to some extent, Hispanic Americans are more likely to be disadvantaged in their later years.

The first disadvantage has to do with life expectancy. Although Asian Americans (and perhaps Hispanic Americans) outlive whites (Markides & Black, 1996), this is not the case for the members of our largest minority group. Recall from Figure 1-2 that the difference in life expectancy between African Americans and whites is substantial. With a life expectancy at birth of only age 65, African American men are especially badly off. More distressing, although the racial gap in life expectancy had been narrowing, a close look at Figure 1-2 reveals that during the mid-1980s it began to widen again. As Table 1-3 shows, African Americans have higher death rates from 11 of the 15 top-ranking causes of death. Growing up in poverty, eating poorer diets, having less access to medical care, and living in dangerous environments, all make it more likely that African Americans, particularly if they are male, either will not make it to old age or will be in poor health during their senior citizen years (Jackson, Antonucci, & Gibson, 1990).

A second disadvantage is economic. In 1988, the median net worth of elderly African Americans was only *one-fourth* that of their white counterparts. Older Hispanic Americans ranked in between the two groups (Chen, 1991; see Figure 1-5). In 1996, elderly African Americans and Hispanic Americans were almost three times as likely to be living below the poverty line as elderly whites.

Rank Order	Cause of Death	Ratio of Black to White
...	All causes	1.61
1	Diseases of heart	1.48
2	Malignant neoplasms, including neoplasms of lymphatic and hematopoietic tissues	1.37
3	Cerebrovascular diseases	1.86
4	Chronic obstructive pulmonary diseases and allied conditions	0.81
5	Accidents and adverse effects	1.27
...	Motor vehicle accidents	1.03
...	All other accidents and adverse effects	1.57
6	Pneumonia and influenza	1.44
7	Diabetes mellitus	2.41
8	Human immunodeficiency virus infection	3.69
9	Suicide	0.58
10	Homicide and legal intervention	6.46
11	Chronic liver disease and cirrhosis	1.48
12	Nephritis, nephrotic syndrome, and nephrosis	2.76
13	Septicemia	2.71
14	Atherosclerosis	1.08
15	Certain conditions originating in the perinatal period	3.21

Ratio of Age-Adjusted Death Rates for the 15 Leading Causes of Death for the Total Population by Race, United States, 1992 — TABLE 1-3

With the exception of lung conditions, pneumonia, and suicide African Americans suffer higher mortality rates from each top-ranking cause of death.

SOURCE: *Monthly Vital Statistics Report 43,* (6) supplement, March 22, 1995.

These differences are a function of income inequalities earlier in life. Because, on average, they earn considerably less and are more likely to be unemployed as young and middle-aged adults, Hispanic Americans and African Americans are more likely to enter old age poor, without savings or pensions to draw on during their retirement years.

Moreover, this situation is likely to continue well into the 21st century because, despite the civil rights progress we have made, substantial earnings differences by race still exist. Although people do move up and down the economic ladder as they approach later life (Crystal & Waehrer, 1996), the best barometer of our economic status when old is our economic status in our younger years (O'Rand, 1996).

As with women, these disadvantages are mitigated by the social and emotional strengths minorities bring to later life. Ethnic minorities have especially close family and community relationships (Mendes de Leon, Glass, George, Evans, & Berkman, 1997). Particularly among immigrant families, norms supporting the care of the elderly are strong (Markides & Black, 1996). When faced with the job of caring full-time for young grandchildren or older family members, African Americans consistently report

FIGURE 1-5   *Median Net Worth of Elderly Families by Race, 1988*

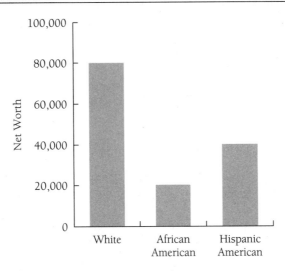

In 1988, the median net worth of an African American household was several times lower than that of a white household. The net worth of Hispanic American households ranked in between the two groups.
SOURCE: Chen, 1991.

lower levels of distress (Anderson-Hanley, Dunkin, Cummings, & Strickland, 1997; Calderon & Tennstedt, 1997). For our largest American minority, the church plays a vital role as a source of spiritual and social support (Taylor, 1993). Moreover, one landmark community survey suggested that African Americans are more psychologically resilient and less likely to suffer from mental disorders than whites (Kessler et al., 1994).

These ethnic and gender distinctions are generalizations. Just as diversity is the number one principle that applies to older people in general, women and minorities differ dramatically in health, in income, in happiness, and in their lifestyles as older adults. Still, as we will see throughout this book, the *statistical* path of later life does differ dramatically depending on gender and race.

A HISTORICAL PERSPECTIVE ON THE FIELD

psychology of aging
Scientific study of behavior in the aging phase of life

Statistics offer an external snapshot. They do not provide insights into the way we behave and change as we age. For these insights we turn to the **psychology of aging—** the scientific study of behavior during the aging phase of life.

The effort to examine aging behavior scientifically is surprisingly recent. Child development is one of psychology's oldest specialties. Among the research areas psy-

Psychologists specializing in aging wear two hats. They are members of the wider community of gerontologists and members of the wider psychological community, too.

The Gerontological Society of America   The main American aging organization. Multidisciplinary group of mainly researchers interested in gerontology. Publishes journals and books, has annual meetings.

American Society on Aging   This organization is newer and includes both researchers and gerontologists working in a wide variety of applied areas. Publishes its own journal, has annual meetings. More likely to highlight innovative practice than research.

American Psychological Association,* Division of Adult Development and Aging   Special-interest division of the American Psychological Association specifically for psychologists interested in adult development and aging. Publishes newsletter and serves as a clearinghouse for other information.

*A section of the special-interest division on clinical psychology of this huge organization is devoted to clinical gerontology.

chologists study, aging ranks as a fairly young field. The following historical information comes from Birren and Birren, 1990, and Birren and Schroots, 1996.

For the first half of the 20th century, development psychology meant only child psychology. (Even today, when psychologists use the term *developmental psychology* they may be referring to children alone.) Although American research in this extremely popular area was underway as early as 1900, child psychology expanded dramatically between the First and Second World Wars. Some leaders of the child development movement made sporadic efforts to study later life during this time. Still, in psychologists James and Betty Birren's words, before the end of World War II, "it is easy to form the impression that most psychologists . . . regard the child as an end product rather than as part of an ongoing course of the human life span" (1990, p. 6).

Interest in the aging process in general was aroused in the middle of the 20th century when scientists returned from World War II and confronted a growing older population. Now that many infectious diseases had been conquered, for the first time in history people were routinely living to later life. In the late 1940s, the National Institutes of Health sponsored an institute on aging. During the same period, the Gerontological Society of America, and the Division of Maturity and Aging, now called the Division of Adult Development and Aging of the American Psychological Association, were formed (See Table 1-4.) In the ensuing decades, spurred on by the explosion in the older population, these organizations flourished, and research on the psychology of aging accelerated (Riegel, 1977). By 1959, enough studies had been published to merit a handbook on the topic. By 1964, the first college textbook appeared.

Today, the psychology of aging is a vigorous, established field. Most psychology departments offer courses in adulthood and aging or gerontology to undergraduates. Graduate students in developmental psychology can get a Ph.D. in this specialty. In 1986, a journal, *Psychology and Aging,* was established devoted exclusively to

clinical gerontology or clinical geropsychology
Assessment and treatment of later-life mental disorders

psychological research on adult development and aging. Besides the many academic researchers, a growing number of practicing psychologists specialize in **clinical gerontology** or **clinical geropsychology,** assessing and treating emotional problems in later life (Zarit & Knight, 1996). In fact, today more psychologists belong to the Division of Adult Development and Aging of the American Psychological Association than to its parent division, Developmental Psychology, which focuses primarily on children.

Although we psychologists who specialize in aging have our own organization, publish our own journal, and get our training "within psychology," we are firmly embedded in a larger enterprise. In fact, the beauty of being in this branch of psychology is that we are *compelled* to branch out to many fields. Because the behavior of older people is shaped by everything from their health status to their place in history, from their finances to the functioning of their brain, at the annual meetings of our main professional organization, the **Gerontological Society of America,** we psychologists may be as likely to attend a lecture by an ethicist, biologist, or historian as one by a colleague in our field (see Table 1-5). This sense of shared enterprise is also evident in our **multidisciplinary** gerontological journals, in the mutual collaboration that is the hallmark of our best research (Musick & Keith, 1997), and at the university-based institutes of gerontology, where researchers and practitioners in various aspects of aging including psychology may be trained and employed. We gerontological psychologists also have the privilege of having some modern pioneers still alive to help nurture our growing field (see Aging in Action 1-2).

Gerontological Society of America
Premier professional organization for scientists who study aging

multidisciplinary
Composed of a variety of different disciplines

So, this branch of psychology is distinguished by its remarkable vigor and breadth. Still, as you read this book, you may note a limitation, too. The main focus of the psychology of aging has been and continues to be probing age-related decline. Even researchers interested in successful aging often couch their studies in terms of "how people manage to stay the same," not the extent to which they evolve or grow. Psychologists are not immune from the stereotype that equates aging with loss. Moreover, the ways we decline with age are much more obvious and easy to chart than the more internal, elusive ways we may improve. Problems of aging such as Alzheimer's disease seem even more pressing because they have such important consequences for society as a whole. The reality is that despite living among this army of vital older people—who often *say* their best years are now—we still know relatively little about whether the poet Robert Browning is correct when he writes, "Grow old along with me; the best is yet to be."

THE PERSPECTIVE AND PLAN OF THIS BOOK

In addition to having this bird's-eye view of the people and our developing field, I want you to be aware of my orientation in writing this book. As should be obvious from its title, this book concerns the psychology of aging. It focuses mainly on behavior in later life.

Within this framework, I will offer a balanced look at the physical, cognitive, emotional, and social sides of life. After these introductory chapters, Part Two explores the physical dimension, providing an overview of Normal Aging and Disease Prevention (Chapter 3); Sensory and Motor Functioning (Chapter 4); and the end-point of

Day 1 At a daylong workshop, "Theories of Aging," I listen to papers by a historian, a biologist, an anthropologist, and several sociologists, in addition to hearing from experts in three core areas of the psychology of aging: a researcher in *cognition* discussing competent performance in the elderly, a specialist in *personality* offering a model of how we regulate our emotions during adult life, and an authority on *psychopathology* (mental disorders) speculating on ideal mental health in old age.

Day 2 *Morning.* At the series of presentations, "Defining and Assessing Quality of Life in Alzheimer's Disease: Recent Advances," focusing on improving the subjective experience of people with this illness, I realize how difficult it is to define, measure, and study high-quality life in this group.

Afternoon. At "Presidential Symposium: Reflections on the Study of Creativity and Aging," once again I am impressed with the unique perspectives experts in various disciplines, from the humanities to sociology to biology, can bring to this important human activity.

Day 3 *(Decide to start my morning with the individual and move to society.)*
8:00–9:45 In "Narrative Gerontology and Late-Life Potentials," presenters discuss how life stories and guided autobiographies can be used to facilitate creativity, help people make sense of their lives, and chart personality during the adult years.

10:15–12:00 At "Critical Gerontology: Implications for Theory and Practice," a demographer, a sociologist, and a gerontologist who specializes in ethical concerns offer provocative critiques of our profession and the wider culture. They touch on topics as different as the disturbing trend to "careerism" (focus on self-advancement) among generation Xers and the lessons we aging professionals can learn from the disability lobby about how to genuinely advocate for impaired older adults.

Day 4
10:45–12:00 At a student-sponsored symposium, "Words from the Wise: Aging Gerontologists Going Reflective," prominent "older gerontologists" offer insights into their own personal pathways to our field.

12:15–1:15 At the Kleemeier Award lecture—an award presented yearly to a gerontologist for outstanding research—the sociologist recipient regales the audience with information about his own family history, presents new data from his ongoing decades-long study of three-generation families, and offers speculations about how family life will be changing in this new century. He predicts that the different generations will be living together once again!

age-related physical change, Disease, Disability, and Health Care (Chapter 5). Part Three concerns cognition: Intelligence (Chapter 6) and Memory and Dementia (Chapter 7). Part Four explores the emotional side of life, Personality (Chapter 8) and Psychopathology (Chapter 9). Part Five concerns the social dimension—that is, our relationships and major roles as older adults. We first look at The Older Family (Chapter 10) and then explore the major late life transitions, Life Transitions: Retirement and Widowhood (Chapter 11). Part Six brings us to the final transition of old age, Death and Dying (Chapter 12), and ends with two brief epilogues: my own comments and some observations by Powell Lawton reflecting on gerontology past and present.

1-2 Powell, PGC, and the Psychology of Aging: The Evolution of a Career, a Center, and a Field

One advantage of being in a relatively young field is being able to speak with some modern pioneers. The elder statesman I interviewed, M. Powell Lawton, has made a dazzling array of contributions to our understanding of disabled older adults. Like many leaders in an emerging discipline, Powell's goal has been both to advance our knowledge and, in 35 years spent as director of research at an innovative facility for the elderly called the Philadelphia Geriatric Center (PGC), to promote the growth of a field. So, in addition to conducting research, over the years he has edited numerous integrative books and journals (including serving as the founding editor of *Psychology and Aging*) and chaired various aging-oriented professional groups. Powell's unfolding career in itself is a mirror tracing our remarkable progress in treating disabled older adults. It is a window on what is possible during the "older years." Powell *embarked* on his career at age 40. Today, at age 74, his energy and passion for research show no signs of slowing down. In listening to this gerontologist, notice also the emphasis on multidisciplinary collaboration that makes our branch of psychology special and how psychological research is being planned to immediately improve the quality of life.

If you think back to the origins of the psychology of aging, Jan, in the middle of the 20th century, most of us fell into this field in a fortuitous way. A friend had met Art Waldman, then the director of the Philadelphia Geriatric Center, at a party. Art was a visionary who wanted PGC to be at the forefront of geriatric care. This was 1960, and I was working as an ordinary clinical psychologist at a psychiatric hospital. Art said, "How would you like to spend a week in San Francisco at the meeting of the Third International Congress of Gerontology?" I said that, while the idea was appealing, I had no interest in leaving my current job, but (and here I think he knew what he was doing) Art urged me to come anyway. I found the meeting very exciting. There were people from all over the world, true pioneers in the field, and it hooked me, but, as I said, at the time I was not looking for another job. Three years later, I got restive, so I recontacted Art, and he made this unusual offer: a clean slate on which to design a research program at our institution. I talked the idea over with a sociologist friend who said, "You'd better take that job. Aging is the coming thing." York House South opened in 1964, one of the first housing facilities for the elderly that incorporated services such as meals and physician visits for people with minor disabilities who did not need nursing home care. So, my first research project was to evaluate the impact of living in York House on our residents. Art's other passion was exploring whether something positive could be done for the mentally impaired elderly—which later became known as Alzheimer's disease. Art was a pioneer in thinking you could do anything more than just warehouse the dementia patient. Our Weiss Institute for dementia, which opened in the early 1970s, was an outgrowth of that vision. I became a member of the small group of behavioral scientists who were

Throughout this book, I will be putting information into historical context, as I feel it is important to understand our past, or where we have come from, in order to appreciate the current research and worldviews we take for granted today. I believe

interested in the impact of the environment on how people functioned, and ultimately, practically all of the leaders in environmental psychology got involved in the planning of Weiss. It was the first treatment setting planned around the dementia patient, and I would say that Weiss is still the best-known treatment environment for dementia. Not that it's still the state-of-the-art. It's been superseded. There are lots of things wrong that we learned. However, the environments that are being built now are the result of the model that we provided. We put forth a cluster of innovations, basic principles about how to approach people with dementia. Things we articulated, such as the use of color and physical aids to enhance memory and movement, all of these features are now standard in the treatment of the cognitively impaired elderly.

In the late 1970s, I was working on my largest study, a national survey of housing sites for older people and my attempt to look at mental health in relation to the environmental features of these settings. Also around that time, I got interested in the way people use time and in the living arrangements of people with disabilities. Elaine Brody [a pioneer researcher in family care for the elderly who was also employed at PGC] and I did some studies of people caring for relatives with disabilities.

My current research with a younger colleague, Kimberly Van Haitsma, involves developing tools to estimate the emotions of Alzheimer's patients with the hope that this knowledge will be useful to family and professional caregivers. We just finished a videotape designed to teach nursing assistants to evaluate these emotions. My other interest has always been in psychological measurement, and so, over the years, we have developed a number of scales to measure emotions and physical functioning in the elderly.

It's always been important for me to get students interested in research. Our approach is to recruit promising people, bring them to PGC, and get them started on research careers. We have new graduates that come here without an interest in aging and they get turned onto becoming researchers. It's been tremendously gratifying to see them go out and establish their own careers. We now have PGC alumni all over the place. At one time, we had 60 people at the institute—anthropologists, psychologists, sociologists, physicians—studying various aspects of aging. Being trained as a clinical psychologist, I've always been an advocate of the development of clinical geropsychology, and so some of my work has been centered around that. However, I consider the environment and aging, emotion and aging, and psychometrics (evaluation) my primary interests.

Right now, foremost in my mind is to go back to some earlier housing work. I have a store of data from 26 years ago, and I want to look at aging in place (how people age in their own homes), but my version of aging in place is not just the tenants getting older but changes in the environment and the joint changes in the individual and environment that affect the quality of life. I have this need for novelty, and so I go on to new projects, but I never give up the old ones. I still have a lot of things I want to do, new things that excite me, and I want to do a good deal of writing.

it is also important to demonstrate how what we learn through research translates into real life. For this reason, I have planned each chapter and major topic to end with an Interventions section describing practical implications of the research. This focus on practical issues pervades the book. In fact, one of my goals is to speak to the aging experience—the actual concerns older people are grappling with as they negotiate life.

For this reason, in the chapters that follow, I will highlight the important social issues facing older Americans today: health care, social security, options in disability, family relationships and concerns. I will pay special attention to how gender, ethnicity, and socioeconomic status shape the quality of later life. My background as a clinical psychologist has shaped another special feature of this book. In addition to surveying the literature, I have taken the step of surveying the people, too.

The vignettes that introduce each chapter and appear in the Aging in Action features are based on the lives of real people. For the most part, they come from interviews I have personally conducted with older adults and professionals who work in our field. While I hope these first-person accounts of aging in operation make the research come alive, please do not read these stories as though they represented *universal reactions* or even feelings typical of most adults. The same is true of every generalization I will make in this book. I cannot emphasize strongly enough that diversity and individual differences are the essence and the beauty of later life.

I hope that this book conveys the excitement of the psychology of aging, this maturing field that speaks directly to your future life. Keep in mind that just as lives develop, the psychology of aging is continually evolving. Perhaps you will become inspired enough by the story in the following pages to decide to help our field grow to a ripe old age.

KEY TERMS

age-irrelevant society
ageism
average life expectancy
baby boom cohort
chronic diseases
clinical gerontology or clinical
    geropsychology
cohort

demography
ethnicity
Gerontological Society of America
gerontology
graying of America
infectious diseases
life expectancy revolution
lifestyle movement

multidisciplinary
old-old
psychology of aging
role
socioeconomic status
young-old

RECOMMENDED READINGS

GENERAL REFERENCES

The following two publications are good sources for facts about older Americans, covering income, illness, disability, the utilization of health care services, living arrangements, minorities, and more.

Administration on Aging. (1997). *Profile of older Americans: 1997.* Washington, DC: Author.

U.S. Senate Special Committee on Aging. (1991). *Aging America: Trends and projections.* Washington, DC: Author.

Birren, J. E., & Schaie, K. W., Eds. (1996). *Handbook of the psychology of aging* (4th ed.). New York: Academic Press.

This edited book, published about every five years, is the definitive reference in the psychology of aging. Glance through the chapters of the latest edition to get a sense of the topics psychologists study.

Gerontologist; Journals of Gerontology, Series B; Generations

These three gerontological journals also offer a first-hand glimpse into the state-of-the-art behavioral science research in aging. *Gerontologist* and the *Journals of Gerontology,* both published by the Gerontological Society of America, cover a broad range of social science–related topics. Each issue of *Generations,* published by the American Society on Aging, offers an in-depth look at a special topic such as grandparenthood, economics, or mental health.

Psychology and Aging

This journal, sponsored by the American Psychological Association, is devoted specifically to research in the psychology of adult development and aging.

SPECIFIC SOURCES

Fischer, D. H. (1977). *Growing old in America.* New York: Oxford University Press.

Minois, G. (1989). *History of old age.* Chicago: University of Chicago Press.

These books offer interesting historical accounts of how the elderly used to be viewed and treated. Fischer covers old age in America. Minois deals with Western culture through the Renaissance.

Jackson, J. S., Chatters, L. M., & Taylor, R. J. (1993). *Aging in black America.* Newbury Park, CA: Sage.

This edited book on the aging experience of African Americans covers topics ranging from crime to self-esteem to family life.

Ory, M., & Warner, H. (1990). *Gender, health, and longevity.* New York: Springer.

This edited book summarizes research relating to gender differences in health and longevity.

Chapter Outline

2

Theories and
Research Methods

"Older people are more spiritual than young adults."
        "Because of his deprived childhood during the Depression, that 80-year-old millionaire watches every penny today."
"That nursing home resident is getting attention when she yells. That is why she acts this way."
Each time we make these types of statements we are using important theories used to understand older adults.

Theories are attempts to organize and explain the "raw data" of behavior. They make sense of the observations we have about older adults. A good theory is clear, is broad in scope, provides new insights, and fits in well with observations. It explains why past events occurred, makes definite predictions about the future, and offers concrete suggestions about how to intervene to improve the quality of life (R. M. Thomas, 1996). Revealing the accuracy of any theory demands research. In this chapter, we survey the two cornerstones of the psychology of aging: theories and research methods.

Throughout this book, you will be introduced to many theories. In this chapter, I offer a preview of some broad theoretical approaches we will encounter repeatedly in the following chapters and sample a few ways psychologists have conceptualized how we change as we age. I will be using the same selective strategy in describing research, focusing mainly on techniques to measure change with age and bringing up issues that loom large in conducting research in our field.

In exploring theories, I've chosen a down-to-earth approach. First, we look at four theories that do not focus specifically on later life. According to these broad, non-age-centered perspectives, the same principles are used to understand behavior at ages 18 and 75. Then, we examine four theories that spell out different types of changes that may occur in our older years.

theories
Systematic efforts to explain behavior within a coherent framework

AGE-IRRELEVANT THEORIES

A Behavioral Perspective on Aging

Behaviorism, perhaps the most influential theory shaping psychology (Kimble, 1993) has a clear position about the aging process and older adults. Behaviorists do not believe there is any such thing as a defined, age-related change. The same principles that explain how a 1-year-old functions explain the functioning of a person of 85. After exploring some basic concepts of this theory, we will look at the interesting insights this *anti*developmental stance offers on development in our older years.

traditional behaviorism
Original behavioral idea that all learning occurs by operant and classical conditioning and that behavior can be understood and predicted by referring to external stimuli and reinforcers alone

classical conditioning
Behavioral process by which humans and animals learn physiological or emotional reactions in new situations

operant (or instrumental) conditioning
Behavioral process by which humans and animals acquire voluntary behavior

reinforce
Behavioral term for reward

extinguish
Behavioral term for disappear

TRADITIONAL BEHAVIORISM   Behaviorists emphasize *nurture* (the environment), not *nature* (genetics). They believe that our actions are determined by our outer-world experiences, not by what we are born with or inherited traits. Behaviorists believe that behavior is predictable and obeys simple laws. According to **traditional behaviorism,** all learning occurs through two basic mechanisms: classical and operant conditioning.

Classical conditioning, the most primitive type of learning, involves involuntary responses—actions or physiological reactions outside of conscious control. In this type of learning, a stimulus that automatically evokes a particular emotion or physiological reaction (the unconditioned stimulus) occurs in conjunction with a neutral stimulus (the conditioned stimulus). After a number of pairings, or one association, a connection is formed and the response is now elicited by the new stimulus alone.

Classical conditioning explains why we salivate when we smell a steak sizzling on the grill. It accounts for that happy feeling that (hopefully) wells up when we approach this class in the morning or turn into our driveway in the evening to see our family. In practice, however, behaviorists most often use classical conditioning to explain why we learn negative emotions in certain situations, such as specific fears. Having an inherently frightening experience, such as being in a car accident, creates a connection between fear and the initially neutral stimulus situation of being in the car. When we next put our key in the ignition, anxiety automatically wells up.

When this experience causes us to change our behavior—perhaps to give up driving and take the bus to work—the second type of learning, called operant conditioning, has occurred.

Operant (or **instrumental**) **conditioning** is the major mechanism explaining our consciously initiated actions. Here the principle is simple. Responses that are rewarded, or **reinforced,** will recur. Responses that are not reinforced will **extinguish,** or disappear. In this case, relief from the anxiety that floods us as we approach our car would be a potent reinforcer, propelling us to avoid the object of our fear.

According to behaviorists, reinforcement drives all behavior. It explains why a 70-year-old widow calls her children daily complaining of chest pains even though there is nothing physically wrong. It makes sense of why her friend the same age, having finally enrolled in college after her husband has died, works long and hard to excel. For the first older adult, the reinforcer motivating her actions seems to be attention. Only by acting ill can this lonely, isolated woman get the caring contact she craves. For the returning student, the reinforcer might be a different kind of attention: "proving to my family that I can make a new life after Jack's death," or possibly, "showing the world that a woman my age can still perform intellectually." Still, in order to prove that these specific reinforcers might be motivating each person's behavior, we would have to chart the conditions surrounding each action. According to behaviorists, we can only determine what is reinforcing by carefully measuring the outcomes linked to performing each response.

We would also want to chart when reinforcement occurs, because different **schedules of reinforcement** (such as being rewarded after every response, at predictable intervals, or irregularly) produce different patterns of behavior.

For instance, if their actions were resistant to extinction, continuing for some time without a current reward, we would expect to find that both women were under some type of *variable reinforcement schedule*. In this common pattern, reinforcement occurs at unpredictable intervals; as a result, people learn persistence—the idea that if they continue responding, at some point they will be reinforced. We would imagine that on certain days her children might be unresponsive, but other times the widow's children gathered around. They worried about her, told her they loved her, and rushed to her side. We would imagine the student as having experienced the hit-or-miss quality of grades. This would teach her a lesson of a superficially different type: "I have to keep studying even when I do not get A's; eventually, my efforts will pay off." In both cases, although the actual content of the learned behavior (industriousness versus incompetence) appears antithetical, the process is the same. Learning is occurring through the identical principle or law.

These simple concepts offer an unusual perspective on important questions in the psychology of aging. Why is it that behavior stays stable over the years? What accounts for age-related change? To explain why we can see much of the older person in the young adult, a traditional behaviorist would invoke operant conditioning and reinforcement. Repeated reinforcement explains why exceptionally creative young adults tend to be unusually accomplished in middle age and why they become increasingly more successful compared to other people in their field as the years pass (see Chapter 6). Reinforcement also accounts for the persistence of negative traits such as hostility. The angry young man provokes a hostile response in other people, solidifying his ill temper. The grumpy, disagreeable 20-year-old is transformed into the hostile, bitter man of 75 (see Chapter 8).

The same behaviorist would use extinction to explain age-related change. Extinction accounts for why, because men no longer see them as sexually attractive, many elderly women report no longer having sexual feelings (see Chapter 10). It offers insights into why, for people in routine jobs, intellectual flexibility declines with age (see Chapter 6). It tells us why, because she is no longer reinforced for being independent and healthy, the elderly widow just described finds that her only chance for human contact lies in acting ill.

BEHAVIORISM'S NEW FACE: THE COGNITIVE/SOCIAL LEARNING APPROACH
For much of this century, behaviorists were satisfied that the principles of classical and operant conditioning could explain all learning. They felt that it was not necessary to make inferences about internal processes such as feelings and thoughts. In fact, behaviorists believed that only studying external, clearly measurable stimuli and responses would make psychology a true "science" of human beings. About 30 years ago, a shift

schedule of reinforcement
Pattern or frequency with which a reward or reinforcing experience occurs

occurred. Many behaviorists realized that operant and classical conditioning could not fully account for behavior. To explain why people acted as they did required widening the focus, venturing beyond what could be externally charted and observed.

The psychologist most responsible for this widened focus was Albert Bandura. In an influential set of studies conducted during the late 1960s and early 1970s, Bandura (1977) and his Stanford University colleagues demonstrated that learning can and often does occur without getting concrete rewards. We also learn by observational learning, or **modeling**—that is, by watching and then imitating what others do. According to Bandura, most learning occurs from observing people. Moreover, we actively *choose* the models and bits of behavior we wish to imitate.

Bandura's ideas were accompanied by other evidence that contradicted traditional behaviorism. Some people continue to act in the same way for months or years when reinforcements seem minimal and there appears to be no reason why extinction has not occurred. The same reinforcing experience, such as repeatedly being praised, may dramatically change the behavior of one individual but have little effect on another. Once again, just focusing on what was objectively happening *to* people seemed inadequate. It seemed necessary to look internally, to the individual's *cognitions,* or thoughts about the world. The cognitive behavioral movement was born.

Cognitive behaviorists still follow many principles of traditional behaviorism. They believe behavior is lawful and predictable and must be systematically charted in order to be understood and changed. Although they do admit that inherited or biological tendencies exist, cognitive behaviorists are still great advocates of nurture. They look to the environment to explain behavior and believe that people can change quite easily in response to environmental interventions. However, there is a central philosophical difference between the way cognitive behaviorists and their traditional counterparts approach human behavior. Rather than viewing people as *reactive*—our behavior is passively determined by the stimuli and reinforcers that happen to exist—cognitive behaviorists view us as *active* agents who shape our own reinforcers. Instead of examining only external events and observable responses, cognitive behaviorists concentrate on identifying, understanding, and changing our perceptions about the world.

Now it is time to introduce two cognitive-behavioral concepts we will encounter repeatedly in this book: self-efficacy and explanatory style.

Self-efficacy refers to our belief in our competence—that is, our conviction that we can perform successfully at a given task. According to Bandura (1989, 1992, 1997), who also developed this concept, efficacy feelings motivate behavior. They determine the goals people set. They predict which activities we engage in as we travel through life. When efficacy expectations are low, we shy away from acting. We choose not to ask a beautiful stranger for a date. We decide that going to medical school is too difficult. When self-efficacy is high, we not only take action, but continue acting long after the traditional behavioral approach suggests extinction should occur. Self-efficacy makes sense of why Grandma Moses continued to paint for decades in obscurity only to emerge world famous in her older years. It tells us why Beethoven persisted when the reinforcers were gone, producing his finest symphony after he had lost his hearing. It explains why the elderly Cezanne persisted in his passion for painting, inventing a whole new art form after being partially paralyzed by a stroke. As Bandura (1997, p. 2) states, "The lives of innovators and social reformers driven by unshakable efficacy

modeling
Learning that occurs through observation rather than direct reinforcement

cognitive behaviorism
Movement in behaviorism stressing the central role that cognitions, perceptions, and thoughts play in behavior

self-efficacy
Internal conviction that one is able to perform successfully at a task

are not easy ones. They are often the objects of derision, condemnation and persecution. . . . Many people who gain recognition and fame shape their lives by overcoming seemingly insurmountable obstacles." If we looked just to standard reinforcement, he argues, most of humanity's greatest achievements would never have occurred.

Although having this sense of personal power is often important, we must not automatically equate high self-efficacy with being happy or even with living a productive life. For one thing, as Bandura (1997) points out, self-efficacy is different from self-esteem. The most "efficacious" people are sometimes immensely self-critical. They succeed *because* they are so demanding, so focused on only reaching the most difficult goals. Others who like themselves a good deal may have low self-efficacy, but languish, contentedly, on the sidelines of life. Unrealistic efficacy feelings can be counterproductive, as when a writer with little talent tries unsuccessfully to "make it" for decades, or a social activist labors for life to reform a political system in which change is impossible to achieve. But in general, Bandura says, self-efficacy is something that we should strive for as we age (and at any age). He may be right. As we will see throughout this book, this simple perception is linked to an amazing array of benefits in later life. The cognitive-behavioral worldview we turn to now has a similar link to aging success.

Explanatory style refers specifically to the perspective that we adopt for viewing nonreinforcing or reinforcing events. Do we see setbacks as temporary, single cases having an external cause? "True, my creative work has been rejected in the past, but this was chance. I always chose galleries without vision. This event says little about my competence or ultimate success." Do we see failures as enduring, global, and internal— signs of incompetence, permanent states that will always occur? "That person's judgment was correct. I'm no good as an artist. I might as well give up."

explanatory style
Specific way a person perceives positive and negative events

Let's illustrate by returning to the college student discussed earlier in describing the concept of reinforcement. Bandura would say that efficacy feelings underlie her drive to study so hard—that is, a conviction that she is competent and intelligent. Furthermore, by examining the strength of these feelings, we can predict what will happen if one semester the student's hopes for making A's are dashed. If self-efficacy is weak, this lack of reinforcement may cause extinction; if robust, the student will work even harder, spending more hours in the library than before.

Explanatory style refers to how the student interprets the disappointing grades. Does she see this failure as global, internal, and stable, reasoning, "This shows I will always do badly; I am incapable of doing well"? Or does she view this event as a temporary, single case, external to the self? "That semester I had a difficult set of professors. I happened to do poorly this term because I was not used to being in school." Table 2-1 shows how different efficacy feelings and explanatory styles would affect an older student's thinking and actions after failing a psychology test.

INTERVENTIONS Traditional behavioral concepts have been used to understand a wide range of later-life behaviors, from societywide early retirement trends, to high suicide rates in widowed men, to why memory and physical abilities erode when people enter a nursing home. According to the theory, when older workers are offered pensions at age 55, and sense that they no longer are really wanted at a company, interest in even the most compelling job evaporates. When a man is deprived of his life companion at age 75 or 80, there may not be enough reinforcers left to motivate continued life. In nursing homes, physical deterioration and memory decline are

TABLE 2-1	Efficacy Feelings and Explanatory Style

EVENT: 70-year-old Mrs. Jones fails her first psychology test the semester she goes back to school

Efficacy Feelings

	Action	Possible Outcomes
HIGH I can succeed	⟶ greater effort, more studying ⟶	success on next test, sense of personal satisfaction, zestful and happy, decides to take honors course or go to graduate school
LOW I can't succeed	⟶ gives up, doesn't study ⟶	Failure on next test, sense of personal inadequacy, demoralized and depressed, drops out of school

Explanatory Style

OPTIMISTIC	Event is (1) temporary, (2) single case, (3) situational or extrinsic to the self. Sample cognitions: (1) This grade was a fluke. (2) I know that I'll do differently from now on. (3) I am intelligent. It's just that I haven't taken a test in so long. I know I'll get A's once I get used to being in school.
PESSIMISTIC	Event is (1) permanent, (2) global, or covering all cases, (3) internal or basic to the self. Sample cognitions: (1) This performance will never change. (2) This will happen in every course. (3) I'm basically incompetent. I don't have the capacity to make it at school at my age.
OBSERVATION:	These different worldviews not only should affect Mrs. Jones's behavior at college but also might have an impact on her general physical and mental health.

predictable because in these settings the reinforcers often promote disability rather than competent functioning (M. M. Baltes, Neumann, & Zank, 1995; M M. Baltes & Wahl, 1992; see Aging in Action 2-1).

The same is true of self-efficacy and explanatory style. These cognitive-behavioral worldviews have been linked to everything from rapid recovery when ill, to having the stamina to search out a late-life career, to coping with the strain of caring for a loved one with Alzheimer's disease. They also offer a unique perspective on age-related

2-1 A Behaviorist in the Nursing Home

How is the behavioral approach used with disabled older adults? What are some issues psychologists face in using traditional behavioral techniques in applied settings such as nursing homes? Insights emerge from this interview with a geriatric behavioral researcher.

I decided to be a clinical psychologist because I wanted to help people. Behavioral approaches, because they are so well documented, were attractive to me. I liked the precision of behaviorism, the idea that by changing the reinforcement contingencies you could make a difference in people's lives.

My interest is in the iatrogenic effects of institutional care—the effect that the environment has on residents even when "good care" is being provided. As my definition of the environment includes the social world, my main focus is the staff. I became interested in care in nursing homes. When you do applied research, you pick a problem that the staff is interested in. I was more interested in deteriorating cognition as a function of being in the institution, but the staff was concerned about incontinence. So, I ran a project to determine the reinforcers controlling incontinence. I was convinced that residents were being incontinent in order to receive attention from the staff, because if you looked at the staff-resident interactions, most social contact was occurring around dressing and changing the person.

My colleague and I set up a procedure whereby residents regularly would be given the chance to go to the toilet and attention would be applied as a consequence of requesting assistance and withheld when the person was wet. An aide went into residents' rooms every hour asking if the person wanted to go to the bathroom. Residents were only taken to the toilet if they requested to go. The purpose of this strategy, which we called prompted voiding, was to put control back into the hands of the residents so they would get assistance only when they wanted it. Over half—and I emphasize half—of the incidents of incontinence are eradicated within two days if you do that. Incontinence is a multibillion-dollar problem, and our idea was that if you could reduce incontinent episodes, you could significantly reduce nursing home costs.

The problem we encountered is that the nursing home aides, while well meaning, are overworked. So a person arrives one day and a coworker is absent, and that individual has 12 people to change and dress rather than 8. Prompted voiding has to be done on the resident's schedule, not the staff's. If there is no reinforcement for asking the resident, the temptation is not to ask. I remain convinced that our techniques are effective. The real need is to shift focus to the powers higher up. We need to change the industrywide reinforcement contingencies that inadvertently can operate to foster less-than-optimal care. *

*I will expand on the issues this gerontologist is addressing when we discuss nursing homes in Chapter 5.

decline. When older people believe that poor memory or illness is inevitable at their age, cognitive behaviorists argue, these age-linked changes in efficacy feelings may lead to withdrawing, avoiding physical or mental activity, and retreating to a rocking chair

(Lachman, 1991). The same is true of age-associated shifts in explanatory style. When a younger person loses his keys or develops a pain, we see the event as temporary, reasoning, "He has too much on his mind. He is not feeling well *today*." In an older person, we interpret the same events in an internal, permanent, global light: "He is suffering from old age."

Now that we have this framework, we can summarize behaviorism's appeal, particularly for psychologists who work clinically with the elderly.

1. **Behaviorism is optimistic.** The theory offers a positive, "easily reversible" perspective on problems that occur in later life. When behaviorists see 70-year-old Mr. Jones who is disagreeable or depressed, they do not nod knowingly about a "characteristic" old-age personality. Instead, they think, "These traits have nothing to do with being at a certain life stage but with the external conditions of living—the fact that since retiring and losing his wife, Mr. Jones has been deprived of the reinforcers necessary to mental health. If this man were reconnected with the world and people, his former 'young' personality would automatically reemerge." When behaviorists see physical deterioration in 80-year-old Mrs. Smith, they think, "How is this problem being maintained by this woman's cognitions? Are negative ideas about what is possible at her time of life causing Mrs. Smith to take to a wheelchair and abandon living a productive life? How can we rearrange this situation to reverse what *seems* to be decline caused by advancing age?"

2. **Behaviorism has wide scope.** Rather than just being a theory of personality, cognition, or physical functioning, behaviorism has global applicability. The principles of learning offer a framework for understanding everything from later-life learning to end-of-life impairments such as incontinence (see Aging in Action 2-1).

3. **Behaviorism is action-oriented.** Behaviorism offers a clear blueprint for change. By using the principles of learning, not only can we understand why older people have certain behaviors, we can immediately intervene to improve the quality of later life.

So, to return to the criteria of good theory at the beginning of this chapter, behaviorism gets high marks for its scope, ability to provide new insights, clarity of predictions, and practical implications. However, despite these attractive features, questions remain. Can the principles of reinforcement really account for why our personality, interests, and attitudes are often so stable over years despite the many changes in the external conditions or reinforcers in our lives? *Why* is it that one person remains confident in the face of repeated failures while for another low self-efficacy is an ongoing burden from youth? Where do these differences in worldviews really come from, and might they not be more resistant to change than behaviorists assume? Perhaps there is more to personality than a collection of isolated, easily charted behaviors and thoughts. The next theory addresses these issues.

psychoanalytic theory
Theory developed by Freud that stresses the primacy of unconscious motivations and early childhood experiences in determining adult personality

A Psychoanalytic Perspective on Aging

If behaviorism has been the most influential theory in psychology, **psychoanalytic theory**, developed by Sigmund Freud during the early decades of the 20th century, is the theory of human behavior that has won in the wider world. Every time we hear statements such as "My problems are caused by traumatic childhood experiences" or "I must have done that unconsciously," we are listening to ideas loosely based on Freud's writings. In fact, although psychoanalytic theory has been heavily criticized, Freud, who wrote extensively from 1900 to the beginning of the Second World War, clearly qualifies as a world-class genius. This man powerfully shaped modern Western culture. He profoundly altered the way people think about human motivations and actions.

THEORY   Freud believed that our basic personality is formed in early childhood and then remains relatively stable. He thought personality has conscious and unconscious aspects. The deepest layer of personality, the unconscious, is the most important determinant of behavior. He also believed that personality has three facets: id, ego, and superego.

The id, present at birth, is the mass of instincts, wishes, and needs we have when entering the world. The ego, the largely conscious, reality-oriented "executive" of personality, is formed when children realize that their needs cannot be immediately satisfied. Ego functions involve logic, reasoning, and planning, getting what we want in an appropriate way. Next, the superego develops, the unconscious internalization of parental and societal prohibitions, norms, and ideals. In other words, during early childhood, Freud believed, we learn the requirements of being human. Our wishes and desires can only be fulfilled by adjusting to reality. Sometimes, these wishes must be abandoned in order to live a moral, ethical life.

Freud and his followers believe that parents are responsible for this learning, and so for our lifelong mental health. If our parents are empathic and sensitive during early childhood, we will develop a strong ego that allows us to adapt to the crises of life. If they are insensitive, or for some reason their care is poor, ego formation will not be optimal and we will be vulnerable, prone to the eruption of impulses from the id, likely to develop problems when encountering the stresses that later life is certain to bring.

So, for Freudian psychoanalysts, the way we behave during old age is stable, determined by a personality that is set in stone from our early years. Later-life stresses, such as becoming ill, being widowed, or retiring, are tests of psychological functioning. These changes strain the capacity of the ego, the executive in charge of mental health, to be firmly in control. It is during these life crises, if our childhood experiences have not been ideal, that we break down and develop psychological symptoms. To understand behavior, it is crucial to look beneath the surface. What unconscious needs, fantasies, and wishes are motivating the person's actions? We now highlight this approach by examining how a psychologist who adopts the traditional psychoanalytic perspective might view the two women described in the section on behaviorism.

In the case of the lonely widow, the psychologist might see the need to be taken care of as a childhood desire that becomes activated in situations of stress. Being isolated and alone might have provoked the eruption of this basic need. Furthermore, believing that personality basically doesn't change, the psychologist would reason that similar episodes probably punctuated the woman's earlier life. In any difficult situation, she would develop psychological problems. In fact, previous life crises would most likely have produced the same symptoms of dependency we observe today. Moreover, the cure for this problem would lie in fully exploring the past. In examining and coming to terms with what happened in the distant years of early childhood, we would find answers to why the widow has this inappropriate way of dealing with life.

The psychoanalytic psychologist would bring the same approach to the student, seeing her pattern of behavior as determined by unconscious childhood needs. However, because the student's behavior seems more appropriate and healthy, the psychologist might put this woman in a different category. Although we could only know for certain by investigating her childhood, the student's actions imply an ego in control, the psychoanalytic criterion of mental health.

INTERVENTIONS   Psychoanalytic theory has made interesting contributions to research in the psychology of aging. The concept of unconscious motivations has added a dimension to our understanding of the way personality is measured and changes during adult life. The idea that there is more to emotions than what people report has enriched our knowledge of how the elderly feel about death. As we will see in Chapter 9, clinical geropsychologists have even used psychoanalytic techniques with institutionalized older adults (Semel, 1996).

However, just from this simple description we can see why *traditional* psychoanalytic ideas have not been very popular in gerontology. Any theory that assumes that nothing important occurs after childhood is bound to seem less than appealing to people committed to exploring the later years! With its exclusive focus on personality and emotional problems, and on who we are as set in stone, psychoanalytic theory lacks the breadth, optimism, and practicality of behaviorism. In fact, traditional psychoanalytic ideas are actively age-hostile, painting older people as incapable of change, describing life's last stage as the season of loss and decline. Moreover, the theory is vague and difficult to prove (or disprove). Like behaviorism, it has trouble explaining the strong differences we often find among people in what look like similar environments. Why is it that one person who grows up in a loving family turns out so badly, while another is a model of mental health? Isn't more than just our upbringing responsible for the ways we act? The effort to answer these questions brings us to a third perspective on older adults.

A Behavioral Genetic Perspective on Aging

Although behaviorism and psychoanalytic theory make different assumptions about what motivates people, the theories are similar in one way. Both stress the importance of our outer-world experiences (or nurture) in determining our mental health and happiness as adults. Now we look at the role that the other category of influence, heredity (or nature), plays in shaping adult life.

THEORY   The effort to study inherited aspects of behavior has a long history in psychology. However, during the first two-thirds of this century, environmental explanations took center stage. During this period in the United States, as we saw in Chapter 1, great advances were occurring in the quality of life. Perhaps it was partly the improvements in life expectancy that helped promote this faith in the power of the environment to erase human problems and accounted for the dominance of behaviorism in American psychology, especially during the middle decades of this century (Kimble, 1993). During the 1950s and early 1960s, psychoanalytic theory was extremely popular. It was widely believed to be a highly effective cure for emotional problems. After the Second World War, we might imagine there would be great resistance to research showing that inborn, hereditary differences have a major impact on behavior. Americans had recently had an object lesson in the costs of this position taken to its extreme in the horrors of the Nazi idea of a master race.

Within a brief period during the 1970s and early 1980s, the pendulum swung the other way. Suddenly, it became routine to emphasize inherited tendencies to explain traits as different as the tendency to become phobic, to bite our nails, or select a spouse. Unless otherwise noted, the material that follows is from Bouchard, 1994; McClearn, 1993; Plomin and McClearn, 1993; and Plomin, DeFries, and McClearn, 1980.

There were important reasons for this shift. One force was the development of medications that were proving as effective as psychotherapy in dealing with many emotional problems. Most important, research in a field called **behavioral genetics**—the influence genetics has on behavior—made the inherited contribution to personality and psychopathology clear.

The basic strategies behavioral geneticists use to examine the influence of heredity on behavior are twin and adoption studies. In **twin studies,** researchers compare identical (monozygotic) twins—who, because they develop from the same zygote, share 100% of their genes—with fraternal (dyzygotic) twins. Fraternal twins, like any brother or sister, develop from separate zygotes and so, on average, share 50% of their genes. Researchers reason that if a trait is highly influenced by genetics, identical twins should be much more alike on that dimension than fraternal twins.

Specifically, in twin studies, researchers select large groups of identical and fraternal twins and **correlate,** or relate, how each group scores along scales measuring particular behavioral dimensions or traits. The statistic used to describe the strength of the association between two measures, called a *correlation coefficient,* can range from $+1$ to -1—showing perfect predictability in either a positive $(+)$ or negative $(-)$ direction—to 0, showing no relationship. However, because even the score the same person would get on different occasions is apt to change, when studies reveal that twin pairs' scores on complex attributes such as intelligence in later life correlate at .8, the strength of these relationships is considered to be remarkably high.

Next, researchers subtract the correlation coefficients for the two groups of twins. Because logically this number automatically omits half of the genetic influence, they double that figure to arrive at a statistic called heritability. **Heritability** refers to the degree to which variations in that trait can be attributed to genetic influences. For instance, twin studies suggest the correlation in height between identical twins is about .9 while that for fraternal twins is about .45; doubling this difference yields a heritability of .9. This does *not* mean that if I am 5'2", my height is due 90% to heredity and 10% to the environment! It means that *on average the differences* we observe in height among Americans today are approximately 90% genetic in origin.

In **adoption studies,** the strategy is to compare adopted children with their biological and adoptive parents. Researchers estimate the impact of heredity on a trait by looking at how closely adopted children resemble their birth parents (with whom they share only genes) or adoptive parents (with whom they share only environment).

These techniques offer a powerful tool for exploring the contribution heredity makes to human differences. However, there is one criticism we might make about the twin-study strategy of comparing identical and fraternal twins who have been raised

behavioral genetics
Field devoted to studying the impact of genetic influences on behavior

twin studies
Behavioral genetic research strategy in which the similarities between identical twins are often compared with the similarities shown by fraternal twins

correlation
A statistical technique designed to show how closely related two variables are to one another

heritability
Statistic describing the genetic contribution of a given behavior or trait

adoption studies
Behavioral genetic research method in which adopted children are compared with their biological and adoptive parents along dimensions or traits

together. Perhaps when researchers find more similarity between identical twins than fraternals, they are really measuring the impact of more similar environments as well as genes. Don't parents treat identical twins more alike, dressing them the same and responding to them more similarly than they do to twins who do not look the same? By finding sets of monozygotic and dyzygotic twins who have been adopted into different families, we would have a way of separating genetics and environment in a pure form. As you might imagine, finding large enough groups of twin pairs in this unusual situation is a heroic task. However, we do have several studies in which researchers have accomplished this feat. Luckily for us, the most comprehensive, the **Swedish Adoption/Twin Study of Aging**, specifically involves people being studied during the aging phase of life.

SwedishAdoption/ Twin Study of Aging
Scandinavian behavioral genetic study in which identical and fraternal twins adopted into different families were reunited and compared in late middle age

In Scandinavia, national registries of births make it easier to find that needle in a haystack: twins adopted into different families. During the early 1980s, researchers tracked down 99 identical and 229 fraternal Swedish twin pairs who had been separated from their biological parents and adopted into different families before age 10. These twins, many of whom were over 50 at the time, were reunited and given an extensive evaluation. They took tests covering personality traits. They were asked about their childhood, the quality of their current relationships, and the major events they had experienced during life. Their physical and intellectual capabilities were probed. The twins' responses on each measure were then compared with one another and contrasted with those of a sample of raised-together twins (Plomin & McClearn, 1990).

These assessments offer a remarkable guided tour of the impact of nature (or heredity) on who we are, allowing psychologists to catalogue and compare the role genetic influences play in shaping everything from temperament, to intelligence test scores, to talents, to our perceptions of the world. Moreover, because the researchers compared heritabilities for middle-aged and elderly twin pairs and asked subjects to return to be retested every three years, the Swedish Adoption/Twin Study has an added bonus. It can tell us whether the hereditary influence on any given behavior changes over time. Just as we would not expect genetics to have an equally powerful impact on personality as on intelligence or physical health, there is no reason to imagine that heritabilities remain stable or constant at every age. Are certain aspects of who we are especially "hereditary" compared to other traits? Might our life experiences become more (or less) influential in shaping our personality, intelligence, or tendency to get ill as we enter and progress through later life? Here are tantalizing, tentative answers to these questions. (This material is from Pedersen, 1996.)

1. **Heritabilities do vary greatly from quality to quality and trait to trait.** As we might expect, the Swedish Adoption/Twin Study shows that the genetic contribution to personality is small compared to that for physical health. Unexpectedly, however, the highest heritabilities turn out to be in *cognition*. Notice, in Figure 2-1, that genetics explains an astonishing 80% of the variability among older adults in IQ!

On the other hand, within each broad category there is variability. We can see this once again by looking at Figure 2-1. For some strange reason, the genetic contribution to memory (the digit span test) is much lower than for our fund of knowledge in old age (the information test). The researchers find the same puzzling differences when they compare different aspects of personality. Although, in general, inherited tenden-

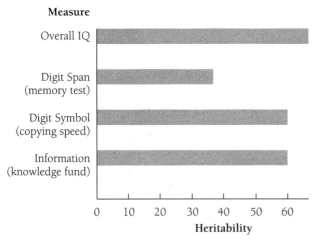

Notice the astonishingly high heritability for overall IQ.
SOURCE: Pedersen, 1996.

cies do have a moderate impact on our personality and attitudes (heritabilities typically hover around 30%), specific traits such as the tendency to believe in luck, to be unassertive, or to erupt easily in anger show no genetic influence at all.

Interestingly, the tendency to develop a pathological extreme of a behavior is more genetically determined than is behavior in the normal range. As we will see in Chapter 7, behavioral genetic studies show that serious late-life cognitive problems such as Alzheimer's disease are quite hereditary. For this frightening illness of aging, fraternal/identical twin comparisons reveal heritabilities as high as 70%—a figure far exceeding the statistics for normal variations in memory shown in Figure 2-1. The same is true of depression. Although there is no evidence of a genetic tendency to develop mild symptoms, serious depressions do have a hereditary link. In other words, as we approach the outer limits of behavior, who we are as people is less determined by our life experiences and more heavily influenced by our genes.

2. **Heritabilities do sometimes wax and wane at different ages.** The most interesting example relates to physical health. When the researchers compared middle-aged and older twins, they found that the heritabilities for illnesses and self-reported health were lower in the older group. In other words, illnesses that crop up earlier (at a more unusual time?) are more "genetic," whereas in old age (a more normal time to get ill), random environmental forces loom larger in determining our physical fate. However, aspects of personality that we might reasonably expect to become more "environmental" as we accumulate more life experiences—extroversion or neuroticism—show no change from later middle age to later life.

INTERVENTIONS   These provocative, puzzling findings offer a lesson in the complexity that we will see throughout this book. Just as there is no simple, single answer to the question of how much of who we are is determined by nurture (the environment) and how much is in our genes, every behavior in later life has multiple, varied causes. Moreover, just as the influence of genetics varies from behavior to behavior and from life stage to life stage, behavioral geneticists find there is even a hereditary influence on the *degree* to which we change and in the relationship between certain traits, such as the contribution that being in good health makes to our overall sense of well-being at different ages.

This research offers lessons in the power and limits of personal control. On the positive side, the finding that genetics is only moderately influential in determining health (and becomes less important over time) suggests that making changes in our lifestyle, such as modifying our eating habits or exercising, does affect our physical fate. On the other hand, because genetics partly determines qualities once believed totally "environmental" (such as personality and emotional problems), there are limits to personal freedom. A variety of self-destructive behaviors are basically more difficult for some people to change. However, we must be careful not to equate "genetically determined" with fatalism or the idea that improvement is impossible or that nothing can be done. Even when something is almost totally genetic, it is also totally dependent on the outer conditions of life.

Let's take the example of the most hereditary quality the researchers found: the extremely high correlations in IQ between older twins who had been raised apart. Suppose the twin pairs lived in a culture where older people were forced out of society at age 40, or at a time in history when there was little education and everyone worked as laborers in the field. In these environments, any differences in intellectual *potential* would probably be irrelevant, as there would be little chance to demonstrate a high IQ at all. Or consider the finding that our tendency to get ill is moderately hereditary in the aging phase of life. If you lived in colonial times, you would be unlikely to live long enough to have the luxury of fulfilling your genetic tendency to develop *any* age-related disease. If you were living even a few decades ago, before the lifestyle revolution, your hereditary tendency to heart disease or another chronic condition might express itself years earlier than today.

These examples show that the quality of our environment is *always* critical. As many observers argue, although it is important to unravel the role genetics plays in behavior, it is even more crucial to provide the outer-world conditions in which our negative genetic tendencies can be inhibited and our positive genetic potential expressed. In a restricted environment, the most brilliant inherited talents may never be fulfilled. In fact, without adequate nurture, or what researchers call an enabling environment, we can never even know what potential talents and gifts our nature (or heredity) holds.

An Information-Processing Perspective on Aging

Behaviorism, psychoanalytic theory, and behavioral genetics have long histories in the behavioral sciences. A fourth influential non-age-centered approach to behavior arrived only during the middle 1960s with the computer. This link is not accidental. Computers are the model for psychologists who use the information-processing approach.

THEORY   The **information-processing perspective**, unlike the theories described previously, is devoted to understanding cognition—that is, *how* we think. It
makes no assumptions about heredity or environment or inferences about what motivates us to behave in certain ways. The basic assumption underlying this approach is
that the mind behaves much like a computer. Just as computers manipulate information, acquiring it and processing it according to rules, human thinking occurs according to similar steps. By proposing models and conducting studies to reveal these steps
and expose how they function, information-processing researchers attempt to understand the operation of the mind.

*information-
processing
perspective*
Approach to
understanding
human cognition
that uses the
operation of
computers as an
analogy to the way
the mind functions

INTERVENTIONS   Information processing, as is true of the other theories in this
section, has been used to understand behavior at every stage of life, from the development of memory in childhood to how memory changes as we grow old. In the psychology of aging, the information-processing approach is the major perspective
researchers use to understand the reasons for age-related cognitive decline. Why is it
that older people react more slowly? What is the source of the losses in various abilities
we often observe in older adults? By setting up diagrams such as the one pictured in
Figure 2-2 and then conducting experiments to localize the problem in one mental
processing phase or component, researchers hope ultimately to improve the quality of
life in old age.

So an information-processing psychologist would have a different interest in looking at the two elderly women described earlier, focusing on the mental processes that
produced each woman's responses. How did the first woman process the information
to make that call to her children? What mental steps occurred between having the idea
to call and picking up the telephone? How exactly does the student manipulate information in memory? Have there been changes in her abilities to process and retrieve
the information she needs to excel at school? By conducting research to uncover these
answers, an information-processing researcher would hope to understand how cognition changes with age.

AGE-CHANGE THEORIES

The theories described previously are general models of behavior. Now we turn to
theories spelling out specific changes during adult life. In this section, we sample the
ideas of just three psychologists because they illustrate very different approaches to
how we can think about age-related change. We start with the best-known life-span
theory: Erik Erikson's idea that there are distinct *stages* of adult life.

Tasks Linked to Age: Erik Erikson's Psychosocial Crises

Erikson was a German psychoanalyst who disagreed with Freud in a few important
respects. Whereas Freud focused on sexual and aggressive impulses, Erikson believed
that *psychosocial concerns,* or issues relating to identity and relationships, are centrally
important in life. Erikson did not accept Freud's pessimistic view of human nature as
"ruled" by the unconscious. Most important, he rejected the traditional psychoanalytic

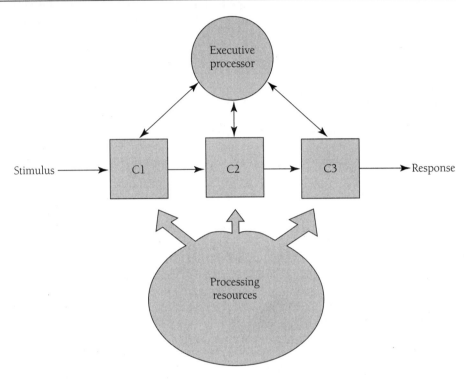

Information-processing theorists typically construct this type of chart, in which thinking is broken down into separate processes or steps (c), an executive processor coordinates the activity, and processing resources are the fuel or energy driving cognitive activity.
SOURCE: Salthouse, 1992.

idea that all growth automatically ends at age 5. Erikson set out to chart the phases of psychological development throughout life.

psychosocial crises
According to Erikson, issues that become salient and must be grappled with at particular life phases

THEORY   According to Erikson (1963), there are eight life tasks or **psychosocial crises** as we journey from birth to old age, each loosely tied to a particular period of life. These tasks build on one another because a person cannot master the issue of a later stage unless the developmental crises of the previous ones have been successfully passed. Except during early infancy, the crises of childhood center around gradually developing a secure, healthy sense of self. Once *identity* is formed in adolescence, we are capable of *intimacy*—the process of merging with another person that is our first task as young adults.

Having made this commitment, Erikson believes, we become capable of giving in a larger sense. **Generativity,** "the concern in establishing and guiding the next generation," is the key to living fully during midlife.

Although generativity can mean giving through raising children, Erikson stresses that we do not need to become parents to feel fulfilled in this task. Generativity involves being committed to furthering the development of our fellow human beings in any area of life. The artist who takes pleasure in creating knowing he will enrich the lives of people who see his paintings, the businesswoman whose joy in work comes from realizing she is producing a helpful product, and the volunteer who serves meals to the homeless experience their middle years differently from the person who focuses only on the self. According to Erikson (1963, p. 267), without being generative we feel "a pervading sense of stagnation and personal impoverishment" because we have not fulfilled the purpose of our middle years.

Not only do we stagnate in the present, we cannot master the final, old-age task, **ego integrity:**

> [t]he acceptance of one's one and only life cycle as something that had to be and that, by necessity, permitted of no substitutions . . . a comradeship with the ordering ways of distant times and different pursuits . . . [but] the possessor of integrity is ready to defend the dignity of his own life style against all physical and economic threats. . . . For he knows that an individual life is the accidental coincidence of but one life-cycle within one segment of history. [Erikson, 1963, p. 268]

As this quotation suggests, older people who have achieved ego integrity feel that their life has meaning. Paradoxically, this sense of personal significance allows them to accept their insignificance in life—that is, the fact that they must soon die. A different fate awaits the older adult who is wracked with regret about mistakes made and dreams left unfulfilled. Frustrated and doomed because it is too late to make amends for the years poorly spent, this person is desperately afraid of dying. In Erikson's words, the emotion that haunts this individual's final years is despair. Table 2-2 summarizes Erikson's last two psychosocial crises, or life tasks, with the positive and negative outcomes of each.

INTERVENTIONS   Erikson's ideas have captured the imagination of social scientists who believe that there is more to growing older than just decline. They have been particularly useful in clinical work with the elderly. For instance, based on Erikson's premise that the task of old age is to come to terms with one's life, a popular activity in senior citizens' centers and nursing homes is **reminiscence** or **life review** sessions, in which older people are encouraged to review their lives in order to ward off depression and enable them to reach the sense of closure that Erikson feels is essential to coming to terms with death.

Interestingly, however, despite the enormous popularity of Erikson's ideas, researchers have only recently begun to test their validity. Are there really distinct stages of development and central issues such as generativity and ego integrity that appear during the aging phase of life? In view of the variations between cohorts and among individuals, is it reasonable to expect that we develop in stages or that certain issues

generativity
Psychosocial task of midlife (roughly ages 35 to 65), involving guiding the next generation

ego integrity
Psychosocial task of later life (65+), involving accepting one's life in order to accept impending death

reminiscence or life review
Promoting late-life ego integrity and mental health through reminiscing about one's past

TABLE 2-2	Erikson's Aging Phase of Life Tasks: Positive and Negative Outcomes	

Middle Adulthood	
As we reach our middle years, our task is to achieve generativity—the sense that in our lives we are benefiting others or being of service through what we do.	
Generativity	**Stagnation**
People feel fulfillment and meaning in daily life.	People feel as though their existence has little meaning. They are stagnating or drifting purposelessly through life.

Later Adulthood	
After having lived generative lives, our task is to review what we have done in life and reach a sense of ego integrity—the feeling that our existence has had meaning and was not wasted.	
Integrity	**Despair**
People feel content, at ease, and unafraid of death.	People feel hopeless, depressed, and terrified of impending death.

become important as every human being ages? We will be discussing these questions when we explore the research on personality in Chapter 8.

One reason why Erikson's ideas became popular so immediately may be that he agreed with much of Freudian theory. Erikson accepted the basic principles of psychoanalysis, including the idea that childhood is important—the foundation for what happens in later life. In contrast, Carl Jung disagreed with Freud in a fundamental way. Jung believed our *older* years are the only truly important time of life.

A Single Shift in Midlife: Carl Jung's Passage toward Maturity

Jung was a colleague of Freud who abandoned the psychoanalytic movement largely because he disagreed with Freud's emphasis on early childhood. Jung believed that who we are as adults cannot be reduced to infantile needs. The present and future are centrally important: our goals and life plans, the person we are now and hope to be. As an outgrowth of this prospective (future-oriented) view of human nature, Jung believed that the second half of life is more important than the first (Mattoon, 1981).

THEORY   Jung divides adult life into two phases, with midlife (about age 40) being a turning point. He begins his discussion with the time of life from puberty to about the mid-30s. During this period, which he calls youth but we would call young adulthood, our main goal is to establish ourselves. We are energetic, passionate, self-absorbed, concerned with satisfying our sexuality, obsessed with carving out our place in the world. In our late 30s, physical and sexual energy begin to decline. We are settled. We know our capacities and the limits of what we can do. We either are successful or have begun to make peace with the idea of not setting the world on fire. So a turning inward occurs. Introspection and contemplation become primary. Relationships, understanding the meaning of life, and giving to others become our main concerns.

According to Jung, making this transition is hazardous. Many people are unable to relinquish "the psychology of the youthful phase" and carry this earlier orientation into middle and later life. They stagnate and become vain, unhappy, and rigid. However, if development occurs in an ideal way, we reach a pinnacle. We can be transformed into spiritual beings.

Jung believes that this **midlife shift to maturity** completes us psychologically. We can accept and integrate all of the facets of our personality, even those we have previously denied. So another consequence of this midlife change is less differentiation between the sexes. Men become more tolerant of the feminine component of their personality, and women give more play to their masculine side.

midlife shift to maturity Jung's idea that in the middle years it is possible to reach an ideally mature psychological state

INTERVENTIONS   Jung's ideas about personality change in aging women and men have some interesting research support. We also can trace the origins of the familiar concept of a midlife crisis to Jung's theory of personality. However, although they have influenced some psychologists (for example, Gutmann, 1987), in general, Jung's speculations are too arcane, too far removed from daily life, and not practical enough to have had a major impact on researchers in aging.

Adapting to Development and Decline: Paul Baltes's Selective Optimization with Compensation

Jung was an early-20th-century philosopher with a mystical worldview that elevated later life. Paul Baltes is a contemporary researcher in adult cognition who has devoted his career to probing often negative age-change. Baltes's theory of **selective optimization with compensation,** though less inspirational, has the virtues of being clear, applicable to many areas of life, and extremely practical. Baltes spells out strategies we can use to cope successfully as we develop and decline during life (Marsiske, Lang, Baltes, & Baltes, 1995).

selective optimization with compensation Baltes's prescription for adapting to age changes, including limiting efforts to areas of top priority, working to optimize performance in these areas, and using external aids to compensate for losses

THEORY   According to Baltes, successful living requires *selection*: Because we cannot do everything, we need to focus our energies on those life activities that are most important personally. Successful living requires *optimization*: In order to perform to our potential, we need to work especially hard in these central areas of life. Successful living requires *compensation*: As none of us is competent to do everything by ourselves, even in these selected domains, we must rely on external supports in the areas where we cannot perform.

INTERVENTIONS   Let's look at how these principles might apply to you, the reader of this book. As you travel through college and realize it is time to select a profession, you decide that your talents lie in psychology. So, among a huge menu of possibilities, you choose that career (selection). Then, you work hard on your grades, giving up other activities, because it is so important to get into graduate school (optimization). In the areas where you are weaker, you compensate. You enlist a friend to help you with the statistics for your senior thesis; you use the spell-check on your

TABLE 2-3	The Mental Activities a Psychology Professor Might Engage in during the "Aging Phase" of Her Career

Selection
Now that I'm 50, I can no longer juggle everything. I'd better think carefully about my priorities. It's time to give up sitting on university committees or giving talks, as teaching and writing are really my main loves.

Optimization
The few seconds I spent scanning my notes before class no longer are sufficient. In order to deliver a good lecture, I need to spend a half hour preparing for each class.

Compensation
I don't trust myself to remember that lecture all by myself. I would feel better bringing a set of notes to class. Those reading glasses are mandatory equipment. It would be nice to have a flashlight on hand so I can see the board when the lights are dim.

computer to make sure your papers are correct (compensation). As this example shows, these strategies are important at any time of life; however, they are critical when people encounter the losses of advancing age.

As older people become aware of their declining capacities, Baltes suggests, they automatically limit themselves to top-priority activities because less can be done as effectively. Because it takes more effort to do just as well, they work harder in those critical areas of life. Finally, when losses become extreme, they rely more heavily on external supports to make up for the functions that have been lost.

Now let's apply these principles to a college professor, perhaps someone much like me, in the aging phase of her career. As she realizes she no longer has the same mental and physical stamina—and a limited time to live—she takes stock of what is important and realizes that teaching and writing are her number one interests in life. So, she focuses on her courses and her writing and reduces her other commitments at work (selection). Because she can no longer count on remembering her lectures as easily, she spends more time going over her notes before class (optimization). Once in the classroom, she compensates. She brings an outline to jog her memory. She takes her reading glasses to make out the notes. She increases the level of lighting in class to more easily read her overheads (see Table 2-3).

Just as they have in my own life, the same processes of selection, optimization, and compensation probably occur with many aging adults. In fact, these three simple principles underlie many of the interventions we will be describing in this book to promote full living during our older years.

Synthesizing the Perspectives: The Contextualist, Life-Span Developmental Approach

By now you may feel overwhelmed by these different points of view. There is the assumption of aging as decline and the opposing belief that we change for the better as we age. There is Erikson's concept of life tasks linked to age and Jung's belief that a single shift to a more integrated state occurs at midlife. There is the principle that personality is unchanged from childhood (psychoanalytic theory) and the opposing idea that our current environment, or perceptions of that environment, determines who we are (behaviorism). There are the different speculations about what causes older people to act the way they do—from reinforcement, to parenting, to heredity. Table 2-4 summarizes the domains of interest of each theory and the kinds of questions it poses in looking at older adults.

The **contextualist, life-span developmental perspective** (P. B. Baltes, 1987; P. B Baltes, Reese, & Lipsett, 1980; P. B. Baltes & Willis, 1977; Dixon, 1992) embraces all of these points of view. This approach to aging is not a defined theory or assumption about the direction of change, but an overall orientation with a single message: Pluralism (a variety of points of view) is the best policy to follow in understanding age change.

Life-span developmentalists believe that pluralism in theories is essential. There are many valid ways of looking at behavior. Our actions *do* have multiple causes. Just as we learned something interesting by examining the aging process through each theoretical perspective or lens, pluralism is essential in describing the path by which we develop and change. Change during adulthood is **multidirectional:** As we age, we gain, we stay the same, and we decline. Change during adulthood is **multidimensional:** Some abilities improve, others remain stable, and others get worse. Finally, people differ greatly from one another; their patterns of aging follow diverse forms.

For instance, wisdom may increase with age while physical stamina decreases. Reading activities may remain stable while other interests, such as going to the theater, may rise to a peak and then decline. Along each dimension people will differ somewhat, depending on their cohort, their ethnic group, their social class, their biological makeup, and their idiosyncratic life experiences. Furthermore, just as we should not always expect consistency between individuals, our personal path is determined by many different factors. How we develop over the years is shaped by a variety of influences, the total **context** of who we are and where we are in time.

As you might imagine, this all-inclusive framework is the guiding approach in this book. In the following chapters, we will be seeing the value of these theories and others in understanding older people, and the many influences that affect how we develop and adapt in later life. We will realize that we do grow better, remain the same, and function less well as the years pass. We will come to appreciate that, despite important underlying patterns we all share, individual variability is also a hallmark of our older years.

The purpose of the life-span approach is to (1) describe, (2) explain, and (3) optimize or improve behavior. So, in covering each aspect of aging, we first look at what happens and why it may happen—that is, we explore the research describing and explaining development. Then, using this knowledge, we focus on specific strategies to improve the quality of our later years.

RESEARCH METHODS

Does our personality really remain unchanged as we age? Is there any truth to Erikson's or Jung's theories? Exactly what abilities rise in which contexts, and which ones decline

contextualist, life-span developmental perspective
All-inclusive orientation to the life span that emphasizes the need to adopt a multifaceted, multidimensional, individual-difference-centered orientation when describing, explaining, and improving development

multidirectional
Changing in different directions

multidimensional
Comprising different components or dimensions

context
The total life situation of the person

TABLE 2-4 **The Different Orientations of Each Theory to the Psychology of Aging**

	Overall Domain of Interest	Specific Interest in Older People
BEHAVIORISM	Any behavior	What are the reinforcers or cognitions explaining the behavior? How can I change this behavior by modifying the environment?
PSYCHOANALYTIC THEORY	Personality	What childhood experiences have caused personality? What unconscious motivations underlie this person's actions?
BEHAVIORAL GENETICS	Any behavior	To what degree is this behavior caused by hereditary predispositions?
INFORMATION PROCESSING	Cognition	How do each person's thought processes occur?
ERIKSON'S THEORY	Development issues at different stages of life	Is this middle-aged person manifesting generativity? Has the older person reached integrity?
JUNG'S THEORY	Personality growth after midlife	Has this person accomplished the midlife transition? Is she showing the androgyny of the second half of life?
BALTES'S THEORY	Any behavior	Is this person using selection, optimization, and compensation to adjust to his losses?

as we advance in years? To answer these questions, we need techniques designed to examine how people differ at different ages. The two strategies that researchers typically use to measure these changes are cross-sectional and longitudinal studies.

Cross-Sectional Studies

cross-sectional studies
Developmental research technique involving testing different age groups at the same time

Because cross-sectional research is easier to carry out, this approach is most often used to measure development (Hertzog, 1996). In **cross-sectional studies,** researchers compare *different age groups at the same time* on the trait or ability that they are interested in—be it muscle strength, maximum cardiac output, motor speed, marital happiness, or mental health. Before testing, the researcher might decide to match the different groups, or make them comparable on important variables other than age that are likely to affect their scores.

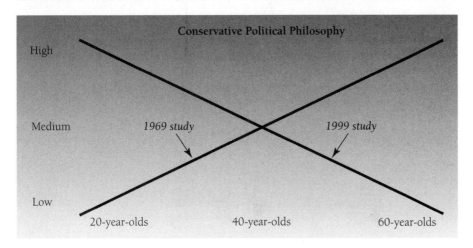

Conservative Political Philosophy

High

Medium   *1969 study*   *1999 study*

Low

20-year-olds   40-year-olds   60-year-olds

Notice how a cross-sectional study conducted with different cohorts can produce opposing results.

For example, if we were interested in finding out whether people become more politically conservative as they age, we might use the following approach. We would randomly select equal numbers of young-adult, middle-aged, and elderly people (for instance, 100 subjects aged 20, 100 aged 40, and 100 aged 60), taking care to match our groups for extraneous influences that might affect their scores, such as social class, educational level, or ethnic background. We would then give a scale of conservatism to each group and compare their scores. If we found a statistically significant trend toward more conservatism in successively older groups, we would conclude that as people grow older, they become more skeptical of government efforts to help its needy citizens or effect social change.

However, our conclusion would be wrong. Because we are not following people over time, we cannot assume that these differences *between* age groups reflect changes that actually occur as people advance in years. For instance, although a study carried out 30 years ago might have shown that young people were the most liberal, today the same hypothetical study might reveal the opposite trend (see Figure 2-3). Because of the political climate in recent years, young adults might have the most conservative views. The most liberal attitudes might be held by the middle-aged and young-old subjects, who developed this political philosophy when they were young adults during the 1960s.

This example points up the crucial problem with cross-sectional studies: They provide information about **age differences**, but they do not reveal **age changes**. In this research strategy, true changes that occur as we advance in years are confounded with differences that result from an extraneous factor—being in a different cohort.

age differences
Differences between groups revealed in cross-sectional studies

age changes
True changes that occur with advancing age

These mid-life photos of me and my grandmother graphically reveal how unalike different cohorts are certain to be at the same stage of life.

1998, age 50   *1953, age 53*

As we learned in Chapter 1, the time in history during which we journey through adult life (our cohort) shapes that journey in crucial ways. We can see this cohort difference immediately by looking at photos of my grandmother and myself taken during the same decade of life. Just as reaching our 50s at a given point during this century obviously influences our external appearance and the way we dress, it is likely to cause striking differences in other areas of life. So what are called **cohort factors** affect not only the results of cross-sectional studies of political attitudes, but also the outcome of almost any study we might carry out.

cohort factors
Biasing effect of being in a certain cohort on the results of cross-sectional studies

Cohort factors are an important bias in cross-sectional studies of physical performance. They also tend to affect the results of studies examining how IQ changes with advancing age. In the past, in these important areas, cross-sectional studies gave us excessively gloomy findings. For years, researchers falsely concluded that more loss occurred with age than really took place.

As we learned in Chapter 1, because of the lifestyle movement and improved health care, over this past century each cohort has been reaching a given age physically healthier than the previous one. The same used to be true of the intellectual environment. Because of regular increases in the number of Americans completing high school and college, particularly during the middle decades of the 20th century, each younger cohort was arriving at a given age better educated and so intellectually better off (see

Chapter 6). These cohort differences in health and years of schooling gave younger groups a built-in advantage on tests of physical functioning and IQ. Older cohorts were handicapped by having been born at their particular time. The *true* extent of the physical or mental loss that age brought was seriously exaggerated.

Cross-sectional studies have another important liability. They tell us only how *groups* differ from one another, not about individual patterns of change. This means they cannot offer answers to some of the most important questions we have about how people change. Even if *on average* sexual activity declines in older age groups, are there some people who become more interested in sex as they age? If we are very physically fit compared to the typical person our age, are we likely to live longer than our contemporaries? If we are especially shy at age 30, will we still be introverted compared to people our age at 65? Is low self-efficacy or a pessimistic explanatory style a burden people carry with them throughout life? Although we can get partial answers to these questions by looking up records or asking people to remember how they used to be, the best strategy is to be on the scene to measure what is going on. This means using the longitudinal approach.

Longitudinal Studies

In **longitudinal studies,** a researcher selects a cohort (or cohorts) and periodically tests this group, ideally using the same measures, over years. For instance, using the previous conservatism example, a researcher might recruit a large group of 20-year-old college juniors and then give them the attitudes questionnaire at regular intervals as they aged. This type of study would give us insights we could never obtain from seeing how different age groups compare. Even if the cohort as a whole grew less accepting of government programs, for example, we might find that people who lost their jobs, or went back to graduate school at age 50, or had a medical crisis behaved differently. Maybe these people would become more in favor of government interventions as they aged. Unfortunately, this informative research technique has liabilities.

Longitudinal studies have practical problems. They require a huge investment of effort, time, and funds. The investigator or research team must remain committed to the study and available to continue it over years or, as in studying aging, decades. Imagine keeping your enthusiasm about a topic for 20 or 40 years. Even if you stayed interested, your question might become outmoded. Even the way you choose to measure conservatism is likely to become obsolete over the years! Imagine getting subjects to make the same demanding commitment. Then, think of the time it would take to search them out each time an evaluation is due. All of these impediments become more serious the longer a study goes on. For this reason, longitudinal studies covering decades are not common. Longitudinal studies spanning all of adult life are very rare.

The difficulty with getting subjects to return over the years is more than just a practical hurdle. It leads to an important bias in itself. Because participating in a longitudinal study requires such a demanding commitment, people who volunteer for this type of research tend to be highly motivated and unusually responsible. Often they are personally invested in the research question. For instance, Mr. Jones volunteers for a study examining physical aging because he is so interested in his health, while Mrs. Smith, who couldn't care less or is embarrassed about revealing her couch-

longitudinal studies
Developmental research technique involving selecting one or more cohorts and periodically retesting the same subjects

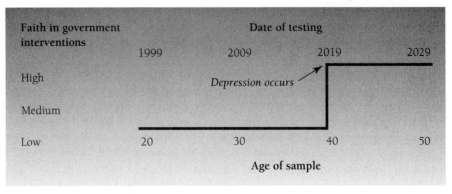

Could we really say this change at age 40 is due to advancing age?

potato habits, quickly declines. Moreover, once in the study, knowing he will be returning helps keep Mr. Jones "on his toes." As the time for each test approaches, he takes care to exercise and watch what he eats. As he gets more comfortable with the procedures, at successive evaluations his blood pressure readings go down and his visual tracking skills become more efficient. Not only has the researcher selected a high-functioning group to begin with, the act of participating in the study has changed subjects. They react differently knowing that they are being tested. Through what are called **practice effects**, over time their scores naturally rise.

These biases are compounded by a process called **selective attrition**, or experimental mortality. In any longitudinal study, people drop out. At each successive evaluation, fewer volunteers remain. But this attrition is not random. The least capable people are likely to leave. People who stay in the study are often an especially well-off group, almost guaranteed to be unlike the average or typical person their age.

For instance, in gerontological research, a main reason people drop out of longitudinal studies is poor health. When they are in their 60s, they mention concerns such as fears about driving to the test site (Golden-Kreutz & Andersen, 1997). When they are in their 70s and above, they are simply too ill to continue or have died (P. B Baltes & Smith, 1997). While health clearly affects how individuals perform on studies examining physical functioning, a moment's thought tells us that good health may also influence how they function in almost every area of life. People who are unusually healthy perform better intellectually. They tend to be happier and more involved in life. They may be aging optimally in almost every way. So, the people who remain in a longitudinal study are likely to be high functioning in many areas investigators choose to measure. Findings based on this group will minimize the negative effects of aging and exaggerate the ways the average person changes for the better as he or she grows old.

practice effects
Biasing effect of being familiar with the testing situation on performance in longitudinal research

selective attrition
Bias that results when a nonrandom group of the original sample— the least capable or most poorly functioning subjects— drops out as a longitudinal study continues; also called experimental mortality

In sum, these influences combine to give longitudinal studies the opposite bias from much cross-sectional research: Longitudinal research provides too *optimistic* a picture of what happens to the typical "randomly selected" adult growing old.

Our ability to make universal statements about development from longitudinal studies is limited in other ways. First, conclusions based on longitudinal studies should be restricted to the particular cohort(s) we are studying. Because each cohort is unique, it is likely to show an idiosyncratic pattern of change as it ages. Moreover, even among this particular cohort, longitudinal studies do not allow us to measure age changes in a pure or isolated way. Here, too, changes that occur due to the advancing years alone are mixed up with an extraneous influence: societal changes occurring at a certain time.

For example, in our study examining conservatism, suppose there was an economic depression between two of our tests. Imagine how that event might affect our cohort's feelings about the mission of government to provide services such as jobs or income to its citizens (see Figure 2-4). In this case, notice that an occurrence around the time of measurement has interfered with our ability to measure "true" age changes. So this type of bias is called a **time-of-measurement effect**.

Sequential Studies

About 40 years ago, K. Warner Schaie (1965), a prominent researcher in adult development, devised what he called **sequential strategies**—techniques designed to compensate for the biases of cross-sectional and longitudinal studies. Schaie's idea was that by conducting several different longitudinal and cross-sectional studies and comparing their results, it would be possible to disentangle time-of-measurement effects and cohort effects from "true" changes that occurred with age (as well as control for biases such as practice effects).

In the longitudinal sequence (P. B. Baltes, Reese, & Nesselroade, 1977), researchers begin longitudinal studies in separate years, tracing how different cohorts perform over the same age range. For instance, they might begin a study of 20-year-olds in 1998, then start a comparable longitudinal study 10 years later in 2008, and compare the results. In the cross-sectional sequence, researchers contrast the results of cross-sectional studies carried out in separate years—comparing, for example, how 20-year-olds, 40-year-olds, and 60-year-olds score on our conservatism questionnaire in 1998 and 2008. By seeing if the change patterns in these studies were similar, or by exploring in what ways they differed, researchers could estimate the extent of bias due to cohort or time-of-measurement effects.

Schaie used these contrasting assessments in an influential study to reveal how intelligence-test performance really changes as we grow old. However, because sequential strategies are so complicated, studies employing this procedure are uncommon. For this reason, throughout this book, when we want to explore development, we will be relying on that precious resource, longitudinal research.

With the caution that they have the problems summarized in Table 2-5, longitudinal studies are invaluable. There is no substitute for the insights we can get by tracing how human beings age. In the following chapters, we will be highlighting the findings of studies covering decades, exploring topics as different as measuring marital

time-of-measurement effect
Biasing effect of societal events occurring around the time of testing on the findings of longitudinal studies

sequential strategies
Developmental research technique designed to uncover true age changes by conducting several longitudinal and cross-sectional studies and comparing the results

1. The studies are expensive, are difficult to carry out, and take decades to complete.
2. The studies offer too optimistic a picture of normal aging.
3. The studies show only how aging occurs in one cohort.
4. The studies confuse changes due to external events occurring around the time of measurement with true age changes.

happiness, charting cognition, and probing personality change. Now we look at one especially comprehensive study of physical aging that we will be mentioning again and again in this book: the Baltimore Longitudinal Study of Aging.

Baltimore Longitudinal Study of Aging
Landmark, ongoing National Institute on Aging–sponsored study of the aging process, focusing mainly on physical functioning

THE BALTIMORE LONGITUDINAL STUDY OF AGING   The National Institute on Aging sponsored the **Baltimore Longitudinal Study of Aging,** beginning in 1959. Subjects ranging in age from their 20s to their 90s were recruited. So far, more than 2,000 men and women have volunteered (not until 1978 was the study extended to women). People who enroll in the study make an intense commitment. Depending on their age, they return either every year or every two years to spend several days at the Gerontology Research Center in Baltimore. At each visit, a medical history is taken. Hundreds of physical capacities are examined, from grip strength, to reaction time, to percentage of body fat, to how deeply a person can breathe. Participants are given tests of memory and learning. Their personalities and methods of coping with stress are probed. The payoff has been worth the investment of effort. As we will see in succeeding chapters, the Baltimore study has contributed greatly to our understanding not just of normal physical aging, but of how we develop in many important areas of life (National Institute on Aging, 1993).

Evaluating the Research

internal validity
Ability to draw accurate conclusions from a study's findings based on the internal quality of the research design

external validity
Ability to generalize accurately from the results of a study to real life

In evaluating any study of aging, it is important to look at two considerations. The first, the **internal validity** of the study, refers to researchers' ability to conclude what they want to based on the design. Can we really say that this hypothesis is true from the particular method used in this study, or are there competing, equally logical reasons why these researchers may have found what they did? The second consideration involves **external validity,** our ability to generalize from that study to the wider world. A study may be elegantly designed, with findings that permit no other interpretation, and still have little meaning if those findings hold only in the highly controlled laboratory situation or apply only to that particular group.

In our critique of longitudinal studies, we saw that practice and time-of-measurement effects represent significant threats to internal validity. When we see a certain change at our next evaluation, we cannot be sure if what we are observing is due to subjects' greater familiarity with the testing situation, to an external event that occurred between the two testings, or really due to age. We also saw that because they

Method　A total of 224 male volunteers aged 55–65 were recruited from several large companies at retirement. The men were randomly assigned to a control (N=111) or an exercise (N=113) group, with stratification by blue- or white-collar job.

　　The exercise group underwent 3 sessions of training per week for a year; these subjects were also encouraged to train 1 additional session each week on their own. The control group carried on retirement without interference. The training consisted of a 10-minute warm-up, approximately 30 minutes of walking or jogging, and then a 10-minute warm-down (the independent variable).

　　At the posttest, the performance of the two groups was compared with their baseline performance on various measures of physical functioning: indexes of cardiorespiratory fitness such as heart rate and breathing capacity, blood lipid (fat) levels, grip strength and flexibility, and body weight changes (the dependent variables).

Results　There were significant increases in some measures of respiratory capacity among the men in the intervention group compared with the controls. There were also significant differences in grip strength favoring the treatment group. However, there were no differences in pretest/posttest body weight or blood lipid levels between the two groups.

Conclusion　Exercise has an impact on some aspects of fitness and little impact on others. In particular, regular exercise may improve respiratory fitness and grip strength.

SOURCE: Cunningham, Rechnitzer, Howard, & Donner, 1987.

---

involve **unrepresentative** or atypical **samples,** the external validity of these studies may be severely compromised. How can we claim our study reflects a universal aging process when we are studying only the most interested subjects, or have only examined how the cohort born in 1920 behaves as they journey through life?

　　With these two types of validity in mind, we now turn to several cautions we will be stressing repeatedly in exploring any type of research in this book.

　　BE CAREFUL TO AVOID THE CORRELATION/CAUSATION MISTAKE　An experiment is the best research technique from a standpoint of internal validity. In a **true experiment,** illustrated in Table 2-6, a researcher systematically varies some prior condition (called the independent variable), then randomly assigns subjects to receive either that treatment or another intervention. The strategy of *random assignment* ensures that any preexisting differences between the subjects "wash out." If the study has been planned correctly, the only factor that makes the groups different is the intervention whose impact the researchers want to assess. If the group exposed to the treatment does differ in the way the researchers predict, then they can conclude that their intervention *caused* the particular result. (The hypothesized result is called the dependent variable because this outcome *depends on,* or must be due to manipulating, the independent variable.)

　　In the psychology of aging, our goal is often to make the statement that "this causes that." However, the experimental approach cannot be used to answer the majority of questions about causes we might have.

　　For example, it would be impossible to do an experiment to test Erikson's idea that reaching integrity causes people not to fear death, or to demonstrate that if the

unrepresentative sample
Subjects selected for study who do not reflect the characteristics of the population that a researcher wants to generalize to

true experiment
Only research method that can truly prove that a specific intervention or prior condition causes a given outcome

student described earlier in this chapter had a pessimistic explanatory style, this attitude might cause her to give up school. We cannot randomly assign subjects to an "integrity group." It would be difficult to manipulate experimentally how people perceive life events. Even questions that we could examine by conducting an experiment might be criticized as impractical or even unethical. For instance, in the study described in Table 2-6, we might legitimately ask how the researchers could really force everyone in the treatment group to exercise four times a week for a year and make sure their behavior did not vary in any other way apart from this specific treatment. Wouldn't you imagine that less healthy people might drop out of the treatment group, or once they got interested in exercising, people exposed to this health-inducing intervention might began to watch their diet too? Certainly, it would be unethical to prevent people in the control group from deciding to exercise on their own. (In fact, in this study there were dropouts from the intervention group, and a few of the control group men did begin to exercise regularly. Moreover, the researchers did not check to see whether *undergoing* the treatment might have induced other lifestyle changes that could have produced their findings apart from exercise.)

Because of these difficulties, in most studies of aging, researchers measure some naturally occurring, preexisting difference between people (such as integrity, explanatory style, or exercising regularly) and relate this attribute to the other quality of interest (such as low death fear, abandoning school, or health and fitness). This type of strategy involves a *correlational approach* because here too we are seeing how one variable relates to another. If a significant correlation exists, then a statement about causality is often made: Reaching integrity makes people fear death less; having a pessimistic explanatory style causes people to abandon their efforts easily; leading an active life promotes health.

This type of conclusion *may* be correct. However, it is equally likely to be wrong. For instance, in the exercise example, the relationship between exercising and health might really be incidental, due to a third underlying cause: genetics. People who are less sickly, more biologically fit, might have more energy during adulthood and so be prone to exercise more. Or we might be confusing cause and effect. People lead a sedentary lifestyle because their body is giving off signals of the underlying illness to erupt later on. Poor health causes physical inactivity, not the reverse.

If we could control for every alternate explanation, we could more confidently make statements about causes by using a simple correlational approach. However, as this degree of control is not often possible, when viewing results of this common research strategy, be on guard: Make assumptions about possible causes with care.

BE CAREFUL TO LOOK AT THE SAMPLE   Because they are easier to recruit, the subjects used to examine many questions in the psychology of aging are selected from settings where older people congregate, such as retirement communities or senior centers. There is always the nagging question of whether the people found in these "special places" are representative of the typical older adult. To make matters worse, in soliciting subjects, researchers often put up advertisements asking people to volunteer. As we saw with longitudinal studies, this practice makes an unrepresentative sample— older people very different from their peers—especially probable.

For instance, let's suppose that you were interested in studying sexual behavior in later life and recruited subjects by putting up flyers at a senior complex in town. Who do you think would respond to the advertisement, people who wanted to make a point about their sexual exploits or those who had no interest in this area of life? Or imagine that you wanted to measure how memory changes with age. Once again it makes sense that the older people whose attention was captured by your notice would be individuals especially proud of how they were performing in this area of life. When you then discovered that most older people have intercourse several times a week or that memory shows no change with age, could you really conclude that your findings reflect the experience of the typical older adult?

We cannot force people into a study. So even when researchers take care to select a representative sample, they must grapple with the question of who volunteers. For this reason, before interpreting the findings of *any* study, it is important to consider the subjects: How were they recruited? What characteristics do they have? Can we generalize from this group to the wider world?

Issues relating to subject selection do more than compromise external validity. They raise questions about internal validity, too. Let's illustrate by returning to our study measuring memory in the elderly and how it compares with memory in the young. If you sample college students and random older people at your senior complex, you have neglected to control for cohort differences in education. But would confining your older sample to people who went to college really make sense? Because college attendance was much rarer in the past, this strategy might result in comparing "intellectually elite" older people with more average young adults.

As this example shows, there are no easy answers about how best to recruit subjects, no truly unbiased way to control for everything but age (Hertzog, 1996). The fact that every strategy has built-in problems applies even more strongly to the next critical choice a researcher must confront: selecting the measures to use.

BE CAREFUL TO LOOK AT THE MEASURES   The validity of a study depends upon its measures—how the investigator defines and assesses sexuality or memory, or to take our earlier example, physical health. Like most concepts in the psychology of aging, these vague entities can be conceptualized and **operationalized,** or translated into concrete measures, in different ways. An investigator's findings can depend on the definition and measurement strategy he or she picks. A researcher who defines sexuality by measuring the frequency of orgasm may get a different impression of sexual behavior and how it changes with age than a colleague who measures this quality by asking how often a man has sexual intercourse or feels aroused. An investigator who measures health by asking people to rate their fitness may get a different response than another who rates health based on objective measures such as tests of cardiorespiratory function or blood pressure. (Notice, for instance, in the study in Table 2-6, how the answer to the question "Does exercise benefit people?" differed for each measure of fitness. In other words, the outcome of this research was dependent on *what* the researchers chose to measure.)

In the psychology of aging, not only must researchers define and measure their concepts with care, they are faced with an additional complication. The defining qualities of what they are measuring may shift with age. The frequency of erection and orgasm may be a reasonable measure of sexuality at age 20 but a poor indicator at 85. For instance, even though by their 60s many men do have trouble performing sexually on occasion, this does not mean they give up intercourse or lose desire. In fact, in one

operationalize
To translate an abstract entity or quality into concrete measures

poll, even some elderly men who were totally incapable of having erections reported having a frequent, satisfying sex life (Brecher et al., 1985)! The blood pressure or blood cholesterol reading that would signal health does differ for someone who is 80 versus 35. Moreover, in their later years, people often report being healthy even when they have some disease. Because their assessments are based on their level of functioning, they tend to be more positive than those of their physicians, who are relying on medical tests (Idler, 1993). Who is correct, the older person or the objective assessment? What *really* is the best measure of health or sexuality in later life?

At a minimum, a researcher's measures must be **reliable;** that is, people must receive the same score if *immediately* administered the test or procedure again. For instance, in the study of fitness, even though we expect long-term changes, we would be in trouble if subjects' rankings on the measures fluctuated widely from minute to minute. In fact, without this short-term consistency, the concept of change would be meaningless, as there would be no way to define fitness at all.

The researcher's measures should be **valid;** that is, they should really measure the quality they are supposed to be measuring. Using the example of our memory study, suppose that how people performed on our measure did not reflect their behavior in the wider world? If people who did poorly on our laboratory test showed superlative scores when asked to recall a similar list of items at the grocery store, we could conclude little from our research.

Questions of measurement reliability and validity are not only critically important in evaluating any particular study. As we will see in the following chapters, they also loom large in basic controversies in the psychology of aging, such as how to define and measure fundamental qualities like memory or intelligence or depression in later life.

Getting Much Bigger and Occasionally Much Smaller: A Final Note on Current Research Trends

In the past few decades, gerontologists have made tremendous strides in grappling with these challenges. To improve external and internal validity, they are likely to use large, representative samples, to employ well-validated scales and multiple measures to operationalize their concepts, and to use sophisticated statistical techniques to disentangle confounding influences that might bias their results (Fried, 1997). This trend to bigger, better-designed research is vital, as it allows us to have confidence in the truth of what we find.

However, amid the cast-of-thousands samples and avalanche of numbers, there is concern. With the emphasis on better quantification (measurement), could it be that something is lost? So, along with the thrust to "bigger studies," there is an emerging minor chord. Some gerontologists are returning to the small, single-person study, exploring the idiosyncratic experience of the individual in depth.

Quantitative research techniques, the strategies described in this chapter, are the foundation of the psychology of aging. In order to make general statements about the aging process, it is important to examine that process across many different people. It is critical to capture vague entities such as health or memory or sexuality through scales having numerical values that can be tallied and compared. Gerontologists who conduct **qualitative research** are not interested in making comparisons between individuals. They are not especially concerned with predicting behavior or with making

---

measurement reliability
Minimum condition for a measure's adequacy, when subjects get roughly the same score if they are retested immediately using that measure

measurement validity
When a scale or measure is really measuring the quality that it is supposed to be measuring

quantitative research
Standard research strategy in which statistical tests, numerical scales, and groups of subjects are used to make general statements about behavior

qualitative research
Alternative research strategy in which interviews, autobiographies, and other personal materials are used to understand an individual person's life in depth

2-2 Taking the Research Road Less Traveled: Interviewing a Gerontological Interviewer

What contribution can qualitative studies make to gerontology? What is the worldview of researchers who adopt this approach? What do gerontologists who conduct qualitative research do? Insights come from anthropologist Robert Rubinstein, a leading figure in this emerging branch of gerontological research.

When I entered graduate school, I wanted to be an archaeologist. Then, I realized that my interest was in people, not things. I did fieldwork in the South Pacific and then got a position at our gerontological institute. When I came here and was exposed to mainstream research in aging, I realized how unfamiliar gerontologists were with what we anthropologists do; I realized the dimension that our approach could add to understanding aging and older adults. Standard gerontological research is narrow, atheoretical, abstract. We measure concepts such as life satisfaction by a number, as if they were entities that could stand on their own, removed from ongoing life. An identical life-satisfaction score has radically different meanings from person to person. It is embedded in that individual's tragedies, his relationships, where he wants to go—the core issues that give purpose to his days. Life satisfaction cannot be divorced from this subjective, ongoing reality. It cannot be studied apart from the rich, multifaceted context of the person's life.

My interest is in life stories—that is, in learning about the experience of aging through having people tell me about their lives. The life story is complex, nuanced, evolving. It captures the heart of what it is to be human, because it reveals how we make meaning out of our life. I go into the community—often into decrepit neighborhoods—visit people in their homes, try to enter into their personal-meaning worlds through intensive interviews. I'm actually a very shy person. After all these years, I still get nervous when I make that first call. I feel immensely gratified when somebody gives me the time of day. But I'm amazed by how receptive people are, how eager they are to tell their story. It's as if they have a hunger to make contact. They leap at the chance to talk. It's heartbreaking how grateful they are to be listened to for the first time. My mission is to give a voice to people that would go unheard and, in the process, help us understand aging as it is really lived.

Over the years, I've seen a change among my gerontologist colleagues, an increased appreciation for the role life stories play in revealing the story of aging. Today, even our most quantitative research often adds on a qualitative component. My main concern is that I see some colleagues attempting to integrate the two techniques, trying to quantify what we do. I feel that's a mistake. The research methods are different. They cannot be blended together. They each stand on their own.

Now that I've left my administrative position at the institute and accepted a university job, I am able to get back to doing research. I may want to do an observational study at a senior center, see how people develop relationships. I'm interested in the experience of ethnic minorities, in particular understudied immigrants such as Hispanic Americans. I'm interested in exploring how families caring for a loved one with Alzheimer's disease cope with managed care. The important thing is that I have the opportunity to start doing what gives me personal meaning in life once again.

statements that apply to most older adults. Their goal is to understand the unique life of the individual, as revealed in journals, through personal observations, or (as described in Aging in Action 2-2) through intensive interviews.

The following chapters are devoted to exploring quantitative research, as this is our scientific strategy for arriving at the truth. However, on occasion we too will stray to this less traveled path, highlighting some interview studies in gerontology and conducting our own interviews to put a human face on the facts about behavior in later life.

KEY TERMS

adoption studies
age changes
age differences
Baltimore Longitudinal Study
   of Aging
behavioral genetics
classical conditioning
cognitive behaviorism
cohort factors
context
contextualist, life-span
   developmental perspective
correlation
cross-sectional studies
ego integrity
explanatory style
external validity
extinguish

generativity
heritability
information-processing
   perspective
internal validity
longitudinal studies
measurement reliability
measurement validity
midlife shift to maturity
modeling
multidimensional
multidirectional
operant (or instrumental)
   conditioning
operationalize a concept
psychoanalytic theory
psychosocial crises
practice effects

qualitative research
quantitative research
reinforce
reminiscence or life review
schedule of reinforcement
selective attrition
selective optimization with
   compensation
self-efficacy
sequential strategies
Swedish Adoption/Twin Study
   of Aging
theories
time-of-measurement effects
traditional behaviorism
true experiment
twin studies
unrepresentative sample

RECOMMENDED READINGS

THEORIES AND THEORETICAL PERSPECTIVES
ON DEVELOPMENT

Baltes, P. B. (1987). Theoretical propositions of life-span developmental psychology: On the dynamics between growth and decline. *Developmental Psychology, 23,* 611–626.
   This article spells out the contextualist, life-span developmental approach.

Baltes, P. B. (1993). The aging mind: Potential and limits. *Gerontologist, 33,* 580–594.
   Baltes spells out his theory of selective optimization with compensation.

Bandura, A. (1997). *Self-efficacy: The exercise of control.* New York: Freeman.
   In this exhaustive tome, Bandura summarizes the decades of research linking self-efficacy to everything from health to societal change.

Erikson, E. H. (1963). *Childhood and society.* New York: Norton.

Erikson describes his eight stages of life.

Plomin, R., DeFreis, J. C., & McClearn, G. E. (1980). *Behavioral genetics: A primer.* San Francisco: Freeman.

Plomin, R., & McClearn, G. E. (1993). *Nature, nurture, and psychology.* Washington, DC: American Psychological Association.

These two books describe the findings and the basic approach of behavioral geneticists. The former is written for the student without much background in the field. The latter book will appeal to advanced students and researchers.

RESEARCH METHODS AND RESEARCH STUDIES

Baltes, P. B., Reese, H. W., & Nesselroade, J. R. (1977). *Life-span developmental psychology: Introduction to research methods.* Monterey, CA: Brooks/Cole.

This book describes research methods in life-span development as well as the contextualist approach.

Thomas, L. E. (Ed.). (1989). *Research on adulthood and aging: The human science approach.* Albany: State University of New York Press.

Contributors to this edited book make the case for conducting qualitative research in aging and discuss their own very different types of qualitative studies.

Chapter Outline

evention

*ık. "At my age a person is old enough to be wise and
ıg about that wisdom." He does not worry about the
is his age or older: his thinning hair, white beard, and
t internals. Joe is committed to rock climbing. The key
to enjoying his passion is defying the physical losses of time.*

In rock climbing, the thrill comes from continually improving, completing more difficult climbs. Every November, on his visit to see family in New Mexico, Joe sets his sights on a higher-rated mountain, then practices daily to master that climb. Planning is crucial. One must know the mountain and rehearse the set of moves it requires. Some climbs require upper-arm strength; toes must balance on the ledge. The body must be positioned just right to avoid a fall. The steepness of the cliff is important, and how far its ledges reach out. While physical stamina and agility are necessary, equally important is knowing oneself. The climber strives for a crucial balance: Push to the limit, but not beyond; combine courage with restraint; avoid fear or being foolhardy; know when to stretch and when to rest. Joe feels that, for a time, his better mental balance may outweigh the physical losses of age. But because, at some point, nature will take over, Joe is preparing, taking role models for his future life. He knows a 65-year-old who is still scaling high-rated mountains, an 80-year-old who water-skis. He also knows a 40-year-old who says he feels too old to run. Joe is comfortable with aging, provided he can remain vigorous. What terrifies him is the idea of incapacity, the thought that someday he may be forced to give in to bodily decline.

AN OVERVIEW OF THE AGING PROCESS

When we think of personality or intelligence, we are likely to see time as a friend. We imagine we will grow, change for the better, mature over the years. In contrast, a biological perspective on aging involves negatives; like Joe, loss in functioning is what many people fear. Early cross-sectional studies of physical aging confirmed these gloomy expectations (Birren & Birren, 1990). Researchers catalogued a depressing list of physical processes that universally declined. These losses set in early, soon after physical maturity. Sometimes, they went back earlier, to the beginning of life.

atherosclerosis
Accumulation of fatty deposits on the walls of arteries

normal aging change
Physical change that is deleterious and progressive and normally occurs as people age

primary aging
Physical changes that are absolutely inevitable in the aging process

secondary aging
Noninevitable, age-related deterioration caused by environmental damage

chronic disease
Long-term, progressive illness, typically without any clear-cut external cause or cure

For instance, **atherosclerosis**—fatty deposits on artery walls—is a predictable physical change that occurs as Americans advance in years. However, beginning atherosclerosis has been found in infants (Moon, 1955). Advanced signs of this process were found in autopsies of Korean War casualties as young as their early 20s (Enos, Holmes, & Beyer, 1955).

Atherosclerosis typifies a **normal aging change** (Elias, Elias, & Elias, 1990). The change is deleterious, making our functioning worse. It is progressive, growing more pronounced over time. While occurring to some degree in almost everyone, the extent to which the change develops varies from person to person, depending on biological predispositions and lifestyle. Atherosclerosis shares another property of many normal aging changes: We do not know whether this change is totally preventable or built into the aging process itself.

Primary aging changes are universal and inevitable. They are basic to the aging process, intrinsic to our makeup as human beings. **Secondary aging** is bodily deterioration caused by noninevitable external damaging forces, such as not taking care of our health. Because studies of physical aging explore what typically happens to people, the two types of aging are intertwined. For this reason, as John Rowe and Robert Kahn (1987) point out, these studies provide an unrealistically gloomy picture of the "true" aging process. Much physical deterioration that normally happens may not *have* to happen. We must be careful to distinguish what typically happens from what ideally can take place.

Making the distinction between typical and ideal aging is crucial. A second basic characteristic of the aging process is that it is intimately linked to disease. Many physical changes we experience as we advance in years, when they occur to a moderate degree, are called normal. When these changes become extreme, they have a different label: chronic disease (Elias, Elias, & Elias, 1990). Even when a physiological change does not shade directly into chronic illness, it weakens us and so makes us susceptible to a variety of diseases (Hayflick, 1987). So the chance of developing illnesses increases with age. In addition, older people are more likely to get certain diseases, the chronic conditions that are part and parcel of normal aging. Once again, atherosclerosis is a perfect example. These fatty deposits, when they block or severely narrow arteries, are what produce the top-ranking age-related chronic illnesses: heart disease and stroke.

Chronic diseases, in contrast to acute, infectious diseases such as the flu or a cold, have certain characteristics. They are long-term, progressive, and typically not curable. While a few chronic illnesses are caused by outside agents such as viruses (AIDS is a perfect recent example), most have no clear-cut external cause. They seem internally generated, produced by a breakdown of the body itself. The emphasis in dealing with these illnesses is on prevention and long-term management, not on an intervention that will produce a dramatic cure (Kart, Metress, & Metress, 1992).

Although children and young adults also suffer from them, chronic diseases are linked to normal aging and are therefore typically illnesses of middle and later life. Eighty-five percent of people over age 65 have at least one chronic illness (U.S. Senate Special Committee on Aging, 1991a). As we advance in years, rates of chronic disease rise dramatically (see Table 3-1).

In fact, heart disease and that other feared illness, cancer, are so closely tied to age that at least one of these diseases has a good chance of being present in the very old

	45–65	65–74	75+
HYPERTENSION (M)	220	307	339
(F)	224	378	417
ARTHRITIS (M)	178.8	430.8	424.9
(F)	297	513.6	604.4
HEARING (M)	191.9	298.8	447.1
IMPAIRMENTS (F)	87	183	307.8
HEART CONDITIONS (M)	162	319	475
(F)	111	250.8	361.4
ORTHOPEDIC (M)	166	144	169
IMPAIRMENTS (F)	173	161	189

Rates of almost every chronic disease rise, often dramatically, in later life.
SOURCE: U.S. Bureau of the Census, 1996, p. 143.

person who dies no matter what the actual cause of death (Manton, Wrigley, Cohen, & Woodbury, 1991). In autopsies performed on the very old, it is typical to find many illnesses that, even though not the immediate cause of death, would have ended the person's life within a matter of months (Comfort, 1979; Hayflick, 1987; Nuland, 1995).

A third fact about the aging process is that it has a fixed end. Though reports of long-lived people continue to tantalize us, as we will see later, they are myths. Almost no one survives beyond about age 105. While scientists argue whether this fixed limit beyond which none of us can live is totally rigid or shifting upward (Manton, 1990; Finch & Pike, 1996), everyone agrees that our **maximum life span** has not changed much since we evolved as human beings (Hayflick, 1987). What has changed dramatically is our *average life expectancy*—the time, on average, we can expect to live.

Our maximum life span is long in comparison with other animals. Although rare species, such as the Galapagos tortoise, do outlive us, human beings survive much longer than any other mammal. The horse lives about 46 years; the goat 20; the mouse slightly more than 3.

While other physical indexes—basal metabolic rate, body temperature, body size—are correlated with mammalian longevity, one theory is that our comparatively large brain is responsible for our long life. A mammal's index of cephalization, or ratio of brain to body weight, is related to its life span. The survival advantage our large brain may offer is that more neurons can function as reserves to replace those lost in the wear and tear of daily life (Birren & Birren, 1990).

Figure 3-1 illustrates how average life expectancy may have varied at different times in American history. As more of us survive to the upper reaches of the possible life span, the life expectancy curve looks increasingly rectangular. The ideal is a rectangle. We have cured all illnesses. All of us fulfill our maximum biological potential, living out the number of years human beings theoretically can (Hayflick, 1987).

maximum life span
Maximum age to which the members of a species can live

FIGURE 3-1 **A Hypothetical Look at the Human Survival Curve at Three Different Times in American History and If We Cured All Diseases**

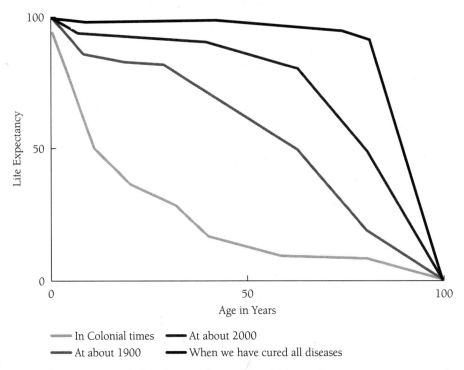

Notice that as more people live closer to the maximum life span, the curve appears increasingly rectangular.

BIOLOGICAL THEORIES OF AGING

Scientists want to understand the reason for these patterns: the association of advancing age with characteristic physical changes and certain diseases, and our maximum life span and its relationship to that of other species. They have devised a variety of hypotheses, or **biological theories of aging**, to account for these mysterious phenomena. One class of theories centers around what is damaging the basic units of our body, our cells.

The body is composed of two basic constituents: (1) cells, either able to divide or nondividing, and (2) intercellular connective tissue, whose main components are proteins called collagen and elastin. Most biologists assume that problems and processes within our cells are the cause of aging and death. However, some argue that changes in the collagen-rich substance surrounding our cells makes a contribution. As we grow old, the normally pliable collagen and elastin molecules link with one another and stiffen. This loss of elasticity is partly responsible for benign signs of aging such as

biological theories of aging
Theories that explain the underlying biological mechanisms involved in aging and death

wrinkled skin. It also causes life-threatening changes such as **arteriosclerosis,** the loss of elasticity of artery walls. Biologist Robert Kohn (1978) suggests that the stiffening of collagen and elastin may in itself be a cause of aging and death, because by making our tissues more rigid, it impairs the passage of materials throughout the body and so prevents nutrients from getting to cells.

arteriosclerosis
Age-related loss of
elasticity of artery
walls

The different cellular hypotheses about why we age are often grouped into two categories: theories that view aging and death as the result of random damage, and theories that suggest a preset biological program oversees the process (Smith, 1990). In reading the following explanations—just a few examples of the many biological theories of aging that have been proposed—understand that one account does not rule out the others. It is just as likely that aging has multiple causes as that a single process is responsible for aging's varied signs.

Random Damage Theories of Aging

DNA DAMAGE   One **random damage theory of aging** points to accumulating faults in cells' ability to produce proteins as the cause of aging and death. Proteins are vital because they are the basis of all cellular reactions and functions. DNA, the genetic material in the nucleus of each cell, programs how bodies develop and work by serving as the blueprint from which these molecules are produced. The DNA molecule uncoils to synthesize RNA, which, in a series of steps, serves as the mold from which the appropriate proteins are formed.

random damage
theories of aging
Theories that view
aging and death as
caused by random
damage

However, in the process of repeatedly uncoiling, the DNA molecule develops changes in its structure. These changes, called mutations, occur continuously in the course of our being exposed to environmental insults and the cells' work. Being responsible for our evolution from one-celled organisms, mutations are not all bad. However, most are deleterious. If their harmful effects are important or widespread enough, they will cause so many defective proteins to be produced that the cell will die.

Our cells have repair mechanisms to correct these spontaneous DNA mistakes; but as we age, the changes may become more frequent and the repair system may not work as efficiently. So, over time, unrepaired damage accelerates.

According to this scenario, physical aging and eventual death are the visible signs of DNA damage (Woodruff & Nikitin, 1997). As more DNA mistakes accumulate, more faulty proteins are produced, and more cells malfunction and die. Eventually, enough cells or enough critical ones are lost from the body to cause death (Orgel, 1973).

FREE RADICAL DAMAGE   A second type of random damage theory pinpoints the by-products of cellular metabolism as the culprits producing cellular damage and death. In the course of their work, cells produce waste products, which are excreted from the cell. These damaging substances may permeate and coat the membranes of other cells, impairing their function and causing their death (see Figure 3-2). They may also do their damage internally, affecting the cells' DNA. One popular candidate to produce this destruction is molecular fragments called **free radicals**, released by the billions into the body by our cells. Evidence supports the idea that free radicals play a role in the aging process. Dietary supplements of antioxidants such as Vitamins

free radicals
Molecules excreted
during cellular
metabolism that
damage the
functioning of cells
and may contribute
to aging and death

FIGURE 3-2 *The Excretion of Free Radicals from a Cell*

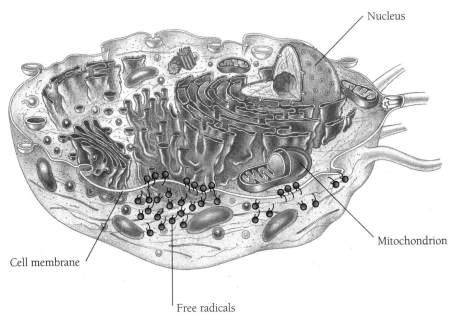

Free radicals, along with other metabolic waste products released into the body, may contribute to aging and death.

C and E, which neutralize these substances, can prolong animals' lives (Kart et al., 1992). In an ongoing study of very old nuns, high body antioxidant levels were associated with lower disability rates (Snowdon, Gross, & Butler, 1996).

Programmed Aging Theories

programmed aging theories
Theories that view aging and death as programmed by a timer or clock

Random damage theories assume that no master plan is responsible for aging and death. There is another, equally reasonable idea: Aging, like growth, is programmed and timed. Advocates of **programmed aging theories** differ as to where the aging timer is located, what sets it off, and what operates it. However, they agree that the orderly, predictable quality of the changes we undergo as we advance in years suggests that aging occurs by a coordinated plan. Furthermore, the fact that every species has a fixed life span strongly implies that aging and death are genetically programmed (Hayflick, 1987).

An aging and death clock may be located in each cell. Perhaps cells are programmed to produce, at a certain time, a protein that inhibits DNA synthesis, causing the cells to self-destruct. Or the clock may be centralized, in a system responsible for coordinating many bodily functions. If a central clock exists, two places with a widespread influence on the body seem likely places for it to reside: the hypothalamus and the immune system.

THE HYPOTHALAMUS AS AN AGING CLOCK   The **hypothalamus** is a tiny structure in the brain responsible for coordinating an amazing list of functions, including eating, sexual behavior, temperature regulation, and emotional expression. It has a key role in regulating physical growth, sexual development, and reproduction, because it is involved in producing hormones. The hypothalamus is definitely responsible for the aging of one body system: By shutting off the production of the ovarian hormone estrogen at about age 50, it ushers in menopause, and so ends a woman's capacity to conceive a child. Its far-ranging effects make it a good candidate to regulate other manifestations of aging, harboring the clock or clocks that time death (Comfort, 1979).

THE IMMUNE SYSTEM AS AN AGING CLOCK   Our **immune system** protects us against foreign invaders such as viruses or bacteria. In response to alien substances— microorganisms or cancer (cancer cells are also foreign to our body's tissues)—the immune system produces "killer cells" and molecules called antibodies to kill the invaders. The thymus, a gland involved in the intricate immune response, slowly disappears during adulthood. Biologist Roy Walford (1969, 1983) has suggested that this gland may be an aging pacemaker, because its disappearance signals a weakening of the immune system that has far-ranging effects.

A well-tuned immune system must make a delicate distinction, recognizing foreign substances and sparing our own cells. As our immune system weakens, Walford reasons, deficiencies develop in both functions. The weakened immune system's ability to fight off foreign attack partly explains why older people recover less easily from infectious illnesses and are more prone to cancer. (It is now believed that our body continuously produces cancer cells, which a strong immune system searches out and destroys.) Deficiencies in the immune system's ability to recognize our own cells may cause it to attack our own tissues, accelerating cell loss. This assault on our own cells, called an *autoimmune response,* may be partially to blame for illnesses as different as diabetes and dementia. Because it can account for so many of the problems that befall older people, a failing immune system seems an especially good candidate for the timer causing us to age.

Extending the Maximum Life Span

If the immune system is responsible for aging, we might be able to slow our aging rate by stimulating immune function. If old age is programmed by the hypothalamus, ways of setting this timer back might be found. If the damaging effect of free radicals causes aging, taking vitamin supplements containing antioxidants might enable us to slow aging and death. So these abstract speculations have profound practical impact. Instead of prolonging our lives a bit by extending our average life expectancy a few years—the most we can hope for by curing any specific disease—the search for why we age has a larger payoff. It may allow us to retard old age for everyone and lengthen our maximum life span.

MINIMIZING YOUR INTAKE   One method of extending the maximum life span has been known for a half century: calorie restriction. In a remarkable series of

hypothalamus
Brain structure responsible for orchestrating many motivational states as well as helping to program physical and sexual development

immune system
System whose function is to destroy foreign substances, either microorganisms or incipient cancer

experiments begun in the late 1930s, researchers have demonstrated that underfeeding rats can increase their maximum life span by as much as 60%. The key is an unusual type of underfeeding, what Roy Walford (1983) calls "undernutrition without malnutrition." The animals are restricted to less food, but given a nutritionally rich diet. They are allowed few empty calories.

It had been thought that to be effective undernutrition had to be started when an animal was weaned. The price of extending the life span was delayed puberty. The rats lived longer, but the diet primarily lengthened the period of life before adult fertility. However, more recent studies suggest that mild caloric restriction begun in adulthood extends longevity too, though its impact is more modest than when this life-extension strategy is begun early on.

Biologists are feverishly exploring the resilience underfeeding produces. Dietary restriction postpones chronic diseases, especially cancer, that lead to death (Higami et al., 1995; Snyder, Pollard, Wostmann, & Luckert, 1990). It increases resistance to infection, by retarding the loss in immune function that normally occurs with age (Effros, Walford, Weindruch, & Micheltree, 1991). It improves the capacity to cope with extreme heat (Hall, Keller, Weindruch, & Kregel, 1997). It slows age-related biochemical changes in organs such as the small intestine (Holt, Heller, & Richardson, 1991) and the liver (Mote, Grizzle, Walford, & Spindler, 1991). It enhances glucose metabolism (Cefalu, Bell-Farrow, Wagner, Miller, & Collins, 1997), thereby postponing the onset of diabetes (Bodkin, Ortmeyer, & Hansen, 1997) and improving muscle strength (Cefalu, Bell-Farrow, et al., 1997); Dean & Cartee, 1996). In other words, underfeeding has widespread anti-aging effects.

There is a qualification. Because of their short lives, this life-extension research has been conducted primarily with rats. In fact, as Richard Weindruch and Edward Masoro (1991) point out, most research on the biology of aging has been done with a single rat strain! Researchers are now studying the impact of underfeeding in our close primate cousins, monkeys (Bodkin et al., 1997), but because these subjects have a life span of about 40 years, it will be decades before we really know if underfeeding them prolongs life (Kemnitz et al., 1993; Ingram et al., 1990). So, be cautious: There is no proof that calorie restriction works for humans (Finch & Pike, 1996). By following this stringent diet, we may be purchasing a protracted, but painfully deprived life.

MOVING TO SHANGRI-LA   What about those people who live, healthy and vigorous, to life's limit and perhaps beyond? If we knew their secrets, we would not need to engage in any draconian life-extension plan.

When researchers visited one remote village, in a mountainous area in Russian Georgia, they speculated that several forces explained these long lives. The Georgians ate a low-calorie diet of fruits and grains. They performed outdoor work until advanced age; and, rather than being devalued, in Georgia, age brought respect. In fact, in this village, living beyond a century was the badge of highest merit, a cause for great acclaim (Kipshidze, Pivovarova, Dzorbenadze, Agadzanov, & Shavgulidz, 1987).

Keeping physically active, not eating fats, and being respected for being old may be life-enhancing. However, as implied earlier, a more objective look at these people uncovers a disappointing fact: There is no evidence that they actually do outlive the rest of us! When researchers visited another area known for long-lived residents, a remote region in Ecuador, *and found census records,* they realized that the villagers typically inflated their ages by at least a decade. None of the supposed centenarians had really reached this age (Mazess & Forman, 1979). In these villages, the publicity and status attached to being long-lived plus the lack of birth records may make inflating one's age an overwhelming temptation. Adding those extra years may not even be fully conscious, because as adults our age becomes unimportant, and so we do "forget" how old we are from time to time.

The practice of adding years to life is not confined to remote villages. In nursing homes, I have noticed residents embellishing on an advanced age to impress listeners, just as a 15-year-old insists he is 18 or a 5-year-old brags that she is really 8. It seems as if only when we leave youth and approach our normal life expectancy is our age a liability. Once we reach our 90s, the years once again become a badge of achievement. They are an emblem of a life well lived.

Scientists predict that during this new century we will have the tools to lengthen the maximum life span, even without depriving ourselves of food (Johnson, Lithgow, & Murakami, 1996). But will this breakthrough be a blessing for humanity as a whole? Imagine the overpopulation problem if we were to increase the life span to 130, or extend a woman's childbearing years by a decade or more. It may be that this "advance" would be a double-edged sword, extending our personal existence at the price of limiting the quality of all of our years.

NORMAL AGING

Although modifying the aging process is not within our grasp, we know more about that process than ever. What is physical aging like? A landmark longitudinal study is unlocking the mystery.

As we have seen, traditional cross-sectional studies of physical aging suggest that, starting right after adolescence, the pattern is decline. However, because each succeeding cohort arrives at a given age healthier, these studies exaggerate the true physical losses that occur over the years. In addition, because they deal with group averages, cross-sectional studies tell us nothing about individual patterns of aging, the very differences *between* people in aging rates that might allow us to shed light on primary aging—the aging process as it can optimally take place (see Aging in Action 3-1).

The Baltimore Longitudinal Study of Aging, begun in 1959 and sponsored by the National Institute on Aging, is our nation's number one effort to probe physical aging in the flesh. As we learned in the last chapter, in this ambitious study, volunteers spend several days at the Gerontology Research Center in Baltimore each year or two having every possible physical function tested and probed. Let's look at some highlights of this research.

Two Basic Principles of Normal Aging

VARIABILITY OF AGING RATES   The first major finding of the Baltimore Study and many others we know from just observing friends and relatives: Individual aging rates vary tremendously. Some 60-year-olds are physically like 40; some 40-year-olds are more like 65. These differences in appearance are mirrored on physiological tests.

3-1 *Aging Optimally over Age 70*

Nowhere are the first-person stories more encouraging than among people who remain vital and athletic in old age. What is optimal physical aging like? Listen to these participants in the Senior Activity and Rejuvenation Project directed by Frank Powell at Furman University.

Eighty-three-year-old Ray Wylie celebrates each birthday by peddling 100 miles on his bike. Besides holding the national championship in bicycle racing in his age group, Ray was a table tennis champion in his younger years. Ray is committed to being a role model, to showing the power fitness has in changing life. However, he is not unidimensional. Before retirement, Ray was the chair of two university math departments. He directed hundreds of graduate theses and wrote a dozen books. He was very involved in raising two boys. Ray's motto is "You can be physically active and still enjoy a full life. Do it when you can. If I can't exercise for a while, the world won't come to an end." How has Ray changed during his old-old years? In Director Powell's words, "I keep waiting to beat him at table tennis, waiting for him to decline. I keep improving, but so does he. His musculature is better today than at age 75."

At age 85, Helen Yockey also belies every stereotype about the old-old. Helen, who began swimming in competitions about a decade ago, consistently wins national meets. Helen too lives a balanced life. In addition to training regularly, Helen works at a soup kitchen and volunteers at Meals on Wheels.

Helen's interest in swimming dates back to her childhood in Akron, Ohio, a city surrounded by lakes. During summer vacation, she used to hitchhike to a local lake with her three brothers, disguised as a boy. She remembers how upset she was the summer her disguise was finally penetrated and she could no longer swim! During her adult life, Helen continued to swim regularly, but for pleasure. Swimming remained her outlet for troubled times. In 1982, in a senior center class, she overheard two men discussing a swim meet. Helen decided to attend, won first place, and was hooked.

Helen's advice is to keep going. A year ago she gave up swimming for a few months, and it was hard getting back. Now she makes sure to lift weights every Monday, Wednesday, and Friday and to swim several miles every day. Helen has had two knee replacements. She wore out the first one, and then used the other up. She is a shoo-in to take the gold in the nationals among the age group over 85.

Abilities as different as lung function, grip strength, and sugar metabolism all vary widely among people the same age.

So, the first principle of normal aging is individual variability (Maddox, 1991). In fact, this variability among people in aging rates becomes *more* dramatic as we travel through life (Harris, Pedersen, McClearn, Plomin, & Nesselroade, 1992).

Even within the person, making generalizations is unwise. Different body systems also vary greatly in their aging rate. The story of "Joe" at the beginning of this chapter

At age 70, Jean Sullivan is the baby in the group. Her sports are the long jump and sprinting. Jean is a newcomer to competitive sports too, although physical activity remains a continual theme in her life. Jean was a physical handful from infancy. Once her parents looked on in horror as she climbed to the top of the high water tower in town. Jean grew up in China, where there were no organized sports. However, she climbed trees, and she loved to run. In eighth grade, she went to boarding school in Shanghai—a turning point in her life. The progressive policy of the school was to allow girls to compete in sports. Jean recalls playing hockey during the Sino-Japanese War while all around the bombs were falling. It taught her that "sports gave a sense of control. In the midst of disaster, life goes on." A year before Pearl Harbor, Jean came to America, where at college she continued to enjoy women's sports. Then she became absorbed in family and work. She became a physician and raised four children. Still, she loved keeping active, and enjoyed just running across the yard because it felt good. In 1987, she heard about a track meet and thought, "Well, I'll give that a try." A few years ago, Jean won the world and national championships in the age group 65–69 in track and field.

According to Jean, "Entering competitions is great fun. Life is more stimulating. I travel the country and meet new friends." According to Jean's husband, Frank, also an athlete in the program, "A lot of the credit for Jean's success belongs to me. I keep her in shape because I chase her around the house!"

These life stories are a perfect introduction to two themes in this book: (1) There is a continuity to adult life. Our interests tend to stay somewhat the same as we age. (2) People who are active physically often age successfully in many areas of life.

At the same time, we must be careful not to equate optimal physical aging with aging success. When I worked in a nursing home, I saw people just as fulfilled as these senior athletes, aging just as successfully even though they were confined to a wheelchair. Think how Jung or Erikson would react to the contemporary idea that the key to aging success is winning the war against physical decline!

SOURCE: Adapted from Furman, F., and Hawkins, M. E. "Positive models of aging: Presentations by members of the Senior Activity and Rejuvenation Project," a symposium at the annual meeting of the Southern Gerontological Society, Charlotte, NC, April 1994.

provides a good example. While to an outside observer Joe looks his age or older, if we look internally at muscle strength, lung capacity, and other functions, he may be younger physiologically than the typical middle-aged adult.

So, even in looking at physical change, we need to adopt the contextual life-span approach. Aging rates differ greatly, both from person to person and within the individual. But even though aging *advances* differently, we can still make generalizations because the *process* occurs in predictable ways.

A participant in the Baltimore Study undergoes a test of cardiorespiratory function.

VARIABILITY OF AGING PATTERNS   The Baltimore Study shows that there are actually several aging paths. One is the pattern found in the cross-sectional studies: Some functions decline in a regular way over time. However, others are stable, either staying unchanged or declining only in the terminal phase of life. Some may actually improve (Shock et al., 1984; National Institute on Aging, 1989, 1993).

In a common pattern, physiological loss occurs, but only when a person develops an age-related illness. For instance, among the high percentage of Baltimore volunteers who showed signs of heart disease, the pumping capacity of the heart declined with age. If a volunteer had no signs of heart disease, his heart pumped as well at age 70 as at age 30 (Shock et al., 1984). Whereas it had been thought that in his middle and later years a man's body generally produced less testosterone (the male sex hormone), the Baltimore researchers found declining testosterone only in their older subjects who were ill.

Interestingly, the Baltimore researchers find that a loss in a normally stable function may be a sign of impending death. Once again, the immune system offers an example. In analyzing blood samples, the researchers found that normally the number of lymphocytes (white blood cells) did not drop as volunteers returned over the years. However, among a minority of people, a decline in lymphocyte count did occur. Although at the time these people reported feeling healthy, and physical examinations revealed no disease, at the next follow-up this group was more likely to have died. These deaths were nonspecific, resulting from a variety of causes. Either because it is a marker of existing illness or because it makes people more prone to disease, declining immune function does seem implicated in aging and death (National Institute on Aging, 1993).

In another pattern, loss occurs, but our body compensates physiologically for the change. The most fascinating example occurs in the brain. As the years pass, we do lose neurons. However, as we will see later in this chapter, in response, some cells grow more robust, adding new dendrites and establishing new connections, helping preserve thinking and memory (National Institute on Aging, 1993.).

The Baltimore Study shows that we cannot think of physical aging only in terms of loss. Stability exists in this important area of life. And even when the years do take a physical toll, our body is resilient. We have the capacity to grow and adapt even in areas such as our brain, where scientists never believed growth after maturity could occur.

Impact of Normal Aging on Daily Life

Despite this upbeat information, the dominant theme of physical aging remains decline. The losses that do take place—in how deeply we can breathe, in the ability of our kidneys to filter wastes, in our muscle mass—affect how we function in specific ways. Over time, our ability to perform at top capacity physically declines. Luckily, most systems have substantial **reserve capacity,** or excess beyond what is normally needed, so these changes are only noticeable when we must stretch ourselves to the limit, or if they have progressed so far that they interfere with daily life.

To a world-class athlete, the physical losses that occur early on are painfully apparent. In his or her 20s, a runner or gymnast worries about being "over the hill." Most of us only think "My body isn't working as well" years later. In our 40s, it is harder to play a strenuous game of tennis. We don't bounce back as fast from surgery.

The physiological losses of aging only become a daily fact of life when they have progressed further. In our 80s, we may have to take our body into account in planning every day. Normal aging has permeated normal life.

Declining reserve capacity explains why elderly people are vulnerable to any stressful situation, be it running for the bus, surgery, or the sweltering summer heat. Age-related physiological losses are most likely to cause problems when a high level of physical performance is needed, when coping depends on having the reserves to meet the challenge.

Until now we have been discussing normal aging in general terms. Now we turn to examine specific aging changes. Because of the behavioral science focus of this text, our tour is selective. I have chosen to describe briefly the most striking external aging signs—hair and skin changes—and then explore aging in two systems especially central to life: the cardiovascular system, our blood vessel lifeline carrying nutrients to the cells; and the nervous system, which regulates every physiological process and

reserve capacity
Built-in extra capacity of organs and systems used only under conditions when maximum physical performance is required

conscious activity of life. In the next chapter, we will explore aging in our sensory and musculoskeletal systems.

The Externals: Hair and Skin

Changes in hair color are perhaps our most obvious sign of advancing age. When you are in your 20s you may look in the mirror, see a few white hairs, and suddenly realize, "I am getting older." Now that I am 50 my graying image localizes me in time the way no other marker can. It is an immediate banner telling outsiders that "Dr. Belsky is not a young adult." Although each of us has our own genetic timetable for this gradual process, eventually everyone undergoes the loss of pigmentation that causes hair to change color.

Hair loses pigment when the cells at the base of the hair follicle that produce the color for each hair die. Interestingly, gray hair is an illusion. Our hair looks gray during those transitional years when hairs that have not lost their pigmentation and nonpigmented hairs are interspersed. Eventually, as more hairs lose pigment, gray hair lightens and eventually appears white. Notice that people with gray hair tend to be in their 40s and 50s, and that in their later years, people have totally white hair. What accompanies this change is the gradual loss of the hair follicles. This leads to the second impression that strikes us about hair in *both* men and women in their older years. The older person's hair seems more sparse and patchy. Hair grows thinner with advancing age.

Skin wrinkling—the creases, furrows, and sagging we also ruefully expect over the years—is another obvious "tip off" of age. We may first notice this wrinkling at about the same time that we find our first white hairs, in our late 20s. However, skin changes are a more variable, less reliable marker of chronological age. The reason is that rather than just being a function of the passing years, wrinkling has an important environmental cause: exposure to the sun.

Wrinkling begins in the areas that we use the most. People who are used to laughing may find their personality fixed in little lines around their face. Those used to frowning suffer the same fate; their mood may be imprinted on their face. So, our skin is more than an envelope covering our body. It can also be the visible reflection of who we are inside.

Wrinkling is the result of a number of changes. In the epidermal layer of the skin, new cells continuously migrate to the surface where they die and are sloughed off (see Figure 3-3). As we age, cell production slows, epidermal turnover rate declines, and our skin begins to look more furrowed and rough. More importantly, the elastic constituents of the skin's thick middle or dermal layer, collagen and elastin, lose their flexibility. As these molecules stiffen, our skin develops creases. A reduction in the activity of the dermal oil glands compounds the problem, drying out our skin and making it rougher and more easily damaged by the wind and sun.

Making matters worse is that as we age, the normally even layer of subcutaneous fat that pads the lower dermis migrates, accumulating in certain areas. This produces the lumpy-looking skin vividly described in Aging in Action 3-2. Because, in our face, one site for this pocketing is beneath the jaw, the "double chin" inevitably materializes in middle age to wreak havoc on vanity in our older years.

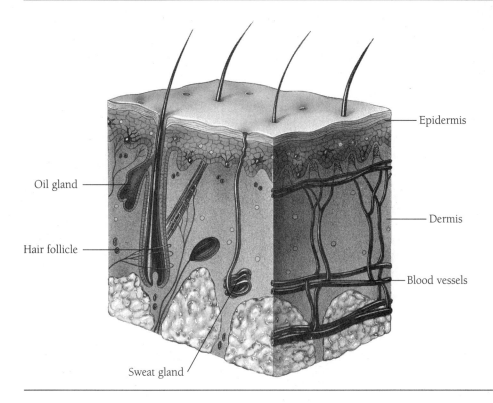

Oil gland

Hair follicle

Sweat gland

Epidermis

Dermis

Blood vessels

Changes in our skin are more than cosmetic. This resilient envelope is what insulates us from insults from the external world. As Figure 3-3 shows, the skin consists of the rapidly replenishing epidermis and a thick dermal layer containing a network of blood vessels and sweat glands. An age-related loss in this blood vessel network, which provides nutrients to the skin, combined with the slower rate of new epidermal cell production, slows wound healing. This blood vessel loss, in addition to a reduction in the activity of the sweat glands, makes older people more vulnerable to extremes of heat and cold. Sweat and blood flow work together to keep our body at a constant internal temperature. In response to a rise in body temperature caused by being in the heat or exercising vigorously, the brain signals the blood vessels of the dermis to dilate and activates sweat production. As the sweat evaporates, it cools the skin's surface and the dermal blood supply, which then flows inward to cool the body. In cold environments, when body temperature begins to decline, the dermal blood vessels constrict, reducing blood flow to the skin, and so conserving body heat. Losses in this regulatory system explain why older people are more susceptible to hyperthermia (heat exhaustion) and hypothermia (reduced body temperature due to being in the cold).

3-2 Confronting an Aging Face

Letty Pogrebin, feminist and founding editor of Ms. magazine, has written a humorous book exposing the female body on "the far side of 50." Here is her frank account of her 55-year-old image revealed in the mirror.

Remember the opening scene from Mommie Dearest, *when the aging . . . Joan Crawford wakes up, takes off her lubricated sleep mask . . . and plunges her face into a bowl of steaming hot water and then into a sinkful of ice cubes? Well, I have what she was trying to prevent.*

Under my eyes are puffy fat pads surrounded by dark circles, each unfortunate feature trying its best to call attention to the other. My wrinkles materialized almost overnight when I was 49. Now the lines in my face remind me of my palms. When I raise my eyebrows, my forehead pleats, and when my eyebrows come down the pleats stay. . . . The cheerful parentheses at the corners of my smile have started looking downtrodden and my top lip is beginning to produce those spidery . . . creases that soak up lipstick. . . .

Just this year, my jaw, the Maginot Line of facial structure, surrendered to the force of gravity. On each side of my chin the muscles have pulled loose from the bone. Once I had a right-angle profile; now there's a hypotenuse between my chin and neck. . . . Which brings me, regrettably, to my neck, with its double choker of lines; and my chest, creased like crepe paper; and my shoulders and arms, which are holding their own for now except for the elbows which are rough enough to shred a carrot. I don't yet have loose skin on the underside of my upper arm—you know, the part that keeps waving after you've stopped—but I can see it coming.

. . .

These days I'm into the truth and the truth is I'm not crazy about my looks but I can live with them. . . . What jolted me out of my low-grade Body Image Blues was the death of friends felled by cancer in the prime of their lives. . . . After the third funeral . . . I saw my body, not as face, skin, hair, figure, but as the vehicle through which I could experience everything my friend would never know again. . . . Ordinary pleasures seemed so precious that I vowed to set my priorities straight before some fatal illness did it for me. Since then I have been trying to focus on the things that really matter. And I can assure you that being able to wear a bikini isn't one of them.

SOURCE: Pogrebin, 1996.

Hyperthermia and hypothermia can be life-threatening because our internal temperature must be maintained at a fairly constant level for our physiological processes to function. The threat to life posed by aging in the skin is minor, however, compared with that caused by age changes in the **cardiovascular system**—the heart and arteries literally at the heart of human life.

cardiovascular system
Circulatory system comprising the heart and arteries

The Cardiovascular System

The heart is the pump for the vascular system, the network of blood vessels bringing vital nutrients to the cells. This four-chambered wonder is resilient, beating roughly 3 billion times in the average life span, pumping the equivalent of about 900 million gallons of blood throughout its miles of arteries and veins.

Heart weight increases with age (Kitzman & Edwards, 1990). For women, the change is pronounced after menopause. The heart walls thicken and narrow. There is a thickening, calcification (hardening), and stenosis (narrowing) of the valves that regulate blood flow through the chambers of the heart. These same changes occur in the blood vessels directly feeding the heart, called the coronary arteries, as well as the vascular system as a whole.

As mentioned earlier, the stiffening and hardening, called arteriosclerosis, is caused by the loss of elasticity in the connective tissue, collagen and elastin, that occurs with age. The narrowing has a different cause. It is due to atherosclerosis, fatty deposits that gradually accumulate in the heart and vessel walls.

The effect of these changes is to impair circulation. The heart pumps less blood at its maximum. The narrower, more rigid blood vessels do not permit as much blood to circulate, so less oxygen and other vital nutrients reach our tissues when "top capacity" is needed. We grow winded more easily. We are less resilient physically to stress (Lakatta, 1987). This circulatory loss, when extreme, affects thinking capacity. As we will see in subsequent chapters, heart disease is the major chronic illness linked to losses in thinking speed in middle and later life (Earles & Salthouse, 1995).

Figure 3-4 shows snapshots of the developing process that ends in death. As plaque formation progresses in the artery, damage occurs to its inner wall, causing swelling and deterioration. Platelets, carried in the blood, adhere to the wall and stimulate its muscle to grow, further narrowing the passageway. Although this arterial debris sometimes clogs the passageway, what happens most often is that a blood clot forms, blocking the artery. If this blockage occurs in a coronary artery, the blood supply to that area of the heart is severely compromised or cut off, and the heart muscle is damaged or dies. The result is the familiar *myocardial infarction,* or heart attack. If this blockage occurs in a blood vessel supplying the brain (a cerebral artery), the brain cells nourished by that vessel will also malfunction and die. The result is another top-ranking cause of death, a *cerebrovascular accident,* or stroke.

In both cases, depending on the degree of damage, either death or disability may occur. However, even in the absence of the dramatic event called a heart attack or stroke, atherosclerosis causes disease. When the coronary arteries become partially obstructed, the person may develop a condition called *angina,* a dull pain that limits physical exertion. When the heart's pumping capacity is diminished by atherosclerosis and other causes, the heart enlarges and its muscle fibers weaken. The symptoms of this condition, called *congestive heart failure,* include shortness of breath and swelling of the ankles and legs, as fluid pools in the lungs and lower extremities.

Is this life-threatening progression inevitable? In the United States, systolic blood pressure, a sign of both atherosclerosis and arteriosclerosis, rises regularly as people age; in Japan, however, where the diet contains less fat, blood pressure normally rises with age only to a minor degree, and people develop heart disease much later in life (Fries, 1990). So, even if atherosclerosis is to some extent primary to aging, the *degree* to which it develops is partly under our control. For this reason, as we saw in Chapter 1, heart disease and stroke (along with lung cancer and accidents) are considered our top-ranking *preventable* causes of death.

FIGURE 3-4   Atherosclerosis Development

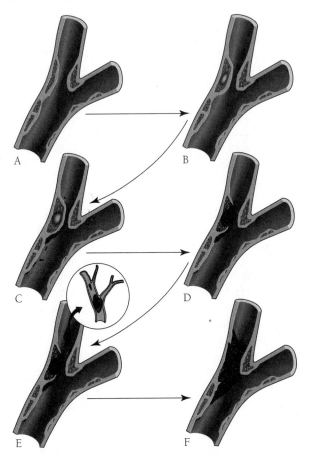

(A) Atherosclerotic plaque at artery branch; (B) ulcer forms in
wall; (C) platelets and other products aggregate on roughened
surface; (D) blood clot forms; (E) emboli form, blocking blood
vessels throughout the artery; (F) clot causes total blockage, resulting in a heart attack.
SOURCE: Kart, Metress, & Metress, 1992.

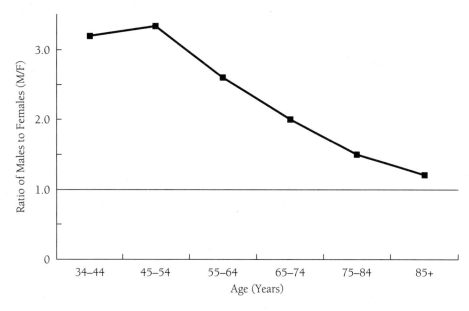

Males die more frequently than females from heart disease at every age, although after menopause, the differences grow less pronounced.
SOURCE: Wingard & Cohn, 1990.

Prospective studies, a type of longitudinal research tracing illness rates in thousands of people, consistently show that certain prior conditions increase the chance of developing heart disease and stroke. These familiar **risk factors**—smoking, high blood pressure, elevated serum (blood) cholesterol, and diabetes—can be modified by diet, exercise, weight control, and medical interventions. Two other risk factors for heart attack and stroke are not under our control: gender and ethnicity.

GENDER AND ARTERIAL CHANGE   Heart disease is the top-ranking killer for both men and women. However, women develop this illness at an older age, and their death rates never equal those of men. Figure 3-5 illustrates the dramatic gender gap in mortality and how it changes with age. Why are men more prone to this killer? Although environmental factors may have some impact (men more often engage in high-risk behaviors such as eating and drinking to excess), compelling evidence suggests the real cause lurks in biological differences (Hazzard, 1990).

prospective studies
Type of longitudinal study following a large population to see what prior conditions predict premature illness

risk factors
Prior conditions that raise the probability of premature disease

The female hormone estrogen protects women against heart disease. At menopause, which typically occurs at about age 50, estrogen levels drop dramatically. As Figure 3-5 shows, it is soon after this age that the gender gap in heart disease mortality begins to decline. Another indirect sign implicating estrogen is that postmenopausal women have higher heart disease rates than premenopausal women of the same age. Most telling is research showing that atherosclerosis formation is related to estrogen and menopause. To understand these studies, it is important to know that the extent to which we develop atherosclerosis is related to our relative ratios of two blood lipids (fats). High risk of heart disease is associated with high levels of low-density lipoproteins (LDL); low risk is associated with high levels of high-density lipoproteins (HDL). Whereas the ratio of "good" to "bad" cholesterol favors women before menopause, after menopause the gender ratio becomes more alike. Moreover, giving estrogen to postmenopausal women raises "good" cholesterol levels, demonstrating that this hormone makes women naturally more resistant to heart disease.

ETHNICITY AND ARTERIAL CHANGE   Although biological predispositions may also play a role in ethnic differences in heart disease and stroke, here the impact of genetics versus lifestyle on illness rates is not as clear. As mentioned previously, Japanese men have less atherosclerosis and lower rates of heart disease than Americans. Japanese and Chinese men living in Hawaii have the same advantage, which may account in part for why, with an average life expectancy of 78, they are among the longest-living U.S. men (Curb, Reed, Miller, & Yano, 1990). Some studies show that, despite having higher disability rates, Hispanic American men may have an advantage with regard specifically to heart disease. When researchers compared Hispanic and Caucasian deaths from heart disease in Texas, they found that men with Spanish last names had lower mortality rates from this illness—a finding that was difficult to explain as these men are more likely to be both diabetic and overweight, both risk factors for heart disease (Markides, Coreil, & Rogers, 1989).

Unfortunately, these advantages do not apply to African Americans. As Figure 3-6 shows, although deaths from heart disease and stroke have declined for both whites and African Americans since 1960, death rates are still significantly higher among African American women and men (see Chapter 1). This **excess mortality**, or higher-than-average risk of death, is most dramatic for stroke. African Americans have 1.8 times the chance of developing this terrifying illness as whites (Anderson, Mullner, & Cornelius, 1989; Braithwaite & Taylor, 1992).

excess mortality
Higher-than-average death rate compared with that of the general population

The main reason is the high rate of hypertension (high blood pressure) among African Americans. Not only are African Americans greatly overrepresented among the 58 million Americans suffering from high blood pressure, they are more likely to develop this problem at a younger age and to have their problem go untreated (Hildrith & Saunders, 1992). Another contributing factor is diabetes. Although, as with blood pressure, diabetes rates normally rise with age, this illness tends to appear earlier in African Americans. African American women in particular are much more prone to diabetes than any other group (Hildrith & Saunders, 1992; Kunkel & Harris, 1997; Murphy & Elders, 1992).

Hypertension and diabetes are extremely dangerous conditions. Not only do both greatly increase the risk of heart attack and stroke, they affect the kidneys, the eyes,

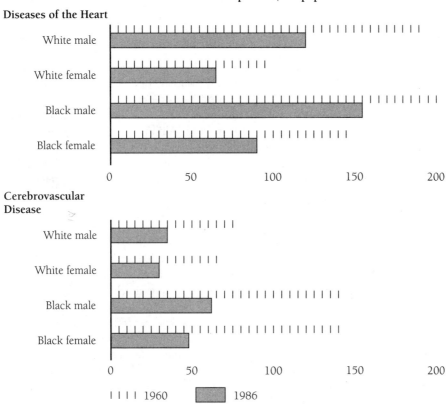

Deaths from heart disease and stroke have declined dramatically since 1960 for both races. African Americans continue to have higher rates of mortality than whites.
SOURCE: U.S. Department of Health and Human Services, 1990a.

and arteries throughout the body. Because these diseases "run in families," Baltimore Study investigators are currently looking at the cellular level at arteriosclerosis formation to see if this stiffening process occurs differently for African Americans. However, even if genetics makes some contribution, lifestyle conditions that promote atherosclerosis formation are more prevalent among African Americans. Being more likely to live in poverty, African Americans often do not have the luxury of buying higher-priced low-fat foods or the time to exercise, or more generally to follow the health-promoting strategies that prevent cardiovascular disease. As we will see in Chapter 5, being poorer, they have less access to good medical care (see also Aging in Action 3-3). The most dramatic impact of this lack of access is in the area of hypertension. This problem, when detected, can be medically treated and controlled; yet there is an alarming rate of untreated hypertension in the African American community (Hildrith & Saunders, 1992), a problem that is causing great public health concern (Savage, McGee, & Oster, 1989).

The Nervous System

The **nervous system** is the seat of every perception, thought, emotion, and response. The nervous system regulates bodily processes outside of conscious awareness too, from respiration, to digestion, to sleep, to the physiological mechanism for maintaining constant body temperature described in the section on the skin. The basic unit of the nervous system is the **neuron.** The billions of neurons in the brain and spinal cord compose the **central nervous system.** The **peripheral nervous system** consists of the billions more neurons fanning out through the body. The command center where the neural signals arrive to be processed, interpreted, and transmitted out is the brain. (Much of the information in this following section is from Scheibel, 1996.)

Gross pictures of the brain show that it gradually decreases in size and weight as we age. Changes begin in the fourth decade of life. The sulci, or ridges, of the brain widen. The cerebral folds narrow. The size of the fluid-filled ventricles (cavities) in the center of the brain increases. Although some of this brain shrinkage, or atrophy, is due to a loss in the supporting glia cells of the nervous system, much of it is caused by the erosion of those basic units of consciousness, the neurons.

The gloomy stereotype we have is true: Neural loss occurs with age. In addition to a falloff in their number, especially with the large neurons, there is a reduction in the size of the cells. Pigmented by-products of cellular metabolism accumulate in the cell bodies of many remaining neurons. When their central space is filled with this waste material, only a small area is left for the protein-synthesizing mechanisms of the cells. Vascular changes discussed earlier also limit the neuron's capacity to make proteins, and so function adequately, by allowing fewer nutrients to get to the cell. Moreover, in old age, especially in the hippocampus (the region of the brain centrally important for memory) mixed in with the normal neurons are abnormal structures, thick bulletlike pieces of matter and long tangles that are the waste product of decay.

This loss cuts a wide swath on behavior. Neural atrophy is an important cause of losses in the ability to see, hear, smell, walk, and stand in later life. It limits the older person's ability to respond quickly, to remember clearly, and to pay attention well. However, unless we develop a genuine brain illness, the majority of our neurons remain intact and functioning until advanced old age.

Recent studies show that the atrophy is more moderate than had been believed, far less than the infamous 100,000 neurons we are supposed to lose every day. Most important, it is far too simplistic to equate how we function with a simple count of neurons. The time of life when we shed the most neurons is infancy! During our first months of life, a programmed reduction of neurons occurs. This loss far outweighs the

3-3 *Personal Responsibility and the Lifestyle Revolution*

At age 62, Chauncy was one of the youngest residents at the nursing home where I worked. A gifted mechanic and avid fisherman who, after suffering a stroke, needed help to eat or get to the toilet, Chauncy's life was a lesson in the costs of this devastating disease. Like a number of African Americans, Chauncy had untreated high blood pressure. He ate a diet high in fat. He gave up taking his blood pressure medication because of the expense. He disliked the side effects and, besides, without health insurance, visits for a condition that produced no symptoms were a luxury he couldn't afford. In a casual conversation, Chauncy's doctor remarked that, while tragic, this man's illness was his own fault: Chauncy would not be in this situation if he had taken better care of his health.

The message of the lifestyle revolution is that illness is preventable and that the key to prevention lies in ourselves. Philosopher Angelo Alonzo (1993) warns against this stance. As we just saw, this emphasis on personal responsibility can shade into a blame-the-victim mentality, in which people who develop "preventable" illnesses are held responsible for their disease. The truth is that all diseases have genetic contributions. We are never totally in control of our physical fate.

Blaming the victim ignores the role that the wider social environment plays in disease. As we will see in Chapter 5, the poor and disadvantaged are more prone to develop age-related illnesses early on (Abeles, 1992). Besides not having ready access to medical care, men such as Chauncy who work 80-hour weeks do not have the time to exercise for leisure. The conditions of their life make it more difficult to avoid the poor health practices that contribute to disease. When we add in the fact that the alcohol and tobacco industries may target the poor, focusing exclusively on personal responsibility may be a way of getting society off the hook. How free is the "choice" to live a healthy lifestyle in order to protect one's future when staying alive day by day must be a first priority?

---

gradual changes that occur as we age. And even though we cannot grow replacements, our brain has mechanisms to compensate for the loss of individual cells.

In a remarkable set of experiments, Stephen Buell and Paul Coleman (1979) compared the neurons of normal elderly people dying at about age 70 with those of middle-aged adults and elderly people who had died with Alzheimer's disease. They were astonished to find the neurons of the normal elderly had more dendrites than those of the middle-aged people. In another study, when Coleman (1986) measured dendrite growth in a part of the brain called the dentate gyrus in young adults, middle-aged people, young-old people, and very old people (aged 90), he found that this growth continued through early later life, although among the very old it stopped. These encouraging findings show that our nervous system is **plastic,** or changeable (Woodruff-Pak & Hanson, 1995). In response to losing neurons, those that remain automatically "sprout" dendrites, and thinking and memory are preserved.

plastic
*Able to be molded
or changed*

Wide variations occur from person to person. In one study (Scheibel, 1996), at age 68, only 50% of people displayed any of the cortical atrophy or ventricular enlargement supposedly typical of later life. In contrast, among those unfortunate people with Alzheimer's disease, the loss is pronounced. As we will see in Chapter 7, the cause of this illness is a deterioration of the neurons and their replacement by the peculiar tangles and thick bullet-shaped material mentioned previously.

In contrast to heart attack and stroke, this devastating chronic disease that is the end point of normal aging cannot be prevented (as far as we know) by changing our lifestyle; nor does its frequency vary by ethnicity or social class (Pearlin, Aneshensel, Mullan, & Whitlatch, 1996). Females are more likely than males to develop Alzheimer's disease, mainly because women live longer and the neural atrophy becomes far more extensive at the uppermost limits of life (Johansson & Zarit, 1995).

These changes show just how intimately linked physical changes considered normal are to chronic disease. Once again, keep in mind the first principle of aging: individual variability. The differences from person to person in aging rates are dramatic; they grow more pronounced as the years advance. These tremendous individual differences, no matter what our gender or social class, are the real message of every study. They are a function of those two factors: what we inherit (our genetics) and what we expose ourselves to in life.

We cannot change our inherited predispositions. Aging and death are inevitable and built into our species. Our own longevity is determined by our genetic makeup to a moderate degree (Mcgue, Vaupel, Holm, & Harvald, 1993; see Chapter 2). Although behavioral genetic research suggests that our tendency to expose ourselves to environmental hazards may also be partly inherited, what we do in the course of living is more amenable to being rearranged. So, in the rest of this chapter, we focus on secondary aging—specifically, the impact our lifestyle makes on aging and disease.

LIFESTYLE, AGING, AND DISEASE

How often have you vowed to watch your diet, drink less, or exercise? When you last got sick, did you question your behavior: "Was I working too hard?" "Was I under too much stress?" These feelings are predictable, automatic, frequent. They are surprisingly contemporary thoughts.

Americans never felt that taking care of their health was unimportant. What has changed, as suggested in Chapter 1, is the *salience* we give to health practices today. Once again, this change occurred in the 1960s and 1970s, a remarkable decade during which the social climate shifted as much in the area of health as in family life. Along with questioning the authority of other social norms, we began to lose faith in traditional medicine to cure our ills. We shifted to a faith in ourselves (Alonzo, 1993). Exercising, eating right, and taking care of our body became the keys to winning the race with disease and death. People who took their health seriously, those who jogged daily or watched what they ate for health reasons, had been the exception. They were viewed as "health nuts" obsessed with their physical state, but today, we have become converts to their way of thinking. What evidence supports our newfound faith?

Health Practices, Social Relationships, and Longevity

The most powerful study showing that lifestyle does affect longevity was a huge prospective investigation begun in Alameda County, California, in 1965. In contrast to studies that focused on risk factors for single illnesses such as heart disease, the Alameda Study was unique; it was the only investigation to focus on how lifestyle *generally* affects disease and death. Thousands of residents of this suburban San Francisco county were questioned about their illnesses, health conditions, and mental health (Berkman & Breslow, 1983). The sample was followed up in 1974 and again in 1983. Although the researchers were also interested in how gender, social class, and race might affect illness rates, their main targets were two "ways of living": health practices and social relationships.

The researchers explored seven health behaviors. As we might expect, keeping physically active, not smoking, maintaining normal weight, and not drinking to excess promoted longevity. In addition, people who slept eight hours a night, ate breakfast, did not snack, and drank moderate amounts of alcohol were more likely to be healthy; they also had lower mortality rates.

Following these good health practices predicted longevity even at older ages (Guralnik & Kaplan, 1989). The life expectancy at age 60 of the men in the study who followed all of these health behaviors was 82, seven years longer than that of men who followed none. Even at age 80, there was a difference between the two groups of one-and-a-half years (Kaplan, 1986). These behaviors increased the chances of living free from disabling chronic disease (Strawbridge, Camacho, Cohen, & Kaplan, 1993). Most encouraging, the researchers found that the motto was "It's never too late." Even over age 50 or 70, people who quit smoking and began to exercise increased their odds of living a longer life (Kaplan, Seeman, Cohen, Knudsen, & Guralnik, 1987; Kaplan, 1992).

The fact that good health practices affect longevity comes as no surprise. The shock was the powerful relationship between social isolation and life expectancy. Based on criteria such as marital status, contacts with friends and relatives, and church attendance, the researchers constructed a social network index—a measure of how involved the men and women were in close relationships. This index was as highly correlated to life expectancy as health practices! People who were the most socially isolated had a mortality rate more than twice as high as those who were most involved (Berkman & Breslow, 1983). Even over age 70, being socially isolated increased the risk of death (Kaplan, 1992).

Because these findings are correlations, we cannot be sure that close social relationships or even following good health practices protects us from becoming ill. As suggested in our discussion of cardiovascular change, people who engage in activities such as exercising for pleasure or not smoking are not a random group. They tend to be middle class and health conscious, the very people who receive the best medical care. They may be biologically advantaged. Who would be a more committed jogger, a person in robust good health or one made lethargic by disease? A perfect example of the danger of assuming causality from correlations concerns the finding that drinking moderately is associated with longevity. New evidence shows that moderate drinking, one or two glasses of wine with dinner, may offer older people protection against heart disease (Schafer, Kubik, & Pelham, 1997). However, in the Alameda Study, the increased risk among nondrinkers was really due to the fact that many people in this group had used alcohol but *because of illness* decided to abstain.

We could make the same argument for social isolation: Mrs. Jones withdraws from people *because* she is ill. However, in the Alameda Study, the relationship between social isolation and longevity held independent of disease. In other words, even when the researchers took initial illness into account, being socially isolated still predicted subsequent death.

Dozens of studies reveal a link between social isolation and premature illness and death (Breschel, 1997). However, be cautious: It is not the quantity of our relationships but their quality that counts. As we all know when entangled in a troubled relationship, overwhelmed by unwanted social demands, or surrounded by critical so-called friends, being with people can just as easily be life-shortening as the reverse. Yes, having relationships is important; but they must be relationships we actively select. They must be supportive relationships, people who uplift us emotionally when they are around (Antonucci & Akiyama, 1995; Antonucci, Fuhrer, & Dartigues, 1997; Ingersoll-Dayton, Morgan, & Antonucci, 1997; Rook, 1997; see also Chapters 10 and 11).

stress buffering
Effect that relationships have in reducing the emotional impact of life stress

If uplifting social ties (close, caring people) protect us against illness, why do they have this effect? Many experts accept some variation of the **stress buffering** hypothesis (Krause, 1989; Markides & Cooper, 1989). Caring relationships offer emotional insulation, cushioning the impact of dramatic downturns in our lives.

Interesting support for this idea comes from a longitudinal study tracing three-generation families over several decades. The University of Southern California research team found that elderly mothers who reported the closest, most affectionate relationships with their children around the time they were widowed lived longer than those with more distant, conflict-ridden family ties (Silverstein & Bengtson, 1991). In other words, while caring relationships are always a blessing, their real power to heal seems to be revealed during times of emotional stress.

Emotional Stress and Illness

The idea that emotional stress causes illness has been a popular belief since ancient times. However, it was only a few decades ago that this idea became scientifically respectable, as enthusiastically embraced by our family doctor as the neighbor next door. One set of studies was particularly influential in convincing a highly skeptical medical community that our psyche can affect our physical state.

LIFE EVENTS AND ILLNESS   In the mid 1960s, Thomas Holmes and Robert Rahe decided to test the "old wives' tale" that stressful life events make people ill. They developed a life-events scale by having a large group of people rank a list of changes according to how great an upheaval each might represent. The scale included both positive and negative events because Holmes and Rahe hypothesized that *any* dramatic change would compromise health. When the researchers correlated illness rates with scores on their scale, they found that people who reported unusually high change ratings within the past six months were more likely to get sick—that is, more prone to illnesses ranging from cancer to colds (Rahe, 1974).

Rahe and Holmes's research was followed by a flood of studies linking illness to life change. In one interesting example, researchers infected undergraduate volunteers with the virus producing the common cold. As Holmes and Rahe had found, the students who came down with symptoms were more likely to have experienced major life changes within the past six months (Stone et al., 1992).

Dramatic life change or stress of any kind may provoke illness through several physiological routes. In situations where we feel threatened, our body is flooded with the stress hormones adrenaline and noradrenaline, neurochemical substances that produce a burst of energy, a state of heightened arousal that allows us to fight or flee from the source of threat. This sympathetic nervous system "fight or flight" response, if prolonged, eventually wears the body down. When the situation is hopeless, the pituitary gland produces cortisol, a hormone known to suppress immune function. Changes in immune function, also measured after people undergo uncontrollable stress (Endresen et al., 1991–1992), may increase our vulnerability to a host of diseases (Vogt, 1992).

The most influential portrayal of the connection between stress and illness was proposed by biologist Hans Selye a half century ago. According to Selye's **general adaptation syndrome,** any organism's response to a stressor occurs in three phases. During the *alarm phase,* the adrenal cortex floods the body with hormones, energizing us to respond. Then we enter the *phase of resistance,* in which output remains high and we are capable of superhuman feats. Finally, in the *exhaustion phase,* our capacities give out and we become ill (Selye, 1976). After the avalanche, a hiker runs miles without feeling the cold and subsists on roots and berries for days. However, unless he is rescued fairly quickly, his resistance dips way down and he falls prey to disease. In the week before our wedding, we find to our amazement that we can finish a full semester's schoolwork and make sure every detail of the ceremony is right. On the honeymoon we develop a 103-degree fever, unable to enjoy the vacation we planned.

general adaptation syndrome Selye's portrayal of the physiological response to stressors, involving an alarm reaction, a phase of resistance, and an exhaustion phase

Unfortunately, the exact physiological path by which stress causes illness is unknown, and the correlations between life events and illness are small. So you must be wary about using major life changes to predict your chances of becoming ill. For one thing, the concept of fixed stress ratings ignores the dramatic differences between people in the stress value of each life event. Getting fired might be a terrible catastrophe to you; to your friend the same event might come as a relief (Costa & McCrae, 1989).

The internal validity of much of the research can be criticized. In demonstrating that life change raises the risk of illness, researchers typically ask people to report on their health and then say what has happened to them within the past six months. However, because memory fades, not all events are recalled over time (Glickman, Hubbard, Liveright, & Valciukas, 1990; Gorman, 1993). Furthermore, this forgetting seems selective, skewed by a person's current emotional state. Whereas most of us may forget less desirable events, wouldn't depressed people be more likely to recall negative life events and also to report disease? In other words, rather than being "real," the link between life change and illness may be incidental, a function of the general worldview of the reporter.

Major personal events are not the only type of stress that can affect health. Today, researchers argue for a much broader conception. Stressful events include a range of experiences, from disasters such as being in that avalanche, to minor everyday hassles, to the strains that we chronically endure. In fact, because their impact does not go away, sociologist Leonard Pearlin (1980) argues that chronic strains such as continually worrying about money, or living with and *not* divorcing an abusive spouse, may be even more life-shortening than major life events. The same applies to little hassles such as losing our keys or forgetting our notebook when we come to class. When Richard Lazarus and his colleagues devised a scale examining these little hassles, they found that these scores were more closely tied to illness than ratings on Holmes and Rahe's scale (Kanner, Coyne, Schaefer, & Lazarus, 1981).

Most important, focusing on outer-world happenings ignores the variations in how people perceive and cope with stress. Some of us fall apart under the smallest setback; others are resilient in the face of the worst tragedy. Some people approach terrible strains, such as living with a chronic illness, by finding joy in every moment. Others create strain when it is not there. Perhaps, argued thoughtful observers, the real reason why the correlations between life events and illness are so small is that what really causes illness lies not outside but within us—in our personality.

TYPE A BEHAVIOR, PAST AND PRESENT   The earliest personality dimension that was linked to illness has become a household word. In a large-scale prospective study that even predated Rahe and Holmes's work, cardiologists Meyer Friedman and Ray Rosenman (1974) made behavioral science history by finding that men with the **Type A behavior pattern**—highly competitive, overachieving, hard-driving, and hostile personalities—were more prone to heart attacks in midlife. Because Type A was an *independent* risk factor for coronary disease, predicting illness even when behaviors such as smoking and exercise were controlled, this research was especially influential in winning over the skeptical medical community to the idea that emotions cause disease.

In the decades that followed, research on Type A has been intense. Books have been published, conferences convened. Researchers have examined the Type A behavior pattern in children and adolescents (Thoresen & Pattillo, 1988), in women, and in different ethnic groups. They have searched for the roots of this behavior in everything from biological predispositions to child-rearing practices fostering narcissism (Fukunishi, Nakagawa, Nakamura, Li, Hua, & Kratz, 1996) and poor self-esteem (Scherwitz & Canick, 1988).

Researchers have speculated about the physiological mechanisms that link Type A and heart disease. When Type A's enter competitive situations or when their self-esteem is threatened, they respond with exaggerated sympathetic arousal, an intense "fight or flight" response (Contrada, Krantz, & Hill, 1988; Houston, 1988). This excessive reactivity raises blood pressure (Scherwitz & Canick, 1988), increases heart rate (Burns, Friedman, & Katkin, 1992; Lyness, 1993), and accelerates blood clotting, increasing the risk of blocked arteries (Markovitz, Matthews, Kiss, & Smitherman, 1996). Type A behavior may increase the risk of heart disease in an indirect way. One study showed that Type A men were more prone to smoke. Women with this trait ate a higher-fat diet than their more relaxed counterparts (Musante, Treiber, Davis, Strong, & Levy, 1992). Because they are so competitive and hostile, Type A's may have poorer relationships (Watkins, Ward, Southard, & Fisher, 1992) and feel more socially

Type A behavior pattern
Competitive, hard-driving, hostile approach to living that may put an individual at risk for premature heart disease

isolated (Malcolm & Janisse, 1991), which in turn may heighten their vulnerability to disease.

Unfortunately, the seemingly solid evidence that Type A personalities have more heart attacks soon began to evaporate. During the 1970s, negative reports began to accumulate, suggesting that the global concept of Type A had to be rethought (Chesney, Hecker, & Black, 1988). First, researchers found that the link between Type A behavior and illness does not apply to every age group. It is only among middle-aged people, not the elderly, that this personality trait predicts heart attacks. Moreover, working too hard does not have health consequences. Only certain dimensions of this personality— excessive hostility accompanied by suspicion—are associated with becoming ill (Haynes & Matthews, 1988; Williams & Barefoot, 1988). The real cause of the problem, some experts feel, is a worldview that is cynical and untrusting, leading the coronary-prone person to feel on guard and respond with anger to imagined threats. It is this distrustful state of angry vigilance that puts the individual at higher risk of heart disease.

PESSIMISM, HELPLESSNESS, AND CONTROL Another aspect of personality thought to produce illness centers around feelings of helplessness and lack of control. This research involves studies probing the impact on health of self-efficacy and explanatory style, those influential cognitive perceptions described in Chapter 2.

In a remarkable study, Martin Seligman and his colleagues set out to show that a pessimistic explanatory style may make us ill. Remember that people who have this hopeless and helpless worldview see positive events as extrinsic and random. Negative life events are viewed as global, internal, and permanent: "Failure will always happen. It shows that I'm incompetent and incapable of success."

Drawing on a longitudinal study of the personalities of Harvard men, Seligman and his coworkers measured explanatory style from interviews recorded in college, then related these ratings to participants' health in their middle 50s. A pessimistic explanatory style in this one interview was associated with poor health and premature death (Peterson, Seligman, & Vaillant, 1994)!

Seligman's research complements an equally remarkable study showing that experimentally enhancing self-efficacy affects longevity. Judith Rodin and Ellen Langer (1977) randomly assigned nursing home residents to two groups. The first was told about the choices and opportunities for decision making in the home. They were encouraged to take on responsibilities, such as planning their meals or caring for a plant. The other group listened to a "benign and caring" lecture that was just as positive but had a different message: "Let the staff take over your care."

This simple control-enhancing communication worked. Over an 18-month period, the death rate for the control group was about 25%; during the same time, only 15% of the residents in the experimental group died! Another study conducted almost two decades later found a similar result. When researchers followed frail older people from the community to a nursing home, even after taking into account age, health, and psychological distress, feelings of control were associated with lower death rates (reported in Carstensen, Hanson, & Freund, 1995).

Bandura (1997) has summarized the research linking self-efficacy to health. People with high self-efficacy are more likely to follow lifestyle recommendations (Gallant,

1997). Interventions enhancing efficacy can improve the ability to stick to a low-fat diet and lower cholesterol. Efficacy-enhancing interventions can even alter the physiological stress response. When phobic people underwent a stress-management training program centered on increasing their sense of control over their fear, their immune competence was higher and their physiological "fight or flight" response less intense when placed in a situation where they had to confront the object of their anxiety.

Again, be cautious. Apart from studies with that special group, nursing home residents, no study has demonstrated directly that high self-efficacy either lengthens life or reduces our susceptibility to disease. We should be equally wary about generalizing from Seligman's compelling study involving explanatory style. When researchers at the National Institute on Aging examined a similar personality dimension, neuroticism, they found no relationship between this trait and illness (Costa & McCrae, 1987). Another study suggests the idea that pessimism causes illness warrants a very close second look. When researchers (Friedman et al., 1993) looked at personality traits measured in childhood in a classic study of gifted children and related them to death rates in middle and later life, they were astonished to find that optimism and cheerfulness were negatively related to longevity. Perhaps because they were less likely to take health risks, dour, conservative, cautious people lived longer than anyone else!

SUMMARY AND CRITIQUE   By now it should be apparent that the effort to demonstrate the "obvious" link between emotional stress and health is more elusive than we might think. Let's summarize what these years of research twists and turns have revealed.

1. Many studies suggest a connection between stressful life experiences and illness. However, the correlation between life events and disease is small, and there is little consensus as to what events are especially illness-producing. An even greater sense of confusion surrounds personality. With the possible exception of hostility, there is no evidence that any personality trait makes us more vulnerable to getting ill.

2. Although hypotheses center around sympathetic arousal and impaired immune function, the physiological response to stress is complex. Researchers have not yet pinpointed the exact physiological changes that occur due to stress, much less demonstrated how these changes make us ill (Leventhal, Patrick-Miller, Leventhal, & Burns, 1998).

3. The route by which emotions cause disease is certain to be complex. Do stressful life events directly cause illness, or do they indirectly affect our health by causing us to eat poorly and neglect our body (Leventhal et al., 1998)? How does our personality influence the impact of life events? How important a role does social support play in buffering us from life's blows?

This ambiguity becomes clear if we look more deeply at the connection between social support and longevity in the study of three-generation families that introduced our discussion of stress. Recall that newly widowed women who reported poor relationships with their children did not live as long as those with close, caring family ties.

But was it really the relationships that promoted longevity, or the mothers' personalities? Mentally healthy women are *both* more likely to have loving family ties *and* to live for a longer time. Or perhaps the real cause for the connection was simply health: Physically fragile women feel more distant from others *and* die sooner.

These complexities suggest that we should pause before automatically labeling a friend's heart attack as due to his "driven" personality. We should be cautious about making statements such as, "His illness was caused by the death of his wife." Not only is the evidence for these assertions shaky, these assumptions may be hurtful. They add insult to injury, because they blame the victim for becoming ill (see Aging in Action 3-3 on page 85).

INTERVENTIONS

As the link between health practices and illness became common knowledge, a tremendous effort was centered on prevention as the cure for disease. From the fitness centers that are now a fixture in most large companies (see Figure 3-7), in hotels, at universities, and in private homes; to the blood pressure machines at your local supermarket; to runs for the heart, health fairs, and public service announcements on television or the local bus, the message is out: Living a healthy life is the key to winning the race with death.

These efforts involve **primary prevention**, preventing risk factors for illness from developing, and **secondary prevention**, changing existing risk factors before they result in disease. They are having an effect. Starting in about 1970, atherosclerosis-related mortality, responsible for most of the deaths in the United States, began to decline at an average rate of 3% a year (Kunkel & Harris, 1997). While no one denies that better medical care is partly responsible, much of this decline is thought to be due to lifestyle changes (Fries, 1990). Since a vigorous public health campaign transformed smoking from a sign of sophistication into a cause for shame, per-capita (per person) cigarette consumption has dropped by 40% (Fries, 1990; Warner, 1989). During the past decade, the number of cases of lung cancer has begun to decline steadily.

Large-scale interventions, such as the stop smoking campaign, can only be evaluated by looking at societywide changes in illness rates. Interventions centered on secondary prevention—changing the behavior of people known to be at high risk for illness—offer direct evidence that changing lifestyle can have an impact on disease. This is why I end this chapter with two such interventions, both involving the number one cause of death in the United States, heart disease.

The Multiple Risk Factor Intervention Trial (Multiple Risk Factor Intervention Trial Research Group, 1982) was our nation's most ambitious effort to make an impact on heart disease rates. More than 100,000 men aged 35 to 57 who smoked, had high blood pressure, and ate a high-fat diet were assigned either to a special intervention group or to regular health care at different centers nationwide. Men in the intervention group received vigorous drug treatment for their hypertension. They participated in group sessions designed to get them to quit smoking and change their diet. They were counseled individually to reduce these risk factors for disease. The participants were followed for seven years.

primary prevention
Efforts to control illness by preventing the development of risk factors for disease

secondary prevention
Efforts to control illness by eradicating existing risk factors for disease

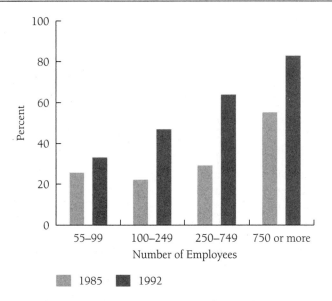

Over the seven years from 1985 to 1992, workplace fitness programs have become increasingly common in the United States. Today, most companies employing more than 100 workers offer this service to their employees.
SOURCE: National Center for Health Statistics, 1995b, p. 6.

The treatment was successful at reducing the risk factors. Blood pressure and cholesterol dropped significantly in the treated men. However, there was no difference in mortality between the groups. Was this because the treatment did not work or because seven years is too short a time to see the benefits of changing behaviors that may have been damaging their arteries for many years? Might the drug therapy to reduce hypertension have had an unintended negative effect? Perhaps there simply was not enough difference between the two groups. Over the course of the study, as the link between heart disease and lifestyle became common knowledge, many men in the control group also stopped smoking and reduced their other risk factors for disease. Whatever the reason, this ambitious "failure" illustrates that interventions to reduce illness do not always have a clear-cut effect.

Another study to prevent heart attack had a different outcome. In the Recurrent Coronary Prevention Project, the goal was to modify Type A behavior, specifically the chronic hostility thought to increase the risk of disease. Men who had had a first heart attack were taught psychological strategies to reduce Type A behavior. They were instructed to change their environment and reduce their tendencies to read personal threat into innocent acts. In situations seen as "threats to my ego," participants learned to substitute more realistic responses. Strategies included direct teaching and modeling the new, more relaxed behavior. The men were told to practice leaving their watch off, smiling, walking slowly. The treatment had an impact. Not only did the men show reductions in type A behavior, the treatment group had fewer second heart attacks over the next four years (Price, 1988).

These two examples illustrate both the promise and the problems with conducting genuine trials to show that prevention works. Although the correlational evidence that lifestyle affects longevity is overwhelming, ethical and practical problems prevent researchers from proving experimentally that changing behavior affects health. The researcher must ask a good deal of the experimental group: Change lifelong behaviors such as not exercising or eating an unhealthy diet, then wait an unknown length of time to see the effects. Not only is it difficult to prevent people in the experimental group from relapsing or dropping out, it is impossible and unethical to keep members of the control group from modifying their lifestyle on their own. When we add in the fact that every illness has many interacting causes, and that these risk factors may vary in surprising ways from group to group (as we saw with Hispanic men and heart disease), it becomes easy to understand why even the best thought-out program can have negative results (Rakowski, 1992, 1994).

In the next two chapters, as we continue to explore the physical dimension of aging, we take the same critical look at the research. In Chapter 4, we look at two broad facets of behavior—sensory and motor functioning—and how they change with age. Once again, we examine what normally happens, explore individual variations, and spell out strategies to reduce the impact of age changes. In Chapter 5, we focus on what happens after illness has struck, looking carefully at the course of disabilities and the health care system in later life.

KEY TERMS

arteriosclerosis
atherosclerosis
biological theories of aging
cardiovascular system
central nervous system
chronic disease
excess mortality
free radicals
general adaptation syndrome
hypothalamus

immune system
maximum life span
nervous system
neuron
normal age change
peripheral nervous system
plastic
primary aging
primary prevention

programmed aging theories
prospective studies
random damage theories of aging
reserve capacity
risk factors
secondary aging
secondary prevention
stress buffering
Type A behavior pattern

RECOMMENDED READINGS

READABLE, NONSCHOLARLY SOURCES ON PHYSICAL AGING

Kart, C. S., Metress, E. K., & Metress, S. P. (1992). *Human aging and chronic disease*. Boston: Jones and Bartlett.
This textbook offers an excellent overview of the aging process in each system.

Nuland, S. (1995). *How we die*. New York: Vintage.
In this popular book, a physician sensitively describes the paths to death, focusing on each major killer, describing how it progresses, and explaining what exactly causes our demise.

Pogrobin, L. (1996). *Getting over getting older*. Boston: Little, Brown.
This book, covering physical aging and more, is also written for a popular audience, but with a very different slant. It offers a humorous, first-person account of what it is like to be a woman over 50 experiencing aging "in the flesh."

Whitbourne, S. K. (1996). *The aging individual: Physical and psychological processes*. New York: Springer.
Another text on physical aging, this time with a psychological bent. This author, a psychologist, offers a lucid account of aging in each body system and its psychological consequences (as well as discussing age changes in memory and personality). I highly recommend this book for readers who want a more comprehensive picture of each body system and how it changes as we age.

MORE SPECIFIC, ACADEMIC SOURCES

Berkman, L., & Breslow, L. (1983). *Health and ways of living: The Alameda County study*. New York: Oxford University Press.

Kaplan, G. A. (1992). Health and aging in the Alameda County study. In K. W. Schaie, D. G. Blazer, & J. S. House (Eds.), *Aging, health behaviors, and health outcomes* (pp. 69–95). Hillsdale, NJ: Erlbaum.
These references offer comprehensive summaries of the Alameda Study.

The biology of aging. (1992, Fall/Winter). *Generations, 16* (whole issue).
The whole issue of this journal is devoted to the biology of aging. Articles review biological theories of aging, cancer in the elderly, and health care, among other topics.

Cristofalo, V. (1988). An overview of the theories of biological aging. In J. E. Birren & V. L. Bengtson (Eds.), *Emergent theories of aging* (pp. 118–127). New York: Springer.
This article provides a more in-depth overview of biological theories of aging.

Hazzard, W. (1990). A central role of sex hormones in the sex differential in lipoprotein metabolism, atherosclerosis, and longevity. In M. Ory and H. R. Warner (Eds.), *Gender, health, and longevity* (pp. 87–108). New York: Springer.
This chapter reviews research implicating estrogen in the gender difference in heart disease.

Leventhal, H., Patrick-Miller, L., Leventhal, E., & Burns, E. (1998). Does stress-emotion cause illness in elderly people? In K. W. Schaie & M. P. Lawton (Eds.), *Annual review of gerontology and geriatrics: Vol 17. Focus on emotion and adult development* (pp. 138–184). New York: Springer.
This chapter, which thoroughly reviews research on the physiology of emotional stress and its links to health, demonstrates just how difficult it is to prove that stress causes disease.

Markides, K. S., & Cooper, C. L. (Eds.). (1989). *Aging, stress, and health*. Chichester, England: John Wiley & Sons.
This edited book reviews the literature on health and stress.

Shock, N. W., Greulich, R. C., Andres, R., Arenberg, D., Costa, P. T., Lakatta, E. G., & Tobin, J. D. (1984). *Normal human aging: The Baltimore Longitudinal Study of Aging* (NIH Pub. No. 84-2450). Rockville, MD: National Institute on Aging.
The Longitudinal Study of Aging, 1984–1990. (1993, September). CD-ROM LSOA.

The book offers a scholarly, comprehensive report of the Baltimore findings and reprints of the journal articles summarizing the study as of 1984. The CD-ROM describes research dating from 1984 to 1990. NIA pamphlets offer regular updates on the Baltimore findings.

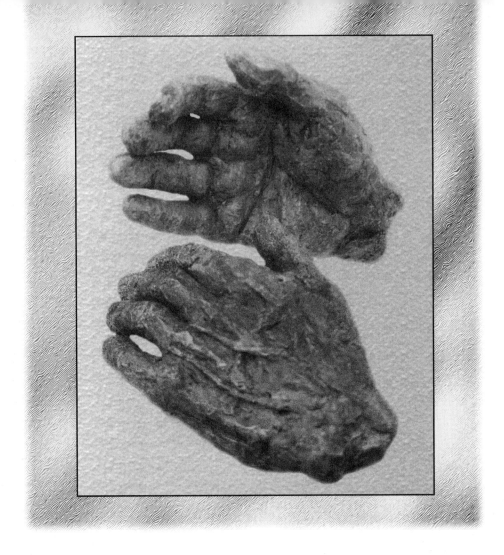

Chapter Outline

4

Sensory and Motor Functioning

 "In my 40s, I prided myself that my vision showed none of the changes supposedly normal at my age," says 58-year-old Nancy. "I did not need bifocals. I had no trouble seeing in dim light. Then, at about age 50, my comfort level driving at night took a dramatic turn for the worse. I have no trouble on well-lit streets, or on familiar roads, or when I can use the lights of the cars ahead as beacons to chart the way. But on a country lane or darkened stretch of highway, I have to squint to make out the contours of the road. Highway ramps are an endurance test. Once I exited, a curve loomed up from a black hole, and I was inches from death. Several times I swerved just in time to avoid a major wreck. A few years ago, more puzzling changes occurred. I have trouble reading when the lights are dim. The print on paperback books is especially hard to make out. On the other hand, the letters on my computer become faint and fade into the screen when my ultrabright office light beams down from above.

"These changes required adjustments. I brought a lamp to work. (At my age, no face should have the misfortune of confronting a fluorescent beam!) I leave early in the morning to make the ten-hour drive to my mother's house. I make sure not to drive after dusk. I let my teenage son find the seats at the movies. I assume the bill on the impossibly faint restaurant tape is correct. However, just this year, I noticed another change. The whine of the office air conditioner is more intrusive. My colleagues at work are murmuring more. Can my hearing be beginning to go?"

Basic to living is our ability to receive information about the environment. Just as crucial is our capacity to respond to the information we receive. Limitations in sensory-motor functioning can have widespread effects. If severe, they may make people less independent, less able to handle life. They may make the elderly feel vulnerable, out of control, less sure of themselves. They may make relationships more difficult and cut off pleasures as simple as enjoying a fragrant rose or a beautiful sunset. For these reasons, sensory and motor losses are among our top-ranking anxieties about old age.

Is it true that age brings dramatic losses in our senses or our ability to move and respond? Answering these questions is not as easy as might appear. People may be reluctant to have their hearing or vision tested, making it difficult to get exact estimates of how prevalent problems are. Moreover, as we just saw in the case of "Nancy," how well people function is surprisingly dependent on the outer world. Because environmental conditions such as lighting or noise levels affect vision or hearing, a small loss under ideal laboratory conditions may represent a genuine handicap in daily life. Or, tests measuring sensory-motor abilities may reveal problems that do not really exist.

A person taking a hearing test is given a series of low-intensity tones and asked to indicate when a sound is heard. The vision test involves identifying the letters or numbers on the familiar eye chart. Sensitivity or acuity on these measures is judged by the faintest stimulus that the person can perceive. But older people tend to be more cautious than the young (Botwinick, 1966; Welford, 1977). When a 70-year-old man is unsure whether he really heard a tone, his impulse is to be cautious, deciding "I'd better not guess." When a psychologist measuring age differences in response speed tells an elderly woman to "push lever A as fast as possible when the green light comes on," she may have a similar mind-set. Younger subjects, being more likely to guess, are at an advantage. They may be judged as more capable in comparison with the elderly than they really are because their strategy maximizes the chance of doing well.

In reading the list of losses that follows, keep these additional thoughts in mind. To measure a loss in the laboratory is not to say that loss presents problems for functioning in the real world (Kline et al., 1992). *Impairing* problems of vision, hearing, or mobility only become common in advanced old age (P. B. Baltes & Smith, 1997). Older people probably adjust naturally to the more minor changes they typically experience and continue to function as fully as before. As with any other physical function, making the distinction between primary and secondary aging is important. Our lifestyle, such as being exposed to high levels of noise or leading an inactive life, accelerates sensory decline and contributes to a slowing and unsteadiness in our responses. So the problems older adults have today might be escaped, in part, by future elderly if they are more health conscious and take better care of their health.

The sensory information we get from the world arrives from a variety of sources. Somatosensory sensors deep within our body give us information about the workings of our organs. Nerve endings directly on our skin respond to pressure, temperature, and pain. Vestibular organs in our interior ear tell us about the location of our body in space. Olfactory nerves and gustatory cells embedded in the nose and tongue allow us to taste and smell. However, vision and hearing are our senses of first rank—those we worry most about losing, those most crucial to daily life. As we might expect, researchers have more information about changes in these primary senses. For these reasons, although we will also consider how age affects the more secondary sensory systems, our main focus will be on vision, hearing, and age.

VISION

Some of the ways age affects our sight are obvious. We notice that we are having more trouble reading smaller print or seeing the time as well on the clock across the street. However, vision also changes in subtle, surprising, and unexpected ways as we grow old.

The Problem

The most basic seeing problem that increases with age is poor **visual acuity,** the inability to see distinctly at distances measured by the eye chart. Impaired acuity, when it cannot be corrected with glasses, affects all our activities; however, uncorrectable problems with acuity affect only a minority of older adults. A second, more limited, type of vision problem is universal in our older years. This is the familiar problem of seeing objects close up, a difficulty whose well-known link to age is indicated by its name, **presbyopia** (old eyes). Interestingly, this classic sign of age does not take place suddenly when people notice it in their 40s. Losses in near vision occur gradually from childhood, growing serious during middle age.

Presbyopia and poor visual acuity are obvious problems; other changes are less apparent. As we saw in the chapter opening, older people have special trouble seeing in dim light. They have problems distinguishing specific colors, in particular blues from greens. They are more bothered by **glare,** being blinded by a direct beam of light. Their field of vision is narrower; they are not as able to see objects at the corner of their gaze. They cannot track or follow moving objects as well. Figure 4-1 illustrates the impact some of these difficulties can have on the ability to perceive the world.

How common are *impairing* problems in vision in middle and later life? To answer this question, the Lighthouse for the Blind, the leading advocacy group for the visually impaired, commissioned a national poll exploring reports of vision difficulties among Americans over age 45 (Harris & Associates, 1996; Brennan, Horowitz, & Reinhardt, 1997). The more than 1200 people questioned in this Louis Harris survey were classified as having a vision impairment if, *when wearing glasses,* they reported having trouble seeing or being unable to recognize a friend from across the room, reading newspaper print, or seeing in one or both eyes. In addition to being asked about their own problems, respondents were questioned about their familiarity with and feelings toward visually impaired people and their knowledge about age-related vision loss. Here are the main findings.

1. **Vision impairments are surprisingly common.**   One in six people report a problem. Moreover, slightly more than half of these people report seriously impaired vision—that is, greater problems seeing or a combination of several problems. On the other hand, more than 9 out of 10 of even these seriously impaired people have *some* vision. Only 2% of the American population is totally blind, unable to see at all.

2. **Rates of vision impairment rise dramatically in advanced old age.**   About 1 in 7 middle-aged and young-old adults have impairments; among the old-old the figure is almost twice as high, slightly more than 1 in 4 (see Figure 4-2). In addition, over age 75, the percentage of people reporting seriously limited vision accelerates.

3. **Although impaired vision cuts across gender, race, and socioeconomic lines, the most vulnerable elderly are at higher risk.**   People with vision impairments are more likely to be female, unmarried, poorly educated, and financially badly off. They are more apt to be nonwhite, living alone, and in poor or fair health. In addition, disadvantaged elderly are more likely to report vision problems that are severe.

4. **Vision impairments are highly visible problems, personally touching the lives of most middle-aged and elderly adults.**   Of the people polled, 16% report a family member is visually impaired; 30% report knowing a person with impaired

visual acuity
Ability to see clearly at distances measured by the eye chart

presbyopia
Age-related impairment in the ability to see close objects distinctly

glare
Blinding effect of a direct beam of light

The upper image illustrates the impact of increased susceptibility to glare; the lower illustrates problems of acuity associated with poor contrast.
SOURCE: Birren & Schaie, 1977.

vision fairly well. More than half of all Americans over age 45 either have a problem themselves or know someone with impaired vision.

5. **Anxiety combined with ignorance about vision impairments is the norm.** While personal familiarity is high, and fears intense—in the Lighthouse Survey, people

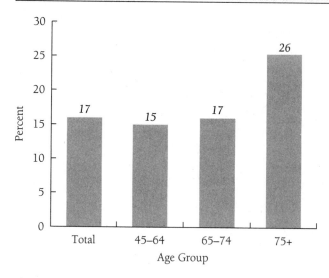

About 1 in 6 people over age 45 has a vision impairment; over age 75, the rate is 1 in 4.

SOURCE: Louis Harris and Associates, 1996.

rated being blind as *worse* than being deaf or losing a limb—people know next to nothing about what causes age-related vision difficulties, how common poor vision is in later life, or what services are available to help the visually impaired. As the researchers conclude, "the mandate to The Lighthouse . . . is expanded public education," ensuring that the public knows more about this feared condition of later life.

In the rest of this section, we follow this mandate. First, we shed light on the reasons why people have the specific difficulties just described, examining the intricate visual system and how it changes with age. Then, we explore strategies for coping when losses in this human function strike.

The Visual System and Age-Related Decline

What causes the specific vision losses that occur with age? Answers lie in looking at how the delicate visual system changes with age.

As Figure 4-3 shows, a variety of specialized structures make up that remarkable organ, the eye. There is the cornea, the eye's tough outer cover; a viscous fluid called the aqueous humor; the pupil, an opening in the iris; the lens, a circular structure in the middle of the eye; and the vitreous humor, a gellike substance that cushions and

FIGURE 4-3   *Anatomy of the Human Eye*

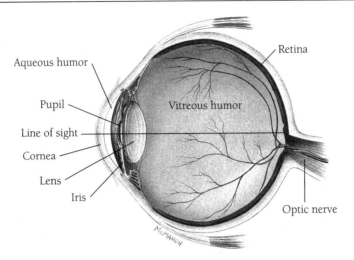

Aqueous humor

Pupil

Line of sight

Cornea

Lens

Iris

Retina

Vitreous humor

Optic nerve

Although all structures can contribute, changes in the pupil/iris and especially the lens are crucial in explaining age losses in vision.

insulates the eye's back rim. This insulation is essential, as it is on this rim, called the retina, that the delicate visual receptors reside.

The purpose of these outer structures is to filter and focus light so the clearest image appears on the receptors: the rods, sensitive to darkness, and the cones, which allow us to see detail and color. The receptors are the link by which we make contact with the visual environment. Here light waves are transformed into the nervous impulses that are carried to the brain. Impulses originating in the rods and cones travel to the brain through the bundle of neurons making up the optic nerve. They arrive at the part of the brain called the visual cortex.

Changes in almost every part of the eye can affect the older adult's ability to see. By about age 70, the cornea becomes more rigid and develops a gray band, which can reduce the visual field, limiting the older person's ability to see out of the corner of the eye. Changes in the quantity, viscosity, and clarity of the fluid-filled aqueous and vitreous humor may occur due to **diabetic retinopathy** and **glaucoma,** two top-ranking late-life vision diseases (see Table 4-1). However, the iris/pupil and especially the lens are particularly important in explaining the normal changes in vision that occur as we age (Fozard, 1990; Kline & Scialfa, 1996).

Iris/pupil changes have a crucial impact on the ability to see well in the dark. The iris is a pigmented, circular structure (our iris color is our eye color) with a hole called the pupil in its center. In bright light, the iris reflexively widens, causing the pupil to constrict. This reduces the amount of light reaching the receptors. In dim light, the iris narrows and the pupil dilates (widens). This allows as much light as possible to get to

diabetic retinopathy
A long-term complication of diabetes in which retinal blood vessels leak or rupture, causing vision loss

glaucoma
A buildup of the fluid within the aqueous humor that can lead to loss of vision

1. Glaucoma   A buildup of the fluid within the aqueous humor (resulting when the normally open passageway that lets the fluid circulate narrows or closes) causes increased pressure within the eye and permanently damages the retinal receptors. With early diagnosis, medications, laser treatments, and sometimes surgery can reopen the passage, preventing blindness. Glaucoma is called the "sneak thief of vision" because it seldom produces early symptoms, so it is important to be tested regularly for this illness in middle and late life.

2. Senile macular degeneration   The neurons in the center part of the retina (called the macula) no longer function effectively. Symptoms include blurred vision and loss of central vision. Early detection is important because occasionally laser surgery can improve vision.

3. Diabetic retinopathy   In this long-term complication of diabetes, the blood vessels that nourish the retina either leak fluid or grow into the eye and rupture, causing serious loss of vision. Laser surgery to seal off leaky blood vessels can sometimes prevent blindness or serious vision loss.

4. Retinal detachment   The inner and outer areas of the retina separate. Detached retinas can often be reattached surgically, restoring sight.

the back of the eye. This rapid change, combined with an increase in the sensitivity of the rods, allows us to see in dim light.

In later life, the iris is less able to constrict. As a result, older people have smaller pupils than the young in both dim and bright light; but the difference is especially great in darkness, when the pupil needs to be as large as possible to permit optimal vision. Having a smaller pupil means having a fixed internal dimmer. In bright light, the dimming does not present many problems, because not much illumination needs to get in. In dim light, however, the impact can be dramatic, explaining why older people have more trouble at the movie theater and driving at night.

The degree of dimming is not minor. Changes in the pupil and iris, along with those in the lens, permit only about 30% as much light to reach the retina at age 60 as penetrated at age 20 (Saxon & Etten, 1978; Pirkl, 1995).

The **lens**, a clear circular structure that looks like a contact lens, plays a central role in several age-related vision changes. As we get older, the lens grows cloudier. In the same way as looking through a dirty window makes it more difficult to see outside, this internal clouding impairs visual acuity. It also explains why older people are especially sensitive to glare. When sunlight hits a dirty window, the rays of light scatter and it becomes impossible to see out. Because older people have a cloudier lens, they experience the same effect, and so are more likely to be blinded by a beam of light shining directly in the eye. At the extreme of this age-related clouding is a partially or completely opaque lens, a **cataract.**

Because little light can reach the retina when the lens is cloudy, cataracts, when severe, cause blindness. However, they do not have to have this devastating effect. Unlike many age-related illnesses, vision loss caused by cataracts can be cured. The physician surgically removes the defective lens and either implants an artificial lens in its place or prescribes contact lenses or glasses. Unfortunately, as we see in Table 4-1,

lens
Normally clear circular structure in the eye that functions to permit close vision and grows more opaque with age

cataract
Chronic condition in which the age-related clouding of the lens has progressed to such a degree that vision is seriously impaired

vision losses caused by the other top-ranking illnesses producing blindness in later life are less easily reversed.

A second change in the lens's transparency affects color vision. Because the clouding has a yellowish tinge, it produces a decrease in sensitivity to hues in the blue-green range. This explains why distinguishing between these two colors is so hard for many older adults.

So far, you may have the impression that the lens is a nonfunctioning window. This is not true. This circular structure, which looks like a contact lens, changes shape to bring objects at different distances into focus on the retina. When we view near objects, the lens bulges (curves outward); when we view distant objects, it flattens and becomes elongated.

This near/far focusing deteriorates with age because of a property of the lens itself. Throughout life the lens grows continuously, adding cells at its periphery without losing old cells. To make way for this growth, the older cells become compacted toward the center of the lens. Over time, this accumulation produces the loss of transparency. It also makes the lens too thick at the center to bend well. This reduction in flexibility makes shifting focus from near to far distances more difficult. Because what is lost is the ability to curve, it is easy to see why poor near vision is a universal age change.

It had been thought that deterioration in these outer structures explained most normal vision loss, but researchers now believe the neural part of the visual system makes a major contribution to vision problems, particularly in later life. As we age, the number of rods and cones decreases. As suggested in the previous chapter, we lose neurons in the optic nerve and visual cortex. This neural atrophy explains why vision difficulties accelerate in advanced old age. It accounts for why older people process or make sense of visual information at a slower rate (Madden, 1990). In other words, vision losses, especially in advanced old age, are due to changes in the nervous system as much as in the eye (P. B. Baltes & Lindenberger, 1997; Kline & Scialfa, 1996; Madden, 1990).

The most dramatic evidence that late-life vision problems reflect overall nervous system deterioration comes from the Berlin Aging Study, a comprehensive investigation probing functioning during the "oldest years" (P. B. Baltes & Smith, 1997). When the researchers gave 516 men and women ranging in age from 70 to 105 an extensive battery of physiological and psychological tests, they found an astonishingly high correlation between how people performed on tests of vision (and hearing and balance/gait) and their scores on an intelligence test—especially, as Figure 4-4 shows, scores on an aspect of intelligence called perceptual speed, believed to closely reflect brain aging (Lindenberger & Baltes, 1997; see also Salthouse, Hancock, Meinz, & Hambrick, 1996). This intimate link between vision and cognition suggests that a common factor, neural deterioration, is causing both types of change. If vision in old age is a barometer of the overall integrity of the brain, this raises the tantalizing possibility that we could use the eye chart as a test of central nervous system functioning. In other words, just as they are our windows *to* the outside world, our eyes—especially in advanced old age—may be a window illuminating who we are inside.

Interventions

Despite these losses, I must emphasize that almost three-fourths of the people in the Lighthouse Survey (even among those over age 75) did not report vision problems

The Relationships of Sensory-Motor Functioning to Intelligence in Advanced Old Age, Berlin Study of Aging (mean age, 85)

FIGURE 4-4

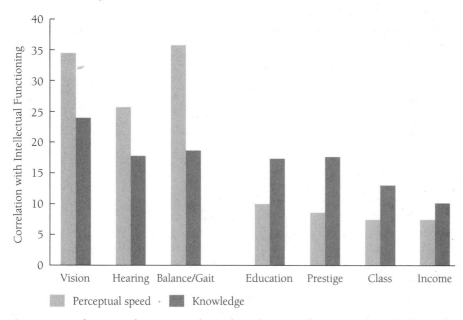

Sensory-motor functioning has an astonishing relationship to intelligence in advanced old age, far outweighing income, education, and social class in predicting scores, particularly on tests requiring speedy responses.

SOURCE: Lindenberger & Baltes, 1997.

serious enough to be classified as an impairment. Older people probably adapt to the changes they gradually notice without much thought. As we saw at the beginning of this chapter, a person gives up night driving. She takes more care when walking into a darkened movie theater. She changes the lighting in her office or house.

Vision difficulties are associated with disability (Rudberg, Furner, Dunn, & Cassel, 1993). In the Berlin Study, people with poor vision were much more likely to have problems with basic activities such as bathing, grooming, or walking up stairs (Marsiske, Klumb, & Baltes, 1997). As we will see later in this chapter, vision looms large in taking any action, from maintaining our balance when we rise from a chair to avoiding trips and falls when we walk (Simoneau & Leibowitz, 1996). However, the real reason why many of the visually impaired people in the Berlin Study were having such *serious* problems handling life was that, at their advanced age, they had other disabling physical problems in addition to not being able to see (Marsiske, Klumb, & Baltes, 1997). In the Lighthouse Survey, which examined vision problems in healthier, younger people as well as in the old-old, only half of the people reporting *extremely* impaired vision said their problems seriously limited their life.

TABLE 4-2	Suggestions for Designing Appliances to Accommodate to the "Older Eye"

1. Isolate graphic information from its background by using sharply contrasting colors.
2. Combine type with graphic symbols (or pictures) in order to provide the person with several cues.
3. Use consistent color coding to facilitate comprehension.
4. Use nonreflective surfaces to eliminate glare.
5. Cluster information to be read on the appliance within a narrow space to minimize age-related problems with poorer peripheral vision.
6. If the product is equipped with lighting, use the gradually adjustable variety so that the person can gradually increase the illumination to an optimal level.

SOURCE: Adapted from J. J. Pirkl, 1995.

To compensate for poorer dark vision, the older person's home should be well lit. Overhead fixtures should be avoided, especially fluorescent bulbs shining down directly on a bare floor, as they magnify glare. Vivid contrasting colors should be used. The strategies listed in Table 4-2 can help increase the visibility of numerals on kitchen appliances, telephones, and other devices around the home that require reading (Pirkl, 1995). To adapt to reductions in the visual field and the ability to process visual stimuli quickly, the elderly should scan their environment when they walk or drive. This strategy is especially important for avoiding accidents. Finally, when a genuine visual disease strikes, people should be aware of the medical interventions and external aids that are available to help the visually impaired.

Although many late-life vision diseases cannot be cured, as we saw in Table 4-1, surgery or medications can sometimes be effective at stemming the damage from even these permanent eye diseases. The accompanying photo shows one of the many devices that have been developed to make life easier for the visually impaired. For the computer user, there are even reading programs that translate written materials that appear on the terminal into synthetic speech.

The social environment is important. Close relationships not only help buffer us against illness, but help us adjust better in the face of chronic disease (see Chapter 5). However, loved ones can add to the problem if, due to anxiety, they withdraw or offer too much support. In the Lighthouse poll, 1 in 4 people admitted that they felt awkward when dealing with a person with vision problems; unfortunately, this was especially true among people who said they had a visually impaired relative. Interestingly, in one study probing factors promoting adjustment in people with serious impairments, friendships, not family relationships, predicted good coping. People who said they had close friends were more optimistic and more motivated to learn compensatory skills (Reinhardt, 1996).

On a positive note, although losing our sight is one of our greatest anxieties about growing old, when this late-life event does occur, it may not be such a devastating emotional blow. Some visually impaired older people—those with other chronic illnesses, living in high-stress environments—do feel overwhelmed and depressed (Wahl, Oswald, Heyl, Zimprich, & Heinemann, 1997). However, in the Lighthouse

The Aladdin Reader is an innovative reading magnification device developed by the Lighthouse for the Blind.

Survey, 90% of the people who reported *extremely* poor vision said they were coping well psychologically with their loss.

HEARING

Late-life vision losses do not typically produce emotional problems, but hearing problems may be more likely to seriously affect our mental health (Eisdorfer, 1970). At first glance, this difference seems puzzling, because we think of vision as our most important sense. However, whereas losing our sight cuts us off from the physical world, poor hearing causes damage in a more important area: It prevents us from using language, the bridge that connects us to other human beings. It is the human world we are deprived from fully entering when we lose the ability to hear.

The Problem

We are correct to link poor hearing with being old. About 4 in 5 Americans with hearing problems are over age 45; more than half are over 65 (Fozard, 1990; Kline & Scialfa, 1996). In a 1994 survey of late-life chronic conditions, poor hearing outdistanced poor vision: Hearing impairments ranked third in frequency; vision impair-

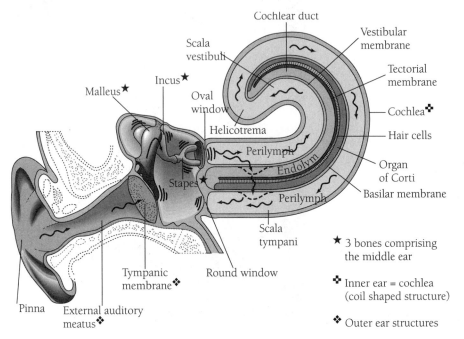

The middle and outer ear amplify sound waves. The hearing receptors are located in the cochlea.

ments ranked ninth (U.S. Bureau of the Census, 1996). We do not need the benefit of statistics to know that poor hearing is more common in older people; we need only to look around. People over 65 are much more likely to wear the visible emblem of this problem—a hearing aid—than any other group.

Hearing begins to decline in our 30s. Losses accelerate in old age. However, there is tremendous variability in the extent of decline. Some people begin losing hearing in their 20s, others later on. For most people, the loss is more extensive for high tones; others do not show this typical age pattern of loss. There also is a gender difference: Men tend to lose their hearing earlier than women and are more likely to develop genuine difficulties at a younger age (Pirkl, 1995).

One reason is that, in addition to being primary to aging, hearing loss has an environmental cause: exposure to noise. People in noisy occupations (who are more likely to be male), such as construction workers or rock musicians, lose hearing earlier and may have serious handicaps by midlife. Prolonged exposure to the chronic noise of simply living in a city also may contribute to age-related hearing difficulties. Since noise pollution is endemic, the prognosis for this problem of aging is grim. The rate of hearing loss increased by 25% from 1971 to 1991—a rise far higher than would be expected based on the aging of the population—at the same time that dramatic declines were occurring in common causes of deafness such as childhood diseases. Experts believe that this alarming increase can only be attributed to higher levels of environmental noise. Notice how loud the sound is in your local movie theater to get an indication of the hearing problems "average people" have today!

Statistics on how many people have hearing problems may err on the low side because people are reluctant to admit they have this difficulty. Poor hearing strikes at our vanity because it is so characteristic of being old. The experience of not being able to hear can easily be rationalized: "Other people are talking too softly. There is too much background noise." Even experts have trouble agreeing on the level of impairment that causes a genuine handicap. The main reason is that a person's hearing varies greatly in different situations, depending on who is speaking and on the level of background noise. As with vision, age-related hearing losses are not a constant, all-or-nothing phenomenon.

Age-related hearing loss has a special name: **presbycusis.** People with presbycusis have special trouble distinguishing high-pitched tones. They have problems hearing the high-pitched voices of children and may miss consonants. They have greater trouble hearing warnings that, even though loud, are shrieked or yelled in a high-pitched voice. They are much more bothered by background noise, such as the hum of traffic on the street or the drone of an air conditioner or fan. Because background noise is lower in pitch than speech sounds, in noisy environments the background seems amplified, making conversation especially hard to hear.

presbycusis
Characteristic age-related hearing impairment involving selective difficulty hearing high-pitched tones

These selective problems can cause misunderstandings. You notice that your uncle can hear on one visit, but not on another. Your natural temptation is to accuse him mentally of pretending, of turning his hearing off deliberately. Everyone is primed to have these suspicions because dealing with hearing problems is so frustrating. It is exhausting having to struggle to achieve something we take for granted, a conversation.

The Auditory System and Age-Related Decline

The ear is a complex structure with outer parts that concentrate, amplify, and prepare sound vibrations for transmission to the brain by receptors located in the inner ear. As Figure 4-5 shows, these sound-wave-amplifying structures include the pinna, the apricot-shaped structure we call the ear; the ear canal, or external auditory meatus; the eardrum, or tympanic membrane; and the three bones of the middle ear. Vibrations amplified by these bones travel to the inner ear. The hearing receptors, called hair cells, are located in the part of the inner ear called the cochlea.

Figure 4-6 shows the coil-shaped cochlea with its fluid-filled compartments. Vibrations set up waves in these compartments, causing the basilar membrane, on which the hair cells sit, to bob up and down. The cells jiggle, shearing against the membrane above. This bending generates the neural firing responsible for our experience of sound. Impulses set off in the hair cells leave the ear and travel to the auditory cortex.

Our perception of a sound—its pitch (highness or lowness), its volume (loudness or softness), and its timbre (complexity)—depends on the way the basilar membrane moves. Different sounds set up varying patterns of motion in the fluid-filled cochlea, which cause different types of displacements of the basilar membrane. For each sound, a unique pattern of hair cells is stimulated to fire. It is through this complicated

FIGURE 4-6   *The Human Cochlea in Cross-Section*

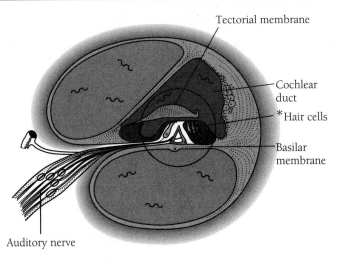

Tectorial membrane

Cochlear duct

*Hair cells

Basilar membrane

Auditory nerve

〜〜 Fluid-filled compartments
  * Hair cells = hearing receptors

The bending of the hair cells against the tectorial membrane generates the neural impulses for sound.

mechanism that we experience the jangle of a jackhammer and the stirring tones of a symphony.

Except for very low frequency tones, the location on the basilar membrane of the hair cells that fire is important to discriminating pitch. Low-frequency tones stimulate the hair cells toward the apex of the cochlea. High-pitched tones cause maximal stimulation of the hair cells at the base of the cochlea. In contrast to age changes in vision, where problems in the more external structures often are partly to blame, presbycusis is typically due to deterioration of the hearing receptors themselves—that is, the atrophy of the actual hair cells. The hair cells at the base of the cochlea (those coding high tones) are most fragile, explaining why people selectively lose hearing for higher-frequency sounds.

Here, too, central nervous system changes are important in explaining hearing problems, especially in advanced old age. Recall that in the Berlin Study, poor hearing as well as poor vision was linked to poor performance on an intelligence test. In one study, researchers simulated hearing loss in young volunteers, making their impairment on a pure-tone hearing test comparable to that of a group of older adults. Then, they gave subjects a test of their ability to understand speech. Although the young-old got similar scores to the young, the old-old still performed worse, suggesting that the difficulties very old people have in understanding conversation involve more than just the problem of hearing individual sounds (Humes & Christopherson, 1991). Their trouble lies in comprehending or making sense of the complex mix of sounds involved in language—a processing deficit, or deficiency at interpreting information, that reflects changes in the brain.

The outer and middle ear contribute to age-related hearing problems. Excessive wax in the ear canal is a common late-life condition that is often overlooked. The bones of the middle ear may have fused together, which requires an operation to cure. When the problem is in these outer parts of the auditory system, the person does not really have presbycusis—that is, selective trouble hearing high-pitched tones. The loss is equal for all tones and so more like what we imagine a hearing difficulty to be. People with this type of hearing loss are more likely to benefit from a device that magnifies all sounds equally: a hearing aid (see Aging in Action 4-1).

Not hearing well increases our physical risk. Sound is a crucial way we learn of environmental dangers. However, the main problem this impairment creates is social.

Friends and family withdraw, defeated by the struggle to communicate. Rather than continually having to say "Please repeat that," the older person may turn silent. In one massive poll of 18,873 nursing home residents, even moderate hearing loss was correlated with social withdrawal (Resnick, Fries, & Verbrugge, 1997). Another strategy is to dominate every conversation because "it's so much easier to talk than to listen" (Souza & Hoyer, 1996, p. 653). The person may grow suspicious, reading betrayal into whispers half-heard. In fact, among people already predisposed to serious emotional problems, hearing disorders may promote paranoid reactions in isolated older adults (see Chapter 9).

Interventions

Because hearing losses affect the quality of life and presbycusis cannot be cured, primary prevention is crucial. The message is clear: Reduce your exposure to environmental noise. According to the Hearing Conservation Amendment of 1982, employers must monitor noise levels in the workplace and, when they exceed a certain level, provide employees with hearing protection devices. They must train workers in the need for hearing conservation and test their hearing at least once a year. They must take steps to reduce noise levels. In other words, government regulations now address what was a major cause of hearing loss: industrial noise.

External controls are not enough. They must be supplemented by vigorous public education. The fact that hearing impairment is one of the few chronic conditions whose frequency is increasing is a testament to the fact that people are not aware of its life-limiting impact. They may not even know that age-related hearing loss can be slowed by taking the simple step of avoiding noise. Mr. Jones, who exercises regularly, does not think to cover his ears when he passes the construction site on his daily jog. He turns his Walkman way up because loud music shuts out the traffic noise and helps pass the time. At the same time that he is helping his heart, he is hurting his hearing. Better cardiovascular function is being purchased at the price of interpersonal isolation a decade down the road.

Once a problem has developed, education is still important. Because people may be reluctant to admit their difficulties, doctors should regularly test patients' hearing in later life. If the problem lies in the noise-amplifying structures described earlier, medical interventions may help. When presbycusis is the cause, people need to overcome their reluctance to consider a hearing aid. Providing information about the latest advances in hearing aid technology (discussed in Aging in Action 4-1) may help. When the problem is serious, **assistive listening devices**—external compensatory aids such as sound amplifiers attached to the phone, the TV, or speakers in the home—may help. Another strategy is to substitute visual stimuli for auditory cues: flashing lights to signal a ringing phone; text telephones that allow typewritten communication by phone; a caption decoder that transcribes the audio signal from the TV set into a written message displayed across the bottom of the screen.

Because a key to improving hearing is limiting background noise, the person's home should be modified. Installing wall-to-wall carpeting and double-paned windows can help muffle extraneous sounds. It is imperative to get rid of noisy appliances such as a rattling air conditioner or fan. Equally important is avoiding extraneous noise when out. Don't take your uncle to that trendy, crowded restaurant, no matter how

assistive listening devices
External aids that compensate for hearing problems

good the food is, or sit in the booth facing the street. Don't eat at the fashionable place with low ceilings or angular walls, as both magnify sound.

Modify the way you act. When talking to a hearing-impaired person, speak slowly and clearly. Make the change to each new subject at a slower rate. Enunciate unfamiliar words distinctly. Face the person so he can simultaneously take advantage of visual clues. Watch the expression on your listener's face for cues to words not being caught. Perhaps even more than with vision, supportive, caring relationships are crucial in coping with hearing problems. Not only is social support related to better emotional adjustment in the face of this debilitating condition, it also will motivate your loved one to use a hearing aid (Souza & Hoyer, 1996).

TASTE AND SMELL

Taste and smell do not have the life-limiting effect hearing and vision problems can cause. However, because they work together to allow us to enjoy food, losses in these senses may make eating less pleasant and so contribute to poor nutrition in the elderly. Smell also serves as an early warning system, alerting us to hazards such as spoiled food, leaking gas, or fire. So poor smell can make life less safe as well as limiting our joy in eating.

The Problem

The elderly have less sensitive taste and smell than younger adults. However, because a variety of illnesses, from nasal problems to Parkinson's disease to head trauma, affect these senses, it is unclear how much of this loss is primary to age. Are the age differences researchers find due to aging itself or to illness? Are they due to the fact that often sick older people are compared with healthy young adults (Bartoshuk, 1989)? Unlike with vision and hearing, taste and smell receptors are located on the tongue and nose and normally are replaced every few days; so, researchers find little falloff in their number with age. However, clear age differences emerge when elderly and young people are asked to use these senses to identify and evaluate foods.

In the first of a series of studies on food sensitivity and preferences, Susan Schiffman (1977) blindfolded college students and elderly people and asked them to identify and rate the pleasantness of blended foods after tasting them. Not only were the older people less able to identify the foods, they were more likely to rate them as weak-tasting.

In her next study, Schiffman and a colleague demonstrated that these changed perceptions were mainly due to impaired smell. The researchers asked subjects to discriminate between the odors of different foods compared in pairs and rate what they smelled for pleasantness. Once again, the elderly were poorer at identifying most odors. However, their sensitivity varied from odor to odor. It was best for fruits. So, as we might expect, the older people gave fruit smells the highest marks for pleasantness (Schiffman & Pasternak, 1979).

More recent research confirms that the reason for the complaint we might hear from an elderly relative, "Food doesn't have as much taste as it used to," is not just nostalgia—the fact that food was fresher in the "good old days"—but altered smell

(Ship, Pearson, Cruise, Brant, & Metter, 1996). It also offers insights into why the elderly prefer heavily spiced foods and why eating preferences change in apparently strange ways in old age. Older people may grow to prefer those foods such as candies or fruits with odors that age impairs the least.

Altered smell sensitivity may partly explain another common complaint older people have: "Food tastes bitter or sour." Foods such as chocolate and some vegetables have a bitter taste that is masked by a pleasant odor. When the sense of smell weakens, these foods may have an unpleasant taste. So, smell, not taste, is the culprit in age-related problems in the ability to enjoy food.

Interventions

These studies suggest that to make eating more pleasurable, we might amplify the odor of foods or have the elderly season their meals heavily. However, as this approach may be unpalatable from the perspective of health, there may be a better way to increase the older person's enjoyment of food. One reason that eating may lose appeal in later life is that dental problems (ill-fitting dentures or gum disease) make chewing painful. By encouraging older people to use a dentist regularly, we may be able to improve the quality of life in this important area of life.

MOTOR PERFORMANCE

Although sensory change is most apparent to the affected person, what others notice first about the elderly are their responses. Older people move more slowly and unsteadily. Most important, the elderly take much *longer* to respond. This loss of response speed is not only one of the most obvious signs of age, but one of the most widely studied processes in the psychology of aging.

Responding quickly is essential to performing basic activities: crossing a street before the light changes, driving, stepping out of the way of environmental obstacles. Slow responding makes older people prone to accidents because it puts them out of sync with the pace that living demands.

Slowness puts the older person out of step with people. It can cause conflict because it is so different from the rate at which the rest of us live. As we have all noticed, when we find ourselves behind the slow older person at the supermarket checkout counter or the older driver going 40 in the 65-mile-per-hour zone, irritation wells up. So the slowing of age puts a damper on relationships and may be one reason that our fast-paced, time-oriented society has prejudices toward the old.

The Pace of Responding

reaction time
Ability to respond quickly and accurately to a stimulus after a signal to act occurs

When psychologists study this slower responding in the laboratory, they measure **reaction time**—the ability to quickly and accurately take action after a signal to respond appears. In a typical reaction time experiment, a subject might be instructed to "press buzzer A as fast as you can when the green light comes on."

A standard finding on these tests is that older groups perform less well. In fact, age differences on these tasks are so universal that slower responding is one of the

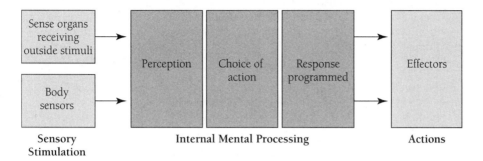

Notice the use of the information-processing diagram type discussed in Chapter 2.

most certain predictions we can make about how our behavior as a young adult will change as the years pass.

However, the extent of the loss depends on the task. Older people do worse when asked to perform complex tasks rather than simple actions; when aiming at a target rather than striking the table as fast as possible; when asked to complete a sequence of steps rather than a simple response. The main reason for these exponential declines in performance as task complexity increases is that more complicated tasks require more thinking. And it is "thinking time" not "acting time" that slows most with age (Salthouse, 1991).

In reaction-time studies, researchers break down responding into two phases: (1) a thinking phase, in which we mentally process incoming information and figure out how to act; and (2) an acting phase, in which we physically carry out the action. When subjects are told to "press buzzer A when the red light comes on," researchers can isolate the thinking phase by measuring the time from when the light appears to when the person begins to lift a hand. They then compare this interval with age differences in movement time—the time it takes to perform the response. Although older people are also slower in the latter phase, the most dramatic differences typically occur in the thinking phase.

What happens during this thinking phase—that is, the time from when the signal to act occurs and the response begins? For hints we turn to the information-processing flowchart in Figure 4-7.

According to Alan Welford (1977), data arriving from the sensory organs are first fed to the brain. The information is perceived, an action is decided on, and the response is programmed. The end point is the action itself, performed by the *effectors*— the voluntary muscles and the involuntary reactors of the autonomic nervous system. According to Welford, this sequence probably takes place many times when we take even the simplest actions:

Performance hardly ever consists of a single run through the chain. . . . Even relatively simple actions such as picking up a glass or opening a door involve a . . . process in which an initial action . . . is followed by a series of smaller adjustments, each of which depends for its precise form on the outcome of the one before. In other words, data from the . . . action and its results on the external world are fed back as part of the sensory input for the next run through the chain. (pp. 450–451)

So what we think of as responding—movement—is only the end of a series of internal events. Where in this chain does the older person's problem lie?

Problems at the last step, taking action, are crucial in explaining slowness in some people—for instance, older adults who suffer from mobility-impairing diseases (discussed in the next section). Problems at the beginning step, sensory input, could account for the slowness of others—people whose sensory difficulties make it a continual struggle to know whether the environment requires action.

However, since the reaction-time studies involve clear signals to respond and leave out the movement part of the chain, the age differences here suggest that the middle, central-nervous-system steps are critical. In other words, the main reason we react more slowly as we age is that our central nervous system is less able to process the information quickly (Cerella, 1990; Salthouse, 1990, 1991).

But if a slower-functioning central nervous system is the problem, then we would not expect the slowing to be limited to physical responses. As we grow older, we should be slower in all our actions, less quick at remembering names or solving puzzles as well as opening doors. Unfortunately, as we will see in exploring cognition, this is the case. Although performance does not fall off as dramatically with verbal responses as with actions that are genuinely physical (Jacewicz & Hartley, 1987), slow responding is typical of advancing age.

This conclusion requires some qualification. Slowness varies greatly from person to person. Being quick is critical to performance only in some activities. Losses are most apparent on complicated tasks. So before assuming that older people are deficient, we need to look carefully at who they are and what they are being asked to do.

For instance, in a job such as air traffic controller, where responding quickly to changing stimuli is essential, losses in reaction time may be noticed early on. In this occupation, people cannot be hired for the control tower if they are over age 30, and they must retire by age 55 (personal communication, supervisor of operations, Nashville International Airport, 1995). Reaction-time losses are less vital in most other jobs. However, whenever work must be done at a fast pace, it presents special problems for older employees.

Even on the assembly line, older workers do not do as poorly as expected on the basis of laboratory tests. Work involves well-practiced activities, and expertise compensates for the slowing that occurs with age. Selective attrition may also be involved. The poorly performing workers retire, leaving only the relatively quick on the job. Who are these hardy older people?

One clue comes from our look at the aging nervous system in Chapter 3. People who respond relatively quickly should be those in good health—in particular, people who do not have brain-impairing diseases. In fact, this is the case. Older people with cardiovascular problems have unusually slow reaction times. Extremely slow responding is typical of people who have strokes, brain tumors, and especially Alzheimer's disease (Hicks & Birren, 1970).

The Act of Taking Action

Slowed reaction time is the most important, widespread change in motor performance that occurs as we age. However, there is another reason for the slowness we observe in older adults. The old-old have problems particularly *performing* actions. They hold a cup of tea more unsteadily. They have more trouble turning on the stove. They take a longer time to rise from a chair or get to the door. These changes involve more than just slowed mental programming. They depend on the integrity of the **musculoskeletal system**—the network of muscles, joints, and bones that carry out our movements.

    In order for us to physically act, our bones must be strong enough to support action. Our muscles must have the power to contract. Our joints must be flexible, able to pivot and bend. Age-related limitations in each of these functions, while they lack the drama of immediate threats to life, loom surprisingly large in the quality of life in old age. They often cause pain and discomfort. At their extreme, they produce the most feared environmental change of later life: Impairments in lower body movement are the number one risk factor for admission to a nursing home (Jette, Branch, & Berlin, 1990; Lawrence & Jette, 1996).

musculoskeletal system
Network of bones, joints, and muscles that carry out movement

    MUSCLES   The muscles are our engine-propelling action. When they contract, exerting force on the adjoining bones, movement takes place. Muscle strength, or the ability to exercise this force effectively, declines gradually beginning in the 40s. After age 70, the losses accelerate (Bemben & McCalip, 1997). Losses are especially apparent in the lower extremities of the body among the "fast twitch" fibers, those muscles that deploy the most powerful contractile force (Whitbourne, 1996) The cause is a loss of muscle mass, or atrophy of the muscle fibers themselves. As is true of many other bodily losses, once gone, the individual fibers cannot regenerate or grow back. However, as we will see later, we can take steps to make the most of what remains.

    BONES   Beginning in our 40s, the density of our bones also begins to decrease. The bones become more porous, brittle, and fragile. The extent to which people are prone to this bone loss, called **osteoporosis,** is influenced by genetics as well as lifestyle, the amount we exercise as well as calcium and vitamin intake in our earlier years. Here gender and ethnicity are important risk factors. Because white women have less dense bones, and the estrogen depletion that occurs at menopause accelerates this skeletal change, the rate of bone loss is much greater for women than for men. An alarming 50 to 80% of women over age 65 suffer from some degree of osteoporosis (Adubifa, LaPalio, Pharm, Lasak, & Lemke, 1997).

osteoporosis
Age-related skeletal disorder in which the bones become porous, brittle, and fragile

    Osteoporosis is a major indirect cause of disability and death. When our bones are porous, they tend to break at the slightest fall. Unlike the many cracks that occur in young adult fractures, the brittle osteoporotic bone tends to break completely. (A good analogy is the difference between what happens when we bend a green stem and a dry twig. The more pliable stem tends to develop fissures, not crack completely, whereas the twig easily snaps in two.) As a result, broken bones heal much less easily in the elderly, so they have more serious consequences. Because many older people never totally recover from a fracture (Magaziner, Simonsick, Kashner, Hebel, & Kenzora, 1990), it may cause a permanent loss of independence (Paier, 1996). If the person is unable to care for herself, she may have to enter a nursing home. This is why preventing this "female" disorder of aging is so important.

osteoarthritis
Age-related skeletal disorder in which the cushion insulating the joints wears away

JOINTS   A third change that limits acting results from **osteoarthritis,** a wearing away of the protective cushion that insulates the joints. Throughout life our joints are subjected to pressure when we move, run, or stretch. This wear and tear causes the protective covering over the ends of the bone to erode. As this protective cartilage is destroyed, bony growths develop, inflammation occurs, and movement is impaired. The exposure of bone on bone causes pain and stiffness. Occasionally, the joints may fuse together, making movement impossible. Not every older person has painful osteoarthritis. However, enough do to make this illness the top-ranking chronic condition of later life (U.S. Bureau of the Census, 1996; see also Chapter 3, Table 3-1).

INTERVENTIONS   Although each of these losses is to some extent permanent, exercise is the main strategy that experts advocate to improve function and prevent further decline. Older people who exercise have faster reaction times. Exercise also helps the muscles, bones, and joints. Exercise increases joint flexibility. It may indirectly stimulate joint repair by improving cardiovascular function and so enabling more blood to get to the joints. Even though we cannot grow new muscle, regular exercise strengthens the fibers that remain (Yarasheski et al., 1997). Although it can be somewhat perilous, experts even recommend exercise to help strengthen osteoporotic bones (Whitbourne, 1996). Not only is exercise helpful for people only moderately disabled by musculoskeletal problems, it can even benefit physically debilitated, institutionalized older adults (Sinacore, Brown, & Hollosy, 1997; Wall, Sullivan, Hite, & Frost, 1997). Finally, aspirin and other medications that reduce inflammation as well as pain are important treatments for the intense discomfort skeletal disorders cause (Ruscin, 1997).

Specifics

Now that we have a sense of why older people move and react slowly, let's look at some specific motor performances and how they change with age. First, we examine the crucial ability to stand and walk (without falling), then that other central activity—the ability to drive with ease. These actions are perfect examples with which to end our discussion because they epitomize Welford's point that many different body systems work in tandem when we perform any life activity.

STANDING, WALKING (AND FALLING)   Input from several sensory systems is needed for us to stand or walk. Vision is important; our eyesight tells us about obstacles in the environment. Standing and walking also depend on the integrity of the vestibular position receptors in our inner ear. When we move our head, liquid in semicircular canals in the cochlea sloshes against hair cells. As with hearing, the deformation of these cells gives us our feeling of balance, our sense of how our body is positioned in space. (The tendency to fall after a whirl on the amusement park ride is due to the

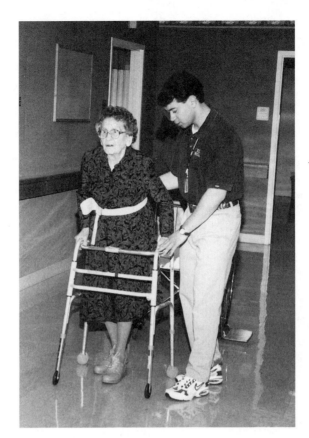

disruption of this inner ear position sense.) When we rise, somatosensory receptors in the joints and muscles fire, providing data about the movement of our limbs. Neurons on the base of our feet, sensitive to pressure and touch, respond. On the output side, standing and walking depend on the integrity of the motor neurons and the adequacy of our muscles, joints, and bones. Coordinating this complex input and output requires continual information processing by our central command center, the brain.

The fact that each of these systems works less efficiently with age causes characteristic differences in the way older people, especially the old-old, stand and walk. In order to remain on our feet and not lose our balance, we must constantly readjust our body's center of mass. When standing with their eyes closed or open, older people exhibit a greater amount of body imbalance, or sway. There are distinctive changes in the person's gait. Older people take shorter steps. They walk at a slower speed. They have a larger stride width. They spend more time in the phase of walking when both feet are on the ground. They make contact with the surface using a more flat-footed approach. All of these changes are compensatory strategies to improve balance and avoid a fall.

Falling, that feared event of later life, becomes much more likely in advanced old age. Moreover, as suggested earlier, falling in old age can be dangerous. Besides causing

Aging in Action

4-2 The Older Sleeper

In college, I was incapable of getting to bed before 2 A.M. My sophomore year, I refused to register for morning classes because they were offered too early in the day. What a difference 30 years makes! Today, staying up until 10 P.M. is a strain. I rise with the sun—often at 5:30 or before. The reason is that the first hint of light awakens me. In fact, everything awakens me at any hour. A cat jumps on the bed, a window creaks, and I am instantly alert, sometimes for an hour or more. Like the other aging people in this book, I have made adjustments to the new, older me. I have a blanket in my office. I take a "cat nap" most afternoons. Those daytime naps are no problem. I am asleep in minutes and wake refreshed for my 3:00 P.M. class.

Why am I experiencing these changes? In large part, the cause is alterations in my biological sleep timer and in my depth of sleep.

Our sleep cycle is controlled by a built-in biological clock. When we are young, this timer is set so that we get drowsy at about 10:00 and sleep until about 7 or 8. As we age, our timer is reset at an earlier point. Even when older people go to bed at 11:00, they are programmed to wake up at 5 or 6. What compounds the problem is a change in the sleep cycle itself. While asleep we descend and then ascend through stages at about 90-minute intervals. Older people spend less time in the deepest phases—sleep stages 3 and 4. Being more often in the fragile "light" sleep stages, people are at risk of waking at the slightest sound. To compound the problem, the length of the wake-resistant dreaming, or REM, phase of sleep declines with age.

Other changes may be affecting my ability to get a good night's sleep. Older people are more likely to manifest disordered breathing when asleep. (My husband tells me that I have begun to snore—often loudly—during the night!) It is possible that I may have a problem called sleep apnea, a condition in which the sleeping person actually stops breathing at times. People with sleep apnea wake up slightly during these episodes and so are excessively sleepy during the day. Sleep apnea (and its symptom, loud snoring) also grows more prevalent with age. In fact, this condition runs in my family. My younger brother has sleep apnea too!

a permanent loss of independence if the person breaks a bone, falling in the elderly is more apt to be life-threatening. In physically fragile older people, falling can cause serious damage, such as the rupture of an internal organ or trauma to the brain (Dunn, Rudberg, Furner, & Cassel, 1992).

Falls are the result of several risk factors: sensory losses that make people less aware of environmental obstacles, losses in muscle mass, foot disorders, and skeletal diseases. Any condition that impairs information processing is crucial (Woolley, Czaja, & Drury, 1997), from Alzheimer's disease to heart conditions (Ho, Woo, Yuen, Sham, & Chan, 1997) to excessive medication use. Even the tendency of older people to sleep less soundly can contribute to falls, by making the person less mentally alert (see Aging in Action 4-2).

DRIVING   Difficulties standing and walking often appear at the upper limits of life. Not so with problems of driving, which, as we saw in the chapter opening, can appear in our vigorous middle years. This is unfortunate because driving can be so important to living a fully independent life. The millions of older people who live in areas without public transportation must sometimes strike a Faustian bargain: drive uncomfortably (and often unsafely); depend on others to drive them around; or move to a place that does not require driving, such as a nursing home.

Driving, too, requires a complex array of skills. As we saw earlier, vision changes such as sensitivity to glare and impaired dark perception make it hard to drive at night. Driving requires good peripheral vision and the ability to quickly process multiple visual cues. Hearing loss affects driving because sound provides information about the location of other vehicles. One must have the bone strength and muscle power to push down on the pedals and the joint flexibility to grasp the wheel. Finally, as we have all noticed when we find ourselves stuck behind an older driver as the traffic light turns from red to green, driving is highly vulnerable to age changes in reaction time.

Most elderly people still drive. In one survey, the majority of people were still driving in their 70s or beyond (Jette & Branch, 1992). However, older people are aware of their problems and take special care to avoid risks (Kosnik, Sekuler, & Kline, 1990; Charness & Bosman, 1995). Compared to middle-aged drivers, the elderly drive less often at night, on expressways, during rush hour, and during poor weather conditions (Stamatiadis, 1996).

Because they drive less often, when we compare age groups, elderly drivers have lower accident rates than young adults. However, when we look at crashes per comparable miles driven, older people are a vulnerable group. Figure 4-8 shows this age/accident relationship clearly. Notice that the accident rates for young-old drivers (especially men) are comparable to those for that other high-risk group, drivers under age 25. However, over age 75, driving is a perilous practice indeed.

This study pinpointed the most dangerous driving situations for elderly women and men. Older people are most likely to have an accident at an intersection, where they must take quick action as the light changes. Turning into oncoming traffic is especially difficult. The elderly are most at risk when performing a maneuver that can be a problem even for excellent drivers, making a left turn into traffic.

There is considerable variability at the same age. Some 60-year-olds are a menace on the road. Some 80-year-olds drive well. Karlene Ball and her associates are devising tests to identify the most dangerous drivers, those most prone to wrecks. Interestingly, the researchers have found that measures of cognition or reaction time, though important, are not fine-tuned enough to distinguish the adequate drivers from the poor. Simple tests of visual acuity are not very good either, although impaired peripheral vision does predict accident rates. The risk of accidents is most closely tied to what Ball calls visual attentional problems: the ability to process visual stimuli quickly, to divide our attention between different visual tasks, and to see a target visual stimulus clearly against its background (Ball & Rebok, 1994).

This research has pressing social importance. We don't want to prevent everyone from driving after a given age, but we want to identify which older drivers should not be on the road. As these studies are still in their infancy, however, let's examine some immediate strategies to make standing, walking, and driving safer in later life.

FIGURE 4-8   *Accident Rates in Urban Areas, by Age and Gender*

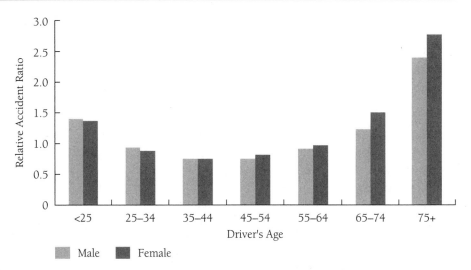

The old-old have an alarmingly greater risk of having an accident, two to three times that of other age groups.
SOURCE: Stamatiadis, 1996.

INTERVENTIONS   As with sensory impairments, for problems of standing and walking, the key is to modify the external world. To prevent falling, furniture in the older person's house should be sparse, and there should be no raised floor areas or throw rugs. A homeowner should consider installing low-pile wall-to-wall carpet even in areas such as the kitchen. Not only will carpeting the whole house help cut down on injuries if a person falls, because it improves both vision and hearing, it also reduces the sensory risk factors for an accident. Doors should open automatically or be light to touch, shelves and storage places should be made easy to reach, and grab-bars should be installed in places like the bathtub where falling is most likely. Finally, when mobility is seriously impaired, classic assistive devices include canes, walkers, and wheelchairs.

According to nurses, older people may be reluctant to use these well-known aids. The issue is their visibility and their symbolic link to decrepitude and decline. In one interview study, nurses described clients so reluctant to use a walker that they tried to hide the device and attempt to inch along grasping onto walls (Rush & Ouellet, 1997). These observations illustrate that, as with a hearing aid, any emblem of old-age dependency can be difficult to accept.

With driving, the research suggests that older people should take special care at intersections. Rather than risk a left turn into traffic, they might go down a block to the light to get on the right side of the street. We as a society should redesign the driving environment to make it genuinely user-friendly for older people, putting adequate lighting on road signs, streets, highways, and especially exit ramps. Even today, an estimated 2 out of 5 drivers are over age 55 (Yee and Melichar, 1997). Making these modifications is mandatory in view of the huge driving group fast traveling the highway to later life—the baby boomers.

A GENERAL STRATEGY FOR ENHANCING SENSORY-MOTOR FUNCTIONING IN OLD AGE

You may have noticed that a major thrust of our discussion has been on modifying the environment to compensate for sensory-motor loss. Now it is time to spell out an approach for handling, in Paul Baltes's framework, the "compensation" phase of age-related decline. These principles were developed several decades ago by psychologist Powell Lawton (see Aging in Action 1-2).

Lawton (1975) first puts forth the following axiom: The more physically impaired the older person, the more crucial is the influence of the outside world. People with disabilities are vulnerable to the environment in a way the rest of us are not because we can perform competently in most settings in our society.

A simple example makes Lawton's point. The lighting in your classroom must be adequate to see the board or take notes, or you would complain vigorously. Your local restaurant would go out of business if the noise level made it impossible to hear. In other words, the environments we are exposed to in the course of living are tailored to fit, or be congruent with, our physical capacities.

However, this fit applies to the dominant group in our society, people without disabilities, not to those who have trouble hearing or seeing or getting around. This brings us to Lawton's second principle: To help people with physical impairments function, we must redesign the world to fit their capacities. This strategy is called enhancing **person/environment congruence.**

According to Lawton (1975), if the environment offers too much support, it may encourage dependency. However, if the outside world is too complex or challenging, it will also promote incapacity. So the most appropriate environment is one that fits the person's capacities or, better yet, slightly exceeds them so the individual is pulled to function at his or her best.

These principles underlie an exciting specialty: designing environments to fit the capacities of people with disabilities. The idea is that the wider environment can serve the same purpose that glasses or a wheelchair do, as a constant support to compensate for an unchangeable condition. Because devices that compensate for permanent impairments are called prostheses, the specially planned housing described next is called **prosthetic environments.**

person/ environment congruence
Adapting the environment to the older person's capacities to enhance independence

prosthetic environments
Environments that function as permanent supports to compensate for chronic disabilities

Designing Housing for the Elderly

In recent decades, researchers have been exploring how architectural design can help promote person/environment congruence. Workshops have been held, books written, and facilities planned through the collaborative efforts of architects and gerontologists.

4-3 Sara, an Architect Who Designs Elderly Housing

When she was in college, Sara used to visit her grandmother in a nursing home. She recalls how the staff members passed by without noticing, and the dimly lit rooms and long halls that contributed to the neglect she observed. Sara was interested in design and also knew she wanted to help older people. She wanted to use architecture to promote the quality of life in old age.

Sara feels design can have a dramatic effect on people who are suffering from memory problems and sensory-motor decline. However, she is frustrated in her current job at a large architecture firm. Few new nursing homes are being built. The bottom line in constructing any health-care setting is cost. The developer controls the shape of the project. The design that looks the most architecturally appealing to the eye at age 30 or 40 may be detrimental to the person of 85. One developer who hired her firm decided that sliding glass doors should set off two symmetrical wings, one for residents with dementia and one for residents who were physically impaired. While everyone complimented the firm for the beauty of its plan, because everything looked identical, the residents bumped into doors or got confused and went the wrong way. To compound the problem, each wing was painted the same color, which, while aesthetically correct, was psychologically wrong. As we will see in our discussion of dementia, contrasting colors alert people to where they are going. They help orient a person to the world. The problem, Sara feels, is that designers and developers don't consider the point of view of the true clients—older people. Without training in gerontology, they have no idea about visual or auditory changes with advancing age. Sara, with her master's in gerontology, sees herself as the advocate for the elderly in her firm. It is a lonely job. Sometimes she can almost hear her coworkers thinking, "There she goes with her obsession again."

This housing for the elderly has a special goal: Through its physical design and the services it offers, it attempts to keep the older person with disabilities living as fully as possible for as long as possible (Lawton, Weisman, Sloane, & Calkins, 1997). Here is a description of one nursing home with this plan.

Set in the rolling landscape of Michigan, Peachwood Inn looks nothing like our image of a nursing home. The front lobby and reception desk resemble a fine hotel. The courtyard offers secure, beautifully landscaped areas for tranquil strolling. Intimate spaces with fireplaces give warm, inviting settings for private visiting. Individually decorated bedrooms in the main building are clustered in self-contained neighborhoods, suggesting a community. The nursing stations located centrally in each wing resemble hotel concierge desks. The effect is to encourage the idea of ownership and individuality.

The space is planned with residents' physical needs in mind. To enhance vision, bright colors and contrasting hues are used. Rather than subjecting residents to the deafening din in a large dining room, the facility has small eating spaces. These cozy dining rooms are light and airy and offer intimate seating. There is a chance for residents who are physically able to cook on their own. Hallways are short and end in flared areas with seating. Another striking feature is the lack of clutter, which encourages mobility. This institution is planned to promote physical independence and serve residents' psychological and social needs (D'Angelo, 1992).

Modifying Public Spaces

Besides building housing specifically for the elderly, about a decade ago the U.S. government took a landmark step toward making *all* buildings person/environment congruent for the physically impaired. On July 26, 1990, Congress passed the **Americans with Disabilities Act,** which stipulates that all new public accommodations must be assessible to the physically impaired or wheelchair-bound. Public facilities must provide services for people with vision or hearing problems, too. The act does not require modifications in existing structures if the expense would be prohibitive. For this reason, many public spaces are still out of bounds to disabled older adults. Still, because of this legislation, millions of elderly people who might otherwise be unable to do so can now visit parks, hotels, or museums and participate fully in our nation's rich cultural life.

Unfortunately, appropriate design is still not the rule where the elderly congregate. Much elderly housing, though built for people with the problems this chapter describes, was designed before gerontologists appreciated the impact architecture could have in promoting independence (Noell, 1995–1996). Other environments, such as retirement communities originally built for active, independent older people, may now have many occupants who, over the years, have become physically impaired (Lawton et al., 1997). As Aging in Action 4-3 suggests, there is resistance to building housing that fits older people's needs. As a result, many facilities today still have the flaws this observer noticed decades ago (Proppe, 1968): poor lighting, long corridors without benches where an older person can rest, bare floors and walls that amplify sound. If anything, these facilities seem designed to promote person/environment *incongruence.*

In fact, most older people, even those with disabilities, do not live in special housing. They live in their own homes, often in the same place where they have lived for decades (Lawton et al., 1997). Contrary to popular opinion, older people are the least mobile segment of society. In one poll, more than one-third had been living in the same place for 20 years or more (American Association of Retired Persons, 1984).

One's own home has a major advantage: It is a familiar setting for negotiating life. The psychological advantages can be considerable, too—the security and link to the past that a home lived in for decades provides. The attachment can be intense even when, viewed by objective standards, the home has few redeeming features:

> Mr. James Devlin is a . . . double amputee who lives on the ground floor of a row house he owns. . . . His living is confined to a small living room and bedroom at the front, a dining room and kitchen behind. . . . Mr. Devlin spends most of his time in the front room. . . . And while his home does have insects, mice, and rats, needs painting, and is feared as a firetrap, it is his, a

Americans with Disabilities Act Landmark legislation stipulating that public facilities (and the work environment) must be fully accessible to people with physical and mental impairments

TABLE 4-3	Sensory-Motor Changes and Interventions: A Summary	
Function	**Change**	**Intervention**
Vision	Poor dark vision; enhanced sensitivity to glare; poor peripheral vision; slower visual processing	1. Use strong indirect lighting, not fluorescent bulbs. 2. Use vivid contrasting colors. 3. Take a flashlight in dimly lit places. 4. Scan the visual environment thoroughly. 5. For severe problems, use low-vision aids.
Hearing	High-pitched tone loss	1. Avoid settings with background noise. 2. Speak distinctly, lower your pitch, face the person. 3. Install wall-to-wall carpeting and double-paned windows. 4. For severe problems, use hearing aids and assistive devices.
Taste and smell	Loss of sensitivity for nonsweet foods; impaired smell	1. Flavor foods more strongly, and chew well. 2. Serve older person fruits. 3. Smoke detectors are essential in an older person's house.
Reaction time	Overall slowing, especially in cases requiring a series of steps or complex actions	1. Avoid high-risk, speed-oriented situations. 2. Keep healthy; exercise.
Movement disorders	Less muscle strength and joint flexibility; bones liable to be broken easily	1. Install low-pile carpeting. 2. Limit the amount of furniture. 3. Doors must swing out easily. 4. Use grab-bars or assistive devices.

place he owns and about which he is in large part satisfied. . . . To an outsider his home is a mess. . . . To Mr. Devlin it expresses . . . a sense of who he is at the present time. (Rubinstein, Kilbride, & Nagy, 1992, pp. 56–57)

Mr. Devlin is poor, seriously disabled, and socially isolated. We might imagine that when older people have adequate financial, physical, and social resources, the situation is different; they remodel their home or decide to move to a more hospitable place. Not so! When I visited my elderly millionaire uncle in his Fifth Avenue apartment, I saw the same inadequate lighting, peeling paint, and bare floors tailor-made for a fall. In fact, this far-too-spacious, 40-year-old home was *less* user-friendly than Mr. Devlin's tiny living space. Because uncounted millions of older people are probably living in housing that magnifies their disabilities, if you have an older relative who has the limitations this chapter describes, your personal mandate is clear. Using the summary information in Table 4-3, take action to increase person/environment congruence!

Americans with Disabilities Act
assistive listening devices
cataract
diabetic retinopathy
glare
glaucoma

lens
musculoskeletal system
osteoarthritis
osteoporosis
person/environment congruence

presbycusis
presbyopia
prosthetic environments
reaction time
visual acuity

Technology and aging: Developing and marketing new products for older people. (1995, Spring). *Generations, 19.*

The whole issue of this journal is devoted to promoting person/environment congruence through environmental design.

Lawton, M. P., Weisman, G. D., Sloane, P., & Calkins, M. (1997). Assessing environments for people with chronic illness. *Journal of Mental Health and Aging, 3,* 83–100.

This article reviews environmental features for the disabled elderly in existing settings.

Chapter Outline

5

Disease, Disability, and Health Care

Mabel began to feel much older 6 years ago. She developed painful arthritis. Opening doors was a problem, as was grasping cabinet doors. Her heart was not pumping efficiently. Her ankles were swollen. She gasped and sweated when she exerted herself. Still, she was able to live in her four-bedroom home. Then, Mabel fell and hurt her back. Her doctor suggested an operation to remove part of the bone in the spine. Unfortunately, the surgery did not help much. Mabel never fully recovered. A year later, on the way to the kitchen, she brushed against a couch and broke another bone. Mabel was frightened. She has no children. Her husband died of a heart attack several decades ago. According to Mabel, "What could I do but enter a nursing home?"

Today, at age 86, Mabel can still get from her bed to the toilet. With effort and creative strategies, she dresses herself. She puts her clothes on the side of her bed so she does not have to walk to the closet. She wears pullovers without buttons instead of dresses. Other problems have developed in recent years. She has needed hip replacement surgery. She wears sunglasses because the light hurts her eyes. Mabel is typical of millions of older people coping with age-related chronic disease.

No matter how much we exercise or watch our diet, unless we die suddenly, we will become acquainted with chronic disease, the type of enduring illness that often cannot be cured. Sometimes this encounter will last a few weeks; sometimes, as in Mabel's situation, it will last for years. Chronic disease accounts for three-fourths of all deaths in America and other developed countries (Jette, 1996; U.S. Bureau of the Census, 1996). It is our nation's major category of health problem, costing billions of dollars in doctors' visits, in days off work, and in home and nursing-home care. In this chapter, we focus on this age-related enemy.

CHRONIC DISEASE VERSUS DISABILITY

Some chronic diseases that strike after midlife occur most often among the young (see Aging in Action 5-1). However, the main characteristic of chronic illness is its intimate link to advancing age. The frequency of almost every chronic condition increases

5-1 *MS in Midlife*

At age 50, Jane was diagnosed with MS, a disabling chronic illness caused by the destruction of the myelin sheath surrounding the neurons in the brain. Because the average age at diagnosis is the early 30s, my friend has what is called a late-onset form of the disease. Although labeled "late," this illness arrived in the center of a vigorous life. Jane, who returned to get her Ph.D. in her middle years, is a committed teacher, a devoted colleague and friend—the person in the department on whom our school psychology students depend.

I didn't plan on this. I expected to live to 100 and die of a stroke. It was sudden. One minute it wasn't there, and the next minute it was. That morning I picked up donuts to take to MTSU, bit into one, and it had a bland taste. So I warned people in the coffee room—but, to my surprise, everyone said the donuts were fine. At lunch, everything tasted strange. During the next 24 hours, my face started getting numb. When you lose your ability to taste, eating is an awful sensation. You taste textures, not food. I made an appointment with a neurologist. When he got the report saying there were spots on my brain significant for MS, I was totally shocked.

My symptoms never go away, but grow more and less intense. It's like you've been to the dentist and had a shot of Novocain and never fully get your feeling back. The numbness in my face has spread out—first to my left arm and, a few months ago, to my left leg. When you lose sensation in your legs, you lose your balance and fall. Your muscles get weaker, and eventually people with MS may have to be in a wheelchair.

More debilitating is the fatigue, the feeling that your body can barely move. This spring, I had to cancel some classes because I could not sit up for two hours. Sometimes, I am so exhausted I can't pull myself out of bed. Heat and stress make the problem worse. For instance, I did an all-day workshop at the end of May. When I got home at 5:00, I went to bed and slept for 14 hours.

in older age groups. By their 80s, the vast majority of people have several chronic diseases.

Table 5-1, listing the top-ranking chronic illnesses in the elderly, highlights another fact: Most age-related chronic conditions are not life-threatening. They limit our ability to function in the world. As we saw in Mabel's case, with chronic illness the enemy is not just death. It is disability.

The National Health Interview Survey, a regular government-sponsored poll, offers an ongoing barometer of disease and disability rates among community-dwelling American adults. The surveys typically show that by age 55, about 8 out of every 10 people has at least one chronic condition. However, an equally high percentage—also 8 in 10—report being disability-free (Jette, 1996). As we ascend the age rungs, the equation changes.

Most terrifying are the cognitive changes. I would read a thesis and couldn't process it. It made no sense. You know Audrey Hamilton. I had a meeting with her about her thesis. I still can't remember a thing we talked about, and she was making decisions about what to do. I was so embarrassed. That's when you and Ginny saw me in the hall, I couldn't stop crying, and you insisted that I see a therapist.

My therapist is wonderful. He works with a lot of MS patients, so he understands the disease. He is getting me to cut down as much as possible, which is hard, because I've always been so active—training me not to get upset if I can't follow through. I gave up the course I was scheduled to teach this summer. Now that I'm resting, I feel better. Thank God, my thinking problems have cleared up. My neurologist tells me that 40% of people with MS develop cognitive changes, but only 10% of those are severe. I hope I'm not in that category. I could take being in a wheelchair, but I don't think I could handle it if there was something wrong with my mind.

Last week, I went back to MTSU. The thesis students were panicking. I had to give it a try. But by the time I got to school, I was so tired that I had to tell a student—a nice girl— that I could only see her for a few minutes. It is hard for people to understand. You don't look impaired. They think you are exaggerating or making things up. Next semester will be a test of how I can function, whether I can continue. I never thought about retirement. Sometimes, I feel like I am dreaming or making this all up. This isn't really happening to me.

In this chapter, we will be discussing age-related chronic conditions, illnesses that often disable people gradually in their later years. With earlier-life chronic diseases such as MS, problems progress at a more episodic, variable rate. People have reprieves in which they function fairly well. However, they too must struggle with the reality that their condition is permanent and will eventually get worse. This sense of inevitable decline—the need to come to terms with an irreversible, gloomy fate—may be the worst torture of living with a disabling chronic disease.

Top-Ranking Chronic Conditions for People 65 and Older*		TABLE 5-1
Arthritis	48.4% of people	
Hypertension	37.2	
Hearing impairment	32.0	
Heart disease	29.5	
Vision disease	23.0	
Orthopedic impairment	17.7	
Diabetes	9.9	
Visual impairment	7.9	

*Most of the top-ranking chronic illnesses among the elderly are not a threat to life.
SOURCE: U.S. Bureau of the Census, 1996.

instrumental
activities of daily
living (IADLs)
*Activities that are
important for
functioning
normally in life
(such as cooking
and cleaning) but
not basic to self-
care*

Disabilities vary in their severity. Some people have trouble with **instrumental activities of daily living** (IADLs). They can function fairly independently, but have difficulties washing their clothes, or running a vacuum cleaner, or shopping for food. Others have impairments in **basic activities of daily living** (ADLs), which are elemental human functions such as the ability to get out of bed, bathe, or feed or dress oneself. Although rates of minor disabilities are always far higher, the alarming news is that limitations in basic ADLs jump dramatically in advanced old age. As Figure 5-1 shows, about 5% of people aged 70 to 74 report one of these problems. Over age 85, the rate quadruples: 1 in 5 people *living in the community* has trouble performing a centrally important activity of life (Crimmins, Saito, & Reynolds, 1997).

**basic activities of
daily living
(ADLs)**
*Elemental self-care
activities such as
walking, bathing,
or feeding or
dressing oneself*

So, although they are linked, chronic disease is not the same as disability. And it is the latter, behavioral index of illness that is most important in later life. This behavioral measure of illness has a special name: **functional impairment.**

Functional impairment is such an important measure of health to gerontologists that they have developed a variety of scales to assess it. Some focus on basic ADLs, such as whether the person can dress herself or rise from a chair. Others measure complex instrumental abilities, such as socializing or raking the yard (deBruin, deWitte, Stevens, & Diederiks, 1992). When older people evaluate their own health, they too look beyond their illnesses to their functional limitations (Stump, Johnson, & Wolinsky, 1995). The reason is that, as we saw vividly with Mabel and Jane, problems in functioning are *the* crucial problems with chronic disease—the toll it takes on human life.

Is Disability the Price of a Ripe Old Age?

**tertiary
prevention**
*Efforts to control
illness once an
individual suffers
from a disease*

Although everyone wants to live to be 80 or 90, far fewer of us would vote to spend these extra years suffering from the impairments that can make life more a burden than a gift. When we look at the growth of these impairments in advanced old age, the clear implication is that our life expectancy progress may be a double-edged sword. By enabling so many people to live to advanced old age, haven't we been purchasing years of suffering from incapacity, not independent life?

This idea becomes more probable when we consider that most medical advances involve **tertiary prevention,** intervening after disease has struck. They postpone death in the face of existing illness, not increase our years of health. Given that as we age, the number of chronic diseases accumulates, most experts see extended **morbidity** (illness) as the price of inching so many people close to the limit of human life (Manton & Suzman, 1992; Verbrugge, 1989, 1990).

There is a more optimistic view. Because the new emphasis on fitness involves primary and secondary prevention, it may be postponing the onset of disease. Therefore, James Fries (1990) argues, the lifestyle revolution has extended **active life expectancy,** our years of healthy life. Furthermore, in Fries's opinion, we are at the brink of witnessing an historic **compression of morbidity:** people living healthy longer, almost until the limit of human life.

**compression of
morbidity**
*Fries's hypothesis
that as a result of
the lifestyle
movement, people
are living healthy
close to the
maximum lifespan.*

The good news is that active life expectancy is increasing. The older population as a whole is healthier than in the past (Crimmins, 1996). However, Figure 5-1 shows little support for the upbeat prediction that we are living healthy to life's outer bounds. Notice that over the 11-year period from 1982 to 1993, *no* clear-cut decline

Percentage of Elderly Males and Females Reporting Problems in a Personal-Care Activity, (National Health Interview Surveys, 1982–1993)

FIGURE 5-1

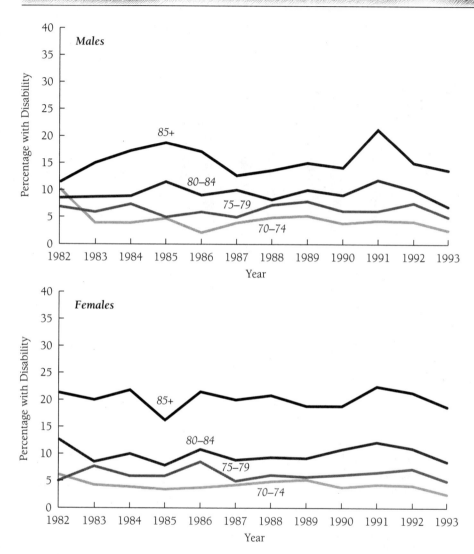

As we advance in years, the chance of being disabled increases. Over age 85, about 1 in 5 people has a limitation in basic personal care.

SOURCE: Crimmins, Saito, & Reynolds, 1997.

FIGURE 5-2

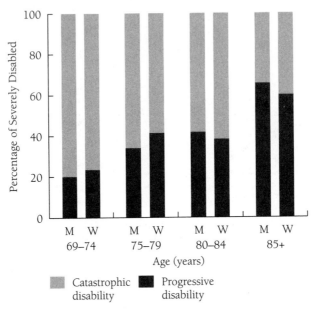

People in their 70s are more likely to be disabled by a catastrophic event. Among the very old, progressive disability is the more common path.
SOURCE: Ferrucci et al., 1996.

in disability occurred. Disability rates fluctuated for both women and men year by year (Crimmins, Saito, & Reynolds, 1997). And we are emphatically not living to life's limits and then dying "with our boots on." Throughout the Western world, ADL limitations accelerate as we ascend the age rungs (P. B. Baltes & Smith, 1997; Femia, Zarit, & Johansson, 1997).

So, yes, when we are in our 60s, we are likely to be healthier than our parents and grandparents were at that age. However, by voting to live to our late 80s, we accept a price: the risk of living disabled for a more extended period of life (Branch et al., 1991).

The Disability Pathway

How does the payment of this unwelcome price occur? How is health transformed into incapacity in our older years? Prospective studies offer a portrayal of the disablement process in the flesh.

There are two main pathways to serious functional decline. Sometimes, a disability occurs suddenly as a consequence of a catastrophic event. Mrs. Smith is fine until the day she breaks her hip. After that, she cannot leave the house. Mr. Jones is working in the yard when he has a stroke. From that time on, he needs help eating or getting out of bed. The second trajectory is gradual and progressive and takes place over years. As their chronic diseases worsen, Mrs. Smith and Mr. Jones gradually do less and less. Two years ago, they had trouble biking or walking to the store. Today, they have trouble moving from their bed to a chair.

How common is each pathway in later life? To answer this question, National Institute on Aging researchers interviewed more than 6,000 older adults in an urban, a suburban, and a rural location at regular intervals over 7 years. If we just consider our overall risk over age 65, we have a greater chance of being disabled by a catastrophic event. As we might expect, the probability of both pathways is far higher in advanced old age. But the relative frequency of the patterns shifts as we ascend the age rungs. As Figure 5-2 shows, at younger ages, severe disability typically follows a catastrophic event; over 85, the gradual downslide to severe ADL problems is the more prevalent path. Finally, when people do became seriously disabled, the researchers found that death tends to occur relatively quickly, in a matter of months (Ferrucci et al., 1996).

What risk factors predict the downslide? To answer this question, Renee Lawrence and Alan Jette (1996) followed another huge group of initially healthy older people over 6 years. The first indicators of what is to come are remarkably similar to those the Alameda study revealed: People who are not overweight and exercise regularly are less likely to develop the chronic illnesses that loom large in producing minor functional limitations and then more severe impairments down the road. Once a person is on that path, lower-body movement problems are the best predictor of more serious declines. As we saw in the last chapter, musculoskeletal disorders (along with vision impairments, cardiovascular problems, and Alzheimer's disease) loom large in predicting serious ADL limitations in our older years.

The flowchart in Figure 5-3 illustrates a probable path from health to disease to disability to death. Besides age and lifestyle, two markers predict the risk of early illness, disability, and death: gender and social class.

Gender, Socioeconomic Status, and Disability

WOMEN, DISEASE, AND DISABILITY   As we saw in Chapter 1, women pay a price for traveling farther on the life expectancy train: more years of disability at the upper limits of life (Verbrugge, 1989, 1990; Jette, 1996).

The main cause, as we saw in Chapter 3, is that one illness spares men from encountering the impairments of advanced old age: Men are more likely to die suddenly of a heart attack. Women survive to develop the nonfatal chronic problems that cause the functional limitations of later life (Jette, 1996; Jette, Branch, & Berlin, 1990; Kosorok, Omenn, Diehr, Koepsell, & Patrick, 1992).

Even when they have potentially fatal illnesses such as heart disease or cancer, women are more likely to live on disabled than to die (Manton, 1990). Women have

FIGURE 5-3   *A Probable Path from Health to Death*

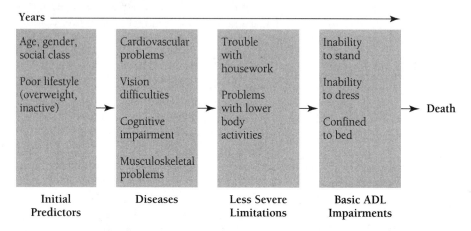

Years ⟶

Age, gender, social class Poor lifestyle (overweight, inactive)	Cardiovascular problems Vision difficulties Cognitive impairment Musculoskeletal problems	Trouble with housework Problems with lower body activities	Inability to stand Inability to dress Confined to bed	→ Death
Initial Predictors	**Diseases**	**Less Severe Limitations**	**Basic ADL Impairments**	

SOURCE: Based on information from Jette, 1996; Lawrence & Jette, 1996; and Rudberg, Sager, & Jie Zhang, 1996.

higher rates of angina, the long-term disabling form of heart disease, than men. When they traced the lives of males and females hospitalized with angina, Jennie Nickel and Thomas Chirikos (1990) found that, even here, women were prone to live on, suffering impairments in their ability to negotiate life. The study tracing catastrophic and progressive disabilities (Ferrucci et al., 1996) reveals the same gender difference in mortality in the face of disabling disease. Recall that in this research, when people developed serious ADL limitations, they were likely to die quickly. However, the researchers found that the transition from serious impairment to death was more extended for women than for men.

It comes as no surprise that disability is the price that women pay for living to their 80s and beyond. However, the phrase "living sicker" applies to women *throughout* adult life. Women visit doctors more often. They report more physical complaints and are more frequently confined to bed by illness. On a variety of measures of morbidity at every point in adulthood, women do worse (Gijsbers Van Wijk, Kolk, Van den Bosch, & Van den Hoogen, 1992).

Although these higher rates are partly due to the reproductive problems and conditions, such as pregnancy and menopausal disorders, that punctuate women's lives, they also reflect a different orientation to health. Women are more likely to admit illness, to be sensitive to their physical state, and to seek professional help early on (Verbrugge, 1989, 1990). In one typical study, older men were more likely to be hospitalized, but elderly women visited the doctor more frequently for preventive visits and minor care (C. Thomas & Kelman, 1990). Do women's higher illness rates reflect differences in *illness-related behavior* or a truly higher rate of disease? Perhaps this tendency to be more sensitive to their body and to take action more quickly in the face of illness actually contributes to women's life expectancy advantage.

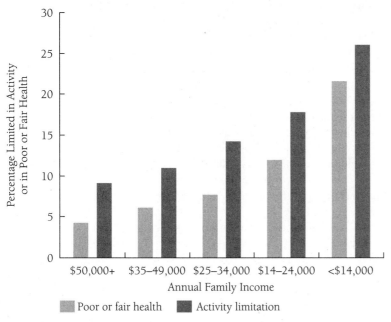

Although the differences between the very poor and other Americans are especially striking, family income is linked to health at all economic levels.
SOURCE: Adapted from National Center for Health Statistics, 1995a, Tables 62 and 63, pp. 153–154.

THE DISADVANTAGED, DISEASE, AND DISABILITY   If the saying that applies to women is "living longer sicker," the phrase that applies to the poor and less educated is "dying sooner, living more ill." Unfortunately, another blow to the compression of morbidity hypothesis is that this aging ideal does not fit the lives of one important group: the poor. Low education and low income, the two commonly used measures of lower socioeconomic status described in Chapter 1, were major risk factors for premature illness and death in the Alameda study. This connection between social class and mortality and morbidity is not confined to the United States. Throughout the world, the poor have higher morbidity and mortality rates than people who are affluent (Kaplan, 1992).

The relationship family income has to morbidity and disability is shown dramatically in Figure 5-4. These statistics are taken from a National Health Interview Survey conducted in 1993. Notice that more than one-fourth of adults with a family income of less than $14,000 per year report being disabled by chronic disease; more than one-fifth report being in fair or poor health. For people earning over $50,000 a year, these rates are much lower: 9.7% and 3.9%, respectively.

Is there a time of life when the social class differences in health are most pronounced? To answer this question, James House and his University of Michigan colleagues decided to break down similar illness/income statistics by age from an earlier National Health Interview Survey. The researchers predicted that social class differences in morbidity should be widest in middle age and early later life. In youth, age-related illnesses would not have had time to develop. As people reach the upper end of life and the biological press toward illness affects everyone, the SES differences in disease should converge.

They were correct. The differences in health between the affluent and the poor were especially striking at ages 45 to 65 (House et al., 1992; see also Crystal & Johnson, 1997). Moreover, because such a high percentage of people in the lowest income group report being disabled by chronic diseases during their middle years, among the poor old-age illnesses are actually diseases of *midlife*.

Social class remains a powerful predictor of disability during our older years. When George Maddox and Daniel Clark (1992) traced the lives of Social Security recipients first studied in their 60s, not only were the poor initially more prone to functional impairments, but during the next decade, this group suffered sharper losses in their ability to negotiate life.

House and his colleagues argue that the reason socioeconomic status is so closely linked to disability is that every risk factor for age-related chronic conditions—from fewer social contacts, to emotional stress, to being overweight, to drinking excessively—is more common in lower socioeconomic groups. The lifestyle revolution may even have heightened the association between SES and disease. Because the most dramatic reductions in smoking have occurred among middle-class people, during the past few decades smoking, especially among women, has become more of a blue-collar practice (U.S. Department of Health and Human Services, 1989).

However, social class is a summary marker that includes a jumble of biological and environmental factors. The statistics in Figure 5-4 are certain to reflect, in part, the fact that low socioeconomic status is often the consequence, not the cause, of poor health. People who are sick are less likely to finish their education, often unable to work, and so more likely to *become* poor. Focusing on lifestyle neglects another environmental reason why the poor are more prone to disease: Poor people are more likely to suffer from age-related illnesses because they get worse medical care.

Medical Care for Disease and Disability

Our first impulse is to assume that the decision to see a doctor is prompted by need—that is, feeling sick. However, **need factors** are only one influence that shapes our choice to get care. According to a widely used framework (Andersen & Newman, 1973), a second category is **predisposing factors**—attitudes we have before illness strikes. As we saw with women, values such as a belief in medicine or sensitivity to one's physical state influence the decision to seek a doctor's help. The third category of influence is **enabling factors**—that is, real-world barriers to getting care. A person will not visit a clinic if he does not know that it exists. He will be less likely to get help if the nearest medical facility is many miles away, if he has no transportation, or if he will lose his job if he takes off from work.

need factors
The impact of one's actual physical state on the decision to seek medical help

predisposing factors
The impact of one's attitude toward medical help-seeking on the decision to seek medical help

enabling factors
The impact of one's access to medical care on the decision to seek medical help

Each of these influences—from fewer physicians in the neighborhood (medically underserved areas tend to be in impoverished urban and rural locations), to greater difficulty getting to the doctor, to cultural values that accept being sick as a normal fact of life—keep poor people from seeing a doctor when ill (Schlesinger, 1989). Another enabling force is also involved: Many poor people cannot pay.

Medical care for every older adult is covered by the government-funded program called **Medicare.** But the United States is the only developed country apart from South Africa that does not have health coverage for *all* its citizens, no matter what their age. Middle-class Americans typically have health insurance through their jobs. People who are very poor have their care paid for by the government program called **Medicaid.** Caught in the middle is a large group of Americans who work but at a job that offers no health insurance.

Even Medicaid, that vital cushion for our nation's poorest Americans, is patchier than we might think. Because eligibility policies differ from state to state, large groups of people living *below* the poverty line are excluded from Medicaid. The result is an astonishing 40 million Americans with no health insurance—1 in 6 people under age 65 (National Center for Health Statistics, 1995a).

People without health insurance, or those who are underinsured, visit doctors less often—even though, being poorer, their health is usually worse. They tend to seek help only when their symptoms have progressed to a serious, less treatable stage (Schlesinger, 1989).

In addition, although the Medicaid program does provide access to a doctor, it does not ensure high-quality care. Many physicians do not accept Medicaid. Because those who do may not offer the best services, poor people may receive less than optimal care (Schlesinger, 1989).

So, simple lack of money puts poor people at risk of becoming disabled and dying before their older years (Manton, Patrick, & Johnson, 1989; U.S. Department of Health and Human Services, 1990a, 1991). But what about the main subject of this book, older adults? After all, their care is paid for by Medicare. Ironically, similar forces make seeing a doctor difficult for less affluent older people, too.

THE ELDERLY AND PHYSICIANS As Figure 5-5 shows, people over 65 are the most frequent consumers of medical care. They are more knowledgeable consumers, too. Middle-aged and elderly people engage in more health-oriented strategies such as watching their diet. They are more health interested and health aware. They even report visiting the doctor for checkups more often than younger adults (Leventhal, Leventhal, & Schaefer, 1992).

However, older people also underutilize services, not visiting doctors as often as they might (Haug, 1981). One reason relates to cost. True, that marvelous umbrella, Medicare, does cover health care for all older adults. This lifesaving program, instituted in 1965, partly explains why, along with Japan and Scandinavia, the United States leads the world in life expectancy over age 65 (Ball, 1996). Still, Medicare has limitations; 85% of private insurance plans offer better coverage. As Table 5-2 shows, older people on Medicare must pay out-of-pocket for a portion of their doctors' visits and hospital care. The program does not cover vital auxiliary services, such as prescription drugs or vision or dental care. Although not directly relevant to our current discussion,

Medicare
Universal paid-for health care for the elderly funded by the federal government

Medicaid
Health care system funded jointly by the federal government and the states in which people below a certain income level get free or reduced-cost health care

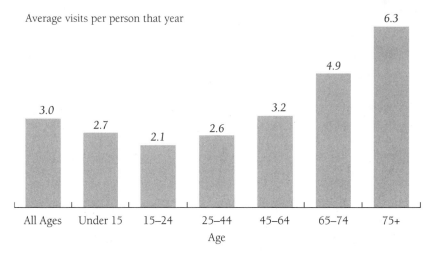

Average visits per person that year

3.0   2.7   2.1   2.6   3.2   4.9   6.3

All Ages   Under 15   15–24   25–44   45–64   65–74   75+

Age

The elderly, in particular the old-old, see a doctor much more frequently than any other group.
SOURCE: U.S. Department of Health and Human Services, 1994.

Medicare has another crucial gap: It does not pay for the ongoing services that are needed to keep older people with disabilities living independently. As a result, even with Medicare, the elderly's out-of-pocket health care expenses are substantial—nearly four times higher than those of people under 65. On average, older people living in the community pay *21%* of their yearly family income for health care. The bulk of this money goes to private insurance to supplement Medicare's gaps or for home health-care services to avoid going to a nursing home (AARP Public Policy Institute, 1995). Medicaid, which covers the elderly poor as well as people under age 65, pays more generously for services. However, poor older Americans pay an even higher fraction out of pocket for their health care than affluent older people do (Driscoll, Jensen, Raetzman, & Staff, 1995). As with younger adults, many older people, even though poor, are not destitute *enough* to quality for Medicaid.

So, even with Medicare and Medicaid, older adults are still deterred from seeing a physician by cost. In addition, to physically get to the office requires another enabling factor: transportation. A person who cannot drive, is isolated and alone, or is too embarrassed to ask for help from family or friends may put off going for help.

Visiting a physician also depends on that important predisposing influence: believing one can benefit from care. Because older people are not immune from the illness stereotypes discussed in Chapter 1, they may conclude that the dizziness or aches and pains that signal serious illness are "normal at my age." At 85 or 90, the idea may seem perfectly reasonable: "At my age, what can any doctor do?" What compounds the situation is that life-threatening illnesses often reveal themselves through

TABLE 5-2

Who is covered?

In 1995, Medicare covered more than 30 million aged persons and approximately 4 million disabled persons.

What is covered?

Part A (Inpatient and Limited Posthospital Care)
1. Inpatient hospital care up to 90 days per benefit period plus 60 lifetime reserve days
2. Care in a skilled nursing facility for 100 days following a 3-day hospitalization; intermittent home care if defined as rehabilitative care
3. Hospice care

Part B (Outpatient Care)
1. Physicians' services
2. Lab and diagnostic tests
3. Outpatient services at hospitals
4. Mental health services

What are the limitations in coverage?
1. The bill charged by hospitals and doctors' visits can exceed the money allotted by Medicare.
2. There is a deductible, meaning the person must pay a certain sum before benefits "kick in."
3. There is no coverage for preventive services, vision or dental care, or prescription drugs.
4. There is no coverage for care not defined as rehabilitative or cure-oriented.*

*This important problem will be discussed later in this chapter.
SOURCE: AARP Public Policy Institute, 1995.

less intense symptoms in later life. For instance, in old age, the intense pain of a heart attack is apt to mask itself as indigestion or heartburn.

Researchers find that older people often use a less stringent standard when they evaluate their health. They tend to be health optimists. They report being in better health than their medical tests indicate (Idler, 1993). The most astonishing example of this inflated optimism occurred in a study exploring self-evaluations of health after experiencing a catastrophic medical event. Six weeks after a heart attack, a stroke, or a broken hip, half of the older men and women in this survey *still* rated their health as excellent or good (Wilcox, Kasl, & Idler, 1996).

This is not to minimize the value of self-ratings. Self-assessments of health are a surprisingly accurate index of physical status in later life. They can be a *better* predictor of longevity and declining function than objective measures such as performance on medical tests (Borawski, Kinney, & Kahana, 1996; Femia et al., 1997). One reason may be that when older people evaluate their health, they take into account nonmedical sources of data such as functional impairments—problems that, as we saw earlier in this chapter, loom large in predicting death (Stump, Johnson, & Wolinsky, 1995). Or perhaps, as Bandura would predict, optimism (or a high sense of self-efficacy) about one's physical state *produces* better health, making people more motivated to fight their disabilities or less vulnerable to dying from disease. These rosy appraisals can be dangerous, however, when they prevent an older person who is genuinely ill from getting care.

Some people may be deterred from seeing a doctor for another reason: They feel unwelcome when they arrive. This brings us to the other side of the relationship between physicians and older adults.

PHYSICIANS AND THE ELDERLY   Older people often complain that doctors give them short shrift because of their age. A study conducted by researchers at the Rand Corporation during the 1970s lent scientific weight to these observations (Kane, Solomon, Beck, Keeler, & Kane, 1981).

These researchers asked physicians in private practice to record the amount of time they spent with each of their patients over a number of days; then they analyzed the figures as a function of the person's age. The researchers predicted that because people over 65 were most likely to be seriously ill, they would receive the most attention. Surely doctors would need to devote more effort to examining their elderly patients. They would have to spend more time explaining the complicated treatments needed to manage chronic disease.

Instead, the reverse was true. Comparing people 45 to 54, 55 to 64, and 65 and over, the researchers found relative stability in the average time spent with the two middle-aged groups, but that significantly less time was spent with patients in the oldest group. These findings held true for office, hospital, and nursing home visits, and for all seven medical specialties the researchers examined.

Do these findings mean that ageism is rampant among doctors? Before assigning all the blame to physicians, let's take a more sympathetic view. Some doctors may avoid treating older patients from simple lack of knowledge. Their training has not equipped them to deal with the functional disabilities of old age.

As suggested earlier, medicine has traditionally emphasized lifesaving cures, dramatic procedures to help people recover from serious disease. As we know, the chronic conditions older people have require a different approach. Dealing with these illnesses requires ongoing management, regularly monitoring the problem and increasing functional abilities despite an unchangeable diagnosis—an illness that never goes away (Kart et al., 1992).

Effectively treating the elderly requires doctors to widen their focus, from attacking disease to waging war against disability. This means not only worrying just about life-threatening illnesses such as cancer or heart disease but also seeing conditions people do not die from as important (Verbrugge, 1989, 1990). Their treatments have to shift. Attacking disability involves using techniques outside the doctor's traditional realm, such as exercise, physical therapy, nutrition, and psychological help. It involves being truly familiar with the community services that exist to keep people out of nursing homes (Damron-Rodriguez et al., 1997). So, to be helpful to their disabled patients, physicians have to work collaboratively, consulting with social workers, dietitians, and physical therapists. They must see these lower-status health-care workers as having important contributions to make. In other words, treating older people with multiple chronic illnesses requires a different model of care.

When we pinpoint exactly when older people visit their doctors, the need for this disability-oriented training becomes clear. In one national survey, it was the onset of ADL impairments that propelled a flurry of visits for medical care (Stump et al., 1995).

INTERVENTIONS   Our discussion suggests that to improve medical care in later life, we must work with the consumer. We must educate older people that aches and pains can signal a treatable illness; they should not be automatically passed off as inevitable signs of old age. On the enabling side, we should offer transportation to doctors' offices when the older person cannot drive. (Some programs providing this service do exist.) Another requirement is to expand Medicare coverage; however, the likelihood of this happening is practically nil. A mushrooming older population and escalating medical costs have put this popular program at risk. The more immediate challenge is to explore ways of *preserving* Medicare at near its current levels as the baby boomers reach their retirement years (AARP, Conference on the Future of Medicare, 1995).

The news is more upbeat from the provider side. Within the past two decades, the medical profession has developed training programs that focus on the special needs of older people suffering from disabling chronic disease (Fortinsky & Raff, 1995–1996). As recently as 1976, only 15 medical schools offered separate courses on aging (Kane et al., 1981); today, almost every medical school offers some training in the special problems of older adults. In 1987, a licensing examination was developed for our nation's youngest medical specialty, **geriatric medicine.**

Specialists in geriatric medicine devote themselves to the medical problems of older adults. They know that in old age disease can present itself differently; for example, the symptoms of a heart attack in an 80-year-old patient can be different from those in a person of 40 or 55. They understand what is physically normal at 80 and so are careful not to pass off treatable illnesses as normal aging or read pathology into normal age changes. They are committed to treating disability and to sharing their authority with other health care professionals. Often, they work as part of a geriatric team at a hospital or clinic. (See Aging in Action 5.2.)

geriatric medicine
Branch of medicine specializing in the problems of elderly people

Do geriatric teams help reduce disabilities? Recent studies evaluating this approach suggest that the answer is yes. Compared with groups given standard medical care, elderly patients assigned to geriatric teams had lower mortality, fewer hospitalizations and nursing home placements, or higher morale and functional health at a later point (Haydar et al., 1997; Stuck, Gerber, Minder, & Beck, 1997).

Geriatric teams serve only a tiny fraction of older adults. For the reasons spelled out in Aging in Action 5-2, there is a serious shortage of doctors who choose this less-than-glamorous specialty (Fortinsky & Raff, 1995–1996). This means that most older adults with functional impairments combine occasional visits to the doctor with the continual emotional and environmental adjustments that must be made to live as fully as possible in the face of disabling chronic disease. They carefully plan around their illness, plotting when to go out and how best to get around. They investigate what devices exist to make their life easier and how they can fit their home to their capacities. They use creative mental strategies to cope emotionally with their fate:

5-2 *The Evolution of a Geriatric Physician*

At medical school, James felt uncomfortable. Being a "people person," he was turned off by the emphasis on organs and analyzing lab values and the neglect of the human being. He disliked the stress on memorization, on becoming proficient in a narrow specialty. He was interested in social policy and felt more at home with philosophy and history. James considered dropping out and going to law school but decided to complete his training: "I felt I could always find work with a medical degree." Geriatrics seemed to fit his interests best.

According to James, because geriatrics is so different, it attracts both the best and the worst medical graduates. The dominant trend in medicine is to focus on single pieces of the person, to master a single operation or devote one's life to being an authority on one organ part. Geriatrics is holistic and process-oriented: You treat the total person and pay attention to the relationship. You consider the overall context within which care occurs. The fact that there is no body of knowledge easily measured by multiple-choice tests disturbs many doctors: "There is little support in a reductionist world for what it is we do." Another problem is the lack of a well-defined role for people who specialize in this field. Being a geriatrician might mean working in a nursing home, doing research, or going out in the community as the head of a geriatric team.

When James took a geriatric fellowship involving community care, he realized another reason why geriatrics will never have broad appeal: The team approach is frustrating. James hated having every medical decision come under scrutiny. He felt threatened when social workers continually questioned what he did. He also understood that he wanted more from his career than only to do patient care. At the same time, this experience convinced him that "the way traditional medicine is practiced offers a warped view. Sure, a patient will comply with medicines in the hospital. When you go into the person's home, you see what the obstacles to compliance are. By teaching only what to prescribe, we miss the boat. We lecture about the anatomy of the heart, not the process of care. We teach what is rationally right, not what's good for the patient. The real truth is in ADL, not hematocrit or coronary status. A person is more than a number on a blood pressure machine."

James's next step was to do a research fellowship, training he hoped would prepare him for an academic career. His research, which involved analyzing large sets of data, on the surface was the farthest point from direct patient care. However, James's interest remained the same: "This young man sublimating his anger into the world of research wanted to get a window on the doctor/patient relationship, to demonstrate how medicine is failing older adults." When he collected data from pharmacies throughout the state on sleeping pill prescribing, James found that physicians were overprescribing sleeping pills for their older patients, putting them at risk for toxic reactions, falls, and confusion.

Today, James conducts research full time. He has a job at a prestigious medical school. He makes a decent salary and does some clinical work consulting to the psychiatry staff. He does not feel at home. The institution has no interest in training geriatric physicians. His colleagues are puzzled at what he does: "Geriatrics is not where the money is in medicine. It is not the stuff of winning a Nobel Prize." James wants to teach and to get back to treating people part time so he is considering a position as a geriatric physician to do 50% research and 50% teaching and patient care. James feels excited by the chance to train students because he believes the geriatric approach is right, not just for older people, but for people of every age. He even finds some critics beginning to admit that he might be correct. Recently, to his surprise, a surgeon colleague asked James to recommend a geriatric physician for his 90-year-old mother.

Sometimes I imagine some place I would like to be . . . or put myself in a picture on TV. I do that sometimes (says a woman confined to a chair in a seventh-floor apartment).

I see people a lot younger than me and all crippled up and living in a wheelchair. . . . I figure I am lucky. . . . You've got to make the best of it, look on the positive side.

I think it was my husband's approach to life . . . that helped me. I think it gave me an inner strength that I couldn't have had, possibly. I don't think I would have been as good. I think I would have been a basket case. (McWilliam, Stewart, Brown, Desai, & Coderre, 1996, pp. 7–8)

This last quotation shows that heroic coping can depend on loved ones. In fact, families are the second heroes in the disability tale. Family members provide 80% of the day-to-day care of our nation's ill and infirm. In the rest of this chapter, we focus mainly on the **formal caregiving supports,** or special services, available to the millions of disabled older Americans and families struggling with their care.

formal caregiving supports
Community services to help disabled people and caregiving families

DEALING WITH DISABILITY

Functional impairments can be helped by strategies such as exercise (Kiyak & Borson, 1992). Having positive family relationships is important. Equally crucial is the wider environment. Mrs. Jones's house is at the top of a steep hill and to get to the front door requires climbing steps. So, although she only has some problems walking, she finds herself housebound, unable to go out. Sally is finding it harder to shop and cook, so her sister takes her in. Soon Sally is much weaker, unable to leave the house. From the purest motives, her sister has artificially created Sally's disability by taking over her life.

It is natural for the most loving person to fall into the trap of doing too much. Who doesn't want to make life as easy as possible for an ill loved one? Who wouldn't rush to help when your father is struggling to feed or dress himself? The temptation to take total care is just as strong in nursing homes. Staff members have no idea of residents' real potential. It is easier to dress or feed the disabled elderly in their care than to wait for them to perform these tasks on their own. When, as we saw in our interview with the behaviorist in Chapter 2, crucial reinforcers such as social contact occur only when a person is being helped, it is no wonder that artificially induced disabilities are such a risk among the old. Gerontologists have a name for these disabilities that do not need to be there—**excess disabilities.**

excess disabilities
Excessive impairment beyond what is inherent in a person's medical state

Excess disabilities tend to occur when there is a mismatch between the person's capacities and the environment. So, this lack of person/environment congruence may happen when an older adult is in a setting that offers too much care. When older people have trouble handling life and families cannot care for them, the knee-jerk reaction is to think of a nursing home. But a nursing home may not be needed. As the studies evaluating geriatric team care show, some nursing home residents do not have to be in an institution. They could live in the community if appropriate alternatives were available or if they took advantage of those that exist. In one project, people at risk of nursing home placement called a special number. Through the use of

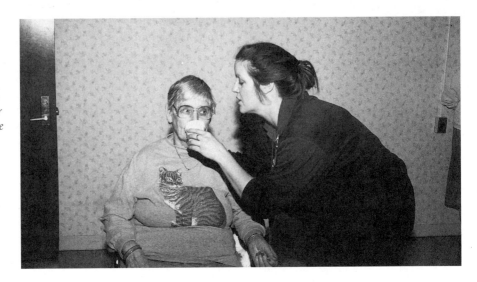

Out of the most loving impulses, this young woman may be promoting excess disabilities by helping her disabled grandmother with an activity she can obviously perform on her own.

community resources, the team operating the project was able to keep 25 to 30% of these callers at home (Hodgson & Quinn, 1980).

Disabilities are sometimes reversible; they can improve. When Thomas Chirikos and Gilbert Nestel (1985) followed several thousand middle-aged men over 15 years, the common pattern was greater loss, but the reverse also occurred. More than 9% of the men who had problems stooping or kneeling in 1976 did not have the same trouble in 1981. More than 8% found their difficulty standing improved. The fear is that putting people in nursing homes when they have these problems may make recovery *less* possible, because the nursing home setting may encourage incapacity, not independence.

Nursing home care is expensive. In 1993, the average yearly cost of a nursing home was $37,000. In some areas of the country, it exceeded $60,000 per year (AARP, 1995). Medicare pays only a tiny fraction of the bill because it covers only acute care. Once care is labeled custodial, or chronic, Medicare will not pay.

Although long-term care insurance does exist, it is too expensive for many older adults. Qualifying for this type of insurance can be hard. Companies impose numerous eligibility restrictions. They may weed out anyone with disabilities or deny coverage if a person answers yes to any health question. Policies have numerous exceptions or only provide coverage for certain types of nursing home care (AARP Public Policy Institute, 1995). Most distressing, many plans only begin to pay 6 months to a year after admission, by which time the resident is apt to have died!

This means that older people not defined as poor are forced to shoulder a huge economic burden. They typically begin by paying the nursing home fees privately. When their savings are gone, they become eligible for Medicaid, which does cover custodial care. As Figure 5-6 shows, in 1993, 85% of the multibillion-dollar nursing home bill was paid for by two sources: older adults themselves and Medicaid (P. Riley, 1995). So, once a person enters long-term care, exiting can be difficult for economic reasons alone (Grenne & Ondrich, 1990).

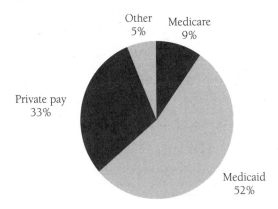

Other
5%

Medicare
9%

Private pay
33%

Medicaid
52%

Older people and Medicaid shoulder 85% of U.S. nursing home costs. People enter long-term care and "spend down" until their assets total less than $2000; then their care is paid for by Medicaid.
SOURCE: Riley, 1995.

Long-term care puts an economic burden on us all. You may be surprised to learn that most of our huge, taxpayer-financed Medicaid bill goes not to health care for poor families but to custodial care—ongoing help to the impaired elderly and disabled adults (Wiener, 1996). Because the thrust of Medicaid is toward inpatient services, much of this money is funneled directly into nursing homes (P. Riley, 1995; Wiener, 1995).

This means that from the perspective of both the older person and society, we need options to keep people outside of institutions when they have functional impairments but do not need to be in a nursing home. Luckily, these community options are expanding (Vladeck & Feuerberg, 1995–1996). They are links in a **continuum of care**—a range of services tailored to the needs of people at all points on the disability spectrum (see Table 5-3).

continuum of care
Range of services tailored to the needs of people with different degrees of disability

Community Options for the Disabled

HOME CARE   The best-known alternative to nursing home placement is **home care**—an array of services involving everything from round-the-clock nursing to a few hours per week helping with housekeeping (see Table 5-4). Because of advances in technology, even people who need 24-hour nursing care can get services in their home if they are willing to pay the enormous bill privately. Generally speaking, however, home care is most appropriate for people who have minor to moderate disabilities, have an involved family, or need short-term care.

home care
Service in which a worker comes into the home to provide care

TABLE 5-3   *Long-Term Continuum of Care*

	Functional Impairment Level	
Minor	*Moderate*	*Severe*
Basically independent, but cannot drive or do heavy work	Instrumental ADL impairments: needs help with activities such as cooking or cleaning; can bathe, dress, get around on one's own	Basic ADL limitations: unable to feed self, toilet, stand, etc.
Specialized services such as transportation, shopping help, chore help as needed	Home care several hours/day; day care; assisted living situation providing meals, housekeeping	Nursing home

Ideally, older people should have services tailored to every functional limitation level.

One barrier to home care or any other community alternative is still cost. Because Medicare only covers care defined as "rehabilitative," unless the service is defined as cure-oriented and a doctor certifies that the patient needs that type of care, Medicare will not pay. This means that while the services of a skilled nurse or physical therapist may be covered, Medicare does not pay for the person most responsible for the disabled person's functioning outside of an institution: the attendant or home health aide.

Although the Medicaid system does cover the services of these workers who provide help with the activities of daily life, how much it pays for varies from state to state. So, although home care was developed to reduce the financial burden of institutionalization, getting ongoing care of this type can be expensive too. It may be an option only when a person needs minor help, is wealthy enough to pay privately for extensive help, or has an income limited enough to qualify for Medicaid.

day care
Service in which the disabled person gets care during the day at a center outside of the home

DAY CENTERS AND PROGRAMS   In a **day care** program, the person goes to a center offering treatment and social activities. Day centers are usually open five days a week, though registrants may vary in the number of days they attend.

Today, a diversity of day care centers exists. Many are for people with Alzheimer's disease; some are for any disabled adult. Some are defined as offering medical care; others focus on social enrichment alone (Coyne, Berbig, Harkey, Swartz, & Vetter, 1997).

Advocates of these centers emphasize their advantages. Day care offers a more stimulating environment than the person might have looking at four walls. It is more cost-effective than one-to-one care. A group of people are getting the services they need in a centralized place. Because the person is not being cared for in an isolated setting, day care may lessen the risk of maltreatment. Home health aides, the primary providers of home care, tend to be older and even more poorly educated than their counterparts in hospitals and nursing homes (Crown, Ahlburg, & MacAdam, 1995).

TABLE 5-4

Home Care Personnel: A Partial List

Personnel	Services
Social workers	Provide counseling and find, coordinate, and supervise home care services.
Registered dietitians	Plan special diets to speed recovery from illness or to manage conditions such as diabetes.
Physical therapist	Use exercise, heat, light, water, and such to treat problems of movement.
Occupational therapists	Teach people how to function at their best with disabilities—for example, how to do housework from a wheelchair.
Nurses	RNs (registered nurses) provide skilled nursing care; LPNs (licensed practical nurses) offer simpler nursing services. The former are more highly trained and are needed mainly to treat complex medical conditions.
Homemakers/home health aides	Usually are the primary caretakers; may do cleaning, housekeeping, bathing, dressing, and other types of personal care. Their job title varies considerably, depending in part on the mix of help provided. For example, "homemaker" or "housekeeper" may be the title when the person mainly does cleaning; "home health aide" or "attendant" may be used when personal care is mainly involved.
Chore workers	Assist with services such as yardwork, home repair, or heavy cleaning.

Home care workers include a variety of professionals. The home health aide, who takes care of activities of daily living, is not reimbursed by Medicare.

Although many provide services above and beyond what they are being paid for (Eustis & Fischer, 1991), there have been alarming reports of abuse with these care providers (Applebaum & Phillip, 1990).

The virtues of day care are offset by certain disadvantages. Day care does not offer the flexibility of home care. The hours are fixed. Centers are not open at night. They cannot be used during an acute illness. Day programs serve a limited group, people who fit the qualifications for the program. It may also be more difficult to convince older people to attend a day center than have someone come to their home.

These serious enabling and predisposing forces limit day care's appeal (Kosloski & Montgomery, 1997). In one national survey, 85% of the day care centers were operating below capacity. On average, they could have taken one-third more people than were enrolled.

CONTINUING-CARE RETIREMENT COMMUNITIES AND ASSISTED LIVING FACILITIES   Whereas day care is for people being cared for at home, other options offer a different approach: Move to a person/environment congruent place. **Continuing-care retirement communities** provide the ultimate person/environment fit, as they offer different levels of care—from independent apartments, to assisted living

continuing-care retirement community Retirement community offering living arrangements for residents in health and later in disability

ing sections with more services, to nursing home care. The idea is that the person arrives at the community healthy and is assured of appropriate services for life. **Assisted living facilities** are free-standing residences providing services for people with impairments not severe enough to warrant a nursing home.

assisted living facilities

Privately paid-for residences that provide services to people who have disabilities

These housing alternatives fill a vital void. They liberate older people from the unpleasant choice of either moving in with children or having to go to a nursing home when disability strikes (Teaford, 1997). Unfortunately, both are costly and so only available to well-off older people. They have other liabilities, too.

On the surface, continuing care seems tailor-made to offer financial as well as emotional peace of mind. The large fee at entry supposedly frees the person from being bankrupted in the event of needing long-term care because that payment partially subsidizes the cost of the nursing home. However, as residents need more services, they typically do incur extra costs. Although these fees may have not been prohibitive when the facility was built and full of healthier residents, they may rise dramatically as a higher fraction of residents age and need more intense care. Many residents who entered these settings in their 60s and 70s when they first opened are now very old (Crews & Harper, 1997). Statistics are used to compute a community's probable health care needs, leaving residents vulnerable to deviations from the illness odds. The community may even go bankrupt if too many of its residents need the nursing home. With assisted living facilities, the problem is that the person is uprooted and then often must be uprooted again in a year or two when the disabilities worsen and warrant a nursing home. So, despite their advantages, these security-promoting housing options are more insecure than they might appear.

Still, continuing care and assisted living are attractive options for older adults with means (R. Morris, 1995–1996). As the brochure in Figure 5-7 shows, these settings offer care one might get in an institution, but in a personal, more user-friendly place. Many nursing home residents are less in need of medical intervention than of ongoing help with personal care. It is better to get this help in a setting where one can live in one's own apartment, in a place that is truly "a home."

SPECIALIZED SERVICES   A variety of services, such as home-delivered meals, transportation, shopping assistance, and home repair, also help keep people out of nursing homes. One innovative program is the Lifeline Emergency Response System. Subscribers to this hospital-based service pay a monthly fee to have their telephone hooked up to a central switchboard. Someone calls daily to check in. If there is no answer, the service contacts a neighbor, who comes by to check. This important service allows the older person living alone the comfort of knowing that help will arrive in a medical emergency when she cannot reach the phone.

These alternatives have performed their mission. In an AARP-commissioned review, Johns Hopkins University researchers concluded that for seriously disabled people, community alternatives do reduce nursing home use. They also have positive emotional effects. Unfortunately, however, especially for these most vulnerable older people, community-based long-term care is *not* more cost-effective than care in a nursing home (Newman & Envall, 1995).

Actually, nursing homes will never be outmoded. Although they may appear different in the future (R. A. Kane, 1995–1996), they will be an enduring fixture on our land. Some people will always require the type of care that only this type of institution

SERVICES & AMENITIES

ADAMSPLACE OFFERS A SPECTRUM OF SERVICES AND AMENITIES TO OUR ASSISTED LIVING RESIDENTS, DESIGNED TO PROVIDE COMFORT, CONVENIENCE, QUALITY CARE AND ENHANCED SAFETY.

Level I

- A choice of five floor plans
- Apartments available (furnished or unfurnished)
- Three chef prepared meals served daily
- Therapeutic diets available
- Beauty/barber shop at an additional fee
- Library area
- Weekly housekeeping/towel and linen service
- Active social, recreational and educational programs, coordinated by our social director
- On-site AdamsPlace management and nursing supervision

- Daily resident safety checks
- On-call assistance with daily living activities
- Round-the-clock emergency call response system
- Regular health and wellness assessments
- Medication counseling
- Telephone message service
- All utilities including telephone (Long distance not included)
- Scheduled transportation for local shopping and other events
- Cable TV at an additional fee

ADAMSPLACE PROVIDES ADDITIONAL SERVICES FOR OUR ASSISTED LIVING RESIDENTS WHO NEED REGULAR PERSONAL ATTENTION AND SUPERVISION WITH MEDICATIONS.

Level II

- All Level I services and amenities
- Assistance with daily living activities
- Supervision of medications

- Occasional reality orientation
- Occasional escort service to meals and community activities

ADAMSPLACE ALSO PROVIDES SUPPLEMENTARY SERVICES FOR OUR ASSISTED LIVING RESIDENTS WHO NEED VERY CLOSE ATTENTION WITH ALL DAILY LIVING ACTIVITIES.

Level III

- All Level I and II services and amenities
- Frequent assistance with daily living activities
- Assistance with manageable incontinence

- Administration of medications
- Escort service to meals and community activities
- Frequent reality orientation

Please consult your AdamsPlace representative for a variety of optional services that are available for residents.

1927 MEMORIAL BLVD.
MURFREESBORO, TN 37129
(615) 904-2449

can provide. In the rest of this chapter, we probe what this enduring feature of our aging landscape is really like.

Nursing Home Care

long-term care facility
Inpatient setting offering care to disabled people over an extended period

Nursing home, or **long-term care facility,** is the name for any inpatient setting that provides shelter and services to people in need of medical and personal care over an extended period. The words *nursing home* strike terror into the hearts of older people. How likely is the average person to suffer this fate? At any given time, only 5% of people over 65 live in these facilities. However, this statistic underestimates the degree to which long-term care touches the lives of older adults.

lifetime risk of placement
Risk of going to a long-term care setting at some point in life

Because it is cross-sectional, the 5% figure does not reveal a person's chance of *ever* being institutionalized—of going to a nursing home at some point in life. This **lifetime risk of placement** is surprisingly high. Experts estimate that almost half of all people who turned 65 in 1990 will enter a nursing home at some time during their remaining years (U.S. Senate Special Committee on Aging, 1991a).

Nursing homes have been described as dumping grounds where people are left to languish unattended as they wait for death. While they may prefer being in an institution to other alternatives, older people often dread the idea of going to a nursing home (Biedenharn & Normoyle, 1991). Are these stereotypes and fears realistic? For answers, let's take a close look at the institutions and the people they serve.

THE INSTITUTIONS   Long-term care facilities vary tremendously. One may be much like a hospital, offering medical services to seriously ill older people. Another may be more like a college dormitory, offering room, board, and personal care to less disabled residents. Institutions differ in size, staff/patient ratio, and philosophy. Their residents vary, too. Even though the law prohibits discrimination in admission, many nursing homes cater to the needs of certain religious or ethnic groups. They serve familiar foods and observe traditional holidays. Some welcome people with Alzheimer's disease or the bedridden. Others confine their occupants to people who are not as severely physically or mentally impaired.

skilled care facilities
Institutions (or units) offering care tailored to the needs of severely disabled people

Despite this diversity, nursing homes are formally categorized in two ways: by the intensity of care they offer and their type of ownership. The first distinction is crucial. To get reimbursed by Medicaid or Medicare, nursing homes must be classified as offering either skilled or intermediate care.

Health-related facilities
Institutions (or units) offering care for people who do not require intensive services but need ongoing help functioning

Skilled care facilities provide the highest level of care, including round-the-clock nursing, physical and occupational therapy, social services, and recreation. **Health-related facilities** are for people who do not need a skilled facility but do require ongoing assistance in functioning. They offer fewer nursing and personal services. Many nursing homes offer both types of care. The advantage of a multilevel facility is that when a resident's physical needs change and a different level of care is needed, that person can get services in the same location.

The ownership categories of nursing homes mirror hospitals. Proprietary homes are owned and run privately for a profit. Voluntary homes are operated by nonprofit organizations such as church groups. Public homes are owned by the city or state.

A third dimension, not formally categorized, is the one we care so vitally about: quality. Visit several nursing homes and you will be struck by the differences in quality. Some facilities are beautifully designed, provide excellent services, and have staff members committed to providing humane care. Others richly deserve the label "snake pit."

One influence affecting the quality of a nursing home is its clientele. Nursing homes that serve more affluent elderly look more appealing, have better services, and tend to provide higher-quality care. Well-off older people get better care for obvious economic reasons, but there is another, less obvious reason they are often better served. Staff members at homes catering to well-off residents are more likely to come under scrutiny because affluent older people are more likely to have friends and relatives who visit and complain if they see mistreatment or neglect. The fact that outside visitors keep nursing homes accountable was suggested when researchers compared how much attention the staff at selected homes paid to different residents. Residents who received the most visits also received the most staff time (Gottesman & Bourestom, 1974).

In evaluating nursing home quality, it is important to consider how a facility physically looks, its services, and its staff. Just as crucial is knowing how much autonomy the home offers residents in their daily life. Although gerontologists almost universally agree that giving disabled older people control is important, even the most humane nursing home must restrict people in basic areas of life. Decisions we take for granted, such as where to live or what meals to eat, are not an option for people living in long-term care. Nursing home residents must wait to be dressed or taken to the bathroom. They often share a room with a person they have never met. As one expert describes it, "Morning starts ridiculously early, dinner is at an unfashionable four-thirty or five. Boredom and a sense of the unnatural prevail" (R. A. Kane, 1995–1996). The truth of this last statement was brought home vividly in an observational study at an Ohio nursing home. In charting the behavior of 23 residents at 5-minute intervals over 12 hours, researchers found that, on average, people spent almost half the day in their room, most often totally alone (VanDyke & Harper, 1997).

Research on other social dimensions of nursing home life is equally disturbing. When Linda Noelker and Walter Poulshock (1984) explored the relationships among residents and staff members of a nursing home that prided itself on offering "personalized care in a familial atmosphere," they found little intimacy and widespread negative feelings toward the residents on the part of the staff. The same distance, disengagement, and lack of respect characterized the residents' relationships with one another, too, though to a smaller degree. Although the average length of time they had lived together was more than 3 years, less than half of these older people reported being close with another resident.

Nursing home residents "live in silence." They keep their complaints to themselves (Kaakinen, 1992). Although, as Aging in Action 5-3 shows, many do have supportive relationships with staff members, most report that their primary relationships lie outside the nursing home (Bitzan & Kruzich, 1990).

Another study reinforces the belief that incidents of patient abuse within nursing homes are not rare. In this survey of nursing home aides (the main caregivers), 10% reported committing a physically abusive act, either using excessive restraint or pushing, hitting, or shoving a resident; 41% admitted committing some act of psychological

**Aging
in
Action**

5-3 Mabel and Bertha

Bertha Holloway, an LPN in the nursing home where Mabel lives, provided some information for this chapter's opening interview. Bertha is familiar with Mabel's history because they are close friends. Every day Bertha makes time to visit with Mabel. She comes in after work and on weekends a few times a month. According to Bertha, "When Mabel's fractures healed, she had the chance to go to another setting offering less intense care. She's an independent woman who likes to care for herself. She stayed here because she felt secure and knew there would be a time when she would need this type of care."

Bertha first sought out a relationship with Mabel as a form of therapy. She had lost a favorite aunt and older sister and there was a void in her life. One day, Mabel mentioned that she had never had a teddy bear. As Christmas was approaching, Bertha bought Mabel the large stuffed animal now proudly displayed in her room, and their friendship began.

Bertha, like Mabel, feels this is her final home. She is almost 60. When she leaves the Health Care Center, it will be to retire. Bertha has been a staff nurse in a variety of hospital settings. She worked on an intensive care unit for years. Why did she switch to nursing home work? According to Bertha, "I was the baby of ten children. My parents had me in their 40s. I had a sister 22 years older than me. So age never meant anything special. However, for years I fought against working in a nursing home because I was afraid I would get upset when my patients died. Then, my oldest sister needed long-term care. I didn't deal with that well. In order to come to terms with the situation, I decided to try out this work."

Bertha made the right choice: "Each one of these people belongs to me. I know their problems. I have a sense of gratification here that I never had in ICU. There, we had young people with hopeless conditions. I went home feeling inadequate, that there was nothing I could do. Now, rarely do I leave feeling dissatisfied. When my patients die, I know that it's their time."

There are a few problems. One of Bertha's peeves is how hard it can be to get some doctors to return phone calls. But Bertha rarely has difficulties with the other staff or the five technicians (aides) she currently supervises: "The patients are my babies. I will not tolerate them being abused."

Mr. Booth, a gentleman in a wheelchair who has been eavesdropping on our conversation, breaks in: "The longer you're in this place, the better you feel about it. I've been here since January and never seen anybody mistreated. When I went to the hospital and came back, the young ladies hugged me because they missed me so much. I am a diabetic, and Mrs. Holloway spends her money to buy me diabetic candy. They baby me. They treat me as good as my mother ever did."

abuse during that year; and 9% admitted they had sworn at or insulted a person in their care (Pillemer & Bachman-Prehn, 1991).

These studies suggest that the grim stereotype of nursing home workers is accurate. Other research contradicts the stereotypes, suggesting that these people care deeply about providing good patient care (Burgio, Engle, Hawkins, McCormick, & Scheve, 1990; see also Aging in Action 5-3). Before blaming nursing home workers, let's look at their job conditions. Like home health aides, nursing home aides are not well educated. The sad fact is that this job is one of the poorest paying, least appreciated occupations society provides. In one poll of more than 140 aides at various New York area nursing homes, workers complained that the nursing staff did not seek their input. Their ideas about residents were often ignored, even though they knew the person's needs best (Burack, Chichin, & Olsen, 1997). Care recipients can be far from appreciative. When I worked as a psychologist in a nursing home, I witnessed patients cursing or becoming physically abusive with no provocation. In fact, in the survey of abusive behaviors on the part of aides, the highest correlate of lashing out at a resident was having been the target of that individual's aggressive act. This suggests that, although not excusable, some of what occurs within nursing homes becomes understandable if we look at the people these institutions serve.

RESIDENTS   Nursing home residents vary in background, ethnicity, temperament, and almost every other characteristic that can differentiate people. Some enter homes for short-term rehabilitation or arrive with a terminal disease to await death. Others live in long-term care for decades, cognitively intact or comatose and needing 24-hour care (R. A. Kane, 1995–1996). Still, a number of general statements can be made about this group.

Nursing home residents tend to be very old. Almost half are over age 85. Because of gender differences in longevity and the fact that women are more likely to have disabling illnesses, they are overwhelmingly female. They are mainly white. Minorities have a lower life expectancy, and institutional care is not as available to nonwhites. Their strong norms to care for the older generation at home also contribute to the relatively low, though growing, numbers of ethnic minorities in nursing homes (Stanford & Schmidt, 1995–1996). As we know from the fact that their care is financed mainly by Medicaid, most residents are currently poor. Most important, people in nursing homes have functional impairments severe enough to warrant institutional placement. To be admitted to a facility offering skilled or intermediate care, a person must be certified as having a level of disability compatible with that type of care.

Placement in a home is associated with deterioration in cognitive capacities and especially severe ADL limitations (Rudberg, Sager, & Zhang, 1996; Wolinsky, Callahan, Fitzgerald, & Johnson, 1992). It is also associated with fewer "social supports." A relatively high proportion of single, divorced, and widowed elderly people live in institutions, and these residents tend to be healthier than their married counterparts. A spouse is the first line of defense against institutionalization. If they are physically able, husbands and wives provide the caregiving when a spouse is having trouble functioning. The second line of defense is children, usually daughters. People with no immediate family members are at much higher risk of entering long-term care (Freedman, 1996).

PERSONALITY AND PSYCHOPATHOLOGY   On almost any measure of mental health, older people living in nursing homes rank as disturbed. More than half suffer from serious cognitive impairments. Apathy, anxiety, and depression are prevalent among the remaining residents of long-term care (German, Rovner, Burton, Brant, & Clark, 1992; Katz & Parmelee, 1997). From our look at what goes on in nursing homes, we might assume that these high levels of emotional disturbance are caused by the institution. Surely the living conditions within many nursing homes would make anyone demoralized and depressed.

A more accurate assumption is that people who have reached the point of applying to nursing homes are already emotionally disturbed. Although the institution may not help matters, emotional problems existed before entering long-term care.

In a classic longitudinal study of adaptation to institutional life, Morton Lieberman and Sheldon Tobin (1983) interviewed three groups of equally disabled older people: nursing home residents, elderly who had applied for admission to the home but were on a waiting list, and a group who had not sought nursing home care. The waiting list group and those in the home had identical symptoms. Compared with the group not seeking institutional care, they were less emotionally responsive and had lower self-esteem.

Every study reveals high rates of mental disorders among residents of nursing homes. However, not *every* nursing home resident is emotionally disturbed. Not only do many people live happily for years within nursing homes, but improvements in mood may occur after entering long-term care (Engle & Graney, 1993; see also Aging in Action 8-2, in Chapter 8 of this book).

Who is more content afterward than before? Researchers find that if a person's life situation is very difficult, placement results in a rise in morale. For older people who genuinely need an institution—those in poor health, with few financial resources, and living alone—placement is a relief. As we saw with Mabel, the nursing home is a haven from the terror of struggling with life outside.

In addition to precarious life circumstances, personality predicts who does well within long-term care. Unfortunately, some not very appealing traits predict adjustment to this way of life.

The main purpose of Lieberman and Tobins's study was to follow their waiting list subjects as they entered and adjusted to the nursing home. The researchers found that residents who declined the least mentally and physically or improved at the end of a year had a set of unpleasant traits. They tended to be aggressive and intrusive. They were likely to blame others rather than themselves. They were low in empathy, and maintained a distrustful distance from other residents.

Given the depressing conditions of institutional life, these findings are no surprise. Aggressive behavior may be an adaptive strategy in a situation where resources are so limited. People who fight are likely to get more of what they need. Keeping emotionally distant from others and unresponsive to their suffering may be helpful in a situation where people have painful disabilities or are near death.

INTERVENTIONS   I hope our discussion has not reinforced more stereotypes than it has erased. In fact, tremendous progress is being made in improving nursing homes. The growth of geriatric medicine, increased attention to the needs of frail older people, studies of the type discussed in this chapter, and media attention to nursing home abuses all have contributed to making the past 15 years an era of exciting change in long-term care.

In 1987, Congress passed the Nursing Home Reform Act (called OBRA '87), a watershed effort to improve nursing home care. OBRA (Omnibus Budget Reconciliation Act) mandates individual assessment of residents on admission, respect for resident rights, and better training of nursing home staff. It discourages the use of

Innovative activities such as this intergenerational program have become much more common in nursing homes in recent years—benefiting both the very young as well as the very old.

dehumanizing physical restraints (the common practice of tying residents to a bed or chair to prevent falling). It stipulates that "the highest practicable physical, mental, and psychological well-being" of residents should be the firm goal in our nation's nursing homes (Lombardo, 1994).

Today, in light of this mandate, the problems of nursing home residents are not swept out of sight. We focus squarely on improving their daily lives. Programs that include ongoing activities, vigorous rehabilitation, and training and upgrading of staff are frequently available at the best nursing homes.

Somewhat more attention is being paid to the diversity of people in long-term care. A few special units house people who arrive for time-limited, Medicare-financed rehabilitative care. Special **Alzheimer's Special Care Units** within general facilities have staff and programs specially devoted to the needs of people with this disease. These units are usually locked or have alarms to prevent patients from wandering. They feature structured activities, and the environment is designed with the needs of the Alzheimer's resident in mind. As of the mid-1990s, more than 3200 Alzheimer's Special Care Units (SCUs) were in operation in the United States (Lane & Lange, 1997).

I must emphasize that many standard nursing homes now have these features (Grant, Kane, & Stark, 1995). It has yet to be proven that just because a unit is labeled "Alzheimer's" it provides superior care (Sloane, Lindeman, Phillips, Moritz, & Koch, 1995). In one comparative study, the staff of a special unit did not score higher on a "knowledge of Alzheimer's" test than their counterparts in other units at the home (Lane & Lange, 1997). Despite decades-long guidelines for how best to plan a unit physically to foster memory and orientation (see the interview with Powell Lawton, Aging in Action 1-2), in another poll, besides complaining about staffing problems, nursing home administrators frequently reported that their Alzheimer's unit was poorly designed physically (Kaplan & Hoffman, 1997). So, although these developments are promising, we still have far to go.

Alzheimer's Special Care Units
Units in nursing homes catering to the needs of residents suffering from cognition-impairing illnesses such as Alzheimer's disease

Grievance Procedure

Your comfort, safety, health and happiness are our concern and we presume that you will give us the opportunity to assist you should a problem arise. We trust that you will feel free to take any action you choose in resolving any problem. The management will not discriminate nor use any coercion or reprisal against you for taking such steps. You may expect the degree of confidentiality that you request.

If at any time you are not being treated fairly, or if you feel that an employee has mistreated you in any way, please take the following steps:

1. Notify the social worker for assistance in resolving the problem. The social worker serves as the center's in-house "ombudsman." An "ombudsman" investigates complaints on behalf of the administrator and reports findings/resolution to the administrator.
2. If you are not satisfied, notify the director of nursing.
3. Should you remain unsatisfied, please take the concern to the assistant administrator or administrator.

You are welcome to present the problem verbally or in writing. You may expect a response at each level as quickly as possible, certainly within 5 working days.

In the event that you choose to describe the concern in writing, especially if the grievance is one addressed by either federal civil rights legislation or Section 504 of the Rehabilitation Act of 1973, you are entitled to a written response within 5 days *at each level.* Section 504 states, in part, that "no otherwise qualified handicapped individual . . . shall, solely by reason of his handicap, be excluded from participation in, be denied the benefits of, or be subjected to discrimination under any program or activity receiving federal financial assistance." The administrator is the designated 504 coordinator for this center and will be happy to address any such issues brought to his/her attention.

In the event that grievances of any sort are not satisfactorily resolved with the center, you may contact an outside representative of your choice:

1. Contact NHC regional or home office staff either directly or through the use of the Patient Care Satisfaction Evaluation provided for your use.
2. File a complaint with the State Survey and Certification agency.
3. Contact your state's ombudsman.
4. File a civil rights or Section 504 grievance.

The names and addresses are available to you upon request to the social worker or administrator and are publicly posted in common areas of the center.

Any of these courses of action is encouraged if you are aware of any patient abuse, either verbal, mental or physical; neglect, misappropriation of property; or discrimination on the basis of race, color, religion, national origin, sex, age or handicap. You, and all other patients, are entitled to protection from such behaviors.

SOURCE: National Health Corporation, Murfreesboro, TN.

We can point to more concrete advances in giving residents greater autonomy and control. Nursing homes have residents councils that meet regularly to discuss residents' complaints and concerns. Nursing home bills of rights are clearly available to residents (see Table 5-5). Increasingly, nursing homes have review boards to guard against abuses in terminal care (T. Miller & Cugliari, 1990; see also Chapter 12).

Well-established programs advocate for residents' rights. In the **nursing home ombudsman** program, residents of nursing homes are visited by a volunteer advocate whose job is to listen to and mediate their complaints. Watchdog organizations complement these efforts. Nursing home rights groups agitate for residents, guide people through applying and selecting a nursing home, and spotlight nursing home reform.

Nursing homes are beginning to pay attention to the anxieties that families continue to feel after placing a loved one in long-term care (Zarit & Edwards, 1996). In questioning 100 family members about their needs, sociologist Peggy Perkinson (1997) found that concerns centered around better collaboration with the staff. Families wanted to be involved in care planning meetings and needed guidelines on how to have "a good visit," especially with a relative with Alzheimer's disease. Based on these interviews, Perkinson is preparing a "Guide to the Nursing Home." The institution where she conducted her research, the Philadelphia Geriatric Center (PGC), is one of our nation's oldest examples of that growing entity, the **teaching nursing home.**

At teaching nursing homes, often affiliated with medical schools, residents and nurses in training get experience in providing care to institutionalized older adults and learn about the problems of the frail elderly firsthand. They are trained in the latest techniques for dealing with disability and chronic disease. Teaching nursing homes are also sites for research on interventions to minimize disease and disability in later life (Lipsitz, 1995–1996).

Despite this progress, more needs to be done. We need more affordable programs to prevent nursing home placement. It is a tragedy that once people need chronic care, they must bankrupt themselves to receive services (or transfer assets to children) or end up going to a nursing home because there is no alternative in between. Much needs to be done to restructure nursing homes. Having little say over one's roommate or meals is still standard. It is possible to give residents many more opportunities to exercise freedom of choice (R. A. Kane & Caplan, 1990). Despite the advances described earlier, a "one size fits all" model still applies in much of long-term care. We need to make a greater effort to tailor institutions to the diverse care needs of the population marooned together in nursing homes (R. A. Kane, 1995–1996). We need to do more to address the special concerns of the increasing number of minorities in long-term care (Stanford & Schmidt, 1995–1996).

Nursing homes need staff members who are better trained and higher paid. They need more of them on each unit or floor. The life of a nursing home aide can be highly frustrating. Imagine having to get an impossibly huge number of people dressed and fed within a given hour. The result must be excess disabilities, offering too much help in the interests of getting things done, or the routine neglect we see exposed on the nightly news.

The pressure to cut Medicaid funds bodes ill for these reforms. One message of this chapter is that this need-based government program is *not* just a service for the poor. It is the bulwark offering middle-class impaired elders quality custodial care. Once people realize that saving Medicaid is in their *own parents'* self-interest, they may be as anxious to preserve this program as they are to save Medicare.

The good news is that as we baby boomers move up the age rungs, we have a personal stake in making living more fulfilling at the end of life. Perhaps as we continue to push life toward our biological maximum, the lifestyle revolution of recent decades

nursing home ombudsman
Volunteer who acts as an advocate for nursing home residents and mediates their complaints

teaching nursing home
Nursing home that serves as a training site for medical and other health care personnel

will be matched by a new health revolution—one providing high-quality health care to people who suffer from the disabilities that are the price of our remarkable life expectancy progress.

KEY TERMS

active life expectancy
Alzheimer's Special Care Units
assisted living facilities
basic activities of daily living
   (ADLs)
compression of morbidity
continuing-care retirement
   communities
continuum of care
day care

enabling factors
excess disabilities
formal caregiving supports
functional impairment
geriatric medicine
health-related facilities
home care
instrumental activities of daily
   living (IADLs)
lifetime risk of placement

long-term care facility
Medicaid
Medicare
morbidity
need factors
nursing home ombudsman
predisposing factors
skilled care facilities
teaching nursing home
tertiary prevention

RECOMMENDED READINGS

PAYING FOR AND RECEIVING HEALTH CARE

The Public Policy Institute of the American Association of Retired Persons is an excellent source for information in this area, offering informational brochures, position papers, and in-depth analyses covering issues relating to financing health care and keeping the frail elderly out of nursing homes. These monographs are highly recommended:

Newman, S., & Envall, K. (1995). *The effects of supports on sustaining older disabled persons in the community.* Washington, DC: AARP.
The authors exhaustively review the studies evaluating the impact of long-term community-based services on health, longevity, quality of life, preventing nursing home use, economic benefits, and other issues for elderly at risk of nursing home placement.

AARP. (1995). *Coming up short: Increasing out-of-pocket health spending by older Americans.* Washington, DC: Author.
This monograph offers a detailed portrait of the out-of-pocket health care costs incurred by the elderly.

AARP. (1995). *Conference on the future of Medicare.* Washington, DC: Author.
This report contains the presentations made at a conference on the future of Medicare. (This is required reading for anyone interested in this vital issue.)

Where is health care headed? (1996, Summer). *Generations, 20.*
The articles in this issue of *Generations* cover the ins and outs of managed care, Medicare, Medicaid, health care reform, and more.

NURSING HOMES

The nursing home revisited. (1995–1996, Winter). *Generations, 19.*
This issue of *Generations* takes a critical look at nursing homes, exploring how they are evolving and the problems that continue to exist in providing quality care.

Kane, R. L., & Caplan, A. (1990). *Everyday ethics.* New York: Springer.

This book, in which prominent experts discuss dilemmas relating to daily life in nursing homes, offers a flavor of the concerns and threats to autonomy that occur in institutional life. Great book!

Sheilds, R. R. (1988). *Uneasy endings: Life in an American nursing home.* Ithaca, NY: Cornell University Press.
This anthropological investigation of life in a nursing home offers an interesting, balanced, true-to-life picture of nursing home life.

Rubinstein, R. L., & Lawton, M. P. (Eds.). (1997). *Depression in long-term and residential care.* New York: Springer.
This book, also recommended in Chapter 9, offers a scholarly overview of depression in institutional care.

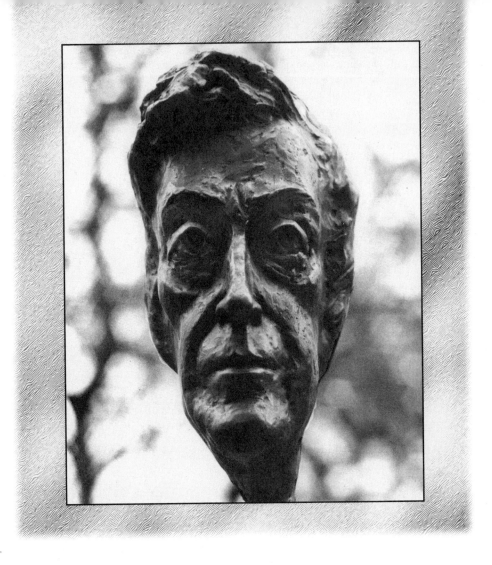

Chapter Outline

6

Intelligence

According to Jean, "When life presents me with problems, my therapy is to challenge my mind." Jean earned both her master's in speech therapy and her doctorate in special education at turning points during her life. At age 64, after her youngest son died, Jean went back to school again to get a Ph.D. in counseling psychology.

Jean finds some differences in her abilities: "I don't switch channels as well as I used to. I can retain at the same rate, but it takes me longer. However, that's no problem because I've always had a bit to spare (I hope that doesn't sound uppity). At the beginning, some students in the program had a patronizing attitude. They seemed reluctant to collaborate on projects because of my age. Now that my 3.8 average is well known, it's no problem. I'm no genius . . . but I always had the feeling that I had enough intelligence. While I may be poor in some areas—such as statistics—being articulate is a big help. Verbal skills go a long way in school and life. Memory is more difficult, but it's surprising how handy the mental strategies I used to teach my learning disabled kids have come in—if I decide to devote the energy to using them! Being more relaxed is an advantage. At my age, a person enjoys the process, focuses on the moment. I have no interest in getting a job or even a degree. I guess this means that in the most important way, I'm a better student today than in my younger years.

Think of adults you admire for their intelligence. What qualities do they have? Most likely, your list will be similar to that of the people in a poll whose responses are shown in Table 6-1. Like Jean, intelligent adults are curious and have an inquiring mind. They have maturity, wisdom, good sense. They have excellent verbal skills and are fluent, articulate, and able to reason with ease (Berg & Sternberg, 1992).

The people in this poll disagreed with the idea that intelligence declines as we age. If anything, they said the reverse. Most often, though, they said we cannot generalize. Some aspects of intelligence increase and others decrease over the years. They rejected the concept of intelligence as being a fixed or unchanging trait. Not only are the defining qualities of an intelligent person different at 20 and at 85, intelligence can and does change. In fact, intelligence at any age can increase depending on our experiences in the world.

1. INTEREST IN AND ABILITY TO DEAL WITH NOVELTY
Is able to analyze topics in new and original ways
Is interested in gaining knowledge and learning new things
Is open-minded to new ideas and trends
Is able to learn and reason with new kinds of concepts
Displays curiosity
Discovers new ideas
Is interested in his or her career
Is able to perceive and store new information
Is inquisitive
Thinks quickly
Is able to comprehend new tasks
Thinks about future and sets goals
Is always trying to better himself or herself
Has an active mind

2. EVERYDAY COMPETENCE
Displays good common sense
Acts in a mature manner
Acts responsibly
Is interested in family and home life
Adjusts to life situations
Deals effectively with problems and stress
Has high moral values
Appreciates young and old individuals
Displays wisdom in actions and thoughts
Makes rational decisions

3. VERBAL COMPETENCE
Displays the knowledge to speak intelligently
Displays good vocabulary
Is able to draw conclusions from information given
Is verbally fluent
Displays clarity of speech

SOURCE: Berg & Sternberg, 1992.

INTELLIGENCE AS MEASURED BY TRADITIONAL TESTS

Wechsler Intelligence Scale for Adults (WAIS)
Most widely used intelligence test for adults

Forty years ago, psychologists disagreed with these ideas. They thought that intelligence declined after youth. They thought the skills involved in being intelligent did not change. Intelligence was a relatively fixed property of the person, one that could be measured by the same set of skills at every age. Curiosity, interest, wisdom, and good sense did not appear among these qualities. Intelligence at every point during adult life was measured by performance on a set of tasks making up standardized intelligence tests—typically the **Wechsler Intelligence Scale for Adults (WAIS).**

TABLE 6-2

Verbal Scale*

Subtest	Measures	Hypothetical item
Information	Fund of knowledge	Who is Bill Clinton?
Comprehension	Social or life knowledge	What do you do when you find an umbrella in your class?
Similarities	Verbal reasoning	Cat is to feline as dog is to ———.
Arithmetic	Mathematical knowledge	Joe had $10.00 and spent $2.50. How much does he have left?
Digit span	Memory	Repeat these digits: 8238910.
Vocabulary	Word definitions	What does *ebullient* mean?

Performance Scale (all tests are timed)*

Digit symbol	Copy the symbols.
Picture completion	What is missing in this picture?
Block design	Given a set of blocks with different patterns on each side, arrange them to look like the pattern on a card.
Picture arrangement	Given a set of pictures, arrange them to tell a story.
Object assembly	Given a set of puzzle pieces, arrange them correctly to form common objects.

*The verbal scale measures a person's knowledge base; the performance scale measures the ability to speedily solve nonverbal problems.
SOURCE: Wechsler, 1981.

The Wechsler Intelligence Scale for Adults, which has now been revised several times, is an example of a **traditional psychometric intelligence test**—a measure in which people are ranked as having more or less of a fixed quantity called "intelligence" based on their performance compared with their peers. This widely used test has a verbal and a performance scale, each composed of different subtests measuring more specific skills. Notice from the examples in Table 6-2 that the verbal part of the test tends to measure factual knowledge—knowledge of historical, literary, or biological facts; of how to function in the world; of mathematics; of word meanings.

The performance tests, which involve copying symbols, arranging or naming pictures, or manipulating puzzles or blocks, measure a different type of skill: the person's ability to solve novel problems. Notice that on this part of the test, speed is essential. Not only are the performance subtests timed, but often bonus points are given for the quickest solution.

Psychologists calculate an intelligence quotient, or IQ, by adding up the number of correct items and comparing that total with how other people of the same age typically score. In other words, the WAIS, similar to any test graded on a curve, depends on performance compared with a reference group. In this case, the reference group is one's age group.

traditional psychometric intelligence test Intelligence test with a series of items in which people are ranked as having more or less intelligence compared with others

During the 1950s, when psychologists tested adults of different ages to get these reference group standards, or *age norms,* they found a depressing fact. Beginning in young adulthood, older groups did worse and worse. The loss was especially dramatic on the performance scale where, starting in the early 20s, scores steadily declined. The decline in verbal scores started somewhat later and only fell off dramatically among people over age 65. This pattern—less loss on verbal measures requiring knowledge and steady decline beginning very early on timed tests of nonverbal skills—was so consistent a research finding that in the early writings it was given a special name: the **classic aging pattern** (Botwinick, 1967).

No matter how much we emphasize that the verbal losses are small, these findings offer little comfort to anyone past youth. However, being from cross-sectional data, they immediately raised suspicions. Even 40 years ago, psychologists knew too much about the difficulties of assuming age changes from differences *between* age groups to take these results as the final word. Would longitudinal studies also reveal this picture of universal decline? Would they confirm the classic aging pattern?

As we might expect, longitudinal studies were more positive. Many showed people improved on the verbal part of the test through middle age (Labouvie-Vief, 1985). However, even here the classic aging pattern showed up. Even when verbal scores improved, decline, though to a smaller degree, still was typical of the performance tests. Longitudinal studies also revealed the pattern in the early cross-sectional research. At the end of life the classic aging pattern broke down. Among very old people, verbal scores dropped dramatically too.

So psychologists were intrigued by these similarities. Both cross-sectional and longitudinal studies revealed the classic aging pattern until old age, followed by universal decline. Then, in 1970, psychologist John Horn made an influential attempt to integrate and make sense of these findings.

Interpreting the Findings: A Two-Factor Theory of Intelligence

Horn (1970) describes two basic types of intelligence. **Crystallized intelligence** reflects the extent to which we have absorbed the knowledge base of our culture. It is the amount of information we have accumulated. This ability is heavily measured by the verbal subtests of the WAIS. The second type of intelligence reflects a central nervous system at its physiological peak. **Fluid intelligence** involves quick reasoning, skills not as dependent on experience. This type of intelligence is what is mainly being measured by the performance tests.

Horn believes that fluid intelligence, as is true of many physiological capacities, reaches its peak in early adulthood and then steadily declines. Because it involves experience and learning, crystallized intelligence follows a different path as we age. This type of intelligence stays relatively stable or increases as the years pass because the rate at which we acquire new information in the course of life tends to balance out the rate at which we forget. In old age, however, crystallized intelligence also declines. At some point in life, the effect of losses—of work, of relationships, and particularly of health—cause the rate of forgetting to exceed the rate at which knowledge is acquired (Horn & Hofer, 1972).

Horn's fluid/crystallized distinction is appealing. It has stood the test of time. The beauty of his two-factor theory is that it not only explains test performance but fits so

classic aging pattern
Typical age finding on IQ tests of relative stability on verbal measures and steady decline beginning early in adult life on timed, nonverbal scales

crystallized intelligence
Category of intelligence reflecting one's knowledge base

fluid intelligence
Category of intelligence reflecting the ability to reason well quickly when presented with novel tasks

many performances in life. As we will see toward the end of this chapter, we can use this framework to explain why in creative fields that depend on solving totally new problems, such as mathematics, people tend to do their best work earlier in life than in those in which high-quality work is more dependent on mastering a body of knowledge, such as history or philosophy. The theory explains why age is more of an enemy to the air traffic controller who must quickly analyze changing information (remember from Chapter 4 the industry ban on hiring people over age 30 to work in the control tower!) than to the CEO of the airline, who by his 50s has accumulated the years of experience to perform at his peak.

More recently, another expert in adult intelligence has expanded on the two-factor theory to explain why performance in many life activities remains stable or improves, despite physiological declines. According to Paul Baltes (1993), as we age, the **mechanics of intelligence** (our fluid abilities, or biologically based "hardware" promoting cognition) falls off, but this loss is compensated for by an increase in the **pragmatics of intelligence,** the "software" or knowledge we accumulate over the years. This gain in the pragmatics of intelligence not only makes up for fluid losses, it powerfully determines performance in the real world. Even with worse cognitive mechanics, Baltes believes, if their crystallized knowledge is extensive, older people can outperform the young.

Can experience, or the pragmatics of intelligence, make up for fluid losses? Marian Perlmutter and her coworkers decided to test Baltes's ideas by focusing on a profession in which we might think fast-paced fluid skills would be especially important: food serving. The researchers consulted experts such as restaurant owners and food critics about the qualities involved in being an excellent food server, constructed a scale measuring these qualities, and gave this test plus standard intelligence tests to people differing in age and years on the job. Older servers did do more poorly on the standard intelligence tests. However, with age and years of experience, scores on the test of "food-server intelligence" rose. So did performance. Older workers were better at what they did, serving more people during both busy and quiet times at work (Perlmutter, Kaplan, & Nyquist, 1990). As Baltes predicts, pragmatics can outweigh mechanics in life!

There is even a neurological basis to the idea that crystallized skills, or the pragmatics of intelligence, grow until late in life. Recall from Chapter 3 that as we age, we gradually lose neurons. However, in reaction to individual cells' being lost, the brain can automatically "sprout" new dendrites so that thinking is preserved—offering a remarkable physical parallel to Baltes's and Horn's idea that crystallized intelligence makes up for fluid declines. The analogy becomes more striking when we remember that at age 70 this compensation takes place, but by age 90 it has stopped, reflecting the decline in crystallized abilities that intelligence tests show takes place in advanced old age.

So by using the fluid/crystallized distinction many of the findings about intellectual change click into place. Still, we are left with nagging questions relating to the tests. When does performance on IQ tests really begin to decline? Is it in middle age or later, as the longitudinal studies show, or in our 20s, as in the cross-sectional research? Because people who volunteer for longitudinal studies tend to be a well-off fraction of the cohort, and, because of selective attrition, only the healthiest volunteers complete these studies, this research is certain to present an overly positive picture of

mechanics of intelligence
Biologically based fluid intellectual skills

pragmatics of intelligence
Experience-based crystallized intellectual skills

age-related losses. Cross-sectional studies, because they confuse cohort factors with genuine age changes, may be biased in the other direction—exaggerating the negative change.

Unraveling the Truth about Change: The Seattle Longitudinal Study

When psychologists thought carefully about what influences other than declining ability due to age might load the test-taking dice against older cohorts, one striking difference stood out: years of formal education. On average, older people have many fewer years of schooling than younger adults. These educational differences were especially great during the 1950s and 1960s, when psychologists were routinely finding that beginning in young adulthood, intelligence steadily declined.

We might imagine that lack of formal education would greatly affect older cohorts' performance on the verbal part of the WAIS, with its emphasis on school skills such as mathematics or vocabulary. A moment's thought suggests that fewer years in the classroom might also affect how well a person scores on the nonverbal scale. Having less experience in school, older cohorts might find any test stranger and more anxiety-provoking. In fact, because it involves such stressful and unusual activities, performance anxiety might even be greater for older people on the nonverbal part of the test.

ability-extraneous influences
Influences apart from intrinsic ability that affect performance on IQ tests

How much impact do **ability-extraneous influences,** such as differences in education, have in explaining age changes on intelligence tests? To answer this important question, during the late 1950s, a research team headed by K. Warner Schaie began a landmark study.

Seattle Longitudinal Study
Classic investigation conducted by Schaie to uncover the true effect of age on IQ

Schaie's **Seattle Longitudinal Study** is *the* central, defining study of intelligence and age. As we learned in Chapter 2, by following cohorts ranging in age from their 20s through their 70s, and by conducting a series of simultaneous longitudinal and cross-sectional comparisons between the groups, Schaie believed he could measure the contrasting biases of each type of research method and so isolate the true impact of age on IQ.

The researchers first selected groups of volunteers, participants in a health organization, 7 years apart in age, and compared their scores. Then, they followed each group longitudinally, testing them at 7-year intervals. At each of these testings, another cross-sectional sample was selected, some of whom were also followed over time (Schaie, 1988, 1990, 1996). Instead of using the WAIS to measure intelligence, Schaie decided to use a test called Thurstone's Primary Mental Abilities Scale (PMA). This scale measures five separate abilities that research suggested were primary or basic to intelligence (see Table 6-3).

In the early 1970s, when most psychologists felt certain that people lose intelligence beginning in their 20s, the publication describing the first 14 years of this study was a ray of light. Cohort factors did turn out to seriously bias cross-sectional studies. The idea that intelligence goes steadily downhill after youth was simply not true!

Schaie's recent analyses, from the fifth wave of this continuing study, offer a good overall picture of how performance on intelligence tests really changes as we grow old. On average, the Seattle study shows gains until the early 40s and stability until the mid-50s or 60s, depending on the test. After age 60, however, 7-year losses are statis-

1. **Verbal meaning**   Subject is asked to pick the synonym of a word
2. **Spatial relations**   Subject is asked to imagine how a figure would look if rotated in space
3. **Inductive reasoning**   Subject is asked to identify a pattern in a series of number or letters by picking the item that should go next in the series
4. **Number**   Subject is asked to add up a series of numbers
5. **Word fluency**   Subject is asked to write as many words as possible beginning with a certain letter

NOTE: The Seattle studies show performance on crystallized tests such as verbal meaning stays stable or rises until the 60s. Scores on tests measuring fluid skills such as inductive reasoning or spatial relations begin to decline by early midlife.
SOURCE: Schaie & Willis, 1993.

tically significant for all five PMA scales (Hertzog & Schaie, 1988; Schaie, 1996). In other words, if we have to generalize, intelligence—as measured by *traditional* tests—increases until midlife, then plateaus, then starts to decline in late middle age.

However, generalizing is hazardous, because different abilities show different patterns of change. As we might expect, the crystallized/fluid distinction is very useful in understanding which abilities "stand up" over time. Whereas scores on tests measuring speed-related fluid skills begin to decline on average by the early 30s, measures of crystallized skills such as verbal abilities remain stable until the 60s. In fact, on two nontimed vocabulary tests, Schaie's volunteers performed at their peak at age 67 (Schaie & Willis, 1993)!

When Schaie (1996) looked at the proportion of people at different ages who had declined on one or more tests over a previous 7-year period, he found more encouraging news. Although, as Figure 6-1 shows, by age 60, virtually everyone experienced a loss on one facet of intelligence, even among the oldest group; virtually no one declined significantly on all five primary abilities. Moreover, loss on most facets of intelligence (that is, three or four out of the five primary abilities) was never typical. Notice that even by the late 80s, only 50% of the volunteers had experienced this type of change.

As Schaie's research team began publishing their results, psychologists changed their thinking about intelligence and age. Today, most experts are careful to point out that intellectual change is multidirectional. Some abilities rise, and some decline. They emphasize the dramatic differences among people in stability and change. Rather than focusing on what generally happens, many have turned their attention to these individual differences. Why do some people seem to lose intelligence early on, whereas others stay alert and intellectually active until the limit of human life? What can keep intelligence fine-tuned? How much can intelligence be improved in later life? Although, as we will see later in this chapter, this multidimensional **contextual perspective on intelligence** has important critics, it dominates how researchers think about age and intelligence today.

contextual perspective on intelligence
Concept that intellectual change is multidirectional and individual-specific, and that, rather than making generalizations, we need to explore the conditions and contexts promoting intelligence in the older years

FIGURE 6-1

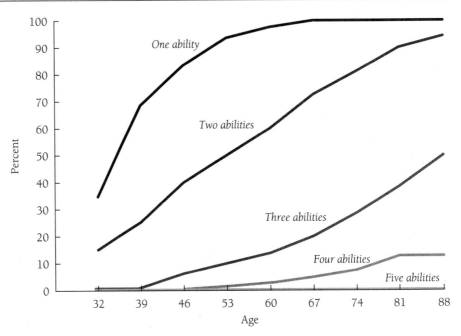

FIGURE 6-1   Cumulative Proportion, by Age, of Individuals Who Showed Significant Decline on One or More Primary Abilities in the Seattle Longitudinal Study

By about age 60, significant losses on one primary ability are practically universal (top line). However, even by age 88, virtually no one declines on all five facets of intelligence (bottom line).
SOURCE: Schaie, 1988.

Speed, Health, Mental Activity, Stability, and Decline

THE IMPACT OF SPEED   The first force that comes to mind in explaining the age-related IQ losses we typically observe on the WAIS and PMA was discussed in the "motor performance" section in Chapter 4: thinking speed. Remember that one of the most predictable generalizations we can make about older people is that they are slower. They are not able to mentally process information as quickly as before. How critical is this overall slowing in accounting for age-related changes in IQ?

According to Timothy Salthouse (1991), it is absolutely critical. Salthouse takes the position that if we cannot think quickly, by definition we cannot think well. Moreover, he argues, age-related slowness is the root cause of age-related IQ decline.

To test this processing-rate interpretation of intellectual change, Christopher Hertzog (1989) measured how rapidly people of various ages could copy correctly marked answers from the PMA booklet onto an answer sheet. He then examined how these copying speed scores correlated with subjects' performance on the various PMA tests. When variations in copying speed were controlled for, the large cross-sectional age declines on each timed PMA test were greatly attenuated. In other words, just as

Salthouse predicts, much of the loss researchers find with age on any fluid IQ test seems to be traceable to slower speed.

Although some slowness is inevitable or primary to growing old, remember from Chapter 4 that reaction times vary from person to person. Older people who are physically active and free from brain-impairing illnesses tend to be quicker than people who are sedentary and ill. This finding brings us to another force that looms large in explaining age changes in IQ and their variations from person to person: health.

THE IMPACT OF ILLNESS   The fact that health might be important in accounting for age-related IQ losses may have entered your mind just by looking at the information about overall change. Why does Schaie's research show that late middle age is the turning point, the time when overall losses first appear? Why does both this study and the WAIS research pinpoint advanced old age as the time of pronounced, accelerated decline? Perhaps the enemy is not just the advancing years, but illness. By late middle age, most people have at least one chronic condition. By the 80s, functional impairments become common (Baltes & Smith, 1997).

Our first hint that poor health might cause IQ losses actually came from one of the earliest studies of the aging process. Because the researchers' original goal was to examine primary aging (the aging process apart from disease) they tried to recruit a very healthy group of elderly men. During their evaluations, they found by accident that their subjects actually fell into two groups: one totally healthy, the other with minor signs of illness such as high blood pressure or beginning heart disease. When the groups were given an intelligence test similar to the WAIS, the totally healthy men outperformed the less-than-ideally healthy group on 10 of 11 subtests (Birren, Butler, Greenhouse, Sokoloff, & Yarrow, 1963).

Older people who report being in poor health and those with a wide range of chronic conditions consistently score lower than their healthier age mates on IQ tests (Field, Schaie, & Leino, 1988; Hultsch, Hammer, & Small, 1993; Perlmutter & Nyquist, 1990; Schaie, 1996). The Berlin Study of Aging, described in Chapter 4, provides dramatic testimony that our physical state is linked to the functioning of our mind. Remember from our earlier discussion how closely correlated sensorimotor capacities—vision, hearing, and the ability to stand and walk—were to scores on a fluid intelligence test (Lindenberger & Baltes, 1997). However, remember also that the Berlin researchers were studying people at the uppermost limits of life. It makes sense that by age 80 or 95, biology is cognitive destiny because in very old age so *many* body systems have broken down. To prove that being ill affects intelligence, we need to study people who are younger, preferably those with just one disease. In addition, to prove that illness causes intelligence to *decline,* we really need longitudinal studies (that is, research tracing how test scores change over the years after becoming ill). Once again, the remarkable Seattle Longitudinal Study gives us the evidence we need, at least for one important illness—heart disease.

We might expect heart disease to be a primary candidate to affect how we function intellectually at any age because poor cardiovascular function reduces the amount of blood getting to the brain. Because we already know that heart disease causes slower reaction times, we can be certain that this illness will affect performance on any fluid intelligence test (Earles & Salthouse, 1995). Actually, Schaie's research team found that men and women with heart disease lost points earlier than healthy volunteers on *all five* PMA abilities. Heart disease even predicted which older people would benefit from a training program to improve IQ.

As part of a series of studies demonstrating that coaching can improve performance on IQ tests, the researchers gave elderly people training in inductive reasoning, then examined their medical records for the previous 7 years. As they suspected, people who benefited most from the training had better medical histories, with fewer diseases and doctors visits; in particular, they were less likely to suffer from cardiovascular disease (Schaie, 1990).

If illness causes IQ scores to decline, could losses beyond what we might normally expect on intelligence tests be a "symptom" of approaching death? This interesting idea, called the **terminal drop hypothesis,** also has a long research history (S. Berg, 1996).

The fact that intelligence test losses could be a sign of approaching death was first discovered almost simultaneously in studies in Germany (Riegel & Riegel, 1972; Riegel, Riegel, & Meyer, 1967) and the United States (Jarvik & Falik, 1963) more than three decades ago. Then, in the late 1980s, Schaie's research team found that dips in normally more stable crystallized skills in later life were an ominous signal of impending death. Elderly people subsequently "lost" to the Seattle study because they died, it turned out, had had especially large declines on the crystallized PMA tests at the previous evaluation (Cooney, Schaie, & Willis, 1988).

In the late 1990s, separate studies, both from Sweden and both measuring cognitive change in the old-old, have added to the mounting evidence that terminal drop exists. In testing men and women in their late 80s three times over a 6-year period, Bo Johansson and Steven Zarit (1997) found that subjects who died before the final evaluation had previously experienced excessive cognitive losses. In following another group of Swedish men and women over age 75, Brent Small and Lars Bäckman (1997) discovered, just as Schaie's research team had a decade earlier, that losses in normally more stable verbal skills were an especially revealing sign of impending death. Perhaps because crystallized abilities should normally remain more stable, changes in this type of intelligence in particular seem to be a marker that something is going very wrong physically.

Our discussion in Chapter 3 of the different aging patterns puts this research into a larger framework. Recall that the Baltimore researchers found that a sudden decline in any normally stable physical function might be a sign of approaching death. So, just as we saw with the immune system, fading crystallized performance may be another indicator of problems—a deviation from a normally relatively steady function signaling a body breaking down. Terminal drop also explains why the classic aging pattern tends to break down in advanced old age. As we approach the biological limit of life, crystallized skills have to slope down too because *everyone* is within a few years of death.

People who are sick and close to death may "lose intelligence" for two reasons: (1) Their physical problems directly impair their thinking; and/or (2) when they take to bed, they lose interest in the world. This second possible reason brings us to the advice that is regularly dispensed to older people today: Keep mentally active.

THE IMPACT OF MENTAL STIMULATION   Elderly people who participate in mentally stimulating activities score comparatively higher on intelligence tests (Hultsch, Hammer, & Small, 1993). A more general atmosphere of environmental

terminal drop hypothesis
Theory that age loss on IQ tests above and beyond what normally should occur is a sign of impending death

1. When you are younger, work at a mentally stimulating job. Marry—and do not divorce—an intelligent, well-educated spouse.
2. As you age, stay physically healthy. In particular, try to avoid developing heart disease.
3. In later life, keep mentally stimulated; but choose activities appropriate to your capacities and pursuits compatible with your interests and abilities.
4. Throughout life, continue to learn and stay intellectually flexible. Be open to new ideas.
5. In very old age, try to preserve your functional capacities. Take care of your vision; keep as physically mobile as possible for as long as you can.

stimulation is linked to high intellectual performance too. Another correlate of staying intelligent as we age is having a long-lasting marriage to a highly educated spouse (Schaie, 1996).

However, because we gravitate to people who are like us, adults who choose mentally stimulating mates are almost certain to be intelligent to begin with. People who read, attend classes, or do crossword puzzles probably select these activities because they are already intelligent or intellectually interested. To demonstrate that mind-stretching activities are helpful in themselves, we need longitudinal research.

For the past 30 years, Carmi Schooler (1990) has been examining how intellectual flexibility, or our ability to approach problems from different perspectives, changes over the years as a function of having certain jobs. Schooler and his coworkers find that complex work, jobs that involve reasoning and thinking, lead to higher intellectual flexibility. Routine work, such as flipping hamburgers, causes intellectual flexibility to decline. The researchers have confirmed these findings for adults of every age in a variety of countries and even extended them to homemakers and children. The more complex our daily life, the more it requires thinking and reasoning, the more flexible intellectually we tend to be (see also De Frias, Schaie, & Willis, 1997).

The most interesting evidence supporting the advice to "keep mentally active" involves experiments in animals. We already know that the brain is able to repair itself and grow by sprouting dendrites. What impact does the environment have in promoting this neural growth? Marian Diamond (1988) has been exploring this question in a series of studies designed to reveal the physical effect on the brains of laboratory rats of being in a highly stimulating environment. Diamond typically puts animals in either a standard environment or an enriched environment (a large cage with other animals and a variety of "toys," such as mazes, wheels, and swings) and then compares the thickness of the cerebral cortex in each group after various periods of time.

In her earliest studies, Diamond found that young rats exposed to the enriched condition had thicker cortexes. Would she see the same effect among older rats? The answer is yes. Though the change is less dramatic and requires being in the stimulating environment much longer, older animals placed in an enriched environment also have thicker, heavier brains.

CONCLUSIONS, CAUTIONS, AND THE IMPORTANCE OF CONTINUITY   The message of this research (offered in summary form in Table 6-4) is that intelligence is plastic—much more environmentally responsive *throughout life* than many psychologists had believed. However, this does not mean we should rush out to become rocket scientists in the name of stimulating our brain. Recall that we must be cautious about generalizing from animal studies. What applies to laboratory rats may not fit human beings. Moreover, as Schooler (1990) points out, exposing ourselves to an environment that is *too* complex may produce anxiety and retreat, and so reduce our ability to deal flexibly with life. The concept of person/environment congruence seems relevant here: The environment must stretch our capacities but also fit who we are.

We need to take the same cautious approach to the studies showing that being ill impairs mental functioning. Although the saying "a sound mind in a sound body" may be accurate to a point, remember that we are describing test score *losses*. Except in extreme cases, such as when we are seriously ill and very old, our enduring abilities, who we are as people, are the most important predictors of how we will function intellectually as we age. As we will see later in this chapter, when we look at that important example of intelligence in action, creative achievements, continuity is the number one theme. People who are highly accomplished earlier in life tend to be creative and high functioning in their later years.

NEW CONCEPTIONS AND TESTS OF ADULT INTELLIGENCE

So far we have been focusing on traditional intelligence tests—exploring their results, the explanations for these results, and the forces affecting these results. Maybe we need to reconsider our basic framework. Are these tests really measuring intelligence in adult life?

The reason for using tests such as the WAIS or PMA is that they are believed valid: How a person performs on these abstract tasks reflects intelligent behavior in the real world. In the past few decades, however, this assumption has been challenged. The argument goes like this: All intelligence tests are constructed to measure behaviors, skills, and attributes deemed signs of intelligence in a particular time and place. There can be no absolutely universal intelligence test because different societies value different behaviors and put a premium on different skills. In a Zulu tribe, being intelligent might include being attuned to nature, being able to sense danger quickly, and being skilled at throwing a spear. In this society, where verbal or mathematical skills are irrelevant, we would be less than intelligent to use the verbal WAIS as our standard for intelligence.

Perhaps we are making the same error in our own society. Our intelligence tests were constructed to measure performance in a particular setting: school. Although they may be good measures of one important aspect of intelligence in childhood and adolescence, they may not apply as well to adulthood, when being intelligent involves making our way in the world (Schaie, 1977–1978, 1989).

IQ tests do their job well for children. They are a very good predictor of performance in school. However, beyond the point necessary to get into an occupation, scores on these tests are less good at discriminating real-world success. The best lawyers, or doctors, or racetrack handicappers (Ceci & Liker, 1986) do not necessarily score higher than other people in their occupation on standard IQ tests, implying that these measures are not measuring the range of skills involved in intelligence in life (Wagner & Sternberg, 1986).

Another fact that should give us pause is that the most responsible jobs in society are held by men and women in the second half of adult life. It is hard to reconcile even Schaie's positive findings of decline starting in the 50s with the fact that the people who run our country, head our corporations, and hold the most responsible positions in society are often at least that age *and beyond*. Although we can explain away the discrepancy between the way middle-aged and older people perform on standard IQ tests and the complexity of the jobs they have by invoking Baltes's assumption that crystallized gains override fluid declines, still what we are saying is the tests are misleading. They are not measuring the *mixture of skills* necessary to being intelligent in adult life.

These thoughts have led psychologists to take a new look at what it means to be an intelligent adult. What qualities are involved in real-world or **everyday intelligence?** Can we construct tests that capture the skills crucial to intelligent behavior in adult life?

everyday intelligence
In contrast to academic knowledge, being intelligent in daily life

Robert Sternberg's Tests of Practical Intelligence

One psychologist who has led this reexamination is Robert Sternberg. Sternberg's ideas have not only transformed how we generally think of intelligence, he has made important contributions to our understanding of creativity and, as we will see in Chapter 10, love. Here we will look at this creative psychologist's efforts to measure **practical intelligence** in adults.

practical intelligence
Being intelligent at negotiating and managing daily life, especially knowing the optimal way to advance in a career

Sternberg and Richard Wagner point out that the items in standard intelligence tests are well defined, are formulated by other people and have little intrinsic interest and only one correct response. Real-world challenges, they argue, have little in common with these artificial tasks. Making intelligent decisions at work and in life involves weighing alternatives, reacting to changing situations, and mastering problems that often do not have clear-cut right or wrong answers. It is no wonder that some people who are good at producing the right answers on an IQ test can fail badly at work and life (Wagner & Sternberg, 1986).

Sternberg and Wagner believe that the knowledge needed to function in the real world differs from the skills measured by IQ tests in another important way. Most often it is never directly taught. We are not formally instructed to choose the career that best fits our personality or told specifically what we have to do to climb the ladder of success at work. We must figure out this "tacit knowledge" for constructing a successful career and life on our own.

According to Sternberg and Wagner, tacit knowledge at work involves separate domains: knowledge at managing oneself, at managing coworkers, and at managing one's career. People who are skilled at managing themselves know how to maximize their own productivity. They understand what will make it easier to begin and continue working and how to approach tasks efficiently. People who shine in the second area have "people skills": They know how to relate to others, to motivate coworkers to do their best. People good at the third domain are attuned to the rules of their profession and sensitive to what exactly is needed to achieve success in their field.

Sternberg and Wagner's next step was to construct tests measuring each domain and to show that these measures could discriminate between people less or more successful in particular fields. The first profession they turned to was one they were familiar with: academic psychology. The second was a field that has been the subject of innumerable how-to books: succeeding as a business manager.

They devised scales of tacit knowledge for both professions and compared the performance of accomplished experts, less successful colleagues, and novices (college undergraduates). In each case, they succeeded. Managers of Fortune 500 companies outperformed business school students, who performed much better than undergraduates on the test of tacit knowledge in business. Scores on the tacit knowledge of psychology test were higher for academic psychologists than for graduate students and were able to distinguish people successful in this field. Quality of publications, rankings of scholarly achievement, and being a professor at a prestigious psychology department were all related to scoring high on the tacit knowledge in psychology scale. Most important, the tests predicted career success *better* than traditional IQ tests. For both professions, performance on the tacit knowledge scales was more related to job success than were scores on a standard intelligence test.

You might be thinking, with reason, that this attempt to devise tests of adult intelligence is *too* specific. Certainly it should be possible to devise measures that have wider applications than a single career. Moreover, Sternberg and Wagner's studies do not speak to the subject of this text, how we *change* as we age. This brings us to Nancy Denney's broader, developmental approach.

Nancy Denney's Unexercised and Exercised Abilities

Unlike Sternberg, Nancy Denney's specialty is adult development, so her main interest has been in examining how people change with age. She has constructed tests that measure everyday intelligence in a more general way. Denney's strategy is to devise problems that people might encounter in daily life, ask adults of different ages to provide solutions, then score these answers for effectiveness. Here is a sample item:

> Let's say that one evening you go to the refrigerator to get something cold to drink. When you open the refrigerator, you notice that it is not cold but rather warm. What would you do?

In Denney's first study, performance on these problems improved until midlife and then declined. Could she make up a test on which younger or older people performed best? To explore this possibility, Denney and her colleagues hit on the idea of devising tests focusing on issues that might crop up at specific ages. They reasoned that young adults should perform best on tests constructed to apply to problems they might encounter. On tests with problems relating to later life, such as retirement, the elderly should perform better than anyone else.

Scores on the young adult test fulfilled their predictions, reaching a peak in youth and declining at older ages. Unfortunately, on the older adult test, middle-aged people still outperformed the elderly. In fact, despite several efforts, on *no* test Denney has designed have older adults done best (Denney, 1989).

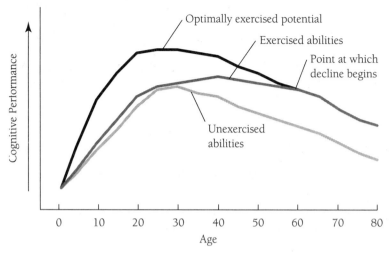

Denney theorizes that unexercised skills peak in the early 20s and then decline, but exercised abilities improve or stay constant through midlife. Once exercised abilities meet one's optimum potential, even performance on these well-practiced activities gradually declines.
SOURCE: Denney, 1989.

I must emphasize that other researchers have had better success at making up tests where the pattern is better performance in later life (Cornelius & Caspi, 1987). Still, Denney was not really alarmed by her findings because they fit in perfectly with her **theory of exercised and unexercised abilities.**

Denney's theory offers a framework for understanding why performance on some activities is best when we are young, other skills are at their peak in midlife, but performance, even on skills people work hard on, often declines before age 65. Central to Denney's thinking is the distinction between abilities we exercise and those we don't exercise, as well as our biological ceiling—the limit we are capable of when our abilities are "optimally exercised."

The bottom curve in Figure 6-2 shows unexercised abilities, or how we perform on an activity that we *never* practice at different ages. Optimally exercised potential, the upper curve, shows how well we *could* perform that activity at our maximum, our limit of reserve capacity, at various ages. Notice that although the two curves greatly differ in height, each has the same slope, reaching its peak at about age 30 and then declining.

Exercised abilities—skills we practice—are shown in the middle curve. Denney reasons that performance on these abilities lies somewhere between our biological

theory of exercised and unexercised abilities
Denney's theory charting the age path of abilities that are practiced during adult life versus those that are not

potential and the lower, unexercised curve. But notice how different the path of this curve is. Because we improve as we practice, performance on continually exercised abilities remains stable or rises over the years, until a certain point. When this curve intersects with the curve for optimal potential, even the most highly practiced ability must slowly wend its way down over time.

Let's illustrate with the interview at the beginning of this chapter. When Jean entered college for the first time, her school skills may have been close to the level of unexercised abilities. With her many educational experiences over the years, she may have been pleased to see her performance improve as it floated closer to her biological optimum. However, because at the same time that optimum is falling, at some point she will hit her biological ceiling (the curves will intersect). Then, no matter how much she continues to practice, her performance will decline. We cannot perform *above* the limit of our reserve capacity.

Denney's theory offers an interesting perspective on the impact of practice on performance at different ages. However, notice that she agrees with the traditional idea that youth is basically our intellectual peak. The psychologists we turn to now disagree with this assumption. In fact, their whole framework for understanding adult intelligence is different: As we mature, our *style,* or manner of approaching problems, totally changes.

A Neo-Piagetian Perspective on Adult Intelligence

neo-Piagetian perspective on adult intelligence
Theory that extends to adult life Piaget's stage approach to intellectual development

The **neo-Piagetian perspective on adult intelligence** grew out of the speculations of philosophers, personality psychologists, and creativity researchers as to what really constitutes mature adult thought. These ideas and findings were synthesized by psychologists specializing in adult cognition to offer a new alternative to thinking about how intelligence develops.

In contrast to the traditional psychometric approach, in which people are ranked as either having more or less of a fixed quantity called intelligence, the basis of this theory is Jean Piaget's idea that as children develop, they go through four different stages of understanding the world. Just as Piaget believed that the child's thinking in each stage is different in form, or qualitatively new, neo-Piagetians believe that adult cognition involves a different way of understanding the world. Piaget believed that the pinnacle of intellectual development occurs in adolescence, with the highly abstract scientific thinking he called formal operations. Neo-Piagetians believe there is a stage after formal operations, called **postformal thought** (Labouvie-Vief, 1992; Rybash, Hoyer, & Roodin, 1986; Sinnott, 1989, 1991).

postformal thought
Type of adult cognition that transcends the highly logical thinking characteristic of formal operations

1. **Postformal thinking is relativistic.** Adolescents in formal operations believe that everything has an answer. They think that by logic we can determine absolute rights and wrongs. As we grow older and have more experience with life, we give up these beliefs. We know that many real-world problems have no clear-cut answers. Making intelligent life decisions means understanding the relativity of all decision making. Postformal thinkers accept conflicting opinions and explore the multiple perspectives from which issues can be seen. They embrace the ambiguities of life.

This awareness of relativity does not mean that postformal thinkers avoid making decisions or having strong beliefs. The ability to *integrate* multiple perspectives is the hallmark of postformal thinking, as wise decisions come from being open to the complexity of life.

2. **Postformal thinking is interpersonal and feeling-oriented.** Adolescents in formal operations believe that by rational analysis they can understand the world. Postformal thinkers go beyond logic to think in a different mode. With the realization that no objective right answer exists, feelings, intuitions, and personal experiences become the basis for making decisions. Postformal thinkers are skilled at empathizing with others and being "in touch" with their inner life.

3. **Postformal thinkers are interested in developing questions and seeing new perspectives rather than finding solutions.** Formal thinkers want to get the "right" answers, have closure, finish or solve tasks. Postformal thinkers are less focused on solutions. They enjoy the process of developing new questions, exploring new perspectives, seeing new frameworks, coming up with different ways of looking at the world.

As we might imagine, testing for this type of thinking (so beautifully described in Aging in Action 6-1) requires a new strategy. Rather than using single-answer tests, researchers measure the *way* a person arrives at answers—the process of decision making itself. Everyday dilemmas are the format. However, unlike in Denney's studies, when given these problems people are asked to describe their thinking in writing or aloud. Do people look at problems from different vantage points? Do they consider the feelings of others in arriving at decisions? Do they understand the subjective nature of their conclusions? Do they refer to their own feelings for guidelines as to what is right? That is how responses to this type of problem are scored.

John is known to be a heavy drinker, especially when he goes to parties. Mary, John's wife, warns him that if he gets drunk one more time, she will leave him. John goes to an office party and comes home drunk. Does Mary leave him? How sure are you of your answer?

According to the theory, adolescents should respond to this dilemma in a logical way. "Mary said she would leave, so of course she should. Yes, I am sure I am right." Older people should weigh the consequences of leaving—for Mary, for John, for the children. They should state that there are no absolute answers. They should realize it is "a judgment call."

On tests of this type, middle-aged and older people typically use more postformal thinking than adolescents. Other research, too, suggests that our sensitivity to feelings grows more intense with age. In exploring age differences in memory for different materials, Laura Carstensen and Susan Turk-Charles (1994) found that older people remembered emotional messages especially well, suggesting that older adults may focus more on the interpersonal dimension of life.

Do these findings mean that postformal thought is a genuine *stage of development*? The answer seems to be no. To qualify as a genuine age-linked stage, postformal thinking would need to satisfy certain criteria: People should progress in sequence, first entering formal operations and then, at a certain age, leaving this stage and entering postformal thought. Once capable of postformal thought, they should not shift back or "regress." They should think only in this stage. Furthermore, if it is really an

6-1 *Postformal Thought in Action*

A wonderful example of postformal thought comes from anthropologist Barbara Myerhoff's description of 93-year-old Jacob, the leader at a senior citizens' center in Southern California serving elderly Jewish immigrants. Like most center members, Jacob immigrated to America in the early 1900s. After retiring, he began a new career helping elderly Jews, giving of himself—as he had throughout his life—to his community.

Looking now at Jacob's life to identify some of the specific features that account for his success, it is at once clear that luck contributed a fair share. Jacob was naturally favored with great energy, good health, intelligence and talent. In addition to these fortunate personal endowments, he was lucky in his successful marriage that produced four healthy, intelligent sons. Jacob had his share of bad luck, too. He had been a political refugee, was jailed, struggled through the major upheaval of immigration, had to learn new occupations and to relocate many times, was cheated out of business by his partner, went bankrupt, made and lost money again and again. Through all his reverses and mistakes, he had no regrets, and he rebounded with more perspective and energy from each setback.

Jacob's autobiographical writings document his active struggle at every stage of his checkered career to integrate conflicting pulls between family obligation and worldly success, and between worldly success and social-political ideals. He struggled also with the contradictions between his internationalist beliefs and his nationalism, in the form of Zionism and American patriotism. And he managed to embrace contradictions generated by his agnostic, even antireligious attitudes, on the one hand, and fervent identification with cultural-ethical Judaism, on the other.

These conflicts, it must be stressed, Jacob integrated. He did not simply resolve and dismiss them—for indeed the contradictions are real. The one who chooses to remain alive to the intrinsic worth of all of these opposing beliefs must continually re-negotiate their alliance. Jacob was able to tolerate ambiguity, and perhaps this trait was a critical contributor to his successful old age. . . .

Jacob's conceptions about and approach to aging were complex and dynamic. He knew how to intensify the present, how to deepen his satisfaction in small rewards and pleasures, how to bring the past into his life for the continuity that gave it intrinsic meaning; yet he never remained fixed on the past nor used it as a negative standard in terms of which to view the present. He knew how to look at the inevitable destiny the future held and accept it without moving toward it with unnecessary speed. Too, Jacob could provide new standards and desires for himself as the old ones became unattainable, generating from within appropriate measures of accomplishment and worth in a continual process of discarding and creating.

SOURCE:Myerhoff, 1978.

age-dependent stage, young people should be incapable of postformal thinking, whereas most (ideally all) middle-aged and elderly adults should think in this way.

None of these conditions holds true. Individuals vary in the extent to which they use postformal thinking at any age. Many young adults can reason in this way; many elderly do not (Labouvie-Vief, Hakim-Larson, & Hobart, 1987). Worse yet, postformal thinkers do not just stay in this stage. With problems that have a correct solution, people use formal reasoning. Only when problems are not well structured, without clear answers, do they adopt a postformal mode (Sinnott, 1989). These findings suggest that, rather than being a genuine stage of development, postformal thinking might more usefully be seen as a skill that some adults have and can draw on as needed in handling life.

Concluding Questions and Criticisms

By now you may have noticed that although these new approaches capture qualities that most of us feel are crucial to intelligence in life, no theory or measure of adult intelligence is totally satisfying. Even the effort to develop these new tests is not universally embraced. Some thoughtful critics believe it is a wrong path (Salthouse, 1991).

Psychologists worry whether, as we saw with Sternberg's scales, tests based in real life will be too situation-specific to be really useful (Scribner, 1986); or if they will be *more* discriminatory, biased in favor of people with certain types of knowledge (Denney, 1989). As you may have noticed in our discussion of postformal thought, tests of life intelligence may be subjective, value-laden, and dependent on the evaluator's own personal idea of what constitutes ideal behavior. Furthermore, measures of everyday intelligence (at least of the type Denney and Sternberg propose) may not even provide information very different from that of traditional psychometric tests. Notice that performance on Denney's tests shows the same pattern as the Seattle research: Scores reach their peak in midlife, then decline. In fact, in exploring how competence in instrumental activities of daily living, such as preparing meals or reading a bus schedule, related to performance on traditional intelligence tests, Sherry Willis (1996) found that older adults' abilities on these everyday tasks were highly correlated with their scores on standard cognitive tests. Should we rush to give up traditional psychometric tests as our main benchmark of intelligence in adulthood and later life? Clearly, the data are not in.

INTELLIGENCE IN ACTION

Now that we have explored how the global entity called intelligence changes as we age (and how difficult it can be to define this central quality), we turn to explore two more specific intellectual skills. First, we look at a type of intelligence we expect to grow with age: wisdom. Then, we examine another highly prized example of intelligence in action: creative work.

Wisdom

The best-thought-out effort to examine wisdom comes, once again, from those innovative life span psychologists, Paul Baltes's research team. In a systematic research

TABLE 6-5	*Two Life Review Problems Used in Measuring Wise Responding*

Young Target

Martha, a young woman, has decided to have a family and not to have a career. She is married and has children. One day, Martha meets a woman friend whom she has not seen for a long time. The friend has decided to have a career and no family. She is about to establish herself in her career.

Old Target

Martha, an elderly woman, had decided to have a family and not to have a career. Her children left home some years ago. One day, Martha meets a woman friend whom she has not seen for a long time. The friend had decided to have a career and no family. She retired some years ago.

> This meeting causes Martha to think back over her life. What might her life review look life?
> Which aspects of her life might she remember?
> How might she explain her life?
> How might she evaluate her life retrospectively?

In this study, a group of older people and young adults were given either the young or elderly Martha vignette and asked to think aloud into a tape recorder. Raters then judged the quality of each subject's responses according to the five wisdom-related criteria.

SOURCE: Staudinger, Smith, & Baltes, 1992.

program, Baltes and his colleagues set out to capture and explore wisdom in depth. As we might imagine, the researchers couch their explorations in Baltes's mechanics-and-pragmatics framework: People who are wise are skilled in the fundamental pragmatics of life.

First, the researchers had to operationalize, or translate, the vague entity called wisdom into concrete characteristics or skills. They came up with five dimensions of **wisdom-related expertise:** People who are wise (1) have rich factual knowledge about life; (2) they have procedural knowledge, an understanding of *how* to implement decisions—when to take action, give advice, evaluate, monitor, and follow up on plans; (3) they possess life span contextualism—a sense of the evolving quality of human relationships and the shifting historical and social environment within which behavior occurs; (4) they are sensitive to the competing perspectives of others and the relative nature of values and goals; and (5) they appreciate life's unpredictability and have backup plans for coping when the inevitable unexpected event occurs (Baltes, Smith, & Staudinger, 1992).

Armed with these criteria, the researchers then needed to devise situations in which older and young adults could demonstrate these qualities or skills. They decided on the technique used in the research designed to reveal postformal thought: Present people with scenarios describing life problems, have them think aloud, and train raters to score these taped protocols. In this case, subjects' responses were rated along each dimension according to a scale ranging from 1 (poor) to 7 (ideally wise). As the

wisdom-related expertise
Baltes's five dimensions measuring skill in the pragmatics of living

examples in Table 6-5 show, older and young adult groups were presented with either a scenario relating to their own life stage or one relating to a similar person at the alternate time of life.

As the researchers expected—under the assumption that wisdom is a rare quality at any age—on average, subjects performed at a low/middle level (about 3) on the tasks. Very few people produced responses at the wise end of the scale (5 or above). Interestingly, people of each age scored somewhat higher if the scenario related to their own time of life. Young adults did better on the vignette describing the younger person; older people performed better when the target person was a 60-year-old. Once again, however, as with postformal thinking, wise responding was more a property of the person than of advancing age. The handful of subjects classified as wise were approximately equally distributed between young and old adults (Baltes & Staudinger, 1993).

If chronological age is not sufficient for wisdom, reasoned the researchers, perhaps experience in activities demanding wisdom-type thinking might produce this expertise. Specifically, if wisdom is a skill involving practice, when a person's life work involves analyzing human relationships, shouldn't wisdom-related knowledge be comparatively high? To explore this possibility, in their next study, the research team compared the performance of a sample of clinical psychologists on their test with that of people in comparable professions (J. Smith, Staudinger, & Baltes, 1994; Staudinger, Smith, & Baltes, 1992).

As predicted, the clinical psychologists scored higher than people whose work did not involve expertise in human relationships. However, their mean wisdom score was still in the average range. Although the numbers favored the older clinical psychologists (4 out of 8 older versus 3 out of 9 young clinicians had total scores qualifying them as wise), even being older *and* in an occupation demanding wisdom was no guarantee of showing a high level of competence in this important area of life.

What qualities converge to produce that rare group, the few adults of *any* age we classify as wise? To answer this question, the researchers gave men and women of various ages the wisdom scenarios and explored how their performance correlated with scores on different measures of personality and cognition (Staudinger, Lopez, & Baltes, 1997). As we might expect, wisdom is somewhat related to cognitive abilities, particularly measures of the pragmatics of intelligence such as vocabulary. Wisdom is more closely associated with certain personality traits. Wise people rank high on a quality called psychological mindedness (being sensitive to one's own and others' feelings) and on openness to experience (being open to exploring different things). Surprisingly, wisdom is equally strongly related to the quality we turn to now: creativity.

Creative Achievements

Ben Franklin invented the bifocal lens when he was 78. The American architect Frank Lloyd Wright completed his greatest masterpiece, the Guggenheim Museum in New York, at age 91. Tolstoy and Picasso are other celebrated examples of geniuses who stayed productive until advanced old age. Yet we often think of age as the enemy of creative work. Older artists complain about the premium put on finding young talent, the fact that few galleries will look at paintings of older artists. In "creative" fields such as advertising, more than other professions, being over 40 is a severe detriment to getting hired. In the sciences and the arts, the general assumption is that most creative breakthroughs happen when people are young.

The reason is that we link creativity with being rebellious, taking risks, adopting new perspectives, and looking at the world in fresh ways—all personality traits and fluid skills that we normally associate with youth. However, to produce high-quality work, doesn't a person need to spend years practicing, perfecting, and refining a craft (Abra, 1989; Simonton, 1997)? Doesn't being *successfully* creative depend on extensive crystallized knowledge, a postformal worldview, and the practical understanding of *how* to be successful measured by Sternberg's scales?

Jacob Rabinow, an elderly inventor who holds more than 200 patents in diverse fields, suggests what it takes to be an original thinker:

> First you have to have a tremendous amount of information—a big database if you like to be fancy. . . . and you do those things which are easy and you don't do those things which are hard, so you get better and better by doing the things you do well . . . and the more you do, the easier it gets . . . and eventually you become very one-sided, but you're very good at it and lousy at everything else. . . . So the small differences at the beginning of life become enormous differences by the time you've done it for 40, 50, 80 years. . . . And then you must have the ability to get rid of the trash which you think of. You cannot think of only good ideas, or write only good music. You must think of a lot of music, a lot of ideas, a lot of poetry. . . . And if you're good you must be able to throw away the junk immediately . . . because you are well-trained and you say, "That's junk." (Csikszentmihalyi, 1996)

Based on the testimony of this expert, creativity should be an age-friendly art, increasing as the years pass. Is Rabinow correct, or does the stereotype that creative abilities erode with age hold?

For answers, we turn to psychologist Dean Simonton's (1989, 1991, 1997) research charting the work of world-class geniuses at different times in their lives. In exploring performance among writers, Simonton finds that the age/creativity relationship varies with the specific literary form. Poets do their best work when youngest, in their late 30s. The peak age for producing fiction is somewhat older, the early 40s. Nonfiction peaks last, at age 50 (Simonton, 1975).

Viewed in terms of fluid and crystallized abilities, these findings make sense. Poets play with language, using words in unexpected ways; in this type of writing, fluid skills seem especially important. Writing a book depends on knowledge, discipline, and years spent perfecting a craft. Writing nonfiction, in particular a scholarly work, depends on having mastered a body of knowledge over a long period of time (Simonton, 1997).

Other research confirms that we can estimate the peak creative age based on the mix of "knowledge" versus "newness" in a given field. Wayne Dennis (1966), for instance, found that dancers tended to reach their peak in their early 30s, but historians and scholars did not reach their creative prime until their 60s.

In these studies of famous people, however, the typical pattern is remarkably similar to Schaie's findings with IQ. Often, as Figure 6-3 shows, people reach their creative peak during their 40s (Simonton, 1997). In examining more average scientists, Stephen Cole (1979) discovered the same pattern. Productivity reaches its peak in the early 40s, levels off until about age 50, and then drops off slowly after that.

This research, however, does not address the issue of most interest to a creative young adult. That person wants to know, "If I, personally, am unusually accomplished today, how likely am *I* to change?" Answering this question requires a longitudinal approach.

In a follow-up to his study of scientists, Cole selected mathematicians who had gotten their PhDs between 1947 and 1950 and traced their careers over the next quarter century, classifying his sample as strong publishers, weak publishers, or non-publishers based on their publications during one five-year period. Then, he looked at whether people maintained the same ranking during other periods. Rarely did a person shift significantly; almost half never changed ranks at all. In a similar study of 1000 academic psychologists, researchers also found that stability was the dominant theme. Although productivity did reach a peak during the 40s, how much a person published was more a function of that individual's enduring characteristics than of being at a certain life stage. People who started out as high publishers continued to be prolific; at 55 to 64, they produced more papers than their less productive contemporaries did at their peak (Horner, Rushton, & Vernon, 1986).

Simonton's elegant research comparing world-class achievers in the sciences with their less accomplished contemporaries offers dramatic testimony that who we are, not what age we are, is the driving force behind creativity. Notice from Figure 6-3 that creative productivity does follow the same age path for everyone, peaking at age 40 or at 50 depending on the time in life when people start producing their creative work. However, world-class figures start out much more prolific. They continue to outshine their peers of *any* age, even in their later years. As we saw with the elderly athletes (see Aging in Action 3-1), with creativity, continuity is a number one theme. Once we start producing creative work, the best key to who we will be creatively lies in our creativity right now.

These insights come from quantitative research—studies statistically charting the number of creative works produced at given ages. Powerful information can also be derived from qualitative research—in-depth interviews with creative adults. When Mihaly Csikszentmihalyi (1996) interviewed a wide range of people over age 60 famous for their innovative work, he came up with compelling insights into the forces fostering creativity at any age.

Csikszentmihalyi believes that, as with intelligence, understanding exceptional creativity requires a contextual approach. Being creative depends on inborn qualities such as talent and drive. Equally important, however, is the outer world. A surprising number of people credited their success to luck—being in the right place at the right time. Csikszentmihalyi believes we should not dismiss these comments as excessively modest. They are accurate assessments of what is needed to achieve. A prominent female physicist enters the sciences at a time when her field is receptive to women, her specialty is expanding, and people are open to her ideas. A famous artist finds his ultra realistic style is just right for the time or, quite by accident, meets an influential gallery owner who loves his work. In other words, Csikszentmihalyi's findings echo the message I conveyed in discussing behavioral genetic research (see Chapter 2): No matter

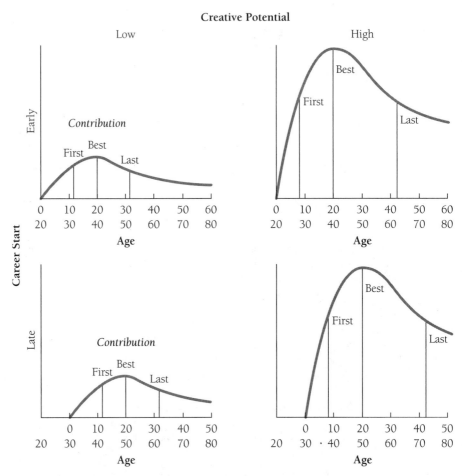

In determining creativity, who we are far outweighs how old we are. Notice that although creative potential follows an identical age pattern for everyone, depending on whether they start their career early or relatively late, the most accomplished people in a given area are always far more creative—outshining everyone else at every time of life.
SOURCE: Simonton, 1997.

how genetically determined the ability, its expression is totally dependent on the environment we are exposed to in the course of life.

Apart from this optimal genetic/environment fit, it was difficult to generalize. Some highly creative people had unhappy childhoods; others were blessed with a

Sigmund Freud (1856–1939) rocked the world in 1900, when at age 44 he published his first major work, The Interpretation of Dreams. *Until his death in advanced old age, Freud continued to put forth masterpieces at an astonishing and steady pace. Freud's work during his "elderly years" shows how true genius may stand undiminished in the face of age.*

loving family life. Some grew up in poverty; others had servants attending to every need. Some showed signs of what was to come quite early; others were indifferent students whose abilities did not emerge until later on. But there were a few traits that made these people special, that set them apart. Exceptionally creative people have a passionate interest in their area of expertise. They have a passion for learning, for improving and expanding themselves. These passions do not dry up after youth; they are as powerful as ever in later life. Seventy-year-old poet Anthony Hecht reflects:

> I probably am a little more trustful in unconscious instincts [today] than I was before. I'm not as rigid as I was. And I can feel this in the quality and texture of the poems themselves. They are freer metrically, they are freer in general design. The earliest poems that I wrote were almost rigid in their eagerness not to make any errors. I'm less worried than that now. (p. 215)

Historian C. Van Woodward, in his 80s, comments:

> Well, [today] I have . . . changed my mind and the reasons and conclusions about what I have written. For example, that book on Jim Crow—I have done four editions of it and I am thinking of doing a fifth, and each time it changes. And they come largely from criticisms that I have received. I think the worst mistake you could make as a historian is to be indifferent or contemptuous of what is new. You learn that there is nothing permanent in history. It's always changing. (p. 216)

Actor Edward Asner, now in his 60s, says his goal is

> demonstrating that that my acting ability is better than it's ever been, doing it across the board, doing it however and whichever way I can, in as many ways as I can—radio, commercials, voice-overs, narrations for documentaries . . . TV, films. . . . It doesn't matter. I thirst to . . . burst at the seams, eager for the chase. (p. 220)

These testimonials are a fitting finale to our research tour. Quantitative studies such as Schaie's must be our basis for understanding the aging process and older adults. It is essential to measure statistically what changes intellectually (and in every other way) as we age. However, we must also remember that, despite the negative generalizations, the highest intellectual achievements can occur at every age.

INTERVENTIONS

Now we conclude by returning to the studies themselves. Is it possible to stave off the IQ losses that often *do* accompany our older years? Through training, can we even enhance that rare quality, wisdom?

Improving Performance on IQ Tests

The Adult Development and Training and Enrichment Project (ADEPT), a systematic program begun by Schaie and his colleagues during the late 1970s, was designed to demonstrate that age-related IQ changes could be reversed. The ADEPT researchers specifically targeted fluid abilities—the more biologically based aspect of cognition—to demonstrate that, in their words, "old dogs can learn new tricks" (Willis, 1989).

cognitive remediation
Training intervention designed to ameliorate or reverse age-related IQ losses

These **cognitive remediation** studies have proved their point. Study after study has shown that training in inductive reasoning or spatial relations improves performance on these fluid tests. The impact of this training is not just immediate. When a person is reminded to use the strategy, gains can be seen even at a long-term follow-up (Hayslip, Maloy, & Kohl, 1995). There also is some very narrow transfer: After being trained on one measure, a person's scores on other tests of the same fluid ability improve (Schaie, 1996).

Training can even wipe out inroads in performance suffered earlier on. In the Seattle sample, after training, most older people who had lost points improved to where they had been 14 years before. Those who had been relatively stable performed at a higher level than in middle age (Willis & Schaie, 1986; Willis, 1989).

However, there are qualifications. As I just implied, transfer is narrow, with improvement mainly limited to that specific ability or skill (Baltes, Sowarka, & Kliegl, 1989). Moreover, although some gains do persist after training, people need periodic booster sessions to maintain their skills (Schaie, 1996; see Figure 6-5). This has led critics to question whether these older people have really become "more intelligent," or have merely been taught a set of intelligence-test-taking skills (Salthouse, 1991).

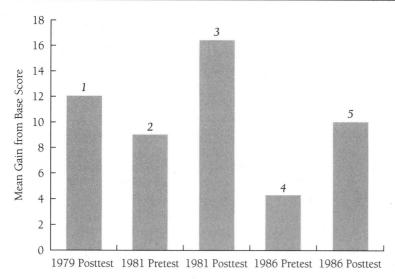

FIGURE 6-5

Mean Change from Baseline Score on Figural Relations for Older Adults (mean age 69, in 1979) after Three Training Sessions over a 7-Year Period

ADEPT results suggest that training can dramatically improve performance on this fluid ability and that some gains do persist over time (see 2 and 4). However, as this elderly group advanced to their mid-70s, the impact of training was not as great (see 5).
SOURCE: Willis & Nesselroade, 1990.

The extent to which people profit from cognitive remediation varies widely (Willis, 1989). Some older people do very well after training; others do not improve. Moreover, whereas the ADEPT researchers have specifically avoided comparing old and young people, other researchers find that young adults benefit as much as or more than the elderly from training to improve IQ (Salthouse, 1991).

In other words, there is a limit to plasticity—an upper boundary beyond which people cannot go. Furthermore, the ceiling for optimum performance seems lower in the old. As Nancy Denney suggests in her theory, and Marian Diamond's studies of neural growth seem to confirm, cognitively as well as physically, older people have a lower reserve capacity than the young.

Baltes's research team advocates an approach called testing the limits to pinpoint that upper boundary. What is the limit of reserve capacity, the ceiling beyond which people cannot go after being trained? Here individual differences in improvement are crucial. In fact, they can be used in a diagnostic way. In one study, Baltes and his colleagues demonstrated that *not* improving after training might be an early marker for Alzheimer's disease (M. M. Baltes, Kuhl, & Sowarka, 1992).

Now that we are confident that, with qualifications, older people can learn new IQ tricks, we turn to an infant effort, also by Baltes's research team, to see if wisdom can be enhanced.

Enhancing Wisdom

The next step for Baltes's team in their evolving exploration was to see if wisdom could be taught. But, in contrast to teaching inductive reasoning or spatial relations, the right approach to teaching wisdom is far from clear. How might this elusive skill be increased?

The researchers reasoned that the main way we become wise is through being exposed to different perspectives and points of view. When we reason things out with another person, or even imagine hashing problems out with someone we respect, our thinking changes. We come to ponder issues in a richer, deeper way. This line of thinking led to an intervention called interactive minds (Staudinger & Baltes, 1996).

First, the researchers gave subjects the wisdom scenarios and measured their scores. Then, they were assigned to one of five groups: two wisdom-promoting inter-active-minds interventions and three control conditions. In one interactive-minds condition, people were paired with a partner and asked to discuss the life task; then, they retreated to another room and were instructed to think through the problem alone. In the second, subjects were told to talk through the issue in fantasy with someone whose ideas they respected and to imagine how that person would respond. In the three control conditions, people were asked to think through the problem silently, or they discussed the problem with someone else but were given no time to reflect, or they received no special instructions.

As predicted, subjects exposed to the interactive-minds treatments improved on the subsequent wisdom task. Interestingly, bouncing ideas off an imaginary person turned out to be as powerful at enhancing wisdom as actually having a partner there. Finally, and perhaps most interesting, although everyone benefited from the interventions, older people exposed to the dialogue with another person improved *more* than the younger adults. So, not only can old dogs learn new tricks, but there are some "tricks" that old dogs may learn even better than the young!

KEY TERMS

ability-extraneous influences
classic aging pattern
cognitive remediation
contextual perspective on
   intelligence
crystallized intelligence
everyday intelligence
fluid intelligence

mechanics of intelligence
neo-Piagetian perspective on adult
   intelligence
postformal thought
practical intelligence
pragmatics of intelligence
Seattle Longitudinal Study
terminal drop hypothesis

theory of exercised and
   unexercised abilities
traditional psychometric
   intelligence test
Wechsler Intelligence Scale for
   Adults (WAIS)
wisdom-related expertise

Csikszentmihalyi, M. (1996). *Creativity: Flow and the psychology of discovery and invention*. New York: HarperCollins.

This fascinating book, which explores creativity in 90 eminent older adults, is highly recommended.

Diamond, M. (1988). *Enriching heredity*. New York: Basic Books.

Diamond offers compelling evidence for the importance of a stimulating environment in fostering mental growth.

Poon, L. W., Rubin, D. C., & Wilson, B. A. (Eds.). (1989). *Everyday cognition in adulthood and late life*. New York: Cambridge University Press.

This edited book describes a variety of new approaches to measuring memory and intelligence in adult life. In one chapter, Denney summarizes her research. In another, Sherry Willis describes the cognitive remediation research.

Rybash, J. N., Hoyer, W. J., & Roodin, P. (1986). *Adult cognition and aging: Developmental changes in processing, knowing, and thinking*. New York: Pergamon Press.

Although this book is somewhat dated, it offers an excellent description of postformal thought.

Salthouse, T. A. (1991). *Theoretical perspectives on cognitive aging*. Hillsdale, NJ: Erlbaum.

This book is only for the aspiring cognitive psychologist but very interesting. Salthouse punches holes in many of the new approaches to intelligence described in this chapter. The message: People do decline dramatically in cognition.

Schaie, K. W. (1996). Intellectual development in adulthood. In J. Birren & K. W. Schaie (Eds.), *Handbook of the psychology of aging* (4th ed) (pp. 266–286). San Diego: Academic Press.

This chapter offers a description and update of the Seattle studies and others.

Sternberg, R. J., & Wagner, R. K. (Eds.). (1986). *Practical intelligence: Origins of competence in the everyday world*. New York: Cambridge University Press.

This edited book describes a variety of creative studies examining life intelligence.

Chapter Outline

7

Memory and Dementia

As I drove to my husband's office for lunch, says Diana Freil McGowen (1993), in a compelling autobiographical account of Alzheimer's disease, *I noticed a shopping center, new to me. It was strange I had not noticed this mall . . . I traveled this route frequently. . . . Near the driveway leading to [the] office, I observed a fire station which was also new to me. . . . "Jack . . . I'm glad to see that new fire station near your entrance." "Diane, that station has always been here," he chided. . . . I started the car and began to pull away. I braked, . . . Where was the exit?*

"Jack," I asked shakily, "how do I get out of here? . . . Just tell me how to get out of this place." Jack . . . pointed straight ahead. . . . I drove from the parking lot. Suddenly . . . nothing was familiar. . . . I drove on with tears . . . streaming down my face. Unfamiliar music blared from the radio. I was hopelessly lost and had no idea how to get home. . . . Suddenly, I saw a sign, "Turkey Lake Park." . . . I turned into the entrance . . . and pulled off the road. My body was shaking with . . . uncontrollable sobs. What was happening? . . . I approached the Ranger Station. The guard smiled. . . . "I appear to be lost." . . . "Where do you need to go?" the guard asked politely. A cold chill enveloped me as I realized I did not remember the name of my street. (pp. 5–9)

In the previous chapter, we explored cognition in a general way. We focused on how that global but elusive quality labeled intelligence changes as we age. Now, we turn to explore two specific topics in cognitive aging. First, we look at that crucial aspect of cognition called memory. Not only is memory loss a central stereotype we have about old age, it is a top-ranking research area for psychologists who study the aging process. Second, we look at the condition we most fear about old age—a disease that has generated thousands of research papers, numerous books and academic reports, and captured the attention of the public to an unparalleled degree. It is the terrible problem Diana suffers from: dementia.

MEMORY

Although most of us believe that in important ways we will grow more intelligent with age, these positive feelings do not extend to memory. When we think of memory,

TABLE 7-1	The Method and Results of a Typical Early Laboratory Memory Study		

A total of 30 elderly and 30 young adult males memorized lists of paired associates. In the paced conditions, the subject had to respond within a certain time period (1.5 or 3 sec.). In the self-paced condition, subjects could control the memory apparatus and learn and answer at their own pace. The table shows that self-paced learning leads to comparatively better performance in the elderly. At the same time, it illustrates the dramatic age differences typically found in standard memory studies. The table measures the mean errors until achieving one perfect list recitation for young and elderly subjects.

	1.5 sec.	3 sec.	Self-Paced
YOUNG	12.52	7.90	6.27
OLD	50.90	25.90	15.30

SOURCE: Adapted from Canestrari, 1963.

almost all of us are likely to believe that our abilities will change for the worse. What exactly are our stereotypes about when these negative changes begin?

When Ellen Ryan (1992) asked visitors to a science museum to evaluate the memory abilities of imaginary "targets" aged 25, 45, 65, and 85, she found that ratings of every facet of memory, from absentmindedness to the ability to memorize information, decreased at each age. In other words, people seem to believe that memory declines steadily with age, not just in old age, and that the loss sets in relatively early, by age 45.

However, although middle-aged people such as myself may complain about our terrible memory (the wonderful description one radio personality uses is "boomer-brain"), memory is not something we regularly think about as we go about daily life. Memory only becomes a *salient* dimension by which people are judged in their older years.

In one study, Judy Rodin and Ellen Langer (1980) filmed three actors, aged 20, 50, and 70, reading an identical speech. Scattered through the monologue were a few references to lapses in memory, such as "I forgot my keys." People then watched the film of either the young, middle-aged, or older actor and were asked to write about what the person was like. Those who saw the 70-year-old frequently described him as forgetful. No one who heard the identical words read by the middle-aged person or the young adult mentioned poor memory.

This study and others have shown that we are primed to look for memory problems in older people. Once someone is over 60 or 70 or 80, we focus on memory lapses. We interpret forgetting in a more ominous light. Joan Erber and her coworkers suggest that the difference lies in our *explanatory style*. Memory failures in younger people are passed off as situational, external to the person, and so irrelevant: "The task was too hard" or "He was preoccupied." In older people, forgetting is viewed as internal, intrinsic, and stable—evidence of a basic problem in the person (Erber, Szuchman, & Rothberg, 1990; Erber & Rothberg, 1991).

This attribution can be costly. If older people avoid mentally stimulating activities based on the idea that their memory is poor and nothing can be done about it, this withdrawal in itself may produce or accelerate decline (Cavanaugh, 1996). If outsiders treat older people as mentally incompetent, which often happens if the individual is old-old or lives in a nursing home, this treatment adds to the problem. As we saw in Chapter 5, lack of reinforcement can lead to excess disabilities. Luckily, because this area has been so well researched in the psychological laboratory, we have good information about memory changes and what can be done about them in our older years.

The Tests and the Findings

In traditional laboratory studies of memory and age, older people and young adults are given a list of words, letters, pictures, or nonsense syllables. After a number of presentations, age differences in performance are examined. When the person is asked to remember the items without hints, the memory test is called *free recall.* When hints are given, such as the first letter of the correct word, the technique is called *cued recall.* Another type of test involves the *recognition* approach. As in multiple-choice tests, the subject must pick out the correct answer from several choices.

As the sample study in Table 7-1 suggests, the elderly almost always perform much more poorly than the young on this type of test. If the task is difficult, age differences show up by middle age (Crook & Larrabee, 1992). For instance, in one study exploring memory change over a 16-year period, although subjects showed little loss on an easier recognition measure, free recall of a list of items declined regularly after age 55 (Zelinski & Burnight, 1997).

This research brings home the pattern we can clearly see in Table 7-1: Varying the difficulty of the memory test produces different degrees of deficiency. Sometimes, older people score very poorly; sometimes, their performance is only slightly worse. Understanding the reasons for these differences has been the real purpose of many studies: "What is the main source of the problem or difficulty that occurs with advancing age?" (Hultsch & Dixon, 1990).

To understand exactly what may be going wrong, let's look at one popular approach to understanding memory: the information-processing perspective.

An Information-Processing Perspective on Memory

As we learned in earlier chapters, psychologists who use an **information-processing perspective** break up mental activity into hypothetical steps, devise studies designed to isolate these steps and confirm their existence, and, in this way, try to shed light on the mystery of how we think. Researchers now believe that, on the way to becoming a "memory," information progresses through three stores, steps, or phases.

First, stimuli arriving from the outside world through the senses is held briefly in a **sensory store** specific to the sense in which it was received. The visual images that impinge on us enter a visual store (or iconic memory); the sounds we hear enter an auditory store (or echoic memory). This first memory stage, somewhat like a photocopy, deteriorates rapidly, within .5 to 2 seconds. Features that we notice or attend to enter the second system called **working memory.**

We can think of this second memory system as a gateway. Working memory is "where the cognitive action is." Here, we keep information in awareness for a temporary period while we make the decision either to discard it or to process it for

information-processing perspective on memory
Theory that information proceeds through three steps, or stores, on the way to becoming a memory

sensory store
Fleeting afterimage of a stimulus reaching a sense organ that rapidly decays

working memory
Gateway memory system containing the limited amount of information that can be kept in consciousness at one time

permanent storage. According to Alan Baddeley (1992), working memory is made up of two limited-capacity holding "bins." As each bin fills to capacity, information is displaced or pushed out. Working memory also includes an executive function that controls attention as well as manipulating the material in these holding areas to prepare it for storage.

A real-life example of the fleeting quality of the information in working memory happens when we get a phone number from the operator and immediately make the call. We know from experience that we can dial the 7-digit number without having to write it down and memory will not fail us, *if the phone rings*. If we get a busy signal and have to try again, memory mysteriously fades. The information has slipped out of this holding place.

To prevent this information loss, we must process the phone number to "memorize" it. Working memory must manipulate or encode the information so that it enters a third, more permanent store called **long-term memory.**

long-term memory
Relatively permanent, large-capacity memory store housing everything that has been learned

When we speak of memory, we are talking about this last system. Long-term memory is the relatively permanent, large-capacity store that is the repository of our past. Researchers find few age differences in tests of sensory memory, but studies clearly show that getting information into and/or out of this permanent warehouse becomes more difficult as we age. Are age-related memory losses due mainly to an encoding/acquisition problem or a retrieval problem? Or, in less technical terms, has the older person inadequately learned the material, or does the problem lie in getting the information out?

These topics were debated for decades as psychologists designed studies to try to isolate the acquisition and retrieval phases of memory and measure the loss. As it became clear that the efficiency of both encoding *and* retrieval seemed to decline, many researchers adopted a different perspective on change.

Timothy Salthouse (1991, 1992) argues that the hundreds of studies of age differences in memory have a similar message: As the task becomes more demanding and complex, older people do worse. These findings suggest that the critical force affecting memory as we age is not the particular type of processing or memory operation (acquisition versus retrieval), but simply *how much* mental processing the task demands. The problem lies in a mechanism powering the system as a whole. Salthouse calls this mechanism **processing resources.**

processing resources
Basic mechanism powering the memory system

What exactly is the processing-resource deficit? What is the bottleneck impairing memory with age? As you might imagine from his perspective on overall intelligence, Salthouse believes that the primary candidate is the loss in thinking speed that underlies so much of the age decline on traditional IQ tests. In support of this position, researchers have found that when they design studies to control for age differences in the speed of responding, the performance of older people is similar to that of young adults on standard memory tests (Luszcz, Bryan, & Kent, 1997; Salthouse, 1996).

Other ideas center more directly on age differences in the capacity of working memory, the gateway for all learning and remembering. Why does working memory grow smaller in our older years? According to Lynn Hasher, the problem lies in the inability to screen out unwanted stimuli. Manipulating and moving material efficiently through working memory requires good concentration. We must attend to the bits of information we need to process and filter out irrelevant information. In older people, Hasher argues, because of physiological changes in the part of the brain promoting attention, task-irrelevant thoughts intrude, leaving less space or energy in working memory for processing what we want to remember and learn (Hasher & Zacks, 1988).

These theories, each of which has support, suggest that with memory, as with reaction time, we must look to the task in understanding how people perform. Any time the memory task is demanding, older people do particularly poorly. As we have seen, one important dimension of difficulty involves speed. Older people do much worse on memory tasks in which the information is presented quickly and/or they have to respond or remember fast (Wingfield, Poon, Lombardi, & Lowe, 1985). Older people also perform more poorly on any task that strains their attentional capacities. They do badly, for instance, when performing two tasks concurrently—either keeping one bit of information in mind while carrying out another task or returning to an activity after being interrupted or attending to something else (A. D. Smith, 1996; Whiting & Smith, 1997). The elderly are particularly deficient when the task involves an unfamiliar activity, such as remembering totally new information, rather than a well-practiced skill.

Now let's look at a different framework on memory that offers other insights into the kinds of remembering that are most difficult for older adults.

A Memory-Systems Perspective on Memory

Think of the amazing resilience of some memories and the equally remarkable vulnerability of others. Why can we automatically remember how to hold a tennis racquet even though we have not been on a court for decades? Why is George Washington, the first U.S. president, locked in our consciousness while it is practically impossible to recall what we had for dinner two days ago? These kinds of memories seem to differ in a way that goes beyond *how much* mental processing went into embedding them into our mind. These types of remembering seem distinct from one another in a more basic way.

The information-processing perspective does not shed light on this question because in that framework, all memory is the same. The only relevant difference is how efficiently the information has been processed, stored, or retrieved. Endel Tulving's **memory-systems theory** offers the answers we need.

Tulving (1985) proposes three different types of memory systems. **Procedural** or **implicit memory** involves information that we learn and remember automatically, without conscious reflection or thought. This memory system includes several categories of learning, such as classically conditioned emotions and many physical skills. Once we have learned a basic skill, such as how to hit a tennis ball or ride a bike, we automatically "remember" that activity, without conscious effort, once confronted with that stimulus again.

Tulving's two other memory systems differ from this "unreflective," situation-linked memory in that they involve conscious recall. **Semantic memory** is our fund of knowledge, such as my knowledge that George Washington was the first U.S. president or what a tennis racquet is. **Episodic memory** is our ability to remember specific ongoing events. My memory of getting on the tennis court last Thursday or what I had for dinner last week would be in this memory system. So would any attempt to recall bits of information in laboratory memory tests. (Table 7-2 offers additional everyday illustrations showing the distinctions among the three memory types.)

memory-systems theory
Tulving's framework dividing memory into discrete systems or categories

procedural or implicit memory
Memory system for information that is learned and/or recalled without conscious effort

semantic memory
Memory system consisting of one's fund of knowledge

episodic memory
Memory system for ongoing life events

TABLE 7-2	Everyday Examples Illustrating the Distinctions among Implicit/Procedural, Semantic, and Episodic Memory

Implicit   You get into your blue Toyota and automatically know how to drive.
Semantic   You know that you have a blue Toyota.
Episodic   You memorize where you left your blue Toyota in the parking lot of the amusement park.

Implicit   You automatically find yourself singing the words to "Jingle Bells" when the melody comes on the radio.
Semantic   You remember that this is a song.
Episodic   You try to remember when you last heard "Jingle Bells."

Implicit   You begin getting excited as you approach your college fall semester senior year.
Semantic   You know that you are a student at X university and that you are a psychology major.
Episodic   You memorize the locations of classrooms and your professors' names during the first week of the new semester.

Implicit   I unconsciously find the letters I am typing now on my computer.
Semantic   I know that I am writing a book, *The Psychology of Aging.*
Episodic   I try not to forget that today I must go to the library and photocopy that article on memory that I will need in preparing this chapter.

As these examples suggest, episodic memory is the most fragile system. A month from now, we will know who George Washington is (semantic memory), and we will remember how to hold the tennis racquet (implicit/procedural memory). However, we are unlikely to remember what we had for dinner two Tuesdays ago. It is recalling the ongoing events of life—from what we ate last Tuesday, to what day last month we decided to play tennis, to the facts you are reading right now—that is most vulnerable to time.

Researchers have conducted ingenious studies demonstrating the independence of these memory types (Schacter, 1992). They have evidence that implicit memory is encoded in a different area of the brain than consciously recalled facts (Squire, 1992). Most important for us, there is a good deal of evidence that the memory systems are affected in different ways as we age.

David Mitchell (1989) examined the performance of older and younger adults on tests designed to reveal the three memory types. To measure semantic memory, Mitchell gave subjects vocabulary tests and asked them to name or identify a series of pictures. (For example, he might show a photo of the White House and ask, "What is pictured here?") During this presentation, Mitchell tested for implicit memory by using a strategy called *repetition priming*. He presented certain pictures in the series once, and others twice. By comparing a person's response latency (rapidity of responding) when a picture had or had not been presented previously, Mitchell measured whether this unconscious learning had occurred. Then, in a second phase of the study, Mitchell tested for episodic memory by showing subjects the original set of pictures embedded in a larger series and asking them to recall which photos they had already seen.

Implicit and semantic memory was as good in the old as in the young. The older people did as well as the young on the repetition-priming task. As we might expect, in view of what we know about age changes in crystallized IQ, they could identify or name as many pictures as the young. However, episodic memory was greatly impaired. The older people were much less able to recall exactly which pictures had been presented previously.

Other researchers have found that implicit memory may also decline a bit with age (Hultsch, Masson, & Small, 1991). Age makes some inroads in semantic memory, too (L. L. Light, 1991). Older people *do* have more trouble recalling familiar facts, such as the names of good friends, vocabulary words, or photos of well-known places (Salthouse, 1991). However, these lapses are far less frequent or pronounced. Any time the task involves "unconscious" responding or recalling well-learned material, older people do very well. Any time the task involves episodic memory—the more difficult task of remembering the events of daily life—the older person's performance will be relatively poor.

How impaired is episodic memory? As we saw in Table 7-1, if we look at traditional memory tests, the answer is a great deal. Young people typically remember about twice as much material as those over 65! Are older people really as deficient as they seem on these tests? Many researchers answer no.

Measuring Everyday Memory

In standard memory studies, as we have seen, young adults and older people are asked to memorize lists of unrelated words, nonsense syllables, letters, or numbers. But learning meaningless words or letters has little in common with the memory demands we face in daily life: "What is that red-haired woman's name?" "How do I get to that person's house?" "I must remember that doctor's appointment at 2." So, as was true of IQ tests, researchers began to wonder: Is how a person performs on these tasks a good index of how memory operates in everyday life?

Researchers had always assumed that by using meaningless stimuli, they could ensure that the situation was equal for everyone—that memory was being measured in an unbiased way. However, this focus on purity and control has problems: It may be *too* removed from real life. As in the old saying, in ridding themselves of the bathwater, were psychologists throwing out the baby?

Moreover, rather than being unbiased, the traditional approach might be especially biased against the old. Imagine that you are an elderly person asked to take a memory test. Not only are you are out of test-taking practice, you probably entered the experiment with high levels of anxiety. "Perhaps the test will show I have Alzheimer's disease!" Although these ability-extraneous factors might operate in any memory experiment, some researchers argued that they were intensified when the material that older people were asked to memorize made no sense (Hulicka, 1967).

Do ability-extraneous influences such as anxiety *differentially* impair older people's performance on memory tests? We do not know for sure (Kausler, 1990). What we do know for certain is that older people often do not perform at their best in these studies.

To take one example, Robert Hill, Martha Storandt, and Claudia Simeone (1990) found that giving incentives (a lottery ticket for free airline travel) improved performance on memorizing a list of words among older adults. Even if they do not discriminate against the old, the traditional studies do not showcase what older people are truly capable of doing.

everyday memory tasks

Memory tasks similar to the memory demands people face in daily life

One way of making the situation more realistic is to use **everyday memory tasks,** or tests that mirror the memory demands that people actually face (Poon, Rubin, & Wilson, 1989). How well can the elderly fit names to faces or remember the location of objects in space (Crook & Larrabee, 1992; Sharps & Gollin, 1988)? How does our ability to recall a conversation, a story, or the message of a written passage change with age (Adams, Labouvie-Vief, Hobart, & Dorosz, 1990; Meyer & Rice, 1989; Zelinski & Miura, 1988)? How well can older adults remember telephone numbers (West & Crook, 1990), television news shows (Stine, Wingfield, & Myers, 1990), or the source of information they have heard (Schacter, Kaszniak, Kihlstrom, & Valdiserri, 1991)?

Using these types of tests does not erase age differences. Older people perform more poorly on most measures of everyday memory, too, but the loss is often less steep and the results more variable than when memory is measured in the traditional way (Hultsch & Dixon, 1990; R. L. West, 1989).

Although the material in these tests is more realistic, the overall situation is just as artificial, "a laboratory test." Reading an article to remember as much as possible for an experimenter is different from reading that article for pleasure at home. Being tested on how well one matches slides of faces to names is not the same as being introduced to a person at a party and then wanting to memorize his name. As memory expert Robin West (1989) points out, any time the conditions are set by the examiner and the expectation is total recall, the situation changes. Just because a test is labeled everyday memory does not mean it reflects how memory really operates in life.

How well does the older person's memory operate in situations more true to life? The following study offers encouraging clues. Jan Sinnott (1986) devised a creative naturalistic (real-life) approach to testing differences in everyday memory among the Baltimore study volunteers. She asked participants of different ages to remember various events that had occurred during their days of being tested at the Gerontology Research Laboratory. Some events were important as a basis for action: "How do you get from your room to the testing area or the cafeteria?" "What are the hours dinner is served?" Others were unimportant: "What materials were on the table while you were solving problems—tissues, pencils, and so on?" "How many problems were you asked to solve?"

In examining memory for both types of events, Sinnott found that young volunteers outperformed the old only on the items measuring unimportant or irrelevant information. For the relevant material—the information that had to be remembered to function—the performance of the older people equaled that of the young.

This study is appealing because it gets to the heart of the problem of making generalizations to life based on laboratory studies. Even if our memory works less well as we grow old, this loss may not matter so much in the real world. As Sinnott points out, one implication of her study is that older people use selection and optimization to flexibly compensate for age-related deficits in the ability to recall. They seem to narrow focus. Rather than remembering "more," they concentrate more on what they really need to remember, so that when it counts, their memory is relatively unimpaired.

Memory for the Future and Memory of the Past

RECALLING WHAT WE PLAN TO DO   The most interesting studies revealing that memory decline may be compensated for by motivation involve **prospective memory**—remembering to take action in the future (Sinnott, 1989): We must remember to bring a pen and notebook to class, to keep a 10 A.M. appointment, to call and remind a spouse to pick up a child at school. At dinner, we cannot forget to take the meat out of the oven on time. These examples show how important prospective memory can be in daily life.

prospective memory
Memory for future actions

In laboratory studies of prospective memory, subjects engaged in a task are told to press a key after a certain number of minutes have elapsed or when a specific cue word appears. Although some studies have found that older people do not remember to take this action as well as the young (Park, Hertzog, Kidder, Morrell, & Mayhorn, 1997), others show no age differences on the word-cue task (Einstein, Smith, McDaniel, & Shaw, 1997).

The most interesting results occur when prospective memory is measured outside of the laboratory, in studies in which subjects of different ages are told to remember to mail back postcards on a given day. Possibly because older people are more motivated, the results are the reverse of what every traditional study shows. The elderly are *better* at remembering than the young (Sinnott, 1989).

So, when we look just at test performance, we neglect to factor in motivation. Heightened attention to memory can compensate for age-related loss. The research on prospective memory also clarifies an inconsistency in our thinking about memory and age: In spite of firmly believing that memory is poor in the elderly, when it comes to asking an adolescent cousin or our 70-year-old grandmother to remember to feed our cat while we are on vacation, we frequently trust the older person more!

RECALLING OUR PERSONAL PAST   There is a second inconsistency in our general belief that memory is worse in the elderly. Granted, older people may have more trouble recalling what they said or did within the past few hours or days, but don't memories from youth become especially vivid in old age? As with memory for future events, this special type of recall of the more distant personal past has its own name: **autobiographical memory.**

autobiographical memory
Memory for one's personal past

Do older people recall their youth especially vividly? To examine the accuracy of this stereotype about memory in the elderly, researchers use an interesting technique. They give older and younger subjects a cue word and ask them to respond with a specific memory, date this personal event, and rate it for vividness. The idea is that if older people "live in the past," their associations should center less often on recent events and more on remote memories from their younger years.

When researchers use this approach, however, they typically find no age differences in the distribution of memories. Recent happenings are equally salient for both the old and the young. The dramatically downward sloping curve as a function of "time since event occurred" found with younger people is equally apparent for older adults (Hess & Pullen, 1996).

There are interesting exceptions. Although recent events are recalled most easily, older people tend to remember events that occurred when they were adolescents and young adults more frequently than those that took place during their middle years

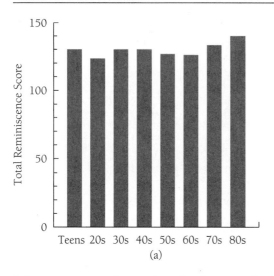

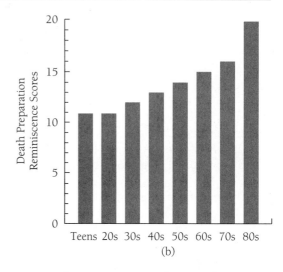

(a)   (b)

Subjects were instructed to rate how often they engaged in the seven types of reminiscence on a scale ranging from never to very frequently. Even though overall reminiscence does not vary by age (a), life review becomes increasingly prevalent in later life (b).
SOURCE: Webster, 1995.

reminiscence peak
In the elderly, tendency to recall events dating from the teens and twenties more readily than events from the middle years.

(Fromholt & Larsen, 1991; Holland, 1995; Rubin & Schulkind, 1997). One hypothesis is that this **reminiscence peak** occurs because our teens and 20s are an especially turbulent time of life. These are the years when we reach puberty, have our first romantic relationships, leave home, get married, and often become parents. As we will see later in this chapter, any event that is emotion-fraught and personally meaningful is apt to be more indelibly etched in mind. Moreover, provided we look only at *certain* older people, there is more truth to the stereotype that the elderly live in the past.

Carol Holland and Patrick Rabbitt (1991) compared the lifetime distribution of memories of nursing home residents with those of a matched group of normal, active elderly. They found that, in contrast to the active elderly, the residents in long-term care *were* most likely to produce memories dating from their earlier years. Holland (1995) reasons that anyone, young or old, who is immersed in living is highly motivated to remember the present because recalling events such as just having gone to the grocery store or meeting one's family is critical to handling life. However, living in a nursing home removes the requirement to remember the ongoing fabric of daily living because the institution takes care of the need to remember what happened yesterday or what will happen next week. Meals arrive, family members visit, life takes place at the whim of others without active effort or control on the older person's part. At the same time as it blots out the motivation to process the present, living in a nursing home heightens the need to recall the distant past. In nursing homes, Holland argues, people may feel compelled to rehearse and recall events relating to who they "really" are (mother or daughter or business executive) because these life review activities allow them to hang onto a sense of their personal identity as human beings.

These findings suggest that by simply exploring age differences in the general tendency to think about the past, we may be missing interesting information. Even if its overall frequency does not change as we age, reminiscing may have a different purpose or meaning for younger and older adults. Specifically, we might expect that the elderly, much more than younger adults, engage in the kind of reminiscence that Erikson calls life review.

To explore this possibility, Jeffrey Webster (1995) first spelled out seven distinct types or categories of thinking about the past. According to Webster, people may talk about events in their lives to teach younger people or simply to keep a conversation going. They may think about their lives to reduce boredom, to understand themselves better, to feel close to loved ones they have lost, or to obsess about old hurts. Finally, they may engage in the kind of behavior Erikson would define as life review—exploring the past in preparation for death.

Using a scale to measure each type of reminiscence, Webster then charted how frequently subjects ranging in age from their teens to their 80s engaged in these different activities. As expected, he found no age differences in the overall quantity of reminiscing that subjects reported (see Figure 7-1a). However, he did find tantalizing differences between the types of reminiscence that were most common at different ages: Younger people were more likely to reminisce to reduce boredom, solve problems, or ruminate about unpleasant events, whereas older people were much more likely to think about their lives to prepare for impending death (see Figure 7-1b).

Interventions

STIMULATING LIFE REVIEW   Our discussion suggests that, although it may not be as crucial as long as older adults are healthy and immersed in life, getting people to recall their lives may be helpful psychologically for the institutionalized or the very old. This is why, as mentioned in Chapter 2, reminiscence or life review activities are used to reduce depression and foster a sense of identity in senior centers and especially in nursing homes. In these sessions, a leader may organize group discussions around specific topics, such as favorite holidays or "jobs I have had," or may simply ask participants to share memories of important events in childhood, as adolescents, or as adults. In one group in a nursing home, 16 residents engaged in this type of reminiscing and were also taught problem-solving skills. After the 10-session treatment, depression rates among participants were significantly lower than before (Dhooper, Green, Huff, & Austin-Murphy, 1993).

Reminiscence is a specialized memory-type intervention focused mainly on emotional health. In the rest of this section, we focus on a much more central topic relating to cognition and age: specific strategies for helping to improve memory in later life.

MEMORY STIMULATING STRATEGIES   As with IQ tests, older people differ widely in their performance on memory tests. This research on individual differences offers lessons for how to minimize age-related memory decline.

7-1 *My Midlife Memory Decline*

Within the past few years, I have had the uneasy sense that my memory has become measurably worse. It is difficult for me to remember a phone number after I call information. I used to be able to dial with no problem; now I have to concentrate carefully. If I have to remember an area code plus the number, two or three digits often slip out of mind. At shopping centers, it has become mandatory to note carefully where I leave my car. Several times I have forgotten this precaution, emerged from a store, and frantically wandered row to row. Most disturbing are the (thankfully) infrequent occasions when I forget information that I absolutely should know: the day I was asked for my zip code and blanked out on the digits (I have lived in the same house for five years!); the time I recommended a good friend's class to a student and totally forgot her name. Am I more distracted these days, or is my feeling that my memory has declined accurate?

One hint might come from looking at research asking the question "Do older people who feel that their memory is poor really perform comparatively poorly on memory tests?" Thankfully, the answer is often no. As I suggest in the text, memory complaints are more diagnostic of low self-efficacy (Lauber & Drevenstedt, 1997) or emotional problems—especially depression—than anything else. But I know that I am not depressed. More important, in order to understand if my impressions of decline are accurate, I cannot trust studies measuring memory at a single point in time. What I need is longitudinal research, studies tracing how self-perceptions about memory relate to deterioration that has actually taken place.

One study fits my requirement, although it explores memory in a very different age group. In their research probing cognitive decline in aged Swedish men and women Steven Zarit and his colleagues looked at whether subjects who felt their memory had seriously declined at the second evaluation were sensing something real (Johansson, Allen-Burge, & Zarit, 1997). Was their intuition tied to greater-than-normal losses since the first testing? The researchers also looked to the future: Would these self-evaluations predict decline at the next test?

Unfortunately, self-perceptions were related to accelerated loss. More ominous, people who evaluated their memory as poor declined more at the next evaluation, too. However, the size of these correlations was small. Moreover, as the researchers point out, the deterioration down the road might have been caused not by physiological changes, but by low self-efficacy. Believing that their memory was bad, people gave up trying to remember, and so their memory got even worse. Still, this study offers troubling hints that the changes I am sensing may be genuine.

1. **Stay in good emotional and physical health.** As we might expect from our discussion of intelligence, people with heart disease and a wide range of other chronic conditions perform particularly poorly on memory tests (Hultsch, Hammer, & Small, 1993; Spiro, Riggs, Elias, & Vokonas, 1997). The same is true of people in poor emotional health, in particular those who are depressed. Not only do older people who are depressed tend to falsely label their memory as worse (Kahn, Zarit, Hilbert, &

Niederehe, 1975; see Aging in Action 7-1), but one symptom of depression in the elderly is memory impairment. Problems with remembering may be so severe they can even be mistaken for Alzheimer's disease. So the first general principle for helping memory in later life is to take care of one's physical and mental health.

2. **Keep mentally stimulated.** As is also true of intelligence, older people who are mentally active (Hultsch et al., 1993) and intellectually interested (Arbuckle, Gold, Andres, Schwartzman, & Chaikelman, 1992) do comparatively better on memory tests. This relationship is especially clear in research examining the type of everyday memory alluded to earlier, remembering the main point of a written passage such as a newspaper article or a page in a book. Although most studies find that older people do more poorly on this task than younger people, with well-read intellectual older subjects the age difference shrinks or disappears (Meyer & Rice, 1989).

Does being skilled verbally help to inoculate people against memory decline? Answers come from a study by Robin West, Thomas Crook, and Kristina Barron (1992) in which subjects of different ages were given various tests of everyday memory. These researchers found that scores on a vocabulary test were a more important predictor of memory for a written passage than a person's age. On the other memory tests, however, age alone was the best predictor of performance. So, as we saw also in Chapter 6, on intelligence, being highly accomplished can overpower changes due to the passing years. However, the impact seems to be specific, limited mainly to the person's area of expertise.

A variety of memory studies have shown that older people who are expert in an activity—be it pilots asked to read an air traffic control message (Morrow, Leirer, Altiteri, & Fitzsimmons, 1994) or elderly bridge players (Clarkson-Smith & Hartley, 1990)—can do as well as or even outperform the young. However, the advantage expertise offers is often limited to tests measuring that type of memory alone. Although the broader benefit on memory of keeping active is unclear, older people should not despair. There are specific techniques that can generally improve memory in later life (and at any age).

3. **Use mnemonic techniques.** We all have noticed that some experiences are indelibly embedded in memory (our graduation day or first day at college) whereas others fade. The main characteristic of the episodic events we remember is their meaningful quality. As I suggested in discussing autobiographical memory, when the details of life are unimportant, memory is apt to be poor. Events that are emotionally important are learned and remembered best. So one key to remembering information more easily is to enhance its memorability.

Mnemonic techniques are strategies to help make information more "memorable." These techniques range from organizing a list of foods into meaningful categories, such as fruits and meats to facilitate recall at the grocery store, to remembering the last four digits of a friend's phone number XXX-1945 by transforming this sequence from a meaningless array of numbers to the year that ended the Second World War. Although researchers disagree as to whether older people spontaneously use these special strategies less frequently than the young (L. L. Light, 1991), it is clear that teaching these techniques can benefit people of any age.

One technique that enhances meaning is using imagery—imagining a striking visual image of the material to be learned. When asked to memorize the paired

mnemonic techniques
Specific techniques used to facilitate learning and recall by making information more vivid or meaningful

TABLE 7-3   *Techniques to Cope with Common Memory Problems*

Problem   Remembering names
Solution   Form a vivid visual image involving the word. To remember Belsky, imagine a huge bell on skis wrapped around my head when we are introduced. To remember "River Road," imagine a huge river overflowing the street.

Problem   Remembering a list of items
Solution 1   First, think of several familiar locations around the house. Then, form a visual image associating each item on the list with a specific place. Next, take a mental walk around your house "stopping" at each location to retrieve each item (this technique is called the method of loci).
Solution 2   Organize the items to be remembered into meaningful categories—for example, shoes, dresses, and so on. Then, when packing for a trip, go category by category down the list.

Problem   Remembering where an item was placed
Solution 1   At home or in familiar settings, have a regular place for each item—perhaps by the front door. Then, when you enter the house, take an extra second to put your keys, your glasses, or your purse in that place.
Solution 2   In unfamiliar places, be alert to where you put an item down. Use a visual image linking the item to that place to facilitate recall. (For example, visualize exactly where your car is when you enter the shopping center.)

Problem   Remembering the material in this chapter (or other written information)
Solution   Take notes on the chapter as you read. The process of organizing the essential points in your mind, then physically writing the material down, helps solidify that information in memory.

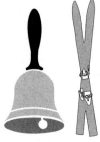

By visualizing these objects, you will more easily remember the name of this textbook's author.

external memory aids
External reminders, such as calendars and lists, used to aid recall

associate *bat–tree,* for example you might imagine a bat sitting in a tree. To recall who wrote this text, you might imagine a large bell on skis wrapped around this book. (Table 7-3 lists additional examples of effective mnemonic techniques.)

Besides these internal techniques, of course, we also have **external memory aids** such as calendars or lists. Some researchers have found that, rather than focusing on the work of internally encoding information, it is more effective to teach older people to rely more heavily on external aids (Wallace & Ratchford, 1997). However, as memory expert Robin West (1989) wisely points out, writing down an appointment on a calendar and then checking that calendar also require remembering!

Not only does writing information avoid the work of internal encoding, this very activity helps embed the material in memory. As I suggest in Table 7-3, if you simply reread this chapter repeatedly before a test, you will not recall the information as well as if you take the time to take notes on what you are reading now. As Orah Burack and Margie Lachman (1996) discovered, giving memory this extra boost seems especially helpful as we grow old.

Using a standard laboratory memory test involving memorizing a list, the researchers instructed groups of elderly and young adult subjects to write the items on paper. Then, in the recall phase of the study, the subjects were told, "Sorry, you cannot refer to what you wrote." When the researchers compared performance in the list-making condition with performance under standard conditions, older subjects were no longer deficient compared with the young. Writing the information was enough to raise the performance of the elderly participants to the level of the young adults.

Older people need to be aware of this immensely relevant information. If they would make the effort to write information, to use imagery, or even to rely more heavily on notes and calendars, their memory would improve greatly (Hultsch & Dixon, 1990; Neely & Backman, 1993; Wallace & Ratchford, 1997). In other words, the key to improving memory in old age (or at any age) is optimization (extra effort) combined with knowledge—an understanding of the specific memory strategies that can compensate for age changes.

4. **Enhance memory self-efficacy.** Simply providing information may not be enough, however. To have a better memory, people must *believe* that change is possible, that older dogs really *can* learn new tricks. So, it is important to focus on improving **memory self-efficacy**—the older person's confidence about being able to improve (Cavanaugh, 1996). As we saw in the research on memory perceptions at the beginning of this chapter, people have a tendency to see loss in this arena of life as an intrinsic, irremediable part of growing old. If older adults believe that they are suffering from a hopeless physiological problem, researchers find, they are less motivated to engage in any memory-enhancing technique (Kwon, 1997). In the grip of this perception of irreversible loss, they may give up even trying to remember, ensuring future decline.

memory self-efficacy
Faith in one's capacity to remember

I must confess that this self-fulfilling spiral has even affected me. Believing that my memory has gotten worse, this summer, for the first time, I stopped making the effort to remember the names of students in my class. If this problem can affect the most knowledgeable middle-aged adult, what about the typical elderly person bombarded with messages that memory declines with age? How much of the age deficit that psychologists find on memory tests might be reduced simply by working to improve memory self-efficacy?

Unfortunately, there is a time when enhancing efficacy feelings is doomed to have less effect and when teaching mnemonic techniques is likely to fail. This is when people have the condition called dementia.

DEMENTIA

Dementia is a label applied to a variety of chronic diseases characterized by severe memory loss. However, although we link this illness with memory, much more than just remembering is involved. Dementia qualifies as the ultimate mental disorder, the total erosion of the person, the complete unraveling of the self. It involves the loss of every human function—reasoning, judgment, personality, emotional control, and the ability to walk, dress, or speak. Although both older and younger people can develop these terrible illnesses, the dementias of old age are almost always progressive. The deficits get progressively worse and end in death.

dementia
Chronic diseases characterized by serious, often irreversible, deterioration in cognition

As seen in the first-person accounts at the beginning of this chapter and in Aging in Action 7-2, even in its early stage, the memory problems associated with dementia go well beyond the episodic, event-related forgetting of normal aging. A woman may not remember how to get home even though she has traveled that route for years. She may forget well-established facts such as the town in which she lives. To qualify for a

7-2 *An Insider's Portrait of Alzheimer's*

Hal is handsome, distinguished, a young-looking 69. He warmly welcomes me into his immaculate apartment at the Assisted Living Facility. Copies of *National Geographic* and *Scientific American* are neatly laid out in stacks on the coffee table. Oil paintings of grandparents and family photos adorn the walls. Index cards organized in piles on the desk list his daughters' names and phone numbers, provide reminders of the city and the state. Hal taught university chemistry for years. After his wife died, he kept active with volunteer work and was very involved in the church. About two years ago, his mind began to unravel. It was not so much the forgetfulness, but the rambling conversations, the disorganized letters, the long-distance calls at all hours of the night. Worried about his ability to live on his own, his daughters planned to move him to Tennessee this coming fall. Their plans were cut short when, one morning, Hal set out to drive across country to Nashville but could not remember the state or his daughters' names. Luckily, he had the presence of mind to check himself into a local hospital, where he learned for certain that he had the illness whose symptoms he graciously consents to describe.

I first noticed that I had a problem giving short speeches. All of a sudden you have a blank and like . . . what do I put in there . . . and I couldn't do it. I can speak. You are listening to me and you don't hear any pauses, but if you get me into something. . . . I just had one of these little pauses. I knew what I wanted to say and I couldn't get into it, so I think a little bit and wait and try to get around to it. It's there. . . . I know it's there . . . but where do I use it? . . . Then, you have to sit down and think and sort. I went to the hospital because I knew there was something wrong. When I got there, they wanted to know about my life. I said, "If you provide me with some information about what you think will happen to me, and if I find that it's a good argument, then I'll tell you about myself." When I was told I had Alzheimer's, I thought, "Oh brother, this is a terrible place to be." The psychiatrist, Dr. West . . . Oh, I got

diagnosis of dementia, the forgetting must be severe enough to impair the person's ability to function in life.

As the illness reaches its middle stage, every aspect of thinking is affected. Abstract reasoning becomes difficult. The person can no longer think through options when making decisions. Language becomes limited. The individual has trouble naming objects. Her speech becomes vague and empty, with excessive uses of referents such as "it" and "thing." She may be unable to recognize familiar objects, such as a chair, or forget how to execute well-practiced actions such as putting on her shoes. Judgment becomes faulty. People may act inappropriately, perhaps undressing in public, running out in traffic, or yelling in the street. They may behave recklessly, unaware of endangering their life or health. Agitation, wandering, insomnia, and paranoia are common (D. Cohen et al., 1993), as are dramatic changes in mood. In fact, experts estimate, at least one-third of all people with this devastating condition are seriously depressed (Teri, 1997).

that right! . . . helped me a lot. Now, I tell everyone what I have. They are kind of shocked, but it doesn't bother me. I'm not ashamed of my Alzheimer's, and I'm not ashamed of anyone else's Alzheimer's.

It's ups and downs; and then one day you are in a deep valley. You can't get tied up in the hills and valleys because they just lead you around and it makes you more frustrated than ever. If I can't get things, I just give up and then try to calm down and come back to it. You have to work very hard to get back to where you were. Like, when I read, I get confused but then I just stop and try again a month later. Or, the people here. I know them by face, by sight, by what they wear; but I cannot get that focus down to memorize any names. I remember things from when I was 5. It's what's happening now that doesn't make a lot of sense. Now, I think it's time for us to stop and let me show you the pictures on my wall and tell you who these people are. . . .

As we walk to my car after this interview, Hal's daughter fills me in:

My father seems a lot happier now that he is here. The big problem is the frustration, when he tries to explain things and I can't understand and neither of us connects. Then he gets angry and I get angry. My father has always been a very organized, very intellectual person, so feeling dependent and out of control is overwhelming for him. We had to get a power of attorney [a legal order declaring guardianship]. I think he understood it conceptually, but he hasn't come to grips emotionally with it. The fact that he can't write checks is devastating. He has days where he gets paranoid, decides that there is a conspiracy out for him. It's tiny things. A letter came to the wrong place and he went down and exploded at the people at the desk. The good news is that we put him on medication that seems to help. Also, they can handle this here. If we get home health services to come in, they will keep him until he gets very bad. For me emotionally, the worst thing is remembering how my father was. You expect a certain response from him and you get this strange response. It's like there's a different person inside.

As the illness progresses to its advanced stage, the person becomes disoriented to time, place, and person. A man may think it is 1943 and he is at sea talking to his commanding officer, when he is actually a resident of Four Acres Nursing Home in 1999. The most basic semantic memories are affected. A woman may forget her name or the fact that she has children. At this point, urinary and fecal incontinence is common. The person may need assistance to walk.

In the final or terminal stage, the patient is totally dependent. The person loses the ability to speak at all and is often unable to perform the most basic human activities such as moving or even swallowing well. Often, it is complications at this stage that lead to death.

Though dementia is often characterized by stages, experts caution that not all people deteriorate in a lockstep way. Some individuals may be able to perform basic tasks such as dressing and going to the toilet in the presence of the most extreme impairments in memory and reasoning. Others whose thinking is much better may need nursing care for these basic activities of daily living (Zarit, Orr, & Zarit, 1985; Wells & Dawson, 1997).

The most heartbreaking variability lies in the time course of these illnesses. Although over time cognition and functional abilities are predestined to worsen, often at an accelerating pace, there are marked individual differences in the rate of decline. If the person is better-educated and the illness develops earlier in life, the deterioration tends to progress at a more rapid rate (Teri, McCurry, Edland, Kukull, & Larson, 1995). On average, however, people have the symptoms of dementia for 7 or so years (Aneshensel, Pearlin, Mullan, Zarit, & Whitlatch, 1995).

The Demography of Dementia

Dementia is less common among people over 65 than many of us believe (Gatz & Pearson, 1988). One community study revealed that it affects only about 5% of Americans this age (Folstein, Bassett, Anthony, Romanoski, & Nestadt, 1991). Although this percentage is not high, it translates into several million older Americans living in the community who have problems handling the basics of life. Moreover, this survey only polled people living outside institutions. Because dementing illnesses frequently result in nursing home admission as the symptoms progress, the number of older people who suffer from this condition is actually higher. It is estimated that at least half of all of the residents in long-term care have this most feared disorder of later life (U.S. Senate Special Committee on Aging, 1991a).

On the positive side, compared with other illnesses of aging, dementia strikes quite late in the life span. It is extremely rare before age 50, rises gradually in frequency during the next three decades, and jumps dramatically in advanced old age. By the mid-80s, about 1 in 4 people living at home suffer from moderate to severe mental loss (Gatz & Smyer, 1992). The fact that dementia does become so much more common at life's uppermost rungs is alarming, however, because of the dramatic growth in the numbers of the oldest-old. By the time the baby boomers enter their 80s and 90s, dementia may be the number one public health problem facing our country.

Although a number of rare illnesses can produce these devastating symptoms (see Table 7-4), usually the person with dementia is suffering from one or a combination of two diseases: vascular dementia and Alzheimer's disease.

Vascular Dementia

vascular dementia
Cardiovascular dementing illness of later life

Vascular dementia is a disease of the cardiovascular system. In this illness, responsible for an estimated one-fourth of cases, the cognitive dysfunction is produced by the death of brain tissue as a result of many small strokes. As we know from Chapter 3, a stroke occurs when an artery feeding the brain becomes blocked by atherosclerosis or other causes, the blood supply to that area is disrupted, and the cells nourished by that vessel die. A large stroke produces symptoms that are difficult to miss, such as paralysis, impaired speech, or death. The person who has vascular dementia has strokes so minor that they may produce few clear symptoms. But as their number increases and more brain tissue dies, cognition deteriorates in a stepwise way.

Because strokes are caused by potentially treatable problems such as high blood pressure, there may be a chance of stemming the progression of this dementing illness

Creutzfeldt-Jakob disease	This rare dementing disease is caused by a slow-growing virus.
Huntington's chorea	In this tragic genetic illness, the offspring of victims have a 50-50 chance of developing it, yet it manifests itself after the peak childbearing years—in the mid-30s. The disease causes not only dementia but involuntary movements that become more pronounced as the illness progresses.
Normal pressure hydrocephalus	This dementing illness is caused by the buildup of pressure in the ventricles of the brain. Treatment, sometimes effective, consists of surgery to drain the fluid.
Pick's disease	Although it produces many of the pathological changes of Alzheimer's, this disease progresses differently, initially affecting different areas of the brain.

SOURCE: Belsky, 1990.

by lowering blood pressure through diet and exercise. Normally, however, the person's deficits become more pronounced because the strokes recur more frequently, affecting larger segments of the brain.

Because of their greater susceptibility to atherosclerosis and cardiovascular disease, males and African Americans tend to have comparatively higher rates of vascular dementia (Cohen et al., 1993). Because of their greater longevity, plus the fact that menopause removes estrogen, a hormone that may protect the integrity of neurons, women are more susceptible to the most common dementing illness, Alzheimer's disease.

Alzheimer's Disease

About 60% of elderly people with dementia have Alzheimer's disease. Another percentage have what is called a mixed dementia: Alzheimer's and vascular dementia combined. **Alzheimer's disease** attacks our humanity at its core. In this illness that has become a synonym for any dementia of old age, the neurons literally wither away.

Normally, a neuron looks like a tree. When a person has Alzheimer's disease, it appears as if the tree is slowly being killed by an infection. First it loses its branches (dendrites); then it swells; then its trunk (axon and cell body) shrivels to a stump (Zarit, Orr, & Zarit, 1985). In place of what had been a normal neuron are wavy filaments called **neurofibrillary tangles,** thick bulletlike bodies of protein called **senile plaques,** and other pathological signs of deterioration.

At first, the destruction is confined mainly to the area of the brain called the hippocampus. As the illness progresses, it cuts a wider swath. More and more healthy neurons are replaced by these pathological structures. The brain of a person with

Alzheimer's disease
Most common dementing illness of later life, involving the deterioration of neurons

neurofibrillary tangles
Wavy filaments of neural tissue characteristic of Alzheimer's disease

senile plaques
Thick bodies of protein characteristic of Alzheimer's disease

advanced Alzheimer's disease may be so studded with abnormal fragments that there are few normal neurons left.

In a classic study, British researchers showed that the memory and thinking problems a person manifests are a direct function of the amount of neural destruction that has taken place. After death, the brains of elderly people with varying degrees of memory loss were autopsied. The researchers found a good correlation between the density of senile plaques and the person's intellectual abilities near the time of death (Blessed, Tomlinson, & Roth, 1968; Roth, Tomlinson, & Blessed, 1966).

Unfortunately, normal older people also show these changes. They, too, have senile plaques and neurofibrillary tangles (Scheibel, 1996). But these structures are fewer in number, and they tend to be confined to limited areas of the brain. In dementia, the damage is extensive and widespread.

The presence of these changes in normal older adults provides a physiological underpinning for the losses in memory and thinking that normally occur in later life. And it shows that the link between normal age changes in cognition and their end point—the chronic illness called Alzheimer's disease—is uncomfortably close. The fact that these changes are part and parcel of normal aging highlights another distressing truth. Although many people do live into their 90s sound in mind (as well as body), not infrequently dementia is the price of living to the ripest old age (Johansson & Zarit, 1995).

CAUSES   What causes the neural decay that results in Alzheimer's disease? Theories center around various agents of destruction. In reading through this list, keep in mind that one lead does not exclude others. Rather than having a single cause, Alzheimer's disease may be the final result of multiple insults to the brain (Gatz, Lowe, Berg, Mortimer, & Pederson, 1994; Gatz et al., 1997).

1. **A virus.**   Because a virus is known to cause the rare type of dementia called Creutzfeldt-Jakob disease, some researchers suggest that a slow-acting virus, one that may take decades to incubate in the body, may be implicated in Alzheimer's disease. (The HIV virus can also produce a dementia that progresses much like Alzheimers' disease.)

2. **Toxic metals.**   Another candidate for an Alzheimer's instigating substance is aluminum because the brain tissue of Alzheimer's patients contains a high concentration of this metal. Does absorbing too much aluminum over a lifetime play a part in causing the disease? Or are the high levels of aluminum a result of the disease process? So far, efforts to link this particular metal definitively to the illness have been inconclusive. In addition to aluminum, speculations also center around the toxic effects of other metals such as lead and mercury.

3. **A deficit in neurotransmitter production.**   Another line of inquiry centers on a prominent feature of the Alzheimer's brain: its striking deficiency of the neurotransmitter acetylcholine. If Alzheimer's disease selectively attacks the acetylcholine-producing (cholinergic) neurons, stimulating the brain's production of this neurotransmitter might be an effective antidote. Although so far researchers have not had clear-cut success, drugs thought to restore acetylcholine are now being prescribed (Hirsch & Charles, 1997).

4. **Amyloid.** An important lead concerns amyloid, an abnormal protein that is a core constituent of both senile plaques and neurofibrillary tangles. Some researchers believe that the buildup of this protein plays a central role in the development of these structures. Does the genetic instruction "Produce amyloid" trigger the disease by causing this toxin to accumulate, producing the neural devastation? This hypothesis was given a boost in 1991 when researchers reported producing tangles and plaques in mice after injecting them with human genetic material fostering amyloid synthesis (Marx, 1991). However, the following year, these findings were discredited (Marx, 1992). Although researchers still are unsure if amyloid is a by-product or true cause of the disease, the search for substances that inhibit this material from being formed is occurring at a feverish pace.

5. **Genetics.** The hottest new research avenue involves genetics, with studies addressing the anxiety-ridden question "If a close relative has Alzheimer's, how likely am I to get the disease?" For years scientists have known that the tendency to develop early-onset Alzheimer's is hereditary: If people develop the illness in midlife, close relatives do have a higher risk of the disease. Interestingly, the Swedish Adoption/Twin Study suggests that the hereditary component to Alzheimer's is powerful even when the illness manifests itself later in life. When researchers compared the concordance rates (or twin pair correlations) for the 64 cases in which one or more fraternal and identical twin subjects had Alzheimer's, they found a remarkably high heritability index of 74% (Gatz et al., 1997).

Studies such as these are fueling the search for an Alzheimer's gene. The first breakthrough occurred more than a decade ago when researchers identified a specific genetic defect in people with the early-onset form of the illness (Barnes, 1987). Interestingly, this genetic marker was located on chromosome number 21, the very one that people suffering from the birth defect Down's syndrome have an extra copy of. For some time, scientists had been intrigued by what they imagined was a connection between these two conditions because victims of Down's syndrome almost universally develop Alzheimer's disease if they live to midlife. This study reveals a reason for the link: Having an extra chromosome 21 may give victims of Down's syndrome a double dose of the Alzheimer's-producing genetic program.

However, Alzheimer's turns out to have multiple genetic pathways. In addition to chromosome 21, as of this writing (1998), mutations in chromosomes 14, 19, and 1 have also been linked to development of the disease.

Another research focus relating to physiology is the link between Alzheimer's disease and vascular dementia. Rather than being independent, these two major mind-impairing diseases may be intertwined. People who have a genetic marker that puts them at higher risk for Alzheimer's also have a higher risk of developing vascular dementia (Slooter et al., 1997). Moreover, the presence of vascular problems seems to bring out the symptoms of Alzheimer's disease. In one study, elderly nuns who had had a brain infarct or stroke exhibited clear-cut symptoms of dementia, even though a subsequent autopsy showed they did not have the required number of plaques and tangles to meet the criteria of Alzheimer's disease (Snowdon et al., 1997).

These findings suggest that interventions to prevent stroke, such as lowering blood pressure, may have the side benefit of helping Alzheimer's patients by postponing the eruption of the distressing behavioral signs of their disease. However, we are

TABLE 7-5	Some Conditions That Can Produce Delirium in the Elderly

Medications: errors in self-administration; polypharmacy (taking different medications simultaneously); abuse of nonprescription drugs; side effects of drugs given appropriately; inappropriate drug dosage for the individual

Diseases and physical conditions: cardiac problems, including heart attack; neurological conditions, such as stroke, encephalitis, or tumors; metabolic disorders of all types; cancer of the pancreas; pneumonia or any illness causing fever; constipation; heat stroke

Environmental changes: death of a loved one; moving; prolonged hospitalization

Poor nutrition: inadequate vitamin or protein intake (older people living alone are at high risk of malnutrition)

Surgery: aftereffects of anesthesia; surgical complications

Accidents or assaults: physical and emotional effects may cause delirium

still far from an Alzheimer's breakthrough. Media hype to the contrary, *no* intervention has any effect on the progression of the pathological brain changes (Pendlebury & Solomon, 1994). For this reason, the diagnosis of Alzheimer's must be made carefully.

DIAGNOSIS   Because no technological advance has enabled physicians to see into the brain and verify neural deterioration, the diagnosis of Alzheimer's is made by exclusion—by taking a careful history, conducting a medical examination, administering psychological tests, and ruling out problems that produce mental impairment but are potentially reversible.

delirium
Any gross disturbance of consciousness that, in contrast to dementia, has a rapid onset and may abate

As Table 7-5 shows, a long list of conditions—from cancer to medication side effects to emotional stress—can produce **delirium,** a state of confusion that is actually quite different from the slow, progressive deterioration of Alzheimer's disease. Delirium develops rapidly. One hour, a rational human being is there; the next, a madman appears. Periods of disorientation may fluctuate with lucid periods when the person shows no impairment. Still, if people are primed to think of dementia, the danger of misdiagnosis is there.

Another problem that can be mistakenly diagnosed as dementia is depression. The reason, as was implied earlier in this chapter, is that depression often causes memory impairment. Unfortunately, memory deficits are common in depressed older people (Lichtenberg, Ross, Millis, & Manning, 1995; Lyness, Eaton, & Schneider, 1994), sometimes making differentiating between the two conditions difficult.

Diagnostic accuracy has improved dramatically. The use of sophisticated psychological tests combined with advances in neuroimaging, or pictures of brain functioning and structure, have made the diagnosis of Alzheimer's disease much easier (Tune, 1993). Until recently, however, people were sometimes labeled demented when they had other diseases. A 90-year-old man arriving in the emergency room with a heart attack is diagnosed as having Alzheimer's disease. Family members assume that their 80-year-old mother's confusion is due to dementia, not remembering that her symptoms began when the doctor prescribed those heart pills. Because mistakes still occur, if Alzheimer's is suspected, get the diagnosis confirmed by a center specializing in this disease.

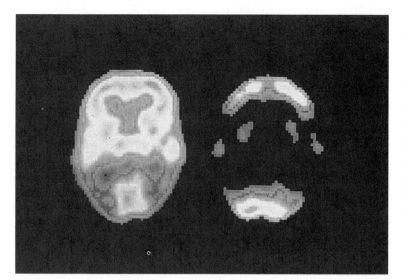

This MRI brain scan is one of the new neuro-imaging techniques that is aiding in the accurate diagnosis of dementing illnesses. Notice the greater activity characteristic of a normal brain (left) compared to that of the brain of a person with dementia (right).

Interventions

Medications can be helpful in reducing the agitation and upsetting personality changes that so often accompany dementia (Cooper & Mungas, 1993), and several drugs that *may* help improve mental functioning have been approved for use (Hirsch & Charles, 1997). However, the main interventions for this set of diseases are environmental. They center around making life easier for the person and for family members. With the understanding that any strategy that makes life easier for patients benefits families and that helping families also benefits the patient, we will look at each side of the equation separately.

HELPING THE PATIENT   As mentioned earlier in this chapter, standard memory-enhancing exercises fall flat in dealing with dementia. However, this does not mean one should abandon strategies to make the most of the cognitive capacities that exist.

With dementing illnesses, as with any age-related disability, a primary goal is to foster person/environment congruence—that is, modify the living situation to fit the person's new capacities. Any external cue or written aid can heighten orientation, from painting the person's room a bright color, to writing the word "restroom" on the bathroom door, to putting up charts in a prominent place to remind the individual of the day of the week.

A primary concern is safety. People need to be protected from harming themselves, particularly during the highly mobile middle stages of the disease. To prevent the person from wandering off, a common strategy is to double-lock or put buzzers on doors to alert caregivers when the person is about to leave. It is important to keep people with dementing illness away from dangerous appliances such as the stove and to put toxic substances such as household cleaners out of reach. Clothing and shoes that slip on rather than needing to be buttoned or laced can help promote functional capacities. A variety of other devices, such as teakettles that whistle when ready or timers that turn the oven off, can help keep the person functioning fairly independently during the early stages of the disease.

Another key is to keep the environment as predictable and familiar as possible. As we saw poignantly at the beginning of this chapter and in Aging in Action 7-2, any challenge to one's cognitive capacities is apt to be overwhelming, especially early in the illness when people are aware of the fact that something is terribly wrong with their mind.

On the other hand, one also must guard against understimulation. Remember from Chapter 5 that excess disabilities can occur when the environment is too bland and unchallenging as well as too complex. Based on the principle that people suffering from dementing illnesses need heightened (but nonthreatening) input, activities from gardening to music to cooking are often used with cognitively impaired older adults. In the following activity, called sensory stimulation, even severely demented people can be reconnected with the outside world using the basic senses of touch, sight, and taste.

> Mr. D. . . . was a severely disabled man who apparently recognized none of his loved ones or caregivers. . . . He no longer fed himself and spent most of his day sleeping or staring into space. . . . It was almost Halloween the first time Mr. D. came to sensory stimulation group. Our department had produced a fine, brilliant orange pumpkin. When his gerichair was wheeled to a place at the table, I gently guided Mr. D.'s hands to the cool, ridged surface of the pumpkin. Contact! His eyes were open, sparkling with life. This man, who hadn't spoken a sentence in weeks, hefted the pumpkin, eyed it approvingly, and said, "Well now isn't that a dandy. Wherever did you get that?" Almost every day thereafter, Mr. D. put in the milk and sugar and stirred his own tea. (Bowlby, 1993, p. 273)

Finally, during the earliest stages, psychotherapy is used to help the person cope and better come to terms emotionally with the disease (see Chapter 9). Reminiscence groups, discussed in our section on memory, may help ward off the depression and paralyzing anxiety that can accompany the terrifying feeling of "losing my mind."

Though it may be possible to talk to the person early in the illness, the reality is that, with dementia, the ability to articulate feelings verbally is rapidly lost. Any intervention to help the person cannot be *proven* to be effective unless we have some method of measuring how people with dementia really feel. Is there a way of entering the inner life of people who have lost human communication, to know if these strategies to help reduce anxiety and confusion, from sensory stimulation to environmental modifications, really work?

Powell Lawton and colleagues say yes. In fact, his research team has developed a measure that will allow us to systematically "read" the emotions of people with this disease (Lawton, Van Haitsma, & Klapper, 1996). As a first step, the researchers had trained raters observe 144 cognitively impaired residents in a nursing home during 10-minute segments, coding their emotions or affect states along basic dimensions such as pleasure, contentment, anger, and fear. Not only could different raters agree on these judgments (the measure was reliable), but preliminary studies also suggest that the scale may be valid (measuring something real). Residents with higher positive

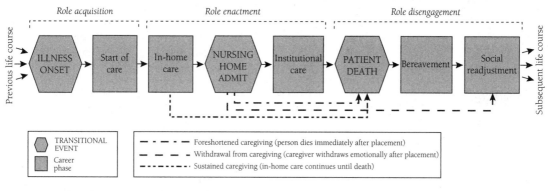

SOURCE: Aneshensel et al., 1995.

affect ratings are more often rated as extroverts by families. Moreover, as expected, positive affect ratings rise when residents are engaged in pleasurable social activities such as the sensory stimulation program just described.

Lawton's research group hopes that eventually this affect rating scale will be used as a tool to assess the quality of care an institution provides. Their goal is to enable nursing home personnel and family members to use the scale to help answer that all-important question: Am I really providing high-quality, loving care?

HELPING FAMILIES   Imagine caring for a loved one with dementia. You know that the illness is permanent. You must helplessly witness your beloved spouse or parent deteriorate. As we saw in Aging in Action 7-2, you must deal with a human being turned alien, where the tools used in normal encounters no longer apply. Your relative may be physically and verbally abusive. She may be agitated and wake and wander in the night (Cohen et al., 1993). As the person becomes incontinent and needs 24-hour care, you are faced with the difficult decision to institutionalize your loved one. At some point afterward, you must cope with the person's death. As the illness progresses, it takes its toll on everyone—your children, even your in-laws (Lieberman & Fisher, 1995). Although some people find transforming meanings in this life experience (Farran, Keane-Hagerty, Salloway, Kupferer, & Wilkin, 1991), in general caregiving is a difficult, upsetting job (George & Gwyther, 1986; see Chapter 10).

In a remarkable 3-year investigation, a team of social scientists set out to intensively trace the lives of 555 caregivers thrust into what they call this "unexpected career" (Aneshensel et al., 1995). As Figure 7-2 illustrates, the researchers found that caregiving follows a path that begins with role acquisition. Next comes role enactment, beginning with care at home and, typically, progressing to placement in a nursing home. Then, there is a phase of institutional care. After the patient dies, there is role

7-3 Designing Dementia Day Care

Tina O'Brian has worked in nursing homes in our area for 18 years. Recently, she and a colleague, Deborah, began the first Alzheimer's day treatment program in town. The morning I visited, I was captivated by the atmosphere of happiness these people provide. Excerpts from this interview with Tina convey some of the magic.

When I was working in the nursing home, I saw residents wandering the halls who could be home. There was no good reason for them to be there except that caregivers had given up. I felt there was a need for a place where people could come and have activities oriented to their capabilities instead of walking around asking, "Where are my folks? When am I going home?" So Deborah and I worked out some figures, approached the higher-ups in our organization, and finally were allowed to start this program. We opened December 16th and this is July the 18th. We thought it was either make it or break it after 6 months, but luckily we got a dispensation to go on for a while longer. We need 12 people to operate in the black, and now only 4 come regularly. It's a continuing struggle to get publicity for our program, to let families know what we offer.

Because these folks have memory deficits, we have to be organized. So between 9 and 9:30 A.M. we go over the date, the weather. We may describe someone's appearance and have the others pick them out. Then, we often have another cognitive exercise. My coworker and I have done these groups for so long that we can't help ourselves. We want to do mental stimulation constantly. So, we may do proverbs. You write a proverb on the board, like "You can't teach an old dog new tricks," omit a word or letter and have people guess what is missing. Tuesday is travel day. We show a video about a country and, prior to the movie, discuss what we know about the place. Afterwards, we make a list of what we learned. We

disengagement, during which the caregiver mourns the loved one and reconstructs a new life. The researchers conclude that interventions need to be tailored specifically to the requirements of each stage.

During the role-acquisition stage, people need education, prevention, and planning. They need to know what they are dealing with—that is, the symptoms, course, and basic characteristics of the disease. They need to understand how to modify the environment and react to the puzzling behavior and learn what community services are available to lighten their load (such as the day program described in Aging in Action 7-3). Even if they are determined to keep the person at home, they need to consider the possibility that institutionalization may be necessary and look into area nursing homes.

Luckily, this education is readily available. Along with the boom in popular and professional interest, an extensive network has arisen to help families coping with dementing diseases. The American Association of Retired Persons and the National Institute on Aging are clearinghouses for information and services. The **Alzheimer's Association** is a vigorous national organization devoted just to this disease. This organization sponsors research, lobbies for funding aimed at prevention and cure, oper-

*Alzheimer's
Association*
*National advocacy,
self-help
organization
addressing concerns
related to
dementing illnesses*

talk about how we would get there, how long it would take to get there. Would you like to go there? One person had been to Holland, and the day after our video about that country she brought in shoes from the trip and we all tried them on. These activities really touch base with people. Every week we do a craft project. We make sure to do some physical exercise each day. Sometimes, we play hot potato or ring toss. Sometimes, we bat a beach ball around. We have great, hilarious fun. We want everybody to feel included, so we celebrate holidays and important dates in their personal lives. We have birthday hoopla, going away hoopla, welcome to our program hoopla.

We did good things around the 4th of July. I brought in a blackberry cobbler, and we told great snake stories and wasp stories. Another day, we churned ice cream. Every day is different. We have our schedule [see Figure 7-3] and then we often say, "Oh, we didn't get to do that thing on the list" because something becomes expanded. It's very creative, very open-ended. There's a lot of exaggeration: "Isn't that wonderful!" clapping people on the back. But we try to treat people as adults—which they are—and I think they feel our expectation that they are competent. At home, families are doing things for them because of the dementia. People, when they are away from home, expect more of themselves.

Our building looks like a log cabin. It's very rustic, so people feel like they have come to a special place. It brings smiles on their faces when they walk in the door. It's been 4 months that this particular group has been coming. These people are great. They have memory loss— one had a stroke—but they are not seriously impaired. They can connect. I only wish there were more people coming, more families that could benefit, because we have a lot of energy and expertise, but very limited funds. Deborah and I really care, and I guess it shows. The main thing is that we try to bring joy into their lives, and love. At times, we've all ended up just holding hands or hugging.

ates information hotlines, and has been the driving force behind the family support groups that have been a lifeline for thousands of caregivers of demented older adults.

Family support groups, in which caregivers meet on a regular basis to share feelings and mutually work to solve problems, come into play during the role-enactment period, the long haul spanning home and institutional care. Interestingly, the researchers found that one important key to coping over this extended period was developing a sense of self-efficacy, a feeling of being on top of the day-to-day stresses. Caregiving-careers researcher Steve Zarit has developed strategies to provide this important sense of control (Zarit & Edwards, 1996; Zarit, Orr, & Zarit, 1985).

Zarit emphasizes that the first step in dealing with a person with a dementing illness is to adopt the correct perspective. When confronted with incessant questions or paranoid accusations, caregivers can easily lose focus, thinking, "Mom wants to annoy me" or "The real human being who hates me is coming out." Family members must view what is happening in its true light: The behavior is not premeditated; it is the disease. People with dementia cannot help how they act. Adopting this nonjudgmental stance then liberates caregivers to come up with workable strategies to cope.

family support groups
Self-help groups for family members caring for loved ones with dementing disorders

January

1998

Sunday	Monday	Tuesday	Wednesday	Thursday	Friday	Saturday
				1 Exercise New Year's Resolutions Deborah Farewell	2 CLOSED	3
4	5 Exercise Xmas UnDecorating **Feelings** Ring Toss	6 Exercise **Travel Video** **Snowbound** Limericks/ Pool	7 CLOSED	8 Exercise Sentence Endings **Library Time** Ocean Target	9 CLOSED	
11	12 Exercise Fun With Music Craft with Betty Bingo	13 Exercise **Travel Video** Touch & Guess A Meditation	14 CLOSED	15 Exercise **Winter Poem** Snowflakes Ocean Target	16 CLOSED	17
18	19 Exercise Taming Squirrels & Other Animals Mixed Proverbs	20 Exercise **Travel Video** "Make a Choice" Pool		22 Exercise Cooking Project Collage Bingo/Puzzles	23 CLOSED	24
25	26 Exercise **Social Bingo** "Quintuplets"	27 Exercise **Travel Video** Feelings Charades		28 Exercise Craft Activity Library Time	30 CLOSED	3

Zarit has clients first monitor the behavior—for instance, noting when the agitation arises or what happens after each angry explosion occurs. Then, they generate a list of possible solutions. Sometimes, the antidote will lie in changing one's own actions: "I need to pay more attention to her when she is being quiet" or "I should give him more exercise or take him out during the day." Sometimes, it may involve getting outside help. Day programs, such as the one described in Aging in Action 7-3, can reduce agitation or outbursts at home because they provide the stimulating contact people crave. Sometimes, as the following comments from two participants in the caregiving-careers study reveal, the key lies less in managing the other person than in changing one's own attitudes and responses (Aneshensel et al., 1995, p. 170):

1. Provide clear cues to aid orientation. Label rooms and objects around the home; use strong contrasting colors; provide plenty of indirect light (see Chapter 4).
2. Protect the person from getting hurt: Double-lock doors; turn off stove.
3. Offer a stimulating yet highly predictable, structured daily routine.
4. Don't take annoying behavior personally. Try to understand its function from the person's point of view.
5. Be nonconfronting. Comments designed to set the person straight, such as "You are not really living at X now" or "Your husband has been dead for 5 years," are certain to be counterproductive.
6. Above all, be calm, caring, and kind.

Accept the fact that the patient won't be able to live up to even minimum standards of etiquette behavior. You can waste a lot of good living time and emotion thinking that they have to meet standards they would have earlier. Let it go. That's the way it is. . . . I realized I never knew what would happen, but I finally decided that wasn't a reason not to do things. He was happier and I was happier if the ordinary standards of life just didn't apply.

My approach to the world is more confident. . . . I used to find my mother terribly embarrassing—you overcome that. . . . Laugh at it. It may seem cruel, but if you didn't see the humor, it would drive you crazy. Understand that the behavior is not voluntary, that they have no control.

Table 7-6 lists some general principles for coping with a loved one with this difficult disease. In Chapter 10, The Older Family, we will be exploring additional caregiving concerns in greater depth.

When they are at the point of considering a nursing home, caregivers need to be aware of the newest trends in institutional care. For instance, they may want to consider one of the special-care dementia units, discussed in Chapter 5, with staff and services devoted to the needs of people with this disease. Families do not make the choice to institutionalize a loved one lightly. The decision is typically made over a period of months, as the caregiver reluctantly comes to understand that it is utterly impossible to continue to keep the person at home (Bennett & Roy, 1997). Interestingly, in spite of their extreme trepidation, most participants in the caregiving-careers study found that once they had taken the step, they were pleasantly surprised with the quality of care their relative received in a nursing home. On the other hand, caregivers need to know that placement is no panacea. It does not totally erase the depression (Zarit & Edwards, 1996). On occasion, it can increase feelings of guilt and pain (Scharlach, Runkle, Midanik, & Soghikian, 1997).

Until we find a cure for dementing illnesses, our best hope for minimizing the pain lies in these studies, interventions, and services for families and patients. We need to make life as easy as possible for the millions of Americans who cope on a daily basis with this difficult disease.

Alzheimer's Association
Alzheimer's disease
autobiographical memory
delirium
dementia
episodic memory
everyday memory tasks
external memory aids
family support groups

information-processing
  perspective on memory
long-term memory
memory self-efficacy
memory-systems theory
mnemonic techniques
neurofibrillary tangles
procedural or implicit memory

processing resources
prospective memory
reminiscence peak
semantic memory
senile plaques
sensory store
vascular dementia
working memory

RECOMMENDED READINGS

MEMORY

Blanchard-Fields, F., & Hess, T. (Eds.). (1996). *Perspectives on cognitive change in adulthood and aging*. New York: McGraw-Hill.
Although this graduate-level text addresses cognition in general, it is particularly strong in its coverage of the latest research on memory.

Poon, L. W., Rubin, D. C., & Wilson, B. A. (Eds.). (1989). *Everyday cognition in adulthood and late life*. New York: Cambridge University Press.
This book, also recommended in the previous chapter, covers memory enhancement techniques and practical memory studies.

DEMENTIA

Aneshensel, C., Pearlin, L., Mullan, J., Zarit, S. H., & Whitlatch, C. (1995). *Profiles in caregiving: The unexpected career*. New York: Academic Press.

The authors follow a sample of 555 caregivers over a 3-year period, charting their stresses and their lives. A landmark in research on caregiving for dementia, this book will be interesting mainly to research-oriented students.

Coons, D. (1991). *Specialized dementia care units*. Baltimore: Johns Hopkins University Press.
This edited book describes special-care dementia units.

McGowen, D. F. (1993). *Living in the labyrinth*. New York: Bantam.
This is a remarkable, first-person account of what it is like to have Alzheimer's disease.

Chapter Outline

8

Personality

 I feel like I have lived six different lives in my six decades of life, says Jane. I was born in Indonesia in 1938. My father was from Tennessee, and my mother was British. When I was a young child, my mother became schizophrenic and was sent to an institution—in those days a death sentence, as there were no drugs. Father took me to my mother's sister in England. Then, a few days later, he was gone, buzzed off, out of my life. I was raised by this aunt who impressed on me how nobody wanted me. I knew my salvation was school, but my aunt and uncle refused to pay. At age 16, I contemplated suicide. Then, quite by accident, I got a position as a nanny at the home of the president of a teachers' college. This wonderful man took me under his wing, provided encouragement, and funded my tuition at this school. At age 20, after graduation, life took another dramatic turn. My father's family invited me to Tennessee to teach in the church. At that time, conditions were primitive in the South. Women were expected to get married and become home-makers. I followed that pattern, marrying and moving to an isolated rural community, where I spent 12 years as a full-time mom. One day, after driving the kids back from school, I thought, "I am a taxi driver." By then it was the 1970s, and the women's movement was going on. I stopped at a local school and said, "I have a teaching background." I just dumped my kids; my youngest was in kindergarten at the time. While working as a teacher, I took my master's in speech and got a job teaching part time at the university. When you are a professor, people look up to you. In my 40s, I was feeling wonderful, very much in control of my life. However, my family was falling apart. My younger child had gotten into drugs and dropped out of college. Tom died of a drug overdose 8 years ago. My son was tall and handsome, with a 150 IQ. Another watershed. I couldn't get over his death, past feeling it was my fault. I couldn't stay in our town. I felt people were saying, "What a shame about Jane's children being such a mess." You see, a few years earlier, my other son told us he was gay.

Last year I turned 60, so I can retire from the system. My son is living in San Francisco with a wonderful partner. They just celebrated their 10th anniversary. Seeing Todd happy has inspired me. I'm going back to get my PhD. I think growing older changes us. You don't have the same fears. You get a perspective about what's important. But we also are the same. You see how, when life has presented me with problems, my salvation has always been to improve my mind. If I look back over my strange life, despite all the changes, I'm basically the same person today as during my teens.

How have this woman's attitudes, emotions, and approach to life changed from youth to late middle age? Has she really become wiser and more mellow as this photo implies or is she basically the same person as the expectant young girl we see on her wedding day? It is questions such as these that the studies in adult personality development described in this chapter are designed to answer.

Think back to the different theories of personality development described in Chapter 2. Do you see evidence in this interview of Jung's idea that women become more assertive and self-confident after midlife? Perhaps you are impressed with the role that historical events, such as the women's movement, and random life experiences, such as finding a mentor or moving to America, played in shaping Jane's interests and goals (the contextualist, life-span approach). Or, in reading this interview, you may be struck with the evidence contradicting traditional psychoanalytic theory: People who have a very unhappy childhood may not be doomed to have serious emotional problems. Jane was able to cope productively even with that most traumatic event, the death of a child. On the other hand, notice that Jane herself agrees with the traditional psychoanalytic idea that there is continuity to personality. She believes that her basic strategy for handling stressful life events has been consistent from her teens.

Like Jane, you may have your own implicit theory of personality—ideas about how people change as they age. Perhaps you have found yourself thinking "I'm acting middle-aged" or, after a visit to an older relative, concluded "She's behaving like an old woman now." Many of us look forward to the person we will be, hoping the years will make us less shy, more mellow, less quick to fly off the handle, more able to compromise. Or we may worry, "Will I be as unhappy and self-centered as Aunt Mary is when I am 75?" How do people such as you and I view personality as changing with age? What issues should we be alert to in evaluating the research on how people *really* do change? These questions set the stage for the main topic of this chapter, the studies examining personality development as we age.

SETTING THE STAGE

Personal Conceptions about Change

To explore our fantasies and thoughts about how people change during adult life, Paul Baltes's research team embarked on a series of studies. First, the researchers asked men and women of various ages to rate the desirability of a long list of adjectives, such as "adventurous," "stingy," "assertive," "curious," and "cynical." Subjects were asked to decide when in life these traits began and ended, and whether each quality increased, stayed stable, or declined over the years.

The results showed that these men and women in the street agreed with the researchers' contextualist, life-span point of view, seeing development as a multifaceted mix of losses and gains. The research team was struck by the consensus among people of every age about the specific ways we change and by the relatively positive views toward aging held by both the old and the young. Although many more negative traits were ranked as increasing in the latter part of life, some desirable qualities were on an upward path until the oldest ages. In fact, gains outnumbered losses almost until the end of life (Heckhausen, Dixon, & Baltes, 1989).

However, we definitely do *not* view our older years as an emotional peak. This became evident when the research team asked young, middle-aged, and elderly people about how they believed their own personality would change during each decade of adult life (Krueger & Heckhausen, 1993). As Figure 8-1 reveals along dimensions as different as extraversion, agreeableness, conscientiousness, and emotional stability, mid life (30s–40s) is seen as the best age. By late life, the balance tips, and undesirable traits outweigh the positive ones.

Worse yet, in later life, our ideas about our future turn negative. Carol Ryff (1991) questioned young, middle-aged, and older adults about feelings of autonomy, self-acceptance, relationships with others, purpose in life, and personal growth: "Do you think you will be improving or declining in these critical areas of life?" Whereas young and middle-aged adults believed they would be changing for the better, 70-year-olds did not share this upbeat view, imagining a downward spiral in the next 10 or 20 years.

A more recent study conducted by Baltes's research team, however, suggests that we do not see late life *just* as a time of decline. When William Fleeson and Jutta Heckhausen (1997) asked young, middle-aged, and older adults to describe themselves now, in the future, and in the past, they found that adults of every age feel good about who they are at the present time. Moreover, people think that each age has special strengths. Youth is viewed as the time of exploration and growth. Productivity and autonomy are characteristic of our middle years. Later adulthood is when feelings of peace and comfort are at their height. Interestingly, everyone expresses similar feelings, showing, once again, that we share clear-cut conceptions of the personality traits that characterize each "season of life."

Are these ideas accurate? Before turning to this question, let's return to Chapter 2— this time to our discussion of research methods.

FIGURE 8-1

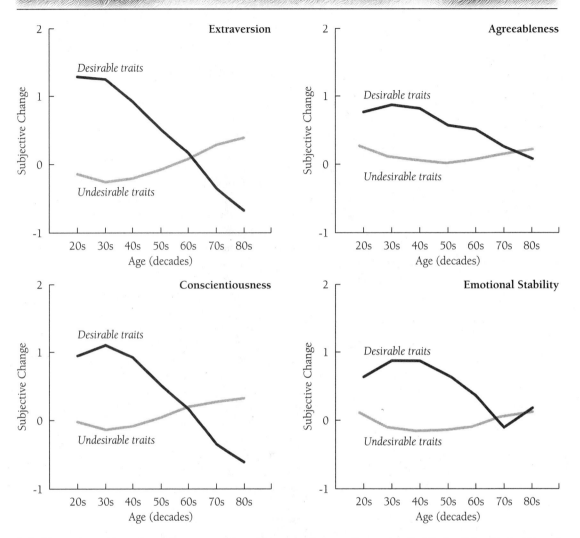

FIGURE 8-1 *Perceived Change on Extraversion, Agreeableness, Conscientiousness, and Emotional Stability across Seven Decades of Adult Life*

In looking at the positive and negative aspects of these dimensions of personality, we view the 30s (or 40s) as the best time of life. By the 70s, undesirable qualities outweigh the positive ones.
SOURCE: Krueger & Heckhausen, 1993.

Problems of Measuring Change

THE ISSUE OF WHAT WE TEST   What do we mean by personality? Under this huge umbrella term lurk incredibly diverse emotions, attitudes, and activities. Personality includes traits such as shyness or assertiveness. It involves our styles of coping with stress, likes and dislikes, values, preferences, and needs. It includes our self-concept, our feelings about the past, our goals, and future plans. It involves unconscious motivations as well as actions and intentions of which we are aware.

So, the first principle in approaching the research is to look carefully at the way each investigator has chosen to operationalize personality. As we saw in our discussion of research methods, we need to be aware that different ways of defining and measuring this vague entity may produce different conclusions about the extent of change. In other words, the answer to the question "How will I change?" is likely to depend on *what* we test.

THE ISSUE OF WHO WE TEST   In exploring personality development, we want to make general statements that will apply to most adults. Although it is easier to get the representative sample needed to make these generalizations in a cross-sectional study, this type of research cannot tell us whether the change we are seeing in a particular aspect of personality is basic to age or simply due to being in a different cohort. A cross-sectional study showing that 70-year-olds are less emotional, for example, may be uncovering a true late-life change, or it may only be showing that today's older people are less likely to be open about their emotions because they grew up before the 1960s when freely discussing personal feelings was more taboo. In addition, because they do not trace the lives of individuals, cross-sectional studies cannot answer some very important questions: If people are especially reserved in youth, do they "grow out" of this tendency? How do experiences such as becoming ill or being widowed change the tendency to be open about our feelings? Longitudinal studies can answer these questions relating to individual change patterns and why they may occur, but they are expensive and take decades to complete. Because they involve a long-term commitment, moreover, they tend to be carried out with "elite" groups—well-educated, upper-middle-class volunteers. Finally, even longitudinal studies do not allow us to make universal statements about people because they only trace development in a particular cohort traveling through time at a given point in history.

So, a second principle in considering the studies is to look carefully at *who* is being tested. Because they are more informative, if possible we should focus on longitudinal research. However, we should be aware that this type of study often tells us about development only within a "special" group.

In this chapter, we will follow this strategy. Although I will mention other research, we will pay special attention to the four comprehensive studies of personality listed and described in Table 8-1. The first, the **Kansas City Studies of Adult Life,** does not fully fit our criterion as longitudinal, because the researchers followed subjects for only a few years. However, as the first attempt to measure personality change systematically in middle and later life, the Kansas City Studies are a landmark in the psychology of aging. Some findings of this research are still being debated today.

The second study fulfills the longitudinal requirement to the utmost extent. The **Berkeley/Oakland Studies** offer a motion picture of personality throughout the *entire life span.* During the late 1920s and early 1930s, psychologists at the University of California at Berkeley selected a large group of children, tested them and their parents periodically through adolescence and again at regular intervals throughout adult life. Today, research is still being carried out on the surviving parents and children. As we

Kansas City Studies of Adult Life
Earliest major study of personality change in middle and later life

Berkeley/ Oakland Studies
Only longitudinal study to cover the entire life span, exploring personality and social development in a cohort born in the late 1920s in Berkeley, California

TABLE 8-1   *The Studies Highlighted in This Chapter: A Preview*

1. **The Kansas City Studies of Adult Life.** Several hundred married middle-class couples, ranging in age from 40 to their 90s, living in Kansas City during the middle 1950s were interviewed and given a variety of measures and tests. *Main personality measure:* The TAT. Subjects are given a series of pictures and asked to tell stories about each. From these story themes, psychologists analyze unconscious motivations.

2. **Berkeley/Oakland Studies.** Several studies of child development begun during the late 1920s and early 1930s were merged and the groups were followed throughout adult life. *Personality measure:* To make the data comparable, researchers adapted the California Q-sort. Based on the personality data, trained raters sort statements on cards referring to personality into three piles as either very characteristic, somewhat characteristic, or not characteristic of each person at different ages.

3. **The Baltimore Longitudinal Study.** Volunteers varying in age take a battery of tests every two years. *Personality measure:* The NEO-PI, a self-report scale measuring broad personality dispositions or traits.

4. **The Mills College Study.** Members of the 1958 and 1960 graduating classes of Mills College for Women were assessed as seniors and periodically reassessed through their early 50s. *Personality measure:* The California Psychological Inventory, a self-report scale asking subjects about their attitudes, traits, and coping styles.

will see in this chapter and others, this one-of-a-kind research project offers insights into everything from personality change and consistency, to the keys to happy, long-lasting marriages, to how friendships and family relationships change during our older years.

The third study, the Baltimore Longitudinal Study of Aging, is already familiar from Chapters 2 and 3. Finally, in the **Mills College Study,** women at a prestigious women's college in California were first evaluated as undergraduates in the late 1950s and then retested several times through middle age.

Although they offer our best information about personality change, notice that each study has its limitations. Not one explores personality development among racial or ethnic minorities. Every study involves mainly middle-class adults. With the exception of the Baltimore Study, each traces the lives of cohorts who reached adulthood or were adults during the middle of the 20th century, a more traditional time in American life. Notice, moreover, that each study defines and measures personality differently. In the Kansas City research, the emphasis was on unconscious processes and coping styles. In the Baltimore and Mills College studies, the focus was on personality traits such as shyness or assertiveness. Some researchers used scales in which people were asked to rate themselves; others measured personality through interviews or the stories a person told.

As we turn now to explore the findings of these studies and others, keep the crucial issue of measurement validity in mind. Are researchers really measuring a given aspect of personality by using a particular strategy or test? Equally important, these *legitimately* different strategies for viewing and measuring personality are central to understanding the great consistency/change debate.

Mills College Study

Classic longitudinal study in which seniors at Mills College for Women were tested and then followed through midlife

THE GREAT CONSISTENCY/CHANGE DEBATE

Phase 1. Focus on Change: The Kansas City Studies of Adult Life

Research on personality change with age began with the Kansas City Studies of Adult Life. In the early 1950s, a research team headed by University of Chicago psychologist Bernice Neugarten chose a group of "typical" middle-aged and elderly white, middle-class American married couples, living in an average American city (Kansas City, Missouri), and interviewed and tested these people over a period of several years (Neugarten & Associates, 1964).

FINDINGS   Because their orientation was psychoanalytic, in addition to their other measures and interviews, the University of Chicago researchers used a test designed to reveal unconscious motivations called the **Thematic Apperception Test (TAT).** In this test, people are shown a series of pictures and asked to tell a story about each scene. The theory is that through these stories, people reveal their unconscious concerns, conflicts, and underlying worldview. Rather than simply letting themes emerge, the researchers categorized the stories their subjects produced along dimensions that they labeled *ego energy* and *mastery style.*

Ego energy (Rosen & Neugarten, 1964) referred to vigorous, passionate, energetic engagement versus withdrawal. If a person told a story that was rich in detail, full of feelings, one in which the characters were passionately involved in life, the idea was that this same passionate involvement would characterize the person's approach to living. Mastery style measured a similar sense of engagement through the story's theme. Was the main character confronting and triumphing over a problem or retreating from the world? Once again, if the message of the story was one of personal triumph and success, this style was believed to reflect the person's approach to the world.

Starting in their late-middle-aged group—men and women in their early 50s—ratings of ego energy and active mastery gradually declined, suggesting to the research team that as people grow old, they tend to become less involved in the world. This internal withdrawal, accompanied by a reduction in the actual number of roles that the researchers found among the men and women in their 60s, caused two members of the team to propose a controversial idea called **disengagement theory.**

According to Elaine Cumming and William Henry (1961), a natural process of disengagement takes place in late middle age. People begin to distance themselves emotionally from society and withdraw from the world. Cumming and Henry proposed not only that this withdrawal is normal, but that disengagement is the *correct* way to age.

The second change the University of Chicago researchers found was equally interesting. When Bernice Neugarten and David Gutmann (1964) gave subjects a TAT card picturing a young man, a young woman, an old man, and an old woman, the younger people (aged 40–54) described the old man and old woman in standard gender stereotypes: He was dominant; she was gentle and submissive. The older men and women (aged 55–70) however, reversed the adjectives: The woman was described as powerful and controlling; the man was seen as passive, submissive, and sweet. The researchers concluded that in later life, personality differences between the sexes blur or reverse.

Thematic Apperception Test (TAT)
Key test used in the Kansas City Studies in which people are thought to reveal their unconscious concerns through telling stories about pictures

disengagement theory
Controversial idea that it is normal and appropriate for older people to withdraw from the world

"Women . . . seem to become more tolerant of their own aggressive egocentric impulses; . . . men . . . of their own nurturant and affiliative impulses" (Neugarten & Gutmann, 1964, p. 89).

Notice that these findings fit in perfectly with Jung's theory. Jung believed that we become more spiritual or "disengaged" and more **androgynous,** or less rigidly masculine and feminine, in middle age. The findings also support our ideas about how people are supposed to change: youth as a time for passionate exploration, midlife as a time of vigorous productivity, and later adulthood as a time of comfort, contemplation, and peace.

androgynous
Having balance between masculine and feminine traits

CRITICISMS   During the late 1960s and early 1970s, however, a barrage of criticism was aimed at the Kansas City results. By that time, a revolution was occurring in women's roles. Could men and women still be described in terms of the gender stereotypes given by the Kansas City 40-year-olds? Psychologists questioned the theory underlying the TAT, that by telling stories about pictures people reveal their unconscious mental processes. Researchers were becoming more sensitive to the problem of assuming age changes from cross-sectional studies and of making generalizations to everyone from only studying a sample of white, married, middle-class adults. Based on disturbing evidence that tests used to reveal personality were often not valid measures of those traits (Campbell & Fiske, 1959; Fiske, 1971), psychologists criticized the inferences the University of Chicago researchers made. Perhaps the finding that older people tell less detailed and imaginative TAT stories does not signify decreasing involvement in life but simply the fact that, as we learned in previous chapters, the elderly are often more uncomfortable taking *any* test and so tend to produce more limited responses.

Most important, many gerontologists disagreed with the idea that disengagement was appropriate in later life. If this idea were allowed to stand, might it not justify discriminatory practices such as mandatory retirement, the idea that older adults should retire to a rocking chair? Isn't it important as we age to keep as active as possible, to stay fully engaged in the world (Lemon, Bengtson, & Peterson, 1972)?

As you may have guessed from previous chapters, this alternative advice for ideal aging, called **activity theory,** easily won out—with important qualifications. Later Kansas City research showed that whether people were happy was really more a function of their personality than their level of activity. Among the best-adjusted men and women, the researchers found a mixture of active and relatively inactive people, all satisfied with life. Among people who were emotionally disturbed, disengagement combined with low morale was the rule (Neugarten, Havinghurst, & Tobin, 1968). In other words, disengagement could be a satisfying way of life, provided it was actively *chosen* by an emotionally healthy individual.

activity theory
Idea that keeping active is the optimum way to age

CURRENT STATUS AND ONGOING ISSUES   For decades, gerontologists were certain that they had closure on the activity/disengagement debate. Granted a few older people could be happy withdrawing, but, in general, keeping as active as possible is the key to aging successfully. Today, however, a familiar theory urges a fresh, second look at this well-worn advice: Baltes's concept of selective optimization with compensation, discussed in Chapter 2.

Recall that Baltes believes that some disengagement *is* critical to aging. As we realize we can no longer do everything as well, we must make the decision to pull back from some activities. But this withdrawal is selective. We have to give up what is less essential in the service of staying engaged in our top-priority areas of life.

Moreover, in contrast to the traditional idea, disengagement does not begin only in our later years. It occurs gradually throughout adult life. Drawing on taped interviews conducted with the Berkeley/Oakland men and women over a 30-year period, Laura Carstensen (1995) discovered that beginning in early adulthood, we start to reduce our number of social interactions. We do not see as many people as before. However, over that same time, people develop more intense relationships with those people they are closest to in life. Just as we cannot care deeply about 50 friends or work our best at ten different pursuits, *selective* disengagement is one key to living fully, both as older people and during the long span of adult life (Carstensen, 1995; Heckhausen & Schulz, 1993; Schulz & Heckhausen, 1996).

It seems logical that disengagement would be automatic when we bump up against the limitations of advancing age. The second finding of the Kansas City Studies is less obvious. Do men and women become more androgynous as they age? David Gutmann, as well as a few other researchers in adult development, believe they do.

Exploring myths, dreams, and anecdotes and pulling together anthropological data from around the world, Gutmann has devoted his career to arguing that a shift toward androgyny is universal during the second half of adult life. However, whereas he originally thought this change was basic to growing old, Gutmann now sees it as due to the different pressures we face as younger versus older adults.

According to Gutmann (1987), personality differences between men and women are needed in the first half of adulthood because of what he calls the **parental imperative.** For optimal child rearing, Guttmann argues, nature has set up a division of labor that, despite the women's revolution, usually follows traditional lines: The man aggressively provides for the family, and the woman handles the interpersonal sphere, taking care of the day-to-day child care and offering the female qualities of understanding, patience, and selflessness. Once children have left the nest, women "reclaim" the masculine qualities they had to dampen to ensure their children's development. At the same time, men relax, giving more play to their nurturing, "feminine" side (Cooper & Gutmann, 1987).

Cross-sectional studies of personality at different ages support the idea that gender roles and attitudes become less sharply distinct at older ages (Feldman, Biringen, & Nash, 1981; Lowenthal, Thurnher, Chiriboga, & Associates, 1975; Sedney, 1985–1986). However, as we know, to really show that Gutmann has a valid point, we must look to longitudinal research.

In the Mills College Study, Ravinna Helson and Paul Wink (1992) gave an adjective checklist to the women they were following at age 27, during the early parental stage, and again at about age 50, when most were in the empty nest. They found that as young parents, the women rated themselves much lower than their husbands on masculine traits such as assertiveness and efficiency, but at the empty nest they ranked themselves as high as their spouses on these traits.

Are these changes really due to the declining parental imperative? Perhaps they are caused by hormonal changes occurring around menopause that affect personality, or by the toughening impact of having coped for decades with life's ups and downs.

parental imperative
Gutmann's hypothesis that parenting evokes defined gender roles during the younger, child-rearing phase of adult life

Postformal researchers might even argue that what Gutmann labels androgyny—more acceptance of both masculine and feminine sides of personality—is actually a sign of a larger process: People become less rigid, more flexible, and generally more open to complexity in themselves and others as they mature (Blanchard-Fields & Chen, 1996; see our discussion of postformal thought in Chapter 6).

Also, these changes may not be as universal as Guttmann thinks. In one interesting comparative study, young adult African American women ranked themselves as more androgynous on a gender-role scale, although just as child-centered, compared with whites (Binion, 1990). In exploring ethnic differences on a general personality test, another group of researchers found that traditional masculine/feminine attitudes were especially strong among Asian American college students, both women and men (Dion & Yee, 1987). In other words, instead of being basic to parenthood, defined gender roles in early adulthood may be partly shaped by our specific cultural group and its norms.

The same dependence on the social environment applies to the shift to androgyny that Guttmann believes occurs automatically after the children are gone. When she first tested the Mills women as they were about to graduate in 1959, Ravinna Helson (1992) gave an identical checklist to their mothers, who were in their early 50s at the time. These empty-nest mothers showed no sign of androgyny!

What accounts for the difference between mothers and their daughters at the same age? Helson believes, once again, that the answer lies in cultural norms, or the experiences each cohort had as it traveled adult life. The Mills daughters were young adults during the 1960s, when women entered the workforce and being assertive became prized. Their mothers lived during a more restricted time in history, when middle-class women were supposed to act in defined, "dependent" ways. Helson argues that the older cohort could not grow more androgynous because their life circumstances stifled any change toward assertion over time. In other words, just as we saw with creative work, the push to become androgynous may depend on having the right environment. It may need a supportive social milieu in which to flower.

Does this mean that our environment is the primary force shaping our personality and that who we become as we age is highly responsive to our specific experiences in life? A good deal of evidence suggests that the answer is no. In contrast to what Erikson, Jung, or indeed, most of us believe, personality during adulthood may be surprisingly enduring and stable, immune to cultural change or life experiences. Paul Costa and Robert McCrae have devoted distinguished careers to arguing this point.

Phase 2. Focus on Stability: Costa and McCrae's Big Five Traits

As the researchers who direct the personality studies for the Baltimore Study, Costa and McCrae have been in a position to analyze how huge numbers of people of every age score on paper-and-pencil personality tests over the years. Many psychologists believe that their findings have put to rest the idea that there are *any* stages of adult development or that people change in predictable ways as they grow old. According to Costa and McCrae, personality stability characterizes adult life. The best prediction about how the years will change us is that they will not (Costa & McCrae, 1980; Costa, McCrae, & Arenberg, 1980, 1983; McCrae & Costa, 1990).

FINDINGS   The evidence that Costa and McCrae have gathered showing that personality stays remarkably stable during adulthood involves the same four global aspects of personality shown in Figure 8-1—dimensions that people predicted would change with age. Costa and McCrae actually identify five general personality tendencies, broad dimensions that underlie all of the specific traits, qualities, and attributes by which we describe people (Costa & McCrae, 1988a; McCrae, Costa, & Piedmont, 1993). How is it possible to reduce the thousands of ways we think about personality into five categories? Costa and McCrae have performed this distilling feat using a statistical technique that showed that all of the adjectives used to characterize personality cluster into the following broad categories:

1. *Neuroticism (N)* is a general tendency toward mental health versus psychological disturbance—that is, anxiety, hostility, depression, self-consciousness, and emotional distress. Is the person stable and well-adjusted or emotionally vulnerable, prone to break down?

2. *Extraversion (E)* reflects outgoing attitudes, such as warmth, gregariousness, activity, and assertion. Is the person at home and happy with others, or does that individual feel more comfortable being alone, living a more reflective, solitary life?

3. *Openness to experience (O)* involves the willingness to take risks, seek out new experiences, and try new things. Does the person love the unbeaten path or the newest thrill? Or is the person cautious and comfortable only with the tried and true?

4. *Conscientiousness (C)* relates to how organized, efficient, and dependable the person is. Is this individual hardworking, self-disciplined, and reliable, or erratic, inconsistent, irresponsible, someone we really can't trust?

5. *Agreeableness (A)* incorporates qualities related to love, such as empathy, caring, friendliness, and cooperation. Is the person caring, sensitive, pleasant, and loving, or contentious, scornful, and rude?

According to Costa and McCrae, measuring how these **big five traits** change over time allows us to test the truth of most theories and stereotypes about personality development. If people become emotionally unstable in later life, neuroticism scores should reach a peak in older adults. If people grow more generative or mature, scores on agreeableness or conscientiousness should rise. If the idea that age makes us rigid is correct, then as people grow old, they should exhibit a decline in openness to experience. If we do pull back from the outer world in our later years, extraversion ratings should decline. But, the volunteers' scores on each of these dimensions are similar at age 35 and age 85.

big five traits
Five overarching dimensions of personality encompassing all smaller descriptions and traits

The Baltimore men and women are an upper-middle-class group. Can we really expect how they change—or, in this case, do not change—to apply to Americans as a whole? It is one thing to say that among highly educated, relatively healthy people, personality remains stable, but what about the less fortunate—people who are poor, uneducated, or ill? To show that the Baltimore findings do apply to Americans in general, Costa and McCrae (1986) decided they needed to show that the Baltimore subjects' scores on neuroticism, extraversion, and openness to experience at each age were similar to those of a more representative group.

Toward this end, the researchers got access to subjects from a national survey involving almost 15,000 respondents and gave these people an abbreviated form of their personality test. They found few differences in the scores of the two samples, suggesting that the Baltimore results can indeed be generalized to most Americans. Furthermore, when they looked at age differences in extraversion, openness, and neuroticism among these thousands of people, here too stability was the dominant theme. Although older age groups did have slightly lower scores on the three dimensions, the differences were not statistically significant.

CURRENT STATUS AND ONGOING ISSUES   Costa and McCrae's research has had an enormous impact on the field of personality. From being uncertain as to whether they could capture and measure personality, many psychologists now agree that the qualities measured by standard personality tests can be distilled to these categories (Ozer & Reise, 1994). These broad dispositions seem to be valid; that is, they seem to be accurately measured by Costa and McCrae's self-report test. When a man rates himself as introverted on Costa and McCrae's scale, his spouse and friends are likely to rate him as introverted too (Costa & McCrae, 1988b). Observers will rate that person as introverted when they meet him in a social situation or watch him at work (McCrae & Costa, 1990). Moreover, other research confirms the consistency of personality over long periods of adult life (Conley, 1984, 1985; West & Graziano, 1989). Even specific pathological ways of viewing the world can be consistent from youth to old age.

Melanie Burns and Martin Seligman (1989) asked elderly men and women to bring in samples of diaries and letters they had written about 50 years earlier, when they were in their late teens and 20s. Then, the researchers instructed their subjects to write about specific recent events in their lives. What they were looking for was similarities in explanatory style. Is the tendency to attribute setbacks to temporary, changeable, external causes a stable trend? When people see failures as global, irreversible, and due to the self, is this an enduring way of perceiving the world? Although they found little consistency in interpretations of positive events, Burns and Seligman found a statistically significant correlation in attributions for negative life happenings between youth and old age. In other words, a pessimistic explanatory style may indeed be a burden some people carry from youth into later life.

FORCES THAT CONTRIBUTE TO STABILITY   While many of us may blame our parents, agreeing with Freud that our upbringing shapes the way we perceive and react as adults, behavioral genetic studies offer a different view. Remember that studies of identical twins raised apart suggest that extraversion and neuroticism are actually heritable traits (Bouchard & McGue, 1990). Even perceptions very similar to explanatory style may have a genetic component.

When Matt McGue, Betsy Hirsch, and David Lykken (1993) asked identical twins who were raised apart to describe how competent and capable they felt in various areas, they found a significant correlation in these assessments. Whether because of actual similarities in ability or inherited tendencies to view oneself in certain ways, the twins tended to share efficacy feelings, agreeing that they were competent or incompetent in each area of life.

The most interesting behavioral genetic studies are those that turn our ideas about personality and environment upside down. Rather than our life experiences' determining our personality, who we are as people shapes our "outer world." Genetic tendencies influence our ideas about the social world. They affect how giving and generous we remember our parents' being during our early years (McCrae & Costa, 1988; Plomin, McClearn, Pedersen, Nesselroade, & Bergemen, 1988). They influence how supportive we see our family and friends as being today (Bergemen, Plomin, Pedersen, McClearn, & Nesselroade, 1990; Chipuer, Plomin, Pedersen, McClearn, & Nesselroade, 1993). There may even be genetic influences on the *objective experiences* we encounter on our journey through adult life.

In the Swedish Adoption/Twin Study of Aging, older twins separated at birth were more likely than chance to report having had similar experiences during adult life (Plomin, Lichtenstein, Pedersen, McClearn, & Nesselroade, 1990). This amazing tendency to report similar life experiences was evident only for life events that we potentially have control over, such as marriage and family conflicts or success or failure at work. It did not appear for uncontrollable events, such as illness of a spouse or the death of a child.

Although at first glance the idea that people who share only genes might have similar life experiences seems ridiculous, if we think more deeply, this relationship makes perfect sense. Think of a young adult who scores low on agreeableness and conscientiousness on Costa's scale, someone who is hostile and unreliable. Wouldn't you imagine this person to be more likely to be fired from her job, to fight with friends, to get divorced, to experience more negative events? Now imagine another young adult who ranks high on these personality dimensions related to being able to love and work effectively. Although not immune from tragedies, wouldn't this person's personality set her up for a smoother, more gratifying life? The Swedish Adoption/Twin Study only reinforces the saying "We make our own luck" (at least, the luck that we can control).

Behavioral genetic research offers a powerful argument that genetics does shape personality. A broad range of personality dimensions, from Costa's big five to more limited attitudes such as conservative political ideas, are much more genetically determined than psychologists ever believed. However, remember that saying a certain trait is *influenced* by inherited tendencies is far different from assuming we are fated to behave in that way. Nor does it mean that what happens to us in life has little impact on who we are. As we saw in Chapter 2, the heritabilities for personality are moderate compared with those for physical health and especially intelligence. In other words, in this important area of life, our life experiences do loom comparatively large in shaping who we are. However, inherited tendencies toward neuroticism or agreeableness may also tend to solidify precisely because heredity and environment are not independent. The two may work in tandem to accentuate who we are for better or for worse.

Berkeley researchers Avishom Caspi, Darrell Bem, and Glen Elder (1989) believe there are two ways in which our experiences during life may interact with our temperamental tendencies to make us "more like ourselves" as we age.

Cumulative consistency occurs when the general consequences of having a certain trait operate to reinforce that attribute. Take Joe Smith, who ranks low on agreeableness at age 20. Because Joe is hostile and unpleasant, he tends to lose jobs repeatedly and to have trouble with relationships. Each failure reinforces his anger, solidifying and heightening his disagreeable worldview. As Joe ages, he grows increasingly more distrustful and angry at the world.

Interactional consistency refers to the immediate social impact of having a certain personality style. Joe's hostile responses evoke a similar response in others; people react angrily to him. In his next encounter, he is even more prone to lash out. Once again, hostility becomes a more entrenched reaction as the years pass.

With the caution that personal examples such as this can never be used to prove or disprove any concept or idea, let me illustrate the process these researchers describe using an acquaintance of mine. This person is abrasive, easily offended, and unwilling to compromise, and so is constantly involved in some fight or feud. About two years ago, his life seemed to come together as he developed his first long-lasting romantic relationship. When he worked up the courage to propose marriage, perhaps scared off by the vision of years of conflict, his girlfriend didn't return his calls. In response, he has concluded that "human beings aren't worth it; they just do you in" and resolved to live life alone. Another familiar saying seems to fit this process: "Paranoid people have enemies."

Caspi, Bem, and Elder (1989) use the principles of cumulative and interactional consistency to explain why certain difficult temperaments measured at about age 10 in the Berkeley/Oakland girls and boys tended to have enduring consequences in midlife. Before you assume that *every* child who is having difficulty in a certain area is destined for a difficult life, let's look at this study in some depth. It tells us that the relationship between temperament and life success is more complex than we might think.

The researchers traced the lives of the girls and boys labeled with three difficult temperaments during middle childhood: children subject to severe temper tantrums (explosive children); children ranked unusually shy; and children judged excessively dependent or too attached to their parents and other adults.

Children with explosive personalities did indeed do more poorly in their travels through life. They were more likely to experience problems at work and to report unhappy marriages or be divorced at midlife (Caspi, Elder, & Bem, 1987). In contrast, the impact of being excessively shy or dependent was less detrimental and differed by gender. Whereas shy boys were somewhat worse off, marrying later and entering careers at older ages than those who were not withdrawn, the researchers could find no long-term consequences of shyness for girls.

The findings for dependency were the most interesting. Although girls in this category did have more problems, boys labeled too dependent or excessively attached had an unusually *happy* adult life! In midlife, they had an impressive list of qualities. They were calm, giving, insightful, and socially poised. They were more likely to have stable marriages, to be nurturing fathers, and to have satisfied wives (Caspi, Bem, & Elder, 1989).

So, even if temperament does endure, we cannot be sure how a given style of approaching the world will play out as we journey through life. Although some aspects of personality, such as being explosive, are pure liabilities, the effect of others, such as shyness, is much less negative. The researchers reasoned that being shy may have been more detrimental for the males in the study because men are expected to take a more active stance in relationships and at work.

But why would the home-oriented tendencies labeled as excessive dependency in childhood turn out to be positive traits for boys? The key may lie in the drive to be close that defines this trait. Perhaps because we as a society expect so much independence from boys, we label healthy levels of dependence as not manly enough. But this same need to be near our **primary attachment figures** (closest loved ones) translates into having especially close marriages and being an involved, caring father during our adult years. In fact, although research in this area is limited, the drive to be attached may even be linked to having close, fulfilling relationships in later life (Magai & Passman, 1998). People who are securely attached—that is, those fully able to reach out in love—not only have happier marriages, they may even cope better with losing their primary attachment figure (being widowed) in their older years.

primary
attachment
figures
Closest loved ones
or "significant
others"

This study is one of my favorites, because it illustrates the power of longitudinal research. Human beings tend to see the moment and assume forever. We agonize about our son who we think of as too dependent or not self-reliant enough. What we really are worrying about is his future life. Only the insights offered by following people can tell us whether our worry is warranted and our fears are correct. As this fascinating research reveals, what appears to be a problem at one point in life may turn out to be a gift!

CAUTIONS ABOUT AND A CRITIQUE OF STABILITY   If the forces propelling personality consistency are so powerful, does this mean that who we are is set in stone? Costa and McCrae themselves caution against this conclusion, stressing that their studies show only that systematic change is unlikely, not that change never occurs. Moreover, even if our basic tendencies to emotional disturbance or openness to experience remain stable, these dispositions may translate into different behaviors at different life stages. A person high in "neuroticism" may be anxiety-ridden at age 20, hostile and bitter at 65. People open to experience may seem to change dramatically as they age, as they shift interests, jobs, and friends in their drive to experience anything new and untried. Without denying that we can see seeds of the 70-year-old in the person of 25, let's look at some other reasons why our crystal ball may be fuzzier than these stability advocates assert.

1. **Change is more likely over longer time periods and over certain periods of life.**   Many of Costa and McCrae's analyses have been cross-sectional. Their longitudinal research covers only about a decade and mainly explores change in people over age 30. Perhaps the evidence for stability would be less impressive if we looked over longer periods of life or explored personality change at different ages.

Once again, the longest-running study of development allows us to adopt this lifespan view. Norma Haan, Roger Millsap, and Elizabeth Hartka (1986) obtained personality ratings from a core group of the original children in the Berkeley/Oakland studies at seven points during their life span: early childhood, late childhood, early adolescence, late adolescence, early adulthood, middle adulthood, and old age.

Interestingly, the researchers found that stability *and* change were both dominant themes. Some aspects of personality shifted dramatically over time; others stayed relatively constant. Some periods of life were times of great change; others produced fewer transformations in the self. Notice in Table 8-2 that the life-span correlations for the different Q-sort components of personality are much lower than the correlations for adjacent time periods, and that these correlations differ at different points in life.

In fact, the compelling finding of this uniquely long longitudinal study was that childhood and adolescence were the periods of greatest stability. In direct contrast to what Freud predicts, adulthood was a time of greater internal change. The years from

TABLE 8-2 **Pattern of Correlations of the Different Facets of Personality Measured by the Q-Sort over Each Period in the Life Span in the Berkeley/Oakland Studies**

	Early to Late Childhood	Late Childhood to Early Adolescence	Early to Late Adolescence	Late Adolescence to Early Adulthood	Early to Middle Adulthood	Middle to Late Adulthood	Life-Span Correlations
MEDIAN CORRELATIONS	.60	.56	.60	.40	.52	.55	.25
PERCENTAGE OF CORRELATIONS THAT EXCEEDED .50	94%	83%	78%	22%	56%	56%	0%

Adolescence to young adulthood is the time when personality changes the most. As we might expect, personality is far less consistent over the entire life span that it is during adjacent life phases.
SOURCE: Haan, Millsap, & Hartka, 1986.

late adolescence through young adulthood (about age 17 to 33) were a time of especially intense flux. Perhaps because this period spanned the transition from childhood dependence to adult maturity, subjects changed more radically over this time period than at any point in the study.

To make sense of their finding that early adulthood, not childhood, is when personality is most changeable, the researchers offered this interesting hypothesis: Changes in the outer fabric of life propel internal change. During childhood and adolescence, the external aspects of our life tend to be relatively stable. We are being cared for in a protected environment and insulated from having to prove ourselves by making our way in the world. In our 20s, our life tends to change radically. Many of us marry, become parents, and establish a career. At this age, we are no longer able to rely on our parents. How we cope depends on us. So, if bumping up against life's challenges causes change, it makes sense that adulthood might be the time of most internal flux.

2. **Change is more likely if we look beyond traits.** The test used to measure personality in the Berkeley/Oakland Studies, the California Q-sort, involves what researchers call an *ipsative approach* to evaluation. Instead of the traditional normative strategy, in which people rank themselves according to defined traits or qualities and their scores are then compared with those of others, people taking this test place statements on cards into piles as either more or less characteristic of themselves, and researchers then examine how this internal organization shifts over time.

This individual-centered measurement strategy may provide different information about change than we would get by seeing how people compare with one another along defined, specific traits (Chaplin & Buckner, 1988; Pelham, 1993). This brings up a question about Costa and McCrae's approach: Although knowing how comparatively neurotic, agreeable, or open to experience a person is tells us a good deal, is it the final word on who we are?

Psychoanalytically oriented psychologists such as Gutmann would argue no. Self-reports and observer ratings of extraversion or agreeableness miss unconscious motivations, the "core" of personality of which we are not aware. For psychologists who believe in the psychoanalytic approach, asking people to report on their own or a friend's personality will never be satisfying. To truly measure personality requires tests of unconscious processes, such as the TAT.

Perhaps the most interesting critique of what traits tell us and what the big five may leave out is that of Northwestern University psychologist Dan McAdams. McAdams (1992) sees personality as having three parallel levels.

Level 1 is the dimension Costa is measuring, traits and dispositions—whether we are shy or outgoing, friendly or rude. These are the aspects of the person we notice when we meet a stranger. We evaluate that person from an external frame of reference. We size up that individual in relation to others we know.

As we get closer and begin to know the person, McAdams suggests, our frame of reference shifts. We fill in the details and learn about that person's specific aspirations and concerns. Now we have entered a new dimension or way of thinking about personality. We are dealing at levels 2 and 3.

Level 2 refers to the themes and concerns that currently organize a person's life. Is Dr. Belsky's family everything? Is writing this book the passion that shapes my days? Level 3 refers to the way these plans and goals are integrated into a life plan over the years. McAdams believes that what is most central in personality is what Erikson calls our identity, and that we are always in the process of constructing a coherent identity or life story as we travel through time.

Level 1 traits may be stable. McAdams agrees that we probably do not change dramatically in extraversion or openness to experience as the years pass. At the second and third levels, however, personality is more likely to evolve. The actual content of what gives meaning to our days is more likely to change as we have new experiences and enter new phases of life.

Because Costa and McCrae's studies focus only on level 1, McAdams believes they are insensitive to level 2 and 3 changes. They cannot measure shifts in life orientation and worldview that occur as we develop, the very changes Erikson and Jung were trying to address in their theories. So it is no wonder that despite people's *feeling* that they have changed dramatically, often in the ways these theorists predict, traditional studies using standard personality tests often show that little change occurs.

Phase 3. Focus on Change: Exploring Life Stories, Goals, Priorities, and Hopes

When we look at levels 2 and 3, we do get a different view of change, as we now see in examining the newest trend in personality research: studies exploring our hopes, goals, and fears.

MCADAMS MEASURES GENERATIVITY   To test Erikson's idea that generativity is a main theme of adult life, Dan McAdams's research team took a series of steps. First, they pinned down or spelled out Erikson's complex concept; then, they devised tests

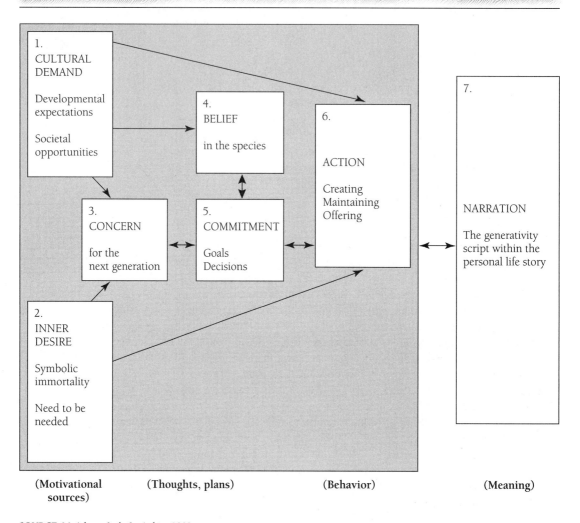

1.
CULTURAL
DEMAND

Developmental
expectations

Societal
opportunities

2.
INNER
DESIRE

Symbolic
immortality

Need to be
needed

3.
CONCERN

for the
next generation

4.
BELIEF

in the species

5.
COMMITMENT

Goals
Decisions

6.

ACTION

Creating
Maintaining
Offering

7.

NARRATION

The generativity
script within the
personal life story

(Motivational
sources)

(Thoughts, plans)

(Behavior)

(Meaning)

SOURCE: McAdams & de St. Aubin, 1992.

to measure these qualities; finally, they looked for the predicted differences at different ages (McAdams & de St. Aubin, 1992).

McAdams and his colleagues see generativity as involving the processes, thoughts, and actions illustrated in Figure 8-2. First, to be generative, people must be at the right stage of life (step 1 in the diagram). "We do not expect 10-year-old children to provide primary care for the next generation. We generally do not expect them to think about

1. I try to pass along the knowledge I have gained through my experiences.
2. I do not feel that other people need me.
3. I think I would like the work of a teacher.
4. I feel as though I have made a difference to many people.
5. I do not volunteer to work for a charity.
6. I have made and created things that have had an impact on other people.
7. I try to be creative in most things that I do.
8. I think that I will be remembered for a long time after I die.
9. I believe that society cannot be responsible for providing food and shelter to all homeless people.
10. Others would say that I have made unique contributions to society.

SOURCE:McAdams & de St. Aubin, 1992.

the legacy they will leave after they die. But as people move into young and middle adulthood, we come to expect an increasing awareness of a commitment to their role as providers" (McAdams, 1994, p. 680). These outer-world expectations must be complemented by inner desire (step 2). This desire has two components: the urge for immortality—that is, to leave something behind of ourselves after death—and the desire to be needed, to be helpful to other human beings. These two conditions evoke generative concern (step 3). When the person has a belief in the species (step 4)—the feeling that human beings are basically good (Van de Water & McAdams, 1989)—concern leads to commitment (step 5), the motivation to act in a generative way. Commitment provokes concrete actions (step 6), such as giving to children or protecting the environment for future generations. Finally, at the third level of personality, this process leads to a personal life story revolving around generative themes (step 7).

Based on this framework, the researchers developed scales to measure the three major dimensions of generativity: generative concern, generative commitment, and generative action. To measure concern, they constructed the measure shown in Table 8-3. They measured generative commitment by asking people to describe ten personal goals: "What plans are most important in your life now?" To assess actions, they used a checklist examining how often within the past month people had engaged in activities such as serving as a role model or teaching someone a skill. They also looked generally at generativity life scripts by asking people to describe the high and low points of their lives.

When they gave their tests to young adult, middle-aged, and elderly people, the researchers found partial support for the idea that generativity reaches a peak in the aging phase of life. Although middle-aged people scored only marginally higher than young adults on generative concern and action, the differences in generative commitment were striking. Young adults scored extremely low on this particular aspect of generativity, with goals that tended to be centered around themselves. For instance, a 20-year-old might say, "I want to make my job more interesting" or "figure out what

8-1 *Life Histories Reveal an Enduring Self*

Anthropologist Sharon Kaufman, in a minor classic called *The Ageless Self*, uses life interviews with very old people not to demonstrate change, but to show that the self is continuous and enduring. Our identity, or the basic themes that organize our life, remain constant despite the changes of old age. Here is an excerpt from her description of Stella, one woman featured in this book.

Whenever I visit Stella in her studio, I am struck by a whirlwind of activity. She is always doing several things at once. I have watched her teach a painting class while at the same time hang a large tapestry on the wall by herself, repair the plumbing under her sink and pay bills. . . . Her energy and determination are remarkable. She happens to be 82 years old.

Stella was born in 1897 on a farm in the Deep South. She looks back on that time, though filled with hard work, as the most peaceful, blissful existence. The independence and self-sufficiency her father sought and apparently achieved during her childhood . . . became a pivotal, driving force in her own life. As a child, Stella was a tomboy. . . . She climbed trees, played with boys, and rode horses. Stella's formal education began at the age of 9 in a "little schoolhouse" located about a mile from the family farm. . . . When Stella finished high school, she moved several hundred miles away so she could establish her own life. . . . She was adventurous; she took vacation trips . . . around the country . . . traveling through places where no roads existed, camping along the way. . . . At the age of 24, she moved to Oregon to marry a man she had known for some years. The marriage was brief; her husband left her shortly after her child was born. In the 1930s she was poor, divorced, and had a child to raise on her own. She met the challenge. She got a secretarial job which she held for 35 years. . . . When Stella was 40, her daughter died from injuries sustained in an ac-

I want to do with my life." Midlife and older people were more likely to say, "I want to be a positive role model," "help my teenage son," or "work for justice and peace in the world."

The most vivid evidence of generativity comes from the third level of personality, how people describe the transforming events in their lives.

I was living in a rural North Dakota town in 1977 and was the mother of a 4-year-old son. One summer afternoon we had discussed going across the street to visit some friends and I went back to the house for something. Jeff left without me and was hit by a car. When I got there, he was lying in the street unconscious and his breath was gurgly. I felt sure he was dying, and I didn't know of anything I could do to preserve his life. My friend did, though, and today Jeff is 18 years old and very healthy. That feeling of being helpless and hopeless while I was sure I was watching my son die was a real turning point. I decided I would never feel it again and I became an EMT [emergency medical technician].

cident. This tragic event changed the course of her life and turned her into a sculptor and painter.

Now the one central theme in her life is her achievement orientation, especially the need to create art. Stella is future oriented . . . and she is driven by the need to accomplish more and be better. . . . "The only time I look back is when I think, 'I used to do better painting and sculptures,' . . . I have to get back to work so I won't have to say that." Not only does she compete with herself, but she also competes with the other artists and art students who come to the studio she owns and operates. . . . Stella needs to be the best at what she does. She needs to have her work highly regarded by others. . . . But she also needs to meet her own standards of creativity.

Stella's achievement orientation and need for recognition apparently have been part of her identity since her early years, long before she became an artist. When she talks about her childhood and youth she emphasizes her accomplishments, successes, and failures. Achievement provides the framework by which Stella describes her clerical work as well. . . . "I had to be absolutely perfect. I never made an error."

Creativity informs a second theme that emerges from Stella's story: her sense of aesthetics and need for perfection. . . . Her role models for perfection are the two most important people in her life, her mother and her daughter. "She [the daughter] was so talented in art. . . . In addition, she was a perfectly behaved child. I never had to criticize her for anything she did." The child is frozen in Stella's memory on the brink of . . . promise. There is only perfection to remember. Stella's sense of productivity, beauty, and perfection was first inspired by her mother, later heightened by the way she viewed her child, and finally given supreme value when the child died.

SOURCE: Kaufman, 1986.

Let's use this interview to illustrate the difference between the trait approach to measuring personality and McAdams's more qualitative technique. Although according to standard personality tests, this woman might have always ranked high in conscientiousness and shown no change in this ranking over the years, the *specific path* her life took was responsive to her life experiences. In McAdams's opinion, once we get beyond "decontextualized traits" and fill in the rich, personal details of human experience, we do see much stability (see Aging in Action 8-1). However, we also see lives being transformed.

Nonetheless, you may be thinking, true identity-transforming experiences such as the one described here probably happen before old age. Yes, Grandma Moses developed a new persona as a famous person in later life, but for most of us, by our 70s the potential to develop fresh, new identities seems limited, in part because so few years are left in which to act on an evolving self. In fact, drawing on our discussion of autobiographical memory, in advanced old age the challenge may be to *hang onto* our old identity—the person we used to be. Reminiscence groups function to reconnect nursing home residents with this identity-at-risk-of-dissipation—the unique human being that was, not an anonymous body in need of care. Can people keep their enduring sense of who they are intact in the face of the identity-eroding losses of advanced old age? The following study offers clues.

Lillian Troll and Marilyn Skaff (1997) interviewed a large group of community-dwelling men and women over age 85 about their identities and then returned to question the same subjects after 30 months. How strong is the sense of a continuous self in later life? How might the feeling of "still being me" change after shattering events such as becoming seriously ill?

Three-fourths of the people said that they felt they were the same person they had always been. None thought they had changed greatly since becoming very old. Moreover, this sense of "me," the same person as ever, was maintained even in the face of dramatic physical changes, such as suffering a stroke. Furthermore, although most subjects reported that they had changed as people during adult life, the watershed identity-transforming events they listed—such as immigration or widowhood—had typically occurred decades earlier.

Although our sense of who we are may endure in the face of the vicissitudes of old age, our ideas about who we *will be* do shift. We see this shift in exploring a second, innovative effort to probe our fantasies, hopes, and dreams.

MARKUS MEASURES SELF-SCHEMAS   In their research, Hazel Markus and her University of Michigan colleagues have examined what they call **self-schemas** or **possible selves**—our personal visions of who we will be in the future. Some possible selves are hoped for; for instance, I might imagine having my book praised as the definitive text on the psychology of aging. Others are feared: A person might imagine herself alone for life or fired, out on the street, unable to support herself.

self-schemas or possible selves
Salient images of who we will be that reflect both our idealized hopes and our dreaded fears

According to Markus, self-schemas drive our personal adult development (Markus & Nurius, 1986). They motivate us to put ourselves into certain situations and avoid others. They offer a framework for interpreting life and tell a good deal about how we will react to specific events. Although theoretically we are free to construct any possible self, the particular schemas we develop are intimately linked to our past experiences and how we see our self behave. A student who has been praised for her abilities in science may develop a hoped-for self as a doctor. Another who remembers being unpopular as a child or feels she doesn't have friends now may develop a feared self as being alone for life. Each type of person will be sensitive to her own schema-relevant events.

For instance, with a friend who has a strong lonely feared self, I am especially solicitous, careful not to break a date. From experience, I know that any breach of what looks like caring activates her unloved possible self and provokes an extreme, often hostile response. With another, who has a strongly competitive self-schema, I downplay any professional success. Signs of achievement in another person evoke her feared self-as-inferior, producing intense pain.

Interestingly, Markus finds that our general satisfaction with ourselves relates to the kinds of possible selves we produce. People low in self-esteem generate more personal hoped-for selves—for instance, they say they "want to be happy or more content." People high in life satisfaction produce hoped-for selves more centered on occupational and family goals. The researchers conclude that when we are basically happy with who we are, we seem freer to direct our energies outward to focus on external, specific, other-directed hopes and dreams (Cross & Markus, 1991).

Possible selves change in interesting ways with age. After adolescence, hoped-for selves become more specific. Whereas an 18-year-old might say "I want to be rich and famous," a middle-aged man might say "I want to be a good father, a better tennis player, and put my children through the college of their choice" (Cross & Markus, 1991). There are age differences in the specific schemas people generate. Though important for everyone, feared selves related to physical functioning become more salient, as we might expect, in middle and later life (Hooker & Kaus, 1994). Most interesting, in later life, our horizons shrink. Hoped-for selves are focused on the present. Older people often wish to be doing more of what they are already doing, such as staying active, useful, and healthy.

Although we might see this narrowed focus as negative, an exciting new theory offers a different view, one charting both our personal priorities and outer-world actions as we journey through life.

CARSTENSEN'S SOCIOEMOTIONAL-SELECTIVITY THEORY   Like McAdams and Markus, Laura Carstensen begins by looking at how our life goals shift as we age. But her aim is all-encompassing: to blanket the whole life span and explore how these priorities affect our social choices—that is, the people we want to be with over the years.

According to Carstensen (1995), during adolescence and young adulthood, we have expansive, future-oriented goals. Our mission is to establish our place on the planet, to understand how the world of people and things works. Spending time with novel social partners, or being with new people, is the best way to fulfill this exploratory, outer-world-centered, information-seeking need. Once we have carved out our place in society, and especially realize that our personal future is limited, we become interested in maximizing the present, more concerned with the emotional quality of our current life. So, our social preferences shift. We prefer to spend as much time as possible with familiar partners, the people we care most deeply about.

Socioemotional-selectivity theory beautifully explains why, just as primary attachment figures are our main focus at life's beginnings, they become increasingly central at life's end. Babies immersed in their immediate emotional states center their lives around the person who is the source of all comfort. They only want to be near their mother. They get upset and agitated when new social partners (unfamiliar people) arrive on the scene. During the exploration phases of the life span—adolescence and young adulthood—we leave these known quantities in favor of unfamiliar social partners, exciting new people who can teach us new things. Then, once we have reached our professional and personal goals (fulfilled our aspirations in life), we return to home base, to reconnect with the people we care most about. In our later years, we recenter our lives around our most gratifying core relationships—spouse, children, and closest friends.

Socioemotional-selectivity theory offers insights into more than just our social self. It provides a perspective on how we manage and treat our emotions at different times of life. According to Carstensen, when our main investment is in the future, we are willing to dampen our immediate feelings and impulses in the service of getting somewhere. Instead of telling off the authority figure who insults us, we hold our tongue because this boss or professor holds the key to getting ahead. We make overtures to that aversive person or engage in social encounters we would rather pass up

TABLE 8-4	How Changing Emotional Priorities Make Sense of Contradictory Old-Age Stereotypes

According to Carstensen, rather than tolerating unpleasant emotions and aversive situations in the service of future goals, when we realize we do not have long to live, maximizing the immediate quality of our current life is our main priority. This emphasis on immediate feelings and living now means that old people may be stereotyped as

1. self-absorbed and focused on their bodily states.
2. cautious and rigid, preferring current activities over risky new pursuits.
3. intolerant and outspoken, unwilling to be "nice" or let things pass.
4. more like their real selves than ever.
5. spiritually oriented and attuned to inner values (less concerned with external achievements such as status, worldly accolades, or accumulating things).
6. more in touch with the most important priorities (wise?).

Old people may also be interested in meeting new people, learning new things, and exploring the world, but only because these activities provide intense, *immediate* pleasure at any time of life.

in order to advance socially or in our career. We accept the anxiety-ridden months of moving to an unfamiliar city or beginning a new job because we know we will feel better than ever in a year or two. As we age, we are no longer interested in where we will be going. So, we refuse to let insulting remarks pass, waste our time with unpleasant people, or choose that uncomfortable situation with future potential over our current, comfortable milieu. Almost unconsciously, we decide: I don't have that long to live. I have to spend my time doing what makes me feel good emotionally *right now*.

This new, landmark theory not only speaks volumes about our priorities and choices, it lets us make sense of many contradictory stereotypes we have about older adults (see Table 8-4). Yes, it is possible for older people to be self-centered (concerned with their own immediate states), cautious (unwilling to try new things), intolerant (quick to reject what they don't like), and outspoken (prone to blurt out what they really feel), as well as being inner-directed, true to themselves, spiritual, and attuned to the real priorities in life. Moreover, the beauty of Carstensen's work is that she grounds her theory firmly in research. Recall from earlier in this chapter that her longitudinal data from the Berkeley/Oakland Studies suggest that beginning in early adulthood, people do grow socially selective, reducing peripheral social contacts in favor of close friends. When asked who they would rather spend time with—a close family member, a recent acquaintance, or the author of an interesting book—her research team finds the same changes: Young people's choices are equally spread among the three possible partners. Older people vote overwhelmingly to be with the family member, the most emotionally central individual in their life. In fact, these choices are not simply due to being a given age. People with AIDS also vote to spend an evening with a familiar close person rather than an interesting stranger. So do people asked to imagine that they are just about to move across the country alone. According to Carstensen, any time we see the future as limited, we recenter our lives around the most immediately gratifying people and experiences in life.

Socioemotional-selectivity theory has offered me insights into the life choices of my cousin Clinton Sheerr, who died of lymphoma at age 50 a few months ago. An exceptionally gifted architect diagnosed in his early 20s with Hodgkin's disease, Clinton gave up his promising career and retired to rural New Hampshire to build houses, hike, and ski for what turned out to be a remaining quarter century of life. Clinton's funeral was an unforgettable celebration—a testament to a person who, although his life was shorter than most, was able to live fully for longer than many people who survive to twice his age.

Socioemotional-selectivity theory makes sense of why, even though normally we are content to live a continent away, when a family member is seriously ill, we suddenly want to be physically close, to spend as much time with our loved one as we possibly can. The theory even accounts for my own behavior during this 50th year of my life—my impulse to revisit old friends, my sudden passion to center my days around my own most meaningful activities in life. Like other people who have reached this birthday milestone, I like to think that having aged a half century has made me more mature. Am I right?

DO WE GROW MORE MATURE WITH AGE?

It is in our personality that we hope to ripen over time. As we grow old, we expect to grow emotionally, expand as people, become more mature. The studies just described do offer hints that this change may take place. Surely having more realistic possible selves, more generative goals, or priorities centered on what is most meaningful does capture some of what we mean by growing more mature. But maturity means more than that.

When we imagine growing mature, we think mainly of our ability to cope with stress. People who are mature have a kind of internal resilience. They are able to flexibly handle the failures, losses, and upsetting life experiences that are the price of being alive. What does the research tell us about this hoped-for self?

Some cross-sectional studies suggest that middle-aged and elderly people handle stress in a more mature, flexible way (Blanchard-Fields & Chen, 1996). However, other research is more ambiguous, and some studies even show the elderly are more defensive and emotionally closed off (Magai & Passman, 1998). What is clearer is that the particular strategies we use to handle frustrations vary in interesting ways at different life stages.

Younger people more often adopt **problem-focused coping** methods in dealing with stress; that is, they work actively to modify or change the unhappy situation in some way. Older people report using more **emotion-focused strategies**; their techniques center more on changing their feelings, making the best of what exists. Although at first glance, problem-focused coping seems more effective and mature, each style may be best suited to the different stressful situations we face at different ages.

In our younger years, the frustrating life conditions we face—such as being in an unpleasant job, a bad living situation, or a relationship going wrong—seem more amenable to change through taking active steps to exert external control. All things being equal, it is better to leave these situations or work to modify their unpleasant features, rather than saying "It's not really that important" or "I'll just adjust emotionally."

problem-focused coping
Taking action to change the situation when faced with a particular life stress

emotion-focused coping
Modifying one's feelings about the situation when faced with a particular life stress

But when we are faced with a disabling chronic illness or widowed at age 85, investing our energies in reversing our life state just won't work. It is better to cope by working on emotionally accepting what we cannot change, learning to accept what is.

In fact, when the situation requires problem-focused coping, older people use this strategy as often as anyone else (Lazarus, 1996). In looking at older women facing two different types of later-life challenges—coping with the ongoing demands of caring for a mentally impaired child or considering a move—Kristen Kling, Marsha Seltzer, and Carol Ryff (1997) found that the people contemplating changing their residence used more problem-focused coping than those facing the unchangeable stress of providing day-to-day care. However, modifying our emotions may sometimes be the best strategy when we are caring for an impaired family member. Recall that in the caregiving-careers study discussed in the previous chapter, people often remarked that the key to handling life lay in changing their *attitudes* about the embarrassing behavior, giving up the idea that they could actively manage the behavior or force their loved one to act in a more appropriate way. In other words, either emotion-focused or problem-focused coping may be appropriate depending on the kind of stress we face (Lazarus, 1996).

So, it is hard to tell by looking at age differences in coping styles whether older people are more or less mature. In addition, notice that this research is cross-sectional. To really examine whether we cope with life in a more mature way as we age, we must look at longitudinal studies, research exploring how people change over time. This brings us, once again, to the Mills study.

When Ravenna Helson and Paul Wink (1992) tested the Mills women from their early 40s to early 50s, they found, as Jung would predict, that the shift toward androgyny described earlier did signal a more mature, more integrated self. The older women were more self-confident, tolerant, and decisive. They showed changes similar to postformal reasoning. They were more tolerant of ambiguity and more open to different points of view. They were also happy. In fact, the Mills women reported feeling better about themselves in their 50s than at any other age.

"It takes a brave poet to claim that [the empty nest] is the prime of life, especially for women," say the researchers (Mitchell & Helson, 1990, p. 452). Yet, that is exactly what Helson and another colleague found when they surveyed life satisfaction in Mills alumnae of different ages. Notice in Figure 8-3 that at age 26, during a time of life we often think of as a woman's best years, subjects are *least* likely to be satisfied. In the 50s, that so-called empty time, twice as many women feel that their lives are first-rate.

Do women have to wait until their older years for these changes? The overall upward trend (with a few valleys) revealed in this cross-sectional survey of happiness implies that the answer is no. In fact, when Helson and Geraldine Moane (1987) followed the study subjects from their late 20s to their early 40s, they found increases in dominance and competence during this earlier adult period, too, suggesting that over the years we gradually do grow more mature.

I must emphasize that this study involves well-educated, upper-middle-class Americans, the very group with the internal and external resources most likely to promote emotional growth. Moreover, the Mills study showed considerable variability. Some people did not change for the better; others declined in maturity and happiness over the years.

Who is most likely to improve? One clue comes from examining maturity earlier in life. In addition to using their standard measure, Ravinna Helson and Brent Roberts

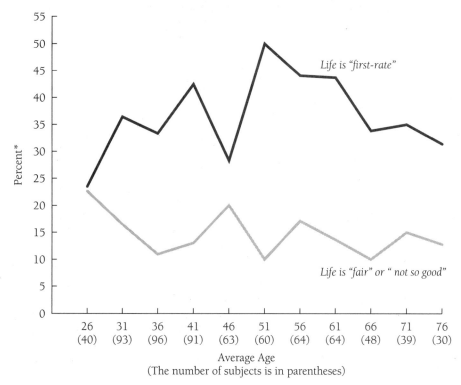

Percent*

Life is "first-rate"

Life is "fair" or " not so good"

| Average Age | 26 (40) | 31 (93) | 36 (96) | 41 (91) | 46 (63) | 51 (60) | 56 (64) | 61 (64) | 66 (48) | 71 (39) | 76 (30) |

Average Age
(The number of subjects is in parentheses)

* Percentages do not add to 100 because responses falling into
an intermediate category have been excluded.

This graph suggests that the early 50s are the optimum age, the time when the highest percentage of women rank their lives as first-rate. (The percentages do not add to 100 because responses falling into an intermediate category have been excluded.)
SOURCE: Mitchell & Helson, 1990.

(1994) used a scale measuring ego development to periodically chart subjects' person-alities. Ego development, scored from a sentence-completion test, is a measure similar to postformal thought or Baltes's wisdom-related expertise that is designed to measure maturity. As is true of the research exploring postformal thinking or wisdom, people do not advance in ego development in a systematic way after about age 30 (Loevinger, 1976; Loevinger & Wessler, 1970). However, Helson and Roberts discovered that if a woman ranked high on this scale compared with her peers in her late 20s, she was most likely to grow in happiness, self-esteem, and competence as she aged.

So, the "good get better" is one defining theme of who will ripen with age. As we might expect from the concepts of cumulative and interactional consistency, people who are initially competent, mature, and psychologically healthy are most likely to grow with age. However, the Mills study only measured growth through the early 50s, so it tells us nothing about later life. Even the most mature 50-year-old may contract emotionally, feeling incompetent, unhappy, and vulnerable when she (or he) comes face to face with the losses of old age.

OLD AGE: SEASON OF STRESS OR PERIOD OF PEACE?

Perhaps you have noticed that we have opposing ideas about our emotional state in later life. On the one hand, we see older people as peaceful, contemplative, and content; on the other, old age is supposed to be the time when we are at our most vulnerable, overstressed, and depressed. It seems natural that in our later years we would feel unhappy and out of control, because at this time of life the reinforcers tilt and losses (or negative events) far outweigh gains. Moreover, the blows we suffer in later life seem especially unnerving because they are irreversible, unable to really be changed (Heckhausen & Baltes, 1991). We can recoup from earlier life losses, such as being divorced or getting fired, by finding a new mate or a new job. There is little chance of finding a new satisfying occupation after retiring at age 70, meeting another life companion at age 80 when our husband dies, or regaining our old healthy self when we develop the functional impairments of old age.

However, there is no evidence that older people are more unhappy or emotionally out of control than the young! In polls taken in countries as different as China, Nigeria, and the United States, the elderly report just as high life satisfaction as anyone else (Diener & Suh, 1998). When Powell Lawton's research group gave a measure of emotional stability to elderly people attending a college course, their middle-aged children, and young adults, they found even stronger results. The elderly people ranked *most* content and in control of their emotions (Lawton, Kleban, Rajagopal, & Dean, 1992). In a similar study, the researchers also found that negative emotions, such as depression, anxiety, and hostility, were at their peak in the younger years (Lawton, Kleban, & Dean, 1993). These studies, however, involved well-educated, young-old adults. What about people grappling with the losses of advanced old age?

Interestingly, even this group seems surprisingly placid and unstressed. When another group of researchers compared perceptions of stress among middle-aged, young-old, and old-old men, they were struck by how difficult it was to elicit *any* reports of problems among the oldest group (Aldwin, Sutton, Chiara, & Spiro, 1996). Despite dealing on a daily basis with the kinds of chronic losses we have been describing in this book, one-fourth of the old-old men said they had "no troubles at all." The study exploring identity among people over 85, discussed earlier, had the same message. Not only did these very old people preserve their sense of who they were in the face of disabling illness, if anything they reported their emotional state had changed for the better, saying that now "I'm calmer," "more tolerant," or more remarkable, "I feel more secure."

Equally amazing, researchers find that, despite their avalanche of uncontrollable losses, older people do not feel more out of control than younger adults. Our sense of self-efficacy stays remarkably robust as we enter later life (Brandtstädter & Rother-

This glowing 93-year-old woman is thoroughly enjoying every minute of her life despite having disabilities and living in an assisted living facility. She is a testament to the fact that advanced old age can be a remarkably problem-free era of life.

mund, 1994). In one survey, people in their late 70s reported *higher* efficacy feelings than people aged 50 to 59 (Wallhagen, Strawbridge, & Shema, 1997).

One strong possibility is that we are seeing cohort differences in the tendency to report negative feelings. Perhaps older adults do feel more vulnerable, but because they lived through the Depression, when people were supposed to be strong in the face of hardship, they shut out their negative feelings and just *report* that they are feeling fine (Magai & Passman, 1998).

But if we look more deeply, there are good reasons why old age may be a surprisingly problem-free time of life. In the same way as they mute the pain of a heart attack or make our senses less sharp, age changes in the nervous system reduce the intensity of our emotions. In stressful situations, older people show less dramatic signs of physiological arousal, such as heart-rate or blood-pressure changes (Filipp, 1996). Another cause may lie, once again, in the types of stresses older people face. The losses we experience in later life, such as widowhood or health problems, are often predictable, expected events. These **on-time** (normal for our age) **events** may be easier to handle than the **off-time** (nonnormative) jolts more typical of our younger years, such as when our boss tells us out of the blue that we are doing poor work or our wife informs us that she wants a divorce. Moreover, being widowed or becoming ill does not signal personal failure; these events do not strike at our self-worth as human beings. During our earlier years, we are continually on the firing line, at risk of failing and feeling bad about ourselves as we make our way through life. In old age, we *should* feel more secure because we no longer have to suffer the slings and arrows that are the price of making our way in the world.

on-time events
Happenings that are predictable and expected at that time of life

off-time events
Happenings that are unpredictable and unexpected at that time of life

Once again, however, there are dramatic individual differences in how content, at peace, or secure elderly people feel. Many of you may know an older adult who is highly discontent and insecure, someone who would vigorously agree with the statement made by one woman at a senior citizens' center where I spoke: "Dr. Belsky, one day you will *really* understand how terrible it is to be old!" Once again, that elusive quality called maturity predicts who rejects these sentiments in later life.

Drawing on Q-sort information from the Berkeley/Oakland parent group, Monika Ardelt (1997) constructed an index of wisdom. In operationalizing this quality, she used a different approach than Baltes's team, placing emphasis on the affective or emotional side of life. According to Ardelt, in addition to being able to see to the heart of problems, wise people have insight into themselves. They have empathy and compassion for their fellow human beings.

As we might imagine, scores on wisdom were associated with life satisfaction. The surprise was how highly related this quality was to well-being. Wisdom was much more critical to later-life happiness than objective life conditions, such as being disease-free or financially well-off. In other words, the message of this study is that the main key to happiness in later life lies not in being healthy and wealthy. It lies in being wise. Are there specific guidelines to follow in engineering a happy, wise old age?

INTERVENTIONS

life-span model of successful aging
Theory of ideal psychological functioning involving using techniques to promote a sense of self-efficacy or feeling of being in control

Erikson and Jung offer guideposts, but they seem difficult to implement, as they involve changing our whole worldview. Jutta Heckhausen and Richard Schulz's **life-span model of successful aging** (Heckhausen & Schulz, 1993; Schulz & Heckhausen, 1996) offers the down-to-earth advice we need.

Drawing on Baltes's theory, Heckhausen and Schulz believe that the key to aging successfully lies in selection, optimization, and compensation. We must put our eggs in the right baskets, optimize performance in centrally important areas of life, and judiciously use external aids. Then, they add an interesting twist: The motivation underlying these activities is the quest for self-efficacy—the drive to enhance our feelings of control.

primary control
Gaining self-efficacy by directly reaching a life goal

secondary control
Gaining self-efficacy by modifying one's emotional reactions and setting new, more easily reachable goals

Drawing on Bandura's ideas, Heckhausen and Schulz argue that feeling in control of our environment is a crucial need at any stage of life. What we really want is what the psychologists call **primary control**—the ability to get concrete reinforcements in the outer world. When we fail at our goals (do not get reinforced), we turn to what Heckhausen and Schulz call **secondary control** strategies, or techniques to internally modify our goals to maintain our sense of control. We decide that going to the prestigious graduate school that rejected us is not that important; we really would be happier at the easier program closer to home. The date who never asked us out again was not worth our time; we are really interested in his handsome roommate, anyway. These secondary control strategies are emotion-focused in that they involve modifying our feelings to accept what is. But they are problem-focused, too. We actively work to change our out-of-control feelings by refocusing our energies on new, more attainable goals.

As Figure 8-4 shows, Heckhausen and Schulz believe that primary control grows steadily through childhood, peaks in midlife, and then declines in old age. At the same

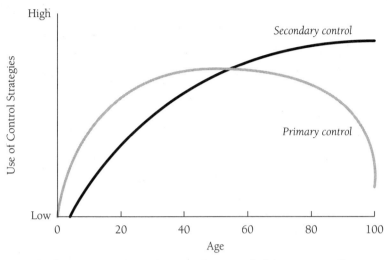

As we develop, primary and secondary control strategies both become more efficient. In later life, however, our ability to exert primary control declines, and secondary control becomes the dominant coping mode.

SOURCE: Schulz & Heckhausen, 1996.

time, as we age and become more cognitively skilled, we grow more proficient at the use of secondary control. As primary control declines in our later years, secondary control strategies loom larger in coping with life.

Our goal still is to achieve primary control. However, we need to do more mental manipulating to get the sense of self-efficacy we need. These manipulations may involve rearranging our activities, turning to new pursuits where we can have control. For instance, at age 60, a committed runner decides to de-emphasize jogging and become more involved with his family; or he takes up bowling or buys a boat. Or it may mean lowering our goals in a given area to fit our new, less capable self. So the runner who at 50 derived his sense of self-efficacy from completing a 5-mile jog at 70 gets a feeling of mastery from taking a brisk, long walk. At 80, he feels in control and upbeat when he can get to the store. At 95, he feels the same robust sense of personal power simply because "at my age" it is a triumph to be able to get from the bed to the chair.

We now have an answer to the puzzle of why efficacy feelings endure in the face of age-related losses: People preserve their sense of control by flexibly changing their priorities and downscaling their goals (Brandtstädter & Rothermund, 1994). By taking pleasure in excelling at what they still can do, some people continue to be models of optimal aging even when suffering from severe limitations of old age. In fact, as the

8-2 Getting It Together in the Nursing Home: A Lesson in the Power of Secondary Control

Last year, I attended an unforgettable memorial service at a Florida nursing home. Person after person rose to eulogize this woman, a gifted poet and playwright, a passionate advocate who worked with immense self-efficacy to make a difference in her fellow residents' lives. Then, Mrs. Alonzo's son told his story: He had never really known his mother. When he was young, she became schizophrenic and was shunted from institution to institution. Found at age 68, dehydrated, curled up in a ball in a tiny apartment, Mrs. Alonzo had been delivered to the nursing home to await death. It was only in this setting, defined by loss of control, that she finally took control of her life. If you think that this story is unique, that personal growth is virtually impossible in an environment this limited, listen to this psychologist friend who also works in a nursing home:

My most amazing success entered treatment two years ago. This severely depressed resident had had an abusive childhood and marriage and suffered from enduring feelings of powerlessness and low self-esteem and yet was very, very bright. I think that being sent to our institution allowed this woman to make the internal changes that she had been incapable of before. Also, I was there to listen—not, like her previous psychiatrists, to dispense drugs. Almost immediately, light bulbs went off. She began to look at her past and see how her experiences had shaped her poor sense of self and then to see her inner strengths. She and I formed a very close, very strong relationship. So, then she decided to work on becoming close with her children. She had been aloof as a mother, and she told me that once her younger child had asked her to say that she loved her and she couldn't get the words out. Now, at age 89, she called this daughter, told her she did love her, and that she was sorry she couldn't say it then. Her daughters said that I had presented them with a miracle, the loving mother they always wanted. The nurses marveled at how my patient had been transformed. She made friends on the floor and became active in the residents' council. In the year and a half we saw one another, she used to tell me "I never believed I could change at this age."

As she finished her story, my friend's eyes filled with tears: "My patient died a few months ago, and I still miss her so much."

Although transformations such as these are clearly rare, these stories offer an interesting twist on Heckhausen and Schulz's assumption that it is basically better to have a high degree of primary control (a wide array of potential reinforcers in our lives). These insights come from a very different psychologist named Victor Frankl, who developed a type of psychotherapy called logotherapy based on witnessing people in an ultimate control-deprived environment grow emotionally. Sent to a Nazi concentration camp as a youth, Frankl saw a few fellow inmates transformed as human beings because they realized, confronted with *no* primary control, that the key to real freedom and power (self-efficacy) lay in transforming their attitudes—that they alone had ultimate power to decide who to "be" emotionally. Frankl would argue that true self-efficacy resides not in primary but in secondary control—not in how easily we can get reinforced in the outside world, but in how well we can take control of who we are inside. (For further information on this existential brand of therapy, see Frankl, 1970. *Man's search for meaning: An introduction to logotherapy.* Boston: Beacon Press.)

remarkable case histories in Aging in Action 8-2 show, sometimes it is even possible to *develop* self-efficacy in an environment epitomizing the loss of primary control.

I think that one message of our discussion is that the key to successful aging lies in having the ability to take pleasure in our current life. Even though they start from different perspectives, use different concepts and terms, and even disagree about whether people are basically better or worse off during their older years, these creative newest life-span theorists (Carstensen and Heckhausen and Schulz) seem to be making this identical point.

Moreover, the research shows that, in contrast to our stereotypes, old age is not the age when we are most unhappy and emotionally distressed. In fact, the reverse may be true. Before accepting this conclusion, however, we need more information. To really know about how the elderly function emotionally, we need to focus on emotional problems—the topic of the next chapter.

KEY TERMS

activity theory
androgynous
Berkeley/Oakland Studies
big five traits
disengagement theory
emotion-focused coping
Kansas City Studies of Adult Life

life-span theory of successful aging
Mills College Study
off-time events
on-time events
parental imperative
primary attachment figures

primary control
problem-focused coping
secondary control
self-schemas or possible selves
Thematic Apperception Test (TAT)

RECOMMENDED READINGS

Caspi, A., Bem, D., & Elder, G. H. (1989). Continuities and consequences of interactional styles across the life course. *Journal of Personality, 57,* 375–406.
Caspi, Bem, and Elder report on the midlife consequences of childhood temperaments in the Berkeley/Oakland Studies.

Gutmann, D. (1987). *Reclaimed powers: Men and women in later life.* Evanston, IL: Northwestern University Press.
Gutmann makes his case for androgyny as a universal change in the older years.

Kaufman, S. R. (1986). *The ageless self: Sources of meaning in late life.* Madison: University of Wisconsin Press.
This beautifully written book is based on interviews illustrating the author's argument that the self is ageless and enduring.

Magai, C. Z., & McFadden, S. H. (Eds.). (1996). *Handbook of emotion, adult development, and aging.* San Diego: Academic Press.

Schaie, K. W., & Lawton, M. P. (Eds.). (1998). *Annual review of gerontology and geriatrics: Vol. 17. Focus on emotion and adult development.* New York: Springer.
These two edited books offer state-of-the-art theories and literature reviews on emotion and emotional change during adult life. Both cover a range of topics and include chapters by Carstensen and Heckhausen and Schulz.

McCrae, J., & Costa, P. T. (1990). *Personality in adulthood.* New York: Guilford Press.
In this book, Costa and McCrae make their case for personality consistency.

Schulz, R., & Heckhausen, J. (1996). A life-span model of successful aging. *American Psychologist, 51,* 702–714.
This article describes the life-span model of aging discussed in the text.

Chapter Outline

9

Psychopathology

 I graduated from college in 1960 and was forced into a family business that was a source of continual fights. One day, I was eating in a cafeteria and my heart began to race. The same thing happened two or three times, and I went to a doctor who gave me Valium, which was a new drug at that time. By then the anxiety attacks would occur several times a day. I was sensitized to them. I could feel them coming. It was complete dread. Very often it was in public places and, of course, you were humiliated. It's happened to me in a commuter train going 50 miles an hour. So, I would jump off at the next stop and take a taxi for miles to get to my destination. The thing has a pattern where you are so worried about it that you begin to avoid everything. I stopped going to the theater or restaurants because I was afraid an attack might occur and I'd have to rush out. The same thing would happen on dates. I'd be heading for a girl's house and I'd have to turn around. I was taking Valium three times a day and going to see a therapist five times a week at a cost of $12,000 a year, which would be $30,000 today. Time dragged on. I was 40. Years of life had gone by, and nothing had happened. I was confined to my parents' home or to my own apartment—and the only thing that cured me were the drugs. For the past 15 years I have been taking Prozac 20 mg a day. Now that I'm 60, I'm pretty much fine, but I still have trouble in certain situations. I can't fly. I have to reserve a low floor at hotels. I try to avoid high bridges. It's life played defensively. Everything is your enemy. With my disease, agoraphobia, you are always hanging onto where you are.

What is your chance of developing agoraphobia or another mental disorder during adult life? Do emotional problems often appear, as in our interview subject, in the early 20s and then persist to wreak their damage into our older years? For answers, we turn to a type of illness survey called an *epidemiologic study*.

Epidemiologic studies examine the prevalence (overall frequency) and incidence (rate of new cases) of diseases within a population during a certain time period. How prevalent (common) was heart disease among Americans during 1998? Did the incidence (number of new cases) of this illness increase during that year? Is heart disease spreading faster among certain groups? Are there gender, racial, or geographic differences in heart-disease rates?

epidemiologic studies
Large-scale surveys designed to reveal the prevalence and incidence of diseases within a population

You may have noticed that our chapters on physical aging often began with epidemiologic studies. Regular surveys, typically conducted by government agencies, offer information about rates of chronic illnesses and disabilities at different ages and among certain groups. By examining these statistics, we know which problems to "target" as a cause for concern. Epidemiologic studies also offer vital clues about what causes diseases. Recall from Chapter 3 that one hint that estrogen might protect women against heart disease came from the epidemiologic finding that before age 50, heart attacks among women are rare.

Epidemiologic studies of mental illness offer the same essential information. However, in psychiatric epidemiology—the field devoted to exploring mental-disorder rates—collecting accurate information on incidence and prevalence presents special challenges.

One hurdle psychiatric epidemiologists face relates, once again, to who is tested. In epidemiologic surveys, it is crucial to have a representative sample. Researchers must ensure that a cross-section of the population agrees to be interviewed and responds honestly. But wouldn't people who abuse alcohol be reluctant to admit engaging in this socially unacceptable behavior? Who would be less happy to welcome an interviewer than the paranoid older person, the person phobic about strangers, or the older adult terrified that she has Alzheimer's disease? In other words, because in psychiatric epidemiology some of the very people most likely to have emotional problems are least likely to volunteer, *minimizing* the true extent of problems is a genuine risk.

A second difficulty psychiatric epidemiologists face relates (again) to what they test. In this case, the concern is fundamental: the reliability and validity of mental-health diagnoses. Mental-health workers must agree on the way they diagnose given people for their labels to have any meaning (reliability). Their system for categorizing people must be measuring real disorders or "diseases" (validity). However, psychological symptoms do not cluster into clear-cut categories. They often occur on a continuum. They cannot be measured and quantified in the same way as readings on a blood pressure machine. What complicates the search for reliable and valid diagnoses is that mental disorders may express themselves through different symptoms at different times of life. For instance, as we will see later, many experts believe that depression is being underdiagnosed among the elderly because this problem tends to manifest itself mainly in memory problems or exaggerated physical complaints (Blazer, Hughes, & George, 1987).

In struggling to improve reliability and validity, the American Psychiatric Association has repeatedly revised the **Diagnostic and Statistical Manual of Mental Disorders,** or **DSM.** The DSM is the labeling system mental-health workers use to put people into diagnostic categories. A landmark occurred in 1980 with the publication of DSM III, which provides lists of *specific* symptoms that qualify for each diagnostic label (American Psychiatric Association, 1980). This more reliable symptom-oriented system allowed epidemiologists to feel confident enough to conduct the first large-scale studies of the prevalence and incidence of emotional problems in the United States.

THE PROBLEMS

In the early 1980s, researchers at the National Institute of Mental Health sponsored the **Epidemiologic Catchment Area Survey (ECA),** the first comprehensive survey

Diagnostic and Statistical Manual of Mental Disorders (DSM) Manual used by mental health workers for categorizing mental disorders

Epidemiologic Catchment Area Survey (ECA) First comprehensive epidemiologic survey of mental disorders in the United States

of mental disorders in the United States. Teams of interviewers examined 20,000 people living in Baltimore, Los Angeles, New Haven, St. Louis, and Durham, North Carolina. These five locations were carefully selected to provide a racial and socioeconomic mix typical of the nation as a whole (Myers et al., 1984). A decade later, from 1990 to 1992, epidemiologists at the University of Michigan conducted similar interviews with more than 8,000 people throughout the United States (Kessler et al., 1994). This National Comorbidity Study (NCS) is more up-to-date and wider in scope. It explores the vital question of **comorbidity,** or the frequency with which people report more than one problem. Its disadvantage for us is that it does not include people over age 54. For this reason, although the NCS will offer important supplementary information, in this chapter we focus mainly on the ECA results.

comorbidity
Coexisting presence of two or more disorders

Scope and Age Patterns

The ECA researchers found that, depending on the location, within any given 6-month period, anywhere from 1 in 5 to 1 in 4 adults suffers from a mental disorder (Myers et al., 1984). This means that our **lifetime prevalence,** or risk of ever developing a problem, is much higher. It is about 1 in 3. When the NCS researchers asked directly about lifetime prevalence—"Have you ever had this set of symptoms before?"—they found more alarming statistics: 1 in 2 Americans will suffer from a mental disorder at some time in life.

lifetime prevalence
Risk of developing a particular disorder at any point in life

On the other hand, mental disorders are youth-oriented. Both polls showed that problems are most prevalent earlier in adult life and decrease with age. In the ECA study, the difference between the youngest and oldest groups was huge: People aged 18 to 24 had almost twice the rate of emotional problems as people over age 65 (Weissman et al., 1985).

As we will see, some disorders are more stable or bimodal, first declining and then rising again in advanced old age. Rates of different problems vary in provocative ways by gender and ethnic group. As we saw in Chapter 7, cognitive impairment is one serious condition that makes a dramatic entry in old age. However, the clear message of the research is that mental disorders are *non-age-oriented* diseases. In fact, the NCS researchers speculated that one reason why their illness statistics were so much higher was that they had included adolescents and ended their survey at middle age (Kessler et al., 1994).

These studies echo the message of the previous chapter: Old age may be a relatively problem-free life stage. But before we get too excited, imagining that as we grow old our emotional problems will magically evaporate or erode, let's subject the statistics to a second, more critical look.

1. **The studies almost certainly underestimate the prevalence of mental disorders in later life.**   Recall that the ECA and NCS are *community* surveys. Whereas younger adults with psychological problems are likely to be living outside of institutions, as we saw in Chapters 5 and 7, older people with serious mental disorders are more apt to be removed from the community and placed in inpatient settings such as nursing homes. So, age comparisons are unfair because many of the most disturbed older adults are not being counted at all.

In addition, "reporting practices" very likely differ in the age groups being polled. This cohort of old-old people grew up during a time when it was shameful to admit emotional problems. In our era of *Oprah,* the situation has changed. We recount our emotional vulnerabilities in depth. So, while a 20-year-old is apt to go overboard in enthusiastically describing symptoms, her 75-year-old grandmother is likely to have the opposite bias, telling an interviewer that she has "no trouble at all."

In fact, the older woman may not even realize that what she is experiencing *are* signs of emotional distress. She may pass off tiredness, trouble sleeping, or lack of interest in life, which we recognize as depression, as "normal for my age." She may misread the churning stomach, palpitations, or dizziness of anxiety as a digestive problem or cardiovascular disease (Gurian & Goisman, 1993). In other words, because they mimic classic signs of old age, late-life mental problems are often missed (Kaszniak, 1996).

2. **The studies may not be revealing genuine developmental changes.** Recall that the NCS and ECA surveys are cross-sectional. So they could be measuring cohort differences in distress, not true age changes. Why, apart from being old, might this elderly cohort be more problem-free than the young?

For one thing, people suffering from paralyzing anxiety, depression, or another mental disorder may be more likely to die at an earlier age (see Chapter 3). So, contrasting the old with the young may be comparing a mentally healthier fraction of the older cohort with an unselected cross-section of the younger group. More ominous, changes in society such as the high divorce rate may have increased the stress on today's young people, making them more susceptible to emotional problems than their parents or grandparents were at the same age. This depressing possibility has led some experts to predict escalating rates of late-life mental disorders in future years (Gatz & Smyer, 1992). Will we be liberated from our emotional problems in later life? The answer is more murky than it first appears.

Specific Disorders

We are on firmer ground when we explore the problems people have—the specific mental disorders that are most prevalent among older adults. Before turning to the actual ECA data, let's scan the problems we *can* develop. What are the major categories of disorders spelled out in the most recent Diagnostic and Statistical Manual, **DSM-IV?**

In DSM-IV, adult mental disorders are grouped into categories based on their defining symptoms and origins. *Organic mental disorders* include a range of conditions that have a clear-cut physiological source and affect either cognition (delirium, dementia, and related disorders) or personality. *Mood disorders* are characterized by disturbances in affect (or mood), and *anxiety disorders* by intense anxiety. *Schizophrenic and other psychotic illnesses* are serious conditions involving a total break with reality. *Substance-abuse disorders* involve the excessive use of alcohol or other social drugs. Some disorders are limited to specific areas of living (sexual and gender identity disorders, eating or sleep disorders, conditions involving the inability to control anger or inhibit the urge to engage in certain destructive activities), whereas *personality disorders* involve one's whole mode of approaching the world (antisocial personalities, dependent personalities). In other conditions, the person develops an imaginary physical illness, either fabricating a medical problem or involuntarily developing symptoms

DSM-IV
Current Diagnostic and Statistical Manual of mental disorders

1. **Alcohol disorders.** Obsessive, destructive use of alcoholic substances. The person must be unable to stop using alcohol even though it causes impairments in social, occupational, or physical functioning.

 Although new cases do occur after midlife, alcohol abuse typically begins in youth, lessens with age, or flares up periodically in response to life stress.

2. **Phobias.** Intense, inappropriate, debilitating anxiety that occurs in certain situations. The anxiety may be connected to a single object (simple phobia); occur in social situations (social phobia); or be more general (agoraphobia).

 Phobias also are most likely to appear in youth, although people also develop these conditions in later life. The biological intensity of the anxiety response wanes with age. However, specific phobias are comparatively enduring, lasting for years or decades. Symptoms of anxiety are dramatically higher among hospitalized and institutionalized older adults.

3. **Depression.** Conditions involving dramatic, long-lasting alterations in mood combined with a range of other physical and psychological symptoms. People who are clinically depressed often have trouble sleeping and eating. They feel apathetic and hopeless, unable to take pleasure in life. They may have trouble concentrating and thinking clearly; they may move slowly or be highly agitated.

 Depressive disorders occur with equal frequency at every age through midlife, dip to a low at about age 60, and rise in advanced old age. Symptoms of depression are also dramatically higher among hospitalized and institutionalized older adults.

SOURCES: Myers et al., 1984; Kessler et al., 1994; Schuckit, Anthenelli, Bucholz, Hesselbrock, & Tipp, 1995.

---

that have no organic cause. Finally, *adjustment disorders* do not really qualify as full-blown mental disorders because they involve time-limited symptoms that occur in reaction to life stress.

If we omit this last category, four disorders overshadow all others in prevalence. Older people are most likely to suffer from cognitive impairment, phobias, and depression. Alcoholism is also a top-ranking later-life disorder, but only for men. With the exception of cognitive impairment, these identical problems—depression, phobias, and alcoholism (for men)—are also the most common mental disorders at every stage of adult life (Kessler et al., 1994; Myers et al., 1984).

Because they loom so large in limiting life in old age, we will focus on these three disorders. First, we look at alcoholism, exploring its characteristics and causes. Next, we examine phobias, especially the most serious phobic condition, agoraphobia. Finally, we turn to depression, a problem often linked with being old. Table 9-1 offers a preview of these problems and how they change during adult life.

Alcoholism

As we know, alcoholic beverages alter our mental state. In the stomach and small intestine, alcohol is absorbed into the bloodstream and carried to the brain. First, there are pleasurable sensations such as a sense of warmth and well-being. Inhibitions are lowered, and anxiety is relieved. Then, negative changes occur. Alcohol causes problems in coordination, balance, judgment, memory, and perception. It makes us irritable, drowsy, and unable to think. At extremely high doses, alcohol causes unconsciousness and, by interfering with breathing, in rare instances, death.

These short-term effects can be life-threatening. Alcohol is implicated in one-half of all fatal traffic accidents. It is a major contributor to deaths by falls, drowning, and from fires and burns. The long-term consequences are equally dangerous. Chronic alcohol abuse, or **alcoholism,** can cause permanent changes in brain function. Alcohol affects other organs such as the heart and kidneys. Alcohol's impact on the liver is well known. Cirrhosis, a condition involving the degeneration of this organ, is most often due to chronic alcohol abuse (U.S. Department of Health and Human Services, 1990b; D. M. Gallant, 1987). Uncontrolled drinking causes havoc in every aspect of life. It interferes with relationships. It impairs the ability to work. These difficulties in functioning are an important criterion used in labeling people as having a genuine mental disorder related to alcohol.

In DSM-IV, disorders involving alcohol are divided into two main categories. Individuals are classified as having alcohol *dependence* when they meet criteria indicating serious signs of addiction, such as experiencing blackouts or withdrawal symptoms, and their pattern of chronic use causes impairments in their ability to function in life. People who do not meet these conditions but who have used alcohol repeatedly even though it causes problems in relationships or at work, or who use alcohol in hazardous situations such as driving, are labeled as having a less severe syndrome called alcohol *abuse*.

alcoholism
Mental disorder characterized by the excessive and/or chronic, impairing use of alcoholic beverages

EPIDEMIOLOGY   Alcoholism is mainly a "male" disease. An alarming 1 in 5 men will develop alcohol dependence; another 1 in 6 will suffer from alcohol abuse at some point in life. For women the risk of having each problem is less than half as great (Kessler et al., 1994). In late life, the gender imbalance is especially great. In the ECA study, elderly men were about 4 times more likely to be diagnosed with an alcohol disorder than women over age 65.

In general, the ECA researchers found alcoholism to be at a low ebb in later life. According to the survey, over a 1-year period, this disorder affected 3% of men over age 65, compared with 8% in the age group 45 to 64 (Myers et al., 1984). In fact, for white males alcohol dependence and abuse are highly youth-oriented conditions. They peak in adolescence and the early 20s and then decline. African American and Hispanic American abuse rates also rise in young adulthood but remain elevated (Bucholz, 1992). This more chronic use pattern may explain the excess mortality from liver disease among African Americans compared with whites.

Once again, we must take these statistics with a grain of salt. After years of abusing their bodies, alcoholics who live to later life may develop dementia or serious physical disorders, and so be more apt to be living in institutions such as nursing homes. As Aging in Action 9-1 suggests, many older alcoholics may not be counted in the statistics because they have other major emotional problems and are disabled and living isolated lives (Ankrom, Thompson, Finucane, & Fingerhood, 1997; Mellor et al., 1996). Selective mortality may also be a factor: As this particular mental disorder is so life-shortening, some severe alcoholics probably die before age 65 from complications of their disease. Although some people begin to abuse alcohol in later life, typically the lure to drink to excess is a tendency that erupts early in adult life (Schuckit, Anthenelli, Bucholz, Hesselbrock, & Tipp, 1995). What causes this enduring lure?

In her 20s, Sylvia was a showgirl. She dated movie stars, went to elegant parties, and had an exciting life. But Sylvia never married. She was too close to her mother to get close to a man.

Now in her late 70s, Sylvia lives alone, in a two-room, cluttered, rent-controlled apartment on New York's Upper West Side. Her mother has been dead for 20 years. Her one living friend is inaccessible, living in faraway Queens. When they last spoke, it was April. Now it is June. Sylvia has a serious hearing problem but refuses to visit a doctor or get a hearing aid. A senior center is out of the question. She feels uncomfortable even leaving the house. Sylvia goes for weeks without talking to anyone but grocery store clerks. Her isolation is self-imposed. Sylvia is a paranoid schizophrenic.

Because she trusts me, Sylvia confides her problem: People are following her on the street. They call out her name and whisper nasty comments as she passes by. Her next-door neighbors are stealing her mail. We must keep our voices low because her apartment walls are bugged. During our conversation, Sylvia opens a half-empty bottle of Scotch. This fragile 95-lb woman will have three drinks in the time we are together. She may have many more after I leave.

Did Sylvia learn to abuse alcohol during her showgirl days? Or did her delusions and problem drinking erupt as she entered her isolation chamber of later life? One thing we know for certain: Sylvia would never be counted in the ECA statistics on elderly female alcohol abuse. She would never let an interviewer in the door.

Sylvia's sad life brings up another problem with the ECA research: Alcohol abuse does not occur in a vacuum. It often coexists with another major mental disorder of adult life. This comorbidity is particularly true of female alcoholics, who typically suffer from other serious emotional problems (Nixon, Tivis, & Parsons, 1995), and are more apt to drink in response to negative moods (Rubonis et al., 1994). Sylvia's primary mental disorder is schizophrenia. By not counting her second problem, how accurate a portrait are the ECA researchers really getting of the prevalence of problems such as alcoholism in later life? How many women (and men) are *really* out there, removed from view, without family and friends, who drink to excess in old age?

CAUSES   Although it has been noticed for centuries that alcoholism "runs in families," this observation offers no clues about whether shared heredity or environment is to blame. Behavioral genetic studies reveal that in the lure to abuse alcohol, inherited tendencies can play a central role.

Figure 9-1 summarizes the findings of studies in which researchers used the adoption method to examine the genetic basis of alcoholism—that is, investigations in which scientists compared the alcoholism rates of adoptees with a biological family history of this problem with those of adoptees without a genetic history of the disease (McGue, 1993).

Notice that the graphs show an interesting gender difference. Whereas adopted males with biological relatives who are alcoholic consistently have higher illness rates,

FIGURE 9-1   *Rates of Alcoholism among Adoptees*

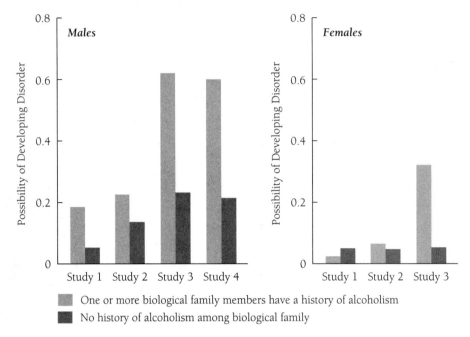

Every study shows that men with a family history of alcoholism face a greater risk of the disorder. However, only one group of researchers found that women with a comparable genetic background have elevated problem rates.
SOURCE: McGue, 1993.

only one group of researchers found that females with this family history have an elevated risk. In other words, the evidence for an inherited component to alcoholism is compelling—but only for men!

Robert Cloninger believes that there are two forms of alcoholism in men, one more clearly genetic than the other. In the nonhereditary type of alcoholism, a man tends to begin drinking after age 25 and is likely to show genuine problems only in middle age. This type of alcoholic can abstain from drinking but tends to lose control once he begins. After remaining sober for months, he periodically goes on a binge. This person tends to be guilty, fearful, and upset by his problem. He is not prone to act out under the influence of alcohol and has comparatively good social adjustment, experiencing fewer chronic problems at home and at work.

In another, more virulent, biologically based form of alcoholism, the onset is earlier, and the difficulty is the inability to inhibit the urge to seek out alcohol. This type of alcoholic tends not to be upset by his condition. He is more likely to be impulsive and hyperactive and to have chronic difficulties with relationships and work.

This man is more likely to become abusive when drinking, to regularly drive while intoxicated, to commit crimes, and to end up in jail (Cloninger, 1987; Cloninger, Bohman, & Sigvardson, 1981).

Even when biological predispositions set the stage, the environment seems to play a role. Don't most of us automatically link drinking to outer-world frustrations and losses? Earlier in adult life, there are the personal rejections: the laid-off worker or scorned lover who blots out his pain at the local bar. In later life, there is the loss of central social roles: the familiar figure of the widower who "turns to alcohol" after his beloved wife dies.

This last observation gains research support from surveys showing that among elderly widowers in particular, alcoholism rates are unusually high (Williams, Takeuchi, & Adair, 1992; Gurland, 1996). The comorbidity of alcoholism with depression and other mental disorders (See Aging in Action 9-1) suggests that people turn to drink to reduce the pain of internal stress. Twin studies suggest that common genetic predispositions play a role in why these diseases cluster (Kendler, Heath, Neale, Kessler, & Eaves, 1993a). Still, older people who enter alcohol treatment programs often report turning to drinking as a "medication" to cope with the painful emotions they feel (Ganzini & Atkinson, 1996).

The urge to drink is related to positive expectations. As we might expect, people who drink to excess tend to believe that alcohol is a magic potion that reduces tension and enhances well-being. During adult life, this connection is solidified through repeated classical conditioning. We celebrate our successes by going out for a drink; we head for the bar at happy hour when we can finally relax after leaving work. This link with relaxation (being irresponsible) may partly explain why alcohol abuse and dependence rates decline so sharply after youth among white males. When men settle down to the responsibilities of a job and family, they have to give up drinking to excess or risk causing havoc in their lives.

This brings us to another *possible* environmental reason for the relatively stable prevalence of alcoholism among minority men and the elevated rates among elderly widowers. Being more likely to be unemployed during their adult years, minorities have fewer brakes to counter the lure of alcohol as they travel through life. In the same way, when a man loses his spouse, any checks on his impulse to abuse alcohol are removed. He no longer has a reason to stay sober "for my wife's sake."

In addition to the inhibiting forces of having a family and holding down a job, this cohort's social norms exert a braking influence. During Prohibition (1920–1933), when the current cohort of old-old Americans were growing up, the stigma against drinking was intense. Women in particular were forbidden to drink. Given that the tendency to abuse alcohol is often a habit developed in youth, some experts reason that today's low prevalence of alcoholism among the elderly is temporary. We will see higher rates of this disorder, and especially more female problem drinkers, as the baby boomers enter their retirement years (Ganzini & Atkinson, 1996).

Whereas the lure to abuse alcohol is a tendency some people battle—with varying success—as they journey through life, with the problem we turn to now the pull to stay ill is not an issue. As we saw in the interview at the beginning of this chapter, phobic disorders cause intense suffering. They make day-to-day life an endurance test.

Phobias

The unpleasant sensations of anxiety are highly adaptive responses. Anxiety allows us to escape from danger. It propels much of the learning that transforms us from unsocialized infants into competent adults. But sometimes anxiety is so intense, pervasive, and inappropriate that it interferes with life. At this point, people are classified as having an anxiety disorder. They have a genuine emotional problem involving anxiety.

phobias
Intense, irrational fears connected to a situation or range of situations

Phobias, the most common anxiety disorders, are intense fears connected to a situation or range of situations. Because they cause avoidance—that is, an unwillingness to encounter the phobic object—their impact varies as a function of the importance of the object to daily life. A phobia of cars is more disabling than a phobia of snakes, unless we earn our living by farming. One woman's fear of airplanes may be mildly incapacitating, robbing her of an enjoyable trip to Hawaii; to another, whose job involves regular flying, that fear may mean the end of a career.

Phobias such as these, because they are confined to a single object or situation, are called simple phobias. Although they can be incapacitating, their specificity limits the impairment they can provoke. Two other types of phobias listed in DSM-IV— social phobia and agoraphobia—are more serious because they involve so *many* situations.

Social phobics become anxious when they perceive themselves as on display. They may be afraid of speaking or eating in public or terrified of talking to authority figures or members of the opposite sex. In these situations, the feeling of being judged or watched evokes anxiety. The visible signs of this fear become a source of embarrassment. Social phobics report that the fear of blushing, stammering, sweating, and twitching solidifies and motivates the avoidance of social situations (Barlow, 1988).

Social phobics suffer because the object of their fear is salient, pervasive, and very important to human life. Imagine being uneasy in many of your interactions. Imagine being so self-conscious that you fail in the very situations, such as dating or dealing with superiors at work, where you most want to succeed. But even the misery social phobics feel can pale compared with the pain suffered by people with the most malignant phobic condition: agoraphobia.

agoraphobia
Most serious phobic condition, in which the person fears a range of outer-world situations

Agoraphobia is the most devastating phobic disorder because, as we saw in the interview at the beginning of this chapter, it *always* severely restricts life. The agoraphobic person is afraid of a wide range of situations, such as elevators, planes, bridges, or other public places. Often the individual is housebound, terrified of venturing out the door.

panic attacks
Intense storms of anxiety that erupt out of the blue

Agoraphobia is also distinctive because it involves **panic attacks**—spells of anxiety that come on out of the blue. To imagine what a panic attack is like, think of a recent situation in which you felt anxious and magnify it tenfold. You feel a sense of terror. You cannot breathe. Your heart is pounding. You are faint and dizzy. You think you are going crazy, having a heart attack, or dying.

Naturally, people who have had a panic attack are terrified of having another. Their fear is magnified because this internal hurricane was unpredictable and so might strike again at any moment. As we saw in the introductory vignette, the result is often retreat: The person vows never to be trapped or stranded in public if a panic attack occurs. Riding on a train, sitting in a movie theater, and going on a date all become situations to be avoided. At this point, the individual has agoraphobia.

People can have repeated panic attacks without developing agoraphobia. They can have agoraphobia without having panic attacks, at least recent ones. However, although experts argue about how frequently agoraphobia occurs without panic, most agree that in this serious type of phobia, panic typically plays a central role (Moras, Craske, & Barlow, 1990).

EPIDEMIOLOGY   Phobias are the top-ranking emotional problem in old age, and at every age (Gurian & Goisman, 1993; Sheikh, 1996). In contrast to alcoholism, phobias are mainly female diseases (Kessler et al., 1994). At the ECA Baltimore site, over a 6-month period, 7.6% of elderly men had this diagnosis. The figure for women was almost twice as high: 14.2% (Myers et al., 1984).

As with alcoholism, phobias are youth-oriented diseases, tending to appear in the teens and 20s. Illness rates decline in old age. However, as we saw in the interview at the beginning of this chapter, this type of mental disorder is comparatively persistent or chronic. Problems with alcohol or depression often remit, perhaps to flare up at another point in life. People who suffer from phobias are apt to be locked in battle with anxiety for years (Kessler et al., 1994).

Because it is the type of phobia that most severely limits life, we now turn to the question of why certain people develop that devastating condition called agoraphobia.

CAUSES   What causes the panic attacks that are so often the trigger provoking agoraphobia? Many experts believe that a physiological abnormality is to blame. One candidate is lactate, a chemical in the blood. Whereas infusing sodium lactate into most people produces no reaction, when agoraphobics are injected with this chemical, they often experience a panic attack. This suggests that a lactate intolerance may cause panic. In certain people, a higher-than-normal sensitivity to blood lactate produces a panic attack (Barlow, 1988).

Another theory implicates dysfunctional breathing patterns in panic attacks. According to this hypothesis, illustrated in Figure 9-2, some people naturally tend to hyperventilate or breathe too deeply in response to even minor stress. This causes CO_2 levels in the blood to decline. To compensate, the heart pumps more rapidly. The rapid beating, or palpitations, causes even deeper breathing. When this happens, people decide they are suffocating or dying, and a full-blown panic attack occurs.

Even if the initial attack is a physiological event, if the outcome is agoraphobia, as Figure 9-2 shows, learning is involved. Once having had a panic attack, as we saw in our beginning interview, the person becomes hypervigilant, alert to any signs of anxiety. However, being in this heightened state of arousal produces the very symptoms the individual fears. In other words, learned anxiety keeps the panic going because the fear of panic makes it more likely that the person will have another attack. This anxiety then turns outward, becoming connected to situations in which a panic attack has occurred or places where escaping is impossible in the middle of an attack. The final step is avoiding all "unsafe" (public) places (Barlow, 1988).

The biological tendency to experience panic attacks seems to subside with age. Among the elderly, experts note, panic symptoms are less intense (Sheikh, 1996). (Recall that emotional arousal in general is lower in later life.) However, mild symptoms of anxiety are fairly common among the elderly and especially prevalent among impaired, institutionalized older adults (Parmelee, Katz, & Lawton, 1993). Moreover,

FIGURE 9-2   *Possible Steps to a Panic Attack and Agoraphobia*

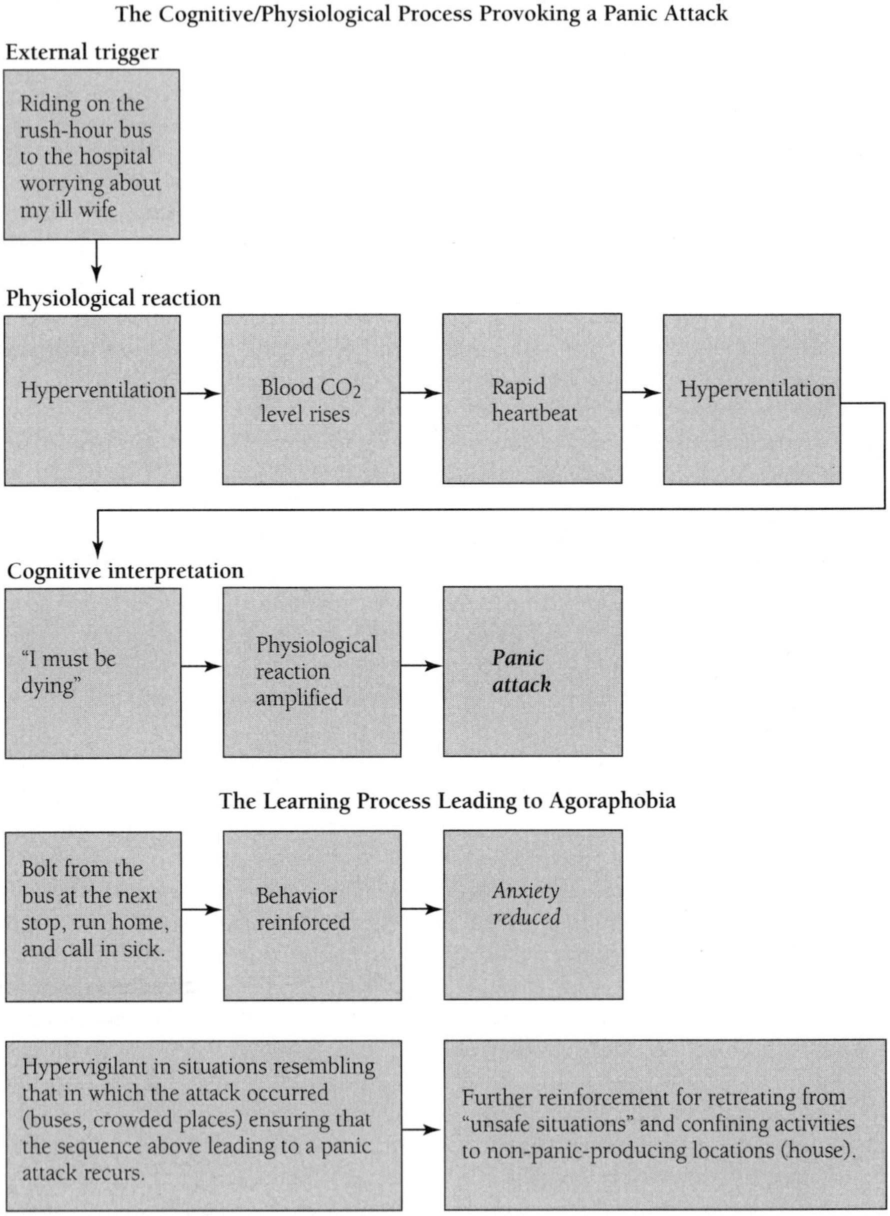

The Cognitive/Physiological Process Provoking a Panic Attack

External trigger

Riding on the rush-hour bus to the hospital worrying about my ill wife

Physiological reaction

Hyperventilation	→	Blood CO_2 level rises	→	Rapid heartbeat	→	Hyperventilation

Cognitive interpretation

"I must be dying"	→	Physiological reaction amplified	→	***Panic attack***

The Learning Process Leading to Agoraphobia

Bolt from the bus at the next stop, run home, and call in sick.	→	Behavior reinforced	→	*Anxiety reduced*

Hypervigilant in situations resembling that in which the attack occurred (buses, crowded places) ensuring that the sequence above leading to a panic attack recurs.	→	Further reinforcement for retreating from "unsafe situations" and confining activities to non-panic-producing locations (house).

This famous painting, The Scream, *by the artist Edvard Munch, conveys some sense of what it feels like to be in the midst of a panic attack.*

agoraphobia remains a problem even in old age (Gurian & Goisman, 1993). The reason may be that, after years of avoidance, the agoraphobic response takes on a life of its own. The person stays imprisoned, and extinction never takes place, because the individual takes care not to encounter what *used* to evoke intense fear.

Although age seems to offer us a biological advantage in our war with debilitating anxiety, this is not true of the emotional problem we turn to now: depression.

Depression

The emotional disorder **depression** is different from the sadness that is the price of being alive. As Aging in Action 9-2 shows, it is a total body/mind alteration, a welter of physical and mental sensations that far transcend just changes in mood.

Depressed people often feel that life has nothing to offer. They have no interest in activities they used to love. Their worldview or cognitions about life and themselves change. They feel worthless and helpless. They may be convinced that no one cares for them and be tortured by voices making terrible accusations and whispering warnings of doom. They are usually indifferent to living. Often, they have recurrent thoughts of suicide.

depression
Mental disorder involving serious, long-lasting low mood accompanied by other defined symptoms

9-2 *A Depression Develops*

In 1986, while in Paris receiving a coveted literary award, the 60-year-old writer William Styron humiliated himself and enraged his hosts by bolting from the luncheon, pleading mental illness. His depression had begun the previous summer at his country house in Martha's Vineyard, a lovely island off Cape Cod. Here is his evocative description of how his condition gradually enveloped his life.

I felt a numbness, an odd fragility—as if my body had become frail, hypersensitive, and disjointed and clumsy. . . . Nothing felt quite right; there were twitches and pains. . . . [The] effect was immensely disturbing, augmenting the anxiety that was never absent from my waking hours and fueling . . . a fidgety restlessness that kept me on the move. . . . By now . . . It was October, and . . . the . . . evening light . . . had none of its familiar loveliness, but ensnared me in a suffocating gloom. . . . I felt an immense . . . solitude. I could no longer concentrate . . . and . . . writing [was] becoming . . . exhausting, stalled, then ceased.

The madness of depression is . . . a storm of murk. Soon evident are the slowed . . . responses, paralysis, psychic energy throttled back to zero. . . . The body . . . feels sapped, drained. . . . As the disorder . . . took possession, I began to conceive that my mind was being . . . inundated by floodwaters. [My voice] underwent a strange transformation, becoming . . . faint, wheezy and spasmodic. The libido . . . made an early exit. . . . Most distressing of all the . . . disruptions was that of sleep.

Exhaustion combined with sleeplessness is a . . . torture. . . . My few hours of sleep were usually terminated at three or four in the morning, when I stared up into the darkness, . . . writhing. . . . Plainly the possibility [of suicide] was around the corner.

SOURCE: Adapted from Styron, 1990, pp. 42–50.

Depression involves physical changes. Depressed people have no energy. They can barely move or get around. There is a disturbance of the sleep cycle. Often, people are tortured by chronic insomnia; sometimes, they sleep for 15 hours a day. Appetite changes. Some people eat excessively; others cannot eat at all. Inability to concentrate and remember and slowed movements or agitated restlessness are also classic signs.

DSM-IV specifies two main types of depression. In a major depression, the symptoms are more serious. The person must have a low mood or be apathetic and have at least five of the other symptoms listed for at least two weeks. In the other type, called dysthymia, the person must have a depressed mood and two or more other symptoms most days for at least two years. Partly because of this requirement involving duration, most depressed people are diagnosed with a major depression.

Diagnostic quarrels about depression are intense. Because depressive symptoms occur on a continuum, some experts believe that categorizing people as having either a depressive disorder or no problem is misleading. This strategy misses people who are depressed but whose symptoms are not severe enough to satisfy the diag-

The dejected expression on this nursing home resident's face is not atypical. Symptoms of depression are rampant among institutionalized older adults.

nostic criteria (George, 1993). The controversy is especially intense regarding depression in later life.

EPIDEMIOLOGY   Depression is the only major emotional disorder that is not a youth-oriented disease. The NCS and ECA epidemiologists found that depression rates were constant through the 40s (Kessler et al., 1994). However, contrary to the common idea that depression is endemic among the elderly, the ECA study found that people over 65 were *less* likely to suffer from this problem than younger adults (Weissman et al., 1985). A decade later, the ongoing Alameda Study, discussed earlier in this book, found the same results. This led the researchers to state categorically: Healthy older people are no more likely to be depressed than anyone else (Roberts, Kaplan, Shema, & Strawbridge, 1997).

Other gerontologists argue that these pronouncements are misleading. Many older people *do* show signs of depression, but their minor symptoms do not qualify for the DSM diagnosis of a psychiatric disorder (Blazer et al., 1987; George, 1993). The prevalence figures for late-life depression are almost certainly artificially low because, as Aging in Action 9-2 reveals, many symptoms of this disorder—loss of libido, impaired sleep, slowed responding—mimic typical old-age changes. In late life, depression can express itself *only* through memory loss and aches and pains. In these masked depressions, the problem appears totally cognitive or physical, not psychological at all.

Once again, it is important to note that the ECA and Alameda studies are community polls. Because depression is a side effect of many later-life illnesses—dementia, some cancers, heart disease—rates of this mental disorder are very high among hospitalized older adults (Gurland, 1996) and especially common in nursing homes (Parmelee et al., 1992). Surveys suggest that 30 to 50% of all residents in nursing homes suffer depressive symptoms at least to some degree (Katz & Parmelee, 1997). When we add in older people in inpatient settings, how common is depression *really* in old age? If we widen our diagnostic umbrella to include depressive symptoms, would rates of this problem skyrocket in later life?

In fact, experts argue, it is wrong to lump together everyone over 65. After dipping to a low in the 60s, rates of depressive symptoms rise again in advanced old age (Kessler, Foster, Webster, & House, 1992; Mirowsky & Ross, 1992). It may be unfair to lump men and women together, too. Actually, the most striking fact about depression is its relationship to gender, not age. In every culture, women are about *twice* as prone to this problem as men. To understand this difference, experts look to hormonal factors, life stresses, temperament, or other forces (McGrath, Keita, Strickland, & Russo, 1990). There may be no one answer, just as there is no one pathway to this debilitating disorder of adult life.

CAUSES   Twin studies show that genetic predispositions are important in the tendency to develop serious depressive illnesses (Kendler, Neale, Kessler, Heath, & Eaves, 1993). However, early experiences and current stresses also contribute to a person's becoming depressed (Kendler, Heath, Neale, Kessler, & Eaves, 1993b; Tsuang & Faraone, 1990). This complexity was revealed in a study in which men and women who reported experiencing childhood family violence had higher rates of depression, but only if they were under current stress (Kessler & Magee, 1994). In other words, childhood experiences may prime us for depression, which is then triggered when our current life is not going well.

Depression rates rise after a variety of earlier life stresses, such as plant shutdowns or divorce. For older men, once again, an important depression-promoting stress is losing a spouse. In a reversal of the typical gender difference, in one epidemiologic study, researchers found that widowed men of any race were more than twice as likely to suffer from a major depression than their female counterparts (Williams, Takeuchi, & Adair, 1992). This brings us to the general class of event that looms large in psychological theories about what triggers depression: loss.

PSYCHOANALYTIC PERSPECTIVE   Freud (1915/1957) was the first person to relate depression to loss, linking this problem to normal mourning. In mourning, Freud reasoned, a person comes to terms with the loss of a loved person by identification. The bereaved person internalizes qualities of the lost loved one; they become part of the mourner's own self. According to Freud, normal mourning turns into depression when the survivor has unconscious negative feelings for the lost person. These negative feelings are also turned inward, resulting in the person's adopting toward the self the unresolved angry feelings once reserved for the other. In Freud's view, then, after a loss of a person who is both loved and hated, anger is turned inward to become self-hate.

Current psychoanalytic views of depression focus on losses of "attachment figures." People are vulnerable to being depressed as adults when the parent/child relationship has been severed in their early years (J. Bowlby, 1980). The child may have been physically abandoned or separated. She may have been emotionally shut out. According to this theory, anytime parents are unavailable, a child is at risk for becoming depressed during adult life.

Psychoanalysts believe that childhood losses cause a sense of failure, inadequacy, and distrust that poisons the person's ability to develop satisfying relationships in adult life. Current losses re-evoke the early trauma and so produce an exaggerated response (Bemporad, 1990). According to Edward Bibring (1953), in the depression-prone person, any loss produces a condition of "ego helplessness." When the person feels hopeless and helpless, that individual is depressed. This emphasis on helplessness and hopelessness also features prominently in behavioral perspectives on depression.

BEHAVIORAL PERSPECTIVE   In the early 1970s, psychologist Martin Seligman noticed that dogs subjected to electric shocks they could not escape developed strange symptoms. They became apathetic, seemed sad, and were unable to think or move quickly. When in a situation where they could avoid the shocks, they froze. This lesson in the futility of acting that had generalized even to events they could control: They had learned to be helpless.

Seligman believed that he had hit on a model for how human depression develops. After a series of inescapable losses, people come to feel that they are helpless or unable to control their destiny. This learned helplessness affects their world outlook and the way they behave. They become apathetic, withdrawn, hopeless—in short, depressed (Seligman, 1975).

Seligman and his colleagues then moved beyond focusing on outer-world events to suggest that it is people's attributions about losses and failures, not the actual experiences, that cause people to become depressed. Depression-prone individuals have a pessimistic explanatory style. Rather than seeing negative events as temporary, situational, and extrinsic to the self, they interpret failures in a global, personal, never-changing light (Abramson, Seligman, & Teasdale, 1978).

Seligman's cognitive behavioral perspective on depression is not the only behavioral point of view. According to Peter Lewinsohn, the depressive process is set in motion when highly reinforcing "scripted" behavior patterns are disrupted. In later life, these disruptions might occur if people are forced to retire from a job they love or to give up a favorite activity because of failing health. According to Lewinsohn, the individual then withdraws, further decreasing the frequency of reinforcing events. According to this traditional behavioral framework, it is simply the lack of adequate reinforcers or pleasurable experiences that produces the depressive symptoms (Hoberman & Lewinsohn, 1989).

Notice that each of these theories makes perfect sense of the high depression rates among institutionalized elderly and the very old. The life conditions of these segments of the older population epitomize the ultimate in lack of human connectedness, reinforcement deprivation, and loss of personal control.

THE WORST CONSEQUENCE: SUICIDE   Although most depressed people are not suicidal, people who contemplate suicide are almost always depressed. Given that depression is so common in advanced old age, does it follow that suicide is relatively prevalent among this group?

The answer is absolutely yes. In contrast to what the media tell us, suicide is not an adolescent issue; *it is a problem of advanced age*. In 1990, 20% of all suicides in the United States were committed by the 12.5% of the population over age 65. Moreover, as Figure 9-3 shows, one group in particular is responsible for this elevated rate: white men. Although the figure does not show it, the suicide risk for males climbs dramatically at the uppermost limits of life. Over age 85, white men commit suicide

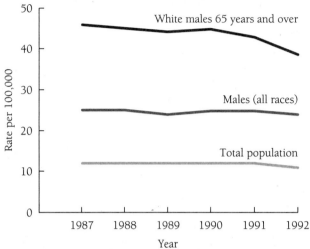

Although we tend to link suicide to adolescence (and women), notice that it is males—particularly elderly white males—who have the highest suicide rates.
SOURCE: National Center for Health Statistics.

three times as frequently as anyone else (Manton, Blazer, & Woodbury, 1987; McIntosh, 1995).

Why is late-life suicide so common specifically in men? Researchers speculate that physical dependency may be one key (Manton et al., 1987). The bodily decay of advanced age is more intolerable for males, because it is so important for men to feel independent and in control.

Another important risk factor for suicide explains why old-old men are especially likely to take their lives: social isolation (see Aging in Action 9-3). Men's emotional eggs all tend be in one basket, their marriage. So, when a man loses his wife, he is left without any other close relationships to cushion the blow. After his wife of 60 years dies, Mr. Jones does not have the energy to look for a new mate. Unmoored from his life anchor, cut adrift from meaningful human attachments or ties, the 80-year-old man shoots himself because there is no logic to continued life.

What can be done to prevent people from taking this drastic step? What help is available for the estimated one-fifth of Americans who suffer from mental disorders in later life (Gatz, Kasl-Godley, & Karel, 1996)? Before exploring the intervention side of the equation, we need to consider the changing context of mental health care.

THE CHANGING CONTEXT OF CARE

Beginning in the late 1960s, a seismic shift took place in the way we approach mental disorders. For much of the 20th century, treatments for psychological problems fell into a single category. As we saw in Chapter 2, mental disorders were believed to be caused by life experiences. Therefore, the main treatment was **psychotherapy**, examining those life experiences to eradicate the pathological attitudes and responses. A *traditional behaviorist* would focus on changing the reinforcers maintaining the behaviors. A *cognitive behaviorist* would concentrate on understanding and changing the person's cognitions or thoughts. A *psychoanalytically oriented* therapist would help the person gain insight into childhood experiences and how they affected current life.

Biological Approaches to Mental Health

Today, these psychotherapies are still used. However, they have been supplemented by a revolution in biological approaches. At the same time as behavioral genetic studies were convincing social scientists about the role of inherited predispositions in determining personality, great strides were being made in **chemotherapy**, or drug treatment

psychotherapy
Any treatment for emotional disorders involving exploring the person's life experiences and unrealistic, pathological perceptions

chemotherapy
Drug treatment for mental or physical disorders

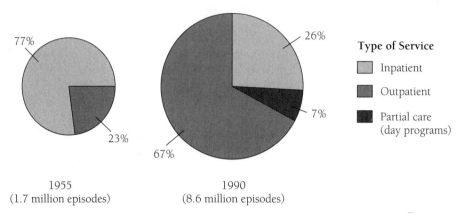

77%

26%

23%

7%

67%

1955
(1.7 million episodes)

1990
(8.6 million episodes)

Type of Service

- Inpatient
- Outpatient
- Partial care (day programs)

The focus of mental health care in the United States clearly has shifted from inpatient to outpatient services. In 1955, about three-fourths of all patient visits for treatment occurred within inpatient settings or mental hospitals. Today, three-fourths of these visits occur in outpatient settings or partial hospitalization programs (day services for the mentally ill).
SOURCE: U.S. Department of Health and Human Services, 1994a, p. 83.

psychotropic medications
Medications used to ameliorate pathological behaviors and mental states

for mental illness. Not only are medications a treatment of first choice for the most serious mental disorders, today **psychotropic** (changing the psyche) **medications** play a central role in the treatment of emotional disorders of almost all kinds.

During the late 1960s, these advances in chemotherapy provided the stimulus for a large-scale emptying of the large psychiatric hospitals that had housed the seriously mentally ill (see Figure 9-4). This push toward "deinstitutionalizing" mental patients was intended to end the practice of "warehousing" seriously mentally ill people for life.

Although the humanitarian impulse to offer outpatient care for these people had unforeseen consequences—many of the mentally disturbed adults we see living on American streets today would have been residents of mental institutions 40 years ago—the **biological revolution in psychiatry** has enabled millions of people whose lives would have been ruined by mental disorders to live a relatively normal life. This focus on alternate treatments such as medications helped to foster another change in the context of mental health care: the effort to extend psychological services to older adults.

biological revolution in psychiatry
Advances in medication therapy during the 1970s and 1980s that led to the use of psychotropic drugs as a central treatment for mental disorders

Older Adults and the Mental Health System

When psychoanalytic therapy was widely thought to be the most effective form of treatment, outpatient mental health interventions were confined to certain groups. People who were young, affluent, verbal, intelligent, and successful were the preferred clients, as they gravitated to and could afford the years of self-reflection believed necessary for this treatment to work. Freud (1924) himself warned that over age 50

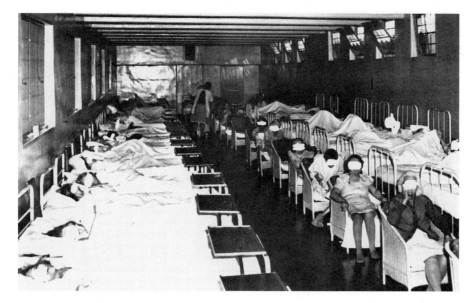

Scenes such as this used to be frequent during the first two-thirds of the 20th century in the large mental hospitals that existed throughout the United States. Today, most of these patients would be living in the community, hopefully with their symptoms controlled by psychotropic drugs.

people were too rigid to profit from psychotherapy. Even when an older person sought treatment, that individual's alien life experiences were thought to interfere with the therapeutic relationship. They would make it more difficult to develop the collaboration and sense of empathy between patient and therapist that was important for treatment to succeed (Sue, 1992).

By the late 1960s, the principles of psychoanalytic theory were under vigorous attack. **Outcome studies**—research measuring the effectiveness of mental health treatments—were revealing that spending years exploring one's childhood was no more effective at curing emotional disorders than time-limited, problem-focused behavioral approaches. An exploding healthy older population was bursting the stereotypes, demonstrating that older dogs could learn new tricks.

As a result, psychologists and other mental health workers (see Table 9-2) turned their attention to older adults. Today, more than a dozen clinical and counseling doctoral psychology programs offer training in geropsychology. Nearly half of all departments of psychiatry offer tracks in geriatric psychiatry. As of 1990, psychiatrists could take an examination and be certified in this field. At least a third of the master's programs in social work allow students to specialize in gerontological social work (Gatz & Finkel, 1996). Textbooks and professional journals are specifically devoted to elderly mental health (Lebowitz, 1993; Logsdon, 1995).

In part, this interest grew out of the boom in anxiety about Alzheimer's disease (Lebowitz, 1993). It was helped along by pioneering psychiatrists who argued that psychotherapy could be effective in people over 65 and by growing concerns that mental disorders in the elderly were being neglected or that psychotropic drugs were indiscriminately overprescribed.

It was aided by changes in the financing of mental health care. Since 1989, Medicare has partially reimbursed outpatient services by psychologists and social workers.

outcome studies
Research designed to demonstrate the effectiveness of treatments for mental and physical disorders

TABLE 9-2

TABLE 9-2   *The Core Mental Health Professionals*

Title	Training	Special additional skills
Psychiatrist	MD, psychiatric residency (usually 3 years in a mental health setting)	Administers drugs; diagnoses and treats medical problems; skilled in the diagnostic interview
Clinical psychologist	PhD in psychology, internship in a mental health setting	Administers and interprets psychological tests; does research
Psychiatric social worker	BA or MSW, supervised field experience in a mental health setting	Works with social agencies and families; knowledgeable about community resources
Psychiatric nurse	RN in nursing plus specialized training in the care and treatment of psychiatric patients	Gives physical care; can assess self-care skills

Medicare and Medicaid also pay in part for mental health services in nursing homes (Lombardo, 1994).

Barriers still exist. As we know, this cohort of elderly did not grow up during the 1960s age of self-disclosure. Especially among the old-old, many people still cling to the idea that emotional problems are shameful, that only "crazy people" seek mental health help. One survey of more than 1000 elderly clinic patients suggests that these predisposing deterrents loom large in the tendency to not get care. People who did use the services were several times more likely to report having seen a mental health worker in their younger years (Aupperle, Coyne, & Pandina, 1997). Adding to the discomfort may be the life stage of the expert dispensing advice: Some older people may feel embarrassed at the thought of getting guidance on how to live from a person half their age.

Enabling factors are also involved. Older people may have trouble physically getting to treatment. They may not even know that services exist. To avoid scaring off potential clients, clinics providing mental health care to older adults sometimes adopt euphemistic names such as "geriatric family services" or "creative aging center," and so render themselves invisible to all but the most aware (Lebowitz, 1993). Another enabling factor is cost. Because Medicare reimburses only 50% of outpatient mental health care, getting treatment may be too expensive for many older adults (Lebowitz, 1993).

Finally, there is the issue of (perceived) need. As we saw earlier, older people may not realize that they have an emotional problem, interpreting their debilitating anxiety or disabling depression as normal aging or a physical disease. In fact, experts estimate, only one-third of older people with mental disorders ever visit a mental health professional. An equal percentage see their primary physician for their symptoms. Another third suffer on their own (Gatz & Finkel, 1996).

Problems from the provider end exacerbate the situation. The number of mental health workers specializing in aging is grossly inadequate to the projected need (Gatz & Finkel, 1996). As we saw in our interview with the geriatric physician in

Chapter 5, working with the elderly is a low-interest area, a professional pathway selected only by a hardy few. Psychologists and others may shy way from treating older clients because they too feel uncomfortable in the role of relationship expert to someone their parents' age. They may have an aversion to dealing with physical or mental disabilities or accept the ageist idea that older people are fixed in their ways. They may feel unable to relate to the concerns of an unfamiliar cohort or an alien life stage. Or they may simply feel inadequate to the task of understanding the older person's needs. Diagnosing emotional problems in older adults can be tricky. Treatments may need to be modified a bit for this special group.

INTERVENTIONS

The first step in treating any mental disorder is to conduct a **diagnostic evaluation**— a far-ranging inquiry into the problem and the person's life. (The following information is from Kaszniak, 1996; and Silver & Herrmann, 1996.)

The Diagnostic Evaluation

The diagnostic evaluation involves a detailed history. What are the person's symptoms? What stresses caused the problem to erupt? How long has the difficulty been going on? What is the person's current life situation like? How has this individual coped with problems before? What are the major milestones in this individual's past?

It includes a careful assessment of the person's behavior—physical appearance, judgment, insight, affect (mood), and interpersonal skills. Is this individual alert or staring vacantly into space? Is she disheveled, dressed in stained clothes? Does he seem out of touch with his feelings or perceptive and aware of his problem, able to connect emotionally?

When an older person arrives for mental health care, this part of the evaluation is identical to that used for an individual of any age. However, in the elderly, a physical examination is mandatory. As we know, in later life, mental and physical problems are often intertwined. It can be difficult or impossible to disentangle a psychological problem from a physical disease. Is the fact that Mr. Jones is listless, unable to eat, and down in the dumps due to depression after his wife's death, or could it signal anemia, a heart problem, or the beginning stages of dementia? Are his symptoms being exacerbated by his heart medication or that sleeping pill the doctor prescribed?

A functional assessment and family interview provide vital additional data. Mr. Jones is having trouble with instrumental activities of daily living, such as driving and doing housework; should he really continue to live all by himself on the family farm? Or would insisting that he move to a assisted living facility in town just multiply his sense of overwhelming loss? How do Mr. Jones's daughter and son view their father's symptoms? Do they seem caring and sympathetic? Can they be counted on to help?

Finally, even if dementia is not suspected, a brief assessment of cognitive capacities is recommended. True, he may appear alert and insightful, but perhaps the **mental status exam** (see Table 9-3) will reveal that Mr. Jones's memory is not all that it seems.

The goal of the assessment is to arrive at a diagnosis and treatment plan for Mr. Jones. If mental health care is suggested, the treatments fall into two basic categories: chemotherapy and psychotherapy.

diagnostic evaluation
Evaluation used to diagnose a mental illness, suggest possible reasons for the problem, and spell out an appropriate treatment(s)

mental status exam
Set of questions designed to reveal basic cognitive functions, such as awareness of self and the world

TABLE 9-3	The Types of Questions Used to Assess Mental Status

1. What is the date? year? season?
2. Where are we now? (hospital, city, state, country)
3. Who am I?
4. Give me the names of your family.
5. What is your address?
6. Name three objects in the room.
7. Write your name.
8. Spell "world."
9. After looking at this sentence, close your eyes and tell me what it says.

Chemotherapy

As we saw earlier, advances in chemotherapy have drastically altered mental health care in the Western world. *Psychotropic medications* have been a godsend to people whose lives, decades earlier, would have been permanently shattered by mental disease. Medications for mental disorders fall into three categories: *Antipsychotic drugs* work to eradicate the symptoms of schizophrenia. *Antidepressant medications* are used for major depression and panic attacks. *Antianxiety drugs* calm minor anxiety symptoms and help induce sleep.

Psychotropic drugs are widely prescribed for adults of every age. Among older people, they rank fifth among the most commonly filled prescriptions in the United States. These later-life mind-savers can be a double-edged sword.

Because the older person metabolizes medicines less effectively, the dosage of a drug that is appropriate at age 20 can have toxic effects at age 85. The risk of unwanted side effects in the elderly is high because older people are more prone to make medication errors and typically take several different medications at the same time (D. E. Barnes et al., 1997). Not only may drugs interact to produce symptoms ranging in severity from dizziness to sudden death, but as noted in our discussion of dementia, toxic reactions may go unrecognized in the elderly because they mimic typical signs of old age. Moreover, psychotropic drugs can be more dangerous in later life because they may exacerbate the symptoms of some important age-related physical problems. For instance, antidepressant and antipsychotic drugs produce heart-rate and blood-pressure changes, and so occasionally cause dangerous arrhythmias in people with heart disease (Beizer, 1994; Young & Meyers, 1996).

Adverse drug effects are an alarming problem in old age. They are implicated in an astonishing one-third of all hospitalizations among the elderly in the United States (J. W. Cooper, 1994)! This means that psychotropic drugs must be used especially carefully in this group (Shorr & Robin, 1994). Physicians need to give the lowest possible dose, be especially alert for side effects, and quickly discontinue the drug if unwanted symptoms crop up. They should make special efforts to ensure that the medication is being taken as prescribed. For the reasons spelled out in Table 9-4, medication errors are a common, almost predictable, event when a person suffers from the multiple physical impairments of advanced old age (Ascione, 1994).

1. **Complexity of the regimen.** Older people with multiple illnesses are likely to be taking several drugs, each with its own dosage schedule. Besides the difficulty of sticking to this complex regimen, they may not be able to get to the store to get each refill on time.

2. **Lack of understanding of drug effects.** Older people may abandon the medicine or take it erratically because they falsely attribute symptoms of another condition to side effects of the drug.

3. **Physical limitations.** Older adults with vision problems may not read the label correctly, or may mistake the yellow pill for the green one. Those with hearing difficulties may miss the verbal instructions a physician gives. People with functional limitations may have trouble physically getting to the medicine cabinet or be deterred from taking their pill because they have trouble opening the bottle and swallowing the medicine.

4. **Poor communication between providers.** People with multiple health problems may visit different health care professionals, each recommending a different medication. If patients do not accurately communicate to each specialist the other drugs they are taking, pills that interact in toxic ways are apt to be prescribed.

SOURCE: Adapted from Ascione, 1994.

Psychotherapy

In contrast to Freud's dire dictum, outcome studies confirm that psychotherapy *is* effective over age 65 (Gallagher-Thompson & Thompson, 1996). In this section, we describe two popular psychotherapies for people of any age and their use in later life: cognitive behavioral and traditional psychoanalytic approaches.

COGNITIVE BEHAVIORAL THERAPY **Cognitive behavioral approaches** are a set of structured, present-focused, action-oriented techniques that seem ideally suited to older people, because they do not involve dredging up childhood memories or lying on a couch for years. The therapy is offered in the form of "classes" or education, so that older adults do not have to define themselves as mentally ill. As we saw in Chapter 2, the behavioral model of the mind is basically age-friendly: Our life stage is irrelevant to understanding and modifying behavior. People can change at any time of life (Zeiss & Steffen, 1996).

cognitive behavioral therapy Structured behavioral treatment for mental disorders involving identifying and changing the pathological cognitions or perceptions believed to be causing the problem

Cognitive behavioral therapy includes a varied set of techniques. These strategies involve working to change the dysfunctional cognitions, the unrealistic thinking patterns, that cognitive behaviorists see as central to making the person ill (Beck, 1973). They also include traditional reinforcement-oriented behavioral approaches. For instance, a cognitive behaviorist may train an alcoholic client to avoid classically conditioned stimuli provoking the urge to drink (such as not taking the route home from work that involves passing his favorite bar). She may have an agoraphobic person gradually venture into "unsafe" places so the fear will extinguish. She may work to get a depressed client to increase the frequency of external reinforcers in his life.

The first step in any cognitive behavioral treatment is to "target" specific goals. These goals must be as behavioral or concrete as possible. For instance, rather than Mr. Jones saying "I want to feel happy like when my wife was alive," the aged widower

TABLE 9-5 *A Dysfunctional Thought Record Constructed by Mr. Jones and the Realistic Responses That He Might Substitute to Break the Depressive Chain*

Situation: Lying in bed, alone at night

Emotions: Sad, miserable, down in the dumps, lonely

Depressive thoughts: I miss Sharon so much. There is no reason to go on living. Nothing gives me pleasure anymore. My life is a total mess. Nobody needs me. I might as well kill myself.

More rational thoughts: (1) Yes, I miss Sharon terribly, but she would want me to go on with life. (2) I still have the farm, and what would my beloved animals do if I died? (3) My daughter and the grandchildren are also relying on me. I'm the only grandpa they have. Last Sunday, Ann told me that visiting the farm to see me was the high point of the children's lives. (4) Maybe I'll invite my daughter and children out this weekend. That would be fun!

would decide "to feel less depressed at night" and "to find activities that give me pleasure." The therapist then gives homework assignments tailored to these goals.

As illustrated in Table 9-5, Mr. Jones might make a record tracing the chain of depression-promoting cognitions and learn to break the spiral by substituting more appropriate thoughts. He might be asked to chart his daily mood to identify what specific activities give him pleasure during the week. These fine-grained observations would help Mr. Jones identify and gain control over the helpless and hopeless cognitions and construct a new, more reinforcing life.

Following is a real-life case of the treatment used with an elderly woman suffering from a chronic disease (Zeiss & Steffen, 1996, pp. 47–50):

> A.T. was a 67-year-old woman with chronic obstructive pulmonary disease who was seen in her home. . . . When she began CBT she spent most of her days at home sitting in the living room. . . . Her best days occurred when the children and grandchildren came to visit. . . . However, most of the time she just complained of shortness of breath. . . . Goals in the first phase of therapy were to (A) improve daily mood, (B) reduce episodes of breathing distress, (C) increase her sense of self-efficacy regarding her ability to be involved in meaningful activities. . . .
>
> A.T. . . . strongly endorsed the opinion that her mood was determined by her physical condition. Furthermore, she argued that variability in her breathing difficulties was determined by variation in air quality; thus she could have no control over her mood. [The therapist accepted this] as potentially valid. . . . Therefore in addition to tracking her daily moods the therapist agreed to note the air quality index from the local paper. After 2 weeks, graphs comparing mood, activity, and air quality index were generated. These graphs showed little relationship between air quality and the client's mood but a strong relationship between mood and activity. . . . This resulted in an enhanced . . . motivation on her part to do the therapy suggestions. . . .
>
> A . . . dysfunctional thought record was used to help A.T. clarify her negative thoughts and learn to challenge them. . . . A.T. was encouraged to think about how to adapt formerly enjoyed activities in accordance with the realities of her health rather than abandoning activities altogether. For example, . . .

she set up a large planter box outside of her living room window to hold her favorite flowers. She was able to do the gardening for this planter although she could not keep up with the whole yard. . . . A.T. had used computers at work and was interested in continuing to use them. . . . After some time she became a consultant to older friends. . . . She and her grandchildren also shared the role of family computer experts and enjoyed computer games together. . . . At the end of 20 sessions A. T.'s depression and anxiety scores had significantly declined.

In addition to careful recording and the emphasis on concretely measuring success, perhaps you were struck with the fact that this psychologist took the unusual step of conducting sessions in the client's home. You may have been impressed with the creative way the therapist addressed that other barrier that, as we saw earlier, makes older people with physical problems resistant to mental health care. Before treatment could proceed, A. T. had to be "taught" that her symptoms were really under her control, not the inevitable consequence of a hopeless physical disease.

Additional socialization for treatment may be required (Gallagher-Thompson & Thompson, 1996). Cognitive behaviorists may allow more time for an older client to learn the ropes, devoting extra sessions to training in articulating behavioral goals or constructing the dysfunctional thought record illustrated in Table 9-5. If an older person has sensory problems, the therapist may present material in different modalities. For instance, with a hearing-impaired individual, she may use a blackboard to help. Flexible tailoring of treatment to the person is the basis of any cognitive behavioral strategy. In fact, this flexible fitting of the therapy to the individual may be what really sets this treatment apart as a psychotherapy of choice in later life (Thompson & Gallagher-Thompson, 1997).

PSYCHOANALYTIC THERAPY Traditional psychoanalysts would shudder at these activities. They would not think of venturing forth from their office or rearranging their whole mode of operation to fit the person's needs. However, even a half century ago, a few psychoanalytic psychotherapists went beyond the traditional setting to use this framework with impaired older adults (Goldfarb, 1953). Psychoanalytically oriented psychologist Vicki Semel continues this tradition today.

In her work with chronically ill people, Semel (1996) focuses less on childhood issues and more on problems in the here and now. She approaches patients from a nonageist perspective, believing that everyone can change. With these modifications, her mode of conducting treatment mirrors classic **psychoanalytic therapy**: The patient is instructed to freely explore his emotions without interference. Through this intense self-exploration, the individual gets insight into the unconscious needs motivating the symptoms and can construct a better life. Here is an excerpt from one of her cases:

psychoanalytic therapy
Treatment for mental disorders involving understanding the unconscious (childhood) motivations believed to be responsible for the problem

My relationship with Mr. F. began after he had a serious stroke, which led him to fixate on the fact that his wife was going to die. He sobbed and was inconsolable about her possible death, yet it was he who was wheelchair bound and more likely to die. Mr. F. had been raised in an immigrant Irish family and became wealthy. . . . Mrs. F. was committed to totally raising their five children. . . . Through his business, Mr. F. had entered a more cos-

9-4 A Psychologist in the Nursing Home

What is working as a psychologist in long-term care like? How do people get interested in this unusual field? Listen to this clinical psychologist who works at a teaching nursing home.

When I was a teenager, I went to Arizona periodically to visit my grandmother. I was struck with the way her friends were aging differently. Some were alert, active, at the peak of their powers; others were in a downslide. That got me intrigued with the forces promoting success-ful aging. The other influence on my interest in geriatrics was working in a psychiatric hospital where I was exposed to elderly patients. I was amazed at how physically compro-mised people were by the time they were hospitalized—how, had there been an intervention earlier, many problems could have been prevented. When I was offered the opportunity to start a psychology department at our comprehensive facility, I leaped at the chance.

I've been at Newman Geriatric Center now for five years and feel just as excited today about what I do as at the beginning. There are few settings where your work is 100% geriatric; where you see a variety of patients, from the severely mentally impaired to people who are extremely sharp; where a psychologist is able to do such an interesting mix of things. You do groups—some with people who are high-functioning and some with people with dementia. Right now a colleague and I are conducting a study to examine the effectiveness of psycho-therapy with dementia and depression. At the early stages of the illness people will say "I'm losing my mind." We see our mission as providing support, enabling residents to deal with a loss. We teach skills to help the person feel more in control. Much of our work involves reinforcing existing strengths, restoring a positive sense of self. Fortunately, the way dementia works is that short-term memory goes but long-term memory remains and so it is possible, through reminiscence sessions, to get residents reconnected to the human being that is still there.

A good deal of my work involves consulting around behavioral management issues— problems staff are having with residents. When I started working here, being the only psy-

mopolitan world. . . . He became a womanizer and enjoyed this aspect of his life. . . . As the years went on and he became physically ill, his freedom to wander became limited. . . . As his health worsened, however, he realized that his wife might well outlive him and that she was in total control of his life. . . . So he cried, unconsciously wishing to mourn his wife's death, his fantasized way to freedom.

In therapy, I helped him to talk. I did not give him any interpretations of his unconscious impulses towards his wife, but waited for him to describe how she wanted him right there under his thumb. Once he was able to express his anger at her, his crying stopped. (pp. 108–109)

Semel is one of the few psychologists who, like your author and the therapist in Aging in Action 9-4, have found gratification and a sense of mission working in a nursing home. We conclude this chapter by briefly exploring why people in our cate-gory are rare.

chologist at our facility, I could only do one-shot consultations on the various units at the center. Now that we have hired additional people, each of us is attached to a particular treatment team. I love my work on the team, having that sense of connectedness, of being on the scene on an ongoing basis to intimately know staff and patients' needs. Another surprisingly gratifying aspect of my job involves sitting on institutional committees. That's where you really get a chance to shape policies—to change things in a basic way for our residents.

My main love, however, is psychotherapy. So, despite my other commitments, I still see individual patients. My basic orientation is psychoanalytic but with this population you have to be flexible. For me, the key lies in the relationship, the bond you form. These people have lost so many relationships. Living in an institution, there's a feeling of vulnerability, of losing the core of who one is. My goal is to restore a sense of integrity and personhood. The patients do not remember what techniques you use, but they do remember feeling cared about, valued, restored. They say things like, "You helped me to find myself again." When I approach a resident for my initial visit, I often use the analogy "It helps to get things off your chest." It's rare that people resist after you couch things like this. Also, residents appreciate talking because they don't want to burden their families with the information that they can share with me.

The high point is the sense that you are making a difference in lives. It's subtle. It's an internal process. You don't see the dramatic shifts you see with younger adults. You cannot change the external circumstances. People get worse; they decline. You can't take away the physical pain. You have to watch people deteriorate and die. What you are really doing is helping people to get worse, or, I should say, helping them cope with getting worse. You have to cope with institutional issues, problems relating to how the residents are being cared for. I don't always get the staff cooperation that I want. It's upsetting, knowing that injustices are being done. Some of it is because there always are people who aren't very nice. Some of it is just the fact of being in an institution. But the gratifications are immense—the feeling that what I do is immensely meaningful.

TOO LITTLE MENTAL HEALTH CARE
IN LONG-TERM CARE

Nursing homes should be a fertile place for mental health services. As we know, the majority of people in long-term care suffer from mental disorders (G. D. Cohen, 1997). The problems these residents have are usually severe. There are the legions of Alzheimer's victims who develop distressing behavioral symptoms or serious depression as a by-product of their dementing disease. There are cognitively intact older residents who become depressed as a consequence of being old and physically impaired. Moreover, with the advent of deinstitutionalization, many chronically mentally ill older people who would otherwise have been in state mental hospitals have been shifted to nursing homes. Woefully few get mental health help.

Recall from Chapter 5 that the Nursing Home Reform Act, called OBRA, signaled a new, humane effort to address nursing homes residents' emotional needs. Still, only an estimated 7% of residents with mental disorders ever get mental health care. Most of those who do get services see a psychiatrist who visits once a month or less to consult with the staff and administer psychotropic drugs. Despite the existence of a growing special interest group called Psychologists in Long-Term Care (Peter Lichtenberg, personal communication, 1997), few psychologists ever set foot in a nursing home (Lombardo, 1994).

Pay is a major deterrent. Medicaid and Medicare do cover mental health services. However, their reimbursement rates are appallingly low. At an average cost of $20 or $30 per session, it simply does not pay for a mental health worker to do nursing home work. Although all states cover services by physicians, only a minority directly reimburse psychologists for mental health care.

In one national survey, half of all nursing home administrators reported that mental health providers were resistant to visiting their facility. If they did agree to offer services, they preferred to see residents at their clinic or office, not on-site. Ironically, in this poll, the areas that administrators identified as special needs require physically being in the facility. Administrators said they could use help teaching staff how to deal with problem behaviors. They needed consultation and training in how to cope with the patient management issues that crop up in long-term care. Not only do these activities require that the consultant be there to watch the behavior, they are not traditionally covered by Medicare or Medicaid.

Psychologists are uniquely qualified to provide this type of guidance. They are the only mental health professionals likely to be skilled in behavioral techniques, a treatment of first choice in managing disruptive behaviors. Far too many nursing home residents are indiscriminately given medications to quiet their symptoms when behavioral interventions would work. Others who could benefit from medications or psychotherapy are not being treated, their symptoms ignored (Monane, Gurwitz, & Avorn, 1993).

This situation is unfortunate. As seen in Aging in Action 9-4, psychologists who work in nursing homes vigorously testify to the usefulness of psychological interventions with these most disabled older adults. In addition to modified behavioral and psychoanalytic treatments and reminiscence groups, one type of treatment that seems especially appropriate for this unusual setting is training in "social skills." In this therapy, the person learns specific techniques for coping with interpersonal issues endemic to nursing home life, such as learning to assert one's needs with the staff and roommates.

A preliminary study at the Philadelphia Geriatric Center has shown social skills training to be *somewhat* beneficial. Although their overall adjustment did not improve, the 12 residents who completed the training were better able to generate constructive responses to problem situations than a comparison group (Frazer, 1997). There is even an outcome study showing that traditional behavior therapy is effective at reducing the depression that often accompanies early Alzheimer's disease (Teri, 1997; Teri, Logsdon, Uomoto, & McCurry, 1997).

This research removes any rationale for a hands-off stance. As our therapy-bred baby boom cohort enters later life, problems getting mental health care for the vital young-old are certain to lessen or erode. But what about that group in especially dire need—people in nursing homes?

agoraphobia
alcoholism
biological revolution in
  psychiatry
chemotherapy
cognitive behavioral approaches
comorbidity
depression

Diagnostic and Statistical Manual
  of Mental Disorders (DSM)
diagnostic evaluation
DSM-IV
Epidemiologic Catchment Area
  Survey (ECA)
epidemiologic studies
lifetime prevalence

mental status exam
panic attacks
phobias
psychoanalytic therapy
psychotherapy
psychotropic medications
outcome studies

RECOMMENDED READINGS

GENERAL REFERENCES

American Psychiatric Association. (1994). *Diagnostic and statistical manual of mental disorders* (4th ed.). Washington, DC: Author.
The current manual for diagnosing mental disorders is required reading for every person in the mental health field.

Birren, J. E., & Sloane, R. B. (Eds.). (1992). *Handbook of mental health and aging* (2d ed.). Englewood Cliffs, NJ: Prentice-Hall.
This is a classic textbook on aging and mental health.

Mental health and aging: Problems and prospects. (1993, Winter/Spring). *Generations, 17.*
The whole issue of this journal is devoted to aging and mental health.

SPECIFIC BOOKS

McGrath, E., Keita, G. P., Strickland, B. R., & Russo, N. (1990). *Women and depression.* Washington, DC: American Psychological Association.
This book thoroughly explores depression in women.

Rubinstein, R. L., & Lawton, M. P. (Eds.). (1997). *Depression in long-term and residential care: Advances in research and treatment.* New York: Springer.
The articles in this edited book cover the characteristics and experience of depression in nursing homes and discuss different treatments for this condition.

Styron, W. (1990). *Darkness visible.* New York: Vintage Books.
This is a beautifully written autobiographical account of the writer's depression and eventual cure.

Zarit, S. H., & Knight, B. G. (Eds.). (1996). *A guide to psychotherapy and aging: Effective interventions in a life-stage context.* Washington, DC: American Psychological Association.
The articles in this edited book summarize a variety of psychological interventions that are used with the elderly.

Chapter Outline

10

The Older Family

The 98-year-old woman in my family is a pioneer. She became a grandparent at age 47 and has been called Grandma for half of her life. She was widowed at age 65 and has lived as an older widow for more than 30 years. She has an adolescent great-grandchild. All of her grandchildren are middle-aged. Ten years ago, she was there to comfort her daughter when she too became a widow at age 65. As she approaches her 100th birthday in the year 2000, this woman can survey her family with knowledge no previous generation ever had. My grandmother has participated in a revolution in intergenerational life.

In 1900, marriage was for child-rearing. The empty-nest phase of married life lasted only a few years. Today, if couples marry at the typical time (their mid-20s) and do not divorce, most can expect their marriage to last for almost a half century (U.S. Bureau of the Census, 1996). If we combine the first childless years of marriage and the empty nest, more than one-third of this time will be spent alone (Aizenberg & Treas, 1985).

In 1900, parents and children were adults together for a small fraction of life. If both sets of parents were present at their wedding, a bride and groom felt blessed. Being a grandparent meant enjoying young children, if a person was lucky enough to see the third generation born. Today, we routinely see several grandparents or even an occasional greatgrandparent walking down the aisle. With three-fourths of Americans in their early 50s having at least one living parent, four-generation families are common (Soldo, 1996). As we travel into this new century, even five generations may no longer be extremely rare (Bengtson, 1993).

In the 1950s, marriage often lasted until death. Children of divorce were looked down on as products of "a broken home." It was unacceptable to have a child outside of the marital bond. When children grew up and had their own families, they lived by themselves. They were not supposed to need their parents' hands-on help.

Today, adults move in and out of marriage as they move through life. With almost one-third of all American children being born to single parents (Council on Families in America, 1995), "unwed motherhood" is becoming an accepted alternate family form.

These changes are due to the 20th-century life expectancy revolution and the 1960s revolution in social roles. Each has left a dramatic imprint on intergenerational life. As life expectancy rose and the time they shared adulthood ballooned, parents and children had to learn to be adults together in new ways. The job of raising children, while still important, has been supplemented by another caregiving concern: caring for a frail parent for years. At the same time, the growth of single-parent families, combined with declining economic prospects for young adults, has meant that older family members have had to increase their involvement with the lower generational rungs. More young adults than ever are sharing households with their middle-aged parents. With an estimated 4 million women now taking primary responsibility for a grandchild's care, the role of grandparent has become more central to family life (Riley & Riley, 1993).

The life expectancy and lifestyle revolutions have also altered couple relationships in the later years. Today, husbands and wives face the challenge of staying committed for an unparalleled length of time. It is more acceptable to express our sexuality at 80, to find a new lover at 90, or to live openly as a homosexual couple.

Ethel Shanas (1984) has described these new families as "pioneers." Uncharted relationships must be negotiated, new paths carved out. What is it like to be married to the same person for more than a half century? Suppose you are a 60-year-old woman with custody of your grandchild who finds yourself suddenly caring full-time for your mother with Alzheimer's disease? How does a 98-year-old woman behave as mother to a 75-year-old daughter or grandmother to a 50-year-old college professor grandchild?

In this chapter, we explore these issues as we focus in depth on three central older family roles: long-married couple, elderly parent/adult child, and grandparent. Keep in mind that, besides leaving out other family relationships, our selective approach cannot reflect the realities of family life in another respect. The family is a mosaic of relationships; it is more than the sum of its parts.

OLDER MARRIED COUPLES

divorce revolution
The dramatic escalation in divorce rates during the last third of the 20th century

U-shaped curve of marital satisfaction
Idea that marital happiness declines during the child-rearing years and rises at the empty nest

Elderly married couples are a varied group. There are the small numbers of late-life newlyweds, people who get married at age 70 or even 85. There are the escalating number of married couples entering their older years having had the earlier life experience of being divorced (Bumpass & Aquilino, 1995). However, because the 1960s **divorce revolution** did not fully hit the pre-baby-boom cohorts, many contemporary elderly couples married in their early 20s and have stayed together for life. In fact, this cohort of elderly married people may be unique—the *only* group in human history with so many members who have mastered the art of being together for 40, 50, or 60 years. This is why I have chosen to focus on these long-lived relationships. What are enduring elderly marriages like?

The Positive Reality: Increasing Harmony

The early research painted a bleak picture: Marital happiness was at its peak during the honeymoon and then steadily declined, reaching a low point in old age. Luckily, recent studies suggest that happiness follows a **U-shaped curve** (Glenn, 1990). Marital satisfaction often drops when a couple has children, but the low is followed by an upswing at the empty nest. Couples can regain some of what they once had when they are free from the pressures of bringing up children and have the luxury of focusing on one another again.

In-depth studies of long-married older couples confirm that marriages can be unusually happy in later life. When Robert Atchley and Sheila Miller (1983) interviewed men and women married an average of 35 years, they found a high degree of harmony. These husbands and wives were very much alike. On a list of goals and favorite activities, they gave identical answers 80% of the time.

In comparing middle-aged couples and an elderly long-married group, Laura Carstensen and her colleagues got the same message. In areas from negotiating finances, to parenting, to where to take a vacation that year, the older couples reported less conflict. The elderly couples experienced more shared pleasure in every area of life (Carstensen, Gottman, & Levenson, 1995; Levenson, Carstensen, & Gottman, 1993).

Why might marriages improve in the older years? One reason is that, rather than drawing a couple closer, becoming parents is more apt to put a wedge between a husband and wife. Researchers find that when couples have children, on average marital satisfaction declines. Feelings of romance lessen. Women in particular tend to withdraw more from their husbands as they center their emotional energies around their child. Arguments tend to flare up around the **division of labor,** or who does what around the house (Belsky, Lang, & Rovine, 1985; Belsky & Pensky, 1988; Cowan & Cowan, 1988, 1992). When the children leave, these sources of conflict are removed. At the empty nest, marital satisfaction improves (White & Edwards, 1990) as couples refocus their attention more fully on one another again. However, more than just being together without the children is involved. Elderly couples seem to relate better. They communicate in a more positive, loving way.

division of labor
Manner in which a couple divides the chores of their married life

COMMUNICATION AND HARMONY   The quality of a marriage is revealed in the way a couple "manages" the relationship—that is, their interactions in daily life. Unhappy couples fight much more often. Worse yet, they exchange blow for blow in an escalating chain. They have trouble expressing loving feelings (Hendrick, 1981). They have a negative explanatory style, misreading hostile intentions into even loving acts (Honeycutt, 1993). Happy couples have fewer intense altercations. They know how to keep their conflicts from getting out of hand. They understand how to express affection lavishly. They regularly make approving, caring comments and freely share feelings of love (Guerrero, Eloy, & Wabnik, 1993).

In videotaping their middle-aged and elderly married subjects discussing issues, Carstensen's research team found that, no matter what the topic, the elderly couples showed more positive, caring communication styles. Even when talking about a defined problem area in the marriage, the elderly couples were more approving and respectful, less prone to lock horns or erupt in anger or disgust.

In may be that, as we saw in Chapter 8, because emotional arousal is less intense in later life, older couples simply *feel* less upset when a difficult marital issue arises. Or, drawing on Heckhausen and Schulz's life-span model of successful aging, elderly couples may be more skilled at secondary control. In a frustrating marital situation, they tend to modulate their feelings, saying "I'll just go on to something else," rather than aggressively trying to exert primary control (change the problem by lashing out

Free from the distractions of working and raising children, this loving couple is clearly relishing the chance to turn their attention fully to one another's needs.

at a partner). As with any crystallized skill, couples may learn to be better conflict managers over the years. However, in her theory of socioemotional selectivity, Laura Carstensen (1995) spells out the most intriguing possibility for why marital conflict is rarer in old age: Older couples fight less often because the motivation to mold the other person in the future is no longer there.

Earlier in a marriage, Carstensen reasons, there is a good payoff in bringing up unpleasant topics, in telling our spouse what we don't like. It is important to get things out on the table to get the other person to change. In our last years together, we become less interested in future improvement and more concerned with the quality of our relationship in the here and now. Moreover, after decades, we know further arguing is fruitless. We have developed strategies to cope with the parts of our partner we don't like.

Let's take Jenny Smith, who dislikes the fact that her husband, Tom, leaves the house a mess. Early in their marriage, the couple has frequent fights centering around this issue as Jenny tries to modify her husband's behavior to improve the quality of her life. When the couple reaches their 70s, it doesn't make sense to waste time arguing. Tom has done all the changing he can. Nagging will only take away from what they have. Moreover, by now Tom picks up his socks more often, and Jenny has learned not to be so anxious about having an immaculate house.

This example may help explain why elderly couples often seem so amazingly alike. When the marriage is going well, each partner gradually adjusts to the other's idiosyncrasies, and eventually a husband and wife reach that beautiful middle ground where their attitudes, interests, and worldviews really mesh.

These studies paint a marvelous portrait of people learning to live as a unit over time. However, I must caution that they involve middle-class, young-old couples. These are the very people with the resources most likely to promote marital bliss. Most important, they are cross-sectional. Without research tracing the course of relationships (longitudinal studies), we do not know if marriages really get *better* in later life or if we are only examining the cream of the crop—couples who have survived the stresses of child rearing to remain together into their older years.

The reality is that selective attrition does occur. As we know, far from all people who get married stay together until later life. The prognosis is really alarming in this age of divorce. Among couples who married in the early 1990s, an estimated two-thirds of these relationships will not endure (Bumpass & Aquilino, 1995). What insights does the research offer you, the unmarried reader, for being that person who can stay married happily for life? Based on the studies just described, one strategy immediately comes to mind: Select a similar mate.

SIMILARITY AND HARMONY   There is a reason why our parents tell us to marry someone who is "like us." Selecting a partner who already shares many of our values, interests, and attitudes, as well as being similar in religion and ethnicity, should reduce the risk of conflicts and make it easier to develop a shared worldview. Research confirms this idea. Marrying a similar person does seem to increase the chance of being happily married as the years pass (Acitelli, Douvan, & Veroff, 1993). In addition, marrying someone very much like ourselves has an interesting side benefit: It may help promote personality consistency on our journey through life.

In tracing the lives of the Berkeley/Oakland couples, Avashalom Caspi and Ellen Herbener (1990) found that people who were initially very much alike not only rated themselves as more happily married 10 years later but also changed less internally over the decade. In other words, not only is it a good policy to marry someone who shares our basic interests and values, this very selection solidifies a stable sense of self as we travel through time.

Clearly, being just like our spouse is not the only important ingredient. Imagine couples who are very much alike in their pathological traits—a terrible temper, an inability to listen, difficulty with compromise. Shouldn't an even more important quality to look for be that elusive quality called maturity or mental health? This brings us to a remarkable study tracing marriages over 45 years.

MENTAL HEALTH AND HARMONY   In the 1930s, Lowell Kelly recruited more than 300 young couples from engagement announcements in the paper, gave them a variety of personality tests, and had friends rate their emotional stability. Then, his research team followed these couples periodically through later life (Kelly & Conley, 1987).

Over the years, 22 couples broke their engagements, and 50 got divorced. Another group stayed unhappily married, together by default. Of the many influences the researchers examined—personality traits, early life history, attitudes about marriage, stressful life events during the marriage, sexual history—these failed relationships were distinguished more by the psychopathology of their participants than anything else. If a man's friends rated him as high in neuroticism at his engagement, he was likely to have marital problems. A women rated as neurotic was set up for an unhappy marriage or future divorce. Once again, we see that broad personality traits such as neuroticism endure and influence the path we follow as we age.

It makes sense that who we are as people would be a critical influence shaping the course of our married life. People who are mature have the emotional flexibility to perform the delicate day-to-day compromising. They are able to fully reach out to a partner in affection, caring, and love. But, so far, you may have noticed, we have been operationalizing marital happiness just in terms of communication, affection, and caring—omitting the sexual side of love. How does marital passion change over the years? Clues come from Robert Sternberg's (1988) **triangular theory of love.**

The Negative Possibility: Decreasing Passion

Sternberg, whose innovative attempt to capture real-world intelligence was described in Chapter 6, breaks love into three basic components: **passion**, **intimacy**, and **decision/commitment.** Sternberg's passion component refers to arousal, the intense longing that has sexual desire as its basis. Intimacy describes love based on genuinely knowing the person, mutual understanding, concern for the other's welfare, loving the person for who he or she really is. Decision/commitment means committing to the other, deciding that this is my life choice.

By combining passion, intimacy, and commitment, Sternberg believes we get a picture of every type of love relationship in life—from the fantasy obsession called a "crush," characterized by intense sexual arousal without any intimacy (knowledge of the individual) at all, to romantic love in which a couple is passionate and intimate but has not yet made a final commitment to be wed. Once they have committed to one another, or are married, love relationships fall into three categories. There are couples united only by commitment; those with commitment plus intimacy; and couples who are experiencing all three facets of love (see Figure 10-1).

Husbands and wives whose relationships involve commitment without passion or intimacy have what Sternberg calls "empty marriages," or "his-and-her unions." A couple stays married but lives sterile, emotionally separate lives. Couples with intimacy and commitment but no passion have **companionate love.** They have the deep loyalty, affection, and closeness of best friends. At the center of the triangle is the ideal relationship, one combining all three components. This type of marriage, in which a husband and wife are sexually attracted, feel emotionally close, and are fully committed to one another, is the kind of relationship we hope for and so rarely can maintain. Sternberg calls this ideal of loving **consummate love.**

By charting the time course of each component, Sternberg implies that among couples married for decades, consummate relationships are rare. Intimacy increases as people get to know one another, then grows at a slower rate, then levels off. When we begin to take the other person for granted and the pressures of real life intrude, a couple tends to grow less intimate as the years pass. A husband and wife don't talk the way they used to. They know one another too well. Work or children become more absorbing. They become "ships passing in the night."

Although it is possible for couples to once again grow intimate, passion is inherently ephemeral. According to Sternberg, passion develops rapidly and declines steeply because the essence of this love is newness. As with any addiction, once the object of our desire becomes familiar, habituation sets in. With predictability, we lose passion because the other person is no longer novel, stimulating, and arousing.

Sternberg's theory gives us another reason why intimacy blossoms after the children are gone. At the empty nest, husbands and wives have the luxury to become more

---

triangular theory of love
Sternberg's categorization of love into different types based on combining three qualities forming the poles of a triangle

passion
Pole of Sternberg's triangle referring to intense sexual arousal

intimacy
Pole of Sternberg's triangle referring to love based on truly knowing the other person

decision/ commitment
Pole of Sternberg's triangle referring to a committed lifetime choice

companionate love
"Best friend" marriage, characterized by intimacy and commitment but no passion

consummate love
Ideal form of love characterized by passion, intimacy, and commitment

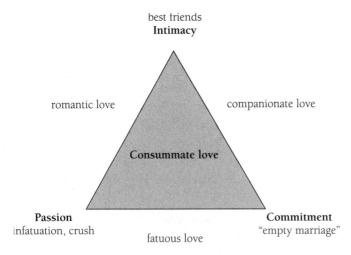

best friends
Intimacy

romantic love   companionate love

Consummate love

Passion   **Commitment**
infatuation, crush   "empty marriage"
        fatuous love

*By combining the components of love, we get the different couple relationships
in life. The types of marriages, in later life and at other ages, are in the center
and on the right side of the triangle.*
SOURCE: Sternberg, 1988.

intimate. They can reconnect with the real human being again. However, the main
message of his analysis is negative: Happily married, long-married older couples have
companionate relationships. They have marriages characterized by deep intimacy but
no passion.

Aging in Action 10-1 suggests that passion is possible in *new* relationships in later
life. But is Sternberg right in assuming that passion is absent even among the happiest
long-married older adults? To answer this question, we need to look more generally at
how growing old affects us in that important area of life—sex.

SEXUALITY IN LATER LIFE

Nowhere are negative stereotypes about aging more powerful than with sexuality. As
we saw in Chapter 1, throughout history human beings have equated youth with
virility and passion and linked age with the end of our sexual life. That this idea is
upsetting is clear when we look at a good index of our fears, humor. During the 1960s,
Erdman Palmore (1971) copied jokes about aging according to subject. He found that
jokes about old age frequently concerned sexuality. A glance at the humorous birthday
cards at your local store will tell you the situation has not changed. Notice that sexual

10-1 *Elderly Lovers*

Joan was 18 when she married Hank. She fondly recalls how she fought for and finally captured the dashing young captain of the football team in her senior year. During their marriage, the intense passion of the early years did wane. However, their affection still "burned just as bright" for more than 50 years. Then, one day, the one love of her life was just not there—dead at age 72 of a sudden, massive heart attack.

When Joan became a widow, she was convinced that her love life was over. Not many men wanted to date a 70-year-old woman. She felt uncomfortable with the few who did ask her out. Joan had been a virgin at marriage. Being with another man was awkward. There were embarrassing encounters. Anyway, she was too old to be interested in a new relationship, much less having sex. Then, she met Henry. He physically resembled Hank. He gave her flowers and told her she was beautiful. Joan found herself involved in a passionate sexual relationship again.

Joan and Henry have been together for almost 7 years. They fly around the world. They have a wonderful time. Joan stays over at Henry's house a few nights a week. Henry has proposed repeatedly or asked Joan to at least move in, but she always says no. She likes having her own "space," a place to be by herself. Futhermore, while "just the right age" for a lover, she is way "too old" for marriage, especially to an 85-year-old man!

In the text, we have been focusing on couples who have been married for decades. However, like Joan and Henry, many people do begin new relationships in their senior-citizen years. What are these "autumn love affairs" like? To answer this question, Kristine and Richard Bulcroft compared a group of elderly lovers with college students in romantic love (Bulcroft & O'Connor-Rudin, 1986).

Being older did not dim the symptoms of passion. The older lovers felt the same heightened sense of reality, awkwardness, heart palpitations, and excitement as the 20-year-olds. It did not weaken the external trappings of romance. Both young and elderly lovers enjoyed candlelit dinners, walks, flowers, and candy. However, among the older lovers, dating was more varied. In addition to going to the movies or out for pizza, the older couples might go camping or fly to Hawaii for the weekend. Interestingly, sex was a vital part of these relationships too.

There was a difference. Few older lovers wanted the romance to end in marriage. As with Joan, the women were especially reluctant. They felt getting married was not necessary as they did not want children. They were afraid remarrying at their age would mean being saddled with the job of nurse. Many had cared for their husband for months during his final illness. They did not look forward to the thought of more time spent as caregiver to a sick spouse.

A national survey of older people offers clues as to why Joan did not even choose to cohabit or move in with Henry. In analyzing data from the Health and Retirement Survey, researchers found that living together in later life may be an alternate lifestyle chosen as much from need as from love. Elderly cohabiting couples, on average, had more limited incomes. Men in particular were in comparatively poor health (Lichter, Pienta, & McLaughlin, 1997). As a healthy, well-off woman in her "vintage years," Joan may see her relationship as offering the best of both worlds—privacy *plus* passionate romance at an unexpected time of life.

loss is still a top-ranking topic in cards announcing another year of living for reluctantly aging adults today.

How does sexuality really change as we grow old? Answering this question is more complicated than it might appear. Sexuality includes different components, from sexual desire to the frequency with which we have sex to the capacity to respond sexually, each of which may change in a different way as we age. Moreover, these complex feelings and activities are heavily dependent on the psychological and social side of life. Age-related physiological changes do affect sexuality. However, sexual feelings and behavior at any age depend on how we feel about ourselves, specifically, our self-concept as attractive, desirable human beings. As we saw in Aging in Action 10-1, these feelings are affected by having an available partner, a person who responds to us sexually. They are also affected by the environment in a more basic sense. Society's ideas about what is appropriate sexual behavior shape sexual feelings and behavior, not only in our older years, but at every stage of life.

The Social Framework

This is why the historic change called the **sexual revolution** must be our framework for discussing age changes in sexuality. Although according to historians, there was a mini-sexual revolution during the first third of the 20th century, during the 1950s the conditions under which "respectable" Americans were supposed to act sexual were once again restricted (Coonts, 1992). Sexual intercourse outside of marriage was prohibited. Campaigns were undertaken against various forms of "abnormal sex," including homosexuality. Although men were given more freedom, sexual expression in women was especially limited. According to the **sexual double standard,** women were not supposed to initiate sex; they were expected to be virgins until marriage; they were not supposed to feel sexual once they reached a "grandmotherly" stage of life.

Then came the decade of the 1960s. Sexuality outside of marriage became acceptable. A vigorous gay rights movement questioned the idea that sexual expression had to be confined to heterosexual love. People rebelled against the idea that sexuality should be more restricted for women or rigidly confined to a particular stage of life (T. W. Smith, 1994). The outcome of this quarter century of sexual liberation is an anti-Victorian society, a culture in which sexuality is graphically displayed in magazines and movies and talk show guests eagerly parade intimate details of their sexual lives.

Notice, however, that these images involve young adults. The media maintain a deafening silence when it comes to sexual expression in the older years. Among the legions of people passing through our living rooms to relate their sexual exploits on TV, we would be hard-pressed to find a single older adult. Steamy sexual encounters among couples in their 60s or 70s are equally conspicuously absent from our movies and magazines.

This absence seems to signal a split in our thinking about elderly sex. Although in theory we celebrate the idea that sexuality can occur at any time of life, we also clearly feel there is something inappropriate or even disgusting about older people having sex (Walz & Blum, 1987). This reluctance to think about later-life sexuality may even apply to the most enlightened observers of sexual life. In the early 1990s, researchers conducted a comprehensive poll probing sexual practices among thousands of American adults (Michael, Gagnon, Laumann, & Kolata, 1994). However, that survey

sexual revolution
Change in mores during the 1960s involving a much more permissive approach to sexuality

sexual double standard
Different norms of appropriate sexual behavior for men and women that traditionally allow much more sexual freedom to men

TABLE 10-1   *Changes in Male Sexuality with Age*

1. Erections take longer to develop.
2. Erections, once achieved, are more apt to be lost.
3. Orgasms are less explosive. Older men experience a seepage of fluid during ejaculation.
4. Penile deflation after orgasm is more rapid.
5. A longer interval is required to resume sexual activity after having had intercourse. By their 50s, after ejaculation, men typically cannot achieve an erection and reach orgasm for 12 to 24 hours.

extended only to age 59—almost as if after the magic birthday 60, nothing important could be said about sex!

This implied message that sex is off-limits after a certain age may operate as a self-fulfilling prophecy, producing the behavior it predicts. Having sexual desires, acting on those feelings, and being able to perform physically in a sexual situation are dependent on our attitudes about ourselves. If older people accept the idea that they are asexual, their interest, activity, and performance will be affected in a negative way. This is why, to have some benchmark for what is possible sexually as we grow old, it is best to turn to research directly exploring changes in the physiology of the sexual response.

Age Changes in Sexual Responsiveness

In the early 1960s, William Masters and Virginia Johnson took the unheard-of step of charting the actual sexual response. Healthy volunteers ranging in age from their 20s to their 50s agreed to have sexual intercourse in their laboratory and so give data for their landmark studies of the physiology of arousal and orgasm.

Masters and Johnson (1966) found several negative changes in their older male volunteers. Erections occurred less spontaneously and required more time and effort to develop. They were more fragile and likely to be lost before ejaculation occurred. There were changes in orgasmic intensity. The older men had less explosive ejaculations. If a man maintained an erection over a long period, ejaculation resulted in a seepage of seminal fluid rather than an expulsion. Penile detumescence (deflation) after orgasm was more rapid. Rather than occurring in two stages as it did among the young, it happened all at once. There was a lengthening of the refractory period, the time after reaching orgasm before another erection (or orgasm) can occur. Unlike the younger men, Masters and Johnson's subjects in their 50s could not develop an erection for 12 to 24 hours after a previous ejaculation.

These studies, summarized in Table 10-1, confirm that there are distinct physiological changes in male sexuality with age. However, they do not mean that middle-aged and elderly men are sexually incapable. Because erections can be maintained longer before the pressure to ejaculate becomes overwhelming, some experts suggest that from the woman's point of view, older men are *better* sexual partners than the young (Corby & Solnick, 1980). And, when Masters and Johnson looked at the opposite sex, a different pattern emerged.

10-2 *Menopause: Minimal Event or Major Change?*

When Barbara was growing up, menopause was something that people didn't talk about. She remembers thinking it would be horrible. At about age 50, Barbara noticed that her periods were growing scanty. She did have a few hot flashes but not often. She said she was too busy to pay attention to them. Although she jokes about having one foot in the grave, today, at age 56, Barbara says she really feels young.

Monica's symptoms started at about age 48. It was hard to pinpoint the time because during those years she was grappling with her husband's fatal illness. She recalls flooding up with infrequent periods and having headaches and feeling edgy, but she says those symptoms had accompanied her menstrual periods too. Being so concerned with her husband, she did not have much time to think about her body during those years. (These vignettes are adapted from J. M. Thompson, 1995.)

The Victorians believed that menopause was a wrenching event, "a change that unhinged the female nervous system and deprives a woman of her personal charm" (Sheehy, 1993, p. 44). We can see echoes of this view in the contemporary biomedical approach, which focuses on menopause as a set of unwelcome symptoms or a "deficiency disease." Most women do have unpleasant sensations. About 90% experience the infamous "hot flash," a sensation of heat in the face and chest. Many report feeling out of sorts or easily triggered to anger and tears. About 10% report symptoms that are very severe (J. M. Thompson, 1995). But for most women menopause is not such a dramatic emotional upheaval. As we saw in Chapter 8, rates of depression and anxiety do not skyrocket around age 50; in fact, in the Mills study, women were most likely to report feeling their lives were "first-rate" during these early menopausal years (V. Mitchell & Helson, 1990). According to feminist writers, the symptoms of menopause have been exaggerated because of ingrained ideas that equate the end of fertility with the end of a woman's productive life (Carolan, 1994). Although we might take issue with this position, notice in our interviews that menopause was simply overshadowed in importance by the events of living that Barbara and Monica were dealing with during their "change of life."

Among the older women, the researchers found minor changes in sexual responsiveness. Breast size did not increase during sexual arousal as it does in young adults. The sex flush, a pinkish rash that occurs during sexual excitement, was not as intense. Contraction of the rectal sphincter during orgasm, an indication of an intense sexual experience, rarely occurred.

All women undergo changes in the reproductive system after menopause that indirectly affect sexuality (Leiblum, 1990). **Menopause** occurs when the body's production of the hormone estrogen, which regulates the menstrual cycle, falls off dramatically. Although its most crucial effect is to end a woman's ability to have children, this estrogen depletion also produces the symptoms described in Aging in Action 10-2, as well as certain changes in the vagina and its surrounding tissues.

menopause
Time in life when estrogen production decreases dramatically and a woman is no longer able to conceive a child

During a woman's childbearing years, the walls of the vagina have thick folds that expand easily to admit a penis or accommodate to childbirth. After menopause, the vaginal walls thin out and become smooth and more fragile. The vagina shortens, and its opening narrows. The size of the clitoris and labia decreases. There is also a decrease in sexual lubrication. It takes longer after arousal for lubrication to begin and not as much fluid is produced. These changes make intercourse more uncomfortable and so may limit sexual enjoyment or force some women to stop having sex.

However, estrogen loss has few effects on sexual desire. The male hormone, testosterone, present in the female body too, regulates the sex drive in both men and women (Campbell & Udry, 1994). Masters and Johnson found the clitoral response to sexual stimulation was identical among their older and younger women. This is important because the clitoris is thought to be the seat of sexual arousal. Also, the older women were just as capable of reaching orgasm as the younger group, though, on average, they did have fewer orgasmic contractions and less prolonged orgasms than the young volunteers. In general, Masters and Johnson concluded with an important statement: "There is no time limit drawn by advancing years to female sexuality" (1966, p. 247).

Even though Masters and Johnson's studies also don't extend past 60, they give us a framework for looking at the topic we turn to now, the few surveys specifically exploring sexual practices in later life.

Age Changes in Sexual Interest and Activity

The only national survey of sexuality after age 50 was sponsored, surprisingly enough, by *Consumer Reports*. In the late 1970s, every *Consumer Reports* subscriber over age 50 was sent a questionnaire covering sexual practices, feelings, and capacities. Because people were encouraged to write about their personal experiences, the book describing this survey is the opposite of a dry statistical report. It is a compelling account of the sexual potential that exists in later life (Brecher & Consumer Reports Book Editors, 1985).

This survey exploded the idea that older people are asexual. A passionate sex life was flourishing even among men and women in their 80s and 90s, golden anniversary couples, and people with serious diseases. The results of this study are echoed in another recent poll of older adults (Wiley & Bortz, 1996). As Table 10-2 shows, most men and women in their 60s reported having sex at least once a week. Even over age 70, one-third did, and the majority desired more frequent sexual relations than that.

Although these studies are interesting, be aware that they do not reflect the experiences and feelings of the "average" older woman or man. Not only are *Consumer Reports* subscribers upper-middle-class and liberal, those who spent hours filling out the questionnaires are probably an especially sexually interested group. The older adults whose responses are shown in the table are even more atypical: people who *chose* to attend a series of lectures on sexuality and age. To supplement these findings, we need research with more representative groups. Ideally, these studies should be longitudinal, so that we can really trace how sexual feelings and behavior change over time. Luckily, we do have these studies: two longitudinal investigations of aging carried

TABLE 10-2

Current Sexual Activity and Desired Sexual Activity as Reported by a Group of Men and Women over Age 60

	Current		Desired	
	Age 60–70	Age 70+	Age 60–70	Age 70+
MALES				
< 1/wk	47	67	3	9
1/wk	41	22	32	44
2+/wk	12	11	66	48
FEMALES				
<1/wk	48	67	12	9
1/wk	32	11	31	36
2+/wk	19	22	57	55

In this poll the majority of men and about half the women were having sex at least once a week. Most wished they could have sex more often.
SOURCE: Wiley & Bortz, 1996.

out at Duke University during the 1960s and 1970s, and the Baltimore Longitudinal Study of Aging.

As part of a psychiatric interview, the Duke volunteers, who ranged in age from their late 40s to their 90s, were asked to estimate how often they had intercourse or, if they had stopped having sexual relations, to say when and explain why. They were told to rate the intensity of their interest in sex and compare it with the strength of their feelings in the past (Verwoerdt, Pfeiffer, & Wang, 1969). Since 1967, the Baltimore men have also been questioned about their sexual feelings and activities when they return over the years. Combining these studies allows us to make the following generalizations about sexuality and age.

1. **People do grow gradually less sexually active as they age, with most men giving up sexual intercourse as they become old-old.** The Duke study pinpoints the decade of the 70s as a sexual watershed for men. About three-fourths of the Duke men in their late 60s reported having intercourse, and an even higher fraction said they still had sexual feelings. During their 70s, most reported giving up intercourse. The number who reported a high or moderate sex drive also declined dramatically over these 10 years. By their 80s, about four-fifths of the men no longer had intercourse. However, even at this age, half reported they still had sexual feelings to some extent.

2. **People vary greatly in the extent of sexual loss and in its emotional importance.** Because their study was longitudinal, the Duke researchers could measure deviations from the general pattern. Do all men become less sexual over time? When they looked at individual subjects over a 3-year period, they discovered that sexual decline is not inevitable. In fact, 20% of the elderly men reported *more* interest in sex and more frequent activity, at least over this short period.

Is the loss men normally experience a terrible blow? According to the Baltimore study, the answer is no. When the researchers asked the older male volunteers if they would prefer having their youthful sexuality restored, only 33% said yes. Few were disturbed enough by their loss to seek medical attention for their difficulties (Martin, 1981). So, although some people are troubled by declining sexuality, as suggested by the responses in Table 10-2, age-related sexual loss may be far from an emotional tragedy to everyone.

3. **At every age, women report less sexual interest and activity than men.**   In the Duke study, the difference was especially great in the 60s, when the majority of men were still reporting an active sex life. As mentioned earlier, 3 out of 4 men aged 65 to 70 reported sexual feelings; however, only 1 in 5 women this age did. Why, in spite of their more stable biological potential, do women experience a dramatic decline in sexuality in middle and later life? For answers, we turn to the predictors of staying sexually active in our older years.

Factors Affecting Sexuality in Middle and Later Life

Because people do differ so much in this central life area, the Duke researchers decided to explore how a variety of factors might relate to sexual age changes. For both men and women, one force stood out: People who reported being highly sexually active in the present said they had been very sexually active in their youth. So, provided we can accept the accuracy of these memories, one key to predicting our sexual future lies in looking at our sexual present and past. People who are extremely interested in sex in youth are likely to remain interested in later life.

For women, however, an external influence looms large: Will there be a partner? The Duke researchers found that the only factor predicting continued sexual activity for women, other than age and past sexual enjoyment, was marital status. More than 40% of the married Duke women over age 65 were sexually active; only 4% of the large group of single and widowed women were. In contrast, 82% of the elderly Duke men without a wife said they were still having intercourse, a fraction that was even higher than for the married volunteers!

So, that important outer-world barrier, not having a partner, seems to explain why female sexual interest dips so deeply with age. As we learned in Chapter 1, at older ages, widowhood and, increasingly, divorce take their toll. As a result, many women are single in their later years. Women are prevented from finding a new partner not only because the field of men their own age shrinks, but because men prefer younger women. As this New York cab driver explains to his female passenger (reported in Michael et al., 1994, p. 84), the sexual odds men face are much different in their later years:

> I asked him if he ever went out with women his own age. . . . The driver . . . replied, "Never. You think that's unfair, right? Well, it's unfair, I don't want to go out with women in their 60s. I'll tell you why—their bodies are just as flabby as mine. And, see, I don't have to settle for that. I've got a good pension . . . on top of what I make driving a cab. Gives me something to offer a younger woman. . . . A woman my age is in a tougher spot. See, she looks just as old as I look but most of the time she's got no money and no job.

Aging women do compensate for not having a partner by increasing the frequency of masturbation (Brecher et al., 1985; Walz & Blum, 1987). Another adaptation many may make is to lose interest in sex. So, as with any behavior that is not reinforced, sexual desire may fade rapidly as women age.

Whereas for older women the limiting factor is external, for older men the barrier to late-life sexuality tends to be internal: health. In the Duke study, for men but not women, both self-reports and objective measures of health were correlated with continued sexual activity. This finding explains the puzzle of why the 70s were such an important decade sexually for the Duke men. During these years, when people become old-old, rates of chronic illness accelerate. When we look at the reasons for male sexual difficulties, we can see why illness has an important effect on aging men.

ILLNESS AND SEXUAL FUNCTION   It is normal for a man to slow down sexually as he ages but still be able to have intercourse. However, **erectile dysfunction,** the chronic inability to have an erection full enough for intercourse, does become a more common problem as men age. Although psychological factors may be important, physical reasons are often responsible. The normal age-related slowing down discussed earlier is compounded by medical problems that inhibit the delicate erection mechanism.

erectile dysfunction Chronic inability to have an erection full enough for intercourse

An erection occurs when the web of blood vessels and blood-containing chambers in the penis becomes engorged. The blood flow into and out of the penis is regulated by hormones, nerves, and valves. A variety of age-related conditions may impair this process and so contribute to impotence: disorders affecting the blood vessels, such as arteriosclerosis, high blood pressure, or diabetes; operations done in the pelvic area, such as bladder, prostate, or rectal surgery; injuries to the pelvic region and spine; and diseases such as kidney ailments or multiple sclerosis.

Being ill may affect a man's sexual performance in a more indirect way: Medications given for chronic illness may have sexual side effects. Drugs taken for common late-life problems such as high blood pressure, heart conditions, or depression often either affect a man's capacity to have an erection or inhibit desire.

Feeling sick can have an indirect impact on sexuality, making any older person too tired or depressed to be interested in sex. There may be an element of fear, the idea sexual excitement is too taxing and can lead to sudden death. This anxiety is especially common when people have that top-ranking chronic illness, heart disease.

When researchers questioned a group of people 11 months after having a heart attack, most reported cutting down the frequency of intercourse dramatically (Bloch, Maeder, & Haissly, 1975). The major cause was emotional, not physical. The person was either depressed, frightened of a relapse, or terrified of having another heart attack during sex.

The fear that intercourse can cause a heart attack prevents both people with heart conditions and their partners from fully enjoying sex (Corby & Solnick, 1980). However, though examples of this experience have captured our imagination, actual cases of people having heart attacks during intercourse are rare (Butler & Lewis, 1973). A general rule is that if a person with heart disease can comfortably climb a few flights of stairs or take a brisk walk around the block, he or she can safely resume having normal sex (Corby & Solnick, 1980).

Interventions

As mentioned earlier, not all older people care about sexual loss or have any interest in having a more active sex life. To decide that every older person should be interested in sex is just as limiting as it is to assume that the elderly are asexual. However, because the barriers against being sexual in later life are still powerful, strategies to promote sexual fulfillment among the elderly have special appeal. Our earlier discussion suggests that a first step is to make visible the fact that older people *are* sexually active—that sexuality does not end at 60 or 95. It will be interesting to see if the media will risk taking this step in a few decades as the huge cohort of baby-boom consumers moves fully into their later years.

However, for older women, the social barriers to expressing sexuality will be hard to erase. The truth is that it is hard to find a partner at age 70 or 80 unless a woman searches for a younger man. The reality is that throughout human history, men have placed emphasis on *youthful* beauty in selecting a sexual mate (Kenrick, Groth, Trost, & Sadalla, 1993). This is why, although their problems tend to be more biological, we can point to more definite advances in enhancing sexuality in older men.

Tremendous progress has been made in treating impotence even when it has a medical cause. Erection-improving medications are available. If the problem has to do with the blood vessels regulating blood flow into the penis, surgery may keep the penis engorged. Even when the person's condition cannot be cured, solutions are possible. Prosthetic devices can be surgically inserted that artificially produce an erection. These devices, called penile implants, enable people still to engage in intercourse. These treatments vary in effectiveness, and they may produce complications. Still, depending on the problem, they can be a great help (Renshaw, 1996).

To offset normal age-related losses in desire and performance (and losses in muscle mass), one controversial strategy is to provide testosterone to older men. Another approach is to use behavioral techniques.

In one study, middle-aged men were given training in fantasizing to erotic stimuli. Half of the subjects got feedback about their erectile responses during the training sessions through a device attached to the penis; the other half did not get this feedback. At the end of the study, both groups of men showed gains in the speed with which they had erections. They reported increasing the time they spent having erotic daydreams and their frequency of intercourse. The changes were most dramatic for the men in the direct feedback group (Solnick, 1978). These results show that even with male sexuality, much decline that normally occurs may not be inevitable or primary to advancing age. (For a summary of suggestions for enhancing sexuality in older men and women, see Table 10-3.)

PARENTS AND CHILDREN AS ADULTS

Notice that much of the research involving elderly couples (and even sexuality) is very upbeat. We get the same message when we look at that other pioneering relationship, elderly parent and middle-aged child. The idea that today's adult children are alienated from their elderly parents is untrue. The bond between the generations is sturdy. Closeness, caring, and a surprising amount of contact are typical.

FOR MEN

1. Understand that some physiological slowing down is normal, and do not be alarmed by occasional problems performing. Sexual relations need to occur more slowly; manual stimulation may be necessary to fully achieve erection and orgasm.
2. Stay healthy and, if possible, avoid sexually impairing medications. Do not be put off by myths about the dangerous consequences of having sex if you suffer from a chronic condition such as heart disease.
3. If troubled by chronic erectile dysfunction, explore the medical and mechanical treatments for this problem.

FOR WOMEN

1. Consider estrogen supplements as an antidote to the loss of lubrication that occurs at menopause.
2. If possible, find a partner.

FOR BOTH GENDERS

Keep physically attractive and feeling desirable. Do not be deterred by negative sexual stereotypes. Remember that many people do have highly fulfilling sexual relationships in their older years.

The first blow to what gerontologists call the **myth of family uninvolvement** was struck by Ethel Shanas in a set of cross-sectional studies conducted decades ago. In 1957, 1963, and 1975, Shanas (1979a, 1979b) examined how many times per week national samples of adult children and their elderly parents visited or called one another. Although we would expect the amount of contact to have declined over this period of shifting family roles, there was little change. Children still lived close to their parents, the vast majority within a 30-minute drive. More than one-third had seen one another either that day or the day before. About 4 in 5 had visited within the past week. Instead of being a nation of isolated nuclear families, the adult child/elderly parent bond was very much intact.

More recent surveys echo this theme. Although family mobility is more common than ever, a surprising amount of face-to-face parent/child contact takes place in the United States. In 1984, 1 out of 3 adults saw an aged parent daily or every other day. Almost two-thirds reported seeing that person once or twice within the past week (Crimmins & Ingegneri, 1990). In another poll, more than one-half of children said they saw an elderly parent at least once a week (Bumpass & Aquilino, 1995). Most said their relationship with this older person was very close (L. Lawton, Silverstein, & Bengtson, 1994). As we enter the new century, then, **intergenerational solidarity** remains an enduring norm (Bengtson, 1993; Bengtson, Rosenthal, & Burton, 1996)

However, one change in the externals of involvement has occurred: Elderly people used to live with their families; now they live alone. Shanas's studies captured the years during which this decline in **coresidence** took place. In 1957, one-third of the elderly parents and their children shared households. By 1975, the figure was 18%.

myth of family uninvolvement
Erroneous idea that children are uncaring and uninvolved with elderly parents today

intergenerational solidarity
Strong, ongoing commitment between different adult generations in a family

coresidence
Living as an extended family in a shared household as adults

The Older Family   ❧   309

This change may partly explain why the myth of family uninvolvement has been so hard to dispel. Older people remember that during *their* childhood, Grandma lived in the house, and they leap to the conclusion that children are less caring today. This interpretation is wrong. It is the older generation that wants it that way. Older people today vigorously reject the idea of moving in with their children (Hamon & Blieszner, 1990). What they want is an arrangement that Shanas calls intimacy at a distance—not living together, but close by.

Our "Walton family" vision of the past is unrealistic. There never was a wonderful time when extended families lived together for decades peacefully. In past centuries, intergenerational households were always fairly rare, simply because the grandparent generation never lived that long. When families did share a residence, their arrangement was caused as much by economic necessity as love. When parents developed disabilities and could not work, they were generally too poor to maintain their own home. As we will see in the next chapter, during the late 1960s and early 1970s Social Security and retirement benefits greatly expanded. The dramatic decline Shanas found in coresidence over those years was mainly due to the fact that older people finally were financially *able* to live on their own.

The push to live separately does not apply equally to every ethnic group. Even controlling for socioeconomic status, elderly African Americans are more likely to live intergenerationally than whites (Choi, 1991; Soldo, Wolf, & Agree, 1990; Taylor & Chatters, 1991). Immigrant status is also related to coresidence. In one study, older unmarried Asian American woman who had migrated to the United States were much more likely to live intergenerationally than their native-born counterparts. As researchers who study these first-generation Americans point out, linguistic and economic barriers force many elderly immigrants to be more dependent on their children than they want. Living apart from family may be an alien idea for some new Americans too.

In analyzing data from six Latin American countries, Susan deVos (1990) found that extended family households were the common pattern. Coresidence did vary from country to country, being most common in the Dominican Republic and least common in Mexico. However, these differences occurred mainly among married older people. In all these countries, it was accepted for a widowed parent to share a residence with an adult child. In contrast, in the United States in 1984, almost 3 out of 4 widowed people with children lived alone.

In summary, the decision to share households seems propelled by cultural norms and especially by financial need. When they are able to live independently, most adults want to live on their own. However, the United States is now at the beginning of another shift in coresidence: The rising number of *young* adults in need means more pressure to share households that is coming this time from the younger generation's side. Between 1965 and 1988, the proportion of middle-aged adults sharing households with their young adult children rose by 6% (Easterlin, Macunovich, & Crimmins, 1993). Moreover, researchers have found that influences associated with need in the younger generation, such as being single or divorced or having limited income, are the primary correlates of sharing a roof (T. A. Dunn & Philips, 1997; Ward, Logan, & Spitze, 1992).

What are the consequences for family harmony? Some signs are troubling. In a national poll of African American families, Robert Taylor and Linda Chatters (1991) found that older people who lived with their children were less satisfied with their family. When University of Chicago researchers interviewed three-generational Chicago families—a young adult grandchild, a middle-aged father and mother, and one aged grandparent—they too found that the families in which the generations shared a household were worse off. In this study, particularly young married daughters living with middle-aged mothers tended to be more unhappy and immature (Cohler & Grunebaum, 1981; Hagestad, 1985).

This research does not prove that living together causes problems. As we know, families who live intergenerationally often choose this arrangement because they are already having difficulties with life. Still, rather than symbolizing more closeness, it makes sense that relationships are at risk of deteriorating when parents and adult children share a roof.

In fact, one message of the Chicago study is that a certain amount of distance is good for parents and children when they live together as adults. To explore what the generations talked about, the researchers showed a set of cards to each person and asked "Do you and _____ talk about this?" If the answer was yes, they then asked whether the person had given or gotten advice about the topic from the other family member. The researchers wanted to discover what issues are "hot" topics for families, and what happens when advising occurs.

The type of advice given varied by gender. Men gave advice about finances, work, or politics; women advised more about children, family relationships, and the social side of life. It was in these very advising areas that conflicts were most prone to erupt. Among men, arguments would flair up about job-related issues. Among women, relationships were a touchy area. It was here that advising had the potential to flow fast and furious among mothers, daughters, and grandmothers, and it was here that disagreements were most intense.

To keep family harmony, parents and children reported that they had to develop conversational demilitarized zones, not revealing too much about their anxieties in these central areas of life. Keeping close meant keeping some separation, knowing when to be silent, and allowing the other generation to make its own mistakes.

There was another interesting pattern. Although advising flowed in all directions, the older generation did most of the advice-giving. Whether a child was 20 or 55, in relation to a parent, he got more advice than he gave. The exception was when a parent was widowed or in bad health. Then, the sides became more equal or even reversed, with the role of main adviser shifting to the child.

This pattern is also revealed in research tracing the flow of **instrumental** (concrete) **services,** such as household or financial help. Although most common when the parent generation is relatively affluent and the grandchildren are very young, parents give to children until they become old and in need. Only then does the giving equalize or flow in the opposite way (Zarit & Eggebeen, 1995).

instrumental services Concrete help, such as financial or caregiving aid

So, the feeling many adult children have about their parents—"They still treat me like a child"—seems to have a grain of truth. Unless they become impaired, parents hold to their role of "nurturer and giver" no matter how old their children are.

The reason that parents stay "parents" makes sense if we think back to what we know about personality during adult life. Remember from Dan McAdams's research in Chapter 8 that generative goals are especially important in the aging phase of life. Parents' priorities center around giving to children. Their main identity as adults is often wrapped up in the nurturer role. Furthermore, because our ongoing sense of

This elderly mother and middle-aged daughter are both thoroughly enjoying their afternoon together but notice the expression of perfect peace on the older woman's face. Do you think that each generation feels exactly the same on this visit? Or does having the chance to see her child have a special meaning in this mother's life?

who we are endures, it stands to reason that we don't give up this central identity in our older years. We hold fast to our role as parent when our child is 50 in the same way as when that child was 5. But this may present a problem that goes beyond the issue of developing a relationship as equals when our child is an adult: Children's mission is to develop their own identity apart from parents. Parents' identity, or primary life attachment, continues to revolve around their child.

A compelling set of studies by Karen Fingerman (1995, 1996, 1997) reveals this imbalanced attachment and the problems it can cause in intergenerational life. In exploring the relationships of 48 elderly mothers and their middle-aged daughters, Fingerman found that 90% of both mothers and daughters rated one another as among their six most important attachments in life. However, whereas 3 out of 4 older women said their daughter was among their top three critical attachments, only half of the younger women said the same about their mother. Half of the mothers rated their child as the person they were most likely to confide in, but for daughters the figure was less than 1 in 6. In other words, elderly mothers may be more involved with their adult daughters than their daughters are with them.

Perhaps because of this "bonding imbalance" in the mother/daughter relationship, Fingerman finds that feelings of disharmony are more intense on the daughter side. Mothers more often minimized problems with their daughters. If they criticized their child, it was in the context of giving praise. Daughters freely mentioned problems in the relationship, openly describing differences of opinion and the mother's faults. This tendency to feel different degrees of negativity was especially striking in another study, in which Fingerman (1995) asked the mother/daughter pairs to think about a specific problem they were having at the time. Mothers were apt to downplay or minimize the conflict. As a result, they misread their daughters' feelings, believing that their child felt better about the issue and the relationship than she really did.

The bottom line of this fascinating glimpse into adult/adult family relationships is that we should not assume that intergenerational solidarity is problem-free. Adult children love and are committed to their elderly parents, but that does not mean that they feel "just close." One interesting implication of Fingerman's research is that the pull to separate or build an identity apart from our parents may not end at adolescence. It may remain locked into our enduring identity as adults. Moreover, simply charting the number of hours parents and children physically spend with one another is probably not the best way to measure closeness—that is, the emotional quality of older family life.

Quantity versus Quality

Actually, older people who see their children very frequently do *not* report feeling closer to their families (Mancini, 1984). There may even be an inverse relationship between the frequency of interaction and feelings of intimacy (Talbott, 1990; Walker & Thompson, 1983). One reason, as we have seen, may be that families come together not just out of a positive emotion, the desire to be close, but out of a negative one, need. A typical example occurs when a child is going through a divorce. In response to this crisis, parent/adult child contact tends to rise dramatically (Aldous, 1995). Grandparents step in, baby-sitting and offering financial and emotional support.

From the older person's end, the situation that causes children to flock around tends to be poor health. Demographers have identified two types of migration among the elderly: the move away from children immediately after retiring—for instance, to a Sunbelt state by middle-class young-old couples in health; and a smaller, reverse migration decades later to be near children when, typically in the 80s, disability strikes (Litwak & Longino, 1987). So, more contact does not automatically signify a family "good." It can just as easily be a sign of a family in trouble.

Joseph Kuypers and Vern Bengtson (1983) believe that family relationships follow a norm of waning involvement. As children grow up, they are supposed to need less ongoing assistance from the older generation. Parents and children should be able to handle life on their own in their adult years. Kuypers and Bengston suggest that relationships are most likely to deteriorate when this unspoken rule is breached and either the parent or child generation needs an excessive amount of help: when a daughter is a single parent, or an elderly parent becomes disabled and needs a child to devote hours to caregiving.

With the younger generation, the norm of waning involvement applies mainly to providing instrumental help. As we saw in Fingerman's research, discussing problems, exchanging confidences, and offering one another psychological support enhances parents' self-esteem (Spitze, Logan, Joseph, & Lee, 1994). In one national survey, parents who engaged in these activities were likely to report the best relationships with their young adult children, whereas providing high levels of financial aid or help with

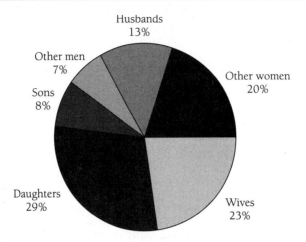

Women provide most of the care for the disabled elderly. Daughters provide most of this care.
SOURCE: U.S. Senate Special Committee on Aging, 1991a.

household jobs was associated with more conflict and distress (Kulis, 1992). This distress can be equally great when the cry for help emanates from the older generation.

Caring for an Ill Parent

The fact that nursing homes are such obvious features on our landscape masks a hidden reality. At least twice as many severely disabled older people live in the community as live in nursing homes. As we learned in Chapters 5 and 7, it is families who are caring for these frail older people, sometimes at great personal cost. The nursing home choice is something families work strenuously to avoid. It is often a last-resort decision, when children become unable to manage the aging parent's care.

Caregiving at the end of the life span, as during life's beginning years, is gender-linked (see Figure 10-2). When the disabled older person is a man, sons do take more responsibility (Lee, Dwyer, & Coward, 1993). Almost always, however, the job of caring for an ill parent falls on a daughter or daughter-in law (Lang & Brody, 1983; Brody, 1985). These **women in the middle** face competing responsibilities. If, as is typical, they are late-middle-aged when the need arises (Soldo, 1996), they may be dealing with illness in their husband or, as we saw earlier, pressures to provide care to a grandchild. More rarely, if they are in their 30s or 40s, they may be active parents themselves.

Today, with most women in the workforce, they often have full-time jobs. Moreover, it has been argued, the job of caring for a frail parent today has become a

women in the middle *Women simultaneously caring for young children—or, more often, adult children and grandchildren—and ill elderly parents*

"normative event" (Brody, 1985). The increase in people living to advanced old age, combined with the tendency for parents to have fewer children, has made this job one that this cohort of middle-aged daughters can expect to assume, sometimes for years.

The term *caregiving* covers a range of activities, from just a bit of occasional help to 24-hour care. Moreover, caring for an older parent is not every contemporary woman's fate (Spitze & Logan, 1990). In fact, in a Canadian survey, even among the age group at highest risk (women in their late 50s), only 7% of the women polled were currently providing hands-on care (Rosenthal, Martin-Matthews, & Matthews, 1996). Even so, the chance of *ever* being in this position is higher today than in the past. In polling women of different ages, Phylis Moen, Julie Robinson, and Vivian Fields (1994) found that almost two-thirds of their subjects aged 55 to 65 reported having been caregivers, compared with less than half of their parents' generation (the cohort born 1905–1917). Despite the growth of services such as home and day care, paid help tends to be used sparingly. Family members, typically daughters, are the main line of defense against a nursing home.

Philadelphia Geriatric Center researcher Elaine Brody (1985) argues that women today ignore the fact that care used to be less intense and feel deficient. No matter how much they are doing for an ill mother or father, they have the nagging sense they should be doing more. They feel even worse when, unlike their own parents, they have to put a disabled parent in a nursing home. Their feelings are based on a false comparison: The burden of caregiving weighs heavier today.

Brody, who has devoted her career to studying these women in the middle, has examined the especially heavy burden on caregivers who work. In comparing employed and nonemployed caregivers, she found that working daughters provided just as much help with shopping, household tasks, and emotional support as the nonworking group, though they did hire home help more often for personal care (Brody & Schoonover, 1986).

This involvement takes a financial toll. In 1982, of the more than 1 million U.S. family caregivers with jobs, 21% reported reducing their hours at work. A similar percentage said they had taken time off without pay. About 9% of a total sample of 2.2 million caregivers reported quitting their jobs to provide care (U.S. Senate Special Committee on Aging, 1991a; see also Pavalko & Artis, 1997).

Study after study has documented the emotional toll of parent care. As we saw in our in-depth look at families coping with a dementing illness, children caring for disabled parents have high rates of depression and anxiety and low levels of morale (George & Gwyther, 1986; Spitze et al., 1994; Zarit & Eggebeen, 1995). Moreover, rather than producing more closeness, just as Kuypers and Bengtson predict, illness in a parent is related to poorer family relationships, increasing the potential for conflict between parent and child (Walker, Martin, & Jones, 1992). A study of spouse caregivers, discussed in the next chapter, highlights the different emotional context of parent care. Whereas Colleen Johnson and Joseph Catalano (1983) found that enmeshing— that is, retreating into the relationship—was a common response if the caregiver was a spouse; if the caregiver was a child, the main reaction was distancing. The older person's demands caused conflict, the relationship deteriorated, competing demands from family added to the friction, and a child would disengage. She would either separate herself from a parent emotionally by going into therapy or decide "I've done all I can" and turn to paid help.

If the parent has emotional problems or Alzheimer's disease, children are especially likely to put distance between themselves and the older person, denying that "my mother is anything like myself" (Albert, Litvin, Kleban, & Brody, 1991). This rejection may be getting through. Dorothy Field and her colleagues traced how the Berkeley/Oakland parent generation felt about their family during their old-old years. Although the researchers found much constancy, one influence associated with a change in feelings was health. Contrary to predictions, older people often reported feeling *more alienated* from their families when they became ill (Field, Minkler, Falk, & Leino, 1993). (As Aging in Action 10-3 reveals, the impact of a child's problems on elderly parents can be even more devastating.)

FACTORS INFLUENCING THE STRESS   The avalanche of testimony that caregiving is stressful involves self-reports of problems, not actual rates of psychiatric disturbance and impaired health (Schulz, Visintainer, & Williamson, 1990). Many studies show that caring for a parent produces mixed emotions. It often provides a sense of meaning in life even while producing strain (B. Miller & Lawton, 1997). Caring for a parent does not weigh equally heavy on everyone. For some people, it is an impossible burden; for others, it is a labor of love.

Once again, the burden people feel is a function of multiple factors, including the intensity of care a parent needs (B. Miller, McFall, & Montgomery, 1991; Mui, 1995) and the number of additional roles, such as mother, wife, or grandparent, a woman must handle at the same time (Franks & Stephens, 1992). Enduring feelings for the older person also play an important role. Warm, loving memories make children more willing to say they will care for ill parents (Whitbeck, Hoyt, & Huck, 1994). The help they do provide feels less burdensome when it is cushioned by this legacy of love (Walker, Martin, & Jones, 1992).

Ethnicity and gender are also relevant factors. Perhaps partly because of their strong tradition of multigenerational caregiving, African Americans report lower levels of caregiving stress (Fredman, Daly, & Lazur, 1995; Hinrichsen & Ramirez, 1992; Kim, Picot, Wykle, & Lee, 1997). Perhaps because they do most of the care themselves, and because of their greater susceptibility to depression, women feel particularly burdened in the caregiving role (Belsky, 1994; Mui, 1995).

The flowchart in Figure 10-3, developed by Leonard Pearlin and his colleagues, highlights the different influences that may interact to produce depression, health problems, and giving up (Pearlin, Mullan, Semple, & Skaff, 1990). Pearlin devised this chart for Alzheimer's disease and used it as a framework to predict and measure family stress in the caregiving-careers study discussed in Chapter 7. However, we can use this same model to apply to any type of parent care.

Pearlin divides stresses into two categories. Primary stressors are directly related to the illness: Is Mrs. Jones's mother incontinent or physically abusive? Does she need 24-hour care? Secondary stressors are the other pressures in the person's life: Does Mrs. Jones have young children? Is she in the middle of a divorce? Background variables such as socioeconomic status, caregiving history, and family network affect the intensity of these secondary stressors, as well as contributing to the sense of overall burden. The person's vulnerability to depression is determined by her personality and coping skills, and the degree of support from family and friends. Is Mrs. Jones someone

10-3 Adult Children as a Source of Stress

When he was growing up, James seemed to be an ideal boy. He was an excellent student, attractive, a good athlete. He was a "loner," but Martha thought that would pass. It made sense that her only child would prefer to stay close to home. James's father had been abusive. He walked out when James was 6.

After college, James began to resemble his father more and more. He was unable to keep a job. He belittled women, went from one failed relationship to the next, and attempted suicide three times. On one occasion, if Martha had not arrived, James would have died. Martha has been trying to show James he is loved no matter what he does. She helps pay the bills. James stays over at the house. She is there to offer support. However, she is becoming afraid of her 33-year-old son. James has a fascination with guns and the martial arts. He gets into rages. Martha sometimes feels like running away, but she knows she could never abandon her "baby." She blames herself for not realizing there was a problem and getting help for James while he was growing up. Mostly, she worries about the future. It's been 15 years of crises. Martha is taking antidepressant drugs. Her son is destroying her life.

Although the text focuses on how parents' problems affect adult children, there is an opposite side. James presents an extreme case, but anxiety about adult children with problems can be an important stress in parents' lives. A telephone survey underlines how crucial this anxiety can be.

Carl Pillemer and Jill Suitor (1991) asked about four signs of trouble. Did a son or daughter have emotional problems, serious health concerns, or problems with alcohol? Had a child been under much stress within the past year? As the researchers expected, those who answered yes to these questions (1 in 4 people) were likely to be more depressed.

However, we cannot equate the anxiety for children with the "burden" that comes from ministering to a parent in need. In contrast to the parent-care research, Pillemer and Suitor found that subjects' distress was unrelated to the amount of caregiving or concrete help provided to the child. In other words, the heartache of a parent for a child is more internal, less tied to *what* is being done. Adults with children who are "failing" feel *they* have failed. Their problem is not ambivalence about an unwanted investment of time but guilt about the past and worry about the future. Where did I go wrong? What will happen to my child?

who reaches out to others, a person with a secure attachment style (Crispi, Schiaffino, & Berman, 1997)? Does her family appreciate what she is doing, or are they critical and full of well-meaning "advice" (Malone-Beach & Zarit, 1995)? Does she personally know others in a similar situation (Pillemer & Suitor, 1996)? Are her brothers and sisters doing their fair share? When a caregiving child feels isolated and alone—no one in her social circle has this burden, siblings have left her to handle the burden alone—she feels especially overburdened, overwhelmed, and distressed (Strawbridge & Wallhagen, 1991).

FIGURE 10-3 *A Conceptual Model of an Alzheimer's Caregiver's Stress*

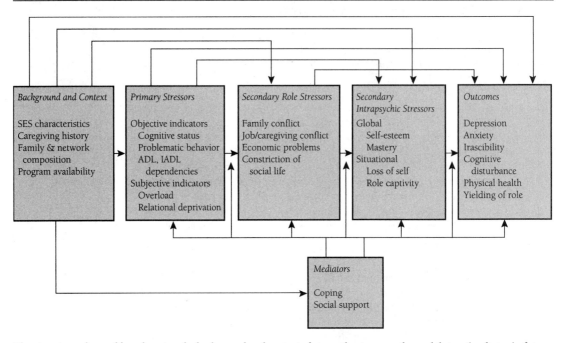

The stress is made up of four domains: the background and context of stress, the stressors, the modulators (mediators) of stress, and the outcomes or manifestations of stress.
SOURCE: Pearlin, Mullan, Semple, & Skaff, 1990.

Interventions

Pearlin's framework illustrates that with caregiving, once again, we need to adopt a contextual approach. The impact of this stress varies dramatically, depending on the total situation within which caregiving occurs. Still, in general, caregiving is a stressful experience. The burden could be lessened if society stepped in to help.

Family and Medical Leave Act
Law requiring companies with more than 50 employees to grant 12 weeks' unpaid leave for care of a newborn or an ill family member

In 1992, society took one helpful step when Congress passed the **Family and Medical Leave Act** stipulating that people who take time off from their jobs to care for an older relative can no longer be arbitrarily fired. However, this law allows only 12 weeks of unpaid leave. It would be more helpful to have formal caregiving supports available on an ongoing basis, because a disabled parent often must have help for months or even years (U.S. Senate Special Committee on Aging, 1991a).

A large-scale outcome study testifies to the impact that one formal support, the day program, can have on caregivers' emotional state. Family caregivers who enrolled an older relative with dementia in a state-subsidized day care program in New Jersey were compared with a control group living in Ohio, which does not offer government-subsidized day care. Three months and one year after participating in the program, depression and feelings of burden were dramatically lower among the day care group. Over the same period, the control-group nonparticipants changed in the opposite direction, becoming more overburdened, depressed, and distressed (Zarit, 1996).

Even when people must pay totally on their own, day care is often surprisingly affordable. It is fairly widely available too. Unfortunately, as we saw in earlier chapters, these services often languish underused. Families may not be aware of the program's benefit or even its existence. They may feel that convincing their relative to come to the program might be too difficult. Or they may interpret the obligation to care for aging parents as "I have to do everything myself." As Susan Selig, Tom Tomlinson, and Tom Hickey (1991) point out, the impulse to care for elderly parents depends on crucial ethical principles: the commandment to "honor thy father and thy mother"—a debt from care given one as a child. Sometimes this moral obligation is interpreted as absolute, so that *every* activity becomes a causality to caregiving.

Even elderly parents don't agree with the idea that children should have absolute responsibility for their care. In one survey, parents, more than children, checked "no" when asked if a daughter should adjust her work schedule to help them (Hamon & Bliezner, 1990). As Elaine Brody suggests, we need to educate this cohort of middle-aged daughters that their situation is different. At no other time in history were people asked to provide care to the older generation for years. We also need to explore ways to offer help that is not too expensive, to the growing numbers of women in the middle.

GRANDPARENTHOOD

As is true of relationships between adjoining generations, there has been an explosion of interest in grandparenthood in recent years. In part, this is because grandparents are becoming much more vital in keeping the more fragile younger family afloat (see "Grandparenting," 1996). In part, this is because researchers have gone beyond quantity, or the frequency of visiting or the number of contacts per day or week, in studying family life.

The actual amount of contact does matter somewhat, but even people who report seeing their grandchildren infrequently still often say that being a grandparent has vital meaning in their life (Wood & Robertson, 1978). One reason may be that grandparenthood is different from practically any other relationship we have. Normally our value is tied to our achievements, what we do. Grandparents are loved for a quality that transcends the visits or the calls—just "being there."

Lillian Troll (1983) calls grandparents the **family watchdogs.** Although they normally wait in the wings, they step in during a crisis to stabilize the family. At these times, their value is illuminated, their hidden importance revealed. Grandparents are the family safety net.

family watchdogs
Function of grandparents to watch over the younger family and step in when a crisis occurs

Troll's idea that grandparents are "guardians" or "watchdogs" is supported by looking at what happens during divorce. When comparing the amount of help a group of midwestern parents gave to their grown-up children, Joan Aldous (1985) found that the amount of support provided varied depending on the child's marital status. Was a daughter or son single or married, divorced with children or not? Although in general parents gave less help to married children, a dramatic exception occurred when a daughter with children was divorced. Then parents stepped in, providing instrumental help, such as baby-sitting and help with housework, and offering much more emotional support. In fact, in examining custody cases referred to a Canadian court over the course of a year, Corinne Wilks and Catherine Melville (1990) found that 3 out of 4 grandchildren had actually lived in a grandparent's home at some point during this time.

Even during calmer times, the job of family stabilizer is important. Grandparents may help their grandchildren indirectly by helping their children become better parents. Grandparents can also be family mediators, helping adolescent children and their parents resolve their differences (Hagestad, 1985; Kennedy, 1990).

Grandparents are the cement that keeps the extended family close. They are the focal point for family get-togethers, one reason sisters and brothers may fly in to see one another at special times such as birthdays and holidays. As summarized by sociologist Guinhild Hagestad (1985, p. 48):

Grandparents serve as symbols of connectedness within and between lives;
as people who can listen and have the time to do so;
as reserves of time, help, and attention;
as links to the unknown past;
as people who are sufficiently varied, flexible, and complex to defy easy categories and clear-cut roles.

Varied and Flexible Grandparent Roles

The stereotypical picture of Grandma is of a white-haired women knitting booties, elderly, disengaged, near death. Today, this image is more likely to fit great- or even great-great-grandparenthood. In an age when most women become grandmothers in their middle years, grandma today might be portrayed in a jogging suit working out or a business suit coming home from the office.

Actually, age is one predictor of grandparenting behavior and style. Younger grandparents are more likely to be active. Grandparents who are older tend to be more peripherally involved (Cherlin & Furstenberg, 1985). Not only may middle-aged grandparents be "younger" in their thinking, they have the energy to participate fully in a grandchild's life. They can play basketball with an 8-year-old or chase around after a toddler for hours.

In a classic study, Bernice Neugarten and Carol Weinstein (1964) classified this relaxed, nonauthoritarian style of relating as "fun seeking." It was one of several ways their middle-class sample of grandparents chose to interpret their free-floating role.

"Formal grandparents," who tended to be older, were more standoffish, more authority figures in their grandchildren's lives. However, they were more involved than the "distant figures," grandparents who rarely saw their grandchildren. At the opposite end of the spectrum were the "surrogate parents," grandparents who assumed day-to-day caretaking responsibilities. Although grandmothers predominated among this group, grandfathers were overrepresented among the last grandparent style, the "reservoir of family wisdom"—grandparents who functioned as guardians of family history, imparting information about the past.

In other studies, researchers have devised different grandparent categories (Robertson, 1977) or discovered that some of Neugarten's and Weinstein's types are absent.

In studying grandparents of teenagers, Andrew Cherlin and Frank Furstenberg (1985) found that the fun-seeking style, a type of relating that Neugarten and Weinstein found to be quite common, did not exist. The reason, the researchers concluded, is that grandparents do not act out their role rigidly, but change the way they behave as their grandchildren grow up. "It's easy and natural for grandparents to treat toddlers as sources of leisure time fun. But no matter how deep and warm the relationship remains over time, a grandmother doesn't bounce a teenaged grandchild on her knee" (p. 100).

How do grandparents act with their teenage grandchildren? In addition to talking, joking, and advising, Cherlin and Furstenberg's national sample of grandparents exchanged help. Some had a major role in how the teenager was being raised. To see how involved grandparents tend to be when their grandchildren are at this stage of life, the researchers developed scales to measure the amount of advising and disciplining and the flow of services between the grandparent and that particular teenage child.

About one-fourth of the grandparents were classified as "detached"—scoring low on measures of closeness and seeing the grandchild less than twice a month. A slightly larger fraction were rated as "passive," seeing the grandchild a bit more often. Surprisingly, "active grandparents" made up almost half the sample. These grandparents not only exchanged help and confidences but were often a major force in how that grandchild was being raised.

Even at an age when we might expect grandparent activity to be at its lowest ebb, the generations remain involved. Among one national sample of young adult grandchildren, 40% reported weekly contact with their closest grandparent. The majority said they called or visited this person several times a month. Most said their relationship with this grandparent was important, enduring, and close (L. G. Hodgson, 1992).

Grandparent Barriers

These studies examine one-to-one relationships. Wouldn't we find different results if we asked these people about their relationships with a different grandparent or grandchild? In other words, perhaps classifying grandparents and grandchildren simply as highly involved or distant is not appropriate. Involvement may vary dramatically depending on the particular "grandparenting pair" we select (J. L. Thomas, 1990b).

When they questioned their respondents about their relationships with other grandchildren, Cherlin and Furstenberg found that classifying a person as active, detached, or passive was often inaccurate. Involvement did differ from grandchild to grandchild. At least 30% of the grandparents reported having favorites. They had a particular grandchild they felt closest to. Closeness depended on physical proximity. A grandparent was more likely to take an active part in the life of a grandchild who lived around the block than one a 6-hour plane ride away. Another factor was compatibility—that is, how appealing or responsive a particular grandchild was. Equally important were the needs and desires of the generation in between.

Grandparents report that loving without having the anxiety of bringing up the younger generation is what makes this role particularly satisfying (Robertson, 1977). Although certain aspects of closeness relate to mental health, having authority over grandchildren does not (J. L. Thomas, 1990a). However, with so many single and full-time working mothers, even if they are not the primary caregiving figure, grandparents often assume a more hands-on role in child rearing than they expect (see

10-4 *Temporarily Parenting Grandparent*

Sally and her husband live in Louisville, about a 3-hour drive from her daughter's home. When her daughter and husband were struggling to build up their business, Sally often took the grandchildren. It was her pleasure to help out the struggling couple during those years. During the divorce, it seemed natural for Sally to take the grandchildren for a few weeks during Christmas. Her daughter needed time to get herself together. It was better if the children were not around. Then, toward the end of the holiday, Sally's daughter called and asked if she could keep Joe and Sara for a few more months. Sally feels she must help her daughter. She wants to be there to provide a sense of security to the grandchildren during this difficult time. However, she never fully appreciated how exhausting having real responsibility for school-age children would be. From 3:00 till bedtime, Sally's time is not her own. She has to help with homework and drive the children to lessons. There is the nightly nagging to get to bed and the anxiety about getting two reluctant children to school on time. Sally no longer has the energy for these battles. Her diabetes has worsened. Although she is responsible, she does not feel like the "true parent" in the sense of having authority to set every rule. Most of all, she worries, "Will the children really go home to their mother this summer?"

Because many more women are being thrust into the position of caregiving grandparent, at least on a temporary basis, Margaret Jendrek (1994) decided to examine what prompts people to take on this active watchdog role. Among a sample of 114 white caregiving grandparents, she uncovered three distinct categories: Day care grandparents watch the children every day while their parents work or go to school. Live-in grandparents have the grandchild residing in their home, most often with the parent but sometimes, as in Sally's situation, without. Custodial grandparents have full legal custody of the child.

As with Sally, the impulse to make life better for the grandchildren was the primary reason all of these women gave for providing care. However, there were differences in the reasons for assuming each type of active watchdog role. Custodial grandparents often were in this situation because of severe dysfunction in the parent: a daughter's mental illness or drug abuse. Live-in grandparents typically were in this arrangement because their daughters could not financially afford to live alone, often because they were unmarried or divorced. Day care grandparents were helping an intact, functional family. They decided to become caregivers because their daughters worked, they were concerned about the expense of a sitter, and felt they could do a better job than paid-for care.

When Jendrek asked, "Did you feel pressured into providing care?" two-thirds of the sample answered no. Grandparents genuinely wanted to assume this job. However, they admitted that caregiving had taken a toll (Jendrek, 1993). There are signs that live-in grandparents feel under the most stress. They do not have custody of the grandchild, and so still operate under the norm of noninterference. They do not have the time-limited commitment of grandparents living outside of the home. As we saw with Sally, their status is more ambiguous. How much care should they really provide?

Older men never had much to do with infants even as young adults. So it is no wonder that my father—like many men in his generation—felt ill at ease when thrust into the caregiving grandfather role. (In fact when this photo was taken, I know he would have felt much more comfortable centering his attention on the other newly arrived object on his lap— the just published first edition of this book!)

Aging in Action 10-4). This role not only conflicts with the norm of waning involvement (Hamon & Cobb, 1993), it goes against another basic grandparenthood principle, the **norm of noninterference:** Grandparents should not meddle in how the grandchildren are being raised (Cherlin & Furstenberg, 1985; C. L. Johnson, 1985a).

A study by Jeanne Thomas (1990a), comparing grandparent perceptions in single and married mothers, illustrates how these rules combined with a daughter's need may create an unsatisfying double bind. In contrast to the married women, the single parents said one of the best things about a grandparent was the help that person offered with child care. However, both groups vehemently agreed that family harmony was threatened when a grandparent interfered with how a grandchild was being brought up. So, at the same time as daughters welcome their mother's help, they seem to reject its predictable outcome: having some say in how the grandchildren are raised!

Grandparents are vulnerable. Not only does the norm of noninterference prevent them from being in authority—and conflict with their natural parental impulse to advise—but the parent generation controls how involved they will be. Although the gates often open too wide, with grandparents pressured into doing excessive child care, at other times the reverse problem occurs. A grandparent feels shut out, condemned to less involvement with the grandchildren than she wants. Most often, the person in this outsider position is the mother of a son.

Grandmothers in general tend to be more emotionally involved with their grandchildren than grandfathers (Cherlin & Furstenberg, 1985; Neugarten & Weinstein, 1964). Often, however, it is the mother's mother to whom grandchildren report being

norm of noninterference *Implicit principle that to have harmonious relationships with the younger family, grandparents must not criticize how the grandchildren are raised*

especially close (Hodgson, 1992; Kennedy, 1990). Although age may be partly responsible (maternal grandmothers are likely to be younger), the main reason is daughters: Women control the family's social relationships, and they naturally want closer contact with their own mothers. This **matrifocal orientation to the family** often consigns a son's mother to being the grandmother of second rank (Hagestad, 1985).

matrifocal
orientation to
the family
Fact that extended
families are closer-
knit on the female
side

One study (Matthews & Sprey, 1985) shows just how vulnerable mothers of sons are. The researchers found that whereas being a highly involved grandparent did not depend on whether a mother's mother got along with her son-in-law, this was not true of the other grandmother. To have a close relationship with her grandchildren, this grandmother had to satisfy two requirements: Be close to her son *and* to his wife. The way the matrifocal tilt works against paternal grandparents is most heartbreaking in divorce. When the wife gets custody, a son's parents may be prevented from seeing the grandchildren at all (Wilson & De Shane, 1982).

A study of middle-class grandparents shows that after a divorce, mothers of sons work hard to avoid this possibility by trying to preserve their relationship with their former daughters-in-law. Colleen Johnson and Barbara Barer (1987) found that 36% of the paternal grandmothers continued to see their former daughters-in-law at least once a week, whereas only 9% of the maternal grandmothers saw their former sons-in-law. In other words, to keep their access to the grandchildren, paternal grandmothers may be unable to side only with their sons after a divorce. They seem to make a special effort to maintain a relationship with the person who controls that access: the custodial parent, their former daughter-in-law.

Johnson and Barer found one benefit for the women who were in this touchy situation. Whereas the family network of maternal grandmothers was likely to shrink after the divorce, because they often cut off relationships with their former sons-in-law, for a paternal grandmother a child's divorce and remarriage was more likely to mean an enlargement in family ties. Not only did many of these women keep close to their former daughter-in-law, they added a new set of relatives when their son married again.

Interventions

Our discussion suggests that although being a grandparent can be very gratifying, grandparents need help in certain situations. One problem is when their child does not have custody after a divorce. Grandparents need safeguards to preserve their relationship with the grandchildren, insurance that they will still be able to visit and call. Until the decade of the 1980s, these safeguards did not exist. Daughters or sons with custody were free to, and sometimes did, shut former in-laws out (Wilson & De Shane, 1982).

Passing laws in this area has pitfalls. Shouldn't parents have final say over their children's welfare? Should the state intrude on a parent's right to determine whom a child sees? However, under pressure from grandparents who had suffered this fate, in 1982 the House of Representatives urged the National Conference of Commissioners on Uniform State Laws to develop a model act on grandparent visitation, one that ensured noncustodial grandparents some rights. Today, in all 50 states, grandparents can petition to see their grandchildren after divorce; although where the children's best

*T*he relationship between grandparents and grandchildren is often a very special one. But for a growing number of grandparents who are the primary caregivers to their grandchildren, this relationship can also be very challenging. Undertaking the full-time responsibility for raising a grandchild means major changes in the lives of these grandparents.

The American Association of Retired Persons (AARP) established the Grandparent Information Center (GIC) to provide information and resources to help grandparents cope with their primary caregiving roles. The Center is working with national and community-based agencies in the child care, aging, legal, and family services fields to address this rapidly emerging phenomenon.

The Center is supported in part by grants from The Ford Foundation and the Freddie Mac Foundation. AARP's nationwide network of regional and state offices and volunteers, as well as its many programs, are focusing attention on the issue of children at risk and their grandparent caregivers.

It is estimated that nearly 4 million children currently live in a household headed by a grandparent. For over one-third of these children (1.5 million) no parent is present and the grandparent assumes the role of primary caregiver to his or her grandchildren or great-grandchildren. This Census Bureau data also indicates that grandparent-headed families represent all socioeconomic levels and ethnic groups.

Grandparents are raising their grandchildren because of: • substance abuse

• teenage pregnancy • death • divorce • parental joblessness • neglect

• incarceration • child abuse • abandonment • AIDS.

Grandparent caregivers may face legal and social problems. They may lack support and respite services, affordable housing, and/or access to medical services and coverage of medical expenses for the grandchildren. They may also have inadequate financial resources to care for their grandchildren. They may find themselves under extreme stress causing physical and mental health problems such as exhaustion or depression.

These problems are exacerbated by the demands of becoming a parent again, coupled with a more violent environment in which the present generation of children is coming of age. Additionally, some of these grandchildren have special medical or learning needs that may put further financial and emotional strain on the family.

The AARP Grandparent Information Center, based in Washington, D.C., was established in 1993 to serve as a national resource center for grandparent-headed families, program providers, professionals, researchers, policymakers, and the public-at-large. The goals of the Center are to:

• Provide grandparents who are raising grandchildren with information and referrals about services and programs that could improve their family's situation;

• Increase public awareness about grandparents raising grandchildren, the grandchildren, and the obstacles facing these families;

• Work with and provide technical assistance to social service agencies, grandparent support groups, and others interested in helping these families;

• Examine issues confronting grandparent-headed families and seek solutions that would address these problems; and

• Facilitate cooperation among the aging, children, family, and legal systems to assist grandparent-headed families.

interests would not be served by seeing a grandparent, these applications can be denied (Aldous, 1995).

Grandparents also need help in the opposite situation. They must reconcile their traditional hands-off stance with the reality that they may be called on to take a more active role with grandchildren than their parents did. Most often, this greater involvement means regular baby-sitting or taking the child for a month or two. However, even by 1992, in a national poll, 1 out of every 10 U.S. grandparents reported having taken primary responsibility for a grandchild's care for at least 6 months (Fuller-Thompson, Minkler, & Driver, 1997). In response to these figures, the American Association of Retired Persons has established a Grandparent Information Center for people thrust into this role. The center's announcement (see Figure 10-4) was followed by newsletters, brochures, and help to people establishing the parenting-grandparents support groups that are springing up nationwide.

Grandparents need to understand their vital role as family stabilizer in this age of divorce and single parenthood. However, many grandparents report feeling partly to blame in this situation (Hamon & Cobb, 1993), adding to their mixed emotions about taking on this active watchdog role. We need to educate grandparents that a child's divorce, or having a baby without being married, does not mean that they have personally failed, just as we need to tell these same women that their responsibilities to the older generation may be more intense. Societywide changes have transformed our generative middle years into a time of genuine giving to more needy generations both ahead of us and behind (Bumpass & Aquilino, 1995). Interventions to take the pressure off younger families, such as affordable child care, will help benefit the grandparent generation too.

KEY TERMS

companionate love
consummate love
coresidence
decision/commitment
division of labor
divorce revolution
erectile dysfunction
Family and Medical Leave Act

family watchdogs
instrumental services
intergenerational solidarity
intimacy
matrifocal orientation to the family
menopause
myth of family uninvolvement

norm of noninterference
passion
sexual double standard
sexual revolution
triangular theory of love
women in the middle
U-shaped curve of marital satisfaction

SEXUALITY

Brecher and Associates (1985). *Sex after 50*. Boston: Little/Brown.
This highly recommended survey describes older Americans' sexual practices.

Masters, W., & Johnson, V. L. (1966). *Human sexual response*. Boston: Little/Brown.
This is Masters and Johnson's classic book on human sexuality.

INTERGENERATIONAL RELATIONSHIPS

Aldous, J. (1995). New views of grandparents in intergenerational context. *Journal of Family Issues, 16,* 104–122.
This review article offers a summary of grandparent research through 1994.

Bengtson, V. L., Rosenthal, C., & Burton, L. (1996). Paradoxes of families and aging. In R. H. Binstock & L. K. George (Eds.), *Handbook of aging and the social sciences* (4th ed.) (pp. 254–282). San Diego: Academic Press.
This review article summarizes the myths and the latest research on aging families.

Grandparenting at Century's end. (1996, Spring). *Generations, 20.*
This issue of *Generations* thoroughly reviews the research on grandparenting. Articles deal with historical conceptions of grandparents, minority grandparents, grandparent visitation, parenting grandparents, and other timely topics.

Zarit, S. H., & Edwards, A. B. (1996). Family caregiving: Research and clinical intervention. In R. T. Woods (Ed.), *Handbook of the clinical psychology of aging* (pp. 333–368). Chichester, England: John Wiley & Sons.
This well-written review article summarizes the research on family caregiving.

Chapter Outline

11

Life Transitions:
Retirement and Widowhood

I've put in a lot of mileage in my 30 years of work, says Mike. In 1968, I dropped out of high school, got married, and got a job with Pizza Hut as a delivery boy. Six years later, I rose to manager. Then, one night, I was robbed and realized, "I've got to look for a calmer job!" I went into the Steel Pipe Industry loading trucks. I sold clothes for J. C. Penney. I worked as a dishwasher. I even had a paper route to make ends meet. In 1976, I got a job at Honeywell selling heating and air-conditioning systems. It's like I was in heaven. I had a secretary, profit sharing, hospitalization. The work was so easy. I could call and within a few months I was being invited for dinner. Then, in 1979, the energy crisis hit, increasing the life expectancy of units already on the market. Sales were down. Honeywell first laid off marginal people. In their next phase, they offered early retirement to people at 55. I was under the impression that if I did a good job I would retire with the company. We'd just had a sales contest, and out of 169 reps, I'd come in second. That Tuesday, I went into the office expecting my boss to commend me. I was devastated when he said, "Mike, there's no easy way to tell you this. I have to lay you off." I was desperate. I had young children to support. A friend who was a commander at the police department helped me get this job.

I've been a police officer now for almost 15 years. In two weeks, on my 53rd birthday, I plan to retire. I can live as well or better than I do now, what with my wife's part-time job and my pensions from Honeywell and the state. If I wait any longer, it will be too late to go back to finish my BA and get a social work degree. There is a real need for someone with my training to work with families. There are some walking time bombs out there. Much of what we police officers do involves domestic violence. When I come into homes, to cool down families throwing furniture, threatening one another with knives or guns, I feel I'm saving lives. The other day, a young kid, about 12, got into my car and said, "Please, Officer, put me in jail." This boy had been kicked out of the house. He had no place to go, nothing to eat. Or a child will call in, "I've seen Daddy beat Mommy." I've had several women say, "Thank you, Officer, for changing my life." I love my job. It's rare to be near 40 and accidentally fall into the perfect field. But we police temporarily put fires out. I want to do something more enduring for these hurting families in the decade or so of productive life I have left.

RETIREMENT

Although Mike's roller-coaster job history ending with retiring to a new career is unusual, it illustrates many themes about how our lives as workers and retirees have shifted in recent years.

Setting the Context

CHANGES IN THE WORK WORLD   In the 1950s, a man finished school, perhaps had one or two trial jobs, and then settled into his lifework (Super, 1980). Once in that job, he would remain, often in the same organization, until he retired. In the large corporations that dominated the economy, such as U.S. Steel, General Motors, and IBM, white-collar workers often rose through the ranks, reaching a pinnacle before they retired. For both the factory worker and the executive, there was a predictable shape to the adult years: on the job, 9 to 5, Monday through Friday, for the 40-year span of a career.

Today, this **traditional stable career** is atypical. People are freer from the constraints of the company, captains of their career. No longer forced to advance through the ranks in a lockstep way or be at a certain career place at a certain age, they can design their own hours, shift in and out of the workforce, or work at home (Bird, 1994; DeFillippi & Arthur, 1994; Miner & Robinson, 1994; Mirvis & Hall, 1994). Some, like Mike, totally change direction, periodically starting over in new fields. Despite its benefits, this liberation is not ideal. It has been purchased at the price of a more vulnerable work life.

In the generation after World War II, America had what writer Tom Wolfe called a "magic economy." In the large corporations, people entered confident of having a secure job and of seeing their standard of living regularly rise. From 1946 to 1970, the income of U.S. workers doubled. Everyone participated in the success, the factory worker and the executive. In fact, the United States was on its way to becoming a genuinely equal society. Thanks to the many high-paying union jobs, the middle class was expanding. The differences between the rich and everyone else were becoming less extreme (P. Peterson, 1993; Reich, 1992).

Then came the rise of global competition and the loss of the industrial jobs that had allowed laborers to construct a middle-class life. As manufacturing fled, people at the lower ends of the income spectrum faltered. Those at the upper rungs were more vulnerable, too. While faring better financially, today managers and even corporation heads are subject to having temporary, time-limited contracts, vulnerable to being suddenly downsized or fired.

One outcome has been **widening income inequality.** During the 1970s and especially the 1980s, the wealthiest fraction of Americans became richer, the middle class shrunk, and more people became poor (P. Peterson, 1993; Reich, 1992). This change was accompanied by a decline in **real income,** or the buying power of the average salary. Two paychecks were now often needed to support the same standard of living, helping to solidify another major change in work: women in the labor force.

For most of the 20th century, work was gender-linked. Employment for middle-class married women was unusual (Betz, 1994). If their husbands could afford it,

---

traditional stable career
Career path in which people spend their whole working life in a single organizational setting

widening income inequality
The growing income gap between rich and poor Americans

real income
Buying power of a salary

women had a defined role during the adult years: Stay home; take care of the children and the house.

Then came the women's movement in the 1970s. For the first time in history, every woman was encouraged to have a career. Today, with almost three-fourths of women under age 64 in the labor force (Gilbert, 1993), staying at home full time has become atypical. Women work because they want to. Most see having a career as important for a fulfilling life (Astin, 1984). This feeling is realistic (Weitzman & Fitzgerald, 1993). Remember from the Mills study that working appears to have had a beneficial effect on women's well-being. Women also work because they have to. Besides the need for two salaries, the increase in single mothers has made staying home to raise children a luxury not many women can still afford (O'Rand, 1996).

These changes have dramatically altered retirement (and work) in the United States and other developed countries. Rather than being a male experience, with approximately half of the older workforce made up of women, issues concerning this central life role have become more gender-neutral events (Moen, 1996; O'Rand, 1996). On the positive side, the shift to a more unstructured work life may offer a more age-friendly environment, one in which the boundaries between work and retirement blur. It becomes more possible for people like Mike to begin a new career in their 50s or for others to wind down gradually as they approach their older years (Quadagno & Hardy, 1996; Mutchler, Burr, Pienta, & Massagli, 1997). On the other hand, the increased vulnerability has the potential to allow more age-*unfriendly* attitudes to emerge. In a more competitive economy, older workers may be the first to be downsized, not just because they are more costly but because they are perceived as being unable to perform. Moreover, because our economic status while working determines how we fare financially as retirees, a more fragile older workforce may translate into escalating old-age poverty rates. How does age affect our abilities at work?

AGE CHANGES IN WORKERS   We hold contrasting stereotypes about age and work: Younger workers are energetic, easy to train, pleased to perform at low-paying jobs. However, they are unreliable and, most important, lack the experience to do a good job. Older workers are responsible and knowledgeable. However, they cost a company more in salary, benefits, and missed work due to health. Worse yet, they are intractable, untrainable, and behind the times.

To see how these potential pluses and minuses balance out, researchers often correlate measures of work performance with employee age. The results are mixed. Some studies show age equals better performance; others, worse; still others reveal no correlation between age and work skill. In synthesizing this research, using a statistical technique called meta-analysis, Harvey Sterns and Michael McDaniel (cited in Rix, 1994) concluded that, overall, being older does offer a slight advantage in work. However, the relationship is so small that it is unfair to make any generalizations at all.

If we think more deeply, the reason for the lack of consistency is clear. It does not make sense to correlate work performance and age because the two should not be related in a linear, one-to-one way. Logic, plus our discussion of intelligence and creativity in Chapter 6, suggests that our work should be best not at the beginning or end of our career, but in the middle.

We intuitively "know" that beginners are poor performers when we shy away from being operated on by the 25-year-old medical school graduate or avoid taking a course from the instructor right out of graduate school: It may take years to perfect that surgery, semesters of painful feedback to learn what does and does not work in the classroom. We want a professor or physician who has reached that point where, as Nancy Denney spells out in her theory, abilities are optimally exercised, expertise is at its peak, and age losses have not set in (see Chapter 6).

Similar feelings make us shun the services of a surgeon near 70 or the professor at the end of a 35-year career: Not only are their physical and mental capacities suspect, these people are probably not up on the latest research. In addition, after so many years on the job, aren't they burned out, bored, indifferent to what they do?

Interestingly, these impressions have a realistic basis mainly at the *beginning* stages of a career. There are clear-cut performance differences between the newly hired person and the individual on the job for five or so years. However, the worker in the middle of his career is not appreciably more competent than his counterpart who is about to retire (Sterns & Miklos, 1995). In fact, at least one desirable quality is probably higher in the older employee: In contrast to our assumption that, after decades, work grows less interesting, job satisfaction is at its peak in our older years (Birdi, Warr, & Oswald, 1995; Clark, Oswald, & Warr, 1996).

Why doesn't the tide turn negative? One clue lies in the work environment. With the loss of factory jobs, most work today does not involve manual labor—the strenuous lifting or hauling that should be most vulnerable to age losses. Jobs totally dependent on speed, such as assembly-line work, have been replaced by machines. In the kinds of work where responding quickly can be important, such as food serving or reservation taking, age-related increases in people skills (how to get along with others) may compensate for the slowing that does take place (see Perlmutter's research in Chapter 6). Selective attrition also occurs. Older workers whose capacities do decline leave. Only the most competent stay on the job (see Sterns and McDaniel in Rix, 1994).

Moreover, in our older years, we *should* feel better about our jobs because we often have better jobs. We have higher-level work offering the creativity and autonomy that researchers find are crucial to being happy in a career (Loscocco & Roschelle, 1991). It also makes sense that work should be more satisfying later on because by that time we know what we don't like, have left unhappy situations, and have found the jobs that emotionally fit us.

However, the main reason for the lack of decline may lie less in our jobs than in the people labeled "older" employees. Older workers are far from old. They are in their late 40s and 50s—around the peak creative years! This brings us to our main topic: the remarkable growth of retirement as a third phase of life.

The Drive to Retire

In 1900, people worked almost until they died. The average person spent 1.2 years being retired. By 1980, the typical man could expect to be retired for 13.8 years, almost one-fifth of his life span (U.S. Senate Special Committee on Aging, 1991a). From a short pause before death, retirement had become a full stage of life.

Figure 11-1 shows that this evolution is continuing. Since 1950, the percentage of men over age 55 in the labor force has been steadily floating downward. The female decline is obscured by the fact that women were simultaneously entering the work

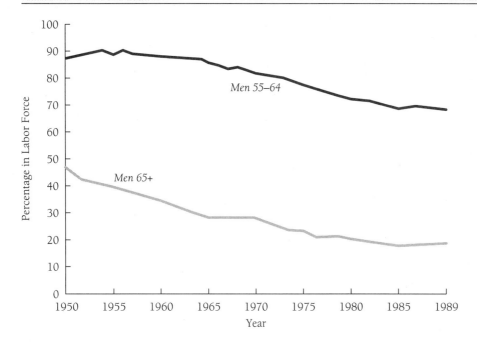

During the same period that late-life life expectancy has been escalating, American men have been leaving the workforce at younger ages.
SOURCE: U.S. Senate Special Committee on Aging, 1991a.

world during much of this time. African American men, because of their lower life expectancy, spend comparatively less of their life span as retirees than whites (Hayward, Friedman, & Chen, 1996). However, the drive to retire is universal, not only in the United States but in France, Sweden, Japan, and every other industrialized country in the world (Guillemard & Rein, 1993). Today, every working person, male or female, in every ethnic and racial group, can expect to live retired for an unparalleled length of time.

In fact, while we still label 65 as the marker, the average retirement age has actually inched down close to 62 (Gendell & Siegel, 1996). This downward drift is remarkable considered against the backdrop of our life expectancy gains. If we were to retire at an equivalent age, in terms of mortality, to what 65 was in 1940, today we should work until age 70.

A variety of influences fuel the retirement drive (Palmore, Burchett, Fillenbaum, George, & Wallman, 1985). Older workers may be pushed to leave their jobs by industry downsizing, age discrimination, or poor health. Another factor is psychological: how much people like their job, their commitment to the work role, the extent to which they are looking forward to leisure activities. However, the main basis is

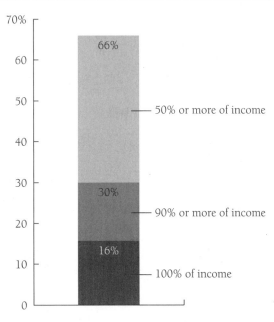

Two-thirds of all retirees rely on Social Security for at half least of their retirement income. For 1 in 6 American retirees, Social Security is their only source of income.
SOURCE: Social Security Administration, 1997.

financial: People are able to retire because they can afford to live without holding down a job. Two economic fuels provide this security: Social Security and private pensions.

Social Security
Government-sponsored old-age insurance program, which people pay into when working and get benefits from when they are incapable of working or during their retirement years

THE ECONOMIC FUELS   **Social Security** is the largest income-maintenance program in the United States. In 1992, about 41.5 million Americans were covered by this program, virtually all of our nation's retirees. As Figure 11-2 shows, Social Security provides the highest fraction of income for the average American retiree (Social Security Administration, 1997). It offers coverage to the families of workers who have died as well as to large numbers of working-age Americans if permanent disability strikes.

Social Security is the number one American mainstay of a decent old age. Before this historic program, when the elderly developed disabilities and could not work, they had to depend on a fragile worker compensation system or their families and charity for help. During the Great Depression of the 1930s, the vulnerability of the aged was laid bare. Millions of older people, left penniless and with families unable to support them, were starving in the streets. Society needed to provide a reliable cushion to protect people when they could no longer work. The result was the **Social Security Act,** signed into law by President Franklin Roosevelt in 1935, which requires working Americans to contribute part of their salary to support current retirees with the guarantee that they too will be taken care of when they reach old age.

At first, Social Security coverage was limited. While benefits gradually became more generous over the years, even with Social Security, poverty among older adults was unacceptably high. So, during the late 1960s and early 1970s, Congress acted again. Benefits were increased 20% and—very important—rose in tandem with the cost of living. The categories of eligible recipients were increased. The age for collecting partial benefits was extended downward. These changes made retiring in relative comfort possible and transformed the early-retirement trickle into a tide.

People retiring at age 62 can collect 80% of the benefits they would get at age 65. This is a major reason why so many people retire in their early 60s today. In addition, between age 65 and 70, workers who collect Social Security are penalized if they earn over a certain amount, forfeiting one dollar in benefits for each three dollars of earnings above this ceiling.

The Social Security system also has incentives to discourage retirement. People over age 70 who work can earn an unlimited amount and still collect all of their benefits. Workers who retire after 65 receive a bonus for each year they delay. And, in an effort to slow what had become a retirement stampede and keep the system solvent, modifications in Social Security were made in 1983. Starting in 2000, the fraction of benefits awarded at age 62 will be gradually reduced to 70%. Most important, the age for collecting full Social Security benefits will rise from 65 to 67 by 2027.

Will these changes delay retirement? The answer is unclear. Although the evidence linking retirement decisions with the generosity of Social Security is indisputable (Quadagno & Hardy, 1996), the picture is complicated by a second financial fuel: private pensions.

Pensions are employer-sponsored funds given to employees when they leave work. Although some companies always offered this benefit, it was not until the 1960s that the practice of giving pensions in industry became widespread. After a trend-setting decision by the Ford Motor Company in the late 1950s, pensions spread to the other major auto companies and then to other large corporations. Soon after, early-retirement benefits were added to the economic package. By the early 1980s, two-thirds of large American companies offered this option to their employees. In addition, many companies today provide health insurance to supplement Medicare and to cover their employees who retire before age 65 (Quadagno & Hardy, 1996).

So, even in the face of cutbacks in Social Security, pensions are a powerful fuel propelling the drive to retire. However, it is mainly workers in higher-status jobs who have pensions (Crystal, 1996; Schulz, 1996). Moreover, to be eligible for this source of income, a person must have worked full time at a company for a number of years. So, the trend toward hiring more temporary and part-time workers may make this source of retirement funds less available in the future. On the other hand, pensions also operate in the opposite way—encouraging people to retire at an unusually young age.

Employers sometimes use pensions to lure older workers to leave their jobs (Schulz, 1996). Strategies such as giving credit for five extra years of work if a person retires at 55, or penalizing employees with lower benefits if they retire beyond age 60,

Social Security Act
Landmark legislation passed by the Roosevelt administration requiring working Americans to contribute part of their salary to support the retired population

pensions
Privately sponsored old-age insurance programs in which individuals and/or their employers set aside funds to be used during retirement

actually make it cost-effective for some workers to retire unusually young (Mehdiza-deh & Luzadis, 1994; Quinn & Burkhauser, 1990). Still, the effectiveness of this lure depends on people's willingness to take the bait.

THE EMOTIONAL LURE   Retirement used to be symbolic of incapacity, the end of productive life. As people became able to retire in relative economic comfort, retire-ment was transformed from a tragedy into the time of life that people were working *toward.*

For the past 30 years, this new emotion has been the winner. The majority of people say they look forward to retirement, even as young adults (Glamser, 1976). Looking forward to the idea in some hazy future, however, is different from giving up a central activity that, as we have seen, seems especially satisfying during the latter part of a person's career. Why are people are so willing to take this step? This brings us to the emotional salience of work in our lives.

In a famous statement, Freud said that the twin keys to adult fulfillment are love and work. One reason that this statement has stood the test of time is because it seems so universally true. However, at least theoretically, we might view the worker role as especially critical to a particular group: upper-middle-class men. Women's identities are often divided between motherhood and career (Barnett, Marshall, & Singer, 1992; Moen, 1996). People in lower-status jobs may not be as likely to define their worth as human beings though their jobs. For men in high-status jobs, however, we would expect that leaving work would be an unusually wrenching blow, as this life role can be the basic underpinning of their identity as adults.

The truth of this statement was vividly revealed in a compelling qualitative study of the inner lives of highly successful men. In the mid-1980s, a research team headed by Robert Weiss intensively interviewed 80 upper-middle-class men, ranging in age from 35 to 55, in several affluent Boston area suburbs. The researchers were impressed with the intensity of their subjects' passion about work, how focal this life role was in their emotional lives. Here is how Weiss (1990, pp. 252–253) describes the men's priorities:

> [Work is] fundamental to having enough self-respect so you feel comfortable with your neighbors. . . . Plus it is truly absorbing. You need self-confidence for your work, because it is challenging and risky. You get the self-confidence by seeing yourself do well and having others recognize that you do well. . . . You care deeply about marriage and your children. That is far and away the part of your life closest to your heart, although not always the part whose demands you put first. . . . "The men of this study want to be men they respect. Being a good man means being able to maintain a respected place among men, being able to serve as the head of one's family."

This quotation offers insights into the multiple meanings career provides. For these men, work was the proving ground for their personal worth as a man. But work meant more than just a forum for personal success. It was their outlet for generativity, too. Notice that the main reason for working was to be "a good provider," to take the best possible care of one's children and wife. But this function of work sheds light on the mystery of why some of these very high achieving men can easily abandon their role as worker in their older years. Once a man reaches retirement age, he has fulfilled his mission to provide for his family. He has put his children through college. He has given his wife a secure life. In other words, as David Gutmann (1987) would say, once having achieved the "parental imperative," a man is able to shift his interests to other aspects of life.

In fact, as they reach retirement age, men may feel that they can express the same basic human needs for challenge and generativity just as effectively through nonwork pursuits. Retirement activities, such as getting involved in community service, fulfilling a long-standing interest in painting, or spending more time with family, satisfy the impulse to be generative. These activities open up new arenas for personal achievement, too. So, a man decides to retire to serve on a foundation, become a master painter, or "get closer to my wife and grandchildren." Proving himself on the job is a challenge that he has already mastered; now it is time to move on to a new challenge in life.

Socioemotional selectivity theory offers another perspective on why retiring might be appealing even for men whose main adult identity has centered on their career. Recall that Carstensen (1995) believes that earlier in life, our mission is to make our mark in the world. Once we have achieved outer-world success, our priorities shift. We recenter our lives around being with the people we care most deeply about.

So when a man is younger, proving his competence at his job is his main aim. But by age 55 or 60, even though his career may still be pleasurable, it is more of a double-edged sword. The time he spends at the office takes him away from his main priority. It prevents him from spending the years he has left with his family, the people he has always been working *for*.

One interesting study (R. M. Cohn, 1979) suggests that this shift in "emotional salience" may really occur as men approach their retirement years. Men of different ages were asked about the satisfaction they got from work and then questioned about their overall self-esteem. Although the older men liked their work just as much or more, it was only for the younger men that work satisfaction was correlated with satisfaction in life. For the older men, the two were disconnected, suggesting that as men age, work does become less psychologically central. How content the older person is in his work life is irrelevant to how content he is generally in life.

This shift may be set in motion surprisingly early on. In a longitudinal study of Boston area men, Linda Evans, David Ekerdt, and Raymond Bosse (1985) examined the intensity of retirement-related activities: How often did a man discuss retirement with his wife, relatives, or retired friends? How often did he read articles about retirement? Although the amount of these activities increased as retirement age drew near, even men who saw leaving work as being 15 years away still did a good deal of informal planning for their retirement life.

Moreover, it is not true that work satisfaction reaches its peak at the very brink of retirement. In the Boston retirement study, David Ekerdt and Stanley DeViney (1993) found that in the year or two before people expected to leave work, job satisfaction dipped. This finding suggests that, besides gradually embracing their new identity, when people are about to retire, they vigorously work to discard their old work skin. They mentally make the transition easier by devaluing the alternative: "I don't like my hours. I hate my boss. It's *really* a good idea that I retire."

Not every worker undergoes these transformations. For many people, work remains their main focus. Their job alone is what gives them real fulfillment. They do equate retirement with emotional death. These sentiments predict actions. Longitudinal studies suggest that people who are reluctant to retire put off the event as long as possible (Palmore et al., 1985). The reverse is also true. People who dislike their work are likely to retire as soon as they can (Hanisch & Hulin, 1991).

THE PUSH TO LEAVE   We already know that employers lure older workers to retire by using the carrot of pensions. To what extent are people forced to retire, actively pushed out of their jobs?

mandatory retirement policies
Now-outlawed company rules that used to require workers to retire at a certain age

Pushing older people out of the workforce was once fully accepted. **Mandatory retirement policies**—company rules requiring employees to retire by age 65—were common in industry. Then, during the late 1960s, just as their counterparts in the civil rights and women's movements fought to outlaw similar practices based on gender or race, a vigorous elderly rights lobby labored to end discrimination based on age. The outcome was the 1967 **Age Discrimination in Employment Act (ADEA)**, which, in its current form, makes mandatory retirement at *any* age illegal, unless a person is working in a profession (such as law enforcement or aviation) where age can be a detriment to public safety, and outlaws age bias of any kind at work. The Americans with Disabilities Act, passed in 1990, also protects older workers because it bans discrimination against prospective and current workers who have disabling conditions unless their impairments directly interfere with their ability to perform.

Age Discrimination in Employment Act (ADEA)
Law banning any form of discrimination in the workplace on the basis of age

These policies make it impossible to discriminate openly on the basis of age. However, employers still may have ageist prejudices that operate in subtle ways.

In one classic study, managers were asked to read vignettes and make decisions about a hypothetical employee. The stories were identical, only in one condition the protagonist was portrayed as age 30 and in the other, 61. Although the managers all said how much they valued their older employees, their "recommended solutions" revealed otherwise. If the employee was older, the managers did not feel he could benefit from retraining and believed he was less adaptable and competent (reported in Rosen & Jerdee, 1995).

Once again, the problem may lie in explanatory style—a different lens for interpreting older workers' performance on the job. Esther Dedrick and Gregory Dobbins (1991) asked management students to imagine that they were the vice president of a company whose task was to make decisions about the head of accounting, who had just completed a computerized billing system for the firm. In one scenario, the accountant took longer than expected, the job was done haphazardly, and morale was low. In another (the "success vignette"), the job was described as having gone well. Here too the stories were identical, differing only in the age of the employee.

Good performance in both young and old accountants was viewed as a function of the person's basic competence. Poor performance by the younger accountant was passed off as temporary: The person did not have enough experience; with more training, he would get the job right. If the accountant was older, however, failure was viewed in stable, global, internal terms: The person was not intellectually "up to the job"; training probably would not be effective. The best solution was to give the accountant simpler, less challenging work.

Other research using simulated vignettes reveals that age biases are most likely to crop up in certain situations: when the job applicant is applying for a low-level, age-incongruent job, such as working at a fast-food chain; when the person making the judgment is too overloaded with other work to have time to make an assessment based on the applicant's personal qualities; or when the individual doing the hiring already holds negative attitudes toward the elderly (Perry, Kulik, & Bourhis, 1996).

Do these impulses operate in life? Here the evidence is less clear. On the positive side, we have the statistic that older workers have the lowest unemployment rates of any group. In 1994, for instance, people in their early 20s were twice as likely to be unemployed as those over age 45 (Rix, 1995). Still, these figures are less reassuring when we consider that the average *duration* of unemployment rises with age. As Aging in Action 11-1 suggests, after months of unsuccessful hunting, some out-of-work older people may get discouraged, give up the job search, and "decide" to retire (Rix, 1995).

The escalating number of age discrimination charges filed with the Equal Employment Opportunity Commission are troubling (Rosen & Jerdee, 1995). So are the figures on **displaced workers**—people who are laid off because of company downsizing. In 1989, people over 55 represented 13% of all workers, but 18% of those who had been downsized (U.S. Senate Special Committee on Aging, 1991a). These figures raise the suspicion that, along with the carrot of pensions, one strategy companies use to get rid of older workers may be to abolish a job slot (or department) when its occupant becomes too senior, and costly, to keep on the payroll.

displaced workers
People who lose their jobs as a result of company downsizing

Here from an engineer at Bell Labs is what it is like to be on the receiving end of the pressure to cut back:

> We were all encouraged to retire at 65 even though the law said it should be 70. It was clear that our work was being produced in Korea at lower cost. We were offered a sweetener with the notion that even if we didn't take retirement at that time our chances would be less favorable next year. And, after all, they could hire young technicians at half the price they were paying us. (Williamson, Reinhart, & Blank, 1992, p. 41)

From a supervisor at Bethlehem Steel:

> They said if we didn't leave the company voluntarily [taking the early-retirement incentive], they would have to reduce the force at their discretion. I chose not to be one of those. Ordinarily we were a two-man office, but when my boss retired a year before he was not replaced . . . After vacation you'd have twice as much work because it wasn't being done by anyone else. (1992, p. 43)

These quotations imply that some "voluntary" early retirement may be surprisingly forced. Moreover, the extent of age discrimination may look more minor because of the legal system. The money awarded for winning this type of suit is small. It is the few years of salary a person would earn by working until the normal retirement time. It may simply be easier for a victim of discrimination to take early retirement rather than waste time and money in court.

11-1 *Older and Underemployed*

For more than 2 years, David, age 51, has been searching for work. David would not be counted in the unemployment statistics. He has a part-time job in a small firm. One or two private clients help pay the bills. The problem is that David is underemployed, not where he should be in relation to his skills and background, especially at this point in life. A lawyer with David's expertise should be earning at least $150,000 a year, enough to support a family at an upper-middle-class level—especially someone with David's résumé. David was a Phi Beta Kappa. He went to a prestigious law school, then worked at some of the city's best law firms. The problem, David argues, is that he is a victim of bad breaks. Now, for a person at his level, there are practically no jobs. Firms generally hire people right out of school. In this profession, the more experienced you are, the less employable you become. David's wife, Anna, believes the problem is her husband. David's job history is suspicious. He never made partner at his first job. Then, he was laid off at his second job when the firm merged and the new partners got rid of David and brought in their own men. They've been forced to borrow money from relatives. Even though she has three teenagers, Anna has to work full time. Other lawyers with worse credentials are making it. When they were laid off in midlife, some of David's colleagues found new full-time jobs. Anna thinks her husband should have seen the signs and started searching for work before his last firm closed its doors. Worse yet, David seems unmotivated—not trying to find a new job. Yesterday, he said, "I'm already in my 50s. Maybe I should give up looking for full-time work."

David is in a difficult situation. As we saw in the text, older people have more trouble in the job market. For men who need to support a family, and who feel their own deficiencies are responsible for their life situation, being out of work is an especially severe blow (Belsky, 1997). However, by blaming her husband, Anna may be fostering the behavior she dislikes. In studying out-of-work older professionals, Brent Mallinckrodt and Bruce Fretz (1988) looked at how depression and the intensity of job seeking varied as a function of an individual's length of unemployment, financial concerns, and a variety of types of social support. Social support was particularly important in predicting both emotional distress and how actively a person continued to search for new work. In particular, the researchers found that a dimension of support they labeled "reassurance of worth" was closely tied to self-efficacy, searching behavior, and self-esteem. In other words, not only do feelings of personal inadequacy multiply the pain, these perceptions may be partly shaped by the messages a laid-off worker gets from the people closest to him. To motivate her husband to continue searching for a job, Anna might be better off focusing on David's abilities rather than blaming him for where he went wrong and how he is failing now.

The Consequences: Life as a Retiree

What are the financial effects of not working? Is being retired good or bad for health? How do people adapt psychologically to this life change?

THE FINANCIAL IMPACT   In the early 1960s, 1 out of every 3 older Americans lived below the poverty line—a poverty rate twice that of younger adults. Then, our

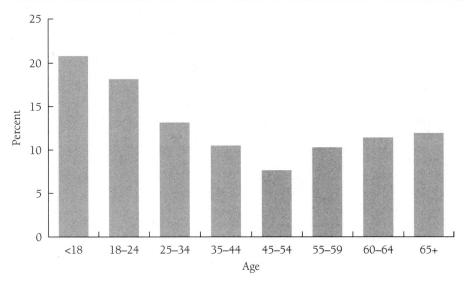

In 1994, children were almost twice as likely as older adults to live in poverty.
SOURCE: U.S. Bureau of the Census, 1996.

nation became sensitized to the elderly poor. That outcry, in a booming economy, produced a remarkable change. Social Security benefits were raised and extended. Medicare was instituted. The impact of these **entitlement programs** has been dramatic. Today, as Figure 11-3 reveals, children have replaced the elderly as our nation's poorest group.

Although far fewer older people live in dire poverty, retirees on average still must cope with less money (Crystal, 1996). In 1993, for instance, the median income of an elderly family was less than half that of a family under age 65 (Wu, 1995). However, in one national poll, younger people reported being more upset than older adults by not having enough money (L. Harris & Associates, 1981).

One reason why retirees may not feel financially strapped is that they pay a smaller portion of the income they do have in taxes. Most important, older people have more assets and fewer expenses (Rendall, 1996). Not only may they own their home, furniture, and other essentials of life, but the tremendous expense of raising children is gone (Crystal, 1996).

Psychological factors may partly account for the lack of pain. Emotionally, retirement is unlike any other economic reversal. The jolt at being unexpectedly forced to belt-tighten is not there. People *expect* to live on a more limited budget after they retire. The pinch may hurt less for another reason. Unlike being fired, retiring does not carry the connotations of having personally failed. As implied in Aging in Action 11-1, when we have the feeling that everyone but us is succeeding, we feel especially resentful and

entitlement programs
Government programs providing financial aid and other services to disadvantaged or other "worthy" segments of the population

TABLE 11-1	*Reasons Why Leaving the Worker Role Can Often Be Pain-Free*

1. **Shifting emotional priorities.** When they are older, people no longer see achievement in the outer world as their main purpose in life. Their goals center around interpersonal concerns—spending time with family and being at home (see Carstensen's and Gutmann's theories).

2. **On-time, planned event.** When they are older, people expect to retire. They do considerable mental planning for this predictable life role before it occurs.

3. **Social support.** Everyone the person's age is in the same boat. Because most people enter this boat healthy and willing, retiring is not seen as a symbol of incapacity or a personal tragedy.

4. **Financial (and emotional) security.** Although retired people have to live on less money, with the growth of pensions and Social Security, more assets, and fewer expenses, the funds they do have are more apt to be adequate to their needs. By providing retired people with a steady (though limited) income for life, Social Security frees them from the earlier adult anxiety of being fired or laid off.

5. **New opportunities for fulfillment.** In our more age-irrelevant society, retirees have many options. They can use this life stage to express their needs for generativity and further challenge. They can see this phase of life as a time to carry out unfulfilled dreams.

6. **Fewer constraints.** Finally, retired people are free from the constraints and hassles that are part and parcel of even the most compelling job.

deprived. In other words, the transition to a nonwork life is less troubling because retiring is an expected, on-time event.

THE EMOTIONAL IMPACT   The same encouraging message relates to retirement's physical and psychological effects. Contrary to myth, people do not die after they retire; they do not become severely depressed. In fact, as we might expect from our earlier discussion, retirement has no effect on health and morale. The study of Boston area men discussed at several points earlier has an even stronger message. When the researchers compared men who had retired during the past year with a group who continued to work, the retirees reported fewer hassles than those still on the job (Bosse, Aldwin, Levenson, & Workman-Daniels, 1991). Another, more recent study has confirmed these results: Retirees felt less stress and reported taking better care of their health than a comparable nonretired group (Midanik, Soghikian, Ransom, & Tekawa, 1995).

This is not to say that retiring has no ups and downs. Retirement researcher Robert Atchley (1977) believes that people go through stages in adjusting to this transition. First, there is a honeymoon period when everything is rosy. A man luxuriates in freedom, goes fishing, travels, packs in activities. A woman makes lunch dates and exercises for hours. Then, a letdown sets in. Something is missing. One person may be doing too much and ends up exhausted. Another feels at loose ends without something productive to do. At this point, the person must consider, "How do I really want the rest of my life to go?" Finally, retirees find their niche and settle down to a predictable routine.

In a longitudinal study of Canadian retirees, researchers found support for these phases (Gall, Evans, & Howard, 1997). High levels of zest were typical in the first year after retirement, followed by an emotional letdown. When David Ekerdt, Raymond Bosse, and Sue Levkoff (1985) compared the happiness, activity levels, and optimism of the Boston retirees at 6-month intervals, they too found that people who had left work more than a year previously were in an emotional slump. Although the inflated optimism of the first months was never fully recaptured, people did emerge from this low. As Atchley would predict, by the second year, happiness levels were higher again.

However, for the reasons summarized in Table 11-1, overall, retirement is a painless transition for many adults. However, as in any area of life, people differ in how they cope, feel, and behave. As we might expect, based on Costa's research, personality continuity is a number one theme. People who feel good about themselves when working feel good about themselves as retirees (Reitzes, Mutran, & Fernandez, 1996). They have the maturity and emotional flexibility to find happiness at any stage of life.

Other factors are also important. As we might imagine, reluctant retirees, such as the managers quoted earlier, tend to be relatively embittered and unhappy. People in poor health and with limited income also tend to be more dissatisfied (Gall, Evans, & Howard, 1997). It makes sense that retirement smiles on people who enter this life stage willingly and basically happy and who have the financial and physical resources to fully enjoy their new life.

Interventions

Despite this generally sunny postwork picture, some dark clouds remain. Perhaps our discussion has left you with the uneasy sense that older workers are vulnerable, prime targets in an economy that puts a premium on cost-effectiveness as the bottom line. Even if we do not buy into the stereotype that our capacities decline with age, the reality is that an employee on the job for 30 years is more expensive. After the 5 or 10 years that it takes that person to get "up to speed," the benefits to the company do not outweigh the costs in terms of salary, insurance, and days off (Clark in Rix, 1994). The impulse to save money by "retiring" older workers may be especially intense during times of rapid technological change. In fact, when the issue is ease of retraining, the age/work performance relationship is less upbeat. Several studies suggest that older workers are less adept at learning new technologies such as computer skills (Sterns & McDaniel in Rix, 1994). What happens when an employer gives into the "bottom line," downsizing an older employee?

HELPING OUT-OF-WORK OLDER WORKERS   A variety of services exist for older people who find themselves out of a job. Perhaps the best-established and most interesting is Operation ABLE. Begun in 1976 in the Chicago area and now operating nationwide, Operation ABLE is a nonprofit, private organization dedicated to providing workers over age 45 with the skills to find new work. Based on the idea that if older workers are to compete in today's job market, they must be versed in technology, the Boston chapter of this organization recently set up a computer skills training center. IBM has contributed the hardware, software, and related equipment; and Digital

FIGURE 11-4 *Age-Differentiated versus Age-Integrated Social Structures*

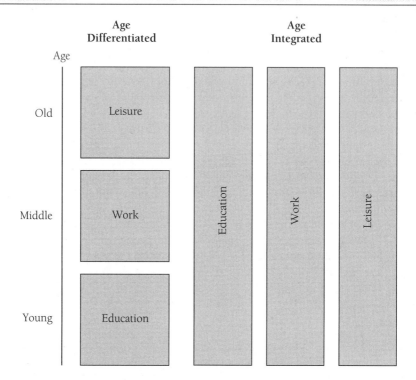

The ideal is to be able to work, retire, or go back to school at any time of life.
SOURCE: Riley & Riley, 1994.

Equipment Corporation has developed the training modules. Both companies provide staff to help the center develop and teach the courses.

Programs such as Operation ABLE have a focused mission: They help laid-off older people go back to work. Another strategy involves a broader, more global approach: Work toward a society in which there is *no* age-linked retirement at all.

WORKING TOWARD AN AGE-INTEGRATED SOCIETY   Matilda White Riley and John Riley (1994) agree that we have gone a long way toward replacing the rigid age structure that used to govern adult life. After the late 1960s, as we saw in previous chapters, it became possible for older people to express their sexuality, to climb mountains, to continue working or retire. Still, they argue, we need to implement a truly **age-integrated society**—a social structure in which people can do what they want at any point during adult life. Abandoning the age separation of education, work, and leisure shown in Figure 11-4 would offer more freedom for people of *any* age to engineer a lifestyle tailored to their own interests, identities, and possible selves. Rather

age-integrated society
Ideal society in which people can perform any activity at any time of life

than just being for retirement, the last third of adult life should be a time to go back to school or start a second career.

GOING BACK TO SCHOOL   Great progress has been made on the education front. Based on the research showing that mental stimulation is good brain cell medicine, educational activities are an integral part of programming at senior centers, retirement communities, and even nursing homes. Increasingly, older people are returning on their own to college for undergraduate or advanced degrees. In fact, a whole group of gerontologists today specialize in lifelong learning, developing and administering educational programs specifically for older adults. Here we discuss two types of educational opportunities that have been set up exclusively for older learners (U.S. Senate Special Committee on Aging, 1991b, 1992).

The best-known older adult education program is **Elderhostel.** In this popular program, open to anyone over age 60, older adults literally go back to college. They enroll in intensive, typically weeklong courses "in residence" at universities, museums, and other educational settings. Since its inception in 1975, Elderhostel has grown at an amazing rate and become widely respected for the quality and diversity of its offerings. As of 1990, 1500 institutions in the United States, Canada, and 40 other countries hosted Elderhostel programs. In that year alone, the 215,000 people who participated in this "adventure of a lifetime" could choose from a dazzling array of options, from examining glacier formations in Alaska, to traveling to Australia to study aboriginal culture, to taking courses in art at the Louvre or studying Mozart in New York. Here is one participant's enthusiastic description:

Elderhostel
Educational program in which people over age 60 take courses on college campuses or in other educational settings around the world

> A week after my program at the University of Notre Dame in Indiana, looking back I have an overwhelming memory: it was simply wonderful. . . . I chose Notre Dame mainly because of three courses offered: "Human Evolution: Prehistory or Poetry," "Pascal on Faith and Reason," and "Wet and Dryland Aerobics." How lucky can you be? Each was better than I had any reason to hope for. . . . Dr. James Ellis was middle-aged, bulky, balding, bronzed. . . . He made mankind come alive, showed us how our species is swiftly and not wisely changing the world. His illustrations were stunning: "We Americans are using 75 percent of the world's calories." (And I didn't want to make him a liar as I passed through the cafeteria line.) We have imported the sweatshop around the world. . . . Next Sandy Vanslager puts us through our paces in the aerobics class. . . . With my damaged ticker I was concerned, but . . . I felt great, even though part of the class dropped out. Dr. Tom Morris was equally outstanding. . . . The quality of the program was so magnificent that I felt I was in heaven. . . . Notre Dame, I won't forget you! (Mills, 1993, pp. 108–111)

The My Turn program at Kingsborough Community College in Brooklyn exemplifies another avenue for getting higher education: the special program for older adults within a traditional college setting. As we saw in our opening interview in Chapter 6, while older people do return to school without benefit of special services, some may be put off by the unfamiliar environment. For others, returning to college is not even possible because they are living on a fixed income or lack the credentials. Many of this cohort of older adults left school before getting a high school diploma. My Turn eliminates these barriers by offering any New York City or state resident over 65 the chance to take courses at this branch of the City University of New York tuition-free, whether or not that person has completed high school. Counseling, tutoring, and peer support while negotiating this new territory are available to the more than 2000 participants from a variety of backgrounds who take advantage of the program every year.

HAVING A POSTRETIREMENT CAREER   Going back to college benefits both the seller (colleges in need of students) and buyer (older adults in need of stimulation). Hiring retired workers requires convincing employers that older people have something special to sell. In addition, as we know, most retirees are happy to leave work. Few want to return, at least full time (D. C. Morris, 1997). What they may be interested in is something in between—to reduce their hours or work at another job part time.

Despite age discrimination, a surprising number of people do find postretirement jobs. In one national poll, almost half of all private-sector firms said that they hired retirees (Hirshorn & Hoyer, 1994). In another survey, one-fourth of all people who retired from a career job went on to other work (Quinn & Burkhauser, 1990). The bad news is that people often take a substantial salary cut in this postretirement career. (Some people may desire this reduction because, if they are in their 60s, they must forfeit Social Security benefits if they earn over a certain amount.)

Sometimes, people seek new jobs after retirement for emotional reasons. They need to work for their mental health. However, the decision is most often prompted by economic need. In analyzing the retirement transitions of a national sample of men ages 55 to 75, researchers found that high income was related to what they called making a crisp (final) exit from the labor force. **Blurred transitions,** in which people retired and then went back to work again, were most closely associated with having no pension and less income coming in, strongly suggesting that many people search out new jobs after retiring to make ends meet (Mutchler et al., 1997). How often are people strapped for income during their retirement years? What is the economic situation of the elderly today?

blurred transitions
Rather than definitively leaving the workforce at the end of a career, winding down slowly or retiring and then returning to work

Old and Rich or Old and Poor?

By this time in the book, you may be wondering about an imbalance: Older people have paid-for medical care; young adults do not. Older people used to live with their families out of financial need; now, young adults are in the position of turning to older parents for help. Older people can live retired for decades. Children are the age group in the most dire economic straits. Have we gone too far as a nation in favoring the old over the young? The question is one of **intergenerational equity**—balancing the needs of competing generations (see Bengtson & Achenbaum, 1993). Let's look first at what economist Peter Peterson (1993) has to say about this controversial topic.

intergenerational equity
Issue of whether government entitlement programs are unfairly benefiting the elderly relative to the young

OLD AND OVERBENEFITED   Peterson argues that today the average retiree can expect to receive Social Security benefits several times in excess of what he or she put in. In addition, the elderly receive free medical care, "senior citizen" rates on airlines, at hotels, and at movies, and a variety of other perks. These old-age benefits are not

means-tested, or dependent on income; they arrive whether the person is a pauper or a millionaire. How fair is it, asks Peterson, to give so much to older citizens when poverty is growing rapidly among the young?

Moreover, Peterson argues, if our current practices continue, this inequity will persist, affecting the current cohort of young people as they travel into old age. As we know, the Social Security and health care benefits enjoyed by retirees are financed by working adults. As the baby boomers retire, the **old-age dependency ratio,** or ratio of working to retired people, will decline. According to Peterson's calculations, if we were to keep Medicare and Social Security benefits at their current levels, one-half the salary of working adults would go to fund these programs in 2040. This group of older adults has benefited from a rising standard of living their children and grandchildren will never see. How fair, Peterson asks, is it to give so much to this particular older cohort at the expense of the cohorts of elderly to come?

Peterson argues that, besides means-testing entitlements such as Social Security and Medicare and generally redirecting support to the working young, we should immediately increase the age for receiving Social Security and eliminate the Social Security earnings test for retirees who work. Forcefully encouraging people to retire later will not only reduce the burden on young adult taxpayers, but benefit everyone. A large, vigorous segment of the older population today is not working. We should capitalize on the wasted talents of retirees (Quinn & Burkhauser, 1990).

Many experts disagree with these forecasts. The tide of young adult immigrants may raise the dependency ratio, allowing future cohorts of elderly to enjoy their retirement years. Today's baby boomers are living longer healthier and, because of the increased numbers of working women, entering retirement with more assets (Easterlin, 1996). They are not as likely to overburden the system as Peterson believes. The idea of a genuine crisis in Social Security is wildly overblown (Kingson & Quadagno, 1995). Relatively minor changes, phased in gradually, such as those suggested Table 11-2, are all that is needed to keep the program afloat. Moreover, would we want to push hard to cut back on this vital old-age safety net if the price is more late-life poverty? Wouldn't forcing older people into the workforce backfire, producing more job competition, lower wages, and greater economic insecurity for younger adults?

OLD AND STILL BADLY OFF Most important, advocates for the elderly vigorously dispute Peterson's portrait of older adults as an affluent, overbenefited class. Recall that with a median income only half that of people under 65, the average older family is still worse off economically. In fact, the percentage of elderly **near poor**— people within striking distance of the poverty line—has barely budged over the past three decades. If we include this group, older adults are much more likely to be living in poverty than people under age 65.

Moreover, by severely cutting Social Security and Medicare, we would be paying a steep price. Without government entitlement programs, one-half of all elderly Americans would be living below the poverty line (Wu, 1995). Pensions, that other financial underpinning of retirement, will not take up the slack. To receive a pension, people have to have worked for the same employer full time for a fixed number of years. The shift to time-limited and part-time employment makes it less likely that contemporary workers will fulfill these requirements and so have this important source of income in their retirement years.

means-tested benefits
Government entitlements that are allotted on the basis of need, only to people under a certain income level

old-age dependency ratio
The ratio of working people to older people collecting Social Security and other benefits

near poor
People living close to the poverty line, with incomes up to 125 or 150% of federal poverty levels

DRACONIAN STRATEGIES

1. Means-test Social Security, putting benefits on a sliding scale related to income and dramatically reducing payouts to more affluent retirees.

   This approach could easily backfire if affluent workers petition to leave the program. Without the participation of this powerful group, the whole old-age social insurance system will fall apart.

2. Reduce Social Security payouts to current recipients, and immediately raise the retirement age.

   Reducing payouts is certain to increase poverty, particularly among the worst-off older Americans, who depend on Social Security as their sole source of income. By increasing the number of people competing for jobs, raising the retirement age could boomerang, flooding the workforce with old workers and so producing more poverty and unemployment among the young.

MILDER STRATEGIES

1. Tax Social Security benefits for the more affluent.
2. Bring state and local government workers into the system.
3. Increase the payroll tax rate for Social Security one percentage point each for employer and employee beginning in 2020.

SOURCE: Kingson & Quadagno, 1995.

These contrasting images illustrate the obvious fact that elderly people cannot be stereotyped. The vigorous, young-old couple on the boat may fit Peterson's portrait of an overbenefited group whereas the woman scrounging for items in this garbage can brings home the fact that old-old women living alone are likely to be poor.

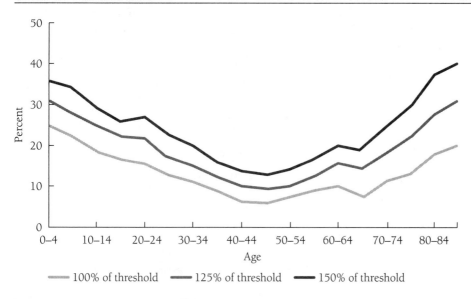

If we take into account the near poor, we get a different picture of life-span poverty, particularly at life's uppermost end.

SOURCE: Radner, 1992, p. 14.

Actually, although young-old, middle-class married couples may be doing well, other parts of the older population are in serious economic straits: women, minorities, and the old-old. The late-life economic troubles women and minorities face are directly tied to their work experiences earlier on. As we saw in Chapter 1, women and minorities earn less, their jobs are less likely to provide pensions, and they tend more often to move in and out of the labor force during their working years—all of which leaves them vulnerable to old-age poverty (Crystal, 1996; O'Rand, 1996; Moen, 1996). The old-old, though they may have entered retirement financially secure, may have spent their assets during their 60s and 70s and have little left at the end of life. Notice in Figure 11-5 the different perspective on life-span poverty we get from looking at the near poor and breaking down the elderly by age. People over age 85 are poorer than children. In fact, old-old women living alone are in worse economic shape than any other group (Burkhauser, 1994).

Our look at these vulnerable groups sounds alarm bells for the elderly to come. The mushrooming numbers of old-old foreshadows more late-life poverty. So does the growth in single parents, women who are likely to enter old age poor. In fact, the real economic problem facing all of us traveling toward later life may lie less in problems with Social Security than in rising income inequality and greater economic vulnerability during our working years (O'Rand, 1996).

WIDOWHOOD

If the loss of the worker role is often remarkably pain-free, this is not true of the central interpersonal loss of later life. Widowhood qualifies as one of life's most wrenching events. In contrast to retirement, which is still more often a male experience, this critical social transition of old age is a female event. In 1995, there were five times as many widows as widowers in the United States. In that year, almost of half of all American women over age 65 were living as widows, whereas widowers made up only 14% of all elderly men (Administration on Aging, 1997). Moreover, as we saw with my grandmother in the previous chapter, a woman's widowhood often lasts for decades. This is because of women's higher life expectancy, plus their tendency to marry older men.

To understand the magnitude of this "attachment loss," once again we begin by taking a step back—exploring our other attachments and the changing quality of this focal adult relationship in recent years.

Setting the Context

OUR CONTINUING CONVOY   Although our spouse is our number one adult attachment figure, we do not enter widowhood in a vacuum. We swim in a sea of social ties as we travel through life.

convoy
Closest social relationships or attachment figures we travel through life with

Gerontologists use the wonderful word **convoy** to describe the salient fish in this social sea, the most important relationships in our lives. The central people in our convoy are immediate family members. However, we also have other relatives and, of course, our friends. Although varying depending on how researchers word the question, studies in a variety of countries suggest that, on average, convoy size is quite constant—hovering between 4 and 8 close attachments in life (Antonucci & Akiyama, 1995). This figure remains fairly stable even at the end of life. In studying community-dwelling people aged 70 to 104, Freider Lang and Laura Carstensen (1994) found that while the *total* social network of this group was about half the size typically reported by younger adults, the number of close convoy members was the about the same. In other words, as the concepts of selective optimization and compensation and socioemotional-selectivity theory predict, in old age we swim in more selective waters: We confine our energies to the most important relationships in life.

Relatives loom large in this convoy in old age and at every age, but friends also remain important fellow travelers even in our oldest years. In longitudinally studying women over 85, Colleen Johnson and Lillian Troll (1994) found that most people still had at least one close friend. However, disability was an impediment, because when a person became ill, it was difficult to maintain the reciprocal giving necessary for friendships to endure. This brings up that interesting relationship distinction—the difference between family and friends (the following is from Antonucci & Akiyama, 1995).

Family members are our first-rank attachments, not only because they are the people we care most about in life but because they are our bottom-line lifeline, the convoy members we depend on for ongoing help in times of need. As we have seen throughout this book, when an older (or younger) person requires ongoing care or instrumental help of any kind, she typically relies on family. Friends are the convoy members selected for pleasant circumstances. They are used for companionship and shared activities, or at most they offer short-term aid.

So, when she needs weekly help with shopping or help paying her bills, a woman turns to her daughter or possibly a sister. When she wants to play cards or have a good long chat, or needs a small loan or a lift to the store, "in a pinch" she calls a friend. In part because of this association with pleasure, the time older people spend with friends is often more uplifting, more unambivalently happy and conflict-free. Another reason why older people (and all people) report more positive experiences with friends is that over time we shed nonfamily convoy members who do not uplift us emotionally. In other words, as in the old saying, we can't choose our family, but we do choose our friends.

We need to keep in mind this convoy cushion and the special functions family and friends serve in exploring how widowed people adjust. In particular, if a person's convoy is unusually small, and especially if it contains few friends, we might predict that the individual will have an especially difficult time coping with the widowed state. In addition, to set the stage for how people cope, we need to look at married life today versus in the past.

CHANGING MARRIAGE   A half century ago, marriage equaled all of adult life. Couples dated briefly and married soon after their teens. Women in particular often went straight to marriage from their parents' home. Once they were wed, a couple stayed together "till death do us part" (Council on Families in America, 1995; Fursten-berg & Cherlin, 1991). Within marriage, gender roles were clearly defined. If a couple was middle class, the wife took care of the housework, and the husband handled the economic side of life (Furstenberg & Cherlin, 1991).

Today, young adults fan out in all directions, typically living on their own for years before they marry. When they do get married, women continue to experience the wider world of work. Although they may not be equal partners (Cowan & Cowan, 1992; Lamb, 1986), particularly when their wives work full time, men share some of the housework and child care. Moreover, with the divorce revolution, more people are entering widowhood having experienced the disruption of marriage at least once already at another point during adult life (Uhlenberg & Miner, 1996).

Today's older people are at an interesting transition point. If they are in their 50s and 60s, they may have been divorced or lived single in their early adult years. Women will have been in the labor force. Men may have much more practice cooking and taking care of the house. However, people who lose a spouse in their 70s or 80s are not likely to have had these training experiences for widowhood. To compound the problem, as we saw in the previous chapter, for many old-old couples a spouse's death ends a shared life that has lasted a half century or more. So, for this segment of older people, widowhood is an unusually wrenching event that involves changing their whole adult way of being.

Being widowed, for everyone, means mourning the loss of a life companion. Even in the most "liberated" relationship, it involves making radical rearrangements in everyday life. Jobs that may have seemed impossible, such as understanding the fi-nances, cooking the meals, or fixing the faucet, fall on the widow or widower. Even waking up takes on new meaning when it is done alone. Relationships with friends may be drastically altered. Many friendships during marriage are based on being part of a couple (Lopata, 1973). Other bonds may weaken, such as relationships with in-laws, the other side of the family. The widowed person must remake an identity whose central focus may have been "married person" for most of adult life. British psychiatrist Colin Parkes (1972), whose research on widows is discussed in the next section, beautifully describes how the world tilts: "Even when words remain the same, their meaning changes. The family is no longer the same as it was. Neither is home or a marriage" (p. 93).

Although the distinction is a bit artificial, widowhood research is often divided into two categories: studies examining the period of active mourning and those probing widowhood as a life state.

Mourning

The first scientific study of mourning was begun after the famous Coconut Grove nightclub fire that suddenly killed several hundred people in Boston in 1942. Psychiatrist Erich Lindemann (1944) decided to interview people who had lost a loved one in the tragedy to explore the symptoms of **normal mourning.**

normal mourning
Typical symptoms of mourning after a loved one has died

In addition to crying or problems eating and sleeping, Lindemann found that mourners were often troubled by guilt, blaming themselves for not doing enough for their loved one. They felt angry at other people, even those they cared about. They were preoccupied by the image of the dead person, at times so intensely they almost hallucinated his or her presence.

These observations were extended by Colin Parkes (1972) in a study of London widows during the first year after losing their spouses. Parkes also found that anger, guilt, and a sense of the loved one's presence were common symptoms of mourning. Some widows showed a total identification with their dead husband. In one woman's words, "My husband is in me right through and through. I can feel him in me doing everything. . . . I suppose he is guiding me all of the time."

Parkes's widows had other unusual symptoms. They were obsessed with the events surrounding the death, repeatedly going over their husband's final hours, his last day. Some reported searching for their spouse, even though they knew intellectually that they were being irrational. British psychiatrist and ethologist John Bowlby (1980) believes this searching behavior is an expression of the instinctive response to separation we see in infancy when the baby crawls after its mother as she is about to leave the room. According to Bowlby, not only is this searching impulse evoked when we lose our most important attachment figure at any time of life, it is not specific to human beings. Consider this poignant observation by the ethologist Konrad Lorenz:

> The first response to the disappearance of the partner consists in the anxious attempt to find him again. The goose moves about restlessly by day and night, flying great distances and visiting places where the partner might be found, uttering all the time the penetrating tri-syllabic call. . . . The searching expeditions are extended further and further and quite often the searcher gets lost; or succumbs to an accident. . . . All the objective, observable characteristics of the goose's behavior on losing its mate are roughly identical with human grief. (as quoted in Worden, 1982, p. 9)

Are these reactions characteristic of mourning? Should we expect them and worry when they do not occur? For answers, we turn to a quantitative investigation probing early widowhood.

In this research, psychologists drew on health department records to recruit several hundred newly widowed people over age 55. Instead of conducting unstructured interviews, they took care to use standard scales of depression and morale and to compare the reactions of their sample with those of a control group of married older adults (Breckenridge, Gallagher, Thompson, & Peterson, 1986).

One of the supposedly normal signs of mourning, intense self-blame, although occurring a certain percentage of the time, was *not* a typical response. Only about one-fourth of the widows and widowers reported any feelings of guilt, and most who did said these feelings were mild. Fewer than 10% showed other signs of anger directed against the self, such as a sense of having failed or feelings of being punished. The three most frequent symptoms people did have were typical reactions to any upsetting experience: crying, a depressed mood, and insomnia.

The researchers suggest their findings show that self-blame is *not* a normal feature of grief. In fact, its presence may indicate that mourning is shading into a true emotional problem, depression. One symptom depressed people may have is irrational guilt, feeling "terrible about myself" (see Chapter 9). These emotions, when intense, suggest that mourning may not be progressing normally, the person is not recovering, and the individual may need professional help. What does progressing normally really mean?

TASK THEORIES OF MOURNING   Counselors who work with bereaved adults traditionally measure the progress of mourning according to certain benchmarks or tasks. Here is psychologist William Worden's (1982) version of the **tasks of mourning**.

tasks of mourning
Benchmarks that must be negotiated to recover from mourning

1. **Accepting the reality of the death.**   Right after the person dies, there is a feeling that it hasn't happened. The new widow may understand the facts intellectually but still feel at any moment she will wake up from a dream. The first task of mourning is to gradually accept the fact that the person has died.

2. **Feeling the pain.**   To get over a loved one's death, the widowed person must accept reality emotionally, confront the painful feelings, mourn deeply and openly.

3. **Adjusting to a new life.**   The person must learn to function in areas the spouse had taken over. A woman must learn how to do the taxes or take out the garbage; a man must learn to prepare his dinner and take care of the house. Eventually, the person must construct a stable, satisfying new life.

4. **Reinvesting emotionally.**   Although it is not necessary to develop a new romantic involvement, it is important to regain the capacity to love in a broader sense. Recovering from mourning means being able to care about life and especially to develop fulfilling attachments to others again.

How long should these tasks take? Worden believes that they should be well under way by the end of one year. Another expert, Therese Rando (1984, 1992–1993), believes that for widows, two or three years is not too long. Still, both thanatologists (death specialists) emphasize that recovery is a relative term. According to Worden, asking when mourning is over is a bit like asking "How high is up?"

Does recovering from mourning depend on feeling the pain? The idea that to recover, a person must do **grief work,** or mourn intensely, has been an accepted principle of bereavement (Rando, 1992–1993; Worden, 1982). On what evidence is this idea based?

In their early studies, Lindemann and Parkes found that people who broke down and experienced the full emotional impact of the death seemed to adjust best to the trauma. People who denied, minimized their feelings, or reacted stoically had the most trouble adjusting to their loss. However, in a more recent study of young widows and widowers, Parkes and Robert Weiss (1983) discovered that people with especially severe emotional reactions had the most trouble recovering. Mourning very intensely was a bad sign!

Margaret Stroebe (1993) argues that our emphasis on the need for grief work is misplaced. In some cultures, giving vent to emotions is seen as pathological. The key to recovering from mourning is dampening grieving, returning quickly to a normal life. In certain situations, as when death was highly traumatic, denial may be the best strategy. At times, distracting the mourner by talking about everything else helps. Counselors need to take a less rigid approach. What works best depends on the situation and the individual.

Bereavement counselors and others may make another error in their efforts to help. Without minimizing the upset, most recent studies show that older widowed people cope quite well (O'Bryant & Hansson, 1995; Pellman, 1992; Zisook & Shuchter, 1991). However, this is not the message we hear from people who actually deal with the bereaved. In comparing widows' and professionals' perceptions of bereavement, Shoshanna Conway, Bert Hayslip, and Ruth Tandy (1991) found that doctors, clergymen, funeral directors, and counselors imagined that widowhood caused incapacitating emotional pain—more difficulty than widows themselves described. Are some people doing the widowed a disservice by assuming they are more devastated and incapable than they really are?

Even the idea that grieving can be fit into defined stages or tasks has been called into question in a longitudinal study of the first two years of bereavement. When researchers interviewed a large sample of elderly widows and widowers at regular times during this period, they found that rather than progressing in an orderly way as task theories imply, mourning was more chaotic. People experienced conflicting emotions and behaviors simultaneously. An example occurred in the tumultuous first few months. At that time, *both* depression and scores on measures of psychological strength were very high. In other words, rather than just feeling "at their worst," people felt a mixture of emotions, both very distressed and also very proud of how they were handling things. Moreover, while there was gradual improvement, there was little truth to the idea there is a defined time when mourning is "complete." At the end of two years, people were still grieving, still actively reconstructing their new life. Along with signs of recovery, some even had symptoms supposedly typical of the first weeks, such as shock, disbelief, and avoidance of the fact (Lund, Caserta, & Dimond, 1986).

Based on these studies, experts now stress the need for a more fluid contextual approach. We must take the concept of stages very loosely. We need to let people grieve in their own best way. It may even be a mistake to use the term recovery from mourning as it implies that people "get over" the relationship or definitively sever the bond with the diseased. The loved one lives on in the emotional life of the survivor, indelibly

Some Influences That May Make Recovery from Mourning Difficult		TABLE 11-3
Previous Factors	**Current Factors**	**Subsequent Factors**
1. Previous convoy losses	1. Mode of death: abrupt	1. Social isolation
2. Weak existing convoy	2. Timing of the death (just when a couple was looking forward to retirement or another happy shared event)	2. Dramatic income loss
3. Being in a highly traditional lifelong marriage		3. Having few new life opportunities
4. Moving to an unfamiliar environment (being an immigrant)		
Ongoing influences include poor mental health, lack of personal resilience, and being male.		

incorporated into that person's identity and evolving life story as she travels through the rest of life (Silverman & Klass, 1996; see also Stella's story in Aging in Action 8-1).

INFLUENCES AFFECTING RECOVERY   This is not to say that we should abandon any effort to chart mourning. After a certain time, we should be concerned if our mother is still setting the table for our dead father, or weeping continually, or unable to find any pleasure in living. It is not appropriate to make mourning a husband a life career.

Table 11-3 suggests that a variety of influences, from previous losses of loved ones (O'Bryant & Straw, 1991) to a history of mental illness (Zisook, Schuchter, & Mulvihill, 1990), may increase the chances that normal mourning will shade into **pathological mourning** or **chronic grief.** Now we turn to two markers that experts have always believed should loom large: gender and the mode or manner of the death.

pathological mourning or chronic grief Active mourning beyond the time when recovery should have occurred

MEN, WOMEN, AND WIDOWHOOD   One widely accepted "widowhood principle" has been that women adjust better than men to the death of a spouse (Rando, 1984; Worden, 1982). The most compelling example has to do with physical health. When Duke University epidemiologists followed several thousand widowed people, they found that whereas widows did not have an elevated death rate, widowers did die more often, both during the first 6 months of bereavement and later on. In fact, a widower's risk of dying returned to normal only if he remarried. In other words, marriage seems critical to health, but only for men!

One reason why widowers in particular may be so vulnerable is that in their role as caregivers, wives guard their husbands' health. Another makes sense in terms of our discussion of the convoy of attachments we carry through life. Recall that social isolation is a risk factor for disease. When men are widowed, they may lose their only really intimate convoy member. Women have closer relationships with family and especially friends to cushion the blow (Antonucci & Akiyama, 1995; Moen, 1996). This is especially true in advanced old age. In longitudinally studying the Berkeley/Oakland parents, Dorothy Field (1997) found that as men reached their old-old years, they became more disinterested in having friends. Not only do friends remain important to older

11-2 Old Friends

The three widows had been close friends for more than 60 years. They met as young parents after the First World War. After the Second World War, as empty-nest couples, they sold their homes and moved to the same apartment complex in town. Rose and Ellie comforted Ann when her husband died in 1964. Ann was there to comfort Rose and Ellie when their husbands passed away. They have supported one another through the deaths of middle-aged children and a daughter's divorce. In recent years, they visited, played cards, and, when they felt up to it, helped one another cook and shop. They called every morning, in Ann's words, to "let each other know we are still alive." Last year, Ann and Rose were worried about Ellie, at 87 the baby. She had had several heart attacks and was in a wheelchair. A few months ago, Ellie died. According to Ann, friends, although never as crucial as family, are important at any age. One of the saddest things about being 96 is that you outlive all your friends.

Gerontologists find that friendships in old age are often enduring relationships, people we have traveled with through decades of life (Antonucci & Akiyama, 1995; Levitt, Weber, & Guacci, 1993). When someone has a friend for 25 or 50 years, that person can really become "like family," there on an ongoing basis to provide help. This is particularly true when an older widowed person's friends are widowed too. In comparing the two types of women, Sally Gallagher and Naomi Gerstel (1993) found that elderly widows reached out more often than wives to offer help to friends. In the researchers' words, marriage "privatizes help-giving" to family. Once they are widowed, women rely on friends to perform the daily nurturing and instrumental functions that had earlier been confined to the marital bond.

women, they can offer a widow special support because they too are likely to be widowed (see Aging in Action 11-2). For elderly women, the widowhood path is predictable, well staked out, smoothed and made easier by those who have gone before. (Recall the high rates of suicide and alcoholism among widowed and old-old men.)

But does widowhood really hit men harder? The longitudinal study of the first 2 years of bereavement discussed previously casts doubt on this belief. When they looked for gender differences in mourning, the researchers were surprised to find that widowers did not have more intense symptoms than widows. Moreover, both men and women recovered at the same rate. Contrary to the idea that men suffer more, this study suggests that the bereavement responses of elderly widows and widowers are identical (Lund et al., 1986). Another large-scale study comparing the grief reactions of several hundred elderly men and women had the same message: *no* gender differences in mourning (Feinson, 1986).

Perhaps, rather than charting overall stress, it may be appropriate to say that men and women have different types of strain. Finances is one area in which women fare worse. Widows have to cope with less income (Bound, Duncan, Laren, & Oleinick, 1991; Holden & Smock, 1991; Holden & Zick, 1997; Morgan, 1991). For widowers, social isolation and loneliness may cause more distress (Umberson, Wortman, & Kessler, 1992). However, as Table 11-3 suggests, with widowhood the best policy is to adopt a contextual approach. Rather than making generalizations, we need to look at the individual person. How flexible emotionally is the widow or widower? Does this woman have enough income to provide a decent life? Does this man's particular convoy offer enough support to cushion the blow? Did the death happen abruptly, or was it an expected event?

ABRUPT VERSUS EXPECTED DEATHS   At the risk of oversimplifying, just as we saw with disability, there are two general pathways to death. Some people die abruptly after a catastrophic event such as an accident, heart attack, or stroke; for others, the end comes expectedly after a period of decline. It seems logical that deaths should be an especially severe blow when they arrive "out of the blue" (O'Bryant, 1990–1991). The bereaved person has no time to prepare emotionally or say good-bye. Fate has swooped in to deliver a random, unexpected blow. With an extended illness, the loss, although painful, is a predictable, on-time event. The person has time to plan for the new, single role. During the final illness, the soon-to-be-widowed spouse can begin emotionally disengaging, retreating from the marriage psychologically in preparation for the loss.

There are compelling reasons why illness in itself would weaken the marital bond. The sick person is self-absorbed, his energy consumed by aches and pains. The well partner's life must totally be rearranged. No longer are a husband and wife fellow travelers sharing life. Their relationship has become stylized, asymmetrical, strained. It is that of patient and nurse. When illness hits a couple, the nursing does fall heavily on the partner's shoulders, even when there are grown children. When a spouse is alive, researchers agree, sons and daughters hold off from really stepping in (Dwyer, 1995; Gatz, Bengtson, & Blum, 1990).

In fact, in their study of older long-married couples discussed in the previous chapter, when Atchley and Miller examined the emotional impact of three changes—retirement, moving (being a recent arrival in the town), and illness—illness was the only stress that had a significant effect. If a husband or wife became ill, the partner's morale declined. Although in this study illness had its greatest impact on men, other researchers have found that having a spouse with health problems is especially likely to affect wives, interfering with their life satisfaction and lowering morale (Quirouette & Gold, 1992).

Notice, however, that these studies are exploring personal happiness, not the intensity of the attachment between a husband and wife. Socioeconomic-selectivity theory would make a different prediction about how these core feelings of closeness change when a spouse becomes seriously ill. Recall that anytime we imagine an important relationship ending, we try to maximize the emotional quality of the here and now. The clear implication is that couples should become *more* attached to one another as they realize that their time together is drawing to a close.

Actually, when a spouse needs caregiving, elderly husbands and wives shoulder the job alone. They are reluctant to rely on formal sources of help (Penning, 1990). Spousal care is extensive, occurring for months or years before placement in a nursing home (Montgomery & Kosloski, 1994). Husbands and wives take on the burden with a freer heart, reporting less ambivalence, conflict, and stress than caregiving daughters or sons (Belsky, 1994). When researchers studied husband and wife caregivers for Alzheimer's patients, one-fourth of the men reported that nursing their wife intensified their feelings of closeness and increased their sense of love (Fitting, Rabins, Lucas, & Eastham, 1986). Colleen Johnson and Joseph Catalano (1983) use the term *enmeshing* to describe this process. As a spouse needs more care, couples reduce their outside involvements, withdraw from friends and relatives, and turn inward to the marriage to satisfy all their needs.

So, knowing in advance may be a double-edged sword. True, it makes planning more possible, but it may also heighten the irreplaceable quality of what will be lost.

Life as a Widowed Person

Mourning, the active phase of grief, tells us little about people who live day to day in "the widowed state." To examine these day-to-day experiences, we have the rich insights of two classic studies by sociologist Helena Lopata (1973, 1979). Lopata studied Chicago widows over age 50, women who had been widows an average of 11 years. Because Chicago has such a rich ethnic mix, many of her subjects were first-generation immigrants; others were more Americanized.

Lopata found that most women were living alone. Widows complained of being lonely but often said they preferred this to moving in with adult children. Not only did they enjoy the freedom, they were afraid conflict would be inevitable if they were to move in with a child. This spirit of self-reliance extended to finances. Although more than half reported their income had dropped dramatically after their husband's death, few widows wanted financial help from relatives.

For many of these widows, their identity as wife had been central to their adult lives. One-fifth felt that they had never really gotten over their husband's death. However, most said they did not want to remarry, mentioning, among other reasons, their age, fear that they would have to take care of a sick husband (1 out of 6 had nursed their husband at home for at least a year before his death), and their belief that they could never find a man as good as their late spouse. This last reason for not marrying is particularly interesting because it demonstrated a process Lopata calls sanctification. Many widows put their late husband on a pedestal, enshrining his memory and idealizing their marriage as total bliss.

Their current attachments were more conflict-ridden. Although children were the most important figures in widows' lives, as we might imagine from what we know about adult/adult family relationships, these relationships were not always close. For many widows, friends were not a support. Half said they never went to places such as movie theaters; 4 in 10 never entertained. The same fraction reported that they always ate lunch alone. Although lack of money probably played a part in restricting these widows, their answers show that many were living isolated, solitary lives.

The least-educated, immigrant widows were most susceptible to social isolation. Lopata suggests that the traditional lifestyle these women had before being widowed was partly to blame because it stressed being totally dependent on the marriage and centering everything around their immediate family. Traditional women, she argues, could only be happy when their environment remained the same. When being widowed meant having to construct a new life, these women were unprepared to cope.

Another study shows that for old-old widowers, life without a spouse can be equally hard. As part of a qualitative exploration of the lives of men over age 70 living alone, anthropologist Robert Rubinstein (1986; see Aging in Action 2-2) questioned 25 widowers about their activities, relationships, life satisfaction, and loneliness. Most were floundering, clinging to the past, unable to form new satisfying relationships. These men had trouble finding focus for their hours, living day by day. In Hazel Markus's framework, the problem was that these men had *no* possible selves. Their whole identity was locked up in the person they used to be.

> Freddy Williams is age 71. . . . Almost all of his time is spent indoors. . . . His grief for his wife [is] . . . very much on the surface. . . . Although he lives in a three-story house . . . he spends most of his day . . . in the living room . . . set up as a . . . day room and museum for her. . . . On one wall is her picture. . . . "Sometimes, even now I'll look up at that and start to cry." . . . My wife . . . she had a good sense of humor. Since she died, that's something I've lost all of. . . . Life stinks sometimes. . . . Day after day, I have nothing to do. . . . I sit here, look out the window. The feelings are real, real deep in you, deep inside" (Rubinstein, 1986, pp. 99–100).

> John O'Brien, 77 years old, has been widowed for about two and a half years. . . . He spends most of his time almost entirely in the downstairs living room because the stairs are difficult for him to climb and, moreover, because "there are too many memories up there." He has left the house "exactly the way it was when my wife died." . . . He is living in a world largely shaped by the memories of his wife. For him much of the meaning of his current life is derived from the past. (p. 103)

For the 11 men Rubinstein judged to be adjusting well, the main key was developing a new relationship—almost always another woman to replace the spouse. In other words, for these widowers, the existing convoy was too fragile to provide the basis for a meaningful life. They had to develop a new, life-reviving attachment to give purpose to their days.

These studies paint an arid portrait, suggesting that many older people never recover from this central life loss. However, remember that Lopata and Rubinstein were examining the most vulnerable people—traditional, old-world women, and old-old widowers living alone. Many men do remarry or develop a satisfying relationship with another woman after being widowed (O'Bryant & Hansson, 1995). Although widowed women are likely to live on without a partner, recent research contradicts the gloomy portrait Lopata paints.

Women get support from other family members to compensate for losing their husband (Avis, Brambilla, Vass, & McKinlay, 1991; Dean, Matt, & Wood, 1992). These family relationships are critically important even though, as we saw with Lopata's women, they cause strain as well as pleasure (Morgan, 1989; O'Bryant & Hansson, 1995). In addition, as we saw in Aging in Action 11-2, friendships endure and may become more instrumental in focus after a husband's death (Connidis & Davies, 1992).

National studies show that many women thrust into poverty by widowhood exit this state even without remarrying, implying that widows today *do* have the skills to enter the work world (Bound et al., 1991). Today's nonimmigrant widows have been socialized differently than Lopata's traditional women. Especially if they are middle-aged or young-old, women often enter widowhood armed with the previous life experiences and inner resources to construct a new life (O'Bryant & Straw, 1991).

Interventions

Our discussion suggests that the best intervention for widowhood is prevention: developing a rewarding, socially rich, multifaceted life. As Paul Costa would say, there is continuity between who we are before being widowed and who we will be afterward.

widowed persons'
services
Supportive services
to aid widows and
widowers

On a more immediate level, **widowed persons' services** ease the transition to this life state. These services, sponsored by churches, human service agencies, and the AARP offer seminars for widows and widowers, operate telephone hotlines, or have widowed volunteers make home visits to the newly bereaved. As described in Aging in Action 11-3, all of these programs sponsor self-help groups in which people come together to discuss their difficulties and concerns.

Michael Caserta and Dale Lund (1993) conducted an outcome study of the effectiveness of these groups. They led sessions for new widows and widowers and examined the mental health of participants before entering and at regular intervals for 2 years after.

Interestingly, the sessions were helpful only for men and women with the lowest competence—people who entered widowhood with the poorest self-esteem, life satisfaction, and mental health. For people with high emotional resilience, during the first 8 weeks, the groups actually produced *more* depression than before. The lesson is that assuming widowhood is an impossible trauma for everyone can have negative effects. It may only be helpful to "prescribe" widowhood counseling when older people have a good deal of trouble coping with this late-life event on their own.

Widowed persons' groups have a focused mission, helping people cope emotionally with this specific life change. Yet Lopata's and Rubinstein's studies reveal that the problem is larger. It revolves around coping with living alone. For this reason, we end our discussion by focusing on that central social condition associated with the transition from marriage: living alone.

Old and Living Alone

In 1995, about 30% of the over-65 population lived alone. Figure 11-6 confirms what we might expect: Far more older women than older men live alone (Administration on Aging, 1997).

There are a variety of pathways apart from being widowed by which older people arrive at living alone. Some older adults live alone because they never married or are divorced (3% and 6% of community-dwelling elders in 1995); some have chosen this lifestyle as a lifelong pattern; others have been thrust into living alone by the death of a parent, child, sibling, or friend. There are rural elders and city dwellers; millionaires in mansions and those living by themselves in poverty and poor health; people enmeshed in close convoys and those who live alone anonymous and isolated, with no visible social supports. All of these contextual influences affect the experience of being old and living alone.

11-3 Widowed Persons' Group

The fourth Sunday of each month, the Widowed Persons' Group meets at a local church. The day I visited, there were a dozen people present: three new widows, a widower, and seven widow volunteers. Florence Johnson, the coordinator, begins the meeting.

We have a few new folks today, so let's go around the room and say our names. Dr. Belsky, the people on the couches are volunteers who have gone through our training program. We send every newly widowed person in the community a letter about a month after the death, tell them about our service, and that a volunteer will contact them. A widowed person who has gone through our training then calls and asks if they want to talk. People are invited to come to this Sunday group or to our informal Friday lunches. We also publish a newsletter every two months. Our program is flexible. People can get fully involved or simply be on our mailing list. Many of the volunteers here were helped by our service and decided that they wanted to help someone else. Now, what do you want to ask us?

What are some things that are hardest for you?

"I've noticed that even when I'm in a crowd, I'm lonely."
"I find the weekends and evenings hard, especially now that it gets dark so early."
"Sundays are my worst. You sit in church by yourself. People avoid you when you are a widow."
"I think the hardest is when you had a handyman and then you lose your handyman. You'd be amazed at how much fixing there is that you didn't know about. My hardest jobs were George's jobs. For instance, every time I have a car problem, I break down and cry."
"I was married to a handyman and a cook. He spoiled me rotten. You don't realize it until they're gone."
"For me, its the incessant doctor bills. I got one yesterday. It's that continual painful reminder of the death."
"And you get all this stuff from Medicare, from Social Security. This year will be the last I file with him."
"They were going to shut my electricity off. They sent me this letter months ahead of time, and then you set it aside and forget it."
"You just don't know what to do. I didn't know anything, didn't know how much money we had, didn't know about the insurance. . . . My friends would help out but, you know it's funny, you don't ask."
"You have friends, but you can't really talk to them. You don't bring him up, and neither does anyone else."
"The thing that upsets me is that I'm scared that no one but me will really remember that he was alive."

Statistically speaking, however, people living alone are a more vulnerable group. Simply by virtue of not being married, they are more likely to be old-old and poor. Although less likely to have functional impairments than their counterparts who live

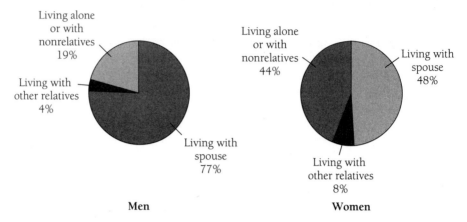

Living alone
or with
nonrelatives
19%

Living with
other relatives
4%

Living with
spouse
77%

Men

Living alone
or with
nonrelatives
44%

Living with
spouse
48%

Living with
other relatives
8%

Women

Women are much more likely to live alone (or with nonfamily members) in later life.
SOURCE: Administration on Aging, 1997.

with children (Coward, Lee, Dwyer, & Seccombe, 1993), people who live alone are more at risk of entering a nursing home when they do get ill. As we saw in Chapter 4, many have lived in the same place for decades, meaning their housing may be ill suited to their needs, no longer person/environment congruent. The wider environment may be far from user friendly. In a rural area, there is the issue of geographic separation, of living too far from family and friends, from shopping and other services. In a city, the outside world may be actively hostile because the neighborhood may have become more dangerous over the years (Pynoos & Golant, 1996).

Once again, anthropologist Robert Rubinstein has gone beyond the statistics to provide compelling insights into the human experience of living alone in later life. Building on his research focusing on elderly men, Rubinstein's research team ventured into some of Philadelphia's worst neighborhoods to conduct interviews with the most disadvantaged elders living alone, people with functional impairments and marginal financial resources. (The average annual income of the people the research team studied was $7000 to $8000.)

These forays uncovered some horrors surpassing the worst institutional abuse. There was Mrs. Kellahan, whose living space was a tiny room filled with cockroaches and mice, who could not use the electricity for fear of a fire or wash herself because the pipes might burst, and who spent her days in a fetal position lying half naked in the bed. There was Mrs. Turner, incontinent, with heart disease and chronic shortness of breath, who had not ventured out of the house for months out of fear and whose drug-dealing next-door neighbors kept her up all hours of the night. However, once we look beyond appearances, the portrait sketched in these riveting case histories is more complex than we might think.

Although their lifestyle was in large part forced, most people said they *wanted* to live alone. Half reported that being alone rarely or never made them feel lonely. A surprising 71% said that living alone did not bother them at all. For one thing, people derived tremendous solace from being in their own home. It is not just that one's home is familiar territory. According to the researchers, these living spaces anchor identity. Photographs, furniture, the well-known spaces make the home a palpable, physical extension of the self. This sense of being "at home" (at one with the environment) was enhanced by the sense of freedom, the opportunity to exercise what Rubinstein beautifully labels "choices writ small." In the words of one man in continual pain from chronic arthritis,

> I hope I can stay independent for the rest of my life. That's the one thing I am hoping for. . . . You're free, you know. You want to lay down, you lay down. You want to sleep, you sleep. You want to go out, you go out. . . . I love it [my home]. There's nothing like it. Like I said, I got everything here. . . . I got my refrigerator. I got food. . . . I got the geri-chair. I got the hospital bed. I got my TV. (Rubinstein et al., 1992, p. 181)

Echoing socioemotional-selectivity theory, this man took pleasure in the immediate moment, enjoying his daily routine, inhaling the textures and sights of his living space. Following Heckhausen and Schulz's life-span model of successful aging, by downscaling his goals and modifying his feelings, despite being almost housebound, he felt an immense sense of self-efficacy, the feeling of being in control of his life.

This is not to whitewash this older adult's circumstances or those of other people the research team interviewed. Their lives were precarious. They could have benefited from much more help. The researchers were particularly disturbed by the noninvolvement of the wider community. When asked to list everyone they relied on, people rarely mentioned neighbors or formal sources of aid. These older adults were coping as best they could, but they were also being forced to go it on their own in their season of need. How fair is it, asked the researchers, for the wider culture to withdraw in the name of individual freedom, to turn its head and let people negotiate life's difficulties alone? Doesn't more attention need to be paid to how we as a society can provide structures that are more responsive to people experiencing life's most stressful events? This same imperative to fit social structures to human needs looms large in the next chapter, as we turn to that final stressful transition of later life: death.

KEY TERMS

Age discrimination in
  Employment Act (ADEA)
age-integrated society

blurred transitions
convoy
displaced workers

Elderhostel
entitlement programs
grief work

intergenerational equity
mandatory retirement policies
means-tested benefits
near poor
normal mourning
old-age dependency ratio

pathological mourning or
   chronic grief
pensions
real income
Social Security
Social Security Act

tasks of mourning
traditional stable career
widening income inequality
widowed persons' services

RECOMMENDED READINGS

RETIREMENT (AND ASSOCIATED TOPICS)

General Sources

AARP Public Policy Institute, Washington, DC
   This arm of the AARP is a veritable treasure trove of information, publishing a host of short "Data Digests" and more in-depth position papers covering topics as diverse as income and poverty in the elderly, discrimination in the workforce, older worker performance, proposals to reform Social Security, and retirement trends.

Social Security Administration, Washington, DC
   This agency is also a terrific general source for information on retirement-related issues ranging from Social Security to labor-force trends to poverty and the economic status of the elderly. One especially interesting publication traces the evolution of Social Security and other income-maintenance programs and clearly spells out the various U.S. entitlement programs.

Specific Publications

Bengston, V. L., & Achenbaum, A. (Eds.). (1993). *The changing contract between generations.* New York: Aldine De Gruyter.
   This book covers intergenerational equity and intergenerational issues from a variety of perspectives. It shows that even gerontologists are divided on the question of whether today's elderly are being unfairly benefited compared with the young.

Financial dimensions of aging. (1997, Summer). *Generations, 21.*
   Once again, this issue is a terrific source for income-related aging issues. Articles cover Social Security, the baby boomers and retirement, the economic status of the elderly, and other topics.

The future of age-based public policy. (1995, Fall). *Generations, 19.*
   This issue of *Generations* covers intergenerational equity and age-based public programs. Different articles explore topics ranging from the evolution of the welfare state, to Social Security, to Medicaid and Medicare, to pension programs.

Morris, R., & Bass, S. (Eds.). (1988). *Retirement reconsidered.* New York: Springer.
   This edited book includes articles relating to social policy, politics, older workers, and retirement.

Peterson, P. (1993). *Facing up: How to restore the economy from crushing debt and restore the American dream.* New York: Simon and Schuster.
   This compelling, readable book is dedicated to the thesis that we are destroying our children's future by deficit spending, middle-class subsidies, and inflated benefits to the old.

Quadagno, J., & Hardy, M. (1996). Work and retirement. In R. H. Binstock, & L. K. George (Eds.). *Handbook of aging and the social sciences* (4th ed.) (pp. 325–345). San Diego: Academic Press.
   This review article thoroughly covers workforce changes affecting older people, the evolution of retirement, and retirement trends. (Other articles in this basic reference in social gerontology cover subjects such as the economic status of the elderly and our increasingly age-integrated society.)

WIDOWHOOD

Klass, D., Silverman, P. R., & Nickman, S. (Eds.). (1996). *Continuing bonds: New understandings of grief.* Washington, DC: Taylor and Francis.
   Chapters in this book, dealing with losses ranging from widowhood to adoption, spell out the new con-

ception of mourning as an individualized process in which the mourner gradually incorporates a continuing attachment to the lost person into ongoing life.

Lopata, H. Z. (1972). *Widowhood in an American city.* Cambridge, MA: Schenkman.

Lopata, H. Z. (1979). *Women as widows: Support systems.* Cambridge, MA: Schenkman.
Lopata's studies of widows are classics in the field.

Rubinstein, R. (1986). *Singular paths: Old men living alone.* New York: Columbia University Press.

Rubinstein, R., Kilbride, S., & Nagy, S. (1992). *Elders living alone.* Hawthorne, NY: Aldine, De Gruyter.
These two books are great favorites of mine. Rubinstein's first book explores that forgotten group, single men living alone; the second offers a vivid portrait of people living poor and disabled by themselves.

Chapter Outline

12

Death and Dying

🌹 *My father seemed to lead a physically charmed life. Unlike many men approaching 80, his mind was sharp; he played golf; he traveled, with no problems, around the world. Though he often joked about being an "old man," he had no infirmities. We joked that he must be immortal when a random checkup revealed just one clogged coronary artery and emergency bypass surgery saved him from a massive heart attack to live on, at 79, with the arteries of "a young man."*

Two years later, my father's luck ran out. For a few months, he had been listless, not his old self, suddenly looking old. Then came the unforgettable call: "The doctor says it's cancer of the liver. Jan, I'm going to die."

Because medicine never immediately admits defeat, the plan was three monthly rounds of chemotherapy, punctuated by "recovery" at home. The recovery never happened. My father got weaker. After a few months, he could barely walk. Then, right before going into the hospital for the third round, my mother called. "Last night your father and I cried together and decided not to continue. We're calling in hospice. I think it's time for you to come down."

The day or two before you die, you go into a coma. It's the week or so before that lasts for years. Everyone has been summoned, to bustle aimlessly around a train that cannot be derailed. First comes the insertion of the catheter that everyone knows will never be re-moved. Then, as if on cue, the disease picks up speed. From the wheelchair to becoming bedfast, the voice that mutates into a whisper, the diapers, hallucinations that make sleep impossible at any hour. Toward the end of the week, you make a final visit to the doctor, who predicts "It will be Monday or Tuesday at most." You hope that the doctor is right. You cannot bear to see those intelligent eyes imprisoned, fully conscious, in that shell hurtling to the end.

When we think of life's most terrifying experiences, nothing seems to equal confronting imminent death. Although my father was certainly not happy during the months from his diagnosis until he died, it was only in the final week or two that the balance tipped, he gave up, and, for him, being dead was preferable to the pain of continued life. In this chapter, we look at how people feel when on their own personal train to death. We focus on the issue of choosing to live or die that looms so large in contemporary discussions about terminal disease. We trace how we as a society got to the point where my father could be informed about what was happening and could die at home rather than in the hospital hooked up to machines. But before discussing these topics relating to the dying process, we take a step back to explore **death anxiety**—the thoughts, fears, and emotions about that final event of living that we experience under more normal conditions of life.

DEATH ANXIETY

To examine how often we think of death when we are healthy, researchers interrupted people of various ages and asked them what they had been thinking about within the past 5 minutes (Cameron, Stewart, & Biber, 1973). Then, they asked directly about death. Had the thought crossed the person's mind? Subjects were approached at different times of day and in different settings, such as in school or at home, and asked to rate their current mood. Would the thought of death occur more frequently in certain situations or at certain times?

The frequency of death thoughts did not vary by time and place. Nor did they occur when people were feeling sad, but they were equally likely to arise in connection with a variety of moods. Age differences appeared only in the percentage of people reporting that the idea of death had fleetingly crossed their minds. In contrast to our belief that older people dwell more on this topic, adolescents and young adults thought just as often about death as the elderly. In fact, an astonishing one-fifth of the men and one-fourth of the women said the idea had crossed their minds at least once during the preceding 5-minute period.

In asking directly about death, perhaps the researchers prompted their subjects to falsely "remember" having this thought. Also, these people were simply being asked about the thought "death." As we saw in exploring life review reminiscing as well as in socioemotional-selectivity theory, even if the *specific* thought may not come to mind more frequently, older adults' overall consciousness seems more death-oriented, more attuned to the finite quality of their lives. But what about the puzzling finding that thoughts of death were associated with positive as well as negative moods? Shouldn't this idea cross our minds mainly when we are upset or depressed? In fact, when other researchers asked adults to rate a wide range of concepts for pleasantness, death ranked dead last (Kogan & Wallach, 1961).

However, in addition to being the worst imaginable thought, death can be viewed, as in Erikson's theory, as an event that is natural and acceptable after having lived a full life. It can even have uplifting connotations: Death is the moment we authentically confront life stripped to its essentials; it is the time to meet God; it is when we are reunited with loved ones that have gone before (Ross & Pollio, 1991).

Research on dreams suggests that joyous feelings can sometimes be associated with images of death. Deidre Barrett (1988–1989) catalogued several hundred college students' dreams relating to death. Although dreams of dying ("A stranger is about to shoot me") were often nightmarish, dreams of *being* dead were usually inspirational:

I begin to float up an arch-like rainbow. . . . it was so beautiful. . . . The whole time the dream was going on, I felt better than I ever have in my whole life.

The clock hands pointed to 12 and suddenly I had a dizzying rush. My mother and I turned into pure energy, pure light. We could go anywhere, free of our bodies. (p. 99)

Barrett's study suggests that, as with any other life event, we cannot take a simplistic approach to death. Feelings about death are multifaceted. They should be measured by multidimensional approaches. As we just saw, one distinction relates to what happens after versus before (Buhler, 1995; Gesser, Wong, & Reker, 1987–1988). Some people may be terrorized by the thought of *being* dead; others of dying, of suffering the pain of terminal disease. Probing death anxiety may require using nontraditional measures such as dreams, because feelings and attitudes revealed through these indirect techniques may offer information we might not get by simply asking people, "How fearful are you of death?" The need for this complex strategy becomes apparent as we look at research specifically exploring the connections among age, illness, religious faith, and anxieties about our own death.

Predicting Death Anxiety

THE IMPACT OF AGE   Do fears of death grow more intense in old age? Our immediate impulse would be to say of course, because older people are so close in life to that event. But remember that Erikson would suggest the reverse: In later life, we have tasted what the world can offer and lived our full share. Older people should view death in a calmer, more accepting way because at their stage in the life cycle dying is natural, appropriate, and right. In one author's words (Rando, 1984):

The dying young adult is filled with rage and anger for the interruption of her life at the moment of its fulfillment. . . . There is frustration, rage, and a sense of unfairness and of being cheated. The patient holds onto life more tenaciously than at any other age. The losses are now especially acute, as the patient will never see the promise for self and significant others (especially children) fulfilled. (p. 246)

Most of us do feel that dying young is more tragic than dying after a full life (Callahan, 1994; Jecker & Schneiderman, 1994; Madey & Chasteen, 1997). When researchers asked subjects to rank imaginary people for priority to receive a life-preserving kidney transplant, this age gradient was clear (Busschbach, Hessing, & Charro, 1993). Notice in Figure 12-1 that after age 10, when we might imagine the recipient could survive for a long time, the young were first in line. Moreover, the older people and the young adults agreed: Preserving life in a young person far outweighs preserving life at age 60, after a full life.

This norm is reflected in what people of different ages say about their own death. Often, as Erikson would predict, elderly people report the least fear (Gesser, Wong, & Reker, 1987–1988; Kastenbaum & Costa, 1977). On the other hand, comparing age groups is misleading. As we know, this cohort of elderly grew up before the 1960s, when openly admitting anxieties became the norm. Particularly when today's old-old adults were young, people were supposed to keep a "stiff upper lip" and not bring up "inappropriate" topics such as death. The biasing impact of this norm of self-disclosure

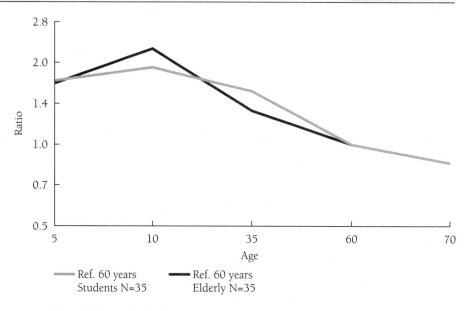

Young adults and older people clearly agree about the value they put on having the chance for a healthy life; the young should be given priority compared with the old.
SOURCE: Busschbach, Hessing, & Charro, 1993.

was highlighted in a study comparing the responses of college students in the 1930s and in 1991 to an *identical* death anxiety scale (Lester & Becker, 1992–1993). The Depression-era students' scores were lower, suggesting that one reason we find age differences in anxiety today may be that this cohort of older adults were *always* less likely to admit being afraid of death.

Older people may not want to admit fear to themselves. Psychoanalysts might say that we are all frightened of dying, but to some people the idea is so intolerable that they deny any fear. To really explore death anxiety, we must go beyond simple, on-the-surface questions to probe fear in a more covert, indirect way (Handal, Peal, Napoli, & Austrin, 1984–1985; Hayslip & Stewart-Bussey, 1986–1987; Guarnaccia & Hayslip, 1997).

When researchers gave three tests of death anxiety, varying from self-report to progressively less conscious fear, to adults of different ages, they did find different degrees of anxiety. When asked directly, most people denied being afraid of death. When instructed to fantasize, their imagery showed mainly ambivalence. On the final, "deepest" scale, a test in which they were asked to give their associations to emotion-laden words, their answers showed frank fear. On the tests of more conscious anxiety, the elderly scored less fearful, but at this most unconscious level, older subjects ranked just as fearful as anyone else (Feifel & Branscomb, 1973). So, especially the elderly may be more apprehensive about death than they admit.

Even if having lived a full life reduces fears about our life's ending, it should do little to touch anxieties about the dying process. Therese Rando (1984) speculates that while the fear of being dead is at a low ebb in old age, the fear of dying becomes more intense: Who will take care of me? Will I suffer greatly? Will I be a burden to those I love? Will I die alone?

In fact, as socioemotional-selectivity theory and the life review concept predict, because they may have thought more deeply about this life event, the elderly have especially rich, varied conceptions centering around death (Tomer, Eliason, & Smith, 1997). Capturing these multifaceted feelings through quantitative scales ranking "anxiety" at a single point in time may not make much sense. Moreover, when older people are healthy, like any one of us immersed in living, we would not expect them to be especially concerned about death. Why, at any age, should we spend time agonizing about a hazy, future event? The day when anxiety should really strike is when that event looms on the horizon as a present reality—when, as with my father, an older person (or any person) has a life-threatening disease. Age may not be a sufficient condition, but surely having a fatal disease must intensify fears of death.

Life-Threatening Illness

Amazingly, even this logical assumption has been difficult to prove. Although some studies do show that people with illnesses such as cancer or AIDS get higher scores on death anxiety scales, often their anxiety ratings are average or even very low (Dougherty, Templer, & Brown, 1986). One reason, as we will see later in this chapter, is that people coping with terminal illness also experience a variety of emotions, from fear to peace to depression to hope. Death anxiety varies as a function of overall personality—whether a person is generally anxious or not (Hintze, Templer, Cappelletty, & Frederick, 1993). Finally, exploring death anxiety even among the seriously ill may require going beyond direct measures of fear.

Bert Hayslip, Debra Luhr, and Michael Beyerlein (1991–1992) examined death anxiety among HIV-positive men through both direct questions and a sentence-completion test of fear. When directly asked, the men did not rank high in anxiety, but on the test exploring less conscious anxiety, their scores were elevated compared with those of a group of healthy men. As the researchers conclude, even when facing death, people seem to deny its emotional impact, making self-reports an inadequate, not genuinely valid method of assessing fear (Earl, Martindale, & Cohn, 1991–1992).

Religious Faith

A third influence that should logically affect death anxiety among the elderly, and people of any age, is religious faith. Although, as Aging in Action 12-1 shows, religion has other vital purposes, isn't one central function of the belief in God to transform death from a hated end into a transition to a better state?

12-1 Religion: Late-Life Medicine for Health?

Mr. Jones, a 102-year-old African American man, attributes his amazingly long life to religious faith. He grew up in the church and attended services several times a week from the time he was a child. Mr. Jones knows he must go to heaven soon. Although appreciative that the Lord has allowed him to reach this age, he is looking forward to the transition to come. (Some of the following ideas are from T. R. Johnson, 1995; Krause, 1997; and McFadden, 1995.)

Fifty years ago, one gerontologist observed that faith in God was second only to good health as the key to aging well. Until recently, however, perhaps because the two seem so incompatible, researchers shied away from using the tools of science to probe the importance of religion in late life. This reluctance is especially strange because, as with Mr. Jones, religion is obviously crucial to many older adults. In a recent survey conducted by the Princeton Religion Center, 76% of older Americans rated religion as very important in their lives, compared with 44% of young adults. Moreover, this difference is not simply a cohort effect. Longitudinal research confirms our intuitive sense that people do grow more religious as they age.

There are many reasons, apart from easing fears of death, why people would turn to religion in their older years. With its emphasis on inner qualities, on looking beyond physical appearances to find the key to human worth, and its injunction to "honor thy father and thy mother," religion is the one institution in society that steadfastly values and elevates later life. People use religion to cope with major life losses—the kinds of problems, such as illness or widowhood, that we experience more often as we grow old. When a person is in the hospital or has lost a spouse, religion reaches out in a visible, concrete sense, offering aid and social support. Religion also provides a forum for older people to be *nonneedy* or involved in the world. Most churches and synagogues sponsor senior citizens groups offering everything from luncheons to exercise to lectures to trips. Church-related charity work gives older members the chance to give to others in need. And if we agree with Laura Carstensen that as we age, we focus more on life's emotional essentials, it makes sense that people would naturally gravitate to religion in their older years. As the setting for critical events in our past—marriage, baptism, our bar mitzvah—and with its familiar rituals, the church or synagogue is rich in emotional meaning, replete with lifelong memories, symbolic of our most emotionally central experiences in life.

Today, now that organizations as scientifically pure as the National Institute on Aging are funding research probing the importance of religion, we are discovering that Mr. Jones and that early gerontologist were right. Religious involvement does seem to be a potent late-life medicine, linked to a wide variety of emotional and physical benefits in old age.

This too makes good scientific sense. Apart from the social support and inspiration regular churchgoing provides, religion offers people built-in emotional armor for coping with life. In other words, using Heckhausen and Schulz's framework, religion provides the ultimate in a sense of secondary control.

Religion becomes especially focal at the end of life. At this Geriatric Center in Florida serving the Jewish elderly, the ritual lighting of the candles offers residents solace, the sense of participating in a timeless tradition, and a feeling of still having control—all emotions that can reduce disability and depression, and possibly even extend life.

Many studies do show that people who are religious report fearing their own and loved ones' deaths less (Powell & Thorson, 1991; P. C. Smith, Range, & Ulmer, 1991–1992). Religious people are more likely to describe death in positive terms as a "portal" rather than a wall (Ross & Pollio, 1991; Westman & Brackney, 1990). The dramatic protection religion can provide against fear was revealed in a study of younger people facing possible death. Among a group of Israeli soldiers serving in a war, having had a life-threatening experience heightened death anxiety if a soldier was not religious; but if the person had a strong religious faith, the same event had a minimal impact on fear (Florian & Mikulincer, 1993).

However, not all studies find that older people who are religious score lower on death anxiety scales! As Lita Buhler (1995) concluded in reviewing this research, to make sense of the contradictions, again it is helpful to distinguish between different components of fear. Buhler found that although older people who were religious reported less fear of what happens *after* death, they were no less afraid of the process of dying.

Our in-depth look at death anxiety once again illustrates the hurdles researchers face in measuring what appear to be the simplest facets of personality. It shows that even in this area of life, it is important to adopt the multifaceted, contextual point of view. The need to avoid sweeping generalizations and prescriptions is even more crucial as we turn to the main topic of this chapter: dying.

DYING

Your university probably has a course devoted to death and dying. You would not have been able to take such a course 30 years ago. As was true of that other taboo topic, sexuality, people used to avoid mentioning or studying death. It took the events of the late 1960s to bring dying out of the shadows (Kastenbaum & Costa, 1977). The revolution that emphasized openness and self-determination in so many areas of life produced an explosion of interest in death.

During the 1970s, death and dying not only became a hot topic at universities, but changing the way we treat the terminally ill became an activist cause. We can see the latest expression of the "death with dignity" movement in Dr. Kervorkian and his suicide machine. We turn now to the research that produced this movement—the classic and more contemporary studies that have altered and continue to shape how we approach the terminally ill. Although much of this research on dying delves into the experiences of people across the age spectrum, it is especially relevant to our age group because it is older adults who typically undergo this final passage of life.

The Person

stages of death theory
Kubler-Ross's idea that the terminally ill go through distinct emotional stages in coping with impending death

KUBLER-ROSS'S STAGES OF DEATH   A watershed in the movement to humanize dying occurred in the late 1960s with Elizabeth Kubler-Ross's famous **stages of death theory,** which suggests that we progress through defined phases in coming to terms with being terminally ill. In working as a psychiatrist in a general hospital, Kubler-Ross became convinced that the medical staff was neglecting the emotional needs of the terminally ill. As part of a seminar for medical students, she got permission to interview dying patients. Whereas the staff was resistant, the interviewees had a different response. Many were relieved to talk openly. To everyone's surprise, many knew their prognosis, even though an effort had been made to conceal the facts. Dr. Kubler-Ross published her discovery that open communication was important to the dying in *On Death and Dying,* a slim best-seller that offered a powerful indictment of terminal care.

Kubler-Ross (1969) believes that people progress through five stages in coming to terms with impending death: denial, anger, bargaining, depression, and acceptance.

When the person first hears the diagnosis, the response is "There must be some mistake." Denial is accompanied by the quest for contradictory evidence, the visit to specialist after specialist searching for a different diagnosis and a new, more positive set of tests. When these efforts fail, denial gives way to anger.

In this stage, the person lashes out, bemoaning fate and railing at loved ones. The patient castigates his doctors as uncaring and insensitive. He gets furious at his father, who is still alive. The idea "I am dying" is so unfair! Eventually, this reaction yields to a more calculating one: bargaining.

In this stage, the person pleads for more time, promising to be "good" if death can be put off a bit, trying to strike a deal with God. Kubler-Ross (1969, p. 83) invokes this example of a woman who begged God to let her live long enough to attend the marriage of her oldest son:

> The day preceding the wedding she left the hospital as an elegant lady. Nobody would have believed her real condition. She . . . looked radiant. I

wondered what her reaction would be when the time was up for which she had bargained. . . . I will never forget the moment she returned to the hospital. She looked tired and somewhat exhausted and before I could say hello, said, "Now don't forget I have another son."

When this reaction subsides, it is replaced by the fourth stage, depression. Then, usually immediately preceding death, this response gives way to acceptance. By this time, the person, quite weak, is neither upset, angry, nor depressed. The patient awaits death calmly, looking forward to the end.

Kubler-Ross never envisioned these stages as a straitjacket, a blueprint for the "correct" way to die. Unfortunately, her theory was sometimes used in this way. Over-enthusiastic counselors might label people abnormal if their responses did not fit into the five-stage sequence. Some even tried to hurry terminally ill people from stage to stage! By now, we should know that human beings do not react in a rigidly patterned way to *any* life stress. In this case, such an approach can be dangerous because it justifies distancing ourselves and negating an ill person's feelings. Rather than under-standing that depression in a person facing death is appropriate, seeing it as a "phase" encourages us to view this emotion through a clinical lens, as somehow not real. Legitimate complaints about doctors, family, or friends can be discounted, passed off as "predictable" signs of the anger stage. So, most experts view this effort to chart the feelings of dying people with mixed emotions. Although it focused attention on a critically important subject, it also fostered its own rigid, judgmental approach to death (Corr, 1993).

Terminally ill people do get angry, deny their illness, and become depressed. However, these emotions do not fall into distinct stages. Steven Antonoff and Bernard Spilka (1984–1985) videotaped terminal patients at random points during the early, middle, and late phases of their disease. Based on Kubler-Ross's thinking, the research-ers predicted that facial expressions should show mainly anger, then sadness, then acceptance as the disease advanced. This was not the case. Expressions of sadness increased in a linear way as death approached. Anger and acceptance (measured by contented expressions) showed no pattern. People were just as likely to look angry in their final days as early on, equally apt to look contented (accepting) right after their diagnosis as in their final days or weeks.

Another comparison of people who told a loved one they knew they were dying also showed few differences between those nearer versus more distant from death. People within days of dying gave no signs of being more accepting. *Everyone* in this study ranked low on calmness and contentment (Baugher, Burger, Smith, & Wallston, 1989–1990).

Psychologist Edwin Shneidman (1976, p. 6) describes "a complicated clustering of intellectual and affective states, some fleeting, lasting for a moment, or a day" as characterizing the emotional life of people coping with this stress. Furthermore, con-trary to what Kubler-Ross implies, even when people know their illness is terminal, the idea "I am dying" may not penetrate in an all-or-none way. People cycle between awareness and denial. Denial and awareness can even be present simultaneously.

Psychiatrist Avery Weisman (1986) uses the term **middle knowledge** to illustrate this suspension between knowing and not knowing, a psychological state he has frequently seen in working with the terminally ill. Weisman believes that middle

middle knowledge
State of being aware on some level yet not fully realizing that one is terminally ill

knowledge tends to manifest itself at transition points, such as when a relapse occurs and the emotional climate shifts. Loved ones turn less optimistic. Doctors avert their eyes when questions about recovery arise. Middle knowledge

> is marked by unpredictable shifts in the margin between what is observed and inferred. Patients seem to know and want to know, yet they often talk as if they did not know and did not want to be reminded of what they have been told. Many patients rebuke their doctors for not having warned them about complications in treatment or the course of an illness even though the doctors may have been scrupulous about keeping them informed. These instances of seeming denial are usually examples of middle knowledge. (p. 459)

As was true of my father, one important emotion people experience even when they "know" that their illness is terminal is hope. As Daniel Klenow (1991–1992) points out, the hope so evident among the terminally ill has various sources: If an individual is religious, he may believe in divine intervention: "God will provide a miraculous cure." Others may put faith in medical science: "Even though liver cancer is incurable, I may be cured by that new drug." Someone may pin her hopes on meditation, alternative therapies, or exercise. As Kubler-Ross suggests, another source of hope is medical fallibility: "True, I have that diagnosis, but I know of cases where a person was told she had 6 months and has been living for 10 years."

A study comparing the dreams of cancer patients and healthy adults reveals how, even on a less conscious level, people wrestle with ambivalence and hope (Coolidge & Fish, 1983–1984). As we might expect, the dreams of the ill people contained more death imagery than those of the healthy older adults. However, only one person dreamed directly about his or her own death. The ill person would dream someone else was dead or dying, sometimes trying to search for that person's identity. This dream is from a young woman one year before she died:

> I went to an outside all-night movie and I was standing in the middle of the street when this car pulled up and dumped out a young pregnant dead woman. . . . I ran over when it was over and I was looking at me on the floor but the girl really didn't look like me. (p. 3)

The researchers believe that this type of dream shows both anxiety and uncertainty. The dreamer's own death, the central concern, is too horrifying to be dreamed about directly. The person is grappling with that crucial question, "Am I really going to die?" Interestingly, as was true in this dream, compared with the control group, the ill people not only dreamed more often about death, but also its opposite. They dreamed about pregnancy, birth, or babies, as if fashioning these themes to compensate for the terror of their waking hours.

This dream is from a middle-aged women one month from death:

> I saw a woman who was very happy. The dream took place in a department store. The woman had a lovely dress and shoes. She was carrying a baby in her arms. She loved the baby very much. When I woke up, I felt very

happy and safe. As I was writing down the dream this fear started all over again. (p. 6)

COPING AND LONGEVITY   This is not to say that making distinctions is unwarranted. People cope in characteristic ways with life-threatening disease. Some try to give their illness meaning by helping others or to maximize the time they have left by becoming closer to loved ones. Others become incapacitated by depression or immobilized by anxiety. Can the way a person copes actually influence the *length* of his remaining time?

In following cancer patients, Avery Weisman and William Worden (1975) discovered that people who lived longer than expected based on the severity of their illness had certain distinctive traits: They maintained responsive relationships with others, especially in the final phase of their illness, and they were more assertive, showing more "fighting spirit" than those who died earlier on. In another study, compared with a group of survivors, people who died early had similar coping styles: They expressed little anger but much self-criticism, guilt, depression, and fear of bodily harm. These nonsurvivors were also less involved in reciprocal social relationships (Viney & Westbrook, 1986–1987).

Other studies, as we might imagine from our review of emotions and health in Chapter 3, show no relationship between the course of a fatal illness and any coping style or personality trait (Schulz & Schlarb, 1987–1988). Even if showing a fighting spirit or having close relationships is correlated with survival, we cannot conclude that this way of responding is causally involved in living a longer time. An equally likely possibility is that people with a fighting spirit are healthier, less temporally close to dying to begin with. (Notice that as my father grew more physically debilitated and drew closer to death, he lost his will to continue battling his disease.) Being assertive may also promote survival in an indirect way: People who "fight" or have involved family and friends tend to get more life-prolonging medical care.

WHAT IS A "GOOD" DEATH?   Even if the way we cope has no impact on the length of our life, we do want, in Avery Weisman's words, an **appropriate death**—one as meaningful and free from anxiety as possible. The need to provide an appropriate death becomes compelling when we realize that most people who undergo their "final passage" are reasonably certain for some period, whether a week or months, of their fate (Schulz & Schlarbe, 1987–1988). What do we mean by an appropriate death?

Charles Corr (1991–1992) spells out one interpretation in his **task-based approach to terminal care.** Unlike the tasks of mourning described in Chapter 11, or Kubler-Ross's stages, Corr's four tasks concern what we hope for when we are terminally ill:

1. We want to minimize physical distress, to be as free as possible from debilitating pain.
2. We want to maximize our psychological security, to reduce fear and anxiety and feel in control of how we die.
3. We want to enhance meaningful social relationships, to be as close as possible to the people we care about most.

appropriate death
When the dying process is as optimal or "correct" psychologically as possible

task-based approach to terminal care
Charles Corr's criteria for an appropriate death

4. We want to foster spirituality and have the sense that there was integrity and purpose to our lives.

In reaching these goals, the primary caregivers of the dying, health care professionals, can play a pivotal role.

Health Care Providers

How do doctors and nurses treat dying patients? How do they feel about dying and death? Researchers have examined these questions through questionnaires as well as by observing how hospital staff members act with the terminally ill.

QUESTIONNAIRE STUDIES   Do doctors withdraw from their dying patients once they know their interventions will not stave off death, acting insensitively and so promoting an inappropriate death?

There are good reasons why they might. It is built into human nature to shy away from tense situations, to avoid other people's emotional pain. Moreover, the thrust of medicine is to get people *physically* better. As we know from our discussion of geriatric medicine, doctors are typically not well trained in dealing with the emotional side of disease. With dying people, not only must doctors encounter this emotional side of illness full-force, they must confront their own painful emotions—their personal sense of impotence, the feeling that they have failed in their mission to heal (Cassel & Capello, 1997). Nurses, because their job is to comfort not to cure, are apt to feel more comfortable around the terminally ill. But doctors would be likely to shy away from the dying if only because these patients stand as a testament to their own *lack* of self-efficacy and primary control.

One study, comparing the emotions of medical residents and nurses, confirms that physicians, in particular those just starting out in their careers, view death in extremely negative terms. The nurses were more apt to describe dying in terms of liberation or peace. The doctors described this event as a disaster, the worst outcome of all (Brent, Speece, Gates, & Kaul, 1992–1993).

Besides not being in a profession devoted to defying death, the more experienced nurses in this study had much more hands-on contact with the terminally ill. This exposure, in itself, may be helpful in muting fear. When researchers explored death anxiety among doctors varying in age and years of practice, they found that, irrespective of specialty, younger, less experienced doctors were more terrorized by the prospect of dealing with death (A. C. Kane & Hogan, 1985–1986). In a parallel study with nursing students, researchers also found that subjects reported feeling more comfortable about dealing with dying patients if they had had previous personal experiences with death. Interestingly, in this study, personal and professional contact with the terminally ill each had a different fear-reducing impact. Professional experience with dying people eased anxiety, reducing a nurse's reluctance to touch or treat the terminally ill. Personal experience with the death of a loved one enhanced the positive pull toward working with this group. Students rated caring for the dying as more rewarding when a person they were close to had died (Brockopp, King, & Hamilton, 1991).

This research offers interesting insights into the emotions that health care providers bring to dying patients. However, to really know how the terminally ill are treated, we need to study actions, not polls probing feelings about death. Physicians' and nurses' attitudes about dying people in the abstract tell us little about how they act when confronted with dying people in the flesh. What *really* happens in hospitals when patients are not expected to live? This brings us to a second study that helped foster the movement to humanize terminal care.

DIRECT OBSERVATIONS   During the late 1960s, sociologists Bernard Glaser and Anselem Strauss (1968) spent several months unobtrusively watching the behavior of nurses, doctors, and aides who worked on different hospital wards in which dying patients were housed. Their lens for interpreting their observations was unique: Caring for the dying was a job, like any other. It was important to understand the way that job was organized.

The work of treating the dying was structured in a clear, though implicit, fashion according to the course the patient's illness was likely to take. Based on the person's diagnosis and physical state at admission, an expectation was set up about how that individual's pattern of dying was likely to proceed. This "dying schedule" governed how the hospital staff acted. Glaser and Strauss used an interesting phrase to refer to this schedule: the **dying trajectory.**

Glaser and Strauss pinpointed several dying trajectories. One frequently found in emergency rooms was the "expected swift death." Someone would arrive whose death was imminent, perhaps from an accident or heart attack, and who had no chance of surviving. "Expected lingering while dying" was another common pattern, one typical of progressive, fatal chronic diseases such as cancer. With an illness of this type, an alternate trajectory might be "entry/reentry": The person would return home several times in between hospital stays. Another trajectory might be "suspended sentence"—discharge for an unknown length of time before readmission in the final crisis before death.

Trajectories could not always be predicted. "Expected swift death" could turn into "lingering while dying" or even "expected to recover" if the patient rallied. "Expected to recover" might become "expected swift death" if the individual took a turn for the worse. These deviations impaired the functioning of the work. The plan became outmoded. Care had to change abruptly. The paradox was that if "off schedule," *living* might be transformed into a negative event:

> One patient who was expected to die within four hours had no money, but needed a special machine in order to last longer. A private hospital at which he had been a frequent paying patient for 30 years agreed to receive him as a charity patient. He did not die immediately but started to linger indefinitely, even to the point where there was some hope he might live. The money problem, however, created much concern among both family members and the hospital administrators. . . . the doctor continually had to reassure both parties that the patient (who lived for six weeks) would soon die; that is to try to change their expectations back to "certain to die on time." (pp. 11–12)

Another miscalculation had the same effect, one in which the patient vacillated between "certain to die on time" and "lingering." In this pattern, loved ones would sadly say good-bye only to find that the person began to improve. Family members, nurses, and doctors sometimes went through this cycle repeatedly. The chaplain might

dying trajectory
The illness path that people follow on the way to death

also be involved. Here too everyone breathed a sigh of relief when the end was really near. (This is not to imply that hospital workers typically wished insensitively for death. The opposite error, a patient expected to recover who then died, was even more upsetting.)

Miscalculated trajectories not only upset the staff, but injured the patient. If someone was "vacillating" or "lingering too long," the doctor and nurses might get annoyed. They could become less responsive, give more perfunctory care, and possibly hasten death. Another type of mistake might also speed up death: assigning the individual to a service unfit for his trajectory. Sometimes a patient needing constant care was put on a ward where only periodic checks were provided and died between observations.

To Glaser and Strauss, their observations suggested that the hospital's mode of approaching the terminally ill was flawed. The goal was efficient work, providing care with a minimum of steps. This focus, when it clashed with the reality that dying is inherently unpredictable, was tailor-made for producing staff frustration and poor patient care.

This indictment, published at about the same time as Kubler-Ross's book, brought home the message that patients were not getting care compatible with having an appropriate death. More humane approaches to dying were required.

INTERVENTIONS (AND ONGOING ISSUES)

The first step in the movement to humanize terminal care was to uncouple dying from traditional medicine, with its emphasis on high-tech machines aimed at defying death. Like birth, death is a natural process. When curative interventions are impossible, the focus should shift to providing a good death.

Hospice Care

hospice
Formal programs offering care tailored to the needs of the terminally ill and their families

This philosophy led to the now well-known alternative to traditional hospital and nursing home care, the **hospice.** Hospice care is for people for whom death is certain, but who may have as much as 6 months to live. Its purpose is different from that of traditional health care settings seeking to cure; its purpose is simply to provide the best care. Hospice personnel are skilled in techniques to minimize physical discomfort and in providing a supportive psychological environment, one that assures patients and family members that they will not be abandoned in the face of approaching death (Cohen, 1979).

Initially, hospice care was delivered in an inpatient setting called a hospice. The current emphasis of the hospice movement, as we saw in our opening vignette, is providing support that allows people to die with dignity at home. As described in Aging in Action 12-2, multidisciplinary hospice teams go into the person's home, providing part-time caregiver relief. They offer 24-hour help in a crisis, giving family caregivers the support they need to allow their relative to spend his final days at home. Their commitment does not end after the person dies. An important component of hospice care is bereavement counseling.

As Corr spells out in his first task, pain control—reducing the physical suffering of the dying—is fundamental to the hospice philosophy. The goal is to decrease pain

12-2 *Hospice Team*

The Murfreesboro Hospice operates from a cozy little house across the street from our local hospital. Here are some excerpts from an interview with the hospice team (nurse, social worker, and volunteer coordinator) in response to the questions, How do you get referrals? Who chooses hospice? and What do you do?

Usually, we get referrals from physicians. People may have a wide support system in the community or be new to the area. Even when there are many people involved, there is almost always one primary caregiver, typically a spouse or adult child.

We see our role as empowering families, giving them the support to care for their loved ones at home. We go into the home as a team to make our initial assessment: What services does the family need? We provide families training in pain control, in making beds, in bathing. A critical component of our program is respite services. Volunteers come in for part of each day. They may take the children out for pizza, or give the primary caregiver time off, or bathe the person, or just stay there to listen.

Families will say initially, "I don't think I can stand to do this." They are anxious because it's a new experience they have never been through. At the beginning, they call a lot. Then you watch them really gain confidence in themselves. We see them at the funeral and they thank us for helping them give their loved one this experience. Sometimes, the primary caregiver can't bear to keep the person at home to the end. We respect that too. The whole thing about hospice is choice. Some people want to talk about dying. Others just want you to visit, ask about their garden, talk about current affairs. We take people to see the autumn leaves, to see Santa Claus. Our main focus is, "What are your priorities?" We try to pick up on that. We had a farmer whose goal was to go to his farm one last time and say good-bye to his tractor. We got together egg crates, a big tank of oxygen, and carried him down to his farm. We have one volunteer who takes a client to the mall. We keep in close touch with the families for a year after, providing them counseling, or referring them to bereavement groups in the community. Some families keep in contact with notes for years. We run a camp each summer for children who have lost a parent [see Figure 12-2]. We have an unusually good support system among the staff. In addition to being with the families at 3 A.M., we call one another at all times of the night. Most us have been working here for years. We feel we have the most meaningful job in the world.

while keeping the patient as alert and independent as possible. Hospice workers are skilled in using medications. They may employ psychological techniques to reduce pain, such as teaching the person to mentally shift focus from the discomfort, emphasizing pleasurable activities, and training families to avoid expressions of anxiety that intensify the pain.

One woman, for example, was in great misery because she wanted to live to see a grandchild about to be born, but knew it was impossible. The controlling of her pain, however, made it possible for her to recover enough strength to knit a gift for the child she would never see, thus helping brighten her last

FIGURE 12-2 *Announcement of a Hospice-Sponsored Summer Camp*

CAMP
FORGET-ME-NOT

Sponsored by
HOSPICE OF MURFREESBORO
a service of Middle Tennessee Medical Center

June 15, 16, 17, and 18, 1998
10:00 a.m. - 2:00 p.m.

For children K - 6th grade, who have
experienced the death of a loved one

Recreation • Lunch • Discussion

Deadline to register: May 22, 1998

There is no charge.
Limited transportation provided, if needed.
Camp will be held at Trinity Methodist Church
Murfreesboro, TN

Hospices around the country offer programs of this type to bereaved children.

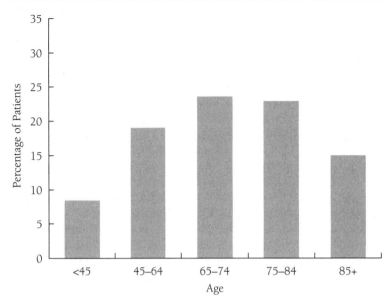

Most patients utilizing hospice care are elderly but not extremely old.
SOURCE: National Center for Health Statistics, 1995a.

days. Another hospice patient had been lying all of the time in a fetal position with a hot water bottle clutched to his chest, staring into space, moaning in his private hell which he said was compounded by pain that was like fire . . . but when the hospice team showed him they could control his pain he became a different person, able to live rather than vegetate during his last days. (Rossman, 1977, p. 126)

Hospice care is not appropriate for everyone. To utilize this service, a person must agree to abandon curative treatments and be judged by a physician as within 6 months of death. Almost always, the individual has family members committed to the physically and emotionally draining task of day-to-day caregiving.

Statistics collected by the Centers for Disease Control offer a portrait of who does enroll. In 1993, of the 50,000 patients per day receiving services from the 1000 hospice agencies in the United States, 71% had cancer. These patients tended to be elderly. In that year, more than 70% of people utilizing this service were over age 65. However, as Figure 12-3 shows, many hospice patients tend to be young-old. One reason may be that in contrast to the very old, this group of older people is "richer" in convoy supports. Hospice patients are typically cared for by a spouse (Bass, Garland, & Otto, 1985–1986). Compared with terminally ill hospitalized older patients, hospice patients have more people living in the home.

Not unexpectedly, physicians are a second, crucial interpersonal force shaping the hospice choice. If they are reluctant to discuss the true nature of the illness, or persist in treating the person heroically, families are not likely to consider hospice when their loved one is terminally ill. In one study with geriatric patients, families utilizing this service tended to have doctors who felt comfortable talking about terminal illness and offered the diagnosis in a matter-of-fact way. Interestingly, possibly because they do not work in a setting full of state-of-the-art death-defying technologies, patients whose physicians were *not* affiliated with large teaching hospitals more often selected hospice care (Prigerson, 1992).

As Aging in Action 12-2 shows, hospice can offer tremendous solace to the dying person and loved ones, allowing families to offer one last demonstration of love. Without minimizing these benefits, so beautifully described by the hospice team, let's focus on some cautions about this still nontraditional choice.

Even with the backup provided by hospice, it may be too anxiety-provoking for some families to be thrust into being responsible for managing the terrifying crises of impending death (Arras & Dubler, 1994). Although polls show that the vast majority of Americans do feel that dying at home is best, even from the ill person's perspective, this may not be totally true.

Ironically, the person may have less privacy at home than in a hospital. In a hospital, care for bodily functions is routinized and impersonal. At home, people are subject to the humiliation of family members' caring for their physical needs. Patients may want to spare their loved ones the vision of themselves incontinent and naked; they may want time alone to cry out, to vent their anger, anguish, and pain. In a hospital, there is the chance to express these emotions in privacy. At home, visiting hours are continuous; patients may feel constrained to act in a certain way.

Just as important, care by strangers can mean care free from guilt. Many people don't want to be a burden to their loved ones. Dying demands 24-hour care. At home, there is the risk of feeling like a burden, a feeling of shame about being needy that may add to the pain of the illness itself. Recall from Chapter 10 that "too much" care can evoke uncomfortable emotions in caregivers too. Family members may feel put upon and then feel guilty. Relationships with the ill person may grow more strained and distant, rather than becoming closer. For these reasons, we should not automatically assume that everyone, even with a supportive family willing to provide care, is better off dying at home.

Hospice programs serve only a small fraction of the terminally ill (Sachs, 1994). Many people do not have family members who can take on this job. Even when loved ones are intent on home care, as we saw in Aging in Action 12-2, anxiety or the physical demands of caregiving may be overwhelming and the person ends up being admitted to a hospital and/or nursing home in the terminal phase of life. So, efforts have also focused on humanizing the primary setting where death still occurs, the hospital or nursing home.

Humanizing Hospital Care

CHANGING INSTITUTIONAL PRACTICES Traditional health care settings have incorporated many hospice strategies. Doctors now are able to give as much medication as necessary to control pain in the terminal phase of life. Patients are sometimes removed from the intensive care unit when they are about to die. They are unhooked from machines and given unlimited time to be with family during their last hours. Hospital administrations routinely bend visiting rules in a person's last days. For instance, a wife may be allowed to sleep in her husband's hospital room, and children can visit at any hour. There is also a push to establish palliative care units within hospitals, similar to inpatient hospices, where patients can go during their last few weeks or days of life (Zuckerman, 1997).

To see if these hospital-based units do help promote a more appropriate death, one group of researchers explored whether terminally ill cancer patients in two of these units were better off emotionally than a comparison group of patients who spent their last days on the traditional ward. After conducting interviews, they coded patients' answers according to the amount of positive versus negative responses. Patients in the palliative care units expressed more positive emotions and less anger. They were less anxious about dying and death (Viney, Walker, Robertson, Lilley, & Ewan, 1994).

CHANGING PEOPLE   Unfortunately, perfunctory care and anxious avoidance still do sometimes characterize traditional terminal care. As we might imagine from our previous discussion, one reason is that health care providers, especially physicians, continue to be uncomfortable in the face of death. Greg Sachs (1994), a doctor who works with the terminally ill, observes, "It is as if the words dying and death have almost disappeared from the vocabulary of physicians entirely. We have heard patients, even those expected to die in a matter of hours or days, described as 'not doing well, having a poor prognosis, or having little chance of making it'" (p. 22). Sachs believes that this reluctance to confront the truth works to the detriment of the terminally ill. To truly humanize hospital care, we must make a systematic effort to change the way traditional health care workers approach dying and death.

This effort is underway. Based on witnessing problems such as Sachs mentions, in 1995, the Institute of Medicine appointed a panel to improve deficiencies in traditional medical end-of-life care (Cassel & Capello, 1997). In their formal recommendations, published in 1997, the committee stressed that providing high-quality terminal care must become a genuine medical priority. One interesting strategy they proposed was to make palliative (comfort) care a full-fledged medical specialty like geriatric medicine or, at the very least, a defined area of medical expertise. Medical schools should offer students systematic training in discussing terminal conditions with patients and their families, so that doctors can better judge when it is appropriate to tell people the facts and when it is most humane *not to reveal the truth*. In addition, we need to pay more attention to reducing the personal anxieties doctors and other health care workers bring to this final event of life.

This is the goal of the **death education courses** now offered at many medical, social work, and nursing schools. Death education can be didactic, focused on imparting information, or experiential, with students role-playing exercises or getting firsthand experience in dealing with the terminally ill. Here we describe one of the first experiential death education courses offered at a medical school (Davis & Jessen, 1980–1981).

In addition to attending a regular seminar, students who enrolled in this course spent one night (from 5:30 P.M. to 8:00 A.M.) "on call" with the chaplain at a community hospital. The on-call chaplain visits the emergency room and the intensive care

death education courses
Formal courses in death and dying offered to students in the health professions

and coronary care units, consulting with the staff and comforting dying patients and their families. When they accompanied the chaplain on these rounds, students were encouraged to discuss the ethical and psychological issues that arose during this experiential introduction to death. They then wrote an essay about what they learned.

> It was perhaps most meaningful that we ended our night with a cesarean section and a live healthy baby! Once again however life was taken for granted and really not much attention was given to it. Procedure was high priority. . . . Doctors examine noses, anuses—in essence every projection or hole in the human body—and yet the very thing that holds these examined parts together—life—is not examined seemingly or fully. . . . It seemed ironic to end our "death" call with a birth—maybe we peeked into the meaning of death. (p. 163)

As this essay reveals, the immediate impact of this experience can be profound. Can a single course produce a lasting change in how students think? A one-shot glimpse of death from a personal perspective can be easily forgotten amid the avalanche of technical-care-oriented courses of medical school.

To determine whether death education is useful, researchers have explored whether having taken this course influences attitudes and ways of treating the terminally ill (Dickinson & Pearson, 1980–1981). They have examined the impact training has on reducing participants' own anxieties about death (Hayslip, Galt, & Pinder, 1993–1994). As we might imagine, in part because of the difficulty of changing (and measuring!) death anxiety, these courses do not affect participants' own anxieties about death. However, when the instruction is experientially focused, death education does seem to make for greater sensitivity toward dying patients (Durlak & Riesenberg, 1991).

Controlling the Timing of Death

The original focus of the "death with dignity" movement was to permit a technology-free, natural death. Today, this principle has been extended one step: Perhaps we should also give terminally ill people more freedom to control *when* they die. In this section, we look at two types of interventions in this second-wave movement to humanize terminal care. The first offers dying patients and their loved ones a mechanism to make their wishes known about artificial, life-prolonging treatment when they are mentally incapacitated; the second is that step embodied by Dr. Kervorkian and his suicide machine. People should be allowed to get help in ending their lives.

ADVANCE DIRECTIVES   Any specific instruction in advance about preferences for life-sustaining treatment is called an **advance directive.** The best-known example is the **living will.** In this document, legal in most but not all states, a person instructs the doctor in advance about his wishes to be kept alive by artificial means should he become permanently comatose (see Figure 12-4). Another document is the **Do Not Resuscitate (DNR)** order frequently found in patients' charts, especially in nursing homes. Here, typically the family or a conservator and the physician direct the hospital or nursing home staff that, should a medical crisis occur in a mentally impaired or

---

Advance directive
Specific instructions in advance about preferences for life-sustaining treatment should individuals be unable to make their wishes known

living will
Document in which people spell out their preferences with regard to life-sustaining treatment in case of incapacity

Do Not Resuscitate (DNR)
Document in an impaired institutionalized person's chart stipulating that CPR not be performed during a medical crisis

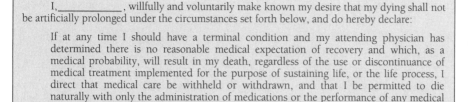

I,_____ , willfully and voluntarily make known my desire that my dying shall not be artificially prolonged under the circumstances set forth below, and do hereby declare:

If at any time I should have a terminal condition and my attending physician has determined there is no reasonable medical expectation of recovery and which, as a medical probability, will result in my death, regardless of the use or discontinuance of medical treatment implemented for the purpose of sustaining life, or the life process, I direct that medical care be withheld or withdrawn, and that I be permitted to die naturally with only the administration of medications or the performance of any medical procedure deemed necessary to provide me with comfortable care or to alleviate pain.

ARTIFICIALLY PROVIDED NOURISHMENT AND FLUIDS: By checking the appropriate line below I specifically:

_____ authorize the withholding or withdrawal of artificially provided food, water, or other nourishment or fluids.

_____ DO NOT authorize the withholding or withdrawal of artificially provided food, water, or other nourishment or fluids.

This is Page 1 of
my Living Will

---

terminally ill person, CPR not be performed to save the person's life. Or, in nursing homes, a **Do Not Hospitalize (DNH)** order may be put in the chart, stipulating that in a medical crisis the resident not be transferred to a hospital for emergency care. Another type of advance directive is called the **durable power of attorney.** In this document, a person designates a specific individual, usually a family member, to make end-of-life decisions at such time as that individual is not capable of deciding on his own. Although we tend to think of advance directives in terms of withholding treatment, these instructions also may stipulate that the person be *given* care.

Advance directives serve an admirable goal. Often, end-of-life care decisions occur in a vacuum because no one knows how the comatose or severely demented person feels about receiving procedures that artificially prolong death. Under the Patient Self-Determination Act, which became law in 1991, all health care institutions receiving Medicare and Medicaid funds are required to provide information to patients at entry to the facility about their right to sign a directive of this type. However, these documents are used less frequently than we might expect. The reason is that advance directives have serious problems too.

For one thing, only a small fraction of people, even those with life-threatening illnesses, take the step of filling out a written directive. People are naturally reluctant to confront their own future incompetence and demise (Sachs, 1994); only about 40% of Americans have a will! As implied earlier, physicians tend to be reluctant to initiate these discussions. They miss opportunities to discuss advance directives when the patient is in the first stages of what looks like a terminal disease (American Medical Association, Council of Ethical and Judicial Affairs, 1991). The idea of advance direc-

Do Not Hospitalize (DNH)
Document in an impaired nursing home resident's chart stipulating that in a medical emergency the person not be transferred to a hospital for care

durable power of attorney
Document in which individuals designate a specific person to make health care decisions in the event of incapacity

tives also flies in the face of some cultural norms. In the traditional Chinese culture, for instance, any talk about death is taboo (Dubler, 1994). Especially when they have not had good access to health care, people are reluctant to sign documents stipulating withholding treatment. As one patient put it, "I've been fighting to get what I need all my life. I'm not going to make it easy for them to hold back care" (reported in Wetle, 1994). People who sign advance directives tend to be well-educated, affluent, and nonminority (Sachs, 1994)—those most at risk of getting "too much" care. Moreover, advance directives were developed as a response to a health care system with strong incentives to overtreat. With the growth of cost-containing efforts in medicine, the climate is shifting away from using expensive technologies to preserve life. When patients perceive that the danger may be in doing too little, they are less likely to be interested in signing a document about what *not* to provide (Wetle, 1994)!

Even when people do sign such a document, there is no guarantee that their preferences will be respected. Many people do not discuss their decision with their family or doctor (Dresser, 1994). The information in the document is vague. What a person says months or years earlier cannot be seen as utterly binding; it cannot cover all situations and circumstances for all time. In one study, patients at hospitals and nursing homes were asked about their preferences for care, which were then placed in the chart. In the subsequent life-threatening episodes examined, one-fourth of the time care was deemed inconsistent with the stated preferences. Most often, a patient wanted *more* aggressive treatment than occurred. For instance, a nursing home resident with end-stage heart failure might request CPR and transfer to a hospital in the case of a cardiac arrest, but after repeated hospitalizations, the family and doctor might decide to forgo another, feeling that nothing more could be done (Danis et al., 1991).

In fact, when mentally competent kidney dialysis patients were asked, almost two-thirds thought that their doctors should have leeway in overriding their own advance directive if they saw the need (Sehgal et al., 1992). How binding can advance directives be? How binding do people really want them to be?

When surrogates (other people) make decisions for the impaired person, different concerns arise. First, there is the question of when exactly a person is mentally incompetent, an issue that often arises in nursing homes. Because only rarely is the person formally judged incompetent by the courts, responsibility for determining competence often rests with the doctor and other health care professionals. Making this determination is not always clear-cut. People may be lucid sometimes, or lucid but incapable of understanding the consequences of certain interventions. As Figure 12-5 shows, some elderly people who might not be able to make informed choices about life-prolonging procedures such as tube feeding can be rendered "competent" by special techniques (Krynski, Tymchuk, & Ouslander, 1994). Because of these difficulties, nursing homes have become sensitive to the need to develop formal guidelines for determining competence. In the 2-year period from 1986 to 1988, for example, the proportion of New York state nursing homes reporting they had or were developing guidelines shot up from a small minority to more than half (T. Miller & Cugliari, 1990).

Then there is the problem of who speaks for the person once it is clear she cannot speak for herself. Few difficulties arise when a specific individual has been given a durable power of attorney in advance. Often, however, there is no clear person in charge, and the doctor either turns to one or another family member or stumbles along

Four Pages from an 11-Page Brochure Designed to Help Elderly People Make Advance Directive Decisions about Enteral Tube Feeding

FIGURE 12-5

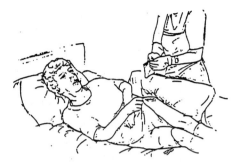

The Problem

Let's think for a minute that you can no longer eat all the food your body needs. From now on, you will need someone to feed you—either by hand or through a feeding tube. You can't eat well because you have a serious disease. This disease is making you lose more and more of your mental and physical abilities. Right now you can't even walk anymore. You can still recognize people and talk to them.

If you don't get enough food, you will become very weak. You could get sores on your skin because you are weak. You could also get infections that might make you very sick or even kill you.

The Good Things about the Feeding Tube

With a feeding tube, you could probably get all the food and fluids your body needs. You would probably live longer than if you didn't have the tube. This way you might not get sores on your skin or infections.

The Bad Things about the Feeding Tube

Some bad things might happen as well. You might get more diarrhea (loose stool) by being fed through the tube. You could also get pneumonia from food getting into your lungs. You could die from pneumonia. You might get pneumonia even *without* the feeding tube, because of the disease that is making you unable to eat well.

SOURCE: Krynski, Tymchuk, & Ouslander, 1994.

12-3 *Hospital-Based Ethicist, an Emerging Role*

Nancy Dubler, director of the Bioethics Department at Montefiore Medical Center in New York City, has been a pioneer in the emerging field of hospital-based medical ethics. Dubler argues that the role of the ethicist in a hospital is to "level the playing field." Families are intimidated by hospitals. They enter overwhelmed by the "maelstrom of personnel." If the staff is primarily people of color, whites may feel excluded. If the staff is white, or male, people of different ethnicities or women may feel shut out. The ethicist acts as mediator and interpreter as much as an actual judge of end-of-life concerns. The following case of a man in congestive heart failure offers a flavor of the issues that arise.

[An elderly man] was admitted to the intensive care unit (ICU). . . . After a week during which [he] became progressively worse, the physician . . . and the nursing staff met with the family and suggested that the patient soon be moved to a regular medical floor. They stated that the ICU was no longer an appropriate locus for care because the patient was dying, and they suggested that he should . . . be permitted to die.

The family . . . insisted that the patient remain in the ICU and be treated with all possible interventions. The opposition to the suggested care plan seemed to the staff to pose a bioethical dilemma and they called me to mediate. . . .

As is my standard process, I first met with the staff to try to understand the patient's history . . . and prognosis. All of the staff were incensed. Mr. Malling's daughters were screaming at the nurses, had refused to talk to the physician and were generally disrupting the unit. A meeting with the family revealed that . . . the sisters felt . . . intimidated by the staff and thought that their lack of education had led to their being ignored. They did not understand the accent of the cardiologist. They had overheard residents saying that medication was "wasted" on Mr. Malling. . . . None of these are bioethical issues. . . . The disagreement seemed to be about whether to transfer the patient. . . . But once the other issues had been uncovered and addressed, that bioethical issue disappeared. Two of the daughters were realistic about their father's chance of recovery. A solution emerged.

SOURCE: Dubler, 1994, p. 7.

---

making critical decisions for the impaired person's care. There is the temptation to overtreat when a doctor feels he might be sued. There is the potential for abuse when family members withhold lifesaving treatment the person might want, or insist on years of expensive, mainly taxpayer-financed, futile care (Callahan, 1987). There is the potential for conflict when the family feels differently than the physician or different family members feel different ways (Kapp, 1991). Suppose you believe that Mom's suffering should no longer be prolonged, whereas your brother insists that treatment continue at all costs? Clearly, these clashes can poison family relationships for years. Because of the potential for conflicts, as illustrated in Aging in Action 12-3, most hospitals and nursing homes now have ethics committees to help mediate end-of-life concerns (Mezey, Ramsey, & Mitty, 1994).

DNR (do not resuscitate) directives deserve special mention because these orders are the most common type of advance directive in nursing homes. While the American Medical Association has emphasized that doctors should discuss this decision with patients when they are competent, most often it is the doctor and family who make the decision to put this order in the chart. For this reason, the AMA has spelled out guidelines for when these orders should apply. Physicians have the ethical obligation to honor the preferences of the patient and his surrogates with regard to resuscitation. They should not permit their own feelings about the person's quality of life to interfere. However, when the doctor feels that prolonging life is futile, he or she may decide to put the order in the patient's chart, provided the family knows and is given ample time to respond or change doctors if they wish. Finally, DNR orders only apply to the decision not to conduct CPR during a cardiac arrest, not to other life-prolonging techniques (American Medical Association, 1991).

PHYSICIAN-ASSISTED SUICIDE   If you think that advance directives pose ethical problems, consider this newest thrust in the "death with dignity" movement. There is a huge leap from letting death proceed naturally when a cure is impossible to allowing physicians to hurry that process along. Should euthanasia (mercy killing) or **physician-assisted suicide** be legal in the United States, as it currently is in Holland? Should it be legal to assist patients who want to kill themselves not only when they are terminally ill but at any time?

physician-assisted suicide
When a physician helps an ill person who desires to die commit suicide

As we just saw, physicians are required by law to honor a patient's wishes to refuse life-prolonging treatment even though this refusal might hasten death. However, as of 1998, in most states it was against the law to actively intervene to help a person who has asked to die. As Bernard Gert, James Bernat, and Peter Mogielnicki (1994) point out, the distinction is between complying with a refusal and actively assisting in a request. The patient has the freedom to be allowed to die. The doctor is prohibited from performing the intervention that ends a person's life.

Killing of any type violates the religious principle that only God can give or take a life. This is why, even though surveys show widespread public support for legalizing physician-assisted suicide (Morrison & Meier, 1994), people who are highly religious, those in the Right-to-Life movement, and people who believe strongly in an afterlife are most loathe to accept this step in self-determination of death (J. Holden, 1993). Religious considerations, however, are not the only arguments against sanctioning physician-assisted suicide.

By agreeing to physician-assisted suicide, critics fear we may be opening the gates to involuntary euthanasia—allowing doctors to "pull the plug" on people who may not really want to die. Even when a person requests help ending his life, the situation may be far from clear. The person may not really be terminally ill. He may have been misdiagnosed or have years of productive life left. As psychiatrist Herbert Hendin (1994) points out, by helping a person die, one is performing an irrevocable act based on what might be a temporary feeling. People who are suicidal are often depressed (see Chapter 9). If the depression were treated, the individual might feel very differently about ending his life. In support of his views, Hendin cites the case of a young man in his 30s diagnosed with leukemia and given a 25% chance of survival. Fearing both the side effects of the treatment and the burden on his family, he begged for assistance in killing himself.

Once the young man and I could talk about the possibility of his dying—what separation from his family and the destruction of his body meant to him—his desperation subsided. He accepted medical treatment and used the remaining months of his life to become closer to his wife and parents. Two days before he died, he talked about what he would have missed without the opportunity for a loving parting. (1994, A19)

There are also excellent arguments on the other side. People who are terminally ill are often in severe pain, suffering that sometimes cannot be fully controlled by medications. Should these patients be forced to unwillingly endure the pain and humiliation of dying when doctors have the tools to mercifully end life? Knowing the agony terminal disease can cause, is it really humane to stand by and let nature gradually take its course (Morrison & Meier, 1994)? Is legalizing physician-assisted suicide a true advance toward humane self-determination or its opposite, the beginning of a "slippery slope" that might end in sanctioning the killing of anyone whose quality of life is impaired?

Age-Based Rationing of Care

You may have noticed an age-component to the "slippery slope" of deciding when not to treat. Many patients with advance directives in their chart are elderly, at the end of their natural life. As we saw earlier in this chapter, there is a societal norm that gives preference to performing heroic measures to preserve life in the young. Should society put limits on the extent to which it marshals the arsenal of life-perpetuating strategies for people who are disabled and at the end of their natural life?

In a controversial book, *Setting Limits,* Daniel Callahan (1987), our nation's most prominent biomedical ethicist, argues that we should not treat the health needs of the disabled elderly as if they were the equal of younger adults. There is a time when the never-to-be-finished fight against death should stop. According to Callahan, waging total war for everyone might be more acceptable if everyone had equal access to health care. However, by putting no controls on Medicare payments for expensive life-prolonging strategies, we implicitly favor older people over the 35 million younger Americans who have no health insurance at all.

Callahan (1994) proposes a **life-cycle approach to medical care,** based on the following principles:

1. **After a person has lived out a natural life span, medical care should no longer be oriented to resisting death.** While stressing that no precise age should be set for this determination, Callahan puts this marker at around the late 70s or 80s. In his view, this does not mean that life at this age has less value. It simply means that at a certain age, death is inevitable and should not be vigorously defied.

2. **Provision of medical care for those who have lived out a normal life span should be limited to the relief of suffering.** At the end of life, the focus should shift from heroic strategies aimed at preserving life to relieving pain.

3. **The existence of medical technologies capable of extending the lives of elderly who have lived out a natural life span creates no presumption whatever that the technologies must be used for that purpose.** Callahan believes that the

life-cycle approach to medical care
Daniel Callahan's controversial idea that heroic, costly life-sustaining treatments should not be performed on people at the end of their natural life

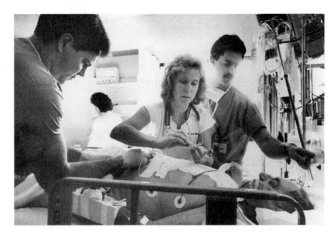

Scenes such as this in which astronomical human and monetary resources are being spent on this comatose elderly man may have prompted Callahan to develop his life-cycle approach to medical care.

proper goal of medicine is to stave off *premature* death. We should not become slaves to technologies developed to further this goal, blindly using each expensive technological advance on every person merely because it exists.

To some extent, doctors follow these prescriptions on an implicit basis today. A physician may decide that an 80-year-old is "too frail" to have a possibly lifesaving operation that he would not hesitate to give a younger adult. A family and the doctor agree that an older nursing home resident be only given comfort care. However, many gerontologists vigorously argue that *formally* adopting age-based rationing will put us on a scary, slippery slope. Granted, intervening to cure cancer in a 90-year-old is not only more dangerous but more futile, because the person is likely to die soon of a heart attack (see Chapter 3). As we saw vividly in Chapter 7, life may seem much less worth living to the person suffering from a dementing disease. At the same time, we need to protect that cognitively impaired person, not presume his life is worth less (Dresser & Whitehouse, 1994). Once we deny treatment based on age or mental incapacity, do we open the door to refusing treatment based on gender, race, or ethnic group? Won't taking one step lead to another and ultimately bring us back to the horrific gerocidal practices of the societies described in Chapter 1 (see Aging in Action 1-1)? As Nancy Jecker and Laurence Schneiderman (1994) put it, health care decision making should be based on considerations of medical futility, not having lived a full life.

Two recent studies focusing on the elderly heighten my personal sense of discomfort with the specter of age-based rationing of care. The first explores variations in the frequency of DNR and other advance directives in different nursing homes. The second explores older adults' own preferences for ending their lives when faced with serious, irreversible diseases.

In looking at how common advance directives were in 60,000 nursing homes, Nicholas Castle (1996–1997) found marked differences from facility to facility in the extent to which "do not treat" orders appeared in patients' charts. Most alarming, he found that the use of advance directives was most common in facilities that we might think would have the greatest incentive to cut costs. For-profit nursing homes were especially likely to have these directives. So were nursing homes with a less adequate patient/staff ratio—that is, those with relatively fewer RNs and other personnel. As Castle points out, these findings do not prove that the impulse to "get rid of" sicker, more costly patients governs end-of-life decisions. (For instance, residents in for-profit homes may have more advance directives because in these settings the staff might be more careful to ask people about their wishes for advance care.) But they do suggest that the decision to forgo heroic treatments could be influenced by the needs of the institution rather than just the wishes of patients and their families.

In fact, when Victor Cicirelli (1997) asked a group of older adults about their own preferences about ending their lives if they were in the kind of physical state that typically merits an advance directive, he discovered that a surprisingly high fraction voted to continue living at all costs. Even when they imagined having terminal illnesses or problems such as having both legs amputated, lying comatose from a stroke, or suffering Alzheimer's disease, only 1 in 10 people said they would actively take measures to end their own life (although one-third said they would like family members to make the decision for them). More than half said they would definitely want to still stay alive.

Taken together, these studies raise a disturbing question. How many older people have "do not treat" orders in their charts that, were they able to voice their preferences, they really would not want? How widespread is *involuntary* age-based rationing of care today?

Notice that our discussion brings us full circle back to issues we have been exploring throughout this book: how the health care system treats older patients; the quality of care in nursing homes; the question of balancing the rights of the young and old; the importance of having a sense of self-efficacy (or control) over our decisions in our older years. In dying as older adults, we see many issues related to living as older adults too.

Age-based rationing of health care is just one of several important social challenges facing the baby boomers as we prepare to enter our senior citizen years. In the following pages, I conclude this extensive tour of what psychologists know about the aging process with two brief personal notes. First, I will offer a few of my own thoughts about our maturing field. Then, I want you to hear from a gerontological psychologist who has been there almost from the beginning. Because, as we saw in Chapter 1, Powell Lawton has been so influential in helping nurture the psychology of aging to vigorous midlife, I think he deserves the final word on where we have come from and how our field can best ripen into its vintage years.

KEY TERMS

advance directives
appropriate death
death anxiety
death education courses
do not hospitalize (DNH)
do not resuscitate (DNR)

durable power of attorney
dying trajectory
hospice
life-cycle approach to medical care
living will

middle knowledge
physician-assisted suicide
stages of death theory
task-based approach to terminal care

DYING PROCESS

Glaser, B., & Strauss, A. L. (1968). *A time for dying.* Chicago: Aldine.

The study of dying trajectories is explained in this interesting and well-written book.

Kubler-Ross, E. (1969). *On death and dying.* New York: Macmillan.

This is the classic book on the dying process

ETHICAL ISSUES

Advance directives. (1994). *Hastings Center Report,* 24(6).

A special supplement to this issue discusses advance care planning and the problems with advance directives. (The *Hastings Center Report,* published bimonthly, is the best single source for information on ethical issues related to death and dying.)

Callahan, D. (1987). *Setting limits: Medical care in an aging society.* New York: Simon & Schuster.

In this book, Callahan gives his argument for age-based rationing of care, proposing that we set "rational limits" on medical interventions to the infirm aged.

Current ethical issues in aging. (1994, Winter). *Generations, 18.*

This issue of the *Generations* is devoted to ethical issues relating to terminal care of the elderly.

JANET BELSKY

We're done! When I finish a book, I feel like many of you at the end of the semester: I can't wait to take some time off and relax. But I am hooked on this writing. The reason is that these books give me a chance to open your eyes and perhaps change the way you think about older people and about your future life. I get to excite you about the challenges of doing research and allow you to step back when someone tells you a "fact" and evaluate critically whether that statement is true. I get to show off the work we psychologists do and the exceptional people I have met who are living life as older adults. Just as important, writing these books is *my* chance to find out what is going on. When you swoop in to get a bird's-eye view of a field every six or so years, you see an evolving entity, just like a living person growing and maturing. You also get the chance to think about areas that are still missing, new directions for development and growth. So, here are a few ideas about information that I would like to see in the fourth edition of this book.

Now that we have made such strides in documenting what can happen in a negative way as we grow old, we need research exploring the ways in which people cope with these changes. This need for further study is particularly striking in that central area in which we psychologists make a unique contribution: cognition. How do people react to and handle the changes in memory and information processing that they are experiencing? Do they really use selection, optimization, and compensation when they go about negotiating life? What *really* happens when people find they are having trouble responding at a traffic light or finding their car in a parking lot?

The new theories charting emotional development do address these issues in a partial, tangential way. Most important, these exciting new theories are finally tackling the challenge of understanding our inner life—how we may change "as people" for the better in our older years. As I hoped to convey in discussing research methods, study-ing emotional development is difficult. It's hard to pin down and measure that elusive entity called personality, much less generalize about change in this important area of life. Just in the past few years, the study of emotion and aging has begun to take off. One thrill for me personally is to see some new Eriksons arrive on the scene. These people, by the way, are often a decade younger than me! The contributions of these theorists are not only exciting on an intellectual level, they also have helped me in understanding other people and making sense of my own life. I hope that we do more thinking in this area and make systematic attempts to link these creative life-span theories to research with older adults in a concrete way.

The same applies to our social relationships and roles. In recent decades, we have made great advances in documenting the negatives: caregiving in disability, what happens to families coping at the extreme. Now it is time to turn to family life during more peaceful, normal times. How do families get along for the decades that they live together in health? What is it like to deal with our attachment figures (both family and friends) during the many years that we share our lives as unimpaired adults?

In this book, I have talked a good deal about person/environment congruence. I have bemoaned the fact that living environments for older adults still often work to promote excess disabilities, in spite of all that we know. I have described the disturbing lack of geriatric physicians and psychologists in nursing homes, the fact that services that could help keep people out of institutions are still unavailable to many older adults. These issues are a real concern. We as a society must do more to make life user-friendly for the millions of older people living in the community who are experiencing the limitations of age. We can do much more to improve the quality of institutional care. But another problem is getting people to accept help that exists. It's a shame to see services such as day programs go underutilized, and that, even when people have the money, they are often reluctant to consider services that they know exist. Being "helped" can be difficult for anyone of any age. We tend to equate it with failure. For older people, the idea of getting services may be especially frightening because it signifies that they have entered the territory of the old. The challenge for we gerontologists is to give people what we know will help them and still keep them feeling independent—to provide needed support and yet preserve that all-important sense of self-efficacy intact.

In recent years, we have made tremendous strides in being sensitive to minority and women's issues in our research. Now, I wonder if we have gone overboard in neglecting men. At the risk of oversimplifying, one message of this book is that, because of their more fragile convoys and the difficulty they often have with being dependent and in need (the "asking directions" problem), men may have special trouble coping with the losses of old age. They will be more at risk in future decades because of the seismic changes in divorce. Once again, it may be difficult to get older men to participate in studies, especially research examining the emotional side of life. We need to confront this challenge and study the inner lives of aging men. Practitioners who serve the elderly, whether at senior citizens' centers or widowed persons' groups, should also make more efforts to reach out to this underserved group.

This is my own personal agenda. But the real function of this book is to lay the groundwork for you to pursue the aging agenda that most interests you. Some of you may want to be researchers; others may decide to make a difference in our field through directly working with older adults. As Baltes points out, it is critical for you to specialize, to carve out your own area of expertise. Selection and optimization are essential to living life in a competent way. But as you follow your own "aging" pathway, I want to urge you to keep one eye on the larger picture. I feel very strongly that we gerontologists must continue to branch out in our reading to other areas of our field to be the best specialists that we can be.

As long as I have you at the beginning point of your selection and optimization, I have a final bit of middle-aged advice. It's easy to see people like me who write books as special or to imagine that the people whose names you regularly read in our journals are basically more intelligent or have some unusual gift. You would be wrong. When I was at your place in my career, I would have laughed if someone told me that one day I would be writing a textbook. (And so would everyone else.) One purpose of this book is to get you to avoid thinking in stereotypes, both about older people and about how people in general are supposed to behave. Now, it's time for me to tell you not to fall into the stereotype we associate with a "name." Not only will making these distinctions limit your personal development, but they are a danger in our field. Setting up hierarchies leads to competition and gets us away from the humanism and mutual collaboration that have historically made gerontology so special. As Powell Lawton will tell you next, this sense of shared collaboration and humanism is really what our field should be all about.

POWELL LAWTON

I count myself in the second generation of 20th-century gerontologists. A few of the first generation (earliest in productivity, that is, not necessarily in age) are still with us, notably James Birren. Others will be difficult to keep in the minds of the new generations. But historians will surely find the work of such people as John Anderson, Oscar Kaplan, and Irving Lorge mixed in with the currently more familiar work of Neugarten and Havighurst. When I came along, there were these people's writings and those of my own cohort—Eisdorfer, Schaie, Botwinick, Riegel, and a limited number of others—plus the Birren *Handbook of Aging and the Individual.* There actually was the chance that one could read everything that had been written about the psychology of aging! Gerontologists constituted a small community. The small numbers ensured that one could come quickly to know those with common interests and also that multidisciplinarity would be the rule in both formal and informal collegial interchange.

It was a lot of fun then. At the time I entered gerontology, I didn't fully appreciate how unusual it was to have a full research department in a geriatric organization. Margaret Blenkner, a research social worker, had just established a research department at the Benjamin Rose Institute in Cleveland and had attracted a great deal of interest in the research that seemed to suggest that giving additional services to frail elders led to more frequent use of institutions and that relocation was associated with excess mortality. She was very impressive in the way she intoned "Service kills!" from the podium. Although these findings were not replicated, she set a high standard for what was then called "applied research." Several others operated from an academic base and a thoroughgoing underpinning of scientific theory while utilizing the instances found in institutional environments for their research. Ruth Bennett and Lucille Nahemow studied the social milieu of the total institution; Sheldon Tobin and Morton Lieberman focused on the stress process in anticipating and becoming a nursing home resident; and Robert Kleemeier wrote the first theoretical account of person/environment interaction as he observed life in a fraternal organization's home for the aged.

My own good fortune at Philadelphia Geriatric Center was due to the vision of its executive vice president, Arthur Waldman. Waldman was a vocational counselor with a bachelor's degree who had yearned to do research but was led by his creative gifts into the administrative route. In less than 20 years, he had created at PGC first-time models of the health-care-oriented nursing home, congregate housing, a care center explicitly for dementia, and small-group homes as satellites to the institution. Each of these became the focus for research that my colleagues and I performed. Close upon the founding of our research institute came the one at the Hebrew Rehabilitation Center for the Aged of Boston, founded by Sylvia Sherwood, and still thriving under her longtime assistant director, John Morris. By now, a network of such applied centers is in operation. My other great good fortune was the string of gifted colleagues with whom I've worked, the first group of whom were Elaine Brody, Morton Kleban, Samuel Granick, and Lucille Nahemow. I can't go beyond that first group because there are far too many. Just as important are the "children" PGC has sent out into the gerontological world. We have had college graduates and master's and doctoral students who have worked for a year or two as research assistants and become firmly committed to careers in various aspects of aging. The "alumni dinner" of former PGC staff at the Gerontological Society of America's annual meeting grows in size each year and has a constantly rotating cast. Although we congratulate ourselves on being able to engage them into gerontology, what they gave PGC during their years of enthusiastic and motivated service is at least of equal value.

Gradually gerontology, and geropsychology specifically, came of age to represent a thriving enterprise with more to read than would be possible in 100 lifetimes, with competing organizations, competing journals, and gerontologists competing for status in these structures and in the academic and grant-funding sectors. As I became an old-timer, rewards seemed sometimes as much automatic as earned. Of course I loved being appointed the first editor of *Psychology and Aging* and being elected president of Division 20 and the Gerontological Society. I date this period (late 1980s) as one in which the change of gerontology from small fraternity to multiplex organization was being completed. I fight the tendency to bemoan the passage of the good old days. What could we have ever wished for that would be better than our present endeavor, with governmental research funding of close to $1 billion, several major federal departments with a gerontological purpose, close to 100 journals, and multiple organizations that draw thousands to their annual meetings? Once the have-not specialty, every day we see psychologists with major accomplishments in other areas moving into geropsychology. It's enough to keep us old-timers giddy with joy.

It is also making me aware that there are risks in size. I am reminded of Roger Barker's classic study *Big School, Small School*. The large school had more resources, great variety, and a level of stimulation impossible in the small school. It also had fewer roles per student and was able to nurture and select top-quality people for athletics, arts, intellectual activities, and governance. The small school had more roles per student and was able to recruit a greater proportion of the student body, including the marginal, into significant types of involvement. I worry that the gerontology of today and the near future may be providing meaningful scientific and educational roles for a lesser proportion of our total than was true when we were smaller.

We need to think of balancing our growth act with some decentralization that increases the level of individual participation, face-to-face contact, and directly shared interests. The proliferation of journals can help decentralize. Our highest-quality journals are at risk of abandoning their nurturing role for younger scientists when they encourage referees not to offer helpful criticism unless the manuscript seems publishable, or if the editor adds little to the process other than making the final decision regarding publication. I count the creation of the interest-group idea to have been my main accomplishment as president of the Gerontological Society of America (GSA). This structure thrives today and consists of usually relatively small groups united by a common scientific interest and the wish to engage in less formal interchange than other GSA program structures provide. The interest groups are all multidisciplinary. The Behavioral and Social Sciences section of the GSA has for several years given an annual Mentoring Award, which helps keep alive awareness of our duty toward students and junior colleagues. The GSA Student Organization has periodically sponsored program material that provides tips to students on ways of becoming fully socialized to gerontology. Such tips include encouraging the student to take the initiative in approaching the senior scientist in correspondence, by telephone, or by trying to arrange a meeting, efforts which more often than not succeed because the senior person enjoys this contact also.

In conclusion, rather than comment on the future of gerontology as a science, I'd like to urge nascent gerontologists not to forget their own early and perhaps isolated times. Geropsychology is intrinsically a humanistic endeavor because it is concerned with people's processes of becoming, across the whole life span. Consistent with this innate humanistic character is a mission to nurture, exchange, and intermingle as we perform our scientific activities.

References

AARP PUBLIC POLICY INSTITUTE. (1994). *Beyond medical price inflation: The continuing case for comprehensive health care reform* (IB no. 18). Washington, DC: Author.

AARP PUBLIC POLICY INSTITUTE. (1995). *Medicare program fact sheet.* Washington, DC: Author.

AARP PUBLIC POLICY INSTITUTE. (1996). *Conference on the future of Medicare.* Washington, DC: Author.

AARP PUBLIC POLICY INSTITUTE. (1996). *The Medicare program.* (Fact sheet no. 45). Washington, DC. Author.

AARP PUBLIC POLICY INSTITUTE AND THE URBAN INSTITUTE. (1994–1995). *Coming up short: Increasing out-of-pocket health spending by older Americans.* Washington, DC: Author.

ABELES, R. P. (1992). Social stratification and aging: Contemporaneous and cumulative effects. In K. W. Schaie, D. G. Blazer, & J. S. House (Eds.). *Aging, health behaviors, and health outcomes* (pp. 33–37). Hillsdale, NJ: Erlbaum.

ABRA, J. (1989). Changes in creativity with age: Data, explanations, and further predictions. *International Journal of Aging and Human Development, 28,* 105–126.

ABRAHAM, J. D., & HANSSON, R. O. (1995). Successful aging at work: An applied study of selection, organization, optimization, and compensation through impression management. *Journals of Gerontology, 50B*(2), P94–P103.

ABRAMSON, L. Y., SELIGMAN, M. E., & TEASDALE, J. D. (1978). Learned helplessness in humans: Critique and reformulation. *Journal of Abnormal Psychology, 87*(1), 49–74.

ACITELLI, L. K., DOUVAN, E., & VEROFF, J. (1993). Perceptions of conflict in the first year of marriage: How important are similarity and understanding? *Journal of Personal and Social Relationships, 10,* 5–19.

ADAMS, C., LABOUVIE-VIEF, G., HOBART, C. J., & DOROSZ, M. (1990). Adult age group differences in story recall style. *Journals of Gerontology, 45*(1), P17–P27.

ADMINISTRATION ON AGING. (1997). *Profile of older Americans: 1997.* Washington, DC: Author.

ADUBIFA, O., LAPALIO, L., PHARM, D. J., LASAK, M., & LEMKE, R. (1997). *Failure to diagnose osteoporosis in elderly women residing in a retirement community.* Paper presented at the 50th Annual Scientific Meeting of the Gerontological Society of America.

ADVANCE DIRECTIVES. (1994). *Hastings Center Report, 24.*

AIZENBERG, R., & TREAS, J. (1985). The family in late life: Psychosocial and demographic considerations. In J. E. Birren and K. W. Schaie (Eds.), *Handbook of the psychology of aging* (2nd ed.) (pp. 169–189). New York: Van Nostrand Reinhold.

ALBERT, S. M., LITVIN, S. J., KLEBAN, M. H., & BRODY, E. M. (1991). Caregiving daughters' perceptions of their own and their mothers' personalities. *Gerontologist, 31,* 476–482.

ALDOUS, J. (1985). Parent–adult child relations as affected by the grandparent status. In V. L. Bengtson & J. F. Robertson (Eds.), *Grandparenthood* (pp. 117–132). Beverly Hills, CA: Sage.

ALDOUS, J. (1995). New views of grandparents in intergenerational context. *Journal of Family Issues, 16*(1), 104–122.

ALDWIN, C. M., SUTTON, K. J., CHIARA, G., & SPIRO, A., III. (1996). Age differences in stress, coping, and appraisal: Findings from the Normative Aging Study. *Journals of Gerontology, 51B*(4), P179–P188.

ALDWIN, C. M., SUTTON, K. J., & LACHMAN, M. (1996). The development of coping resources in adulthood. *Journal of Personality, 64,* 837–871.

ALONZO, A. A. (1993). Health behavior: Issues, contradictions, and dilemmas. *Social Science and Medicine,* 37(8), 1019–1034.

AMERICAN ASSOCIATION OF RETIRED PERSONS (1984). *Data gram: Housing satisfaction in older Americans.* Washington, DC: Author.

AMERICAN MEDICAL ASSOCIATION, COUNCIL OF ETHICAL AND JUDICIAL AFFAIRS. (1991). Guidelines for the appropriate use of do-not-resuscitate orders. *Journal of the American Medical Association, 265,* 1868–1871.

AMERICAN PSYCHIATRIC ASSOCIATION (1980). *Diagnostic and statistical manual of mental disorders* (3rd ed.). Washington, DC: Author.

AMERICAN PSYCHIATRIC ASSOCIATION. (1994). *Diagnostic and statistical manual of mental disorders* (4th ed.). Washington, DC: Author.

ANDERSEN, R., & NEWMAN, F. (1973). Societal and individual determinants of medical care utilization in the United States. *Milbank Memorial Fund Quarterly, 51,* 95.

ANDERSON, R. M., MULLNER, R. M., & CORNELIUS, L. J. (1989). Black-white differences in health status: Methods or substance? In D. P. Willis (Ed.), *Health policies and black Americans* (pp. 72–99). New Brunswick, NJ: Transaction.

ANDERSON-HANLEY, C., DUNKIN, J., CUMMINGS, J. L., & STRICKLAND, T. L. (1997). *Ethnic variability in dementia caregiver process variables.* Paper presented at the 50th Annual Scientific Meeting of the Gerontological Society of America.

ANESHENSEL, C. S., PEARLIN, L. I., MULLAN, J. T., ZARIT, S. H., & WHITLATCH, C. J. (1995). *Profiles in caregiving: The unexpected career.* San Diego: Academic Press.

ANGEL, J. L., & HOGAN, D. P. (1991). The demography of minority aging populations. In *Minority elders: Longevity, economics, and health* (pp. 1–13). Washington, DC: Gerontological Society of America.

ANKROM, M., THOMPSON, J., FINUCANE, T., & FINGERHOOD, M. (1997). *Gender differences in alcohol use and abuse in the homebound elderly and their caregivers.* Paper presented at the 50th Annual Scientific Meeting of the Gerontological Society of America.

ANTONOFF, S. R., & SPILKA, B. (1984–1985). Patterning of facial expressions among terminal care patients. *Omega: Journal of Death and Dying, 15,* 101–108.

ANTONUCCI, T. C., & AKIYAMA, H. (1995). Convoys of social relations: Family and friendships within a life-span context. In R. Blieszner & V. H. Bedford (Eds.), *Handbook of aging and the family* (pp. 355–372). Westport, CT: Greenwood Press.

ANTONUCCI, T. C., FUHRER, R., & DARTIGUES, J.-F. (1997). Social relations and depressive symptomatology in a sample of community-dwelling French older adults. *Psychology and Aging, 12,* 189–195.

APPLEBAUM, R., & PHILLIP, P. (1990). Assuring the quality of in-home care: The "other" challenge for long-term care. *Gerontologist, 30,* 444–450.

ARBUCKLE, T. Y., GOLD, D. P., ANDRES, D., SCHWARTZMAN, A., & CHAIKELMAN, T. (1992). The role of psychosocial context, age, and intelligence in memory performance of older men. *Psychology and Aging, 7,* 25–36.

ARDELT, M. (1997). Wisdom and life satisfaction in old age. *Journals of Gerontology, 52B*(1), P15–P27.

ARRAS, J. D., & DUBLER, N. N. (1994). Bringing the hospital home: Ethical and social implications of high-tech home care. *Hastings Center Report, 24*(5), S19–S28.

ARTHUR, M. B. (1994). The boundaryless career: A new perspective for organizational inquiry. *Journal of Organizational Behavior, 15*(4), 295–306.

ASCIONE, F. (1994). Medication compliance in the elderly. *Generations, 18*(2), 28–33.

ASTIN, H. S. (1984). The meaning of work in women's lives: A sociopsychological model of career choice and work behavior. *Counseling Psychologist, 12,* 117–126.

ATCHLEY, R. C. (1977). *The social forces in later life* (2nd ed). Belmont, CA: Wadsworth.

ATCHLEY, R. C., & MILLER, S. (1983). Types of elderly couples. In T. H. Brubaker (Ed.), *Family relationships in later life* (pp. 77–90). Beverly Hills, CA: Sage.

AUPPERLE, P. M., COYNE, A. C., & PANDINA, G. (1997). *Factors affecting utilization of outpatient mental health services by the elderly.* Paper presented at the 50th Annual Scientific Meeting of the Gerontological Society of America.

AVIS, N. E., BRAMBILLA, D. J., VASS, K., & MCKINLAY, J. B. (1991). The effect of widowhood on health: A prospective analysis from the Massachusetts Women's Health Study. *Social Science and Medicine, 33,* 1063–1070.

BADDELEY, A. D. (1992). Working memory: The interface between memory and cognition. *Journal of Cognitive Neuroscience, 4*(3), 281–288.

BALL, K., & REBOK, G. (1994). Evaluating the driving ability of older adults. *Journal of Applied Gerontology, 13*(1), 20–38.

BALL, R. M. (1996). Medicare's roots: What Medicare's architects had in mind. *Generations, 20,* 13–18.

BALTES, M. M., KUHL, K., & SOWARKA, D. (1992). Testing for limits of cognitive reserve capacity: A promising strategy for early diagnosis of dementia? *Journals of Gerontology, 47,* P165–P167.

BALTES, M. M., NEUMANN, E. M., & ZANK, S. (1994). Maintenance and rehabilitation of independence in old age: An intervention program for staff. *Psychology and Aging, 9,* 179–188.

BALTES, M. M., & WERNER-WAHL, H. (1992). The behavior system of dependency in the elderly: Interaction with the social environment. In M. G. Ory, R. P. Abeles, & P. D. Lipman (Eds.), *Aging, health, and behavior* (pp. 83–108). Newbury Park, CA: Sage.

BALTES, P. B. (1987). Theoretical propositions of life-span development psychology: On the dynamics between growth and decline. *Developmental Psychology, 23,* 611–626.

BALTES, P. B. (1993). The aging mind: Potential and limits. *Gerontologist, 33,* 580–594.

BALTES, P. B., & LINDENBERGER, U. (1997). Emergence of a powerful connection between sensory and cognitive functions across the adult life span: A new window to the study of cognitive aging? *Psychology and Aging, 12,* 12–21.

BALTES, P. B., REESE, H. W., & LIPSETT, L. P. (1980). Life-span developmental psychology. *Annual Review of Psychology, 31,* 65–110.

BALTES, P. B., REESE, H. W., & NESSELROADE, J. R. (1977). *Life-span developmental psychology: An introduction to research methods.* Monterey, CA: Brooks/Cole.

BALTES, P. B., & SMITH, J. (1997). A systematic-wholistic view of psychological functioning in very old age: Introduction to a collection of articles from the Berlin Aging Study. *Psychology and Aging, 12,* 395–409.

BALTES, P. B., SOWARKA, D., & KLIEGL, R. (1989). Cognitive training research on fluid intelligence in old age: What can older adults achieve by themselves? *Psychology and Aging, 4,* 217–221.

BALTES, P. B., & STAUDINGER, U. M. (1993). The search for a psychology of wisdom. *Current Directions in Psychological Science, 2*(3), 75–80.

BALTES, P. B., & WILLIS, S. L. (1977). Toward psychological theories of aging and development. In J. E. Birren & K. W. Schaie (Eds.), *Handbook of the psychology of aging* (pp. 128–154). New York: Van Nostrand Reinhold.

BANDURA, A. (1977). Self-efficacy: Toward a unifying theory of behavioral change. *Psychological Review, 84,* 191–215.

BANDURA, A. (1989). Human agency in social cognitive theory. *American Psychologist, 44,* 1175–1184.

BANDURA, A. (1992). Exercise of personal agency through the self-efficacy mechanism. In Ralf Schwarzer (Ed.), *Self-efficacy: Thought control of action* (pp. 3–38). Washington, DC: Hemisphere.

BANDURA, A. (1997). *Self-efficacy: The exercise of control.* New York: Freeman.

BARLOW, D. H. (1988). *Anxiety and its disorders: The nature and treatment of anxiety and panic.* New York: Guilford.

BARNES, D. E., BERO, L., FLESHMAN, R., GUGLIELMO, J., KISHI, D., & REED, D. (1997). *Medications use among residents of Marin County, CA, aged 55 and older.* Paper presented at the 50th Annual Scientific Meeting of the Gerontological Society of America.

BARNES, D. M. (1987). Defect of Alzheimer's is on chromosome 21. *Science, 235,* 846–847.

BARNETT, R. C., MARSHALL, N. L., & SINGER, J. P. (1992). Job experiences over time, multiple roles, and women's mental health: A longitudinal study. *Journal of Personality and Social Psychology, 62,* 634–644.

BARRETT, D. (1988–1989). Dreams of death. *Omega: Journal of Death and Dying, 19,* 95–101.

BARTOSHUK, L. M. (1989). Taste: Robust across the age span? *Annals of the New York Academy of Sciences, 561,* 65–75.

BASS, D. M., GARLAND, T. N., & OTTO, M. E. (1985–1986). Characteristics of hospice patients and their caregivers. *Omega: Journal of Death and Dying, 16,* 51–68.

BAUGHER, R. J., BURGER, C., SMITH, R., & WALLSTON, K. A. (1989–1990). A comparison of terminally ill persons at various time periods to death. *Omega: Journal of Death and Dying, 20,* 103–115.

BECK, A. T. (1973). *The diagnosis and management of depression.* Philadelphia: University of Pennsylvania Press.

BEIZER, J. L. (1994). Medications and the aging body: Alteration as a function of age. *Generations, 18*(2), 13–18.

BELSKY, JAY, LANG, M., & ROVINE, M. (1985). Stability and change in marriage across the transition to parenthood: A second study. *Journal of Marriage and the Family, 47,* 855–865.

BELSKY, JAY, & PENSKY, E. (1988). Marital change across the transition to parenthood. *Marriage and Family Review, 12*(3–4), 133–156.

BELSKY, J. K. (1990). *The psychology of aging: Theory, research, and interventions* (2d ed.). Pacific Grove, CA: Brooks/Cole.

BELSKY, J. K. (1994). The research findings on gender issues in aging women and men. In B. Wainrib (Ed.),

Gender issues across the life cycle (pp. 163–171). New York: Springer.

BELSKY, J. K. (1997). *The adult experience.* St. Paul, MN: West.

BEMBEN, M. G., & MCCALIP, G. (1997). *Alterations in strength and power as a function of age.* Paper presented at the 50th Annual Scientific Meeting of the Gerontological Society of America.

BEMPORAD, J. R. (1990). Psychoanalytic therapy of depression. In B. B. Wolman & G. Stricker (Eds.), *Depressive disorders: Facts, theories, and treatment methods* (pp. 296–309). New York: Wiley.

BENGTSON, V. L. (1989). The problem of generations: Age group contrasts, continuities, and social change. In V. L. Bengtson & K. W. Schaie (Eds.), *The course of later life: Research and reflections* (pp. 25–54). New York: Springer.

BENGTSON, V. L. (1993). Is the "contract across generations" changing? Effects of population aging on obligations and expectations across age groups. In V. L. Bengtson & W. A. Achenbaum (Eds.), *The changing contract across generations* (pp. 1–2). New York: Aldine de Gruyter.

BENGTSON, V. L., & ACHENBAUM, W. A. (EDS.). (1993). *The changing contract across generations.* New York: Aldine de Gruyter.

BENGTSON, V. L., ROSENTHAL, C., & BURTON, L. (1996). Paradoxes of families and aging. In R. H. Binstock & L. K. George (Eds.), *Handbook of aging and the social sciences* (4th ed.) (pp. 254–282). San Diego: Academic Press.

BENNETT, V. M., & ROY, C. A. (1997). *Placement decision processes among Alzheimer's disease caregivers.* Paper presented at the 50th Annual Scientific Meeting of the Gerontological Society of America.

BERG, C. A., & STERNBERG, R. J. (1992). Adults' conceptions of intelligence across the adult life span. *Psychology and Aging, 7,* 221–231.

BERG, S. (1996). Aging, behavior, and terminal decline. In J. E. Birren & K. W. Schaie (Eds.), *Handbook of the psychology of aging* (4th ed.) (pp. 323–337). San Diego: Academic Press.

BERGEMAN, C. S., PLOMIN, R., PEDERSEN, N. L., & MCCLEARN, G. E. (1991). Genetic mediation of the relationship between social support and psychological well-being. *Psychology and Aging, 6,* 640–646.

BERGEMAN, C. S., PLOMIN, R., PEDERSEN, N. L., MCCLEARN, G. E., & NESSELROADE, J. R. (1990). Genetic and environmental influences on social support: The Swedish Adoption/Twin Study of Aging. *Journals of Gerontology, 45*(3), P101–P106.

BERKMAN, L., & BRESLOW, L. (1983). *Health and ways of living: The Alameda County study.* New York: Oxford University Press.

BETZ, N. E. (1994). Basic issues and concepts in career counseling for women. In W. B. Walsh & S. H. Osipow (Eds.), *Career counseling for women* (pp. 237–261). Hillsdale, NJ: Erlbaum.

BEYERLEIN, M. M., HAYSLIP, B., & LUHR, D. D. (1992). Levels of death anxiety in terminally ill men: A pilot study. *Omega: Journal of Death and Dying, 24,* 13–19.

BIBRING, E. (1953). The mechanism of depression. In P. E. Greenacre (Ed.), *Affective disorders* (pp. 13–48). New York: International Universities Press.

BIEDENHARN, P. J., & NORMOYLE, J. B. (1991). Elderly community residents' reactions to the nursing home: An analysis of nursing home–related beliefs. *Gerontologist, 31,* 107–115.

BINION, V. J. (1990). Psychological androgyny: A black female perspective. *Sex Roles, 22*(7–8), 487–507.

BINSTOCK, R. H., & GEORGE, L. K. (EDS.). (1996). *Handbook of aging and the social sciences* (4th ed.). San Diego: Academic Press.

THE BIOLOGY OF AGING. (1992, Fall/Winter). *Generations, 16.*

BIRD, A. (1994). Careers as repositories of knowledge: A new perspective on boundaryless careers. *Journal of Organizational Behavior, 15*(4), 325–344.

BIRDI, K., WARR, P., & OSWALD, A. (1995). Age differences in three components of employee well-being. *Applied Psychology: An International Review, 44*(4), 345–373.

BIRREN, J. E., & BIRREN, B. A. (1990). The concepts, models, and history in the psychology of aging. In J. E. Birren & K. W. Schaie (Eds.). *Handbook of the psychology of aging* (3rd ed.) (pp. 1–20). San Diego: Academic Press.

BIRREN, J. E., BUTLER, R. N., GREENHOUSE, S. W., SOKOLOFF, L., & YARROW, M. R. (1963). *Human aging: A biological and behavioral study.* Washington, DC: U.S. Public Health Service.

BIRREN, J. E., & SCHAIE, K. W. (EDS.). (1996). *Handbook of the psychology of aging* (4th ed). San Diego: Academic Press.

BIRREN, J. E., & SCHROOTS, J. F. (1996). History, concepts, and theory in the psychology of aging. In J. E. Birren & K. W. Schaie (Eds.). *Handbook of the psychology of aging* (4th ed.) (pp. 3–23). San Diego: Academic Press.

BIRREN, J. E., & SLOANE, R. B. (EDS.). (1992). *Handbook of mental health and aging* (2nd ed). Englewood Cliffs, NJ: Prentice-Hall.

BITZAN, J. E., & KRUZICH, J. M. (1990). Interpersonal relationships of nursing home residents. *Gerontologist, 30,* 385–390.

BLANCHARD-FIELDS, F., & CHEN, Y. (1996). Adaptive cognition and aging. *American Behavioral Scientist, 39*(3), 231–248.

BLANCHARD-FIELDS, F., & HESS, T. (EDS.). (1996). *Perspectives on cognitive change in adulthood and aging.* New York: McGraw-Hill.

BLAZER, D., HUGHES, D. C., & GEORGE, L. K. (1987). The epidemiology of depression in an elderly community population. *Gerontologist, 27,* 281–287.

BLESSED, G., TOMLINSON, B. E., & ROTH, M. (1968). The association between quantitative measures of dementia and of senile changes in the cerebral grey matter of elderly subjects. *British Journal of Psychiatry, 114,* 797–811.

BLIESZNER, R., & BEDFORD, V. H. (EDS.). (1995). *Handbook of aging and the family.* Westport, CT: Greenwood Press.

BLOCH, A., MAEDER, J., & HAISSLY, J. (1975). Sexual problems after myocardial infarction. *American Heart Journal, 90,* 536–537.

BODKIN, N. L., ORTMEYER, H. K., & HANSEN, B. C. (1997). *Age and the onset of Type II diabetes in monkeys: Implications for effective intervention in humans.* Paper presented at the 50th Annual Scientific Meeting of the Gerontological Society of America.

BOOTH, A., & AMATO, P. (1994). Parental marital quality, parental divorce, and relations with parents. *Journal of Marriage and the Family, 56,* 21–34.

BORAWSKI, E. A., KINNEY, J. M., & KAHANA, E. (1996). The meaning of older adults' health appraisals: Congruence with health status and determinant of mortality. *Journals of Gerontology, 51B*(3), S157–S170.

BOSSE, R., ALDWIN, C. M., LEVENSON, M. R., & WORKMAN-DANIELS, K. (1991). How stressful is retirement? Findings from the Normative Aging Study. *Journals of Gerontology, 46*(1), P9–P14.

BOTWINICK, J. (1966). Cautiousness in advanced age. *Journal of Gerontology, 21,* 347–353.

BOTWINICK, J. (1967). *Cognitive processes in maturity and old age.* New York: Springer.

BOTWINICK, J., & BIRREN, J. E. (1963). Mental abilities and psychomotor responses in healthy aged men. In J. E. Birren, R. N. Butler, S. W. Greenhouse, L. Sokoloff, & M. R. Yarrow (Eds.), *Human aging: A biological and behavioral study* (pp. 97–110). Washington, DC: U.S. Public Health Service.

BOUCHARD, T. J. (1994). Genes, environment, and personality. *Science, 264,* 1700–1701.

BOUCHARD, T. J., & MCGUE, M. (1990). Genetic and rearing environmental influences on adult personality: An analysis of adopted twins reared apart. *Journal of Personality, 58,* 263–292.

BOUND, J., DUNCAN, G. J., LAREN, D. S., & OLEINICK, L. (1991). Poverty dynamics in widowhood. *Journals of Gerontology, 46*(3), S115–S124.

BOWLBY, C. (1993). *Therapeutic activities with persons disabled by Alzheimer's disease.* Gaithersberg, MD: Aspen.

BOWLBY, J. (1980). *Loss.* New York: Basic Books.

BRAITHWAITE, R., & TAYLOR, S. (1992). African American health: An introduction. In R. Braithwaite & S. Taylor (Eds.), *Health issues in the black community* (pp. 3–5). San Francisco: Jossey-Bass.

BRANCH, L. G., GURALNIK, J. M., FOLEY, D. J., KOHOUT, F. J., WETLE, T. T., OSTFELD, A., & KATZ, S. (1991). Active life expectancy for 10,000 men and women in three communities. *Journals of Gerontology 46*(4), M145–M150.

BRANDTSTÄDTER, J., & ROTHERMUND, K. (1994). Self-percepts of control in middle and later adulthood: Buffering losses by resealing goals. *Psychology and Aging, 9,* 265–273.

BRECHER, E. M., & CONSUMER REPORTS BOOK EDITORS. (1985). *Love, sex, and aging.* Boston: Little, Brown.

BRECKENRIDGE, J. N., GALLAGHER, D., THOMPSON, L. W., & PETERSON, J. (1986). Characteristic depressive symptoms of bereaved elders. *Journal of Gerontology, 41,* 163–168.

BRENNAN, M., HOROWITZ, A., & REINHARDT, J. (1997). *Factors associated with risk of self-reported vision impairment in later life.* Paper presented at the 50th Annual Scientific Meeting of the Gerontological Society of America.

BRENT, S. B., SPEECE, M. W., GATES, M. F., & KAUL, M. (1992–1993). The contribution of death-related experiences to health care providers' attitudes toward dying patients: Medical and nursing students with no professional experience. *Omega: Journal of Death and Dying, 26,* 181–205.

BRESCHEL, E. F. (1997). *Social integration, sense coherence, and mortality among the elderly.* Paper presented at the 50th Annual Scientific Meeting of the Gerontological Society of America.

BROCKOPP, D. Y., KING, B., & HAMILTON, J. E. (1991). The dying patient: A comparative study of nurse caregiver characteristics. *Journal of Death Studies, 15,* 245–258.

BRODY, E. M. (1985). Parent care as a normative family stress. *Gerontologist, 25,* 19–29.

BRODY, E. M., KLEBAN, M. H., JOHNSEN, P. T., HOFFMAN, C., & SCHOONOVER, C. B. (1987). Work status and parent care: A comparison of four groups of women. *Gerontologist, 27,* 201–208.

BRODY, E. M., & SCHOONOVER, C. B. (1986). Patterns of parent care when adult daughters work and when they do not. *Gerontologist, 26,* 372–381.

BUCHOLZ, K. K. (1992). Alcohol abuse and dependence from a psychiatric epidemiologic perspective. *Alcohol Health and Research World, 16*(3), 197–208.

BUELL, S. J., & COLEMAN, P. D. (1979). Dendritic growth in the human aged brain and failure of growth in senile dementia. *Science, 206,* 854–856.

BUHLER, L. K. (1995). *The relationship between intrinsic religiosity and death anxiety in the elderly.* Unpublished master's thesis, Middle Tennessee State University, Murfreesboro, TN.

BULCROFT, K. A., & BULCROFT, R. A. (1991). The timing of divorce: Effects on parent–child relationships in later life. *Research on Aging, 13*(2), 226–243.

BULCROFT, K. A., & O'CONNOR-RUDIN, M. (1986, June) Never too late. *Psychology Today,* 66–71.

BUMPASS, L., & AQUILINO, W. S. (1995, March). *A social map of midlife: Family and work over the middle life course.* Available from the John D. & Catherine T. MacArthur Foundation Research Network on Successful Midlife Development, Gilbert Brim, Director, 1625 Tenth Ave., Vero Beach, FL 32963.

BURACK, O. R., CHICHIN, E., & OLSEN, E. (1997). *Overlooking the nursing assistant: A qualitative and quantitative study.* Paper presented at the 50th Annual Scientific Meeting of the Gerontological Society of America.

BURACK, O. R., & LACHMAN, M. E. (1996). The effects of list making on recall in young and elderly adults. *Journals of Gerontology, 51B*(4), P 226–P233.

BURGIO, L. D., ENGLE, B. T., HAWKINS, A., MCCORMICK, K., & SCHEVE, A. (1990). A descriptive analysis of nursing staff behaviors in a teaching nursing home: Differences among NAs, LPNs, and RNs. *Gerontologist, 30,* 107–112.

BURKHAUSER, R. V. (1994). Protecting the most vulnerable: A proposal to improve Social Security insurance for older women. *Gerontologist, 34,* 148–149.

BURNS, J. W., FRIEDMAN, R., & KATKIN, E. S. (1992). Anger expression, hostility, anxiety, and patterns of cardiac reactivity to stress. *Behavioral Medicine, 18*(2), 71–78.

BURNS, M. O., & SELIGMAN, M. E. (1989). Explanatory style across the life span: Evidence for stability over 52 years. *Journal of Personality and Social Psychology, 56,* 471–477.

BUSSCHBACH, J. J., HESSING, D. J., & CHARRO, F. T. (1993). The utility of health at different stages in life: A quantitative approach. *Social Science and Medicine, 37,* 153–158.

BUTLER, R. N. (1980). Ageism: A forward. *Journal of Social Issues, 36,* 8–11.

BUTLER, R. N., & LEWIS, M. I. (1973). *Aging and mental health.* St. Louis: Mosby.

CALDERON, V., & TENNSTEDT, S. (1997). *Meaning of caregiver burden: Differences and similarities among African American, Puerto Rican, and White caregivers.* Paper presented at the 50th Annual Scientific Meeting of the Gerontological Society of America.

CALLAHAN, D. (1987). *Setting limits: Medical care in an aging society.* New York: Simon & Schuster.

CALLAHAN, D. (1994). Aging and the goals of medicine. *Hastings Center Report, 24,* 39–41.

CAMERON, P., STEWART, L., & BIBER, H. (1973). Consciousness of death across the life span. *Journal of Gerontology, 28,* 92–95.

CAMPBELL, B. C., & UDRY, J. R. (1994). Implications of hormonal influences on sexual behavior for demographic models of reproduction. In K. L. Campbell & J. W. Wood (Eds.), *Human reproductive ecology: Interactions of environment, fertility, and behavior* (pp. 117–127). New York: New York Academy of Sciences.

CAMPBELL, D., & FISKE, D. (1959). Convergent and discriminant validation by the multitrait-multimethod matrix. *Psychological Bulletin, 56,* 81–105.

CANESTRARI, R. E. (1963). Paced and self-paced learning in young and elderly adults. *Journal of Gerontology, 18,* 165–168.

CANTOR, M. H. (1983). Strain among caregivers: A study of the experience in the United States. *Gerontologist, 23,* 597–604.

CAROLAN, M. T. (1994). Beyond deficiency: Broadening the view of menopause. *Journal of Applied Gerontology, 13*(2), 193–205.

CARSTENSEN, L. L. (1995). Evidence for a life-span theory of socioemotional selectivity. *Current Directions in Psychological Science, 4*(5), 151–156.

CARSTENSEN, L. L., GOTTMAN, J. M., & LEVENSON, R. W. (1995). Emotional behavior in long-term marriage. *Psychology and Aging, 10,* 140–149.

CARSTENSEN, L. L., HANSON, K. A., & FREUND, A. M. (1995). Selection and compensation in adulthood. In R. A. Dixon & L. Bäckman (Eds.). *Compensating for psychological deficits and declines: Managing losses and promoting gains* (pp. 107–126). Mahwah, NJ: Erlbaum.

CARSTENSEN, L. L., & TURK-CHARLES, S. (1994). The salience of emotion across the adult life span. *Psychology and Aging, 9,* 259–264.

CASERTA, M. S., & LUND, D. A. (1993). Intrapersonal resources and the effectiveness of self-help groups for bereaved older adults. *Gerontologist, 33,* 619–629.

CASPI, A., BEM, D., & ELDER, G. H. (1989). Continuities and consequences of interactional styles across the life course. *Journal of Personality, 57,* 375–406.

CASPI, A., ELDER, G. H., & BEM, D. J. (1987). Moving against the world: Life course patterns of explosive children. *Developmental Psychology, 23,* 308–313.

CASPI, A., & HERBENER, E. S. (1990). Continuity and change: Assortative marriage and the consistency of personality in adulthood. *Journal of Personality and Social Psychology, 58,* 250–258.

CASSEL, C. K., & CAPELLO, C. (1997). Easing the pain of death. *Hospital Practice, 32,* 13–19.

CASTLE, N. (1996–1997). Advance directives in nursing homes. Resident and facility characteristics. *Omega: Journal of Death and Dying, 14,* 321–332.

CAVANAUGH, J. C. (1989). The importance of awareness in memory and aging: Issues of structure and function. In L. W. Poon, D. C. Rubin, & B. A. Wilson (Eds.), *Everyday cognition in adulthood and late life* (pp. 59–73). New York: Cambridge University Press.

CAVANAUGH, J. C. (1996). Memory self-efficacy as a moderator of memory change. In F. Blanchard-Fields & T. M. Hess (Eds.), *Perspectives on cognitive change in adulthood and aging* (pp. 488–507). New York: McGraw-Hill.

CECI, S. J., & LIKER, J. (1986). Academic and non-academic intelligence: An experimental separation. In R. J. Sternberg & R. Wagner (Eds.), *Practical intelligence* (pp. 119–143). New York: Cambridge University Press.

CEFALU, W. T., BELL-FARROW, A., WAGNER, J. D., MILLER, L., & COLLINS, J. (1997). *Caloric restriction maintains an increased insulin sensitivity and reduced intra-abdominal fat and may alter muscle morphology in non-human primates.* Paper presented at the 50th Annual Scientific Meeting of the Gerontological Society of America.

CERELLA, J. (1990). Aging and information-processing rate. In J. E. Birren & K. W. Schaie (Eds.), *Handbook of the psychology of aging* (3rd ed.) (pp. 201–221). San Diego: Academic Press.

CHAPLIN, W. F., & BUCKNER, K. E. (1988). Self-ratings of personality: A naturalistic comparison of normative, ipsative, and idiothetic standards. *Journal of Personality, 56,* 509–530.

CHARNESS, N., & BOSMAN, E. A. (1995). Compensation through environmental modification. In R. A. Dixon & L. Bäckman (Eds.), *Compensating for psychological deficits and declines: Managing losses and promoting gains* (pp. 147–168). Mahwah, NJ: Erlbaum.

CHEN, Y.-P. (1991). Improving the economic security of minority persons as they enter old age. *Minority elders: Longevity, economics, and health* (pp. 14–23). Washington, DC: Gerontological Society of America.

CHERLIN, A. J., & FURSTENBERG, F. F. (1985). Styles and strategies of grandparenting. In V. L. Bengtson & J. F. Robertson (Eds.), *Grandparenthood* (pp. 97–116). Beverly Hills, CA: Sage.

CHESNEY, M. A., HECKER, M. H. L., & BLACK, G. W. (1988). Coronary-prone components of Type A behavior in the WCGS: A new methodology. In B. K. Houston & C. R. Snyder (Eds.), *Type A behavior pattern: Research, theory, and intervention* (pp. 168–188). New York: Wiley.

CHILDREN'S DEFENSE FUND. (1994). *The state of America's children: Yearbook, 1994.* Washington, DC: Author.

CHIPUER, H. M., PLOMIN, R., PEDERSEN, N. L., MCCLEARN, G. E., & NESSELROADE, J. R. (1993). Genetic influence on family environment: The role of personality. *Developmental Psychology, 29,* 110–118.

CHIRIKOS, T. N., & NESTEL, G. (1985). Longitudinal analysis of functional disabilities in older men. *Journal of Gerontology, 40,* 426–433.

CHOI, G. N. (1991). Racial difference in the determinants of living arrangements of widowed and divorced elderly women. *Gerontologist, 31,* 496–504.

CICIRELLI, V. G. (1997). Relationship of psychosocial and background variables to older adults' end-of-life decisions. *Psychology and Aging, 12,* 72–83.

CLARK, A., OSWALD, A., & WARR, P. (1996). Is job satisfaction U-shaped in age? *Journal of Occupational and Organizational Psychology, 69*(1), 57–81.

CLARKSON-SMITH, L., & HARTLEY, H. (1990). The game of bridge as an exercise in working memory and reasoning. *Journals of Gerontology, 45,* P233–P238.

CLONINGER, C. R. (1987). Neurogenetic adaptive mechanisms in alcoholism. *Science, 236,* 410–416.

CLONINGER, C. R., BOHMAN, M., & SIGVARDSSON, S. (1981). Inheritance of alcohol abuse: Cross-fostering analysis of adopted men. *Archives of General Psychiatry, 38,* 861–868.

COHEN, D., EISDORFER, C., GORELICK, P., PAVEZA, G., LUCHINS, D. J., FRELS, S., ASHFORD, J. W., SMELA, T., LEVY, P., & HIRSCHMAN, R. (1993). Psychopathology associated with Alzheimer's disease and related disorders. *Journals of Gerontology, 48*(6), M255–M260.

COHEN, G. D. (1997). Gaps and failures in attending to mental health and aging in long-term care. In R. L. Rubinstein & M. P. Lawton (Eds.), *Depression in long-*

term and residential care: *Advances in research and treatment* (pp. 211–222). New York: Springer.

COHEN, K. P. (1979). *Hospice: Prescription for terminal care*. Germantown, MD: Aspen.

COHLER, B. J., & GRUNEBAUM, H. V. (1981). *Mothers, grandmothers, and daughters: Personality and child care in three-generation families*. New York: Wiley.

COHN, B. A., & WINGARD, D. L. (1990). Variations in disease-specific sex morbidity and mortality ratios in the United States. In M. G. Ory & H. R. Warner (Eds.), *Gender, health, and longevity: Multidisciplinary perspectives* (pp. 25–40). New York: Springer.

COHN, R. M. (1979). Age and the satisfactions from work. *Journal of Gerontology, 34,* 264–272.

COLE, S. (1979). Age and scientific performance. *American Journal of Sociology, 84,* 264–272.

COLEMAN, P. D. (1986, August). *Regulation of dendritic extent: Human aging brain and Alzheimer's disease*. Paper presented at the 94th annual meeting of the American Psychological Association, Washington, DC.

COMFORT, A. (1979). *The biology of senescence* (3rd ed). New York: Elsevier/North Holland.

COMSTOCK, B. S. (1992). Decision to hospitalize and alternatives to hospitalization. In B. Bongar (Ed.), *Suicide: Guidelines for assessment, management, and treatment* (pp. 204–217). New York: Oxford University Press.

CONLEY, J. J. (1984). Longitudinal consistency of adult personality: Self-reported psychological characteristics across 45 years. *Journal of Personality and Social Psychology, 47,* 1325–1333.

CONLEY, J. J. (1985). Longitudinal stability of personality traits: A multitrait-multimethod-multioccasion analysis. *Journal of Personality and Social Psychology, 49,* 1266–1282.

CONNIDIS, I. A., & DAVIES, L. (1992). Confidants and companions: Choices in later life. *Journals of Gerontology, 47(3),* S115–S122.

CONTRADA, R. J., KRANTZ, D. S., & HILL, D. R. (1988). Type A behavior, emotion, and psychophysiologic reactivity: Psychological and biological interactions. In B. K. Houston & C. R. Snyder (Eds.), *Type A behavior pattern: Research, theory, and intervention* (pp. 254–274). New York: Wiley.

CONWAY, S. W., HAYSLIP, B., & TANDY, R. E. (1991). Similarity of perceptions of bereavement experiences between widows and professionals. *Omega: Journal of Death and Dying, 23,* 37–51.

COOLIDGE, F. L., & FISH, C. E. (1983–1984). Dreams of the dying. *Omega: Journal of Death and Dying, 14,* 1–8.

COONEY, T. M., SCHAIE, K. W., & WILLIS, S. L. (1988). The relationship between prior functioning on cognitive and personality dimensions and subject attrition in longitudinal research. *Journals of Gerontology, 43,* P12–P17.

COONS, D. (1991). *Special care dementia units*. Baltimore: Johns Hopkins University Press.

COONTS, S. (1992). *The way we never were*. New York: Basic Books.

COOPER, J. K., & MUNGAS, D. (1993). Alzheimer's disease drug treatment. *Journal of Geriatric Drug Therapy, 8(2),* 5–18.

COOPER, J. W. (1994). Drug-related problems in the elderly patient. *Generations, 18(2),* 19–27.

COOPER, K. L., & GUTMANN, D. L. (1987). Gender identity and ego mastery style in middle-aged pre– and post–empty nest women. *Gerontologist, 27,* 347–352.

CORAZZINI, K. N. (1997). *Living arrangements of elderly African Americans: What we can learn from the health and retirement study*. Paper presented at the 50th Annual Scientific Meeting of the Gerontological Society of America.

CORBY, N., & SOLNICK, R. L. (1980). Psychosocial and physiological influences on sexuality in the older adult. In J. E. Birren & R. B. Sloane (Eds.), *Handbook of mental health and aging* (pp. 893–921). Englewood Cliffs, NJ: Prentice-Hall.

CORNELIUS, S. W., & CASPI, A. (1987). Everyday problem solving in adulthood and old age. *Psychology and Aging, 2,* 144–153.

CORR, C. A. (1991–1992). A task-based approach to coping with dying. *Omega: Journal of Death and Dying, 24,* 81–94.

CORR, C. A. (1993). Coping with dying: Lessons that we should and should not learn from the work of Elisabeth Kubler-Ross. *Death Studies, 17,* 69–83.

COSTA, P. T., & MCCRAE, R. R. (1980). Influence of extraversion and neuroticism on subjective well-being: Happy and unhappy people. *Journal of Personality and Social Psychology, 38,* 668–678.

COSTA, P. T., & MCCRAE, R. R. (1986). Cross-sectional studies of personality in a national sample: Development and validation of survey measures. *Psychology and Aging, 1,* 140–143.

COSTA, P. T., & MCCRAE, R. R. (1987). Role of neuroticism in the perception and presentation of chest pain symptoms and coronary artery disease. In J. W. Elias & P. H. Marshall (Eds.), *Cardiovascular disease and behavior* (pp. 39–66). Washington, DC: Hemisphere.

COSTA, P. T., & MCCRAE, R. R. (1988a). From catalog to classification: Murray's needs and the five-factor model. *Journal of Personality and Social Psychology, 55,* 258–265.

COSTA, P. T., & MCCRAE, R. R. (1988b). Personality in adulthood: A six-year longitudinal study of self-reports and spouse ratings on the NEO Personality Inventory. *Journal of Personality and Social Psychology, 54,* 853–863.

COSTA, P. T., & MCCRAE, R. R. (1989). Personality, stress, and coping: Some lessons from a decade of research. In K. S. Markides & C. L. Cooper (Eds.), *Aging, stress, and health* (pp. 269–285). Chichester, England: Wiley.

COSTA, P. T., MCCRAE, R. R., & ARENBERG, D. (1980). Enduring dispositions in adult males. *Journal of Personality and Social Psychology, 38,* 793–800.

COSTA, P. T., MCCRAE, R. R., & ARENBERG, D. (1983). Recent longitudinal research on personality and aging. In K. W. Schaie (Ed.), *Longitudinal studies of adult psychological development* (pp. 222–225). New York: Guilford.

COUNCIL ON FAMILIES IN AMERICA. (1995, March). *Marriage in America: A report to the nation.* New York: Institute for American Values.

COWARD, R. T., LEE, G. R., DWYER, J. W., & SECCOMBE, K. (1993). *Old and alone in rural America.* Washington, DC: American Association of Retired Persons.

COWAN, C. P., & COWAN, P. A. (1988). Who does what when parents become partners: Implications for men, women, and marriage. *Marriage and Family Review, 12,* 105–132.

COWAN, C. P., & COWAN, P. A. (1992). *When partners become parents.* New York: Harper and Row.

COYER, J. L., PARISI, J. D., & SLOTTERBACK, C. S. (1997). *Intergenerational relations: What children think are the "best" and "worst" things about being old.* Paper presented at the 50th Annual Scientific Meeting of the Gerontological Society of America.

COYNE, A. C., BERBIG, L. J., HARKEY, J. R., SWARTZ, L. S., & VETTER, D. J. (1997). *Medical vs. social day care: Patterns of health care complaints.* Paper presented at the 50th Annual Scientific Meeting of the Gerontological Society of America.

CREWS, D. E., & HARPER, D. E. (1997). *Congregate care retirement communities: A case study of current directions.* Paper presented at the 50th Annual Scientific Meeting of the Gerontological Society of America.

CRIMMINS, E. M. (1996). Mixed trends in population health among older adults. *Journals of Gerontology: Social Sciences, 51B,* S223–S225.

CRIMMINS, E. M., & INGEGNERI, D. G. (1990). Interaction and arrangements of older parents and their children: Past trends, present determinants, future implications. *Research on Aging, 12*(1), 3–35.

CRIMMINS, E. M., SAITO, Y., & REYNOLDS, S. L. (1997). Further evidence on recent trends in the prevalence and incidence of disability among older Americans from two sources: The LSOA and the NHIS. *Journals of Gerontology: Social Sciences, 52B*(2), S59–S71.

CRISPI, E. L., SCHIAFFINO, K., & BERMAN, W. H. (1997). The contribution of attachment to burden in adult children of institutionalized parents with dementia. *Gerontologist, 37,* 52–60.

CRISTOFALO, V. (1988). An overview of the theories of biological aging. In J. E. Birren & V. L. Bengtson (Eds.), *Emergent theories of aging* (pp. 118–127). New York: Springer.

CROOK, T. H., & LARRABEE, G. J. (1992). Changes in facial recognition memory across the adult life span. *Journals of Gerontology, 47*(3), P138–P141.

CROSS, S., & MARKUS, H. (1991). Possible selves across the life span. *Human Development, 34*(4), 230–255.

CROWN, W. H., AHLBURG, D. A., & MACADAM, M. (1995). The demographic and employment characteristics of home care aides: A comparison with nursing home aides, hospital aides, and other workers. *Gerontologist, 35,* 162–170.

CRYSTAL, S. (1996). Economic status of the elderly. In R. H. Binstock & L. K. George (Eds.), *Handbook of aging and the social sciences* (4th ed.) (pp. 388–409). New York: Academic Press.

CRYSTAL, S., & JOHNSON, R. W. (1997). *Health inequality, age of onset of disability, and financial consequences.* Paper presented at the 50th Annual Scientific Meeting of the Gerontological Society of America.

CRYSTAL, S., & WAEHRER, K. (1996). Later life economic inequality in longitudinal perspective. *Journals of Gerontology, Series B: Social Sciences, 51,* S307–S318.

CSIKSZENTMIHALYI, M. (1996). *Creativity: Flow and the psychology of discovery and invention.* New York: HarperCollins.

CUMMING, E., & HENRY, W. (1961). *Growing old.* New York: Basic Books.

CUNNINGHAM, D. A., RECHNITZER, P. A., HOWARD, J. H., & DONNER, A. P. (1987). Exercise training of men at retirement: A clinical trial. *Journal of Gerontology, 42,* 17–23.

CURB, J. D., REED, D. M., MILLER, F. D., & YANO, K. (1990). Health status and life style in elderly Japanese men with a long life expectancy. *Journals of Gerontology, 45*(5), S206–S211.

CURRENT ETHICAL ISSUES IN AGING. (1994, Winter). *Generations, 18.*

DAMRON-RODRIGUEZ, J., LIU, D., SHRAGUE, S., OSTERWEIL, D., FRANK, J., CRUISE, P., & HECK, E. (1997). *Physician knowledge of community-based care.* Paper presented at the 50th Annual Scientific Meeting of the Gerontological Society of America.

D'ANGELO, C. (1992). Cartello. In A. Bush-Brown & D. Davis (Eds.), *Hospitable design for health care and senior communities* (pp. 160–161). New York: Van Nostrand Reinhold.

DANIS, M., SOUTHERLAND, L. I., GARRETT, J. M., SMITH, J. L., HIELEMA, F., PICKARD, G., EGNER, D. M., & PATRICK, D. L. (1991). A prospective study of advance directives for life-sustaining care. *New England Journal of Medicine, 324,* 882–888.

DAVIS, G., & JESSEN, A. (1980–1981). An experiment in death education in the medical curriculum: Medical students and clergy "on call" together. *Omega: Journal of Death and Dying, 11,* 157–166.

DE FRIAS, C. M., SCHAIE, K. W., & WILLIS, S. L. (1997). *Complexity of the work environment and cognitive functioning.* Paper presented at the 50th Annual Scientific Meeting of the Gerontological Society of America.

DEAN, A., MATT, G. E., & WOOD, P. (1992). The effects of widowhood on social support from significant others. *Journal of Community Psychology, 20*(4), 309–325.

DEAN, D. J., & CARTEE, G. D. (1996). Brief dietary restriction increases skeletal muscle glucose transport in old Fischer 344 rats. *Journal of Gerontology: Biological Sciences, 51A*(3), B208–B213.

DEBRUIN, A. F., DEWITTE, L. P., STEVENS, F., & DIEDERIKS, J. P. (1992). Sickness Impact Profile: The state of the art of a generic functional status measure. *Social Science and Medicine, 35*(8), 1003–1014.

DEDRICK, E. J., & DOBBINS, G. H. (1991). The influence of subordinate age on managerial actions: An attributional analysis. *Journal of Organizational Behavior, 12*(5), 367–377.

DEFILLIPPI, R. J., & ARTHUR, M. B. (1994). The boundaryless career: A competency-based perspective. *Journal of Organizational Behavior, 15*(4), 307–324.

DENNEY, N. A. (1989). Everyday problem solving: Methodological issues, research findings, and a model. In L. W. Poon, D. C. Rubin, & B. A. Wilson (Eds.), *Everyday cognition in adulthood and late life* (pp. 59–73). New York: Cambridge University Press.

DENNIS, W. (1966). Creative productivity between the ages of 20 and 80 years. *Journal of Gerontology, 21,* 1–8.

DEURRESTI, M., BROOKS, M., TRIPLETT, J., HAMDAN, K., BEBER, C., & SILVERMAN, M. (1997). *Monitoring for polypharmacy in a frail elderly home-bound population: An integral part of case management.* Paper presented at the 50th Annual Scientific Meeting of the Gerontological Society of America.

DEVOS, S. (1990). Extended family living among older people in six Latin American countries. *Journals of Gerontology, 45*(3), 87–94.

DHOOPER, S. S., GREEN, S. M., HUFF, M. B., & AUSTIN-MURPHY, J. I. (1993). Efficacy of a group approach to reducing depression in nursing home elderly residents. *Journal of Gerontological Social Work, 20*(3–4), 87–100.

DIAMOND, M. C. (1988). *Enriching heredity.* New York: Free Press.

DICKINSON, G. E., & PEARSON, A. A. (1980–1981). Death education and physicians' attitudes towards dying patients. *Omega: Journal of Death and Dying, 11,* 167–174.

DIENER, E., & SUH, M. E. (1998). Subjective well-being and age: An international analysis. In K. W. Schaie & M. P. Lawton (Eds.), *Annual review of gerontology and geriatrics: Vol. 17. Focus on emotion and adult development* (pp. 304–324). New York: Springer.

DION, K. L., & YEE, P. H. (1987). Ethnicity and personality in a Canadian context. *Journal of Social Psychology, 127*(2), 175–182.

DIXON, R. A. (1992). Contextual approaches to adult intellectual development. In R. J. Sternberg & C. A. Berg (Eds.), *Intellectual development* (pp. 350–380). New York: Cambridge University Press.

DOUGHERTY, K., TEMPLER, D. I., & BROWN, R. (1986). Psychological states in terminal cancer patients over time. *Journal of Counseling Psychology, 33,* 357–359.

DRESSER, R. (1994). Advance directives: Implications for policy. *Hastings Center Report, 24*(6), S2–S5.

DRESSER, R., & WHITEHOUSE, P. J. (1994). The incompetent patient on the slippery slope. *Hastings Center Report, 24,* 6–12.

DRISCOLL, L. (1995). *The Medicare program.* Washington, DC: American Association of Retired Persons, Public Policy Institute.

DRISCOLL, L., JENSEN, D., RAETZMAN, S., & STAFF FROM THE URBAN INSTITUTE. (1995). *Coming up short: Increasing out-of-pocket health spending by older Americans.* Washington, DC: American Association of Retired Persons, Public Policy Institute.

DUBLER, N. (1994). Introduction. *Generations, 18,* 2–7.

DUNN, J. E., RUDBERG, M. A., FURNER, S. E., & CASSEL, C. K. (1992). Mortality, disability, and falls in older persons: The role of underlying disease and disability. *American Journal of Public Health, 82*(3), 395–400.

DUNN, T. A., & PHILLIPS, J. W. (1997). *Co-residence and children's income*. Paper presented at the 50th Annual Scientific Meeting of the Gerontological Society of America.

DURLAK, J. A., & RIESENBERG, L. A. (1991). The impact of death education. *Death Studies, 15*(1), 39–58.

DWYER, J. W. (1995). The effects of illness on the family. In R. Blieszner & V. H. Bedford (Eds.), *Handbook of aging and the family* (pp. 401–421). Westport, CT: Greenwood Press.

EARL, W. L., MARTINDALE, C. J., & COHN, D. (1991–1992). Adjustment: Denial in the styles of coping with HIV infection. *Omega: Journal of Death and Dying, 24*(1), 35–47.

EARLES, J. L., & SALTHOUSE, T. A. (1995). Interrelations of age, health, and speed. *Journals of Gerontology, 50B*(1), P33–P41.

EASTERLIN, R. A. (1996). Economic and social implications of demographic patterns. In R. H. Binstock & L. K. George (Eds.), *Handbook of aging and the social sciences* (4th ed.) (pp. 73–93). New York: Academic Press.

EASTERLIN, R. A., MACUNOVICH, D. J., & CRIMMINS, E. M. (1993). Connections: Kin and cohort. In V. L. Bengtson & W. A. Achenbaum (Eds.), *The changing contract across generations* (pp. 67–88). New York: Aldine de Gruyter.

EFFROS, R. B., WALFORD, R. L., WEINDRUCH, R., & MITCH-ELTREE, C. (1991). Influences of dietary restriction on immunity to influenza in aged mice. *Journals of Gerontology, 46*(4), B142–B147.

EINSTEIN, G. O., SMITH, R. E., MCDANIEL, M. A., & SHAW, P. (1997). Aging and prospective memory: The influence of increased task demands at encoding and retrieval. *Psychology and Aging, 12,* 479–488.

EISDORFER, C. (1970). Developmental level and sensory impairment in the aged. In E. Palmore (Ed.), *Normal aging* (pp. 238–242). Durham, NC: Duke University Press.

EKERDT, D. J., BOSSE, R., & LEVKOFF, S. (1985). An empirical test for phases of retirement: Findings from the Normative Aging Study. *Journal of Gerontology, 40,* 95–101.

EKERDT, D. J., & DEVINEY, S. (1993). Evidence for a pre-retirement process among older male workers. *Journals of Gerontology, 48*(2), S35–S43.

ELIAS, M. F., ELIAS, J. W., & ELIAS, P. K. (1990). Biological and health influences on behavior. In J. E. Birren & K. W. Schaie (Eds.), *Handbook of the psychology of aging* (3rd ed.) (pp. 79–102). San Diego: Academic Press.

ENDRESEN, I. M., RELLING, G. B., TONDER, O., MYKING, O., WALTHER, B. T., & URSIN, H. (1991–1992). Brief uncontrollable stress and psychological parameters influence human plasma concentrations of IgM and complement component C3. *Behavioral Medicine, 17*(4), 167–176.

ENGLE, V. F., & GRANEY, M. J. (1993). Stability and improvement of health after nursing home admission. *Journals of Gerontology, 48*(1), S17–S23.

ENOS, W., HOLMES, R., & BEYER, J. (1955). Pathogenesis of coronary disease in American soldiers killed in Korea. *Journal of the American Medical Association, 158,* 192.

ERBER, J. T., & ROTHBERG, S. T. (1991). Here's looking at you: The relative effect of age and attractiveness on judgments about memory failure. *Journals of Gerontology, 46*(3), P116–P123.

ERBER, J. T., SZUCHMAN, L. T., & ROTHBERG, S. T. (1990). Age, gender, and individual differences in memory failure appraisal. *Psychology and Aging, 5,* 600–603.

ERIKSON, E. H. (1963). *Childhood and society*. New York: Norton.

EUSTIS, N. N., & FISCHER, L. R. (1991). Relationships between home care clients and their workers: Implications for quality of care. *Gerontologist, 31,* 447–456.

EVANS, L., EKERDT, D. J., & BOSSE, R. (1985). Proximity to retirement and anticipatory involvement: Findings from the Normative Aging Study. *Journal of Gerontology, 40,* 368–374.

FARRAN, C. J., KEANE-HAGERTY, E., SALLOWAY, S., KUP-FERER, S., & WILKIN, C. S. (1991). Finding meaning: An alternative paradigm for Alzheimer's disease family caregivers. *Gerontologist, 31,* 483–489.

FFIFFI, H., & BRANSCOMB, A. B. (1973). Who's afraid of death? *Journal of Abnormal Psychology, 81,* 282–288.

FEINSON, M. C. (1986). Aging widows and widowers: Are there mental health differences? *International Journal of Aging and Human Development, 23*(4), 241–255.

FELDMAN, S. S., BIRINGEN, Z. C., & NASH, S. C. (1981). Fluctuations of sex-related self attributions as a function of stage of family life cycle. *Developmental Psychology, 17,* 24–35.

FEMIA, E. E., ZARIT, S. H., & JOHANSSON, B. (1997). Predicting change in activities of daily living: A longitudinal study of the oldest old. *Journals of Gerontology, 52B*(6), P294–P302.

FERBER, M. A., O'FARRELL, B., & ALLEN, L. R. (EDS.). (1991). *Work and family: Policies for a changing work force*. Washington, DC: National Academy Press.

FERRUCCI, L., GURALNIK, J. M., SIMONSICK, E., SALVE, M., CORTI, C., & LANGLOIS, J. (1996). Progressive versus catastrophic disability: A longitudinal view of the disablement process. *Journals of Gerontology 51A,* M123–M130.

FIELD, D. (1997). *A longitudinal study of friendships in old age.* Paper presented at the 50th Annual Scientific Meeting of the Gerontological Society of America.

FIELD, D., MINKLER, M., FALK, R. F., & LEINO, E. V. (1993). The influence of health on family contacts and family feelings in advanced old age: A longitudinal study. *Journals of Gerontology, 48B*(1), P18–P28.

FIELD, D., SCHAIE, K. W., & LEINO, E. V. (1988). Continuity in intellectual functioning: The role of self-reported health. *Psychology and Aging, 3,* 385–392.

FILIPP, S. H. (1996). Motivation and emotion. In J. E. Birren and K. W. Schaie (Eds.), *Handbook of the psychology of aging* (4th ed.) (pp. 218–235). San Diego: Academic Press.

FINCH, C. E., & PIKE, M. C. (1996). Maximum life span predictions from the Gompertz Mortality Model. *Journals of Gerontology, 51A*(3), B183–B194.

FINGERMAN, K. L. (1995). Aging mothers' and their adult daughters' perceptions of conflict behaviors. *Psychology and Aging, 10,* 639–649.

FINGERMAN, K. L. (1996). Sources of tension in the aging mothers and adult daughters relationship. *Psychology and Aging, 11,* 591–606.

FINGERMAN, K. L. (1997). Being more than a daughter: Middle-aged women's conceptions of their mothers. *Journal of Women and Aging, 9*(4), 55–72.

FISCHER, D. H. (1977). *Growing old in America.* New York: Oxford University Press.

FISKE, D. (1971). *Measuring the concepts of personality.* Chicago: Aldine-Atherton.

FITTING, M., RABINS, P., LUCAS, M. J., & EASTHAM, J. (1986). Caregivers for dementia patients: A comparison of husbands and wives. *Gerontologist, 26,* 248–252.

FLEESON, W., & HECKHAUSEN, J. (1997). More or less "me" in past, present, and future: Perceived lifetime personality during adulthood. *Psychology and Aging, 12,* 125–136.

FLORIAN, V., & MIKULINCER, M. (1993). The impact of death-risk experiences and religiosity on the fear of personal death: The case of Israeli soldiers in Lebanon. *Omega: Journal of Death and Dying, 26,* 101–111.

FLOYD, M., & SCOGIN, F. (1997). Effects of memory training on the subjective memory functioning and mental health of older adults: A meta-analysis. *Psychology and Aging, 12,* 150–161.

FOLSTEIN, M. F., BASSETT, S. S., ANTHONY, J. C., ROMANOSKI, A. J., & NESTADT, G. R. (1991). Dementia: A case ascertainment in a community survey. *Journals of Gerontology, 46*(4), M132–M138.

FORTINSKY, R. H., & RAFF, L. (1995–1996). The changing role of physicians in nursing homes. *Generations, 19*(4), 30–35.

FOZARD, J. L. (1990). Vision and hearing in aging. In J. E. Birren & K. W. Schaie (Eds.), *Handbook of the psychology of aging* (3rd ed.) (pp. 150–170). San Diego: Academic Press.

FRANKL, V. E. (1970). *Man's search for meaning: An introduction to logotherapy.* Boston: Beacon Press.

FRANKS, M. M., & STEPHENS, A. P. (1992). Multiple roles of middle-generation caregivers: Contextual effects and psychological mechanisms. *Journals of Gerontology, 47,* S123–S139.

FRAZER, D. W. (1997). Psychotherapy in residential settings: Preliminary investigations and directions for research. In R. L. Rubinstein & M. P. Lawton (Eds.), *Depression in long-term and residential care: Advances in research and treatment* (pp. 185–210). New York: Springer.

FREDMAN, L., DALY, M. P., & LAZUR, A. M. (1995). Burden among white and black caregivers to elderly adults. *Journals of Gerontology, 50B*(2), S110–S118.

FREEDMAN, V. A. (1996). Family structure and the risk of nursing home admission. *Journals of Gerontology, 51B*(2), S61–S69.

FREUD, S. (1924). On psychotherapy. *Collected papers* (vol. 1). London: Hogarth.

FREUD, S. (1915/1957). *Mourning and melancholia.* In J. Strachey, *Standard edition of the complete psychological works of Sigmund Freud.* London: Hogarth.

FRIED, L. P. (1997). *Quantitative methods in aging research.* Paper presented at the 50th Annual Scientific Meeting of the Gerontological Society of America.

FRIEDMAN, H. S., TUCKER, J. S., TOMLINSON-KEASEY, C., SCHWARTZ, J. E., WINGARD, D. L., & CRIQUE, M. H. (1993). Does childhood personality predict longevity? *Journal of Personality and Social Psychology, 65,* 176–185.

FRIEDMAN, M., & ROSENMAN, R. (1974). *Type A behavior and your heart.* New York: Knopf.

FRIES, J. F. (1990). Medical perspectives upon successful aging. In P. B. Baltes & M. M. Baltes (Eds.), *Successful aging: Perspectives from the behavioral sciences* (pp. 35–40). New York: Cambridge University Press.

FROMHOLT, P., & LARSEN, S. F. (1991). Autobiographical memory in normal aging and primary degenerative dementia (dementia of Alzheimer type). *Journals of Gerontology, 46*(3), 85–91.

FUKUNISHI, I., NAKAGAWA, T., NAKAMURA, H., LI, K., HUA, Z. Q., & KRATZ, T. S. (1996). Relationships between Type A behavior, narcissism, and maternal closeness for college students in Japan, the United States of America, and the People's Republic of China. *Psychological Reports, 78*(3, Pt. 1), 939–944.

FULLER-THOMPSON, E., MINKLER, M., & DRIVER, D. (1997). A profile of grandparents raising grandchildren in the United States. *Gerontologist, 37,* 406–411.

FURMAN, F., & HAWKINS, M. E. (1994, April). *Positive models of aging: Presentations by members of the senior activity and rejuvenation project.* Symposium of the annual meeting of the Southern Gerontological Society, Charlotte, NC.

FURSTENBERG, F. F., JR., & CHERLIN, A. J. (1991). *Divided families: What happens to children when parents part?* Cambridge, MA: Harvard University Press.

THE FUTURE OF AGE-BASED PUBLIC POLICY. (1995, Fall). *Generations, 19.*

GALL, T. L., EVANS, D. R., & HOWARD, J. (1997). The retirement adjustment process: Changes in the well-being of male retirees across time. *Journals of Gerontology, 52B*(3), P110–P117.

GALLAGHER, S. K., & GERSTEL, N. (1993). Kinkeeping and friend keeping among older women: The effect of marriage. *Gerontologist, 33,* 675–681.

GALLAGHER-THOMPSON, D., & THOMPSON, L. W. (1996). Applying cognitive-behavioral therapy to the psychological problems of later life. In S. H. Zarit & B. G. Knight (Eds.), *A guide to psychotherapy and aging: Effective clinical interventions in a life-stage context* (pp. 61–83). Washington, DC: American Psychological Association.

GALLANT, D. M. (1987). *Alcoholism: A guide to diagnosis, intervention, and treatment.* New York: Norton.

GALLANT, M. (1997). *Gender differences in the predictors of daily health practices.* Paper presented at the 50th Annual Scientific Meeting of the Gerontological Society of America.

GANZINI, L., & ATKINSON, R. M. (1996). Substance abuse. In J. Sadavoy, L. W. Lazarus, L. F. Jarvik, & G. T. Grossberg (Eds.), *Comprehensive review of geriatric psychiatry II* (2nd ed.) (pp. 659–692). Washington, DC: American Psychiatric Press.

GATZ, M., & BENGTSON, V. L., & BLUM, M. J. (1990). Caregiving families. In J. E. Birren & K. W. Schaie (Eds.), *Handbook of the psychology of aging* (3rd ed.) (pp. 405–427). San Diego: Academic Press.

GATZ, M., & FINKEL, S. I. (1996). Education and training of mental health service providers. In M. Gatz (Ed.), *Emerging issues in mental health and aging* (pp. 282–302). Washington, DC: American Psychological Association.

GATZ, M., KASL-GODLEY, J., & KAREL, M. J. (1996). Aging and mental disorders. In J. E. Birren & K. W. Schaie (Eds.), *Handbook of the psychology of aging* (4th ed.) (pp. 365–383). San Diego: Academic Press.

GATZ, M., LOWE, B., BERG, S., MORTIMER, J., & PEDERSON, N. (1994). Dementia: Not just a search for the gene. *Gerontologist, 34,* 251–255.

GATZ, M., & PEARSON, C. G. (1988). Ageism and the provision of psychological services. *American Psychologist, 47,* 184–187.

GATZ, M., PEDERSEN, N. L., BERG, S., JOHANSSON, K., MORTIMER, J., POSER, S. F., VIITANE, M., WINBLAD, B., & ANLBOM, P. (1997). Heritability for Alzheimer's disease: The study of dementia in aging twins. *Journals of Gerontology, 52A,* M117–M125.

GATZ, M., & SMYER, M. A. (1992). The mental health system and older adults in the 1990s. *American Psychologist, 47,* 741–751.

GEKOSKI, W. L., & KNOX, V. J. (1990). Ageism or healthism? Perceptions based on age and health status. *Journal of Aging and Health, 2,* 15–27.

GENDELL, M., & SIEGEL, J. S. (1996). Trends in retirement age in the United States 1955–1993, by sex and race. *Journal of Gerontology: Social Sciences, 51B*(3), S132–S139.

GEORGE, L. K. (1993). Depressive disorders and symptoms in later life. *Generations, 17,* 35–38.

GEORGE, L., & GWYTHER, L. (1986). Caregiver well-being: A multidimensional examination of family caregivers of demented adults. *Gerontologist, 26,* 253–259.

GERMAN, P. S., ROVNER, B. W., BURTON, L. C., BRANT, L. J., & CLARK, R. (1992). The role of mental morbidity in the nursing home experience. *Gerontologist, 32,* 152–158.

GERT, B., BERNAT, J. L., & MOGIELNICKI, R. P. (1994). Distinguishing between patients' refusals and requests. *Hastings Center Report, 24,* 13–15.

GESSER, G., WONG, P. T., & REKER, G. T. (1987–1988). Death attitudes across the life span: The development and validation of the death attitude profile (DAP). *Omega: Journal of Death and Dying, 18,* 113–128.

GIJSBERS VAN WIJK, C. M., KOLK, A. M., VAN DEN BOSCH, W. J., & VAN DEN HOOGEN, H. J. (1992). Male and female morbidity in general practice: The nature of sex differences. *Social Science and Medicine, 35,* 665–678.

GILBERT, L. A. (1993). *Two careers, one family: The promise of gender equality.* Beverly Hills, CA: Sage.

GLAMSER, F. D. (1976). Determinants of a positive attitude towards retirement. *Journal of Gerontology, 31,* 104–107.

GLASER, B., & STRAUSS, A. L. (1968). *A time for dying.* Chicago: Aldine.

GLENN, N. D. (1990). Quantitative research on marital quality in the 1980s: A critical review. *Journal of Marriage and the Family, 52,* 818–831.

GLICKMAN, L., HUBBARD, M., LIVERIGHT, T., & VALCIUKAS, J. A. (1990). Fall-off in reporting life events: Effects of life change, desirability, and anticipation. *Behavioral Medicine, 16*(1), 31–38.

GOLDEN-KREUTZ, D. M., & ANDERSEN, B. L. (1997). *Older adults in longitudinal clinical trials: Issues of recruitment and retention.* Paper presented at the 50th Annual Scientific Meeting of the Gerontological Society of America.

GOLDFARB, A. I. (1953). Recommendations for psychiatric care in a home for the aged. *Journal of Gerontology, 8,* 343–347.

GONYEA, J. (1997). *America's shifting social contract and women's economic security.* Paper presented at the 50th Annual Scientific Meeting of the Gerontological Society of America.

GORMAN, D. M. (1993). A review of studies comparing checklist and interview methods of data collection in life event research. *Behavioral Medicine, 19,* 66–71.

GOTTESMAN, L. E., & BOURESTOM, N. C. (1974). Why nursing homes do what they do. *Gerontologist, 14,* 501–506.

GRANDPARENTING AT CENTURY'S END. (1996, Spring). *Generations, 20.*

GRANT, L. A., KANE, R. A., & STARK, A. J. (1995). Beyond labels: Nursing home care for Alzheimer's disease in and out of special care units. *Journal of the American Geriatrics Society, 43,* 569–576.

GRENNE, V. L., & ONDRICH, J. I. (1990). Risk factors for nursing home admissions and exits: A discrete-time hazard function approach. *Journals of Gerontology, B 45*(6), S250–S258.

GUARNACCIA, C., & HAYSLIP, B. (1997). *Overt and covert death anxiety: An empirical test of a blended psychometric and projective measurement model.* Paper presented at the 50th Annual Scientific Meeting of the Gerontological Society of America.

GUERRERO, L. K., ELOY, S. V., & WABNIK, A. I. (1993). Linking maintenance strategies to relationship development and disengagement: A reconceptualization. *Journal of Social and Personal Relationships, 10,* 273–283.

GUILLEMARD, A. M., & REIN, M. (1993). Comparative patterns of retirement: Recent trends in developed societies. *Annual Review of Sociology, 19,* 469–503.

GURALNIK, J. M., & KAPLAN, G. A. (1989). Predictors of healthy aging: Prospective evidence from the Alameda County study. *American Journal of Public Health, 79,* 703–708.

GURIAN, B., & GOISMAN, R. (1993, Winter/Spring). Anxiety disorders in the elderly. *Generations, 17,* 38–43.

GURLAND, B. (1996). Epidemiology of psychiatric disorders. In J. Sadavoy, L. W. Lazarus, L. F. Jarvik, & G. T. Grossberg (Eds.), *Comprehensive review of geriatric psychiatry II* (2nd ed.) (pp. 3–41). Washington, DC: American Psychiatric Press.

GUTMANN, D. (1987). *Reclaimed powers: Men and women in later life.* Evanston, IL: Northwestern University Press.

HAAN, N., MILLSAP, R., & HARTKA, E. (1986). As time goes by: Change and stability in personality over fifty years. *Psychology and Aging, 1,* 220–232.

HACKER, A. (1992). *Two nations.* New York: Scribners.

HAGESTAD, G. (1985). Continuity and connectedness. In V. L. Bengtson & J. Robertson (Eds.), *Grandparenthood* (pp. 31–48). Beverly Hills, CA: Sage.

HALL, D. M., KELLER, E. T., WEINDRUCH, R. H., & KREGEL, K. C. (1997). *Caloric restriction ameliorates declining thermotolerance with age: Involvement of reactive oxygen species and oxidative stress.* Paper presented at the 50th Annual Scientific Meeting of the Gerontological Society of America.

HAMEL, M., GOLD, D. P., ANDRES, D., REIS, M., DASTOOR, D., GRAUER, H., & BERGMAN, H. (1990). Predictors and consequences of aggressive behavior by community-based dementia parents. *Gerontologist, 30,* 206–211.

HAMON, R. R., & BLIESZNER, R. (1990). Filial responsibility expectations among adult child–older parent pairs. *Journals of Gerontology, 45*(3), P110–P112.

HAMON, R. R., & COBB, L. L. (1993). Parents' experience of and adjustment to their adult children's divorce: Applying family stress theory. *Journal of Divorce and Remarriage, 21*(1–2), 73–94.

HANDAL, P. J., PEAL, R. L., NAPOLI, J. G., & AUSTRIN, H. R. (1984–1985). The relationship between direct and indirect measures of death anxiety. *Omega: Journal of Death and Dying, 15,* 245–262.

HANISCH, K. A., & HULIN, C. L. (1991). General attitudes and organizational withdrawal: An evaluation of a causal model. *Journal of Vocational Behavior, 39*(1), 110–128.

HARRIS, J. R., PEDERSEN, N. L., MCCLEARN, G. E., PLOMIN, R., & NESSELROADE, J. (1992). Age differences in genetic and environmental influences for health from the Swedish Adoption/Twin Study of Aging. *Journals of Gerontology, 47*(3), P213–P220.

HARRIS, L., & ASSOCIATES. (1981). *Aging in the eighties: America in transition.* Washington, DC: National Council on the Aging.

HARRIS, L., & ASSOCIATES. (1996). *Executive summary: The Lighthouse national survey of vision loss.* New York: The Lighthouse Inc.

HASHER, L., & ZACKS, R. T. (1988). Working memory comprehension and aging: A review and a new view. In G. H. Bower (Ed.), *The psychology of learning and motivation: Advances in research and theory* (vol. 22, pp. 193–225). New York: Academic Press.

HAUG, M. (ED.). (1981). *Elderly patients and their doctors.* New York: Springer.

HAYDAR, Z., EDMONDSON, T., LOWE, J., BROCK, K., BRIGGS, E., & LEFF, B. (1997). *A randomized trial of home-based comprehensive geriatric assessment: The value of longitudinal care through house calls.* Paper presented at the 50th Annual Scientific Meeting of the Gerontological Society of America.

HAYFLICK, L. (1987). The human life span. In G. Lesnoff-Caravaglia (Ed.), *Realistic expectation for long life* (pp. 17–34). New York: Human Services Press.

HAYNES, S. G., & MATTHEWS, K. A. (1988). The association of Type A behavior with cardiovascular disease: Update and critical review. In B. K. Houston & C. R. Snyder (Eds.), *Type A behavior pattern: Research, theory, and intervention* (pp. 51–82). New York: Wiley.

HAYSLIP, B., GALT, C. P., & PINDER, M. M. (1993–1994). Effects of death education on conscious and unconscious death anxiety. *Omega: Journal of Death and Dying, 28,* 101–111.

HAYSLIP, B., LUHR, D. D., & BEYERLEIN, M. M. (1991–1992). Levels of death anxiety in terminally ill men: A pilot study. *Omega: Journal of Death and Dying, 24,* 13–19.

HAYSLIP, B., MALOY, R. M., & KOHL, R. (1995). Long-term efficacy of fluid ability interventions with older adults. *Journals of Gerontology, 50B*(3), P141–P149.

HAYSLIP, B., & STEWART-BUSSEY, D. (1986–1987). Locus of control–levels of death anxiety relationships. *Omega: Journal of Death and Dying, 17,* 41–48.

HAYWARD, M. D., FRIEDMAN, S., & CHEN, H. (1996). Race inequities in men's retirement. *Journals of Gerontology, 51B,* S1–S11.

HAZZARD, W. (1990). A central role of sex hormones in the sex differential in lipoprotein metabolism, atherosclerosis, and longevity. In M. Ory & H. R. Warner (Eds.), *Gender, health, and longevity: Multidisciplinary perspectives* (pp. 87–108). New York: Springer.

HECKHAUSEN, J., & BALTES, P. B. (1991). Perceived controllability of expected psychological change across adulthood and old age. *Journals of Gerontology, 46B,* P165–P175.

HECKHAUSEN, J., DIXON, R. A., & BALTES, P. B. (1989). Gains and losses in development throughout adulthood as perceived by different adult age groups. *Developmental Psychology, 25,* 109–121.

HECKHAUSEN, J., & SCHULZ, R. (1993). Optimization by selection and compensation: Balancing primary and secondary control in life-span development. *International Journal of Behavioral Development, 16,* 287–303.

HEDRICK, S., JOHNSON, J. R., INUI, T. S., & DIEHR, P. (1991). Factors associated with participation in a randomized trial of adult day health care. *Gerontologist, 31,* 607–610.

HELSON, R. (1992). Women's difficult times and the rewriting of the life story. *Psychology of Women Quarterly, 16,* 331–347.

HELSON, R., & MOANE, G. (1987). Personality change in women from college to midlife. *Journal of Personality and Social Psychology, 53,* 176–186.

HELSON, R., & ROBERTS, B. W. (1994). Ego development and personality change in adulthood. *Journal of Personality and Social Psychology, 66,* 911–920.

HELSON, R., & WINK, P. (1992). Personality change in women from the early 40's to the early 50's. *Psychology and Aging, 7,* 46–55.

HENDIN, H. (1994, December 16). Scared to death of dying. *New York Times,* pp. A19–A20.

HENDRICK, S. S. (1981). Self-disclosure and marital satisfaction. *Journal of Personality and Social Psychology, 40,* 1150–1159.

HERTZOG, C. (1989). Influences of cognitive slowing on age differences in intelligence. *Developmental Psychology, 25,* 636–651.

HERTZOG, C. (1996). Research design in studies of aging and cognition. In J. E. Birren & K. W. Schaie (Eds.), *Handbook of the psychology of aging* (4th ed.) (pp. 24–37). San Diego: Academic Press.

HERTZOG, C., & SCHAIE, K. W. (1988). Stability and change in adult intelligence: 2. Simultaneous analysis of longitudinal means covariance structures. *Psychology and Aging, 2,* 122–130.

HESS, T. M., & PULLEN, S. M. (1996). Memory in context. In F. Blanchard-Fields & T. M. Hess (Eds.), *Perspectives on cognitive change in adulthood and aging* (pp. 387–427). New York: McGraw-Hill.

HICKS, L. H., & BIRREN, J. E. (1970). Aging, brain, damage, and psychomotor slowing. *Psychological Bulletin, 74,* 377–396.

HIGAMI, Y., YU, B. P., SHIMOKAWA, I., BERTRAND, H., HUBBARD, G. B., & MASORO, E. J. (1995). Anti-tumor action of dietary restriction is lesion-dependent in male Fischer 344 rats. *Journals of Gerontology, 50A*(2), B72–B77.

HILDRETH, C. D., & SAUNDERS, E. (1992). Heart disease, stroke, and hypertension in blacks. In R. Braithwaite & S. E. Taylor (Eds.), *Health issues in the black community* (pp. 90–105). San Francisco: Jossey-Bass.

HILL, R. D., STORANDT, M., & SIMEONE, C. (1990). The effects of memory skills training and incentives on free recall in order learning. *Journals of Gerontology* 45(6), P227–P232.

HINRICHSEN, G. A., & RAMIREZ, M. (1992). Black and white dementia caregivers: A comparison of their adaptation, adjustment, and service utilization. *Gerontologist, 32,* 375–381.

HINTZE, J., TEMPLER, D. I., CAPPELLETTY, G. G., & FREDERICK, W. (1993). Death, depression, and death anxiety in HIV-infected males. *Death Studies, 17,* 333–341.

HIRSCH, C., & CHARLES, J. (1997). *How should clinicians assess the effectiveness of drug treatment for Alzheimer's disease?* Paper presented at the 50th Annual Scientific Meeting of the Gerontological Society of America.

HIRSHORN, B. A., & HOYER, T. D. (1994). Private sector hiring and use of retirees: The firm perspective. *Gerontologist, 34,* 50–58.

HO, S. C., WOO, J., YUEN, Y. K., SHAM, A., & CHAN, S. G. (1997). Predictors of mobility decline: The Hong Kong old-old study. *Journals of Gerontology: 52A*(6), M356–M362.

HOBERMAN, H., & LEWINSOHN, P. (1989). Behavioral approaches to the treatment of unipolar depression. In American Psychiatric Association (Ed.), *Treatment of psychiatric disorders* (vol. 3, pp. 1846–1862). Washington, DC: American Psychiatric Association.

HODGSON, J. H., & QUINN, J. L. (1980). The impact of the triage health care delivery system on client morale, independent living, and the cost of care. *Gerontologist, 20,* 364–371.

HODGSON, L. G. (1992). Adult grandchildren and their grandparents: Their enduring bond. *International Journal of Aging and Human Development, 34*(3), 209–225.

HOLDEN, J. (1993). Demographics, attitudes, and afterlife beliefs of right-to-life and right-to-die organization members. *Journal of Social Psychology, 133,* 521–527.

HOLDEN, K. C., & SMOCK, P. J. (1991). The economic costs of marital dissolution: Why do women bear a disproportionate cost? *Annual Review of Sociology, 17,* 51–78.

HOLDEN, K. C., & ZICK, C. D. (1997). *The economic impact of widowhood in the 1990s: Health and disability precursors.* Paper presented at the 50th Annual Scientific Meeting of the Gerontological Society of America.

HOLLAND, C. A. (1995). Memory changes in older people. In F. Glendenning & I. Stuart-Hamilton (Eds.), *Learning and cognition in later life* (pp. 74–94). Brookfield, VT: Ashgate.

HOLLAND, C. A., & RABBITT, P. M. A. (1991). Ageing memory: Use versus impairment. *British Journal of Psychology, 82,* 29–38.

HOLT, P. R., HELLER, T. D., & RICHARDSON, A. G. (1991). Food restriction retards age-related biochemical changes in rat small intestine. *Journals of Gerontology, 46*(3), B89–B94.

HONEYCUTT, J. M. (1993). Marital happiness, divorce status, and partner differences in attributions about communication behaviors. *Journal of Divorce and Remarriage, 21*(1–2), 177–201.

HOOKER, K., & KAUS, C. R. (1994). Health-related possible selves in young and middle adulthood. *Psychology and Aging, 9,* 126–133.

HOPPER, J. (1993). The rhetoric of motives in divorce. *Journal of Marriage and the Family, 55,* 801–813.

HORN, J. L. (1970). Organization of data on life-span development of human abilities. In L. R. Goulet & P. B. Baltes (Eds.), *Life-span development psychology: Research and theory* (pp. 423–466). New York: Academic Press.

HORN, J. L., & HOFER, S. M. (1992). Major abilities and development in the adulthood period. In R. J. Sternberg & C. A. Berg (Eds.), *Intellectual development* (pp. 44–99). New York: Cambridge University Press.

HORNER, K. L., RUSHTON, J. P., & VERNON, P. A. (1986). Relation between aging and research productivity of academic psychologists. *Psychology and Aging, 1,* 319–324.

HOUSE, J. S., KESSLER, R. C., HERZOG, A. R., MERO, R. P., KINNEY, A. M., & BRESLOW, M. J. (1992). Social stratification, age, and health. In K. W. Schaie, D. G. Blazer, & J. S. House (Eds.), *Aging, health behaviors, and health outcomes: Social structure and aging* (pp. 1–32). Hillsdale, NJ: Erlbaum.

HOUSTON, B. K. (1988). Cardiovascular and neuroendocrine reactivity, global Type A, and components of Type A behavior. In B. K. Houston & C. R. Snyder (Eds.), *Type A behavior pattern research, theory, and intervention* (pp. 212–253). New York: Wiley.

HOWARD, D. V. (1996). The aging of implicit and explicit memory. In F. Blanchard-Fields & T. M. Hess (Eds.), *Perspectives on cognitive change in adulthood and aging* (pp. 221–254). New York: McGraw-Hill.

HULICKA, I. M. (1967). Age differences in retention as a function of interference. *Journal of Gerontology, 22,* 180–184.

HULTSCH, D. F., & DIXON, R. A. (1990). Learning and memory in aging. In J. E. Birren & K. W. Schaie (Eds.), *Handbook of the psychology of aging* (3rd ed.) (pp. 258–274). San Diego: Academic Press.

HULTSCH, D. F., HAMMER, M., & SMALL, B. J. (1993). Age differences in cognitive performance in later life: Relationships to self-reported health and activity life style. *Journals of Gerontology, 48*(1), P1–P11.

HULTSCH, D. F., MASSON, M. E., & SMALL, B. J. (1991). Adult age differences in direct and indirect tests of memory. *Journals of Gerontology, 46*(1), P22–P30.

HUMES, L. E., & CHRISTOPHERSON, L. (1991). Speech identification difficulties of hearing-impaired elderly persons: The contributions of auditory processing deficits. *Journal of Speech and Hearing Research, 34,* 686–693.

HUMMERT, M. L., GARSTKA, T. A., & SHANER, J. L. (1997). Stereotyping of older adults: The role of target facial cues and perceiver characteristics. *Psychology and Aging, 12,* 107–114.

IDLER, E. L. (1993). Age differences in self-assessments of health: Age changes, cohort differences, or survivorship? *Journals of Gerontology, 48*(6), S289–S300.

INGERSOLL-DAYTON, B., MORGAN, D., & ANTONUCCI, T. (1997). The effects of positive and negative social exchanges on aging adults. *Journals of Gerontology: Social Sciences, 52B*(4), S190–S199.

INGRAM, D. K., CUTLER, R. G., WEINDRUCH, R., RENQUIST, D. M., KNAPKA, J. J., APRIL, M., BELCHER, C. T., CLARK, M. A., HATCHERSON, C. D., MARRIOTT, B. M., & ROTH, G. S. (1990). Dietary restriction and aging: The initiation of a primate study. *Journals of Gerontology, 45*(5), B148–B163.

INGRAM, L. A., & WILLIAMSON, G. M. (1997). *Activity restriction and depression in elderly caregiver–care recipient spousal pairs.* Paper presented at the 50th Annual Scientific Meeting of the Gerontological Society of America.

IRION, J. C., & BLANCHARD-FIELDS, F. (1987). A cross-sectional comparison of adaptive coping in adulthood. *Journal of Gerontology, 42,* 502–504.

JACEWICZ, M. M., & HARTLEY, A. A. (1987). Age differences in the speed of cognitive operations: Resolution of inconsistent findings. *Journal of Gerontology, 42,* 86–88.

JACKSON, J. S., ANTONUCCI, T. C., & GIBSON, R. C. (1990). Cultural, racial, and ethical minority influences on aging. In J. E. Birren & K. W. Schaie (Eds.), *Handbook of the psychology of aging* (3rd ed.) (pp. 103–123). San Diego: Academic Press.

JACKSON, J. S., CHATTERS, L. M., & TAYLOR, R. J. (1993). *Aging in Black America.* Newbury Park, CA: Sage.

JANTZ, R. K., SEEFELDT, C., GALPER, A., & SEROCK, K. (1976). Children's attitudes towards the elderly: Final report. College Park: University of Maryland.

JARVIK, L. F., & FALIK, A. (1963). Intellectual stability and survival in the aged. *Journal of Gerontology, 18,* 173–176.

JECKER, N. S., & SCHNEIDERMAN, L. J. (1994). Is dying young worse than dying old? *Gerontologist, 34,* 66–72.

JENDREK, M. P. (1993). Grandparents who parent their grandchildren: Effects on lifestyle. *Journal of Marriage and the Family, 55,* 609–621.

JENDREK, M. P. (1994). Grandparents who parent their grandchildren: Circumstances and decisions. *Gerontologist, 34,* 206–216.

JETTE, A. M. (1996). Disability trends and transitions. In R. H. Binstock & L. K. George (Eds.), *Handbook of aging and the social sciences* (4th ed.) (pp. 94–117). New York: Academic Press.

JETTE, A. M., & BRANCH, L. G. (1992). A ten-year follow-up of driving patterns among the community-dwelling elderly. *Human Factors, 34*(1), 25–31.

JETTE, A. M., BRANCH, L. G., & BERLIN, J. (1990). Musculoskeletal impairments and physical disablement among the aged. *Journals of Gerontology, 45,* M203–M208.

JOHANSSON, B., ALLEN-BURGE, R., & ZARIT, S. H. (1997). Self-reports on memory functioning in a longitudinal study of the oldest old: Relation to current, prospective, and retrospective performance. *Journals of Gerontology: Psychological Sciences, 52B*(3), P139–P146.

JOHANSSON, B., & ZARIT, S. H. (1995). Prevalence and incidence of dementia in the oldest old: A longitudinal study of a population-based sample of 84 90-year-olds in Sweden. *International Journal of Geriatric Psychiatry, 10*(5), 359–366.

JOHANSSON, B., & ZARIT, S. H. (1997). Early cognitive markers of the incidence of dementia and mortality: A longitudinal population-based study of the oldest old. *International Journal of Geriatric Psychiatry, 12,* 53–59.

JOHNSON, C. L. (1985a). Grandparenting options in divorcing families: An anthropological perspective. In V. L. Bengtson & J. Robertson (Eds.), *Grandparenthood* (pp. 81–96). Beverly Hills, CA: Sage.

JOHNSON, C. L. (1985b). The impact of illness on late-life marriages. *Journal of Marriage and the Family, 47,* 165–173.

JOHNSON, C. L., & BARER, B. M. (1987). Marital instability and the changing kinship networks of grandparents. *Gerontologist, 27,* 330–335.

JOHNSON, C. L., & CATALANO, D. (1983). A longitudinal study of family supports to impaired elderly. *Gerontologist, 23,* 612–618.

JOHNSON, C. L., & TROLL, L. E. (1994). Constraints and facilitators to friendships in late late life. *Gerontologist, 34,* 79–87.

JOHNSON, T. E., LITHGOW, G. J., & MURAKAMI, S. (1996). Hypothesis: Interventions that increase the response to stress offer the potential for effective life prolongation and increased health. *Journals of Gerontology, 51A*(6), B392–B395.

JOHNSON, T. R. (1995). The significance of religion for aging well. *American Behavioral Scientist, 39*(2), 186–208.

KAAKINEN, J. R. (1992). Living with silence. *Gerontologist, 32,* 258–264.

KAHN, R., ZARIT, S. H., HILBERT, H. M., & NIEDEREHE, G. (1975). Memory complaint and impairment in the aged: The effect of depression and altered brain function. *Archives of General Psychiatry, 32,* 1569–1573.

KANE, A. C., & HOGAN, J. D. (1985–1986). Death anxiety in physicians: Defensive style, medical specialty, and exposure to death. *Omega: Journal of Death and Dying, 16,* 11–22.

KANE, R. A. (1995–1996). Transforming care institutions for the frail elderly: Out of one shall be many. *Generations, 19,* 62–68.

KANE, R. A., & CAPLAN, A. L. (EDS.). (1990). *Everyday ethics: Resolving dilemmas in nursing home life.* New York: Springer.

KANE, R. L., SOLOMON, D. H., BECK, J. C., KEELER, E., & KANE, R. A. (1981). *Geriatrics in the United States: Manpower projections and training considerations.* Lexington, MA: Heath.

KANNER, A. D., COYNE, J. C., SCHAEFER, C., & LAZARUS, R. S. (1981). Comparison of two modes of stress measurement: Daily hassles and uplifts versus major life events. *Journal of Behavioral Medicine, 4,* 1–39.

KAPLAN, G. A. (1986, August). *Aging, health, and behavior: Evidence from the Alameda County study.* Paper presented at the 94th annual meeting of the American Psychological Association, Washington, DC.

KAPLAN, G. A. (1992). Health and aging in the Alameda County study. In K. W. Schaie, D. G. Blazer, & J. S. House (Eds.), *Aging, health behaviors, and health outcomes* (pp. 69–95). Hillsdale, NJ: Erlbaum.

KAPLAN, G. A., SEEMAN, T. E., COHEN, R. D., KNUDSEN, L. P., & GURALNIK, J. (1987). Mortality among the elderly in the Alameda County study: Behavioral and demographic risk factors. *American Journal of Public Health, 77,* 307–312.

KAPLAN, M., & HOFFMAN, S. (1997). *Problems involved in the implementation of dementia care programs.* Paper presented at the 50th Annual Scientific Meeting of the Gerontological Society of America.

KAPP, M. B. (1991). Health care decision making by the elderly: I get by with a little help from my family. *Gerontologist, 31,* 619–623.

KART, C. S., METRESS, E. K., & METRESS, S. P. (1992). *Human aging and chronic disease.* Boston: Jones and Bartlett.

KASTENBAUM, R., & COSTA, P. (1977). Psychological perspectives on death. *Annual Review of Psychology, 28,* 225–249.

KASZNIAK, A. W. (1996). Techniques and instruments for assessment of the elderly. In S. H. Zarit & B. G. Knight (Eds.), *A guide to psychotherapy and aging: Effective clinical interventions in a life-stage context* (pp. 163–219). Washington, DC: American Psychological Association.

KATZ, I. R., & PARMELEE, P. A. (1997). Overview. In R. L. Rubinstein & M. P. Lawton (Eds.), *Depression in long-term and residential care: Advances in research and treatment* (pp. 1–28). New York: Springer.

KAUFMAN, S. R. (1986). *The ageless self: Sources of meaning in late life.* Madison: University of Wisconsin Press.

KAUSLER, D. H. (1990). Motivation, human aging, and cognitive performance. In J. E. Birren & K. W. Schaie (Eds.), *Handbook of psychology of aging* (3rd ed.). (pp. 171–182). San Diego: Academic Press.

KELLY, E. L., & CONLEY, J. J. (1987). Personality and compatibility: A prospective analysis of marital stability and marital satisfaction. *Journal of Personality and Social Psychology, 52,* 27–40.

KEMNITZ, J. W., WEINDRUCK, R., ROECKER, E. B., CRAWFORD, K., KAUFMAN, P. L., & ERSHLER, W. B. (1993).

Dietary restriction of adult male rhesus monkeys: Design, methodology, and preliminary findings from the first year of study. *Journals of Gerontology, 48*(1), B17–B26.

KENDLER, K. S., HEATH, A. C., NEALE, M. C., KESSLER, R. C., & EAVES, L. J. (1993a). Alcoholism and major depression in women: A twin study of the causes of comorbidity. *Archives of General Psychiatry, 50,* 690–698.

KENDLER, K. S., HEATH, A. C., NEALE, M. C., KESSLER, R. C., & EAVES, L. J. (1993b). The prediction of major depression in women: Toward an integrated etiologic model. *American Journal of Psychiatry, 150,* 1139–1148.

KENDLER, K. S., NEALE, M. C., KESSLER, R. C., HEATH, A. C., & EAVES, L. J. (1993). A longitudinal twin study of 1-year prevalence of major depression in women. *Archives of General Psychiatry, 50,* 843–852.

KENNEDY, G. E. (1990). College students' expectations of grandparent and grandchild role behaviors. *Gerontologist, 30,* 43–48.

KENRICK, D. T., GROTH, G. E., TROST, M. R., & SADALLA, E. K. (1993). Integrating evolutionary and social exchange perspectives on relationships: Effects of gender, self-appraisal, and involvement level on mate selection criteria. *Journal of Personality and Social Psychology, 64,* 951–969.

KESSLER, R. C., FOSTER, C., WEBSTER, P. S., & HOUSE, J. S. (1992). The relationship between age and depressive symptoms in two national surveys. *Psychology and Aging, 7,* 119–126.

KESSLER, R. C., & MAGEE, W. (1994). Childhood family violence and adult recurrent depression. *Journal of Health and Social Behavior, 35*(1), 13–27.

KESSLER, R. C., MCGONAGLE, K. A., ZHAO, S., NELSON, C. B., HUGHES, R., ESHLEMAN, S., WITTCHEN, H., & KENDLER, K. S. (1994). Lifetime and 12-month prevalence of DSM III-R psychiatric disorders in the United States. *Archives of General Psychiatry, 51,* 8–19.

KIM, J., PICOT, S., WYKLE, M., & LEE, H. (1997). *Contributions of obligations, assets, perceived rewards and race to social health of female caregivers of elders.* Paper presented at the 50th Annual Scientific Meeting of the Gerontological Society of America.

KIMBLE, G. A. (1993). Evolution of the nature-nurture issue in the history of psychology. In R. Plomin & G. E. McClearn (Eds.), *Nature, nurture, and psychology* (pp. 3–25). Washington, DC: American Psychological Association.

KINGSON, E., & QUADAGNO, J. (1995). Social Security: Marketing radical reform. *Generations, 19*(3), 43–49.

KINSELLA, K. (1995). Aging and the family: Present and future demographic issues. In R. Blieszner & V. H. Bedford (Eds.), *Handbook of aging and the family* (pp. 32–56). Westport, CT: Greenwood Press.

KIPSHIDZE, N. N., PIVOVAROVA, I. P., DZORBENADZE, D. A., AGADZANOV, A. S., & SHAVGULIDZ, N. A. (1987). The longevous people of Soviet Georgia. In G. Lesnoff-Caravaglia (Ed.), *Realistic expectations for long life.* New York: Human Sciences Press.

KITZMAN, D. W., & EDWARDS, W. D. (1990). Minireview: Age-related changes in the anatomy of the normal heart. *Journals of Gerontology, 45,* M33–M39.

KIYAK, H. A., & BORSON, S. (1992). Coping with chronic illness and disability. In M. G. Ory, R. P. Abeles, & P. D. Lipman (Eds.), *Aging, health, and behavior* (pp. 141–173). Newbury Park, CA: Sage.

KLASS, D., SILVERMAN, P. R., & NICKMAN, S. L. (EDS.). (1996). *Continuing bonds: New understandings of grief.* Washington, DC: Taylor & Francis.

KLENOW, D. J. (1991–1992). Emotion and life-threatening illness: A typology of hope sources. *Omega: Journal of Death and Dying, 24,* 49–60.

KLINE, D. W., KLINE, T. J., FOZARD, J. L., KOSNIK, W., SCHEIBEL, A., & SECKULER, R. (1992). Vision, aging, and driving: The problems of older drivers. *Journals of Gerontology, 47*(1), P27–P34.

KLINE, D. W., & SCIALFA, C. T. (1996). Visual and auditory aging. In J. E. Birren & K. W. Schaie (Eds.), *Handbook of the psychology of aging* (4th ed.) (pp. 181–203). San Diego: Academic Press.

KLING, K. C., SELTZER, M. M., & RYFF, C. D. (1997). Distinctive late-life challenges: Implications for coping and well-being. *Psychology and Aging, 12,* 288–295.

KOGAN, N., & WALLACH, M. A. (1961). Age changes in values and attitudes. *Journal of Gerontology, 16,* 272–280.

KOHN, R. (1978). *Principles of mammalian aging* (2nd ed). Englewood Cliffs, NJ: Prentice-Hall.

KOSLOSKI, K., & MONTGOMERY, R. (1997). *How perceptions of access, quality, and utility affect the use of respite services.* Paper presented at the 50th Annual Scientific Meeting of the Gerontological Society of America.

KOSNIK, W. D., SEKULER, R., & KLINE, D. W. (1990). Self-reported visual problems of older drivers. *Human Factors, 32,* 597–608.

KOSOROK, M. R., OMENN, G. S., DIEHR, P., KOEPSELL, T. D., & PATRICK, D. L. (1992). Restricted activity days among older adults. *American Journal of Public Health, 82,* 1263–1267.

KRAUSE, N. (1989). Issues of measurement and analysis in studies of social support, aging, and health. In

K. S. Markides (Ed.), *Aging and health: Perspectives on gender, race, ethnicity, and class* (pp. 43–66). Newbury Park, CA: Sage.

KRAUSE, N. (1997). Religion, aging, and health: Current status and future prospects. *Journals of Gerontology, 52B*(6), S291–S293.

KRUEGER, J., & HECKHAUSEN, J. (1993). Personality development across the adult life span: Subjective conceptions versus cross-sectional contrasts. *Journals of Gerontology, 48B*(3), P100–P108.

KRYNSKI, M. D., TYMCHUK, A. J., & OUSLANDER, J. G. (1994). How informed can consent be? New light on comprehension among elderly people making decisions about enteral tube feeding. *Gerontologist, 34,* 36–43.

KUBLER-ROSS, E. (1969). *On death and dying.* New York: Macmillan.

KULIS, S. S. (1992). Social class and the locus of reciprocity in relationships with adult children. *Journal of Family Issues, 13,* 482–504.

KUNKEL, S. R., & HARRIS, K. M. (1997). *Recent trends in mortality by gender, race, and age: 1985–1991.* Paper presented at the 50th Annual Scientific Meeting of the Gerontological Society of America.

KUYPERS, J. H., & BENGTSON, V. C. (1983). Toward competence in the older family. In T. H. Brubaker (Ed.), *Family relations in late life* (pp. 211–228). Beverly Hills, CA: Sage.

KWON, S. (1997). *Two-year change of participation motivation for cognitive interventions: The role of control beliefs, self-efficacy, and perceived deficits.* Paper presented at the 50th Annual Scientific Meeting of the Gerontological Society of America.

LABOUVIE-VIEF, G. (1985). Intelligence and cognition. In J. E. Birren & K. W. Schaie (Eds.), *Handbook of the psychology of aging* (2nd ed.) (pp. 500–530). New York: Van Nostrand Reinhold.

LABOUVIE-VIEF, G. (1992). A neo-Piagetian perspective on adult cognitive development. In R. J. Sternberg & C. A. Berg (Eds.), *Intellectual development* (pp. 197–228). New York: Cambridge University Press.

LABOUVIE-VIEF, G., HAKIM-LARSON, J., & HOBART, C. J. (1987). Age, ego level, and the life-span development of coping and defense processes. *Psychology and Aging, 2,* 286–293.

LABUS, J. G., & DAMBROT, F. H. (1985–1986). A comparative study of terminally ill hospice and hospital patients. *Omega: Journal of Death and Dying, 16,* 225–233.

LACHMAN, M. E. (1991). Perceived control over memory aging: Developmental and intervention perspectives. *Journal of Social Issues, 47*(4), 159–175.

LAKATTA, E. G. (1987). The aging heart: Myths and realities. In J. W. Elias & P. H. Marshall (Eds.), *Cardiovascular disease and behavior: Series in health psychology and behavioral medicine* (pp. 179–193). Washington, DC: Hemisphere.

LAMB, M. E. (1986). The changing role of fathers. In M. E. Lamb (Ed.), *The father's role: Applied perspectives* (pp. 4–29). New York: Wiley.

LANE, W. C., & LANGE, C. D. (1997). *Comparing the knowledge of Alzheimer's between SCU and regular nursing unit staff: Implications for interdisciplinary training.* Paper presented at the 50th Annual Scientific Meeting of the Gerontological Society of America.

LANG, A. M., & BRODY, E. M. (1983). Characteristics of middle-aged daughters and help to their elderly mothers. *Journal of Marriage and the Family, 45,* 193–202.

LANG, F., & CARSTENSEN, L. (1994). Close emotional relationships in later life: Further support for proactive aging in the social domain. *Psychology and Aging, 9,* 315–324.

LAUBER, B., & DREVENSTEDT, J. (1997). *An investigation of older adults' memory complaints.* Paper presented at the 50th Annual Scientific Meeting of the Gerontological Society of America.

LAWRENCE, R. H., & JETTE, A. M. (1996). Disentangling the disablement process. *Journals of Gerontology, 51B*(4), S173–S182.

LAWTON, L., SILVERSTEIN, M., & BENGTSON, V. (1994). Affection, social contact, and geographic distance between adult children and their parents. *Journal of Marriage and the Family, 56,* 57–68.

LAWTON, M. P. (1975). *Planning and managing housing for the elderly.* New York: Wiley.

LAWTON, M. P. (1997). Positive and negative affective states among older people in long-term care. In R. L. Rubinstein & M. P. Lawton (Eds.), *Depression in long-term and residential care: Advances in research and treatment* (pp. 29–54). New York: Springer.

LAWTON, M. P., KLEBAN, M. H., & DEAN, J. (1993). Affect and age: Cross-sectional comparisons of structure and prevalence. *Psychology and Aging, 8,* 165–175.

LAWTON, M. P., KLEBAN, M. H., RAJAGOPAL, D., & DEAN, J. (1992). Dimensions of affective experience in three age groups. *Psychology and Aging, 7,* 171–184.

LAWTON, M. P., VAN HAITSMA, K., & KLAPPER, J. (1996). Observed affect in nursing home residents with Alzheimer's disease. *Journals of Gerontology: Psychological Sciences, 51B,* P3–P14.

LAWTON, M. P., WEISMAN, G. D., SLOANE, P., & CALKINS, M. (1997). Assessing environments for older people with chronic illness. *Journal of Mental Health and Aging, 3*(1), 83–100.

LAZARUS, R. S. (1996). The role of coping in the emotions and how coping changes over the life course. In C. Magai & S. H. McFadden (Eds.), *Handbook of emotion, adult development, and aging* (pp. 289–306). San Diego: Academic Press.

LEARY, W. E. (1988, February 25). The new hearing aids: Nearly invisible devices filtering sound. *New York Times*, p. B6.

LEBOWITZ, B. D. (1993). Mental health and aging: Federal perspectives. *Generations, 17*(1), 65–68.

LEE, G. R., DWYER, J. W., & COWARD, R. T. (1993). Gender differences in parent care: Demographic factors and same gender preferences. *Journals of Gerontology, 48B*, S9–S16.

LEIBLUM, S. R. (1990). Sexuality and the midlife woman. *Psychology of Women Quarterly, 14*, 495–508.

LEMON, B. W., BENGTSON, V. L., & PETERSON, J. A. (1972). An exploration of the activity theory of aging, activity types and life satisfaction among in-movers to a retirement community. *Journal of Gerontology, 27*, 511–523.

LESNOFF-CARAVAGLIA, G., & KLYS, M. (1987). Lifestyle and longevity. In G. Lesnoff-Caravaglia (Ed.), *Realistic expections for long life*. New York: Human Sciences Press.

LESTER, P., & BECKER, P. (1992–1993). College students' attitudes toward death today as compared to the 1930s. *Omega: Journal of Death and Dying, 26*, 219–222.

LEVENSON, R. W., CARSTENSEN, L. L., & GOTTMAN, J. M. (1993). Long-term marriage: Age, gender, and satisfaction. *Psychology and Aging, 8*, 301–313.

LEVENTHAL, H., LEVENTHAL, E. A., & SCHAEFER, P. M. (1992). Vigilant coping and health behavior. In M. G. Ory, R. P. Abeles, & P. D. Lipman (Eds.), *Aging, health, and behavior* (pp. 109–140). Newbury Park, CA: Sage.

LEVENTHAL, H., PATRICK-MILLER, L., LEVENTHAL, E. A., & BURNS, E. A. (1998). Does stress-emotion cause illness in elderly people? In K. W. Schaie & M. P. Lawton (Eds.), *Annual review of gerontology and geriatrics: Vol. 17. Focus on emotion and adult development* (pp. 138–184). New York: Springer.

LEVITAN, S., & CONWAY, E. (1990). *Families in flux: New approaches to meeting workforce challenges for child, elder, and health care in the 1990s*. Washington, DC: Bureau of National Affairs.

LEVITT, M. J., WEBER, R. A., & GUACCI, N. (1993). Convoys of social support: An intergenerational analysis. *Psychology and Aging, 8*, 323–326.

LICHTENBERG, P. A., ROSS, T., MILLIS, S. R., & MANNING, C. A. (1995). The relationship between depression and cognition in older adults: A cross-validation study. *Journals of Gerontology, 50*(1), P25–P32.

LICHTER, D., PIENTA, A., & MCLAUGHLIN, D. (1997). *Cohabitation among older adults: An alternative lifestyle or financial strategy?* Paper presented at the 50th Annual Scientific Meeting of the Gerontological Society of America.

LIEBERMAN, M. A., & FISCHER, L. (1995). The impact of chronic illness on the health and well-being of family members. *Gerontologist, 35*, 94–102.

LIEBERMAN, M. A., & TOBIN, S. S. (1983). *The experience of old age: Stress, coping, and survival*. New York: Basic Books.

LIGHT, K. E., & SPIRDUSO, W. W. (1990). Effects of adult aging on the movement complexity factor of response programming. *Journals of Gerontology, 45*(3), P107–P109.

LIGHT, L. L. (1991). Memory and aging: Four hypotheses in search of data. *Annual Review of Psychology, 42*, 333–376.

LINDEMANN, E. (1944). Symptomatology and management of acute grief. *American Journal of Psychiatry, 101*, 141–148.

LINDENBERGER, U., & BALTES, P. B. (1997). Intellectual functioning in old and very old age: Cross-sectional results from the Berlin Aging Study. *Psychology and Aging, 12*, 410–432.

LIPSITZ, L. A. (1995–1996). The teaching nursing home: Accomplishments and future directions. *Generations, 19*(4), 47–51.

LITWAK, E., & LONGINO, C. F. (1987). Migration patterns among the elderly: A developmental perspective. *Gerontologist, 27*, 266–272.

LIU, K., & MANTON, K. G. (1991). Nursing home length of stay and spend-down in Connecticut, 1977–1986. *Gerontologist, 31*, 165–173.

LOEVINGER, J. (1976). *Ego development: Conceptions and theories*. San Francisco: Jossey-Bass.

LOEVINGER, J., & WESSLER, R. (1970). *Measuring ego development*. San Francisco: Jossey-Bass.

LOGSDON, R. G. (1995). Psychopathology and treatment: Curriculum and research needs. In B. G. Knight, L. Teri, P. Wohlford, & J. Santos (Eds.), *Mental health services for older adults: Implications for training and practice in geropsychology* (pp. 41–51). Washington, DC: American Psychological Association.

LOMBARDO, N. E. (1994). *Barriers to mental health services for nursing home residents*. Washington, DC: American Association of Retired Persons, Public Policy Institute.

LOPATA, H. (1973). *Widowhood in an American city*. Cambridge, MA: Schenkman.

LOPATA, H. (1979). *Women as widows: Support systems*. Cambridge, MA: Schenkman.

LOSCOCCO, K. A., & ROSCHELLE, A. R. (1991). Influences on the quality of work and nonwork life: Two decades in review. *Journal of Vocational Behavior, 39*(2), 182–225.

LOWENTHAL, M. F., THURNHER, M., CHIRIBOGA, D., & ASSOCIATES (1975). *Four stages of life: A comparative study of women and men facing transitions*. San Francisco: Jossey-Bass.

LUND, D. A., CASERTA, M. S., & DIMOND, M. F. (1986). Gender differences through two years of bereavement among the elderly. *Gerontologist, 26*, 314–320.

LUSZCZ, M. A., BRYAN, J., & KENT, P. (1997). Predicting episodic memory performance of very old men and women: Contributions from age, depression, activity, cognitive ability, and speed. *Psychology and Aging, 12*, 340–351.

LYNESS, S. (1993). Predictors of differences between Type A and B individuals in heart rate and blood pressure reactivity. *Psychological Bulletin, 114*, 266–295.

LYNESS, S., EATON, E. M., & SCHNEIDER, L. S. (1994). Cognitive performance in older and middle-aged depressed outpatients and controls. *Journals of Gerontology, 49B*(3), P129–P136.

MADDEN, D. J. (1990). Adult age differences in the time course of visual attention. *Journals of Gerontology, 45*(1), P9–P16.

MADDOX, G. L. (1991). Aging with a difference. *Aging Well, 1*, 7–10.

MADDOX, G. L., & CLARK, D. O. (1992). Trajectories of functional impairment in later life. *Journal of Health and Social Behavior, 33*(2), 114–125.

MADEY, S. F., & CHASTEEN, A. (1997). *Belief in a just world and the perceived injustice of dying young or old*. Paper presented at the 50th Annual Scientific Meeting of the Gerontological Society of America.

MAGAI, C., & MCFADDEN, S. (1996). *Handbook of emotion, adult development, and aging*. San Diego: Academic Press.

MAGAI, C., & PASSMAN, V. (1998). The interpersonal basis of emotional behavior and emotional regulation in adulthood. In K. W. Schaie & M. P. Lawton (Eds.), *Annual review of gerontology and geriatrics: Vol. 17. Focus on emotion and adult development* (pp. 104–137). New York: Springer.

MAGAZINER, J., SIMONSICK, E. M., KASHNER, T. M., HEBEL, J. R., & KENZORA, J. E. (1990). Predictors of functional recovery one year following hospital discharge for hip fracture: A prospective study. *Journals of Gerontology, 45*(3), M101–M107.

MALCOLM, A. T., & JANISSE, M. P. (1991). Additional evidence for the relationship between Type A behavior and social support in men. *Behavioral Medicine, 17*(3), 131–133.

MALLINCKRODT, B., & FRETZ, B. R. (1988). Social support and the impact of job loss on older professionals. *Journal of Counseling Psychology, 35*(3), 281–286.

MALONE-BEACH, E. E., & ZARIT, S. H. (1995). Dimensions of social support and social conflict as predictors of caregiver depression. *International Psychogeriatrics, 7*(1), 25–38.

MANCINI, J. A. (1984). Research on family life in old age: Exploring the frontiers. In W. H. Quinn & G. A. Hughston (Eds.), *Independent aging: Family and social systems perspectives* (pp. 58–71). Rockville, MD: Aspen.

MANTON, K. G. (1990). Population models of gender differences in mortality, morbidity, and disability risks. In M. G. Ory & H. R. Warner (Eds.), *Gender, health, and longevity: Multidisciplinary perspectives* (pp. 201–253). New York: Springer.

MANTON, K. G., BLAZER, D. G., & WOODBURY, M. A. (1987). Suicide in middle age and later life: Sex- and race-specific life-table and cohort analyses. *Journal of Gerontology, 42*, 219–227.

MANTON, K. G., PATRICK, C. H., & JOHNSON, K. W. (1989). Health differentials between blacks and whites: Recent trends in mortality and morbidity. In D. P. Willis (Ed.), *Health policies and black Americans* (pp. 129–199). New Brunswick, NJ: Transaction Publishers.

MANTON, K. G., & SUZMAN, R. (1992). Forecasting health and future societies: Implications for health care and staffing needs. In M. G. Ory, R. P. Abeles, & P. D. Lipman (Eds.), *Aging, health, and behavior* (pp. 327–357). Newbury Park, CA: Sage.

MANTON, K. G., WRIGLEY, J. M., COHEN, H. J., & WOODBURY, M. A. (1991). Cancer mortality, aging, and patterns of comorbidity in the United States: 1968 to 1986. *Journals of Gerontology, 46*(4), S225–S234.

MANUCK, S. B., MULDOON, M. F., KAPLAN, J. R., ADAMS, M. R., & POLEFRONE, J. M. (1989). Coronary artery atherosclerosis and cardiac response to stress in cynomolgus monkeys. In A. W. Siegman & T. M. Dembroski (Eds.), *In search of the coronary prone behavior: Beyond Type A* (pp. 207–223). Hillsdale, NJ: Erlbaum.

MARKIDES, K. S., & BLACK, S. A. (1996). Race, ethnicity, and aging: The impact of inequality. In R. H. Binstock & L. K. George (Eds.), *Handbook of aging and the social sciences* (4th ed.) (pp. 153–170). New York: Academic Press.

MARKIDES, K. S., & COOPER, C. L. (EDS.). (1989). *Aging, stress and health.* Chichester, England: Wiley.

MARKIDES, K. S., COREIL, J., & ROGERS, L. P. (1989). Aging and health among Southwestern Hispanics. In K. S. Markides (Ed.), *Aging and health: Perspectives on gender, race, ethnicity, and class* (pp. 177–210). Newbury Park, CA: Sage.

MARKOVITZ, J. H., MATTHEWS, K. A., KISS, J., & SMITHERMAN, T. C. (1996). Effects of hostility on platelet reactivity to psychological stress in coronary heart disease patients and in healthy controls. *Psychosomatic Medicine, 58*(2), 143–149.

MARKUS, H., & NURIUS, P. (1986). Possible selves. *American Psychologist, 41,* 954–969.

MARSISKE, M., KLUMB, P., & BALTES, M. M. (1997). Everyday activity patterns and sensory functioning in old age. *Psychology and Aging, 12,* 444–457.

MARSISKE, M., LANG, F. B., BALTES, P. B., & BALTES, M. M. (1995). Selective optimization with compensation: Life-span perspectives on successful human development. In R. A. Dixon & L. Bäckman (Eds.), *Compensating for psychological deficits and declines: Managing losses and promoting gains* (pp. 35–79). Mahwah, NJ: Erlbaum.

MARTIN, C. E. (1981). Factors affecting sexual functioning in 60–79-year-old married males. *Archives of Sexual Behavior, 10,* 399–420.

MARX, J. (1991). New clue found to Alzheimer's. *Science, 253,* 857–858.

MARX, J. (1992). Major setback for Alzheimer's models. *Science, 255,* 1200–1202.

MASTERS, W. H., & JOHNSON, V. E. (1966). *Human sexual response.* Boston: Little, Brown.

MATTHEWS, S. H., & SPREY, J. (1985). Adolescents' relationships with grandparents: An empirical contribution to conceptual clarification. *Journal of Gerontology, 40,* 621–626.

MATTOON, M. A. (1981). *Jungian psychology in perspective.* New York: Free Press.

MAZESS, R. B., & FORMAN, S. H. (1979). Longevity and age exaggeration in Vilcabamba, Ecuador. *Journal of Gerontology, 34,* 94–98.

MCADAMS, D. P. (1992). The five-factor model in personality: A critical appraisal. *Journal of Personality, 60,* 329–361.

MCADAMS, D. P. (1994). *The person: An introduction to personality psychology* (2nd ed.). San Diego: Harcourt Brace Jovanovich.

MCADAMS, D. P., & DE ST. AUBIN, E. (1992). A theory of generativity and its assessment through self-report, behavioral acts, and narrative themes in autobiography. *Journal of Personality and Social Psychology, 62,* 1003–1015.

MCCLEARN, G. E. (1993). Behavioral genetics: The last century and the next. In R. Plomin & G. E. McClearn (Eds.), *Nature, nurture, and psychology* (pp. 27–49). Washington, DC: American Psychological Association.

MCCRAE, R. R., & COSTA, P. T. (1988). Recalled parent-child relations and adult personality. *Journal of Personality, 56,* 418–433.

MCCRAE, R. R., & COSTA, P. T. (1990). *Personality in adulthood.* New York: Guilford Press.

MCCRAE, R. R., COSTA, P. T., & PIEDMONT, R. L. (1993). Folk concepts, natural language, and psychological constructs: The California Psychological Inventory and the five-factor model. *Journal of Personality, 61,* 1–26.

MCCULLOUGH, B. J. (1995). Aging and kinship in rural context. In R. Blieszner & V. H. Bedford (Eds.), *Handbook of aging and the family* (pp. 332–354). Westport, CT: Greenwood Press.

MCDERMID, S., HUSTON, T., & MCHALE, S. M. (1990). Changes in marriages associated with the transition to parenthood: Individual differences as a function of sex-role attitudes and changes in the division of household labor. *Journal of Marriage and the Family, 52,* 475–486.

MCFADDEN, S. H. (1995). Religion and well-being in aging persons in an aging society. *Journal of Social Issues, 51*(2), 161–175.

MCGOWEN, D. F. (1994). *Living in the labyrinth.* New York: Bantam.

MCGRATH, E., KEITA, G. P., STRICKLAND, B. R., & RUSSO, N. F. (EDS.). (1990). *Women and depression: Risk factors and treatment issues.* Washington, DC: American Psychological Association.

MCGUE, M. (1993). From proteins to cognitions: The behavioral genetics of alcoholism. In R. Plomin & G. E. McClearn (Eds.), *Nature, nurture, and psychology* (pp. 245–268). Washington, DC: American Psychological Association.

MCGUE, M., HIRSCH, B., & LYKKEN, D. T. (1993). Age and the self-perception of ability: A twin study analysis. *Psychology and Aging, 8,* 72–80.

MCGUE, M., VAUPEL, J. W., HOLM, N., & HARVALD, B. (1993). Longevity is moderately heritable in a sample of Danish twins born 1870–1880. *Journals of Gerontology, 48*(6), B237–B244.

MCINTOSH, J. L. (1992). Suicide of the elderly. In B. Bongar (Ed.), *Suicide: Guidelines for assessment, management, and treatment* (pp. 106–124). New York: Oxford University Press.

MCINTOSH, J. L. (1995). Suicide prevention in the elderly (age 65–99). In M. M. Silverman & R. W. Maris (Eds.), *Suicide prevention: Toward the year 2000* (pp. 180–192). New York: Guilford Press.

MCWILLIAM, I., STEWART, N., BROWN, J., DESAI, K., & CODERRE, P. (1996). Creating health with chronic illness. *Advances in Nursing Science, 18*, 1–15.

MEHDIZADEH, S. A., & LUZADIS, R. A. (1994). The effect of job mobility on pension wealth. *Gerontologist, 34*, 173–179.

MELLOR, M. J., ALFREDO, C. T., KENNY, E., LAZERUS, J., CONWAY, J. M., RIVERS, L., VISWANATHAN, N., & ZIMMERMAN, J. (1996). Alcohol and aging. *Journal of Gerontological Social Work, 25*(1–2), 71–89.

MENDES DE LEON, C. F., GLASS, T. A., GEORGE, L. K., EVANS, D. A., & BERKMAN, L. F. (1997). *Social participation, social ties, and social support in relation to functional decline in older blacks and whites.* Paper presented at the 50th Annual Scientific Meeting of the Gerontological Society of America.

MENTAL HEALTH AND AGING: PROBLEMS AND PROSPECTS. (1993, Winter/Spring), *Generations, 17*.

METTS, S., & CUPACH, W. R. (1990). The influence of relationship beliefs and problem-solving responses on satisfaction in romantic relationships. *Human Communication Research, 17*(1), 170–185.

MEYER, B. J. F., & RICE, G. E. (1989). Prose processing in adulthood: The text, the reader, and the task. In L. W. Poon, D. C. Rubin, & B. A. Wilson (Eds.), *Everyday cognition in adulthood and late life* (pp. 59–73). New York: Cambridge University Press.

MEZEY, M., RAMSEY, G. C., & MITTY, E. (1994). Making the PSDA work for the elderly. *Generations, 18*(4), 13–18.

MICHAEL, R. T., GAGNON, J. H., LAUMANN, E. O., & KOLATA, G. (1994). *Sex in America.* Boston: Little, Brown.

MIDANIK, L. T., SOGHIKIAN, K., RANSOM, J. J., & TEKAWA, I. S. (1995). The effect of retirement on mental health and health behaviors: The Kaiser Permanente retirement study. *Journals of Gerontology, 50B*(1), S59–S61.

MILLER, B., & LAWTON, M. P. (1997). Positive aspects of caregiving: Introduction. Finding balance in caregiver research. *Gerontologist, 37*, 216–217.

MILLER, B., MCFALL, S., & MONTGOMERY, A. (1991). The impact of elder health, caregiver involvement, and global stress on two dimensions of caregiver burden. *Journals of Gerontology, 46*(1), S9–S19.

MILLER, S., BLALOCK, J., & GINSBERG, H. (1984–1985). Children and the aged: Attitudes, contact, and discriminative ability. *International Journal of Aging and Human Development, 19*, 47–53.

MILLER, T., & CUGLIARI, A. M. (1990). Withdrawing and withholding treatment: Policies in long-term care facilities. *Gerontologist, 30*, 462–468.

MILLS, E. S. (1993). *The story of Elderhostel.* Hanover, NH: University Press of New England.

MINER, A. S., & ROBINSON, D. F. (1994). Organizational and population level learning as engines for career transitions. *Journal of Organizational Behavior, 15*, 345–364.

MINOIS, G. (1989). *History of old age.* Chicago: University of Chicago Press.

MIROWSKY, J., & ROSS, C. E. (1992). Age and depression. *Journal of Health and Social Behavior, 33*, 187–205.

MIRVIS, P. H., & HALL, D. T. (1994). Psychological success and the boundaryless career. *Journal of Organizational Behavior, 15*, 365–380.

MITCHELL, D. B. (1989). How many memory systems? Evidence from aging. *Journal of Experimental Psychology: Learning, Memory, and Cognition, 15*(1), 31–49.

MITCHELL, V., & HELSON, R. (1990). Women's prime of life: Is it the 50s? *Psychology of Women Quarterly, 14*, 451–470.

MOEN, P. (1996). Gender, age, and the life course. In R. H. Binstock & L. K. George (Eds.), *Handbook of aging and the social sciences* (4th ed.) (pp. 171–187). New York: Academic Press.

MOEN, P., ROBINSON, J., & FIELDS, V. (1994). Women's work and caregiving roles: A life course approach. *Journals of Gerontology, 49B*(4), S176–S186.

MONANE, M., GURWITZ, J. H., & AVORN, J. (1993), Winter/Spring). Pharmacotherapy with psychoactive medications in the long-term-care setting. *Generations, 17*, 56–61.

MONTGOMERY, R. J. V., & KOSLOSKI, K. (1994). A longitudinal analysis of nursing home placement for dependent elders cared for by spouses versus adult children. *Journals of Gerontology, 49*(2), S62–S74.

MONTHLY VITAL STATISTICS REPORT. (1995, March 22). *43*(6).

MOON. (1955). Coronary arteries in fetuses, infants, and juveniles. *Circulation, 15*, 366.

MOR, V., BANASZAK-HOLL, J., & ZINN, J. (1995–1996). The trend toward specialization in nursing care facilities. *Generations, 19*(4), 24–29.

MORAS, K., & CRASKE, M. G., & BARLOW, D. H. (1990). Behavioral and cognitive therapies for panic disorder. In M. Roth, R. Noyes, & G. D. Burrows (Eds.), *Handbook of anxiety* (vol. 4, pp. 311–323). New York: Elsiever.

MORGAN, L. A. (1989). Economic well-being following marital termination: A comparison of widowed and divorced women. *Journal of Family Issues, 10,* 86–101.

MORGAN, L. A. (1991). *After marriage ends: Economic consequences for midlife women.* Newbury Park, CA: Sage.

MORRIS, D. C. (1997). *Retirement satisfaction and the subjective well-being of older adults in Middletown, U.S.A.* Paper presented at the 50th Annual Scientific Meeting of the Gerontological Society of America.

MORRIS, R. (1995–1996). The evolution of the nursing home as an intermediary institution. *Generations, 19*(4), 57–61.

MORRIS, R., & BASS, S. A. (EDS.). (1988). Toward a new paradigm about work and age. In R. Morris & S. Bass (Eds.), *Retirement reconsidered* (pp. 3–15). New York: Springer.

MORRISON, R. S., & MEIER, D. E. (1994). Physician assisted dying: Fashion public policy with an absence of data. *Generations, 18*(4), 48–53.

MORROW, D., LEIRER, V., ALTITERI, P., & FITZSIMMONS, C. (1994). When expertise reduces age differences in performance. *Psychology and Aging, 9,* 134–148.

MOTE, P. L., GRIZZLE, J. M., WALFORD, R. L., & SPINDLER, S. R. (1991). Influence of age and caloric restriction on expression of hepatic genes for xenobiotic and oxygen metabolizing enzymes in the mouse. *Journals of Gerontology, 46*(3), B95–B100.

MUI, A. C. (1995). Caring for frail elderly parents: A comparison of adult sons and daughters. *Gerontologist, 35,* 86–93.

MULTIPLE RISK FACTOR INTERVENTION TRIAL RESEARCH GROUP. (1982). Multiple risk factors intervention trial: Risk factor changes and mortality results. *Journal of the American Medical Association, 248,* 1465–1477.

MURPHY, F. C., & ELDERS, M. J. (1992). Diabetes and the black community. In R. Braithwaite & S. E. Taylor (Eds.), *Health issues in the black community* (pp. 121–131). San Francisco: Jossey-Bass.

MUSANTE, L., TREIBER, F. A., DAVIS, H., STRONG, W. B., & LEVY, M. (1992). Hostility: Relationship to lifestyle behaviors and physical risk factors. *Behavioral Medicine, 18*(1), 21–26.

MUSICK, M., & KEITH, E. (1997). *Interdisciplinary research and the young scholar.* Panel discussion presented at the 50th Annual Scientific Meeting of the Gerontological Society of America.

MUTCHLER, J. E., BURR, J. A., PIENTA, A. M., & MASSAGLI, M. P. (1997). Pathways to labor force exit: Work transitions and work instability. *Journals of Gerontology, 52B*(1), S4–S12.

MYERHOFF, B. (1978). *Number our days.* New York: Meridian.

MYERS, J. K., WEISSMAN, M. M., TISCHLER, G. L., HOLZER, C. E., III, ORVASCHEL, H., ANTHONY, J. C., BOYD, J. H., BURKE, J. D., JR., KRAMER, M., & STOLTZMAN, R. (1984). Six-month prevalence of psychiatric disorders in three communities. *Archives of General Psychiatry, 41,* 959–967.

NATHANSON, C. A. (1990). The gender-mortality differential in developed countries: Demographic and sociocultural dimensions. In M. G. Ory & H. R. Warner (Eds.), *Gender, health, and longevity: Multidisciplinary perspectives* (pp. 3–23). New York: Springer.

NATIONAL ACADEMY ON AGING. (1995, November). *The public policy and aging report* (vol. 7, no. 1). Washington, DC: Gerontological Society of America.

NATIONAL CENTER FOR HEALTH STATISTICS (1995a). *Health, United States, 1994.* Hyattsville, MD: Public Health Service.

NATIONAL CENTER FOR HEALTH STATISTICS (1995b). *Healthy People 2000: Review, 1994.* Hyattsville, MD: Public Health Service.

NATIONAL INSTITUTE ON AGING. (1989). *Older and wiser* (NIH Pub. No. 89-2797). Bethesda, MD: National Institutes of Health.

NATIONAL INSTITUTE ON AGING. (1993). *With the passage of time: The Baltimore Longitudinal Study of Aging* (NIH Pub. No. 93-3685). Bethesda, MD: National Institutes of Health.

NEELY, A. S., & BACKMAN, L. (1993). Long-term maintenance of gains from memory training in older adults: Two 3½-year follow-up studies. *Journals of Gerontology, 48B*(5), P233–P237.

NEUGARTEN, B. L. (1977). Personality and aging. In J. E. Birren & K. W. Schaie (Eds.), *Handbook of the psychology of aging* (pp. 626–659). New York: Van Nostrand Reinhold.

NEUGARTEN, B. L., & ASSOCIATES (EDS.). (1964). *Personality in middle and late life.* New York: Atherton.

NEUGARTEN, B. L., & GUTMANN, D. L. (1964). Age-sex roles and personality in middle age: A thematic apperception study. In B. L. Neugarten & Associates (Eds.), *Personality in middle and late life* (pp. 58–89). New York: Atherton.

NEUGARTEN, B. L., HAVIGHURST, R. J., & TOBIN, S. S. (1968). Personality and patterns of aging. In B. L. Neugarten & Associates (Eds.), *Middle age and aging: A reader in social psychology* (pp. 173–177). Chicago: University of Chicago Press.

NEUGARTEN, B. L., & WEINSTEIN, C. (1964). The changing American grandparent. *Journal of Marriage and the Family, 26,* 199–204.

NEWMAN, S. J., & ENVALL, K. (1995). *The effects of supports on sustaining older disabled persons in the community.* Washington, DC: AARP.

NICKEL, J. T., & CHIRIKOS, T. N. (1990). Functional disability of elderly patients with long-term coronary heart disease: A sex-stratified analysis. *Journals of Gerontology, 45*(2), S60–S68.

NIXON, S. J., TIVIS, R., & PARSONS, O. A. (1995). Behavioral dysfunction and cognitive efficiency in male and female alcoholics. *Alcoholism Clinical and Experimental Research, 19,* 577–581.

NOELKER, L. S., & POULSHOCK, S. W. (1984). Intimacy: Factors affecting its development among members of a home for the aged. *International Journal of Aging and Human Development, 19,* 177–190.

NOELL, E. (1995–1996). Design in nursing homes: Environment as a silent partner in caregiving. *Generations, 19*(4), 14–19.

NULAND, S. (1995). *How we die.* New York: Vintage.

THE NURSING HOME REVISITED. (1995–1996, Winter), *Generations, 17.*

O'BRYANT, S. L. (1990–1991). Forewarning of a husband's death: Does it make a difference for older widows? *Omega: Journal of Death and Dying, 22,* 227–239.

O'BRYANT, S. L., & HANSSON, R. O. (1995). Widowhood. In R. Blieszner & V. H. Bedford (Eds.), *Handbook of aging and the family* (pp. 440–458). Westport, CT: Greenwood Press.

O'BRYANT, S. L., & STRAW, L. B. (1991). Relationship of previous divorce and previous widowhood to older women's adjustment to recent widowhood. *Journal of Divorce and Remarriage, 15,* 49–67.

O'RAND, A. M. (1988). Convergence, institutionalization, and bifurcation: Gender and the pension acquisition process. In G. L. Maddox & M. P. Lawton (Eds.), *Annual review of gerontology and geriatrics: Vol. 8. Varieties of aging* (pp. 132–155). New York: Springer.

O'RAND, A. M. (1996). *The cumulative stratification of the life course.* In R. H. Binstock & L. K. George (Eds.), *Handbook of aging and the social sciences* (4th ed.) (pp. 188–207). New York: Academic Press.

ORGEL, L. (1973). The maintenance of the accuracy of protein synthesis and its relevance to aging. *Proceedings of the National Academy of Science, 67,* 1496.

ORTHNER, D. K. (1990). The family in transition. In D. G. Blankenhorn, S. Bayme, & J. B. Elshtain (Eds.), *Rebuilding the nest: A new commitment to the American family* (pp. 93–118). Milwaukee: Family Service America.

ORY, M. G., & WARNER, H. R. (EDS.). (1990). *Gender, health, and longevity: Multidisciplinary perspectives.* New York: Springer.

OZER, D. J., & REISE, S. P. (1994). Personality assessment. *Annual Review of Psychology, 45,* 357–388.

PAIER, M. S. (1996). Specter of the crone: The experience of vertebral fracture. *Advances in Nursing Science, 18*(3) 27–36.

PALMORE, E. B. (1971). Attitudes towards aging as shown by humor. *Gerontologist, 11,* 181–186.

PALMORE, E. B. (1990). *Ageism: Positive and negative.* New York: Springer.

PALMORE, E. B., BURCHETT, B., FILLENBAUM, G. G., GEORGE, L. K., & WALLMAN, L. M. (1985). *Retirement: Causes and consequences.* New York: Springer.

PARK, D. C., HERTZOG, C., KIDDER, D. P., MORRELL, R. W., & MAYHORN, C. B. (1997). Effects of age on event-based and time-based prospective memory. *Psychology and Aging, 12,* 314–327.

PARKES, C. M. (1972). *Bereavement: Studies of grief in adult life.* New York: International Universities Press.

PARKES, C. M., & WEISS, R. S. (1983). *Recovery from bereavement.* New York: Basic Books.

PARMELEE, P. A., KATZ, I. R., & LAWTON, M. P. (1992a). Depression and mortality among institutionalized aged. *Journals of Gerontology, 47*(1), P3–P10.

PARMELEE, P. A., KATZ, I. R., & LAWTON, M. P. (1992b). Incidence of depression in long-term care settings. *Journals of Gerontology, 47*(6), M189–M196.

PARMELEE, P. A., KATZ, I. R., & LAWTON, M. P. (1993). Anxiety and its association with depression among institutionalized elderly. *American Journal of Geriatric Psychiatry, 1*(1), 46–58.

PAVALKO, E. K., & ARTIS, J. E. (1997). Women's caregiving and paid work: Causal relationships in late midlife. *Journals of Gerontology, 52B*(4), S170–S179.

PEARLIN, L. (1980). Life strains and psychological distress among adults. In N. J. Smelser & E. H. Erikson (Eds.), *Themes of love and work.* Cambridge, MA: Harvard University Press.

PEARLIN, L. I., ANESHENSEL, C. S., MULLAN, J. T., & WHITLACH, C. J. (1996). Caregiving and its social support.

In R. H. Binstock & L. K. George (Eds.), *Handbook of aging and the social sciences* (4th ed.) (pp. 283–302). New York: Academic Press.

PEARLIN, L. I., MULLAN, J. T., SEMPLE, S. J., & SKAFF, M. M. (1990). Caregiving and the stress process: An overview of concepts and their measures. *Gerontologist, 30,* 583–594.

PEDERSEN, N. (1996). Gerontological behavioral genetics. In J. E. Birren & K. W. Schaie (Eds.), *Handbook of the psychology of aging* (4th ed.) (pp. 59–77). San Diego: Academic Press.

PELHAM, B. W. (1993). The idiographic nature of human personality: Examples of the idiographic self-concept. *Journal of Personality and Social Psychology, 64,* 665–677.

PELLMAN, J. (1992). Widowhood in elderly women: Exploring its relationship to community integration, hassles, stress, social support, and social support seeking. *International Journal of Aging and Human Development, 35*(4), 253–264.

PENDLEBURY, W. W., & SOLOMON, P. R. (1994). Alzheimer's disease: Therapeutic strategies for the 1990s. *Neurobiology of Aging, 15,* 287–289.

PENNING, M. J. (1990). Receipt of assistance by elderly people: Hierarchical selection and task specificity. *Gerontologist, 30,* 220–227.

PERKINSON, M. A. (1997). *Information needs of families of nursing home residents.* Paper presented at the 50th Annual Scientific Meeting of the Gerontological Society of America.

PERLMUTTER, M., KAPLAN, M., & NYQUIST, L. (1990). Development of adaptive competence in adulthood. *Human Development, 33*(2–3), 185–197.

PERLMUTTER, M., & NYQUIST, L. (1990). Relationships between self-reported physical and mental health and intelligence performance across adulthood. *Journals of Gerontology, 45*(4), P145–P155.

PERRY, E. L., KULIK, C. T., & BOURHIS, A. C. (1996). Moderating effects of personal and contextual factors in age discrimination. *Journal of Applied Psychology, 81,* 628–647.

PETERSON, C., & SELIGMAN, M. E. P. (1987). Explanatory style and illness. *Journal of Personality 55,* 237–265.

PETERSON, C., SELIGMAN, M. E. P., & VAILLANT, G. E. (1994). Pessimistic explanatory style is a risk factor for physical illness: A thirty-five-year longitudinal study. In A. Steptoe & J. Wardle (Eds.), *Psychosocial processes and health: A reader* (pp. 235–246). Cambridge, England: Cambridge University Press.

PETERSON, P. (1993). *Facing up: How to restore the economy from crashing debt and restore the American dream.* New York: Simon and Schuster.

PILLEMER, K., & BACHMAN-PREHN, R. (1991). Helping and hurting: Predictors of maltreatment of patients in nursing homes. *Research on Aging, 13*(1), 74–95.

PILLEMER, K., & SUITOR, J. J. (1991). Will I ever escape my child's problems? Effects of adult children's problems on elderly parents. *Journal of Marriage and the Family, 53,* 585–594.

PILLEMER, K., & SUITOR, J. J. (1996). It takes one to help one: Effects of similar others on the well-being of caregivers. *Journals of Gerontology, 51B*(5), S250–S257.

PIRKL, J. J. (1995). Transgenerational design: Prolonging the American dream. *Generations, 19,* 32–36.

PLANEK, T. W., & FOWLER, R. C. (1971). Traffic accident problems and exposure characteristics of the older driver. *Journal of Gerontology, 26,* 224–230.

PLOMIN, R., DEFRIES, J. C., & MCCLEARN, G. E. (1980). *Behavioral genetics: A primer.* San Francisco: Freeman.

PLOMIN, R., LICHTENSTEIN, P., PEDERSEN, N., MCCLEARN, G., & NESSELROADE, J. R. (1990). Genetic influence on life events during the last half of the life span. *Psychology and Aging, 5,* 25–30.

PLOMIN, R., & MCCLEARN, G. E. (1990). Human behavioral genetics of aging. In J. E. Birren & K. W. Schaie (Eds.), *Handbook of the psychology of aging* (3rd ed.) (pp. 67–77). San Diego: Academic Press.

PLOMIN, R., & MCCLEARN, G. E. (1993). *Nature, nurture, and psychology.* Washington, DC: American Psychological Association.

PLOMIN, R., MCCLEARN, G. E., PEDERSEN, N. L., NESSELROADE, J. R., & BERGEMEN. (1988). Genetic influence on childhood family environment perceived retrospectively from the last half of the life span. *Developmental Psychology, 24,* 738–745.

POGREBIN, L. (1996). *Getting over getting older.* Boston: Little, Brown.

POON, L. W., RUBIN, D. C., & WILSON, B. A. (EDS.). (1989). *Everyday cognition in adulthood and late life.* New York: Cambridge University Press.

POPENOE, D. (1988). *Disturbing the nest: Family change and decline in modern societies.* New York: Aldine de Gruyter.

POWELL, F. C., & THORSON, J. A. (1991). Constructions of death among those high in intrinsic religious motivation: A factor-analytic study. *Death Studies, 15*(2), 131–138.

PRICE, V. A. (1988). Research and clinical issues in treating Type A behavior. In B. Kent & C. R. Snyder

(Eds.), *Type A behavior pattern research, theory, and intervention* (pp. 275–311). New York: Wiley.

PRIGERSON, H. G. (1992). Socialization to dying: Social determinants of death acknowledgment and treatment among terminally ill geriatric patients. *Journal of Health and Social Behavior, 33,* 378–395.

PROPPE, H. (1968). Housing for the retired and aged in southern California: An architectural commentary. *Gerontologist, 8,* 176–179.

PYNOOS, J., & GOLANT, S. (1996). Housing and living arrangements for the elderly. In R. H. Binstock & L. K. George (Eds.), *Handbook of aging and the social sciences* (4th ed.) (pp. 303–325). New York: Academic Press.

QUADAGNO, J., & HARDY, M. (1996). Work and retirement. In R. H. Binstock & L. K. George (Eds.), *Handbook of aging and the social sciences* (4th ed.) (pp. 326–345). New York: Academic Press.

QUINN, J. F., & BURKHAUSER, R. V. (1990). Work and retirement. In R. H. Binstock & L. K. George (Eds.). *Handbook of aging and the social sciences* (3rd ed.) (pp. 307–323). San Diego: Academic Press.

QUIROUETTE, C., & GOLD, D. P. (1992). Spousal characteristics as predictors of well-being in older couples. *International Journal of Aging and Human Development, 34*(4), 257–269.

RADNER, D. (1992, Fall). The economic status of the aged. *Social Security Bulletin, 55,* 14.

RAHE, R. H. (1974). Life change and subsequent illness reports. In E. K. Gunderson & R. H. Rahe (Eds.), *Life stress and illness* (pp. 58–78). Springfield, IL: Charles C. Thomas.

RAKOWSKI, W. (1992). Disease prevention and health promotion with older adults. In M. G. Ory, R. P. Abeles, & P. D. Lipman (Eds.), *Aging, health, and behavior* (pp. 239–275). Newbury Park, CA: Sage.

RAKOWSKI, W. (1994). The definition and measurement of prevention, preventive health care, and health promotion. *Generations, 18,* pp. 18–23.

RANDO, T. A. (1984). *Grief, dying, and death: Clinical interventions for caregivers.* Champaign, IL: Research Press.

RANDO, T. A. (1992–1993). The increasing prevalence of complicated mourning: The onslaught is just beginning. *Omega: Journal of Death and Dying, 26,* 43–59.

REICH, R. (1992). *The work of nations.* New York: Knopf.

REINHARDT, J. P. (1996). The importance of friendship and family support in adaption to chronic vision impairment. *Journals of Gerontology, 51 B*(5), P268–P278.

REITZES, D. C., MUTRAN, E. J., & FERNANDEZ, M. E. (1996). Does retirement hurt well-being? Factors influencing self-esteem and depression among retirees and workers. *Gerontologist, 36,* 649–656.

RENDALL, M. S. (1996). Aggregating poor and near-poor elderly under different resource definitions. *Journals of Gerontology 51B*(4), S209–S216.

RENSHAW, D. C. (1996). Sexuality and aging. In J. Sadavoy, L. W. Lazarus, L. F. Jarvik, & G. T. Grossberg (Eds.), *Comprehensive review of geriatric psychiatry* (2nd ed.) (pp. 713–729). Washington, DC: American Psychiatric Press.

RESNICK, H. E., FRIES, B. E., & VERBRUGGE, L. M. (1997). Windows to their world: The effect of sensory impairments on social engagement and activity time in nursing home residents. *Journals of Gerontology, 52B*(3), S135–S144.

RIEGEL, K. F. (1977). History of psychological gerontology. In J. E. Birren & K. W. Schaie (Eds.), *Handbook of the psychology of aging* (pp. 7–10). New York: Van Nostrand Reinhold.

RIEGEL, K. F., & RIEGEL, R. M. (1972). Development, drop, and death. *Developmental Psychology, 6,* 306–319.

RIEGEL, K. F., RIEGEL, R. M., & MEYER, G. (1967). A study of the dropout rates in longitudinal research on aging and the prediction of death. *Journal of Personality and Social Psychology, 5,* 342–348.

RILEY, M. W., & RILEY, J. W. (1993). Connections: Kin and cohort. In V. L. Bengston & W. A. Achenbaum (Eds.), *The changing contract across generations* (pp. 167–168). New York: Aldine de Gruyter.

RILEY, M. W., & RILEY, J. W. (1994). Age integration and the lives of older people. *Gerontologist, 34,* 110–115.

RILEY, P. (1995). *Long-term care: The silent target of the federal and state budget debate.* Washington, DC: Gerontological Society of America.

RIX, S. (1994). *Older workers: How do they measure up?* Washington, DC: American Association of Retired Persons, Public Policy Institute.

RIX, S. (1995). *The older worker in 1994: New survey questions limit comparisons with earlier years.* Washington, DC: American Association of Retired Persons, Public Policy Institute.

ROBERTS, R. E., KAPLAN, G. A., SHEMA, S. J., & STRAWBRIDGE, W. J. (1997). Prevalence and correlates of depression in an aging cohort: The Alameda County study. *Journals of Gerontology, 52B*(5), S252–S258.

ROBERTSON, J. F. (1977). Grandmotherhood: A study of role conceptions. *Journal of Marriage and the Family, 39,* 165–174.

RODIN, J. (1986). Aging and health: Effects of the sense of control. *Science, 233,* 1271–1276.

RODIN, J., & LANGER, E. (1977). Long-term effects of a control relevant intervention with the institutionalized aged. *Journal of Personality and Social Psychology, 35,* 897–902.

RODIN, J., & LANGER, E. (1980). Aging labels: The decline of control and the fall of self-esteem. *Journal of Social Issues, 36,* 12–29.

ROOK, K. S. (1997). Positive and negative social exchanges: Weighing their effects in later life. *Journals of Gerontology: Social Sciences, 52B*(4), S167–S169.

ROSEN, B., & JERDEE, T. H. (1995). *The persistence of age and sex stereotypes in the 1990s: The influence of age and gender in management decision making.* Washington, DC: American Association of Retired Persons, Public Policy Institute.

ROSEN, J. L., & NEUGARTEN, B. L. (1964). Ego functions in the middle and later years: A thematic apperception study. In B. L. Neugarten & Associates (Eds.), *Personality in middle and late life.* New York: Atherton.

ROSENTHAL, C., MARTIN-MATTHEWS, A., & MATTHEWS, S. (1996). Caught in the middle? Occupancy in multiple roles and help to parents in a national probability sample of Canadian adults. *Journals of Gerontology, 51B*(6), S274–S283.

ROSS, L. M., & POLLIO, H. R. (1991). Metaphors of death: A thematic analysis of personal meanings. *Omega: Journal of Death and Dying, 23,* 291–307.

ROSSMAN, P. (1977). *Hospice.* New York: Fawcett Columbine.

ROTH, M., TOMLINSON, B. E., & BLESSED, G. (1966). Correlation between scores for dementia and counts of "senile plaques" in cerebral grey matter of elderly subjects. *Nature, 209,* 109–110.

ROWE, J. W., & KAHN, R. L. (1987). Human aging: Usual and successful. *Science, 237,* 143–149.

RUBIN, D. C., & SCHULKIND, M. D. (1997). Distribution of important and word-cued autobiographical memories in 20-, 35-, and 70-year-old adults. *Psychology and Aging, 12,* 524–535.

RUBINSTEIN, R. L. (1986). *Singular paths: Old men living alone.* New York: Columbia University Press.

RUBINSTEIN, R. L., KILBRIDE, J. C., & NAGY, S. (1992). *Elders living alone: Frailty and the perception of choice.* New York: Aldine de Gruyter.

RUBINSTEIN, R. L., & LAWTON, M. P. (EDS.). (1997). *Depression in long-term and residential care: Advances in research and treatment.* New York: Springer.

RUBONIS, A. V., COLBY, S. M., MONTI, P. M., ROHSENOW, D. J., GULLIVER, S. B., & SIROTA, A. D. (1994). Alcohol cue reactivity and mood induction in male and female alcoholics. *Journal of Studies on Alcohol, 55,* 487–494.

RUDBERG, M. A., FURNER, S. E., DUNN, J. E., & CASSEL, C. K. (1993). The relationship of visual and hearing impairments to disability: An analysis using the longitudinal study of aging. *Journals of Gerontology, 48A,* M261–M265.

RUDBERG, M. A., SAGER, M. A., & ZHANG, J. (1996). Risk factors for nursing home use after hospitalization for medical illness. *Journals of Gerontology, 51A*(5), M189–M194.

RUDDICK, W. (1994). Transforming homes and hospitals. *Hastings Center Report, 24*(5), S11–S14.

RUSCIN, M. (1997). *Management of medications in patients with osteoarthritis.* Paper presented at the 50th Annual Meeting of the Gerontological Society of America.

RUSH, K. L., & OULLET, L. L. (1997). Mobility aids and the elderly client. *Journal of Gerontological Nursing, 24* 7–15.

RYAN, E. B. (1992). Beliefs about memory changes across the adult life span. *Journals of Gerontology, 47*(1), P41–P46.

RYBASH, J. N., HOYER, W. J., & ROODIN, P. (1986). *Adult cognition and aging: Developmental changes in processing, knowing, and thinking.* New York: Pergamon Press.

RYFF, C. D. (1991). Possible selves in adulthood and old age: A tale of shifting horizons. *Psychology and Aging, 6,* 286–295.

SACHS, G. A. (1994). Improving care of the dying. *Generations, 18*(4), 19–22.

SALTHOUSE, T. A. (1990). Cognitive competence and expertise in aging. In J. E. Birren & K. W. Schaie (Eds.), *Handbook of the psychology of aging* (3rd ed.) (pp. 310–319). San Diego: Academic Press.

SALTHOUSE, T. A. (1991) *Theoretical perspectives on cognitive aging.* Hillsdale NJ: Erlbaum.

SALTHOUSE, T. A. (1992). The information-processing perspective on cognitive aging. In R. J. Sternberg & C. A. Berg (Eds.), *Intellectual development* (pp. 261–278). New York: Cambridge University Press.

SALTHOUSE, T. A. (1996). General and specific speed mediation of adult age differences in memory. *Journals of Gerontology: Psychological Sciences, 51B*(1), P30–P42.

SALTHOUSE, T. A., HANCOCK, H. E., MEINZ, E. J., & HAMBRICK, D. Z. (1996). Interrelations of age, visual acuity, and cognitive functioning. *Journals of Gerontology, 51B*(6), P317–P330.

SAVAGE, D. D., MCGEE, D. L., & OSTER, G. (1989). Reduction of hypertension-associated heart disease and stroke among Black Americans: Past experience and new perspectives on targeting resources. In D. P. Willis (Ed.), *Health policies and Black Americans* (pp. 297–321). New Brunswick, NJ: Transaction.

SAXON, M. J., & ETTEN, S. V. (1978). *Physical change and aging: A guide for the helping professions.* New York: Tiresias Press.

SCHACTER, D. L. (1992). Understanding implicit memory: A cognitive neuroscience approach. *American Psychologist, 47,* 559–569.

SCHACTER, D. L., KASZNIAK, A. W., KIHLSTROM, J. F., & VALDISERRI, M. (1991). The relation between source memory and aging. *Psychology and Aging, 6,* 559–568.

SCHAFER, D., KUBIK, M., & PELHAM, A. (1997). *Is moderate drinking beneficial? A comparison of drinkers and abstainers.* Paper presented at the 50th Annual Scientific Meeting of the Gerontological Society of America.

SCHAIE, K. W. (1965). A general model for the study of developmental problems. *Psychological Bulletin, 64,* 92–107.

SCHAIE, K. W. (1977–1978). Toward a stage theory of adult cognitive development. *International Journal of Aging and Human Development, 8,* 129–138.

SCHAIE, K. W. (1988). The impact of research methodology in theory building in the developmental sciences. In J. E. Birren & V. L. Bengtson (Eds.), *Emergent theories of aging* (pp. 41–57). New York: Springer.

SCHAIE, K. W. (1989). The hazards of cognitive aging. *Gerontologist, 29,* 483–493.

SCHAIE, K. W. (1990). Intellectual development in adulthood. In J. E. Birren & K. W. Schaie (Eds.), *Handbook of the psychology of aging* (3rd ed.) (pp. 291–309). San Diego: Academic Press.

SCHAIE, K. W. (1996). Intellectual development in adulthood. In J. E. Birren & K. W. Schaie (Eds.), *Handbook of the psychology of aging* (4th ed.) (pp. 266–286). San Diego: Academic Press.

SCHAIE, K. W., & LAWTON, M. P. (1997). *Annual review of gerontology and geriatrics: Vol. 17. Focus on emotion and adult development.* New York: Springer.

SCHAIE, K. W., & WILLIS, S. L. (1993). Age difference patterns of psychometric intelligence in adulthood: Generalizability within and across ability domains. *Psychology and Aging, 8,* 44–55.

SCHARLACH, A., RUNKLE, M. C., MIDANIK, L., & SOGHIKIAN, K. (1997). *Transitions in the lives of caregivers.* Paper presented at the 50th Annual Scientific Meeting of the Gerontological Society of America.

SCHEIBEL, A. B. (1996). Structural and functional changes in the aging brain. In J. E. Birren & K. W. Schaie (Eds.), *Handbook of the psychology of aging* (4th ed.) (pp. 105–128). San Diego: Academic Press.

SCHERWITZ, L., & CANICK, J. C. (1988). Self-reference and coronary heart disease risk. In B. K. Houston & C. R. Snyder (Eds.), *Type A behavior pattern: Research, theory, and intervention* (pp. 146–167). New York: Wiley.

SCHIFFMAN, S. (1977). Food recognition by the elderly. *Journal of Gerontology, 32,* 586–592.

SCHIFFMAN, S., & PASTERNAK, M. (1979). Decreased discrimination of food odors in the elderly. *Journal of Gerontology, 34,* 73–79.

SCHLESINGER, M. (1989). Paying the price: Medical care, minorities, and the newly competitive health care system. In D. P. Willis (Ed.), *Health policies and Black Americans* (pp. 270–296). New Brunswick, NJ: Transaction.

SCHMIDT, D. F., & BOLAND, S. M. (1986). Structure of perceptions of older adults: Evidence for multiple stereotypes. *Psychology and Aging, 1,* 255–260.

SCHOOLER, C. (1990). Psychological factors and effective cognitive functioning in adulthood. In J. E. Birren & K. W. Schaie (Eds.), *Handbook of the psychology of aging* (3rd ed.) (pp. 347–358). San Diego: Academic Press.

SCHUCKIT, M. A., ANTHENELLI, R. M., BUCHOLZ, K. K., HESSELBROCK, V. M., & TIPP, J. (1995). The time course of development of alcohol-related problems in men and women. *Journal of Studies on Alcohol, 56,* 218–225.

SCHULZ, J. H. (1996). Economic security policies. In R. H. Binstock & L. K. George (Eds.), *Handbook of aging and the social sciences* (4th ed.) (pp. 410–427). New York: Academic Press.

SCHULZ, R., & HECKHAUSEN, J. (1996). A life-span model of successful aging. *American Psychologist, 51,* 702–714.

SCHULZ, R., & SCHLARB, J. (1987–1988). Two decades of research on dying: What do we know about the patient? *Omega: Journal of Death and Dying, 18,* 299–317.

SCHULZ, R., VISINTAINER, P., & WILLIAMSON, G. M. (1990). Psychiatric and physical morbidity effects of caregiving. *Journals of Gerontology, 45*(5), P181–P191.

SCRIBNER, S. (1986). Thinking in action: Some characteristics of practical thought. In R. J. Sternberg & R. K. Wagner (Eds.), *Practical intelligence* (pp. 13–31). New York: Cambridge University Press.

SEDNEY, M. A. (1985–1986). Growing more complex: Conceptions of sex roles across adulthood. *International Journal of Aging and Human Development, 22,* 15–29.

SEHGAL, A., GALBRAITH, A., CHESNEY, M., SCHOENFELD, P., CHARLES, G., & LO, B. (1992). How strictly do dialysis patients want their advance directives followed? *Journal of the American Medical Association, 267*, 59–63.

SELIG, S., TOMLINSON, T., & HICKEY, T. (1991). Ethical dimensions of intergenerational reciprocity: Implications for practice. *Gerontologist, 31*, 624–630.

SELIGMAN, M. E. P. (1975). *Helplessness: On depression, development, and death.* San Francisco: W. H. Freeman.

SELYE, H. (1976). *The stress of life.* New York: McGraw-Hill.

SEMEL, V. G. (1996). Modern psychoanalytic treatment of the older patient. In S. H. Zarit & B. G. Knight (Eds.), *A guide to psychotherapy and aging: Effective clinical interventions in a life-stage context* (pp. 101–120). Washington, DC: American Psychological Association.

SHANAS, E. (1979a). The family as a social support system in old age. *Gerontologist, 19*, 169–174.

SHANAS, E. (1979b). Social myth as hypothesis: The case of the family relations of old people. *Gerontologist, 19*, 3–9.

SHANAS, E. (1984). Old parents and middle-aged children: The four- and five-generation family. *Journal of Geriatric Psychiatry, 17*(1), 7–19.

SHARPS, M. J., & GOLLIN, E. S. (1988). Aging and free recall for subjects located in space. *Journal of Gerontology, 43*, 8–11.

SHEEHY, G. (1993). *The silent passage.* New York: Pocket Books.

SHEIKH, J. I. (1996). Anxiety and panic disorders. In E. W. Busse & D. G. Blazer (Eds.), *The American Psychiatric Press textbook of geriatric psychiatry* (2nd ed.) (pp. 279–289). Washington, DC: American Psychiatric Press.

SHEILDS, R. (1988). *Uneasy endings: Life in an American nursing home:* Ithaca, NY: Cornell University Press.

SHIP, J. A., PEARSON, J. D., CRUISE, L. J., BRANT, L. J., & METTER, E. J. (1996). Longitudinal changes in smell identification. *Journals of Gerontology 51A*(2), M86–M91.

SHNEIDMAN, E. S. (1976). Death work and stages of dying. In E. S. Schneidman (Ed.), *Death: Current perspectives* (pp. 443–451). Palo Alto, CA: Mayfield.

SHOCK, N. W., GREULICH, R. C., ANDRES, R., ARENBERG, D., COSTA, P. T., LAKATTA, E. G., & TOBIN, J. D. (1984). *Normal human aging: The Baltimore Longitudinal Study of Aging* (NIH Pub. No. 84-2450). Washington, DC: U.S. Public Health Service.

SHORR, R., & ROBIN, D. (1994). Rational use of benzodiazepines in the elderly. *Drug Therapy, 4*, 9–20.

SIEBERT, D. C., MUTRAN, E. J., & REITZES, D. C. (1997). *Meaning of friendships and attitudes toward retirement.*

Paper presented at the 50th Annual Scientific Meeting of the Gerontological Society of America.

SILVER, I. L., & HERRMANN, N. (1996). Comprehensive psychiatric evaluation. In J. Sadavoy, L. W. Lazarus, L. F. Jarvik, & G. T. Grossberg (Eds.), *Comprehensive review of geriatric psychiatry* (2nd ed.) (pp. 223–249). Washington, DC: American Psychiatric Press.

SILVERMAN, P. R., & KLASS, D. (1996). Introduction: What's the problem? In D. Klass, P. R. Silverman, & S. L. Nickman (Eds.), *Continuing bonds: New understandings of grief* (pp. 3–30). Washington, DC: Taylor & Francis.

SILVERSTEIN, M., & BENGTSON, V. L. (1991). Do close parent-child relations reduce the mortality risk of older parents? *Journal of Health and Social Behavior, 32*, 382–395.

SIMONEAU, G. G., & LEIBOWITZ, H. W. (1996). Posture, gait, and falls. In J. E. Birren & K. W. Schaie (Eds.), *Handbook of the psychology of aging* (4th ed.) (pp. 204–217). San Diego: Academic Press.

SIMONTON, D. K. (1975). Age and literary creativity: A cross-cultural and transhistorical survey. *Journal of Cross Cultural Psychology, 6*, 259–277.

SIMONTON, D. K. (1989). The swan song phenomenon: Last works effects for 172 classical composers. *Psychology and Aging, 4*, 42–47.

SIMONTON, D. K. (1991). Emergence and realization of genius: The lives and works of 120 classical composers. *Journal of Personality and Social Psychology, 62*, 829–840.

SIMONTON, D. K. (1997). Creative productivity: A predictive and explanatory model of career trajectories and landmarks. *Psychological Review, 104*(1), 66–89.

SINACORE, D. R., BROWN, M., & HOLLOSY, J. O. (1997). *Effects of low-intensity exercise followed by weight-lifting on frailty.* Paper presented at the 50th Annual Scientific Meeting of the Gerontological Society of America.

SINNOTT, J. D. (1986). Prospective/intentional and incidental everyday memory: Effects of age and passage of time. *Psychology and Aging, 1*, 110–116.

SINNOTT, J. D. (1989). General systems theory: A rationale for the study of everyday memory. In L. W. Poon, D. C. Rubin, & B. A. Wilson (Eds.), *Everyday cognition in adulthood and late life* (pp. 59–73). New York: Cambridge University Press.

SINNOTT, J. D. (1991). What do we do to help John? A case study of postformal problem solving in a family making decisions about an acutely psychotic member. In J. D. Sinnott & J. C. Cavanaugh (Eds.), *Bridging paradigms: Positive development in adulthood* and *cognitive aging* (pp. 203–219). New York: Praeger.

SLOANE, P. D., LINDEMAN, D. A., PHILLIPS, C., MORITZ, D. J., & KOCH, G. (1995). Evaluating Alzheimer's special care units: Reviewing the evidence and identifying potential sources of study bias. *Gerontologist, 35,* 103–111.

SLOOTER, A. J., TANG, M. X., VAN DUIJN, C. M., STERN, Y., OTT, A., BELL, K., BRETELER, M. M., VAN BROECKHOVEN, C., TATEMICHI, T. K., TYCKO, B., HOFMAN, A., & MAYEUX, R. (1997). Apolipoprotein E epsilon4 and the risk of dementia with stroke: A population-based investigation. *Journal of the American Medical Association, 277,* 818–821.

SMALL, B. J., & BÄCKMAN, L. (1997). Cognitive correlates of mortality: Evidence from a population-based sample of very old adults. *Psychology and Aging, 12,* 309–313.

SMITH, A. D. (1996). Memory. In J. E. Birren & K. W. Schaie (Eds.), *Handbook of the psychology of aging* (4th ed.) (pp. 236–250). San Diego: Academic Press.

SMITH, J., & BALTES, P. B. (1990). Wisdom-related knowledge: Age/cohort differences in response to life-planning problems. *Developmental Psychology, 26,* 494–505.

SMITH, J., & BALTES, P. B. (1997). Profiles of psychological functioning in the old and oldest old. *Psychology and Aging, 12,* 458–472.

SMITH, J., STAUDINGER, U. M., & BALTES, P. B. (1994). Occupational settings facilitating wisdom-related knowledge: The sample case of clinical psychologists. *Journal of Consulting and Clinical Psychology, 62,* 989–999.

SMITH, J. R. (1990). Minireview: DNA synthesis inhibitors in cellular senescence. *Journals of Gerontology, 45 A*(2), B32–B35.

SMITH, P. C., RANGE, L. M., & ULMER, A. (1991–1992). Belief in afterlife as a buffer in suicidal and other bereavement. *Omega: Journal of Death and Dying, 24,* 217–225.

SMITH, T. W. (1994). Attitudes toward sexual permissiveness: Trends, correlates, and behavioral connections. In A. S. Rossi (Ed.), *Sexuality across the life course* (pp. 63–97). Chicago: University of Chicago Press.

SNOWDON, D. A., GREINER, L. H., MORTIMER, J. A., RILEY, K. P., GREINER, P. A., & MARKESBERY, W. R. (1997). Brain infarction and the clinical expression of Alzheimer's disease: The Nun Study. *Journal of the American Medical Association, 277,* 813–817.

SNOWDON, D. A., GROSS, M. D., & BUTLER, S. M. (1996). Antioxidants and reduced functional capacity in the elderly: Findings from the Nun Study. *Journal of Gerontology: Medical Sciences, 51A*(1), M10–M16.

SNYDER, D. L., POLLARD, M., WOSTMANN, B. S., & LUCKERT, P. (1990). Life span, morphology, and pathology of diet-restricted germ-free and conventional lobundwistar rats. *Journals of Gerontology, 45A*(2), B52–B58.

SOCIAL SECURITY ADMINISTRATION. (1997). *Fast facts and figures about Social Security.* Washington, DC: U.S. Government Printing Office.

SOLDO, B. J. (1996) Cross pressures on middle-aged adults: A broader view. *Journals of Gerontology, 51B*(6), S271–S273.

SOLDO, B. J., WOLF, D. A., & AGREE, E. M. (1990). Family, households, and care arrangements of frail older women: A structural analysis. *Journals of Gerontology, 45B*(6), S238–S249.

SOLNICK, R. L. (1978). Sexual responsiveness, age, and change: Facts and potential. In R. L. Solnick (Ed.), *Sexuality and aging.* Los Angeles: University of California Press.

SOUZA, P. E., & HOYER, W. J. (1996). Age-related hearing loss: Implications for counseling. *Journal of Counseling and Development, 74,* 652–653.

SPEAS, K., & OBENSHAIN, B. (1995). *Images of aging in America.* Washington, DC: American Association of Retired Persons.

SPIRO, A., III, RIGGS, K., ELIAS, M., & VOKONAS, P. (1997). Does coronary heart disease affect cognitive abilities? Paper presented at the 50th Annual Scientific Meeting of the Gerontological Society of America.

SPITZE, G., & LOGAN, J. (1990). More evidence on women (and men) in the middle. *Research on Aging, 12,* 182–198.

SPITZE, G., LOGAN, J. R., JOSEPH, G., & LEE, E. (1994). Middle generation roles and the well-being of men and women. *Journals of Gerontology, 49*(3), S107–S116.

SQUIRE, L. R. (1992). Memory and the hippocampus: A synthesis from findings with rats, monkeys, and humans. *Psychological Review, 99,* 195–231.

STAMATIADIS, N. (1996). Gender effect on the accident patterns of elderly drivers. *Journal of Applied Gerontology, 15,* 8–22.

STANFORD, E. P., & SCHMIDT, M. G. (1995–1996). The changing face of nursing home residents: Meeting their diverse needs. *Generations, 19*(4), 20–23.

STAUDINGER, U. M. (1996). *Interactive minds: A facilitative setting for wisdom-related performance.* Unpublished manuscript.

STAUDINGER, U. M., & BALTES, P. B. (1996). Interactive minds. A facilitative setting for wisdom-related performance. *Journal of Personality and Social Psychology, 71,* 746–762.

STAUDINGER, U. M., LOPEZ, D., & BALTES, P. B. (1997). The psychometric location of wisdom-related performance: Intelligence, personality, and more? *Personality and Social Psychology Bulletin, 23,* 1200–1234.

STAUDINGER, U. M., SMITH, J., & BALTES, P. B. (1992). Wisdom-related knowledge in a life review task: Age differences and the role of professional specialization. *Psychology and Aging, 7,* 271–281.

STEPHEN, D. L. (1991–1992). A discussion of Avery Weisman's notion of appropriate death. *Omega: Journal of Death and Dying, 24,* 301–308.

STERNBERG, R. J. (1988). Triangulating love. In R. J. Sternberg & M. L. Barnes (Eds.), *The psychology of love* (pp. 119–138). New Haven, CT: Yale University Press.

STERNBERG, R. J., & BARNES, M. L. (EDS.). (1988). *The psychology of love.* New Haven, CT: Yale University Press.

STERNBERG, R. J., & WAGNER, R. K. (1986). *Practical intelligence.* New York: Cambridge University Press.

STERNS, H. L., BARRETT, G. V., CZAJA, S. J., & BARR, J. K. (1994). Issues in work and aging. *Journal of Applied Gerontology, 13,* 7–19.

STERNS, H. L., & MIKLOS, S. M. (1995). The aging worker in a changing environment: Organizational and individual issues. *Journal of Vocational Behavior, 47,* 248–268.

STINE, E. A. L., WINGFIELD, H., & MYERS, S. D. (1990). Age differences in processing information from television news: The effects of bisensory augmentation. *Journals of Gerontology, 45,* P1–P8.

STONE, A. A., BOVBJERG, D. H., NEALE, J. M., NAPOLI, A., VALDIMARSDOTTIR, H., COX, D., HAYDEN, F. G., & GWALTNEY, J. M. (1992). Development of common cold symptoms following experimental rhinovirus infection is related to prior stressful life events. *Behavioral Medicine, 18*(3), 115–120.

STRAWBRIDGE, W. J., CAMACHO, T. C., COHEN, R. D., & KAPLAN, G. A. (1993). Gender differences in factors associated with change in physical functioning in old age: A six-year longitudinal study. *Gerontologist, 33,* 603–609.

STRAWBRIDGE, W. J., & WALLHAGEN, M. I. (1991). Impact of family conflict on adult child caregivers. *Gerontologist, 31,* 770–777.

STROEBE, M. (1993). Coping with bereavement: A review of the grief work hypothesis. *Omega: Journal of Death and Dying, 26,* 19–42.

STUCK, A. E., GERBER, E. E., MINDER, C. E., & BECK, J. C. (1997). *A randomized trial of in-home comprehensive assessments in older persons: Final results.* Paper pre-

sented at the 50th Annual Scientific Meeting of the Gerontological Society of America.

STUMP, T. E., JOHNSON, R. J., & WOLINSKY, F. D. (1995). Changes in physician utilization over time among older adults. *Journals of Gerontology 50B*(1), S45–S58.

STYRON, W. (1990). *Darkness visible.* New York: Random House.

SUE, S. (1992). Ethnicity and mental health: Research and policy issues. *Journal of Social Issues, 48,* 187–205.

SUPER, D. E. (1980). A life-span, life-space approach to career development. *Journal of Vocational Behavior, 16,* 282–298.

TALBOTT, M. M. (1990). The negative side of the relationship between older widows and their adult children: The mothers' perspective. *Gerontologist, 30,* 595–603.

TAYLOR, R. J. (1993). Religion and religious observances. In J. S. Jackson, L. M. Chatters, & R. J. Taylor (Eds.), *Aging in black America* (pp. 101–123). Newbury Park, CA: Sage.

TAYLOR, R. J., & CHATTERS, L. M. (1991). Extended family networks of older black adults. *Journals of Gerontology, 46*(4), S210–S217.

TEAFORD, M. (1997). *Assisted living for moderate income older adults.* Paper presented at the 50th Annual Scientific Meeting of the Gerontological Society of America.

TECHNOLOGY AND AGING: DEVELOPING AND MARKETING NEW PRODUCTS FOR OLDER PERSONS. (1995, Spring). *Generations, 19.*

TERI, L. (1997). The relation between research and depression and a treatment program: One model. In R. L. Rubinstein & M. P. Lawton (Eds.), *Depression in long-term and residential care: Advances in research and treatment* (pp. 129–153). New York: Springer.

TERI, L., LOGSDON, R. G., UOMOTO, J., & MCCURRY, S. M. (1997). Behavioral treatment of depression in dementia patients: A controlled clinical trial. *Journals of Gerontology, 52B*(4), P159–P166.

TERI, L., MCCURRY, S. M., EDLAND, S. D., KUKULL, W. A., & LARSON, E. B. (1995). Cognitive decline in Alzheimer's disease: A longitudinal investigation of risk factors for accelerated decline. *Journals of Gerontology, 50A*(1), M49–M55.

THOMAS, C., & KELMAN, H. R. (1990). Gender and the use of health services among elderly persons. In M. G. Ory & H. R. Warner (Eds.), *Gender, health, and longevity: Multidisciplinary perspectives* (pp. 137–156). New York: Springer.

THOMAS, J. L. (1990a). The grandparent role: A double bind. *International Journal of Aging and Human Development, 31,* 169–177.

THOMAS, J. L. (1990b). Grandparenthood and mental health: Implications for the practitioner. *Journal of Applied Gerontology, 9,* 464–479.

THOMAS, L. E. (ED.). (1989). *Research on adulthood and aging: The human science approach.* Albany: State University of New York Press.

THOMAS, R. M. (1996). *Comparing theories of child development* (4th ed.). Pacific Grove, CA: Brooks/Cole.

THOMPSON, J. M. (1995). *A case study analysis of the social behavioral aspects of menopause.* Unpublished master's thesis, Middle Tennessee State University, Murfreesboro.

THOMPSON, L. W., & GALLAGHER-THOMPSON, D. (1997). Psychotherapeutic interventions with older adults in outpatient and extended care settings. In R. L. Rubinstein & M. P. Lawton (Eds.), *Depression in long-term and residential care: Advances in research and treatment* (pp. 169–184). New York: Springer.

THORESEN, C. E., & PATTILLO, J. R. (1988). Exploring the Type A behavior pattern in children and adolescents. In B. K. Houston & C. R. Snyder (Eds.), *Type A behavior pattern: Research, theory, and intervention* (pp. 98–145). New York: Wiley.

TOMER, A., ELIASON, G., & SMITH, J. (1997). *The structure of death anxiety in young and old adults: A structural equation models analysis.* Paper presented at the 50th Annual Scientific Meeting of the Gerontological Society of America.

TOWER, R. B., KASL, S. V., & MORITZ, D. J. (1997). The influence of spouse cognitive impairment on respondents' depressive symptoms: The moderating role of marital closeness. *Journals of Gerontology 52B*(5), S270–S278.

TROLL, L. E. (1983). Grandparents: The family watchdogs. In T. Brubaker (Ed.), *Family relationships in later life* (pp. 63–74). Beverly Hills, CA: Sage.

TROLL, L. E., & SKAFF, M. M. (1997). Perceived continuity of self in very old age. *Psychology and Aging, 12,* 162–169.

TSUANG, M. T., & FARAONE, S. V. (1990). *The genetics of mood disorders.* Baltimore: Johns Hopkins University Press.

TULVING, E. (1985). How many memory systems are there? *American Psychologist, 40,* 385–398.

TUNE, L. (1993). Neuroimaging: Advances and new directions. *Generations, 17*(1), 79–80.

UHLENBERG, P., & MINER, S. (1996). Life course and aging: A cohort perspective. In R. H. Binstock & L. K. George (Eds.), *Handbook of aging and the social sciences* (4th ed.) (pp. 208–228). New York: Academic Press.

UMBERSON, D., WORTMAN, C. B., & KESSLER, R. C. (1992). Widowhood and depression: Explaining long-term gender differences in vulnerability. *Journal of Health and Social Behavior, 33,* 10–24.

U.S. BUREAU OF THE CENSUS. (1993). *Statistical abstract of the United States 1993.* Washington, DC: U.S. Government Printing Office.

U.S. BUREAU OF THE CENSUS. (1994). *Statistical abstract of the United States 1994.* Washington, DC: U.S. Government Printing Office.

U.S. BUREAU OF THE CENSUS. (1995). *Statistical abstract of the United States 1995.* Washington, DC: U.S. Government Printing Office.

U.S. BUREAU OF THE CENSUS. (1996). *Statistical abstract of the United States 1996.* Washington, DC: U.S. Government Printing Office.

U.S. DEPARTMENT OF HEALTH AND HUMAN SERVICES. (1989). *Reducing the health consequences of smoking: Twenty-five years of progress: A report of the surgeon general: Executive summary.* Rockville, MD: Author.

U.S. DEPARTMENT OF HEALTH AND HUMAN SERVICES. (1990a). *Health status of the disadvantaged: Chartbook 1990.* Washington, DC: U.S. Government Printing Office.

U.S. DEPARTMENT OF HEALTH AND HUMAN SERVICES. (1990b). *Seventh special report to the U.S. Congress on alcohol and health.* Rockville, MD: National Institute on Alcohol Abuse and Alcoholism.

U.S. DEPARTMENT OF HEALTH AND HUMAN SERVICES. (1991). *Health status of minorities and low income groups.* Washington, DC: U.S. Government Printing Office.

U.S. DEPARTMENT OF HEALTH AND HUMAN SERVICES. (1994a). *Mental health, United States, 1994.* Rockville, MD: Author.

U.S. DEPARTMENT OF HEALTH AND HUMAN SERVICES. (1994b). *National health care survey, 1994.* Atlanta: Centers for Disease Control and Prevention.

U.S. PUBLIC HEALTH SERVICE. (1995). Advance report of final mortality statistics, 1995. *Monthly Vital Statistics Report, 43*(6).

U.S. SENATE SPECIAL COMMITTEE ON AGING. (1991a). *Aging America: Trends and projections.* Washington, DC: Author.

U.S. SENATE SPECIAL COMMITTEE ON AGING. (1991b). *Lifelong learning for an aging society* (DHHS Publication No. 102-J). Washington, DC: U.S. Government Printing Office.

U.S. SENATE SPECIAL COMMITTEE ON AGING. (1992). *Lifelong learning for an aging society (Annotated)* (DHHS Publication No. 102-R). Washington, DC: U.S. Government Printing Office.

VALENTE, S. M. (1993–1994). Suicide and elderly people: Assessment and intervention. *Omega: Journal of Death and Dying, 28,* 317–331.

VAN DE WATER, D. A., & MCADAMS, D. P. (1989). Generativity and Erikson's "belief in the species." *Journal of Research in Personality, 23,* 435–449.

VANDYKE, S., & HARPER, G. J. (1997). *Daily activity patterns of residents in nursing home settings.* Paper presented at the 50th Annual Scientific Meeting of the Gerontological Society of America.

VERBRUGGE, L. M. (1989). Gender, aging, and health. In K. S. Markides (Ed.), *Aging and health: Perspectives on gender, race, ethnicity, and class* (pp. 23–78). Newbury Park, CA: Sage.

VERBRUGGE, L. M. (1990). The twain meet: Empirical explanations of sex differences in health and mortality. In M. G. Ory & H. R. Warner (Eds.), *Gender, health, and longevity: Multidisciplinary perspectives* (pp. 159–200). New York: Springer.

VERWOERDT, A., PFEIFFER, E., & WANG, H. S. (1969, February). Sexual behavior in sensescence: 2. Patterns of sexual activity and interest. *Geriatrics,* 137–154.

VINEY, L. L., WALKER, B. M., ROBERTSON, T., LILLEY, B., & EWAN, C. (1994). Dying in palliative care units and in hospital: A comparison of the quality of life of terminal cancer patients. *Journal of Consulting and Clinical Psychology, 62,* 157–164.

VINEY, L. L., & WESTBROOK, M. (1986–1987). Is there a pattern of psychological reactions to chronic illness which is associated with death? *Omega: Journal of Death and Dying, 17*(2), 169–181.

VLADECK, B. C., & FEUERBERG, M. (1995–1996). Unloving care revisited. *Generations, 19*(4), 9–13.

VOGT, T. M. (1992). Aging, stress, and illness: Psychobiological linkages. In M. G. Ory, R. P. Abeles, & P. D. Lipman (Eds.), *Aging, health, and behavior* (pp. 207–238). Newbury Park, CA: Sage.

WAGNER, R., & STERNBERG, R. (1986). Trait knowledge and intelligence in the everyday world. In R. J. Sternberg & R. Wagner, *Practical intelligence* (pp. 51–83). New York: Cambridge University Press.

WAHL, H. W., OSWALD, F., HEYL, V., ZIMPRICH, D., & HEINEMANN, H. (1997). *Age-related visual impairment: Aspects of adaptation in a longitudinal view.* Paper presented at the 50th Annual Scientific Meeting of the Gerontological Society of America.

WALFORD, R. (1969). *The immunologic theory of aging.* Baltimore: Williams & Wilkins.

WALFORD, R. (1983). *Maximum lifespan.* New York: Avon.

WALKER, A. J., MARTIN, S. S., & JONES, L. L. (1992). The benefits and costs of caregiving and care receiving for daughters and mothers. *Journals of Gerontology, 47*(3), S130–S139.

WALKER, A. J., & THOMPSON, L. (1983). Intimacy and intergenerational aid and contact among mothers and daughters, *Journal of Marriage and the Family, 45,* 841–848.

WALKER, N., PHILBIN, D. A., & FISK, A. D. (1997). Age-related differences in movement control: Adjusting submovement structure to optimize performance. *Journals of Gerontology, 52B*(1), P40–P52.

WALL, P. T., SULLIVAN, D. H., HITE, R., & FROST, M. (1997). *Effects of muscle strength training in severely debilitated elderly.* Paper presented at the 50th Annual Scientific Meeting of the Gerontological Society of America.

WALLACE, J., & RATCHFORD, A. (1997). *Prospective memory strategies in older adults.* Paper presented at the 50th Annual Scientific Meeting of the Gerontological Society of America.

WALLHAGEN, M. I., STRAWBRIDGE, W., & SHEMA, S. (1997). *Perceived control: Mental health correlates in a population-based aging cohort.* Paper presented at the 50th Annual Scientific Meeting of the Gerontological Society of America.

WALZ, T. H., & BLUM, N. S. (1987). *Sexual health in later life.* Lexington, MA: Lexington Books.

WARD, R. A., LOGAN, J., & SPITZE, G. (1992). Consequences of parent–adult child coresidence: A review and research agenda. *Journal of Family Issues, 13,* 553–572.

WARNER, K. E. (1989). Effects of the antismoking campaign: An update. *American Journal of Public Health, 79*(2), 144.

WATKINS, P. L., WARD, C. H., SOUTHARD, D. R., & FISHER, E. B. (1992). The Type A belief system: Relationships to hostility, social support, and life stress. *Behavioral Medicine, 18*(1), 27–32.

WEBSTER, J. D. (1995). Adult age differences in reminiscence functions. In B. K. Haight & J. D. Webster (Eds.), *The art and science of reminiscing: Theory, research, methods, and applications* (pp. 89–102). Washington, DC: Taylor & Francis.

WEBSTER, P. S., & HERZOG, A. R. (1995). Effects of parental divorce and memories of family problems on relationships between adult children and their parents. *Journals of Gerontology 50B*(1), S24–S34.

WECHSLER, D. (1981). *WAIS-R manual* (rev. ed.). New York: Harcourt Brace Jovanovich.

WEINDRUCH, R., & MASORO, E. J. (1991). Concerns about rodent models for aging research. *Journals of Gerontology, 46*(3), B87–B88.

WEISMAN, A. D. (1986). Denial and middle knowledge. In E. Schneidman (Ed.), *Death: Current perspectives* (pp. 452–469). Palo Alto, CA: Mayfield.

WEISMAN, A. D., & WORDEN, J. W. (1975). Psychological analysis of cancer deaths. *Omega: Journal of Death and Dying, 6,* 61–75.

WEISSMAN, M. M., MYERS, J. K., TISCHLER, G. L., HOLZER, C. E., III, LEAF, P. J., ORVASCHEL, H., & BRODY, J. A. (1985). Psychiatric disorders (DSM III) and cognitive impairment among the elderly in a U.S. urban community. *Acta Psychiatrica Scandinavica, 71,* 366–379.

WEISS, R. (1990). *Staying the course.* New York: Basic Books.

WEITZMAN, L. M., & FITZGERALD, L. F. (1993). Employed mothers: Diverse lifestyles and labor force profiles. In J. Frankel (Ed.), *The employed mother and the family context* (pp. 7–30). New York: Springer.

WELFORD, A. T. (1977). Motor performance. In J. E. Birren & K. W. Schaie (Eds.), *Handbook of the psychology of aging* (pp. 450–496). New York: Van Nostrand Reinhold.

WELLS, D. L., & DAWSON, P. (1997). *Description of retained human abilities in persons with dementia.* Paper presented at the 50th Annual Scientific Meeting of the Gerontological Society of America.

WEST, R. L. (1989). Planning practical memory training for the aged. In L. W. Poon, D. C. Rubin, & B. A. Wilson (Eds.), *Everyday cognition in adulthood and late life* (pp. 59–73). New York: Cambridge University Press.

WEST, R. L., & CROOK, T. H. (1990). Age differences in everyday memory: Laboratory analogues of telephone number recall. *Psychology and Aging, 5,* 520–529.

WEST, R. L., CROOK, T. H., & BARRON, K. L. (1992). Everyday memory performance across the life span: Effects of age and noncognitive individual differences. *Psychology and Aging, 7,* 72–82.

WEST, S. G., & GRAZIANO, W. G. (1989). Long-term stability and change in personality: An introduction. *Journal of Personality, 57,* 175–193.

WESTMAN, A. S., & BRACKNEY, B. E. (1990). Relationships between indices of neuroticism, attitudes toward and concepts of death, and religiosity. *Psychological Reports, 66*(3, Pt. 1), 1039–1043.

WETLE, T. (1994). Individual preferences and advance directives. *Hastings Center Report, 24*(6), S5–S8.

WHITBECK, L. B., HOYT, D. R., & HUCK, S. M. (1994). Early family relationships, and support provided to parents by their adult children. *Journals of Gerontology, 49B*(2), S85–S94.

WHITBOURNE, S. K. (1996). *The aging individual: Physical and psychological processes.* New York: Springer.

WHITE, L., & EDWARDS, J. N. (1990). Emptying the nest and parental well-being: An analysis of national panel data. *American Sociological Review, 55,* 235–242.

WHITING, W. L., & SMITH, A. D. (1997). Differential age-related processing limitations in recall and recognition tasks. *Psychology and Aging, 12,* 216–224.

WIENER, J. M. (1995). Current approaches to integrating acute and long-term care financing and services. Washington, DC: AARP Public Policy Institute.

WILCOX, V. L., KASL, S., & IDLER, E. L. (1996). Self-rated health and physical disability in elderly survivors of a major medical event. *Journals of Gerontology, 51B*(2), S96–S104.

WILEY, D., & BORTZ, W. M., II. (1996). Sexuality and aging: Usual and successful. *Journals of Gerontology, 51A,* M140–M146.

WILKS, C., & MELVILLE, C. (1990). Grandparents in custody and access disputes. *Journal of Divorce, 13*(3), 1–14.

WILLIAMS, D. R., TAKEUCHI, D. T., & ADAIR, R. K. (1992). Marital status and psychiatric disorders among blacks and whites. *Journal of Health and Social Behavior, 33,* 140–157.

WILLIAMS, R., JR., & BAREFOOT, J. C. (1988). Coronary-prone behavior: The emerging role of the hostility complex. In B. K. Houston & C. R. Snyder (Eds.), *Type A behavior pattern: Research, theory, and intervention* (pp. 189–211). New York: Wiley.

WILLIAMSON, R. C., REINHART, A. D., & BLANK, T. O. (1992). *Early retirement: Promises and pitfalls.* New York: Plenum.

WILLIS, S. L. (1989). Improvement with cognitive training: Which old dogs learn what tricks? In L. W. Poon, D. C. Rubin, & B. A. Wilson (Eds.), *Everyday cognition in adulthood and late life* (pp. 59–73). New York: Cambridge University Press.

WILLIS, S. L., & NESSELROADE, C. S. (1990). Long-term effects of fluid ability training in old-old age. *Developmental Psychology, 26,* 905–910.

WILLIS, S. L., & SCHAIE, K. W. (1986). Practical intelligence in later adulthood. In R. J. Sternberg & R. Wagner (Eds.), *Practical intelligence* (pp. 236–270). New York: Cambridge University Press.

WILLIS, S. L. (1996). Everyday problem solving. In J. E. Birren & K. W. Schaie (Eds.). *Handbook of the psychology of aging* (4th ed.) (pp. 287–308). San Diego: Academic Press.

WILSON, K. B., & DE SHANE, M. R. (1982). Legal rights of grandparents: A preliminary discussion. *Gerontologist, 22,* 67–71.

WINGARD, D. L., & COHN, B. A. (1990). Variations in disease-specific sex morbidity and mortality ratios in the United States. In M. G. Ory & H. R. Warner (Eds.), *Gender, health, and longevity: Multidisciplinary perspectives* (pp. 25–37). New York: Springer.

WINGFIELD, A., POON, L. W., LOMBARDI, L., & LOWE, D. (1985). Speed of processing in normal aging: Effects of speech rate, linguistic structure, and processing time. *Journal of Gerontology, 40,* 579–585.

WOLINSKY, F. D., CALLAHAN, C. M., FITZGERALD, J. F., & JOHNSON, R. J. (1992). The risk of nursing home placement and subsequent death among older adults. *Journals of Gerontology, 47*(4), S173–S182.

WOO, J., HO, S. C., CHAN, S. G., YUEN, Y. K., & SHAM, A. (1996). Risk factors for falls in the Chinese elderly. *Journals of Gerontology, 51A*(5), M195–M198.

WOOD, V., & ROBERTSON, J. F. (1978). Friendship and kinship interaction: Differential effect on the morale of the elderly. *Journal of Marriage and the Family, 40,* 367–375.

WOODRUFF, R. C., & NIKITIN, A. G. (1997). *Evidence in support of the somatic mutation theory of aging: Transposable DNA element movement in somatic cells reduces life span in drosophila.* Paper presented at the 50th Annual Scientific Meeting of the Gerontological Society of America.

WOODRUFF-PAK, D. S., & HANSON, C. (1995). Plasticity and compensation in brain memory systems in aging. In R. A. Dixon & L. Backman (Eds.), *Compensating for psychological deficits and declines: Managing losses and promoting gains* (pp. 191–218). Mahwah, NJ: Erlbaum.

WOOLLEY, S. M., CZAJA, S. J., & DRURY, C. G. (1997). An assessment of falls in elderly men and women. *Journals of Gerontology 52A*(2), M80–M87.

WORDEN, J. W. (1982). *Grief counseling and grief therapy: A handbook for the mental health practitioner* (2nd ed.). New York: Springer.

WOROBEY, J. L., & ANGEL, R. J. (1990). Functional capacity and living arrangements of unmarried elderly persons. *Journals of Gerontology, 45*(3), S95–S101.

WU, K. B. (1995). *Income and poverty in 1993: How did older Americans do?* Washington, DC: AARP Public Policy Institute.

YARASHESKI, K. E., GISCHLER, J., PAK-LADUCA, J. Y., HASTEN, D. L., SINACORE, D. R., & BINDER, E. (1997). *Weight-lifting exercise training increases muscle protein synthesis rate in physically frail 84-year-old women.* Paper presented at the 50th Annual Scientific Meeting of the Gerontological Society of America.

YEE, D., & MELICHAR, J. (1997). *Driver safety and health promotion for a culturally diverse, elderly population in the Bay Area.* Paper presented at the 50th Annual Scientific Meeting of the Gerontological Society of America.

YOUNG, R. C., & MEYERS, B. S. (1996). Psychopharmacology. In J. Sadavoy, L. W. Lazarus, L. F. Jarvik, & G. T. Grossberg (Eds.), *Comprehensive review of geriatric psychiatry* (2nd ed.) (pp. 755–817). Washington, DC: American Psychiatric Press.

ZARIT, S. H. (1996). *Adult day care and the relief of caregiver strain.* Paper presented at the 49th Annual Scientific Meeting of the Gerontological Society of America.

ZARIT, S. H., & EDWARDS, A. B. (1996). Family caregiving: Research and clinical intervention. In R. T. Woods (Ed.), *Handbook of the clinical psychology of aging* (pp. 331–368). Chichester, England: Wiley.

ZARIT, S. H., & EGGEBEEN, D. J. (1995). Parent-child relationships in adulthood and old age. In M. H. Bornstein (Ed.), *Handbook of parenting: Vol. 1. Children and parenting* (pp. 119–140). Mahwah, NJ: Erlbaum.

ZARIT, S. H., & KNIGHT, B. G. (EDS.). (1996). *A guide to psychotherapy and aging: Effective clinical interventions in a life-stage context.* Washington, DC: American Psychological Association.

ZARIT, S. H, ORR, N., & ZARIT, J. (1985). *The hidden victims of Alzheimer's disease: Families under stress.* New York: New York University Press.

ZEISS, A. M., & STEFFEN, A. (1996). Behavioral and cognitive-behavioral treatments: An overview of social learning. In S. H. Zarit & B. G. Knight (Eds.), *A guide to psychotherapy and aging: Effective clinical interventions in a life-stage context* (pp. 423–450). Washington, DC: American Psychological Association.

ZELINSKI, E. M., & BURNIGHT, K. P. (1997). Sixteen-year longitudinal and time lag changes in memory and cognition in older adults. *Psychology and Aging, 12,* 503–513.

ZELINSKI, E. M., & MIURA, S. A. (1988). Effects of thematic information on script memory in young and old adults. *Psychology and Aging, 3,* 292–299.

ZISOOK, S., & SHUCHTER, S. R. (1991). Early psychological reaction to the stress of widowhood. *Psychiatry, 54,* 320–333.

ZISOOK, S., SHUCHTER, S. R., & MULVIHILL, M. (1990). Alcohol, cigarette, and medication use during the first year of widowhood. *Psychiatric Annals, 20,* 318–326.

ZUCKERMAN, C. (1997). *The hospital palliative care initiative: Developing palliative care services in a consortium* of New York City hospitals. Symposium held at the 50th Annual Scientific Meeting of the Gerontological Society of America.

Name Index

Corti, C., 136, 137, 138
Costa, P. T., 89, 92, 236, 237, 238, 239, 241, 242–243, 369, 374
Council on Families in America, 12, 293, 351
Cowan, C. P., 295, 351
Cowan, P. A., 295, 351
Coward, R. T., 314, 362
Coyer, J. L., 4
Coyne, A. C., 150, 282
Coyne, J. C., 89
Craske, M. G., 271
Crews, D. E., 152
Crimmins, E. M., 134, 135, 136, 309, 310
Crispi, E. L., 317
Crook, T. H., 197, 202, 207
Cross, S., 248, 249
Crown, W. H., 150
Cruise, L. J., 116
Crystal, S., 17, 140, 335, 341, 349
Csikszentmihalyi, M., 186, 187
Cugliari, A. M., 160, 388
Cumming, E., 233
Cummings, J. L., 18
Cunningham, D. A., 55
Curb, J. D., 82

Daly, M. P., 316
Damron-Rodriguez, J., 144
D'Angelo, C., 127
Danis, M., 388
Dartigues, J.-F., 88
Davies, L., 359
Davis, G., 385
Davis, H., 90
Dawson, P., 212
Dean, A., 70, 359
Dean, J., 254
Debruin, A. F., 134
Dedrick, E. J., 338
Defillippi, R. J., 330
De Frias, C. M., 175
Defries, J. C., 37
Denney, N. A., 178, 180, 183, 191, 332
Dennis, W., 186
Desai, K., 147
De Shane, M. R., 324
de St. Aubin, E., 244
DeViney, S., 337
DeVos, S., 310
deWitte, L. P., 134
Dhooper, S. S., 205
Diamond, M. C., 175, 191
Dickinson, G. E., 386

Diederiks, J. P., 134
Diehr, P., 137
Diener, E., 254
Dimond, M. F., 354
Dion, K. L., 236
Dixon, R. A., 47, 197, 202, 209, 229
Dobbins, G. H., 338
Donner, A. P., 55
Dorosz, M., 202
Dougherty, K., 371
Douvan, E., 297
Dresser, R., 388, 393
Drevenstedt, J., 206
Driscoll, L., 142
Driver, D., 326
Drury, C. G., 122
Dubler, N., 388, 390
Dubler, N. N., 384
Duncan, G. J., 356
Dunkin, J., 18
Dunn, J. E., 107, 122
Dunn, T. A., 310
Durlak, J. A., 386
Dwyer, J. W., 314, 357, 362
Dzaja, S. J., 122
Dzorbenadze, D. A., 70

Earl, W. L., 371
Earles, J. L., 79, 173
Easterlin, R. A., 13, 310, 347
Eastham, J., 358
Eaton, E. M., 216
Eaves, L. J., 269, 276
Edland, S. D., 212
Edwards, A. B., 161, 221, 223
Edwards, J. N., 295
Edwards, W. D., 79
Effros, R. B., 70
Eggebeen, D. J., 311, 315
Einstein, G. O., 203
Eisdorfer, C., 109
Ekerdt, D. J., 337, 343
Elder, G. H., 239–240
Elders, M. J., 82
Elias, J. W., 64
Elias, M., 206
Elias, M. F., 64
Elias, P. K., 64
Eliason, G., 371
Eloy, S. V., 295
Endresen, I. M., 89
Engle, B. T., 156
Engle, V. F., 158
Enos, W., 64
Envall, K., 152

Erber, J. T., 196
Erikson, E. H., 41–44
Etten, S. V., 105
Eustis, N. N., 151
Evans, D. A., 17
Evans, D. R., 343
Evans, L., 337
Ewan, C., 385

Falik, A., 174
Falk, R. F., 316
Faraone, S. V., 276
Farran, C. J., 219
Feifel, H., 371
Feinson, M. C., 356
Feldman, S. S., 235
Femia, E. E., 136, 143
Ferber, M. A., 12
Fernandez, M. E., 343
Ferrucci, L., 136, 137, 138
Field, D., 173, 316, 355
Fields, V., 315
Filipp, S. H., 255
Fillenbaum, G. G., 333
Finch, C. E., 65, 70
Fingerhood, M., 266
Fingerman, K. L., 312, 313
Finkel, S. I., 281, 282
Finucane, T., 266
Fischer, D. H., 8, 9
Fischer, L., 219
Fischer, L. R., 151
Fish, C. E., 376–377
Fisher, E. B., 90
Fiske, D., 234
Fitting, M., 358
Fitzgerald, J. F., 157
Fitzgerald, L. F., 331
Fitzsimmons, C., 207
Fleeson, W., 229
Florian, V., 373
Foley, D. J., 136
Folstein, M. F., 212
Forman, S. H., 71
Fortinsky, R. H., 146
Foster, C., 276
Fozard, J. L., 104, 109
Frankl, V. E., 258
Franks, M. M., 316
Frazer, D. W., 290
Frederick, W., 371
Fredman, L., 316
Freedman, V. A., 157
Fretz, B. R., 340
Freud, S., 34–35, 41, 189, 276, 280–281, 336

Mitchell, V., 252, 253, 303
Mitcheltree, C., 70
Mitty, E., 390
Miura, S. A., 202
Moane, G., 252
Moen, P., 14, 315, 331, 336, 349, 355
Mogielnicki, R. P., 391
Monane, M., 290
Montgomery, A., 316
Montgomery, R., 151
Montgomery, R. J. V., 357
Moon, 64
Moras, K., 271
Morgan, D., 88
Morgan, L. A., 356
Moritz, D. J., 159
Morrell, R. W., 203
Morris, D. C., 346
Morris, R., 152
Morrison, R. S., 391, 392
Morrow, D., 207
Mortimer, J., 214
Mote, P. L., 70
Mui, A. C., 316
Mullan, J. T., 86, 212, 316, 318
Mullner, R. M., 82
Multiple Risk Factor Intervention Trial Research Group, 93
Mulvihill, M., 355
Munch, Edvard, 273
Mungas, D., 217
Murakami, S., 71
Murphy, F. C., 82
Musante, L., 90
Musick, M., 20
Mutchler, J. E., 331, 346
Mutran, E. J., 343
Myerhoff, B., 182
Myers, J. K., 263, 265, 266
Myers, S. D., 202

Nagy, S., 127–128
Nakagawa, T, 90
Nakamura, H, 90
Napoli, J. G., 370
Nash, S. C., 235
Nathanson, C. A., 14, 15
National Center for Health Statistics, 94, 139, 141, 278, 383
National Health Interview Survey, 132, 139
National Institute on Aging, 54, 74, 75, 92, 137, 372
Neale, M. C., 269, 276

Neely, A. S., 209
Nesselroade, C. S., 191
Nesselroade, J. R., 53, 72, 239
Nestadt, G. R., 212
Nestel, G., 148
Neumann, E. M., 32
Newman, F., 140
Newman, S. J., 152
Nickel, J. T., 138
Niederehe, G., 206–207
Nikitin, A. G., 67
Nixon, S. J., 267
Noelker, L. S., 155
Noell, E., 127
Normoyle, J. B., 154
Nuland, S., 65
Nurius, P., 248
Nyquist, L., 169, 173

Obenshain, B., 5
O'Bryant, S. L., 354, 355, 357, 359, 360
O'Connor-Rudin, M., 300
O'Farrell, B., 12
Oleinick, L., 356
Olsen, E., 157
Omenn, G. S., 137
Ondrich, J. I., 148
O'Rand, A. M., 7, 13, 17, 331, 349
Orgel, L., 67
Orr, N., 212, 213, 221
Ortmeyer, H. K., 70
Ory, M. G., 15, 81
Oster, G., 84
Ostfeld, A., 136
Oswald, A., 332
Oswald, F., 108
Otto, M. E., 383
Oullet, L. L., 124
Ouslander, J. G., 388, 389
Ozer, D. J., 238

Paier, M. S., 120
Pak-Laduca, J. Y., 120
Palmore, E. B., 4, 10, 299, 333, 338
Pandina, G., 282
Parisi, J. D., 4
Park, D. C., 203
Parkes, C. M., 352, 354
Parmelee, P. A., 157, 271, 275
Parsons, O. A., 267
Passman, V., 241, 251, 255
Pasternak, M., 115

Patrick, C. H., 141
Patrick, D. L., 137
Patrick-Miller, L., 92
Pattillo, J. R., 90
Pavalko, E. K., 315
Peal, R. L., 370
Pearlin, L. I., 86, 90, 212, 316, 318
Pearson, A. A., 386
Pearson, C. G., 212
Pearson, J. D., 116
Pedersen, N. L., 38, 72, 239
Pelham, A., 88
Pelham, B. W., 242
Pellman, J., 354
Pendlebury, W. W., 216
Penning, M. J., 357
Pensky, E., 295
Perkinson, M. A., 161
Perlmutter, M., 169, 173, 332
Perry, E. L., 339
Peterson, C., 92
Peterson, J., 353
Peterson, J. A., 234
Peterson, P., 330, 346–347
Pfeiffer, E., 305
Pharm, D. J., 119
Phillip, P., 151
Phillips, C., 159
Phillips, J. W., 310
Picot, S., 316
Piedmont, R. L., 237
Pienta, A., 300
Pienta, A. M., 331
Pike, M. C., 65, 70
Pillemer, K., 156, 317
Pinder, M. M., 386
Pirkl, J. J., 105, 108, 110
Pivovarova, I. P., 70
Plomin, R., 37, 38, 72, 239
Pogrebin, L., 78
Pollard, M., 70
Pollio, H. R., 368, 373
Poon, L. W., 179, 202
Poulshock, S. W., 155
Powell, F., 72
Powell, F. C., 373
Price, V. A., 95
Prigerson, H. G., 384
Proppe, H., 127
Pullen, S. M., 203
Pynoos, J., 362

Quadagno, J., 331, 335, 347, 348
Quinn, J. F., 336, 346, 347
Quinn, J. L., 148
Quiroette, C., 357

Subject Index

hospice care, 380–384
humanizing medical care, 384–386
physician-assisted suicide, 391–392
Death education courses, 385–386
Decision/commitment, 298
Delirium, 216
Dementia, 195, 209–213. *See also* Alzheimer's disease
and care rationing, 393
and demography, 212
and depression, 210, 216
and nursing homes, 159, 212, 223
rare causes, 213
stereotypes, 6
vascular, 212–213, 215
Demography, 7, 9–18. *See also* Gender differences; Racial differences; Role revolution
baby boom cohort, 7, 11–12, 308
and decline stereotype, 20
defined, 7
and dementia, 212
and family, 293–294
hospice care, 383
life expectancy revolution, 9–11, 36, 65, 134, 294, 333
and Medicare, 146
racial differences, 14, 16–18
retirement, 332–333
role revolution, 11–13
Denney exercised/unexercised ability theory, 178–180
Dental problems, 116
Depression, 273–278
and alcoholism, 269
behavioral genetics on, 39
and caregiving, 315, 316–317
and cognitive behavioral therapy, 286
and death/dying, 375
defined, 265, 273
and dementia, 210, 216
and memory, 206–207, 216, 275
psychoanalytic theory on, 276–277
and suicide, 277–278, 279
and widowhood, 276, 354
Detached grandparenthood, 321
Developmental psychology, 19
Diabetes, 70, 82, 104, 105

Diabetic retinopathy, 104, 105
Diagnostic and Statistical Manual of Mental Disorders (DSM), 262, 264, 266, 274, 275
Diagnostic evaluation, 283
Disability. *See also* Nursing homes
excess, 147–148, 161, 218
extent of, 132
and friendships, 350
gender differences, 137–138
and life expectancy, 134–136
measurement of, 134
medical care for, 140–147
and osteoporosis, 119–120
pathway of, 136–137, 138
and socioeconomic status, 139–140
and vision impairments, 107
Disadvantaged people. *See* Socioeconomic status
Disease. *See* Chronic disease; Disability; Medical care
Disengagement theory, 233, 234
Displaced workers, 339
Distant figure grandparenthood, 320
Division of labor, 295
Divorce, 297
and caregiving, 13
and grandparenthood, 313, 319–320, 324–325
and parent-adult child relationships, 13, 313
revolution in, 12, 13, 294
and stress, 264
DNA damage, 67
Do not hospitalize (DNH) order, 387
Do not resuscitate (DNR) order, 386–387, 391
Double standard, 301
Downsizing, 339, 343
Driving, 123, 124–125
DSM. *See* Diagnostic and Statistical Manual of Mental Disorders
Duke study, 305, 306
Durable power of attorney, 387
Dying trajectory, 379–380

Eating, 115–116. *See also* Nutrition
ECA. *See* Epidemiologic Catchment Area Survey
Economic status. *See* Socioeconomic status
Education, 345–346
Effectors, 117–118

Efficacy. *See* Self-efficacy
Ego, 35
Ego development, 253
Ego energy, 233
Ego helplessness, 277
Ego integrity, 43, 44
Elastin, 66–67
Elderhostel, 345
Emotional states, 254–256
Emotional stress hypothesis, 88–91, 92
Emotion-focused coping strategies, 251, 252, 256
Enabling factors, 140, 282
Enmeshing, 358
Entitlement programs, 334–335, 341, 346–347
Environmental influences. *See also* Cohort factors; Interventions; Nature/nurture argument
and alcoholism, 269
and androgyny, 236
and creative achievement, 187–188
and hearing impairments, 110–111, 114–115
and heart disease, 81, 83–84
and life expectancy, 13–14
and personality, 242, 247
wrinkling, 76
Epidemiologic Catchment Area Survey (ECA), 262–263, 264, 266, 267, 271, 275
Epidemiologic studies, 261–262, 266, 271, 275–276
Episodic memory, 199, 200–201
Erectile dysfunction, 307, 308
Eriksonian theory, 41–44, 243–247
and death/dying, 368, 369
and personality, 44, 243–247
Estrogen, 82
Ethicists, 390
Ethnicity, 5. *See also* Racial differences
Everyday intelligence, 177
Everyday memory, 201–202
Excess disability, 147–148, 161, 218
Excess mortality, 82
Exercised/unexercised ability theory, 178–180
Experience. *See* Environmental influences
Explanatory style, 31, 32, 34
and depression, 277

Explanatory style (*continued*)
and marriage, 295
and personality, 238
and retirement, 338
External memory aids, 208–209
External validity, 54
Extinction, 28–29
Extraversion, 237. *See also* Big five traits

Falling, 121–122
Family. *See also* Caregiving; Parent-adult child relationships; Relationships; Role revolution
and convoy, 350
and death/dying, 384
stereotypes, 6
Family and Medical Leave Act (1992), 318
Family support groups, 221
Family uninvolvement myth, 309
Family watchdogs, 319–320, 322
Family wisdom reservoir grandparenthood, 320
Fixed life span. *See* Maximum life span
Fluid intelligence, 168–170, 186
Forced retirement, 338–339, 343
Formal caregiving supports, 149–154. *See also* Caregiving; Nursing homes
assisted living facilities, 152
continuing-care retirement communities, 151–152, 153
continuum of, 149, 150
day care, 150–151, 220–221, 222, 318–319
home care, 149–151
specialized services, 152
Formal grandparenthood, 320
Free radical damage, 67–68
Free recall, 197
Freudian theory. *See* Psychoanalytic theory
Friendships. *See also* Relationships
and convoy, 350–351, 355–356
and vision impairments, 108
and widowhood, 352
Functional impairments, 134, 143, 147
Fun-seeking grandparenthood, 320, 321

Gender differences. *See also* Gender roles
agoraphobia, 271

alcoholism, 266, 267–268
Alzheimer's disease, 86
and androgyny, 45, 233–234
depression, 276
disability, 137–138
grandparenthood, 323–324
health orientation, 14, 138
hearing impairments, 110
heart disease, 81–82, 137–138
life expectancy, 12, 13–14, 15, 86, 137
living alone, 362
and midlife maturity shift, 45
nursing home residents, 157
osteoporosis, 119
parent-adult child relationships, 311, 316
and parental imperative, 235–236
personality, 240–241
retirement, 330–331, 332–333
sexuality, 306–307
suicide, 277–278
vascular dementia, 213
widowhood, 355–357
Gender roles, 278. *See also* Gender differences; Role revolution
androgyny, 45, 233–234, 235–236
and grandparenthood, 323
parental imperative theory, 235–236, 337
and personality, 240–241
and sexuality, 301
and widowhood, 355
General adaptation syndrome, 89
Generativity, 43, 44
and parent-adult child relationships, 311
and personality, 243–247
and retirement, 337
Geriatric medicine, 145, 146
Gerontological Society of America, 19, 20, 21
Gerontology. *See also* Psychology of aging field
defined, 4
professional organizations, 19, 21
Glare, 101, 102
Glaucoma, 104, 105
Gradual disability onset, 136, 137
Grandparenthood, 319–326
barriers, 321, 323–324
custodial, 322, 325–326

and divorce, 313, 319–320, 324–325
flexible roles, 320
interventions, 324–326
"Graying of America," 7, 9
Grief work, 354

Hair, 76
Hair cells, 112
Health. *See* Physical health
Health care. *See* Medical care
Health insurance, 141
Health orientation, 140, 142–144
gender differences, 14, 138
Health-related facilities, 154
Hearing aids, 113
Hearing Conservation Amendment (1982), 114
Hearing impairments, 109–115, 123, 126
Heart attacks, 79
Heart disease, 64–65. *See also* Chronic disease
and aging process, 78–84
and dementia, 212–213, 215–216
gender differences, 81–82, 137–138
and intelligence, 173–174
interventions, 93–95
and reaction time, 118–119
and sexuality, 307
and Type A behavior pattern, 90, 91, 94–95
Heredity. *See* Nature/nurture argument
Heritability, 37
Historical perspectives
ageism, 8
demography, 9
gerontology, 18–20
life expectancy, 65, 66
retirement, 334–335
HIV, 214, 371
Home care, 149–151
Home health-care services, 142
Hormones, 82, 303–304
Hospice care, 380–384
Hospital-based ethicists, 390
Housing, 125–128
Huntington's chorea, 213
Hypertension, 84
Hypothalamus, 69

IADLs (instrumental activities of daily living), 134

Id, 35
Identity, 42, 246–248
    and parent-adult child
        relationships, 311–312,
        313
    and widowhood, 358
Illness. *See* Chronic disease;
    Disability; Physical health
Imagery, 207–208
Immigrant status, 310
Immune system, 69, 70, 74–75
Impairments. *See* Physical health;
    Sensory-motor functioning
Implicit (procedural) memory, 199,
    200, 201
Income inequality. *See*
    Socioeconomic status
Incontinence, 210
Infectious diseases, 9
Information-processing
    perspective, 40–41, 42
    on memory, 197–199
    on reaction time, 117–118
Instrumental activities of daily
    living (IADLs), 134
Instrumental conditioning. *See*
    Operant (instrumental)
    conditioning
Instrumental services, 311,
    313–314, 319–320
Integrity. *See* Ego integrity
Intellectual flexibility, 175
Intelligence, 165–192
    behavioral genetics on, 38, 39,
        40
    behaviorism on, 29
    and chronic disease, 173–174
    and cohort factors, 50–51,
        170
    and creative achievement,
        185–190
    exercised/unexercised ability
        theory, 178–180
    interventions, 190–192
    measurement of, 166–168
    and mental stimulation,
        174–175
    neo-Piagetian perspective,
        180–183, 236, 253
    practical, 177–178
    and processing speed, 172–173
    and relationships, 175
    Seattle Longitudinal Study,
        170–172, 173
    and sensory-motor functioning,
        173

traditional test limitations,
    176–177
two-factor theory, 168–170
and vision impairments, 106
and wisdom, 183–185
and work stereotypes, 331–332
Interactional consistency. *See*
    Cumulative/interactional
    consistency theory of
    personality
Intergenerational equity, 346–349
Intergenerational solidarity, 309,
    313
Internal validity, 54
Interventions. *See also* Death/dying
    interventions
    Alzheimer's disease, 217–223
    behavioral genetics, 39–40
    behaviorism, 31–34
    caregiving, 318–319
    Eriksonian theory, 43–44
    grandparenthood, 324–326
    hearing impairments, 113,
        114–115
    information-processing
        perspective, 41
    intelligence, 190–192
    and lifestyle revolution, 93–95
    medical care, 146–147,
        384–386
    memory, 205–209
    motor performance, 124–125
    nursing homes, 158–162
    personality, 256–259
    prosthetic environments,
        125–128
    psychoanalytic theory, 36,
        280–281, 287–288
    psychopathology, 283–289
    retirement, 343–346
    selective optimization with
        compensation, 45–46
    sensory-motor functioning,
        124–128
    sexuality, 308, 309
    vision impairments, 106–109
    widowhood, 360, 361
Interviews. *See* Qualitative research
Intimacy, 42, 298–299
IQ. *See* Intelligence
Iris, 104–105

Jungian theory, 44–45, 234

Kansas City Studies of Adult Life,
    231, 232, 233–234

Kübler-Ross stage theory of dying,
    374–375, 377

Laws
    Age Discrimination in
        Employment Act, 338
    Americans with Disabilities Act,
        127
    Family and Medical Leave Act,
        318
    grandparenthood, 324–325
    Hearing Conservation
        Amendment, 114
    Nursing Home Reform Act,
        158–159
    Patient Self-Determination Act,
        387
    Social Security Act, 335
Lens, 105
Life-cycle approach to medical
    care, 392–393
Life expectancy. *See also* Life
    expectancy revolution
    and disability, 134–136
    extending, 69–71
    gender differences, 12, 13–14,
        15, 86, 137
    historical perspectives, 65, 66
    racial differences, 13, 16–17
    and relationships, 87, 88, 92–93
Life expectancy revolution, 9–11,
    65
    and behavioral genetics, 36
    and lifestyle revolution, 134
    and relationships, 294
    and retirement, 333
Lifeline Emergency Response
    System, 152
Life review. *See* Reminiscence
Life span. *See* Life expectancy;
    Maximum life span
Life-span perspective, 46–47, 228,
    256
Lifestyle revolution, 9, 40, 86–95
    and active life expectancy, 134
    Alameda Study, 87–88
    and blaming the victim, 85
    emotional stress hypothesis,
        88–91, 92
    and interventions, 93–95
    and personality, 92–93
    self-efficacy, 91–92
Lifetime prevalence, 263
Lifetime risk of placement, 154
Lighthouse Survey, 101–103,
    106–107, 108–109

Lipoproteins, 82
Live-in grandparenthood, 322
Living alone, 14, 127–128, 360–363
Living wills, 386. *See also* Advance directives
Logotherapy, 258
Longitudinal studies, 51–54. *See also specific studies*
Long-term care facilities. *See* Nursing homes
Long-term care insurance, 148
Long-term memory, 198
Loyola Generativity Scale, 245

McAdams level theory of personality, 243
Mandatory retirement policies, 338
Marriage, 294–299. *See also* Divorce; Relationships; Role revolution; Widowhood
changes in, 293–294, 351–352
and chronic disease, 357–358
harmony in, 294–298
and intelligence, 175
and sexuality, 298–299, 306
and triangular theory of love, 298–299
Mastery style, 233
Masturbation, 307
Matrifocal family orientation, 324
Maturity, 45, 251–254, 256
Maximum life span, 65, 68, 69–71
Means-tested benefits, 347, 348
Measurement
of disability, 134
of intelligence, 166–168
of memory, 197
of personality, 230–232
of psychopathology, 261–264, 267
Measurement reliability, 58
Measurement validity, 54, 58
Measures, 57–58
Mechanics of intelligence, 169
Media, 301
Medicaid, 141, 142, 148, 161
and advance directives, 387
and mental health care, 282, 290
Medical care, 140–147. *See also* Health orientation; Mental health care; Terminal care
age-based rationing, 392–394
cost of, 141–142
and death/dying, 378–380, 384–386

and health orientation, 14, 138, 140, 142–144
interventions, 146–147, 384–386
problems with, 144–146
Medicare, 141–142, 143, 146
and advance directives, 387
and intergenerational equity, 347
and mental health care, 281–282, 290
Memory, 195–209. *See also* Dementia
autobiographical, 203–205
behaviorism on, 31–32
and depression, 206–207, 216, 275
everyday, 201–202
information-processing perspective on, 197–199
interventions, 205–209
measurement of, 197
memory-systems theory, 199–201
prospective, 203
reminiscence (life review), 43–44, 205, 218, 247–248
and self-efficacy, 209
stereotypes, 6, 196–197, 201, 203, 209
Memory-systems theory, 199–201
Men. *See* Gender differences; Gender roles
Menopause
and androgyny, 235
and heart disease, 79, 81, 82
and sexuality, 303–304
Mental disorders. *See* Psychopathology
Mental health. *See* Personality; Psychopathology
Mental health care, 278–284. *See also* Psychotherapy
changes in, 278–279, 280–282
chemotherapy, 279–280, 284, 285
diagnostic evaluation, 283
in nursing homes, 289–291
problems with, 282–283
Mental status exam, 283, 284
Mental stimulation, 174–175, 207, 218
Middle knowledge, 375–376
Midlife maturity shift, 45
Mills College Study, 232, 235, 236, 252, 303, 331

Minority people. *See* Racial differences
Mnemonic techniques, 207–208
Modeling, 30
Mood disorders, 264
Morbidity, 134
Motor performance, 116–125
driving, 123, 124–125
interventions, 124–125
and prosthetic environments, 127
reaction time, 116–120
standing/walking, 120–122, 124
Mourning, 352–358
gender differences, 355–357
and mode of death, 357–358
task theories, 353–355, 377
MS (multiple sclerosis), 132–133
Multidimensional/multidirectional nature of change, 47, 171
Multidisciplinary research, 20, 22
Multiple Risk Factor Intervention Trial, 93
Multiple sclerosis (MS), 132–133
Muscles, 119
Musculoskeletal system, 119–110
Myocardial infarctions. *See* Heart attacks
My Turn program, 345–346

National Comorbidity Study (NCS), 263, 264, 275
Nature/nurture argument. *See also* Environmental influences
and behavioral genetics, 36, 37–38, 238–239
and behaviorism, 28, 30
and psychoanalytic theory, 35
NCS (National Comorbidity Study), 263, 264, 275
Near poor, 347
Need factors, 140
Neo-Piagetian perspective on intelligence, 180–183, 236, 253
Nervous system, 84–86. *See also* Cognition; Dementia
and alcoholism, 266
and Alzheimer's disease, 213–214
and emotional states, 255
and hearing impairments, 112–113
and intelligence, 169
and motor performance, 117–119

Physical health (*continued*)
and widowhood, 355–356
and young-old vs. old-old,
10–11
Physician-assisted suicide,
391–392
Piagetian theory. *See* Neo-Piagetian
perspective on intelligence
Pick's disease, 213
Plasticity, 85, 176, 191
PMA. *See* Thurstone's Primary
Mental Abilities Scale
Possible selves (self-schemas),
248–249
Postformal thought, 180–183, 236,
253
Postretirement careers, 346
Poverty. *See* Socioeconomic status
Practical intelligence, 177–178
Practice effects, 52, 54
Pragmatics of intelligence, 169
Predisposing factors, 140. *See also*
Health orientation
Presbycusis, 111
Presbyopia, 101
Prevention, 93, 134
Primary aging, 64
Primary attachment figures, 241,
249, 312–313, 352
Primary control strategies,
256–257
Primary prevention, 93, 134
Problem-focused coping strategies,
251–252, 256
Procedural (implicit) memory, 199,
200, 201
Processing resources, 198
Processing speed, 41, 172–173,
198
Programmed aging theories, 68–69
Prospective memory, 203
Prospective studies, 81
Prosthetic environments, 125–128
Psychoanalytic theory, 34–37
on depression, 276–27
and Eriksonian theory, 41–42,
44
on personality, 35, 228, 238,
241, 243
and psychotherapy, 280–281,
287–288
on work, 336
Psychology and Aging, 19–20
Psychology of aging field,
18–20, 21, 22. *See also*
Gerontology

Psychopathology, 261–273,
278–290. *See also* Depression
alcoholism, 265–269
behavioral genetics on, 39, 267–
269
interventions, 283–289
measurement of, 261–264, 267
and memory, 206–207
mental health care, 278–283
and nursing homes, 157–158,
263, 282
and parent-adult child
relationships, 316
and personality, 238
phobias, 265, 270–273
racial differences, 18
stereotypes, 6, 264, 280–281
Psychosocial crises. *See* Eriksonian
theory
Psychotherapy, 279, 280–281,
285–289. *See also* Mental
health care
clinical geropsychology field, 20,
36
cognitive behavioral approaches,
285–287
and dementia, 218
and psychoanalytic theory,
280–281, 287–288
Psychotropic medications, 280,
281, 284, 285
Pupil, 104–105

Qualitative research, 58–60
Quantitative research, 58. *See also*
Research methods

Racial differences
alcoholism, 266, 269
androgyny, 236
coresidence, 310
demography, 14, 16–18
and heart disease, 82–84
life expectancy, 13, 16–17
nursing home residents, 157
osteoporosis, 119
parent-adult child relationships,
17–18, 316
retirement, 333
suicide, 277–278
vascular dementia, 213
Random damage aging theories,
67–68
Reaction time, 116–120, 123
Real income, 330

Recurrent Coronary Prevention
Project, 94–95
Reinforcement, 28–29
Relationships. *See also* Caregiving;
Grandparenthood; Marriage;
Parent-adult child
relationships; Sexuality
convoy, 350–351, 355–356,
383
and disability, 147, 148
and hearing impairments,
113–114, 115
and intelligence, 175
and life expectancy, 87, 88,
92–93
and nursing homes, 155, 157,
161
and role revolution, 12
socioemotional-selectivity theory,
249–251, 296
stress buffering hypothesis, 88
and suicide, 278
and Type A behavior pattern,
90–91
and vision impairments, 108
Reliability, 58
Religion, 18, 371, 372, 373, 391
Reminiscence (life review), 43–44.
See also Autobiographical
memory
and death/dying, 371
and dementia, 205, 218
and personality, 247–248
Reminiscence peak, 204
Research methods, 47–60
behavioral genetics, 37
collaboration, 20, 22
cross-sectional studies, 48–51
current trends, 58, 60
evaluating, 54–58
longitudinal studies, 51–54
sequential studies, 53
Reserve capacity, 75, 191
Resilience, 14
Retinal detachment, 105
Retirement, 330–349
behaviorism on, 31
context changes, 13, 330–332
demography, 332–333
economic motivations, 334–336
emotional impact, 342–343
emotional motivations, 336–338
financial impact, 340–342
forced, 338–339, 343
and intergenerational equity,
346–349

Credits

These pages constitute an extension of the copyright page. We have made every effort to trace the ownership of all copyrighted material and to secure permission from copyright holders. In the event of any question arising as to the use of any material, we will be pleased to make the necessary corrections in future printings. Thanks are due to the following authors, publishers, and agents for permission to use the material indicated.

Chapter 1
page 11: John Eastcott/Yva Momatuk/Photo Researchers Inc.

page 15: Figure 1-3 from "The gender mortality differential in developed countries: Demographic and sociocultural dimensions," by C. A. Nathanson. In M. Ory and H. R. Warner (Eds.) *Gender, health and longevity,* p. 9, figure 1.4. Copyright © 1990 Springer Publishing Company Inc., New York NY 10012. Used with permission.

page 16: Figure 1-4 from "The demography of minority aging populations" by J. L. Angel and D. F. Hogan, *Minority elders: Longevity, economics and health,* p. 4, figure 1. Copyright © 1991 The Gerontological Society of America. Reprinted with permission.

page 18: Figure 1-5 from "Improving the economic security of minority persons as they enter old age" by Y. P. Chen, *Minority elders: Longevity, economics and health,* p. 19, table 10. Copyright © 1991 The Gerontological Society of America. Reprinted with permission.

Chapter 2
page 39: Figure 2-1 from "Gerontological Behavioral Genetics" by N. L. Pedersen, *Handbook of the Psychology of Aging,* 4th ed., p. 63, table 1. Copyright © 1996 Academic Press, Inc. Reprinted by permission of the publisher and author.

page 42: Figure 2-2 from "The information-processing perspective on cognitive aging" by T. A. Salthouse. In R. J. Sternberg and C. A. Berg (Eds.), *Intellectual Development,* p. 263, figure 9-1. Copyright © 1992, reprinted with permission of Cambridge University Press.

page 50 (left and right): Courtesy of the author.

Chapter 3
page 74: Courtesy of the National Institute on Aging.

page 78: Excerpt from *Getting over getting older* by L. C. Pogrebin, pp. 128–129, 153. Copyright © 1996 by Letty Cottin Pogrebin. By permission of Little, Brown and Company (Inc.).

page 80: Figure 3-4 from *Human aging and chronic disease* by C. S. Kart, E. K. Metress, & S. P. Metress, p. 201, figure 12.3. Copyright © 1992 Boston: Jones and Bartlett Publishers. Reprinted with permission.

page 81: Figure 3-5 from "Variations in disease-specific sex morbidity and mortality ratios in the United States" by D. L. Wingard & B. A. Cohn. In M. Ory and H. R. Warner (Eds.), *Gender, health and longevity,* p. 30, figure 2-2. Copyright © 1990 Springer Publishing Company Inc., New York NY 10012. Used with permission.

Chapter 4
page 102: Figure 4-1 from *Handbook of the Psychology of Aging* by J. E. Birren & K. W. Schaie, p. 516, figure 15. Copyright © 1977 by Van Nostrand Reinhold Company. Reprinted with permission.

page 103: Figure 4-2 from *The Lighthouse national survey on vision loss* by Louis Harris and Associates, p. 13.

Copyright © 1995 The Lighthouse, Inc. Reprinted with permission.

page 107: Figure 4-4 from "Intellectual functioning in old and very old age" by U. Lindenberger & P. B. Baltes, *Psychology and Aging, 12,* p. 427, figure 6. Copyright © 1997 American Psychological Association. Reprinted with permission.

page 109: Courtesy of The Lighthouse Inc.

page 121: Southern Photography.

page 124: Figure 4-8 from *Journal of Applied Gerontology, 15,* by N. Stamatiadis, p. 17. Copyright © 1996, Reprinted by permission of Sage Publications.

Chapter 5

page 135: Figure 5-1 from "Proportion with personal care disability" by E. Crimmins, Y. Saito, & S. L. Reynolds, *Journals of Gerontology Social Studies, 52B,* S59–71. Copyright © 1997 The Gerontological Society of America. Reprinted with permission.

page 136: Figure 5-2 from "Progressive versus catastrophic disability: A longitudinal view of the disablement process" by Ferrucci, Guralnick, Simonsock, Salve, Corti, and Langlois, *Journals of Gerontology Social Studies, 52B,* M126. Copyright © 1996 The Gerontological Society of America. Reprinted with permission.

page 148: Southern Photography.

page 149: Figure 5-6 from "Long term care: The silent target of the federal and state budget debate" by P. Riley, *The National Academy on Aging, Public Policy and Aging Report,* Nov. 1995, p. 4. Copyright © 1995 The Gerontological Society of America. Reprinted with permission.

page 159: Courtesy of Joseph L. Morse Geriatric Center, West Palm Beach, Florida.

Chapter 6

page 166: Table 6-1 from "Adults' conceptions of intelligence across the adult life span" by C. J. Berg & R. J. Sternberg, *Psychology and Aging, 2,* pp. 221–231, table 1. Copyright © 1992 American Psychological Association. Adapted with permission.

page 172: Figure 6-1 from "Hazards of cognitive aging" by K. W. Schaie, *Gerontologist, 29,* p. 40, figure 6. Copyright © 1988 The Gerontological Society of America. Adapted with permission.

page 179: Figure 6-2 from "Everyday problem solving" by N. A. Denny (1989). In L. W. Poon, D. C. Rubin & B. A. Wilson (Eds.) *Everyday cognition in adulthood and late life,* pp. 59–73. New York: Cambridge University Press. Reprinted by permission of Cambridge University Press.

page 182: Excerpt from *Number our days* by Barbara Myerhoff. Copyright © 1978 by Barbara Myerhoff. Used by permission of Dutton Signet, a division of Penguin Books USA, Inc.

page 184: Table 6-5 from "Wisdom-related knowledge in a life review task: Age differences and the role of professional specialization" by U. M. Staudinger, J. Smith, & P. B. Baltes, *Psychology and Aging, 7,* p. 275, table 2. Copyright © 1992 American Psychological Association. Reprinted with permission.

pages 186–190: Excerpts from *Creativity: Flow and the psychology of discovery and invention* by M. Csikszentmihalyi. Copyright © 1996 by Mihaly Csikszentmihalyi. Reprinted by permission of HarperCollins Publishers, Inc.

page 187: Figure 6-3 from "Creative productivity: A predictive and explanatory model of career trajectories and landmarks" by D. Simonton, *Psychological Review, 104,* pp. 66–89, figure 5. Copyright © 1997 American Psychological Association. Reprinted with permission. Originally published in Developmental Psychology, 1991.

page 191: Figure 6-5 from "Long-term effects of fluid ability training in old-old age" by S. L. Willis & C. S. Nesselroade, *Developmental Psychology, 26,* p. 908, figure 2. Copyright © 1990 American Psychological Association. Reprinted with permission.

Chapter 7

page 196: Table 7-1 from "Paced and self-paced learning in young and elderly adults" by R. Canestrari, *Journal of Gerontology, 18,* p. 166. Copyright © 1963 The Gerontological Society of America. Adapted with permission.

page 204: Figure 7-1 from "Age differences in reminiscence functions" by J. D. Webster (1995). In B. K. Haight & J. D. Webster (Eds.) *The art and science of reminiscing: Theory, research methods and applications,* p. 93, figure 1; p. 96, figure 2. Washington D.C.: Taylor & Francis Publishers. Reproduced by permission. All rights reserved.

page 217: Science Source/Photo Researchers.

page 219: Figure 7-2 from *Profiles in Caregiving: The Unexpected Career* by Aneshensel, Pearlin, Mullin, Zarit, & Whitlatch, p. 24, figure 2-1. Copyright © 1995 Academic Press, Inc. Reprinted by permission of the publisher and author.

Chapter 8

page 228: Deborah Kahn Kalas/Stock, Boston.

page 230: Figure 8-1 from *Journals of Gerontology: Psychological Science, 48* by J. Krueger & J. Heckhausen,

p. 104. Copyright © 1993 The Gerontological Society of America. Reprinted with permission.

page 242: Table 8.2 from "As time goes by: Change and stability in personality over fifty years" by Haan, Millsap, & Hartka, *Psychology and Aging, 1,* pp. 220–232, table 2. Copyright © 1986 American Psychological Association. Reprinted with permission.

page 244: Figure 8.2 and **page 245:** Table 8-3 from "A theory of generativity and its assessment through self-report, behavioral acts, and narrative themes in autobiography" by D. P. McAdams & E. D. St. Aubin, *Journal of Personality and Social Psychology, 62,* p. 1005, figure 1; p. 1015. Copyright © 1992 American Psychological Association. Reprinted with permission.

page 246: Excerpt from "Stella" by S. R. Kaufman, *The ageless self: Sources of meaning in late life,* pp. 62–66. Copyright © 1986. Reprinted by permission of The University of Wisconsin Press.

page 253: Figure 8-3 from "Women's Prime of Life, Is It the 50s?" by V. Mitchell & R. Helson, *Psychology of Women Quarterly, 14,* p. 456. Copyright © 1990 Cambridge University Press. Reprinted with permission.

page 255: Courtesy of Adams Place.

page 257: Figure 8-4 from "A life span model of successful aging" by R. Schulz & J. Heckhausen, *American Psychologist, 51,* p. 709, figure 2. Copyright © 1996 American Psychological Association. Reprinted with permission.

Chapter 9

page 268: Figure 9-1 from "From proteins to cognitions: The behavioral genetics of alcoholism" by M. McGue. In R. Plomin & G. E. McClearn (Eds.) *Nature, Nurture, and Psychology,* p. 251. Copyright © 1993 American Psychological Association. Reprinted with permission.

page 273: *The Scream* by Edvard Munch. Foto Marburg/ Art Resource, New York.

page 275: Southern Photography.

page 281: UPI/Corbis-Bettmann.

pages 286 and **287:** Excerpt from "Behavioral and cognitive-behavioral treatments: An overview" by A. Zeiss & A. Steffen, *A guide to psychotherapy and aging: Effective clinical interventions in a lifestage context,* pp. 47–50. Copyright © 1996 American Psychological Association. Reprinted with permission.

Chapter 10

page 296: Courtesy of Muriel Kaplan.

page 299: Figure 10-1 from "Triangulating love" by R. J. Sternberg (1988). In R. J. Sternberg & M. L. Barnes (Eds.) *The Psychology of Love,* figure 6.2. Reprinted by permission of Yale University Press.

page 305: Table 10-2 from "Sexuality and aging: Usual and successful" by Wiley & Bortz. In *Journal of Gerontology, Medical Sciences, 51A,* p. 143. Copyright © 1996 The Gerontological Society of America. Reprinted with permission.

page 312: Courtesy of Adams Place.

page 318: Figure 10-3 from "Caregiving and the stress process: An overview of concepts and their measures" by L. I. Pearlin, J. T. Mullan, S. J. Semple & M. M. Skaff, *Gerontologist, 30,* p. 143. Copyright © 1990 The Gerontological Society of America. Reprinted with permission.

page 323: Courtesy of Muriel Kaplan.

Chapter 11

page 344: Figure 11-4 from "Age integration and the lives of older people" by M. W. Riley & L. W. Riley, *Gerontologist, 33,* p. 445. Copyright © 1994 The Gerontological Society of America. Reprinted with permission.

page 348 (left): Courtesy of Muriel Kaplan.

page 348 (right): Peter Menzel/Stock, Boston.

Chapter 12

page 370: Figure 12-1 from "The utility of health at different stages of life: A quantitative approach" by J. J. Busschbach, D. J. Hessing, F. T. Charro, *Social Science and Medicine, 37,* pp. 153–158. Copyright © 1993 Elsevier Science Ltd., the Boulevard, Langford Lane, Kidlington, OX 5, 1GB, U.K. Reprinted with permission.

page 373: Courtesy of Joseph L. Morse Geriatric Center, West Palm Beach, Florida.

page 389: Figure 12-5 from "How informed can consent be? New light on comprehension among elderly people making decisions about enteral tube feeding" by M. D. Krynski, A. J. Tymchuk, & J. G. Ouslander, *Gerontologist, 34,* p. 38, figure 1. Copyright © 1994 The Gerontological Society of America. Reprinted with permission.

page 393: Nubar Alexanian/Stock, Boston.